AUG 2006

W9-AVT-414

HISTORICAL DICTIONARIES OF
RELIGIONS, PHILOSOPHIES, AND MOVEMENTS
Jon Woronoff, Series Editor

1. *Buddhism,* by Charles S. Prebish, 1993
2. *Mormonism,* by Davis Bitton, 1994. *Out of print. See No. 32.*
3. *Ecumenical Christianity,* by Ans Joachim van der Bent, 1994
4. *Terrorism,* by Sean Anderson and Stephen Sloan, 1995. *Out of print. See No. 41.*
5. *Sikhism,* by W. H. McLeod, 1995. *Out of print. See No. 59.*
6. *Feminism,* by Janet K. Boles and Diane Long Hoeveler, 1995. *Out of print. See No. 52.*
7. *Olympic Movement,* by Ian Buchanan and Bill Mallon, 1995. *Out of print. See No. 39.*
8. *Methodism,* by Charles Yrigoyen Jr. and Susan E. Warrick, 1996. *Out of Print. See No. 57.*
9. *Orthodox Church,* by Michael Prokurat, Alexander Golitzin, and Michael D. Peterson, 1996
10. *Organized Labor,* by James C. Docherty, 1996. *Out of print. See No. 50.*
11. *Civil Rights Movement,* by Ralph E. Luker, 1997
12. *Catholicism,* by William J. Collinge, 1997
13. *Hinduism,* by Bruce M. Sullivan, 1997
14. *North American Environmentalism,* by Edward R. Wells and Alan M. Schwartz, 1997
15. *Welfare State,* by Bent Greve, 1998
16. *Socialism,* by James C. Docherty, 1997
17. *Bahá'í Faith,* by Hugh C. Adamson and Philip Hainsworth, 1998
18. *Taoism,* by Julian F. Pas in cooperation with Man Kam Leung, 1998
19. *Judaism,* by Norman Solomon, 1998
20. *Green Movement,* by Elim Papadakis, 1998
21. *Nietzscheanism,* by Carol Diethe, 1999
22. *Gay Liberation Movement,* by Ronald J. Hunt, 1999
23. *Islamic Fundamentalist Movements in the Arab World, Iran, and Turkey,* by Ahmad S. Moussalli, 1999
24. *Reformed Churches,* by Robert Benedetto, Darrell L. Guder, and Donald K. McKim, 1999
25. *Baptists,* by William H. Brackney, 1999
26. *Cooperative Movement,* by Jack Shaffer, 1999
27. *Reformation and Counter-Reformation,* by Hans J. Hillerbrand, 2000

28. *Shakers,* by Holley Gene Duffield, 2000
29. *United States Political Parties,* by Harold F. Bass Jr., 2000
30. *Heidegger's Philosophy,* by Alfred Denker, 2000
31. *Zionism,* by Rafael Medoff and Chaim I. Waxman, 2000
32. *Mormonism,* 2nd ed., by Davis Bitton, 2000
33. *Kierkegaard's Philosophy,* by Julia Watkin, 2001
34. *Hegelian Philosophy,* by John W. Burbidge, 2001
35. *Lutheranism,* by Günther Gassmann in cooperation with Duane H. Larson and Mark W. Oldenburg, 2001
36. *Holiness Movement,* by William Kostlevy, 2001
37. *Islam,* by Ludwig W. Adamec, 2001
38. *Shinto,* by Stuart D. B. Picken, 2002
39. *Olympic Movement,* 2nd ed., by Ian Buchanan and Bill Mallon, 2001. *Out of Print. See No. 61.*
40. *Slavery and Abolition,* by Martin A. Klein, 2002
41. *Terrorism,* 2nd ed., by Sean Anderson and Stephen Sloan, 2002
42. *New Religious Movements,* by George D. Chryssides, 2001
43. *Prophets in Islam and Judaism,* by Scott B. Noegel and Brannon M. Wheeler, 2002
44. *The Friends (Quakers),* by Margery Post Abbott, Mary Ellen Chijioke, Pink Dandelion, and John William Oliver Jr., 2003
45. *Lesbian Liberation Movement: Still the Rage*, by JoAnne Myers, 2003
46. *Descartes and Cartesian Philosophy,* by Roger Ariew, Dennis Des Chene, Douglas M. Jesseph, Tad M. Schmaltz, and Theo Verbeek, 2003
47. *Witchcraft,* by Michael D. Bailey, 2003
48. *Unitarian Universalism,* by Mark W. Harris, 2004
49. *New Age Movements,* by Michael York, 2004
50. *Organized Labor,* 2nd ed., by James C. Docherty, 2004
51. *Utopianism,* by James M. Morris and Andrea L. Kross, 2004
52. *Feminism,* 2nd ed., by Janet K. Boles and Diane Long Hoeveler, 2004
53. *Jainism,* by Kristi L. Wiley, 2004
54. *Wittgenstein's Philosophy,* by Duncan Richter, 2004
55. *Schopenhauer's Philosophy,* by David E. Cartwright, 2005
56. *Seventh-day Adventists,* by Gary Land, 2005
57. *Methodism,* 2nd ed., by Charles Yrigoyen Jr. and Susan E. Warrick, 2005
58. *Sufism,* by John Renard, 2005
59. *Sikhism,* 2nd ed., by W. H. McLeod, 2005
60. *Kant and Kantianism,* by Helmut Holzhey and Vilem Mudroch, 2005
61. *Olympic Movement,* 3rd ed., by Bill Mallon with Ian Buchanan, 2006
62. *Anglicanism,* by Colin Buchanan, 2006

Historical Dictionary of the Olympic Movement

Third Edition

Bill Mallon,
with Ian Buchanan

*Historical Dictionaries of Religions,
Philosophies, and Movements, No. 61*

The Scarecrow Press, Inc.
Lanham, Maryland • Toronto • Oxford
2006

SCARECROW PRESS, INC.

Published in the United States of America
by Scarecrow Press, Inc.
A wholly owned subsidiary of
The Rowman & Littlefield Publishing Group, Inc.
4501 Forbes Boulevard, Suite 200, Lanham, Maryland 20706
www.scarecrowpress.com

PO Box 317
Oxford
OX2 9RU, UK

Copyright © 2006 by Bill Mallon and Ian Buchanan

All rights reserved. No part of this publication may be reproduced, stored
in a retrieval system, or transmitted in any form or by any means, electronic,
mechanical, photocopying, recording, or otherwise, without the prior permission
of the publisher.

British Library Cataloguing in Publication Information Available

Library of Congress Cataloging-in-Publication Data

Mallon, Bill.
  Historical dictionary of the Olympic movement / Bill Mallon with Ian
Buchanan.— 3rd ed.
      p. cm. — (Historical dictionaries of religions, philosophies, and
movements ; no. 61)
  Includes bibliographical references.
  ISBN 0-8108-5574-7 (hardcover : alk. paper)
  1. Olympics—History—Dictionaries. 2. Olympics—Records. I. Buchanan,
Ian, 1932–II. Title. III. Series.

GV721.5.B83 2006
796.48'03—dc22
                                                            2005016706

Second edition by Ian Buchanan and Bill Mallon, Historical Dictionaries of
Religions, Philosophies, and Movements, No. 39, Scarecrow Press, Lanham,
Maryland, 2001   ISBN 0-8108-4054-5

♾™ The paper used in this publication meets the minimum requirements of
American National Standard for Information Sciences—Permanence of Paper
for Printed Library Materials, ANSI/NISO Z39.48-1992.
Manufactured in the United States of America.

Dedicated to Ian Buchanan
for his friendship over the years

Contents

Editor's Foreword   *Jon Woronoff* ... ix

Preface ... xi

Acronyms and Abbreviations ... xv

Chronology of the Olympic Movement ... xxvii

Chronology of the Olympic Games and Olympic
Winter Games ... xxxvii

Introduction ... xciii

THE DICTIONARY ... 1

Appendixes

A   Presidents of the International Olympic Committee ... 331

B   The Games of the Olympiads: Sites, Dates, Nations,
and Athletes ... 332

C   The Olympic Winter Games: Sites, Dates, Nations,
and Athletes ... 333

D   Members of the International Olympic Committee ... 334

E   Awards of the International Olympic Committee ... 346

F   Final Olympic Torchbearers within the
Olympic Stadium ... 352

G   Speakers of the Olympic Oath ... 355

H   Official Openings of the Olympic Games ... 357

I   Most Olympic Medals Won: Summer, Men ... 359

J   Most Olympic Medals Won: Summer, Women   360

K   Most Olympic Gold Medals Won: Summer, Men   361

L   Most Olympic Gold Medals Won: Summer, Women   362

M   Most Olympic Medals Won: Winter, Men   363

N   Most Olympic Medals Won: Winter, Women   364

O   Most Olympic Gold Medals Won: Winter, Men   365

P   Most Olympic Gold Medals Won: Winter, Women   366

Q   Positive Drug Tests at the Olympic Games   367

R   Attempts at Olympic Revival Prior to 1896   375

Bibliography   377

About the Authors   411

Editor's Foreword

Of the many movements included in this series, there is nothing quite like the Olympic movement in scope. The original Olympic Games were held about three millennia ago, and the next Olympic Games are never more than two years away. The flame from the old to the new Games was carried by dedicated individuals—Pierre de Coubertin and other pioneers—and is now borne by tens of thousands of organizers, athletes, trainers, sponsors, and fans, and observed by a public that numbers in the billions. Whereas only Greeks participated in the original Olympic Games, participation has now spread around the world, including 202 countries at latest count. Despite a need for organized bodies and institutions, this remains a vibrant peoples' movement in many ways.

But the Olympic movement is also often something more and occasionally something less. The participants are not only competing in their own interest, or that of the country they represent, to win highly coveted awards and trophies but also to show how sport can enrich humanity. They are imbued, to some extent at least, with the ideals of the Olympics, and even the spectators go away better than they arrived. But these ideals, some so lofty that they simply cannot be fulfilled, contrast with the nitty-gritty of the Olympics: which city and country to choose, which sports to include, how to make the athletes abide by the rules, how to organize and run the biggest show on Earth, and how to have that show cover its costs and perhaps turn a profit. Even the more ordinary day-to-day activities of what has become a vast and complex set of organizations are sometimes less than inspiring. Thus, on occasion, there are grounds for complaint.

Given the exceptional scope of the Olympic movement, this book had to cover an unusually broad range of persons, places, and events as well as an extended time horizon. It has done so extremely well with an extensive chronology and concise recapitulation of the modern Olympic Games and with dictionary entries on Olympic bodies, significant pioneers, organizers and athletes, the various sporting events and federations, and a multitude of countries. These have all been revised and expanded to produce a more up-to-date dictionary. And, for this new edition, more athletes have been added and some of the complaints and the important reforms they resulted in have been analyzed. The appendixes provide handy information on leading figures and the most outstanding athletes. And a brief but useful bibliography suggests further reading.

This is now the third edition of *Historical Dictionary of the Olympic Movement*. It is written by Bill Mallon on the basis of the previous editions coauthored with Ian Buchanan. Both have an abiding interest in sports and have actively supported the Olympic movement. Among other things, they helped found the International Society of Olympic Historians (ISOH), of which Ian Buchanan was the first president and Bill Mallon the immediate past-president. They have already written an impressive number of significant works on the Olympic Games and combined their knowledge and insight in a book that is informative and readable and will be an excellent guide for those who want to know more about the movement in general or are just hunting for information on specific games or athletes.

Jon Woronoff
Series Editor

Preface

Since 1896, the Olympic Games have become one of the most watched and publicized spectacles in the world. Jim McKay, longtime sportscaster who covered many Olympic Games, once noted that they constitute the largest peacetime gathering of humanity in the history of the world. One former U.S. Olympic competitor, Elliott Denman (a walker), reflected on the Olympic Games: "[The Olympics] bring the world together. They are a remarkable cause for the good of mankind. In a planet beset with divisiveness, the Games continue to promote both the magnificent diversity of mankind, and the commonality of all."

Although the world watches the Olympic Games every four years and marvels at the feats of the athletes, the Olympic movement and its philosophy of "Olympism" go on daily and are the cornerstones of the work of the International Olympic Committee (IOC). The Olympic movement does not receive the publicity received by the Games themselves, but it has the ability to serve and has served as a major force for international goodwill. Former U.S. vice president Al Gore correctly pointed out that "the IOC is the oldest multi-national, non-governmental continuous organization in the world."

The first edition of *Historical Dictionary of the Olympic Movement* was published by Scarecrow Press in 1995 and the second edition in 2001. We have been gratified by the response to the book and pleased that this response allowed us to produce a second, and now a third edition. When we began the original work, we thought it might be a rehashing of work we had done together on earlier projects. Quickly, we realized it was not, and that the need for a complete dictionary of the Olympic movement was a real one. Though we have both studied the Olympic Games and Olympic movement extensively, we do not think a comparable work exists that allows the student of the Olympics to find background references on all aspects of the Olympic Games and

Olympic movement in one source. This book is not intended to be an encyclopaedic study of the Olympic movement and Olympic Games, but an introductory text allowing readers to gain insight into the history, politics, and fascinating events that have surrounded the Olympics since their inception in Ancient Greece and their modern resurrection in 1896. To this end, we hope we have been successful.

Since the first edition of this book, a great deal has happened in the Olympic world. Specifically, in 1999, the International Olympic Committee was rocked by scandal relating to the process of selecting host cities for the Olympic Games. Reports of bribery were rampant, and revelations relating to this scandal were in the media almost daily during 1999. We have dealt with this problem in some detail. Further, the problems of drugs in sports has expanded and become the leading headline dealing with the Olympic movement, at least in the United States. This problem is addressed at some length. But we hope to emphasize that the Olympic movement is related to much more than just the holding of sports events, and the negative publicity engendered by scandals should not blind people to all the good that is done by the Olympic movement and the International Olympic Committee. Moreover, we hope that the recent Sydney Olympics, an exemplar of Olympic Games, and the Athens Olympic Games, returning the Olympics to their roots, will help people realize this.

We would like to thank Jon Woronoff, the series editor of Scarecrow's Historical Dictionaries of Religions, Philosophies, and Movements. We have been helped in our research particularly by Karel Wendl of the IOC, who first suggested our names to Jon Woronoff. We would also like to thank Patricia Eckert (IOC), Wolf Lyberg (SWE), Joachim K. Rühl (GER), Howard Stupp (IOC), Ture Widlund (SWE), and David Young (USA). Lyberg, Rühl, Wendl, Widlund, and Young are all members of the International Society of Olympic Historians (ISOH), an organization devoted to studying the Olympic Games and Olympic movement. We also extend special thanks to IOC and ISOH member Dick Pound (CAN), who wrote the foreword to the first edition and also carefully edited many sections of the original book.

We again thank the many loyal Olympic followers worldwide who have assisted us in our research. Our thanks go out especially to the over 300 members of the International Society of Olympic Historians, many of whom have lent their knowledge. ISOH members continue to be at the forefront of the study of the Olympic Games and Olympic movement, and we are both proud to be involved in the organization. Special thanks again go to Jon Woronoff and Scarecrow Press for their support and guidance in allowing us to produce this third edition.

Further, the junior author (Mallon) would like to thank the senior (Buchanan) for his help, support, and mentoring over the years.

We hope you like it.

Ian Buchanan
Burgh Next Aylsham, Norwich, England

Bill Mallon
Durham, North Carolina, United States

January 2005

Acronyms and Abbreviations

THREE-LETTER SPORT ABBREVIATIONS

ARC	Archery
ASK	Alpine Skiing
ATH	Athletics (Track and Field)
BAS	Basketball
BDM	Badminton
BIA	Biathlon
BOB	Bobsledding
BOX	Boxing
BSB	Baseball
CAN	Canoeing and Kayaking
CUR	Curling
CYC	Cycling
DIV	Diving
EQU	Equestrian Events
FEN	Fencing
FKL	Freestyle Skiing
FSK	Figure Skating
FTB	Football, Association (Soccer)
GYM	Gymnastics
HAN	Team Handball
HOK	Hockey (Field)
ICH	Ice Hockey
JUD	Judo
LAX	Lacrosse
LUG	Luge
MOP	Modern Pentathlon
MSP	Military Ski Patrol

MTB	Motorboating
NSK	Nordic Skiing
POL	Polo
ROW	Rowing and Sculling
RUG	Rugby Football
SAI	Sailing
SHO	Shooting
SKE	Skeleton
SSK	Speed Skating (Long-track)
STK	Short-Track Speed Skating
SWI	Swimming
TEN	Tennis (Lawn Tennis)
TKW	Taekwondo
TMP	Trampoline
TOW	Tug-of-War
TRI	Triathlon
TTN	Table Tennis
VOL	Volleyball
WAP	Water Polo
WLT	Weightlifting
WRE	Wrestling
YAC	Yachting

THREE-LETTER NATIONAL ABBREVIATIONS

AFG	Afghanistan
AHO	Netherlands Antilles
ALB	Albania
ALG	Algeria
AND	Andorra
ANG	Angola
ANL	Antilles (West Indies)
ANT	Antigua and Barbuda
ARG	Argentina
ARM	Armenia
ARU	Aruba
ASA	American Samoa

AUS	Australia
AUT	Austria
AZE	Azerbaijan
BAH	The Bahamas
BAN	Bangladesh
BAR	Barbados
BDI	Burundi
BEL	Belgium
BEN	Benin
BER	Bermuda
BHU	Bhutan
BIH	Bosnia-Herzegovina
BIR	Burma
BIZ	Belize
BLR	Belarus
BOH	Bohemia
BOL	Bolivia
BOT	Botswana
BRA	Brazil
BRN	Bahrain
BRU	Brunei
BUL	Bulgaria
BUR	Burkina Faso
CAF	Central African Republic
CAM	Cambodia (Kampuchea)
CAN	Canada
CAY	Cayman Islands
CEY	Ceylon
CGO	Congo
CHA	Chad
CHI	Chile
CHN	China
CIS	Commonwealth of Independent States (aka EUN)
CIV	Côte d'Ivoire (Ivory Coast)
CMR	Cameroon
COD	Democratic Republic of the Congo
COK	Cook Islands
COL	Colombia

COM	Comoros Islands
CPV	Cape Verde
CRC	Costa Rica
CRO	Croatia
CUB	Cuba
CYP	Cyprus
CZE	Czech Republic
DEN	Denmark
DJI	Djibouti
DMA	Dominica
DOM	Dominican Republic
ECU	Ecuador
EGY	Egypt
ERI	Eritrea
ESA	El Salvador
ESP	Spain
EST	Estonia
ETH	Ethiopia
EUN	Unified Team (aka CIS)
FIJ	Fiji
FIN	Finland
FRA	France
FRG	Federal Republic of Germany
FSM	Federated States of Micronesia
GAB	Gabon
GAM	The Gambia
GBR	Great Britain
GBS	Guinea-Bissau
GDR	German Democratic Republic
GEO	Georgia
GEQ	Equatorial Guinea
GER	Germany
GHA	Ghana
GRE	Greece
GRN	Grenada
GUA	Guatemala
GUI	Guinea
GUM	Guam

GUY	Guyana
HAI	Haiti
HKG	Hong Kong
HON	Honduras
HUN	Hungary
INA	Indonesia
IND	India
IOP	Independent Olympic Participant
IRI	Iran
IRL	Ireland
IRQ	Iraq
ISL	Iceland
ISR	Israel
ISV	U.S. Virgin Islands
ITA	Italy
IVB	British Virgin Islands
JAM	Jamaica
JOR	Jordan
JPN	Japan
KAZ	Kazakstan
KEN	Kenya
KGZ	Kyrgyzstan
KIR	Kiribati
KOR	Korea (South)
KSA	Saudi Arabia
KUW	Kuwait
LAO	Laos
LAT	Latvia
LBA	Libya
LBR	Liberia
LCA	Saint Lucia
LES	Lesotho
LIB	Lebanon
LIE	Liechtenstein
LTU	Lithuania
LUX	Luxembourg
MAD	Madagascar
MAR	Morocco

MAS	Malaysia
MAW	Malawi
MDV	Maldives
MEX	Mexico
MGL	Mongolia
MKD	Macedonia
MLD	Moldova
MLI	Mali
MLT	Malta
MON	Monaco
MOZ	Mozambique
MRI	Mauritius
MTN	Mauritania
MYA	Myanmar
NAM	Namibia
NCA	Nicaragua
NED	The Netherlands
NEP	Nepal
NFL	Newfoundland
NGR	Nigeria
NIG	Niger
NOR	Norway
NRU	Nauru
NZL	New Zealand
OMA	Oman
PAK	Pakistan
PAN	Panama
PAR	Paraguay
PER	Peru
PHI	The Philippines
PLE	Palestine
PLW	Palau
PNG	Papua-New Guinea
POL	Poland
POR	Portugal
PRK	Democratic People's Republic of Korea (North)
PUR	Puerto Rico
QAT	Qatar

RHO	Rhodesia
ROM	Romania
RSA	South Africa (current abbreviation)
RUS	Russia
RWA	Rwanda
SAF	South Africa (former abbreviation)
SAM	Samoa (Western)
SCG	Serbia and Montenegro
SCO	Scotland
SEN	Senegal
SEY	Seychelles
SIN	Singapore
SKN	St. Kitts and Nevis
SLE	Sierra Leone
SLO	Slovenia
SMR	San Marino
SMY	Smyrna
SOL	Solomon Islands
SOM	Somalia
SRI	Sri Lanka
STP	São Tomé and Princípe
SUD	The Sudan
SUI	Switzerland
SUR	Suriname
SVK	Slovakia
SWE	Sweden
SWZ	Swaziland
SYR	Syria
TAN	Tanzania
TCH	Czechoslovakia
TGA	Tonga
THA	Thailand
TJK	Tajikistan
TKM	Turkmenistan
TLS	Timor l'Este (East Timor)
TOG	Togo
TPE	Chinese Taipei
TRI	Trinidad and Tobago

TSL	Thessalonika (Thessalonikí)
TUN	Tunisia
TUR	Turkey
UAE	United Arab Emirates
UAR	United Arab Republic
UGA	Uganda
UKR	The Ukraine
URS	Soviet Union
URU	Uruguay
USA	United States
UZB	Uzbekistan
VAN	Vanuatu
VEN	Venezuela
VIE	Vietnam
VIN	St. Vincent and the Grenadines
VOL	Upper Volta
YAR	Yemen Arab Republic (North)
YEM	Yemen
YMD	Yemen Democratic Republic (South)
YUG	Yugoslavia
ZAI	Zaire
ZAM	Zambia
ZIM	Zimbabwe

OTHER ABBREVIATIONS USED

AAU	Amateur Athletic Union (USA)
ACNO	Association des Comités Nationaux Olympiques
ACNOA	Association des Comités Nationaux Olympiques d'Afrique
ACNOE	Association des Comités Nationaux Olympiques d'Europe
ACOM	Association of Collectors of Olympic Memorabilia
AGFIS	Association Générale des Fédérations Internationales de Sports
AIBA	Association Internationale de Boxe Amateur
AIOWF	Association of the International Olympic Winter Sports Federations

ANOC	Association of National Olympic Committees
ARISF	Association of the IOC-Recognized International Sports Federations
ASOIF	Association of Summer Olympic International Federations
CAS	Court of Arbitration for Sport
CMAS	Confédération Mondiale des Activités Subaquatiques
CMSB	Confédération Mondiale des Sports de Boules
COJO	Comité d'Organisateur des Jeux Olympiques
EOC	European Olympic Committees
FEI	Fédération Équestre Internationale
FIA	Fédération Internationale de l'Automobile
FIBA	Fédération Internationale de Basketball Amateur
FIBT	Fédération Internationale de Bobsleigh et de Tobogganing
FIC	Fédération Internationale de Canoë
FIDE	Fédération Internationale des Échecs
FIE	Fédération Internationale d'Éscrime
FIFA	Fédération Internationale de Football Association
FIG	Fédération Internationale de Gymnastique
FIH	Fédération Internationale de Hockey
FIL	Fédération Internationale de Luge de Course
FILA	Fédération Internationale de Luttes Associées (formerly Fédération Internationale de Luttes Amateurs)
FIM	Fédération Internationale de Motocyclisme
FIMO	International Olympic Memorabilia Federation
FINA	Fédération Internationale de Natation Amateur
FINO	Fédération Internationale de Numismatic Olympique
FIPO	Fédération Internationale de Philately Olympique
FIPV	Fédération Internationale de Pelote Basque
FIQ	Fédération Internationale de Quilleurs
FIRS	Fédération Internationale de Roller Sports
FIS	Fédération Internationale de Ski
FISA	Fédération Internationale des Sociétés d'Aviron
FIT	Fédération Internationale de Trampoline
FITA	Fédération Internationale de Tir à l'Arc
FIVB	Fédération Internationale de Volleyball
FMK	Fédération Mondiale de Karaté

FSFI	Fédération Sportive Feminine Internationale
GAISF	General Association of International Sports Federations
GANEFO	Games of the New Emerging Forces
IAAF	International Amateur Athletic Federation
IBA	International Baseball Association
IBF	International Badminton Federation
IBF	International Boxing Federation
IBU	International Biathlon Union
ICFP	International Committee for Fair Play
IDSF	International Dance Sport Federation
IF(s)	International Federation(s)
IFBB	International Federation of Body Builders
IFNA	International Federation of Netball Associations
IHF	International Handball Federation
IIHF	International Ice Hockey Federation
IJF	International Judo Federation
IKF	International Korfball Federation
IOA	Independent Olympic Athletes
IOA	International Olympic Academy
IOC	International Olympic Committee
IOF	International Orienteering Federation
IOP	Individual Olympic Participants
IOTC	International Olympic Truce Centre
IOTF	International Olympic Truce Foundation
IPC	Institut Pierre de Coubertin
IPC	International Paralympic Committee
IRB	Independent Review Board
ISA	International Surfing Association
ISAF	International Sailing Federation
ISF	International Softball Federation
ISOH	International Society of Olympic Historians
ISSF	International Shooting Sport Federation
ISU	International Skating Union
ITF	International Tennis Federation
ITTF	International Table Tennis Federation
ITU	International Triathlon Union
IWF	International Weightlifting Federation

IWSF	International Water Ski Federation
IWUF	International Wushu Federation
NBA	National Basketball Association (USA)
NGB	National Governing Body
NGO	Non-Governmental Organization
NOA(s)	National Olympic Academy(ies)
NOA(s)	National Olympian Associations
NOC(s)	National Olympic Committee(s)
OCA	Olympic Council of Asia
OCOG	Organizing Committee of the Olympic Games
ODECABE	Organización Deportiva Centroamericana y del Caribe
ODEPA	Organización Deportiva Panamericana
ODESUR	Organización Deportiva Sudamericana
OGKS	Olympic Games Knowledge Services
ONOC	Oceania National Olympic Committees
OPNMC	Olympic Philately, Numismatic, and Memorabilia Commission
PASO	Pan American Sports Organization
SANOC	South African National Olympic Committee
SCSA	Supreme Council for Sport in Africa
SIRC	Sport Information Resource Centre
TOP	The Olympic Programme
TWIF	Tug-of-War International Federation
UCI	Union Cycliste Internationale
UIAA	Union Internationale des Associations d'Alpinisme
UIM	Union Internationale Motonautique
UIPMB	Union Internationale de Pentathlon Moderne et Biathlon
UN	United Nations
USOC	United States Olympic Committee
WADA	World Anti-Doping Agency
WBA	World Boxing Association
WBF	World Bridge Federation
WCBS	World Confederation of Billiards Sports
WCF	World Curling Federation
WOA	World Olympians Association
WSF	World Squash Federation
WTF	The World Taekwondo Federation
YMCA	Young Men's Christian Association

Chronology of the Olympic Movement

12th century BCE   Classics scholars consider that the ancient Olympic Games may have been held as early as this century, although no definite evidence of the competitions exists until 776 BCE.

776 BCE   First recorded Ancient Olympiad celebrated in Olympia on the Peloponnesus Peninsula in Ancient Greece. The Olympic Games initially consist of a single race of about 190 meters in length, termed a *stadion* race. The first winner is Coroebus, a cook from the city-state of Elis.

582 BCE   The first Pythian Games are held at Delphi in Ancient Greece.

582 (?581) BCE   The first Isthmian Games are held at the Isthmus of Corinth in Ancient Greece.

573 BCE   The first Nemean Games are held at Nemea in Ancient Greece.

393 AD   The ancient Olympic Games end after 12 centuries when they are prohibited by the imperial decree of Roman Emperor Theodosius I.

1612–1642   Robert Dover's Games, an early attempt at revival often called the Cotswold Olimpick Games, are held annually in the Cotswolds (England) on Thursday and Friday of Whitsun Week. They stop shortly after Dover's death in 1641 but are revived during the reign of King Charles II in the 1660s.

1850   22 October: The Much Wenlock Olympian Games, the brainchild of British sports enthusiast Dr. William Penny Brookes (1809–1895), are held for the first time in Much Wenlock, England, a small town in rural Shropshire. The Much Wenlock "Olympics" are a major influence on Pierre de Coubertin, who visits them in 1889.

1859   15 November: The first Zappas Olympic Games, an early attempt at revival of the Olympics, are held in Athens. The Games were initiated and financed by a wealthy grain dealer, Evangelis Zappas (1800–1865).

1863   1 January: Pierre Frédy, the Baron de Coubertin, is born in Paris, France, to Charles Louis Frédy, the Baron de Coubertin, and the former Agathe Marie Marcelle Gabrielle de Grisenoy de Mirville.

1870   15 November: The second Zappas Olympic Games are held in Athens. They are considered the most successful of the Zappas Olympics.

1875   18 May: The third Zappas Olympic Games are held in Athens.

1889   18 May: The fourth Zappas Olympic Games are held in Athens.

1891 The first Panhellenic Gymnastic Society Games, modeled after the Zappas Olympics, are held in Athens.

1892   25 November: Meeting of sports dignitaries at the Sorbonne celebrating the fifth anniversary of the Union des Sociétés Françaises de Sports Athlétiques (USFSA), at which Coubertin first broached the idea of the revival of the Olympic Games. His speech ended with the now famous summons, "Let us export rowers, runners, and fencers; there is the free trade of the future, and on the day when it is introduced within the walls of old Europe the cause of peace will have received a new and mighty stay. This is enough to encourage your servant to dream now about the second part of his program; he hopes that you will help him as you have helped him hitherto, and that with you he will be able to continue and complete, on a basis suited to the conditions of modern life, this grandiose and salutary task, the restoration of the Olympic Games."

1893 The second Panhellenic Gymnastic Society Games, modeled after the Zappas Olympics, are held in Athens.

1894   16–24 June: The Paris International Athletic Congress is organized by Coubertin at the Palais de la Sorbonne in Paris. Although it was purported to be a congress with amateurism as its main theme, the program lists 10 points to be discussed, the last three of which concern the reestablishment of the Olympic Games. This is later regarded as the 1st

Olympic Congress. **23 June:** The International Olympic Committee (IOC) is formed at the end of the Sorbonne Congress and consists mostly of sports dignitaries who had attended the congress; Demetrios Vikelas of Greece elected as the first president of the International Olympic Committee at the end of the 1st session of the IOC.

1896 6–15 April: Athens, Greece—Celebration of the Games of the Ist Olympiad of the modern era. **10 April:** Baron Pierre de Coubertin of France elected as the second president of the International Olympic Committee at the 2nd session of the IOC.

1897 23–31 July: Le Havre, France—2nd Olympic Congress celebrated at the Town Hall of Le Havre with "Sports Hygiene and Pedagogy" as the theme.

1900 20 May–28 October: Paris, France—Celebration of the Games of the IInd Olympiad.

1904 1 July–23 November: St. Louis, Missouri, USA—Celebration of the Games of the IIIrd Olympiad.

1905 9–14 June: Brussels, Belgium—3rd Olympic Congress celebrated at the Palais des Académies with "Sport and Physical Education" as the theme.

1906 22 April–2 May: Athens, Greece—Intercalated Olympic Games are held in Athens during the interim between the celebrations of the Olympiad. No longer officially recognized by the IOC, they were, nonetheless, the best Olympic Games to date and may have helped save the Olympic Games after debacles of 1900 and 1904. **23–25 May:** Paris, France—4th Olympic Congress celebrated at the Comédie Française et Touring Club with "Art, Literature, and Sport" as the theme.

1908 27 April–31 October: London, England—Celebration of the Games of the IVth Olympiad.

1912 5 May–27 July: Stockholm, Sweden—Celebration of the Games of the Vth Olympiad.

1913 7–11 May: Lausanne, Switzerland—5th Olympic Congress celebrated at the Palais de l'Université with "Sports Psychology and Physiology" as the theme.

1914   15–23 June: Paris, France—6th Olympic Congress celebrated at the Palais de la Sorbonne with "Olympic Regulations" as the theme.

1915–1917   December (1915)–February (1917): Baron Godefroy de Blonay of Switzerland is appointed interim IOC president by Coubertin, who enlists to help the French war effort. Coubertin felt that the IOC should not be headed by a soldier.

1916   Summer: The Games of the VIth Olympiad, scheduled to be held in Berlin, Germany, are canceled due to World War I.

1917   February: Baron Pierre de Coubertin resumes his post as president of the International Olympic Committee.

1920   23 April–12 September: Antwerp, Belgium—Celebration of the Games of the VIIth Olympiad.

1921   2–7 June: Lausanne, Switzerland—7th Olympic Congress celebrated at the Casino de Montbenon with "Olympic Regulations" as the theme.

1924   25 January–4 February: Chamonix, France—Celebration of the "Semaine internationale des sports d'hiver" (International Winter Sports Week), which was later designated retroactively as the 1st Olympic Winter Games. **4 May–27 July:** Paris, France—Celebration of the Games of the VIIIth Olympiad.

1925   28 May: Count Henri de Baillet-Latour of Belgium elected as the third president of the International Olympic Committee at the 24th session of the IOC in Prague. **29 May–4 June:** Prague, Czechoslovakia—8th Olympic Congress celebrated at the Prague Town Hall with "Sports Pedagogy and Olympic Regulations" as the theme. The congress is notable for Coubertin's retirement as IOC president.

1928   11–19 Feburary: St. Moritz, Switzerland—Celebration of the 2nd Olympic Winter Games. **17 May–12 August:** Amsterdam, the Netherlands—Celebration of the Games of the IXth Olympiad.

1930   25–30 May: Berlin, Germany—9th Olympic Congress celebrated at the Aula of the Friedrich Wilhelm University with "Olympic Regulations" as the theme.

1932 **4–15 February:** Lake Placid, New York, USA—Celebration of the 3rd Olympic Winter Games. **30 July–14 August:** Los Angeles, California, USA—Celebration of the Games of the Xth Olympiad.

1935 **15 September:** At a rally in Nuremburg, Hitler announces the enactment of the Nuremburg Laws, stripping Jews of their German citizenship and their rights under German law. This gives new impetus to consideration to boycott the 1936 Olympics, both to be based in Germany.

1936 **6–16 February:** Garmisch-Partenkirchen, Germany— Celebration of the 4th Olympic Winter Games. **7 March:** Hitler orders three battalions of the German army into the Rhineland, violating the Treaty of Versailles. In response, France considers the possibility of a boycott of the 1936 Olympics. **1–16 August:** Berlin, Germany—Celebration of the Games of the XIth Olympiad. Despite calls for a boycott from many nations, almost all IOC member nations participate at Berlin.

1937 **2 September:** Pierre de Coubertin dies while walking through Lagrange Park in Geneva, Switzerland.

1938 **26 March:** At a ceremony in ancient Olympia, the heart of Pierre de Coubertin, which had been removed from his body shortly after his death, is placed for perpetuity in a marble stele at the base of the Kronos Hill, near the ancient Olympic stadium.

1940 **Winter:** The 5th Olympic Winter Games are canceled due to World War II. The Games were originally awarded to Sapporo, Japan, which withdrew on 16 July 1938. They were reassigned to St. Moritz, Switzerland, which withdrew as host on 9 June 1939. The Games were then reassigned to Garmisch-Partenkirchen, Germany. **Summer:** The Games of the XIIth Olympiad, originally scheduled to be held in Tokyo, Japan, and later (after the withdrawal of Tokyo on 16 July 1938) awarded to Helsinki, Finland (awarded 3 September 1938), are canceled due to World War II.

1942 **6 January:** IOC president Count Baillet-Latour dies. The International Olympic Committee presidency will remain vacant during the remainder of World War II, although Sweden's J. Sigfrid Edström assumes the position of de facto president.

1944   Winter: The 5th Olympic Winter Games, tentatively scheduled for Cortina d'Ampezzo, Italy, are canceled due to World War II. **Summer:** The Games of the XIIIth Olympiad, originally scheduled to be held in London, England, are canceled due to World War II.

1946   4 September: J[ohannes] Sigfrid Edström of Sweden elected as the fourth president of the International Olympic Committee at the 40th session of the IOC in Lausanne.

1948   30 January–8 February: St. Moritz, Switzerland—Celebration of the 5th Olympic Winter Games. **29 July–14 August:** London, England—Celebration of the Games of the XIVth Olympiad.

1952   14–25 February: Oslo, Norway—Celebration of the 6th Olympic Winter Games. **16 July:** Avery Brundage of the United States elected as the fifth president of the International Olympic Committee at the 48th session of the IOC in Helsinki. **19 July–3 August:** Helsinki, Finland—Celebration of the Games of the XVth Olympiad.

1956   26 January–5 February: Cortina d'Ampezzo, Italy—Celebration of the 7th Olympic Winter Games. **10–17 June:** Stockholm, Sweden—Celebration of the Equestrian Games of the XVIth Olympiad. The Equestrian Games were made necessary because of Australia's highly restrictive animal quarantine restrictions. **29 October:** Israel invades the Sinai Peninsula, a part of Egypt. Egypt, Lebanon, and Iraq withdraw from the Melbourne Olympics in protest. **4 November:** Soviet troops enter Budapest, Hungary, in an effort to stop rising political insurgency. This eventually leads to boycotts of the Melbourne Olympics by Spain, Switzerland, and the Netherlands, protesting the Soviet action. **22 November–8 December:** Melbourne, Victoria, Australia—Celebration of the Games of the XVIth Olympiad. In an attempt to solve the problem of the two Germanys, a unified German team representing both East (GDR) and West (FRG) Germany competes at the International Olympic Committee's behest.

1960   18–28 February: Squaw Valley, California, USA—Celebration of the 8th Olympic Winter Games. **25 August–11 September:**   Rome, Italy—Celebration of the Games of the XVIIth Olympiad.

1963   November: GANEFO (the Games of the New Emerging Forces) are held in Djakarta, Indonesia. GANEFO refuses to admit athletes from Israel or Taiwan (Chinese Taipei), and the International Federations for track and field athletics, swimming, and shooting ban all athletes who competed at GANEFO from competing at the Tokyo Olympics in 1964. The IOC did not support this as a blanket ban on all athletes competing at GANEFO.

1964   29 January–9 February: Innsbruck, Austria—Celebration of the 9th Olympic Winter Games. **10–24 October:** Tokyo, Japan—Celebration of the Games of the XVIIIth Olympiad.

1968   6–18 February: Grenoble, France—Celebration of the 10th Olympic Winter Games. **2 October:** Student protests against the Mexico City Olympics come to a head in the capital city. On this day, student protesters hold a rally in the Plaza of Three Cultures, and government troops open fire, killing almost 300, with thousands injured and imprisoned. **12–27 October:** Mexico City, Mexico—Celebration of the Games of the XIXth Olympiad.

1972   3–13 February: Sapporo, Japan—Celebration of the 11th Olympic Winter Games. **21 August:** Sir Michael Morris, the Lord Killanin of Dublin and Spiddal (Ireland) elected as the sixth president of the International Olympic Committee at the 73rd session of the International Olympic Committee in Munich. **26 August–11 September:** Munich, Federal Republic of Germany—Celebration of the Games of the XXth Olympiad. **5 September:** Terrorists representing the Black September group forever change the Olympic Games when they take hostage and then savagely murder 11 members of the Israeli Olympic team. The deaths occur at the Fürstenfeldbruck airport on the outskirts of Munich.

1973   30 September–4 October: Varna, Bulgaria—10th Olympic Congress, the first in 43 years, celebrated at the Sports Palace with the theme of "Sport for a World of Peace: The Olympic Movement and Its Future."

1976   4–15 February: Innsbruck, Austria—Celebration of the 12th Olympic Winter Games. **17 July–1 August:** Montreal, Quebec, Canada—Celebration of the Games of the XXIst Olympiad. **25–26 November:** The two-China question is finally resolved. On 25 November 1979, mainland China, the People's Republic of China, is recognized officially by the IOC. The next day, the Chinese Taipei Olympic Committee is given official International Olympic Committee recognition under that name, agreeing to compete using only that name, and not as the Republic of China. This clears the way for both Chinese Olympic Committees to compete together at the Olympic Games. **25–27 December:** The Soviet Union invades Afghanistan, precipitating an eventual boycott of the Moscow Olympics.

1980 4 January: In retaliation for the Soviet invasion of Afghanistan, U.S. president Jimmy Carter announces, for the first time, the possibility of a U.S. boycott of the 1980 Moscow Olympics. **13–14 February:** Lake Placid, New York, USA—Celebration of the 13th Olympic Winter Games. **16 July:** Juan Antonio Samaranch [Torello] elected as the seventh president of the International Olympic Committee at the 83rd session of the IOC in Moscow. **19 July–3 August:** Moscow, USSR—Celebration of the Games of the XXIInd Olympiad. Approximately 60 countries boycott the Olympics in protest of the Soviet Union's invasion of Afghanistan.

1981 23–28 September: Baden-Baden, Federal Republic of Germany—11th Olympic Congress celebrated at Baden-Baden's Kurhaus with "United By and For Sport" as the theme, with three subthemes: 1) The Future of the Olympic Games; 2) International Cooperation; and 3) The Future Olympic Movement.

1984 8–19 February: Sarajevo, Yugoslavia—Celebration of the 14th Olympic Winter Games. **8 May:** The Soviet Union announces it will not attend the Los Angeles Olympic Games, citing concerns over the safety of its athletes in Los Angeles, and because of "anti-Communist activities" in the United States. **28 July–12 August:** Los Angeles, California, USA—Celebration of the Games of the XXIIIrd Olympiad. Fourteen invited countries join the Soviet-inspired boycott. Of the Soviet-bloc nations, only Romania defies the boycott and competes.

1988 13–28 February: Calgary, Alberta, Canada—Celebration of the 15th Olympic Winter Games. **17 September–5 October:** Seoul, Republic of Korea—Celebration of the Games of the XXIVth Olympiad. A small boycott of six nations occurs, because certain countries support only North Korea (People's Democratic Republic of Korea) and do not recognize South Korea (Republic of Korea), refusing to compete in that nation.

1992   8–23 February: Albertville, France—Celebration of the 16th Olympic Winter Games. **25 July–9 August:** Barcelona, Spain—Celebration of the Games of the XXVth Olympiad. For the first Olympics since 1960, no politically inspired boycott or other serious political problems mar the Games.

1994   12–27 February: Lillehammer, Norway—Celebration of the 17th Olympic Winter Games. **23 June:** The 100th Anniversary of the founding of the modern Olympic Games is celebrated with a ceremony at the Sorbonne, where Coubertin held the 1st Olympic Congress that reestablished the modern Olympic Games. **29 August–3 September:** Paris, France—12th Olympic Congress celebrated with four main themes: 1) The Olympic Movement's Contribution to Modern Society; 2) The Contemporary Athlete; 3) Sport in Its Social Context; and 4) Sport and the Media. The 12th Olympic Congress is held in celebration of the 100th anniversary of the Olympic movement.

1996   6 April: The 100th Anniversary of the opening of the Games of the Ist Olympiad, the first Olympic Games of the modern era. **19 July–4 August:** Atlanta, Georgia, USA—Celebration of the Games of the XXVIth Olympiad, the Centennial Olympic Games. **27 July:** During the Atlanta Olympics, a bomb explodes in Centennial Olympic Park, killing two people and injuring many more. In late 2004, Eric Rudolph was caught and found in the mountains of North Carolina. He later admitted his guilt in the bombing, as well as in the bombings of several abortion clinics.

1998   7–22 February: Nagano, Japan—Celebration of the 18th Olympic Winter Games. **24 November:** Salt Lake City television station KTVX reveals that the Salt Lake City Bid Committee had been paying tuition and expenses for the daughter of an IOC member. The Olympic bribery scandal begins.

1999   8 February: First report related to the Olympic bribery scandal released by the Board of Ethics of the Salt Lake Organizing Committee for the Olympic Winter Games of 2002. **1 March:** Release of the Mitchell Commission Report. **17–18 March:** Extraordinary session of the IOC relating to the Olympic bribery scandal. The Pound Commission Report was released during this meeting. At the end of the session, 10 IOC members had either resigned or been expelled relating to findings of the various commissions. **11–12 December:** 110th IOC session in Lausanne, Switzerland, at which the 50 recommendations of the IOC 2000 Commission were discussed and, eventually, implemented in full.

2000   16 September–1 October: Sydney, New South Wales, Australia—Celebration of the Games of the XXVIIth Olympiad.

2001   16 July: Dr. Jacques Rogge elected as the eighth president of the International Olympic Committee at the 112th IOC session in Moscow.

2002   8–24 February: Salt Lake City, Utah, USA—Celebration of the 19th Olympic Winter Games.

2004   13–29 August: Athens, Greece—Celebration of the Games of the XXVIIIth Olympiad.

2005   July: Selection of London as the host city for the Games of the XXXth Olympiad (2012); other final candidate cities: Madrid, Moscow, New York, Paris.

2006   11–26 February: Torino (Turin), Italy—Scheduled Celebration of the 20th Olympic Winter Games.

2008   8–24 August: Beijing, China—Scheduled celebration of the Games of the XXIXth Olympiad.

2010   12–28 February: Vancouver, British Columbia, Canada—Scheduled celebration of the 21st Olympic Winter Games.

Chronology of the Olympic Games and Olympic Winter Games

The Games of the Ist Olympiad (1896) The Games of the Ist Olympiad were held in Athens, Greece, from 6 through 15 April 1896. (At the time, Greece recognized the Julian calendar, not the Gregorian calendar used by much of the world then and now used almost universally. In Greek terms, the Games were held from 25 March to 3 April 1896.) London was initially to have been the site, but the Sorbonne Congress of 1894 elected Athens as the host city, by acclamation. The only other city seriously considered was Paris.

Fourteen nations competed at Athens, with approximately 235–255 athletes—it cannot be determined with certainty. No women competed. The first Olympic champion of the modern era was James Connolly of the United States who won the hop, step, and jump in track and field athletics (now called the triple jump). Greece won the most medals with 50, while the United States won the most gold medals with 11, including most of the track and field athletics events. The highlight of the Games was the marathon victory of Spyridon Louis of Greece. When he neared the stadium, messengers came into the ancient stadium and cried out, "Hellas! Hellas! (A Greek! A Greek!)," sending the crowd into a frenzy. The Olympic pride based on millennia of Olympic tradition was then realized by the home crowd, which had been rather disappointed by the results of the Greek athletes. Loues won the race and became a hero, offered gifts and riches by many different Greek merchants. But he asked only for a cart to help him carry and sell his water, and he returned to being a shepherd in his small town of Amarousi.

Many people wanted the Games to remain permanently in Athens, and in 1896 the American athletes wrote a letter to the *New York Times* asking that this be done. But Coubertin insisted that the Games be spread to various countries to emphasize the international flavor of the Olympic Games.

The Games of the IInd Olympiad (1900) The Games of the IInd Olympiad were held in Paris, France, from 20 May through 28 October 1900. They were a disaster. If one had to nominate the "worst modern Olympics" ever, 1900 and 1904 would surely lead the voting.

In 1900, Paris hosted a great World's Fair, the Exposition Universelle Internationale de 1900 à Paris. Coubertin made plans to hold the Olympics as part of the fair and planned to organize the events. But the organizers of the fair relegated Coubertin to a relatively minor administrative position and took over the organization of the sporting events connected with the fair. Most of the events we today consider "Olympic" were not even labeled as such in 1900, often being called the "Championnats d'Exposition," or "Championnats Internationaux." Years later, many athletes did not know that they had competed in the Olympic Games, believing that their sport had been only a part of the World's Fair. Only the athletics (track and field) events were really publicized in the media as being part of the Olympics.

The Games were stretched out over five months (May–October) and formal opening and closing ceremonies were not held. It is difficult to know, because of the confusion over titles, and the many, many events held at the fair, what events should actually be considered "Olympic" and which should not. The IOC had no real control over this, and thus one sees various listings. Many unusual sports and events were contested, such as motorboating, balloon racing, underwater swimming, and an obstacle swimming race. So the number of nations and athletes competing is completely conjectural.

Women made their Olympic début, with the first known competitors being a yachtswoman, Countess Hélène de Pourtalès of Portugal, and two croquet players listed only as Mme. Brohy and Mlle. Ohnier. Charlotte Cooper (GBR) won the first championships by a woman, in tennis singles and mixed doubles. Margaret Abbott (USA) won the "Olympic" golf championship in early October. Neither of those two sports was labeled as Olympic by the organizers. Years later, Abbott's relatives did not know for certain that the title she won that day had been for the Olympic championship. In many sports, medals were not awarded. Most of the listed prizes were cups and other similar trophies. In several sports, notably fencing and shooting, professional events were held and yet were considered later by the IOC to be of "Olympic" stature.

The Games of the IIIrd Olympiad (1904)   The Games of the IIIrd Olympiad were held in St. Louis, Missouri, USA, from 1 July through 23 November 1904. After the debacle of 1900, Coubertin was hoping for better from the United States in 1904, but did not see his hopes realized. The Games were awarded to Chicago. However, St. Louis was to host a major world's fair in 1904, the Louisiana Purchase International Exposition, and the St. Louis organizers wanted the Olympics as part of the fair. They threatened to hold competing Olympics if Chicago did not allow them to have the Games. Chicago eventually acquiesced.

The Games were very similar to 1900—they lasted almost five months, many of the events were not labeled as Olympic but only as championships of the fair, it is difficult to know which sports and events were definitely on the Olympic program, a number of unusual sports and events saw their way to the program, and the Games were mostly an afterthought to the fair. Again, the number of competing nations and athletes cannot be determined with any accuracy.

Coubertin vowed after 1904 that he would never again hold the Olympics as a sideshow to a fair. Notably, he did not even attend the Olympics in 1904, sending two IOC delegates from Hungary and Germany in his place. He was appalled when he heard of the happenings in St. Louis, but never more so than when he heard about the "Anthropological Days." The fair organizers included several days of "Olympic" competitions among several so-called primitive tribes that were being exhibited at the exposition. Among these were Pygmies, Patagonians, Filipinos, Native American Indian tribes, Japanese Ainus, and certain Asian tribes. Events included throwing bolos, mud fighting, and climbing a greased pole.

Again, only the athletics (track and field) received any great publicity as being an Olympic sport. These events were virtually an American club championship, and, in fact, Albert Spalding donated a trophy to be awarded to the American club scoring the most points in the event. Though surpassed by athletes in other sports, the American foursome of Archie Hahn, Harry Hillman, James Lightbody, and Ray Ewry won three gold medals each in track and field and received the bulk of the media attention. In other sports, American dominance was almost as complete, owing to the fact that only a few other countries attended the Games, and very few foreign athletes competed.

Two black Tswana tribesmen who were part of the Boer War exhibition at the fair, Len Tau and Jan Mashiani, also competed in the marathon. Ironically, they are considered to be the first Olympic competitors from South Africa.

The Intercalated Olympic Games of 1906   The Olympic Games of 1906 were held in Athens, Greece, from 22 April through 2 May 1906. Twenty nations attended with 842 athletes competing (836 men and 6 women). (Fifteen Danish women also gave a gymnastics exhibition in 1906.)

Today, the IOC and some historians do not consider the 1906 Intercalated Olympics to be "true" Olympic Games. By doing so, they neglect the Games that may have helped save the Olympic movement. After the debacles of 1900 and 1904, the Olympics were in desperate straits. The Greeks had wanted to host more Olympics, and they proposed holding "interim" Olympics, every four years in the even year between the Olympics. The first of these was scheduled in 1906. The Greeks later scheduled interim Olympics for 1910 and 1914, but political and economic events in Greece prevented those from being held.

The Games of 1906 were not of the caliber of many Olympics of later years, but they were the best Olympics to that date. Again, many of the facilities were not of the highest quality. However, as in 1896, the Greeks approached their responsibility with enthusiasm, and the most international field to date competed in these Olympics. A true opening ceremony was conducted for the first time, with the athletes marching with their teams following a flag bearer from their own country.

The newspapers considered these Games to be the Olympics and labeled them as such. Coubertin, at first opposed to the idea, subsequently embraced them as Olympics when he saw that the Greeks were organizing the best "Olympics" of the modern era. The IOC made no official determination of the status of these events at first, but in 1948 declared them not to be official based on the findings of the Brundage Commission. The Olympics of 1906 deserve that title much more so than do the farces that were 1900 and 1904. They resurrected the flagging Olympic movement.

The Games of the IVth Olympiad (1908)   The Games of the IVth Olympiad were held in London, England, from 27 April through 31 October 1908. Twenty-two nations attended with 2,024 athletes competing (1,980 men and 44 women). The Games were originally awarded to Rome, Italy, which was chosen over Berlin, Germany, at the 6th IOC session in London on 22 June 1904. Historically, it has usually been stated that the Italians relinquished the 1908 Olympics because of the 1906 explosion of Mt. Vesuvius, which erupted near Naples, and the Italians felt that they needed the money to rebuild the area around the volcano. However, it is now established that the Italians were preparing to give up their rights to the IVth Olympiad even before the explosion. London gladly accepted the chance to host the 1908 Olympics after the Italians told the IOC of their plans.

These Olympics were easily the best organized to date. They also had the most international flavor of any Olympics yet held. By now the Olympics were becoming "known" to the world, and athletes everywhere wanted to compete, and managed to find ways to do so. Still, the Games, though superbly run, are best known for multiple political arguments and other bickering that occurred.

The problems began at the opening ceremony. The Swedish and United States flags did not fly over the stadium, as the organizers stated that they could not find them. This so infuriated the Swedes that when a dispute arose over wrestling rules later in the Games, they threatened to withdraw from the competition. The Finns marched in the ceremony without a flag. Finland was a territory of Russia in 1908, but Russia allowed them to compete separately, provided they did so under the Russian flag. The Finns, in protest, marched under no flag. The United States later protested the officiating in multiple track and field athletics events.

Two of the best-known controversies involved the 400 meter race and the marathon. In the 400 meters, American John Carpenter won the initial running of the final, but was disqualified when it was ruled that he had run out of his lane in the final straight to impede Britain's Wyndham Halswelle. The other two Americans in the final, William Robbins and John Taylor, refused to run in the second final and Halswelle walked over to the gold medal. In the tug-of-war, the Americans pulled a team of London policeman in the first round and were easily defeated. But the Americans protested the footwear of the London constables, stating that they were specially prepared to give them better traction during the pull. The protest was disallowed.

The final controversy and the most memorable event of the 1908 Olympics was the marathon. The race was to start at Windsor Castle so that Queen Alexandra's grandchildren could watch the beginning. The distance from there to the finish line at the Shepherd's Bush stadium was 26 miles, 385 yards. This was the first time this distance was chosen for a marathon, and it later became the standard.

The leader for most of the second half of the race was Dorando Pietri, a candymaker from Capri, Italy. But when Pietri entered the stadium, he was totally exhausted. Like a drunken sailor, he staggered and fell several times before the finish line. He also turned in the wrong direction twice during the last lap. Officials, urged on by sympathetic fans, helped him to his feet and directed him to the finish line. He finished the race first and was declared the winner. A few hundred meters behind him finished Johnny Hayes of the United States. An immediate protest was lodged, and Pietri was disqualified, with Hayes winning the gold medal.

The Games of the Vth Olympiad (1912)   The Games of the Vth Olympiad were held in Stockholm, Sweden, from 5 May through 27 July 1912. After the problems and controversies of 1908, the pseudo-Olympics of 1900 and 1904, and the meager international participation of 1896 and 1906, Stockholm should be credited with the first truly modern Games of Olympic proportions. No other city was seriously considered as host for 1912, and Stockholm was elected by acclamation at the 10th IOC session in Berlin on 28 May 1909. Twenty-seven nations attended, with 2,381 athletes competing (2,328 men and 53 women).

The Games were marvelously organized. The only significant political problems concerned the entries of Finland and Bohemia. Both nations wished to compete as independent nations, but in 1912, Finland was a part of Russia, and Bohemia was a part of the Austro-Hungarian Empire. As in 1908, both were allowed to compete but were not allowed to use their own flags.

But probably more than any other Olympics, the 1912 Games belonged to one person, Jim Thorpe. Jim Thorpe was a Sac and Fox Indian from Oklahoma who had attended the Carlisle Indian School. In 1912, Thorpe decided to compete in the two new Olympic events testing the all-around abilities of the track and field athletes—the decathlon of 10 events, and pentathlon of five events. He won by enormous margins. When awarded his prizes by King Gustav V, the king reportedly said, "Sir, you are the greatest athlete in the world." Thorpe's reply was supposedly, "Thanks, King." But, in 1913, it was discovered that

Thorpe had played minor league professional baseball in 1909 and 1910, and he was stripped of his medals. Seventy years later, in 1982, the IOC finally relented and restored the medals to Thorpe's family — he had died in 1953.

Hannes Kolehmainen of Finland, the first of the great Flying Finn distance runners, also made his début at the 1912 Olympics. He won four medals: three gold in the 5,000 meters, 10,000 meters, and individual cross-country, and a silver in the team cross-country. When Kolehmainen won, the Russian flag was raised because of Finland's subjugation to the Russians at that time. "I would almost rather not have won, than see that flag up there," he said (Lord Killanin and John Rodda, eds., *The Olympic Games 1984*: *Los Angeles and Sarajevo* [Salem, N.H.: Michael Joseph, 1983, 77]).

One tragedy did occur at the 1912 Olympic Games when the Portuguese marathoner Francisco Lazaro collapsed during the race and died early the next morning. He was the first Olympic athlete to die during the competition. This has occurred only one other time, in 1960 when the Danish cyclist Knut Enemark Jensen died during the cycling road race.

The 1912 Olympics were also noteworthy for the first swimming events for women. Previously, women had competed at the Olympics to any degree only in tennis, with minor appearances in archery, golf, yachting, and croquet in 1900, 1904, and 1908. There were only two swim events for women in 1912, a 100 meter freestyle and a freestyle relay, as well as a high diving event, but they were important as they were the first truly "athletic" events in which women were allowed to compete at the Olympics. The list of events in which women compete would increase with each Olympiad.

The Games of the VIth Olympiad (1916)   The Games of the VIth Olympiad were originally awarded to Berlin, Germany, which was chosen at the 15th IOC session in Stockholm on 4 July 1912 over Budapest, Hungary. Other cities that expressed an interest to host the 1916 Olympics were Alexandria, Egypt; Amsterdam, the Netherlands; Brussels, Belgium; and Cleveland, Ohio, USA. Because of World War I, the Games were not celebrated.

The Games of the VIIth Olympiad (1920)   The Games of the VIIth Olympiad were held in Antwerp, Belgium, from 23 April through 12

September 1920. Other cities that had expressed an interest in hosting the 1920 Olympic Games were Amsterdam, the Netherlands; Atlanta, Georgia, USA; Budapest, Hungary; Cleveland, Ohio, USA; Havana, Cuba; and Philadelphia, Pennsylvania, USA. The offer from Lyon was seriously considered during World War I when Belgium was being ravaged by the effects of the war, but Antwerp was officially chosen at the 18th IOC session in Lausanne on 5 April 1919. However, 29 nations eventually attended the Games in Antwerp, with 2,663 athletes competing (2,586 men and 77 women).

The war was only over a year when the 1920 Olympics were finally awarded to war-ravaged Belgium. Coubertin decided that, although the war would have been over less than two years, the VIIth Olympiad should be celebrated as scheduled. Although the Games were decidedly austere, the Belgian people and organizing committee did an amazing job in preparing for the Games on such short notice.

The opening ceremonies were notable for the first use of the Olympic flag at the Olympics, the first time the Olympic oath was taken by a competitor (Victor Boin), and the first release of homing pigeons as a symbol of peace. Of the 29 countries competing, Germany, Austria, Hungary, and Bulgaria were missing—the IOC barred them because they were aggressor nations in World War I.

The Olympics were most notable for the début of Paavo Nurmi of Finland, probably the greatest distance runner ever. Nurmi competed in four events, losing only in the 5,000 meters. His countryman, Hannes Kolehmainen, returned eight years after his Stockholm victories in the 5,000 and 10,000 meters, and won the marathon. The shooting program contained 20 events, including 10 team events, allowing Willis Lee and Lloyd Spooner of the United States to win seven medals, and Carl Osburn (USA) to win six. Nedo Nadi (ITA) was also much decorated as he won five gold medals in fencing.

The Antwerp Olympics helped the world recover from the Great War. Coubertin summarized them in the Antwerp Town Hall when he addressed the IOC in the presence of King Albert of Belgium:

This is what the seventh Olympiad has brought us: general comprehension; the certainty of being henceforward understood by all. . . . These festivals . . . are above all festivals of human unity. In an incomparable synthesis the effort of muscles and of mind, mutual help and competition, lofty patriotism and intelligent cosmopolitanism, the personal interest in the champion and the abnegation of the team-member, are bound in a sheaf for a common task.

The 1st Olympic Winter Games (1924)   The 1st Olympic Winter Games were held in Chamonix, France, from 25 January through 4 February 1924. Sixteen nations attended with 291 athletes competing (278 men and 13 women).

In June 1922, the French Olympic Committee held a congress in which representatives of skiing, skating, and ice hockey were present. They arranged to hold an International Winter Sports Week in Chamonix in early 1924. The contests were not originally called the Olympic Games, but the opening speech, while not using the word Olympic in the title, did state that they were under the "high patronage of the International Olympic Committee." Their original official title was the "Semaine internationale des sports d'hiver" (International Winter Sports Week). On 27 May 1925, the IOC amended its charter to begin a cycle of Olympic Winter Games. The Chamonix events were never officially mentioned as the 1st Olympic Winter Games in this proclamation. It is felt, however, that this was an error of the secretary taking the minutes, as the IOC has long since recognized the 1924 Chamonix events as the 1st Olympic Winter Games.

The politics of declaring these as Olympic Games may have been more interesting than the Games themselves. The 1924 Winter Olympics saw Clas Thunberg and Thorleif Haug crowned as multiple champions in skating and skiing, respectively. Gillis Grafström repeated his title in men's figure skating that he had won at the Summer Games in Antwerp in 1920. In women's figure skating, Herma Planck-Szabó of Austria won the title, but the eighth- and last-place finisher would later become the greatest women's figure skater ever, Sonja Henie.

The Games of the VIIIth Olympiad (1924)   The Games of the VIIIth Olympiad were held in Paris, France, from 4 May through 27 July 1924. Other cities considered as hosts were Amsterdam, the Netherlands; Barcelona, Spain; Los Angeles, California, USA; Prague, Czechoslovakia; and Rome, Italy. Forty-four nations attended the 1924 Olympics, with 3,068 athletes competing (2,933 men and 135 women). After the difficulties of the 1900 Olympics in Paris, Coubertin fervently desired to see his home city host another Olympics. Paris was elected to host the 1924 Olympics at the 20th IOC session in Lausanne on 2 June 1921, and redeemed itself nicely.

The 1924 Olympics are today most famous as the Olympics of Harold Abrahams and Eric Liddell, the Olympics of *Chariots of Fire*. In 1981, the movie *Chariots of Fire* was made, celebrating the lives of Abrahams and Liddell and their route to the 1924 Olympic Games. The movie won the Academy Award for Best Picture of the Year. It was an excellent movie, but much of the story was apocryphal, with ample use of poetic license.

Besides its heralded stars, the 1924 Olympics unveiled several other notable firsts. The Olympic motto—"Citius, Altius, Fortius"—was used for the first time at the Olympic Games themselves, although Coubertin had used it as early as 1894 in the *Revue Olympique*. And at the closing ceremony the practice of raising three flags—one for the IOC, one for the host nation, and one for the succeeding host nation—was instituted for the first time. For the first time, there was also a small Olympic Village at Paris in 1924.

In swimming, Johnny Weissmuller (USA) made his first Olympic appearance and showed why he would someday become known as the world's greatest swimmer. He later competed in the 1928 Olympics as well, and then turned to Hollywood where he became famous as Tarzan, portraying that character in 19 movies.

The Games themselves were the personal playground of Paavo Nurmi, who took up where he left off in 1920. Nurmi won five gold medals and could have won more had the schedule allowed him time to compete in more events.

The 2nd Olympic Winter Games (1928)   The 2nd Olympic Winter Games were held in St. Moritz, Switzerland, from 11 through 19 February 1928. Other cities considered by the IOC as possible hosts were Davos, Switzerland, and Engelberg, Switzerland, but St. Moritz was awarded the Games at the 28th IOC session in Lausanne on 10 April 1929. Twenty-five nations attended with 463 athletes competing (435 men and 28 women). The 1928 Olympic Winter Games were highly successful, but the organizers had to contend with poor weather. The föhn, a strong wind coming down the leeward side of a mountain and carrying warm weather with it, postponed several events and forced the cancellation of one. On the morning of the 50 kilometer cross-country skiing, the temperature was about 0° C. (32° F.), but during the competition, the föhn came in, and temperatures rose to 25° C. (77° F.) by mid-day, playing havoc with the snow and waxing conditions.

Later that night, the warm weather brought rain that poured down and ruined the ski courses. Fortunately, snow and frost over the next few days rescued the organizers. But the föhn affected several other events as well. In the 10,000 meter speed skating, the United States' Irving Jaffee had the best time after the first few runs. But the föhn was bringing in warm weather and melting the rink, so the event was halted because of the conditions, and it was never restarted. Jaffee is listed by some American sources, incorrectly, as having won the event, but it actually was never contested to a conclusion. The five-man bob race also suffered the wrath of the föhn, when the bob course thawed and the four-run contest was shortened to only two runs.

The individual stars of the Games were Clas Thunberg, who won two more golds in speed skating; Johan Grøttumsbråten, who won two nordic skiing golds; Gillis Grafström, who won his third consecutive figure skating title; and Sonja Henie, who won her first of three Olympic figure skating championships. But perhaps the real star of the 1928 Winter Olympics was the Canadian ice hockey leviathan, which in the absence of American participation, was unchallenged in winning the title with a goal margin of 38-0.

The Games of the IXth Olympiad (1928)   The Games of the IXth Olympiad were held in Amsterdam, the Netherlands, from 17 May through 12 August 1928. The only other city seriously considered as a host was Los Angeles, California, USA. Amsterdam was chosen as host of the 1928 Olympics at the 19th IOC session in Lausanne on 2 June 1921. Forty-six nations attended with 2,867 athletes competing (2,593 men and 274 women).

The 1928 Olympic Games were remarkable for the return of Germany to the Olympic Games for the first time since 1912, after the country had not been invited in 1920 or 1924. In addition, an Olympic flame burned at the Olympic stadium for the first time ever. It burned atop the marathon tower, although it was not lit at the end of a torch relay.

The 1928 Olympics were an unusual event in that no single athlete dominated. Paavo Nurmi was back, and he won three more medals, but only one of them was gold. Johnny Weissmuller was back and again won two gold medals. But the biggest story of the 1928 Olympics was probably the emergence of women.

The ancient Olympic Games did not allow women as competitors, or even as spectators. If they were found to be watching, they were supposedly put to death. Baron de Coubertin did not want women in the Olympics, and he explicitly said so several times in his writings. In the modern Olympics, probably because of Coubertin's opposition, women were admitted slowly and only grudgingly.

Women had competed at the Olympics since 1900 but in small numbers and never in the showcase sport of track and field athletics. Women were not allowed to compete in this sport until the 1928 Olympics. Track and field is governed by the IAAF (International Amateur Athletic Federation), and it did not initially support the admission of women's track and field to the Olympics, so the women formed a separate organization, the FSFI (Fédération Sportive Féminine Internationale). The FSFI held its own events, the Women's "Olympics" in 1922 in Paris, and the 1926 "2nd International Ladies' Games" in Göteborg, Sweden.

It was only after these games proved the success of women's athletics that the IAAF acquiesced and allowed the sport into the Olympics. However, in 1928, only five events were held for women. The 1928 Olympic track and field events were so few and in such varied disciplines that no single woman could dominate. They were marred when several women finalists were on the verge of collapse after the 800 meters, which was also a common sight among men. The IOC reacted by barring women from running distances over 200 meters, and this was not changed until 1960.

The 1928 Olympics were one of the last truly peaceful and fully attended Olympics. The Depression had not yet occurred, which would mar the 1932 Olympics. Hitler was still in prison, and the post–World War II boycotts had not yet occurred. They were missing the single standout athlete and one other thing. Because of illness, Coubertin missed his first Olympics since 1906. He did not get to see women compete in track and field.

The 3rd Olympic Winter Games (1932)   The 3rd Olympic Winter Games were held in Lake Placid, New York, USA, from 4 through 15 February 1932. Seventeen nations attended with 252 athletes competing (231 men and 21 women). Several other U.S. cities also submitted candidatures to the IOC, as well as Montreal, Quebec, Canada, but Lake Placid was chosen to host at the 27th IOC session in Lausanne on 10 April 1929.

The biggest news of these Games was the controversy over the manner in which the speed skating events were contested. For the first time in Olympic history, the European method of skating time trials in pairs was not used. Instead the American method of pack racing was used to determine the Olympic champions. (It became a separate indoor discipline of the sport again in 1992 at Albertville.) The Europeans, unaccustomed to the style, fared badly, and the great Clas Thunberg, still a viable competitor at age 39, refused to compete in protest of the change. Norway's Ivar Ballangrud did compete, but managed only a silver medal in the unfamiliar style.

One innovation that débuted at the Olympics in 1932 was the use of the three-level victory podium for presentation of the medals. It had first been used at the 1930 British Empire Games in Hamilton, Ontario, Canada.

The pack style did make heroes of two U.S. skaters. Hometown boy Jack Shea returned from Dartmouth College and won the 500 and 1,500 meter races. He also delivered the oath of the athletes and, in 1980, would be a member of the organizing committee when the Winter Olympics returned to Lake Placid. Irving Jaffee won the other two events, the 5,000 and 10,000 meters. A few years later, during the depths of the Depression, he pawned the gold medals and never saw them again.

In figure skating, Gillis Grafström competed again but was finally defeated as Austrian Karl Schäfer won the title with Grafström second. Sonja Henie repeated in the women's competition. In bobsledding, U.S. teammates Billy Fiske and Clifford Grey repeated as gold medalists from 1928.

The Games of the Xth Olympiad (1932)   The Games of the Xth Olympiad were held in Los Angeles, California, USA, from 30 July through 14 August 1932. It was the only city that applied to host the Olympics, as the world was in the midst of a terrible economic depression. Los Angeles was awarded the Games by acclamation at the 22nd IOC session on 8 April 1923. Only 37 nations attended, the first time the number of competing nations had not increased at an Olympics. There were 1,326 competing athletes (1,200 men and 126 women). The Depression and the travel distance from Europe kept the international turnout low. Less than half as many athletes competed as in 1928, as many nations sent only small squads.

The 1932 Olympics also saw the unveiling of a woman to rival the feats of Jim Thorpe. Mildred Ella "Babe" Didrikson was a 21-year-old Texas tomboy in 1932. She was from Dallas and was heralded even before the Olympics. Restrictions on women's participation prevented Babe from showing her true colors. She was allowed to enter only three events, though no such restriction existed for men. She won the javelin throw, and the 80 meter hurdles, but in a virtual dead heat with Evelyne Hall (USA). Babe was second in the high jump, losing in a jump-off after she tied for first with Jean Shiley. Had she been able to compete in more events, it is likely that Didrikson could have won several more medals. After the Olympics, Babe Didrikson took up golf and became the greatest women's player in that sport.

Paavo Nurmi also attempted to compete at the 1932 Olympics but was not allowed to do so. Shortly before the Games the IOC declared him a professional for having received money for a tour of Germany. He had planned to run the marathon in 1932, and it is almost certain that he would have won that race, had he been allowed to compete.

The United States dominated what was close to a domestic Olympics, winning 41 gold medals and 103 medals in all. This was more than the winning totals of the next four best nations combined.

The 4th Olympic Winter Games (1936) The 4th Olympic Winter Games were held in Garmisch-Partenkirchen, Germany, from 6 through 16 February 1936. Garmisch-Partenkirchen was chosen by the IOC at its 32nd session in Vienna on 8 June 1933. Other candidate cities were Montreal, Quebec, Canada, and St. Moritz, Switzerland. Twenty-eight nations attended with 668 athletes competing (588 men and 80 women).

The 1936 Olympic Winter Games were held under the Nazi regime of Adolf Hitler. When IOC president, Henri de Baillet-Latour, was traveling to Garmisch to see the Games, he was astonished to see road signs en route declaring "Dogs and Jews not allowed." Baillet-Latour demanded an audience with Der Führer and demanded that the signs be taken down. Hitler replied that he thought it usual, when a guest entered a person's home, that the guest followed the wishes of the host. Baillet-Latour responded that when the flag of Olympia flew over the area, he became the host and Hitler was only invited guest. Hitler acquiesced and had the signs removed.

The Games were opened in a blinding snowstorm. They ended with the ski jump being watched by a record attendance of 150,000 people.

In between, Ivar Ballangrud won three more gold medals in speed skating. Sonja Henie won her third consecutive gold medal in figure skating, but the victory was a bit controversial. Henie had become a favorite of Der Führer, and it was thought that he wished her to win. She was not undeserving, but Britain's Cecilia Colledge was much improved, and some thought that her second-place finish was less than it could have been.

The biggest upset of the 1936 Olympic Winter Games occurred in ice hockey when the British team defeated the Canadians. The victory was aided by the scheming of J. F. "Bunny" Ahearne, general secretary of the British Ice Hockey Federation. Ahearne had a "mole" working in the Canadian Amateur Hockey Association and by 1934 had a complete list of all Canadian registered players who had been born in the British Isles. He contacted many of them and the team that won in Garmisch was led by eight ersatz Brits, several of whom had been imported from Canada. The Canadians howled in protest but to no avail.

The Games of the XIth Olympiad (1936) The Games of the XIth Olympiad were held in Berlin, Germany, from 1 through 16 August 1936. The IOC considered at least 11 other cities as possible hosts, but Berlin was chosen in the final vote over Barcelona, Spain, by 43-16 at the 30th IOC session in Barcelona on 26 April 1931. Forty-nine nations attended, with 3,955 athletes competing (3,626 men and 329 women).

Because of Nazi policies against Jews and their aggressive national tendencies, there were many protests against the Olympics being held in Berlin in 1936. The Americans came the closest to boycotting in protest, although the British and French both considered the option. At the IOC session in Vienna on 7 June 1933, the membership discussed the discrepancy between Nazi doctrine and Olympic principles, with two American members questioning the German members about their country's policies. At the 33rd IOC session in Athens on 15 May 1934, Lord Aberdare, a British member, then expressed concerns about reports from Germany. He pointedly asked the German IOC members if their government's pledges were trustworthy. In September 1934, future IOC president Avery Brundage traveled to Germany to inspect the country and its policies. He later recommended that the Games go on in Germany, but calls for a boycott continued, although they were never realized.

And the Games were magnificently staged, as Hitler spared no expense and used them as a propaganda tool to demonstrate the beauty and efficiency of the Third Reich. He had Leni Riefenstahl, a renowned German filmmaker, produce a wondrous movie, *Olympia*, to ensure that the propaganda would not end at the closing ceremonies.

No other Olympics belonged to a single noncompetitor as much as the 1936 Olympics with Adolf Hitler. But these Olympics were actually dominated by Jesse Owens. He showed up Hitler's Aryan supremacy theories and ruled the Berlin Olympic Games. Owens, a black American, won four gold medals in track and field athletics, winning the 100 meters, the 200 meters, the long (broad) jump, and the 4 × 100 meter relay. He was the most heralded and popular athlete of the 1936 Olympics.

The greatest innovation of the 1936 Olympics was conceived by Dr. Carl Diem, head of the organizing committee. He proposed that a torch relay be instituted to carry a flame from ancient Olympia to the Berlin Stadium and then to light the Olympic flame at the stadium. On 20 July 1936, 15 Greek maidens clad in short, belted smocks representing the robes of priestesses, gathered on the plain at ancient Olympia, and the flame was lit there by the rays of the Greek sun off a reflector. The high priestess presented the flame to Kyril Kondylis, the first Greek runner, to begin a torch relay. After several thousand miles, the flame arrived in Berlin where it was lit in the stadium by Fritz Schilgen. Thus it was that the first flame of Olympia burned over a Reich that later used flames to incinerate millions of Jews, and other "undesirables," in World War II.

The 1940 Olympic Winter Games   The 5th Olympic Winter Games, scheduled for 3 through 14 February 1940, were originally awarded to Sapporo, Japan, at the 37th IOC session in Warsaw on 9 June 1937. Sapporo withdrew on 16 July 1938, and the Games were awarded to St. Moritz at the IOC Executive Board meeting in Brussels on 3 September 1938. St. Moritz withdrew on 9 June 1939 at the 39th IOC session in London, and the 1940 Olympic Winter Games were then awarded to Garmisch-Partenkirchen, which eventually also withdrew. The Games were not held because of World War II.

The Games of the XIIth Olympiad (1940)   The Games of the XIIth Olympiad were to have been held from 22 September through 6 October 1940, but did not take place because of the onset of World War II. At the 36th IOC session in Berlin on 31 July 1936, the Games were awarded to Tokyo, Japan, in a vote of 36-27 over Helsinki, Finland.

Other cities that had expressed interest in hosting the 1940 Olympics were Alexandria, Egypt; Buenos Aires, Argentina; Dublin, Ireland; Athens, Greece; Rio de Janeiro, Brazil; Barcelona, Spain; Budapest, Hungary; and either Toronto or Montreal, Canada. On 16 July 1938, Tokyo withdrew as host. On 3 September 1938, at the IOC Executive Board meeting in Brussels, the Games were awarded to Helsinki, but the Games were canceled late in 1939.

The 1944 Olympic Winter Games   Although the 1940 Olympic Winter Games were not held, the 5th Olympic Winter Games were scheduled for 1944 and were awarded to Cortina d'Ampezzo, Italy (16 votes in round two), which was chosen over Montreal, Quebec, Canada (12 votes in round two); and Oslo, Norway (2 votes in round two) at the 39th IOC session in London on 9 June 1939. The Games were not celebrated because of World War II.

The Games of the XIIIth Olympiad (1944)   The Games of the XIIIth Olympiad were to have been held in 1944, but did not take place because of World War II. The Games had been awarded to London, England, which won the IOC nomination with 20 votes over Rome, Italy (11 votes); Detroit, Michigan, USA (2 votes); and Lausanne, Switzerland (1 vote) at the 39th IOC session in London on 9 June 1939.

The 5th Olympic Winter Games (1948)   The 5th Olympic Winter Games were held in St. Moritz, Switzerland, from 30 January through 8 February. Twenty-eight nations attended with 668 athletes competing (591 men and 77 women). The only candidate that opposed St. Moritz for 1948 was Lake Placid, New York. St. Moritz was chosen by the IOC Executive Board, which met in Lausanne on 4 September 1946 and made its decision.

St. Moritz hurriedly put together excellent arrangements for the Games that were again disturbed, though less severely, by the föhn. Ice hockey matches (held outdoors) and the 10,000 meters speed skating had to be delayed, but no events were canceled this time.

Alpine skiing made its true Olympic début. A few combined events had been held in 1936, but this time there were three events for both men and women. Two athletes won a second "St. Moritz" Olympic medal, as "Bibi" Torriani played on the Swiss ice hockey team to match his bronze from 1928; and John Heaton (USA) also repeated his silver medal from the skeleton race in 1928. The skeleton race, a form of tobogganing unique to the St. Moritz resort, was held at the Olympics for the second time to date. Skeleton returned to the Olympic program in 2002 at Salt Lake City.

The Games of the XIVth Olympiad (1948)   The Games of the XIVth Olympiad were held in London, England, from 29 July through 14 August 1948. For the only time in Olympic history, the Games were awarded by a postal vote after the IOC recommended London as the site to its members. The vote was confirmed by the IOC membership at its 40th session in Lausanne on 4 September 1946. Other candidate cities were Baltimore, Maryland, USA; Lausanne, Switzerland; Los Angeles, California, USA; Minneapolis, Minnesota, USA; Philadelphia, Pennsylvania, USA. Fifty-nine nations attended with 4,073 athletes competing (3,680 men and 393 women).

As in 1920, the IOC decided that it was necessary to resurrect the Olympic movement at the earliest scheduled time. Thus, although England had been ravaged by Hitler's air raids, the Games of the XIVth Olympiad were awarded to London in 1948. In spite of years of difficulties caused by rationing of food, clothes, and other essential materials, the English organizing committee did an outstanding job.

No great innovations accompanied the Games themselves, as most of the protocols of the opening, closing, and victory ceremonies were by now established. However, these Games were significant as they were televised for the first time, although only to small local audiences. Television sets were still quite rare.

One country that was missed was the Soviet Union. The USSR had competed in 1946 at the European Championships in track and field athletics, and it was thought that perhaps it would return to the Olympics in 1948. This was not to be, and the reasons for its failure to compete have never been fully revealed.

As a very popular sport in England, track and field was truly the focus of these Olympics, as it is so often. Three athletes stood out in the athletics stadium. "Fanny" Blankers-Koen (NED), a 30-year-old mother of three children in 1948, won the 100 meters, 200 meters, 80 meter high hurdles, and helped win gold in the 4 × 100 meter relay. Bob Mathias (USA), a 17-year-old schoolboy, won the decathlon despite a torrential downpour throughout much of the two-day event. In the next few years he would prove that it was not a fluke. He would win again in 1952 at Helsinki and was never defeated in his decathlon career. Finally, Emil Zátopek (TCH) won the 10,000 meters and finished second in the 5,000. It was only a prelude to his heroics of 1952.

The 6th Olympic Winter Games (1952)   The 6th Olympic Winter Games were held in Oslo, Norway from 14 through 25 February 1952. Thirty nations attended with 693 athletes competing (584 men and 109 women). At the 41st IOC session in Stockholm on 21 June 1947, Oslo was chosen by the IOC with 18 votes over Cortina d'Ampezzo, Italy (9 votes) and Lake Placid, New York, USA (1 vote).

The Olympic Winter Games were finally held in a Nordic country, and an Olympic flame was first lit at the Olympic Winter Games. Unlike the summer flame, however, this flame was originally lit from the hearth of the house in Morgedal, Norway, where Sondre Norheim, the pioneer of modern skiing, was born. At the end of a ski relay, Eigil Nansen, grandson of the explorer Fridtjof Nansen, lit the flame in the Bislett stadium.

Norway's athletes dominated the events, especially so Hjalmar Andersen who won three gold medals in speed skating. In alpine skiing, the handsome Stein Eriksen of Norway seemed the embodiment of a modern ski hero. He won the giant slalom and was second in the slalom. Dick Button of the United States won his second consecutive men's figure skating championship. In women's skiing, Andrea Mead-Lawrence (USA) won two events by upsetting the European women.

In bobsledding, Germany won both the two-man and four-man events. Its "athletes" in this event were so large that their momentum helped them win by increasing their speed. This caused the International Bobsleigh Federation to change its rules to place a weight limit on bobsled teams.

The Games of the XVth Olympiad (1952)   The Games of the XVth Olympiad were held in Helsinki, Finland, from 19 July through 3 August 1952. At the 41st IOC session in Stockholm on 21 June 1947, Helsinki won the vote in the second round over Los Angeles, California, USA; Minneapolis, Minnesota, USA; Amsterdam, the Netherlands; Detroit, Michigan, USA; Chicago, Illinois, USA; and Philadelphia, Pennsylvania, USA. Sixty-nine nations attended with 4,916 athletes competing (4,395 men and 521 women).

In 1952, the biggest news from Helsinki was that the Soviets were there. After the Bolshevik Revolution of 1917, the USSR had not competed in the Olympics until the Helsinki Games. The world braced for the athletic battles between the Soviet Union and the United States—in effect, a cold war Olympics. The Soviets were accorded one rather unusual allowance. They were housed in a separate Olympic Village, and stayed only with athletes from the Eastern bloc countries of Hungary, Poland, Bulgaria, Romania, and Czechoslovakia.

It is always an exciting moment when the Olympic torch enters the stadium. In 1952, the excitement was palpable when the Finnish crowd realized that the torchbearer was the Finnish hero of heroes, Paavo Nurmi. Although by then 55 years old, Nurmi carried the torch on high and still had his very familiar stride. Not only the crowd but even the athletes were excited. They broke ranks to run to the side of the track to get closer to the distance running legend. Some Finnish football players then brought the torch from the track to the top of the tower, handing it to Hannes Kolehmainen, second only to Nurmi in the Finnish pantheon of sporting heroes. The 62-year-old Kolehmainen lit the Olympic flame at the top of the tower.

Given that the Games were opened by two of the greatest distance runners ever, it was fitting that the 1952 Olympics were dominated by a distance runner who even surpassed a few of their feats. Emil Zátopek, the Czech who had won the 10,000 meters in 1948, was by now the greatest distance runner in the world. He entered the 5,000 and 10,000 meters and won both of them rather easily. He then entered the marathon, a race he had never before run. Still, the extra distance did not deter Zátopek. He was running with the favored Jim Peters of Great Britain for the first half of the race when he turned to Peters and asked him if the pace wasn't a bit slow. With no reply, Zátopek took off and was never seen again by Peters. Zátopek won the race by over 2½ minutes, while Peters failed to finish.

The Americans and the Soviets met several times in these Olympics, most notably in the boxing ring. In 1952, the Americans had the best of it, though the Soviets would improve in the coming years. The press made a big thing out of the medal counts, which were led early by the Soviet Union, although the United States eventually won the most medals and gold medals. This too would change in later Olympics.

The 7th Olympic Winter Games (1956) The 7th Olympic Winter Games were held in Cortina d'Ampezzo, Italy, from 26 January through 5 February 1956. Thirty-two nations attended with 821 athletes competing (689 men and 132 women). Cortina d'Ampezzo was chosen at the 44th IOC session in Rome on 28 April 1949 with 31 votes over Montreal, Quebec, Canada (7 votes); Colorado Springs, Colorado, USA (2 votes); and Lake Placid, New York, USA (1 vote).

The Cortina Olympics began ominously when the torch bearer at the opening ceremonies, speed skater Guido Caroli, tripped over a microphone wire and fell. However, he was not harmed and the torch did not go out. After that initial difficulty, the Games were a wonder.

The big news was the entrance of the Soviets into the Winter Olympics. The Soviet Union immediately excelled at speed skating and, in an upset, began its domination of ice hockey when its team defeated the Canadians.

The hero of the Cortina Olympics was movie-idol-handsome Toni Sailer of Austria, "The Blitz from Kitz" (Kitzbühel). Sailer won all three alpine skiing events by large victory margins each time. In ski jumping, the Finns introduced a new aerodynamic style when they placed their arms against their sides rather than forward in front of their heads. With the new method Antti Hyvirinen and Aulis Kallakorpi took first and second, respectively. The figure skating competitions saw two very close contests as Americans swept the men's medals, with Hayes Alan Jenkins winning. Among the women, Tenley Albright barely defeated Carol Heiss. Heiss and Jenkins would later marry.

The 1956 Equestrian Olympic Games   After the IOC awarded the Games of the XVIth Olympiad to Melbourne, Australia, they learned that Australian quarantine laws would not allow the importation of horses for the equestrian events without an extended quarantine period. This precluded Melbourne from being able to host the equestrian events at the 1956 Olympic Games. It was decided, actually in violation of the Olympic Charter, to hold separate Equestrian Olympic Games in Stockholm, Sweden, from 10 through 17 June 1956. At the 50th IOC session in Athens on 13 May 1954, Stockholm was chosen with 25 votes over Paris, France (10 votes); Rio de Janeiro, Brazil (8 votes); Berlin, Germany (2 votes); and Los Angeles, California, USA (2 votes).

The Equestrian Games of 1956 were held without major incidents and were contested by 29 nations and 159 athletes (146 men and 13 women). The opening ceremony was quite unusual as all competitors came in on their mounts, including the flag bearers. Hans Wikne brought the Olympic flame into the stadium on horseback and lit the main torch.

Karin Lindberg and Henry Eriksson held lighted torches, ran toward the stadium tower with the torches, and lit flames there. Sweden's Henri Saint Cyr recited the oath of the athletes while on his horse, and later won two gold medals in individual and team dressage. This was matched by Germany's Hans Günter Winkler, who won gold medals in the individual and team show jumping events. The only controversy of the 1956 Equestrian Games came in the three-day event when one horse broke his leg and had to be destroyed. The SPCA (Society for the Prevention of Cruelty to Animals) was very upset and a lengthy debate followed.

The Games of the XVIth Olympiad (1956)   The Games of the XVIth Olympiad were held in Melbourne, Victoria, Australia from 22 November through 8 December 1956. At the 44th IOC session in Rome on 28 April 1949, Melbourne was awarded the Olympics by a single vote in the fourth round over Buenos Aires, Argentina. Other candidate cities were (with round of elimination from voting): Los Angeles, California, USA (third round); Detroit, Michigan, USA (third round); Mexico City, Mexico (second round); Chicago, Illinois, USA (first round); Minneapolis, Minnesota, USA (first round); and Philadelphia, Pennsylvania, USA (first round). Sixty-seven nations and 3,188 athletes eventually competed in Melbourne (2,818 men and 370 women).

This was the first time that the Games were held in the Southern Hemisphere and necessitated the Olympic Games being held very late in the year to take advantage of the early part of the Australian summer. Because of Australian quarantine laws, it was decided, in violation of the Olympic Charter, to hold separate Olympic Equestrian Games in Stockholm, Sweden, from 10 through 17 June 1956. (See The 1956 Equestrian Olympic Games.)

But between June and the Melbourne Olympics, the world was thrown into turmoil. On 29 October, Israel invaded Egypt's Sinai Peninsula. Then on 4 November 1956, 200,000 Soviet troops entered Budapest, Hungary, to quell political uprisings in that country. Egypt, Lebanon, and Iraq withdrew in protest at Israel's action. The Netherlands, Spain, and, somewhat surprisingly, Switzerland withdrew in protest at the Soviet action. Switzerland kept alive its record of competing in every modern Olympics only because it had already been represented by athletes in Stockholm. These protests constituted the first true boycott in modern Olympic history, though the scene would be repeated many times in the coming decades.

With that background, water polo had the unusual distinction of being perhaps the most awaited event of the Olympics. In a final round match, the Soviet Union met the Hungarians, usually a water polo power. The athletes from both countries wasted no time in breaking all known rules and niceties of water polo. The water was literally blood red in several areas during the match, and several players had to be helped out of the water because of bleeding. Hungary achieved some measure of revenge for the invasion of their country when it won, 4-0.

The Games were less well attended than those of other years because of the travel distance to Australia. Still, all the major sporting countries were represented. In a precursor of problems to come, the People's Republic of China (Beijing, then Peking) withdrew because the Republic of China (Taiwan) was allowed to compete. The question of the two countries' representation would not be resolved for 28 years.

The 8th Olympic Winter Games (1960)   The 8th Olympic Winter Games were held in Squaw Valley, California, USA from 18 through 28 February 1960. Thirty nations attended with 664 athletes competing (520 men and 144 women). At the 51st IOC session in Paris on 14 June 1955, Squaw Valley won a close contest by two votes over Innsbruck, Austria (32-30 in the second round). Garmisch-Partenkirchen, Germany, and St. Moritz, Switzerland, were also candidate cities, but were eliminated in the first round of voting.

When the 1960 Olympic Winter Games were awarded to Squaw Valley, all that existed there was a hotel. The ski village was the dream of Alexander Cushing, and he succeeded in convincing the IOC to hold the Olympics based on his dream. After the award the Europeans verbally attacked the site for various reasons. The ski courses were not up to FIS caliber in the alpine competitions, while in the nordic races, the altitude (2,000 meters [6,650 feet]) was felt to be too stressful for the competitors. The Squaw Valley organizers polled the Winter Olympic nations and found that only nine would send a bobsled team so they elected to save the expense by not building a run and not contesting the sport. In all, despite the initial misgivings about the site, the Games were well run with few problems. And U.S. television was present, showing the events to the American people for the first time.

Biathlon was introduced as a sport for the first time. Women's speed skating also made its Olympic début and saw the arrival of Lidiya Skoblikova (URS) who won two gold medals. In figure skating, Hayes Alan

Jenkins's brother, David Jenkins, won the men's titles, while David Jenkins's future sister-in-law, Carol Heiss, avenged her 1956 defeat to easily win the women's title. In the nordic combined event, Georg Thoma (FRG) became the first non-Scandinavian to win a nordic Olympic event. In ice hockey, the United States pulled a major upset when it defeated the Soviet Union in the semifinal match. The U.S. went on to defeat Czechoslovakia in the finals and win the gold medal. Not as well publicized as the miracle of 1980, the U.S. victory in 1960 was equally astonishing.

The Games of the XVIIth Olympiad (1960) The Games of the XVIIth Olympiad were held in Rome, Italy, from 25 August through 11 September 1960. At the 51st IOC session in Paris on 16 June 1955, Rome was awarded the Games in the third round over Lausanne, Switzerland, by a vote of 35-24. The other candidate cities (with round of elimination from voting) were Detroit, Michigan, USA (second round); Budapest, Hungary (second round); Brussels, Belgium (first round); Mexico City, Mexico (first round); and Tokyo, Japan (first round). Eighty-three nations attended the Games, with 5,337 athletes competing (4,725 men and 612 women).

Rome had been awarded the 1908 Olympics but eventually relinquished their right to host them. Fifty-two years later the Olympics would return to the eternal city. Never before, and possibly never again, were the ancient and modern civilizations so intertwined at an Olympics. The 1960 Olympics were a wonder. With the boycotts, massacres, and political problems that were to come, many Olympic afficionados would later yearn for the glory that was Ancient Greece and the grandeur that was modern Rome.

Many of the events took place in settings thousands of years old. Wrestling was held in the Basilica of Maxentius, where similar competitions had taken place two millennia previously. Gymnastics events were held in the Terme di Caracalla. The marathon began in front of the ancient Roman capitol, on Capitoline Hill, and finished along the Appian Way beneath the Arch of Constantine. For modern facilities the Italians provided Stadio Olimpico, a beautiful track and field complex, the Sports Palace for boxing, and the Velodrome for cycling.

A number of heroes emerged from the Games. In women's athletics, the Italians and the world thrilled to the feats of Wilma Rudolph, an American sprinter from Tennessee. Long-legged and attractive, she was dubbed by the European press as "La Gazelle Noire"—the black gazelle. She won the women's 100 meters and 200 meters, and anchored the sprint relay.

In basketball and boxing, two of the greatest ever practitioners of those sports were on display. In basketball, the U.S. men's team won very easily as the team was led by Oscar Robertson, Jerry West, Jerry Lucas, Walt Bellamy, and Terry Dischinger. Certainly the greatest amateur team ever, it rivals many of the great NBA teams. In boxing, the light-heavyweight gold medal was won by Cassius Marcellus Clay, who as Muhammad Ali would thrill the world for the next two decades as "The Greatest."

The 1960 Olympics were the first Summer Olympics televised in the United States, although all events were shown on tape delay after the film was flown from Rome to New York. And also for the first time since the 1912 marathon (Portuguese runner Francisco Lazaro), the Olympics saw the death of a competitor. In the cycling road race, Knut Enemark Jensen (DEN) collapsed and later died. He was found to have taken amphetamines, and his death was partially responsible for the institution of drug testing in the mid-1960s.

The 9th Olympic Winter Games (1964)   The 9th Olympic Winter Games were held in Innsbruck, Austria, from 29 January through 9 February 1964. Thirty-six nations attended with 1,093 athletes competing (894 men and 199 women). At the 56th IOC session in Munich, Germany, on 26 May 1959, Innsbruck (49 votes) was chosen over Calgary, Alberta, Canada (9 votes); and Lahti, Finland (0 votes).

Innsbruck was an almost unanimous choice to host the 1964 Olympic Winter Games, and the IOC has made few better choices. Innsbruck became the first Olympic host city since World War II, winter or summer, to spread the Olympic events around geographically a bit, with some events being held 30 kilometers (20 miles) from Innsbruck center. Because of this and the central location of the city, well over a million spectators saw these Olympics. In addition, television now transmitted them to over a billion viewers. Computers were also present for the first time at the Olympics, as the electronic age came to Olympia.

With all this, there were a few problems. The organizing committee forgot to order snow for the events. In the last few days, the Austrian army hauled 20,000 cubic meters of snow to the ski courses so they would be well packed. In practice before the Games, two athletes were killed—Ross Milne, an Australian skier, and Kazimierz Skrzypecki, a Polish-born British luger.

Soviet women were the biggest winners at Innsbruck. Lidiya Skoblikova produced one of the great performances of the Olympic Winter Games when she won all four women's speed skating gold medals in four days. In women's cross-country skiing, Klavdiya Boyarskikh won gold medals in all three women's events. The Soviets also ensured there would be no repeat of 1960 and won the ice hockey title easily. But in bobsledding, both events produced big upsets. Britain's Tony Nash and Robin Dixon won the two-man title, while Vic Emery drove the four-man champion sled from Canada. Neither country had a bobsled run in 1964.

The Games of the XVIIIth Olympiad (1964)   The Games of the XVIIIth Olympiad were held in Tokyo, Japan, from 10 through 24 October 1964. At the 56th IOC session in Munich, Germany, on 26 May 1959, Tokyo (34 votes) won the final vote in the first round over Detroit, Michigan, USA (10 votes); Vienna, Austria (9 votes); and Brussels, Belgium (5 votes). Ninety-three nations attended with 5,132 athletes competing (4,452 men and 680 women).

For the first time, the Olympic Games were celebrated in an Asian country. The Japanese were eager to prove that they had recovered from the horrors of World War II, and to emphasize the point, they chose as the final torchbearer Yoshinori Sakai, who had been born in Hiroshima on the day the atomic bomb immolated that city.

Before the Games began, there was a minor controversy when Indonesia and North Korea withdrew because several of their athletes were declared ineligible. The affected athletes had competed in the Games of the New Emerging Forces (GANEFO) in Jakarta, Indonesia, in November 1963. Indonesia did not allow Taiwan or Israel to compete at those Games, so the International Federations for athletics, swimming, and shooting banned any athlete from the Tokyo Olympics who had competed at GANEFO. Because this affected several of their athletes, Indonesia and North Korea withdrew from Tokyo in protest. The only significant athlete missing was Dan Sin-Kim of North Korea, the women's world record holder in the 400 and 800 meters.

In athletics, Billy Mills of the United States pulled off one of the biggest upsets in Olympic history when he won the 10,000 meter run. The most decorated hero of the Games was swimmer Don Schollander who won four gold medals in men's swimming. Schollander could have won a fifth gold medal, but the U.S. coaches left him off the medley relay team, although he was America's fastest freestyler.

The Japanese were gracious hosts, but they were helped in their own efforts by two new Olympic sports: judo and volleyball. In volleyball the Japanese women, coached by the martinet-like Hirofumi Daimatsu, were easily victorious. In judo, the Japanese won three of the four gold medals. But the one they lost, in the open class to Holland's Anton Geesink, was a crushing blow to the hosts.

The Games were beautifully run, and the minor boycott had no effect. The 1964 Olympics were the last Olympics to be held for 28 years without major political overtones and boycotts.

The 10th Olympic Winter Games (1968)   The 10th Olympic Winter Games were held in Grenoble, France, from 6 through 18 February 1968. Thirty-seven nations attended with 1,158 athletes competing (947 men and 211 women). At the 62nd IOC session in Innsbruck on 28 January 1964, Grenoble was chosen on the third ballot over a large field of candidate cities, which included Calgary, Alberta, Canada (third round); Lahti, Finland (second round); Sapporo, Japan (first round); Oslo, Norway (first round); and Lake Placid, New York, USA (first round).

The controversy so often associated with the Olympic Games began to reach Winter Olympia in 1968 at Grenoble. Though the Games went fairly well, there were many problems. It began before the Olympics when the IOC decided it wished to curb advertising on skis and clothing by the alpine skiers. They threatened to expel certain skiers, while the skiers threatened to withdraw en masse in revolt if that were done. A compromise was eventually reached in which the skiers agreed to remove all equipment with advertising prior to being photographed or interviewed.

The 1968 Winter Games' hero of heroes was Jean-Claude Killy who had grown up and learned to ski in the neighboring mountains. He was favored in all three alpine events, and all France expected Killy to duplicate Toni Sailer's 1956 feat and win the three alpine skiing gold medals. He succeeded but not without a major controversy in the slalom. The race was held in fog, and both Karl Schranz (AUT) and Håkon Mjøn (NOR) initially posted faster times, but both were disqualified for missing gates. Schranz appealed, stating that he had been interfered with, and replays showed that he had. He was allowed a restart and again posted a winning time. But he was then disqualified when further investigation revealed that the interference on the first run occurred after Schranz had missed his gates. And Killy had his third gold medal, and France had its hero.

In the bobsled events, held on l'Alpe d'Huez, the site of so much heroism and suffering during the Tour de France, Eugenio Monti of Italy finally succeeded in winning an Olympic gold medal. In fact he won two. In pairs figure skating, the almost lyrical team of Lyudmila Belousova and Oleg Protopopov won their second consecutive championship.

The Games of the XIXth Olympiad (1968)   The Games of the XIXth Olympiad were held from 12 through 27 October 1968 in Mexico City, Mexico. At the 61st IOC session in Baden-Baden, Germany, on 18 October 1963, Mexico City had been awarded the Games on the first ballot with 30 votes over Detroit, Michigan, USA (14 votes); Lyon, France (12 votes); and Buenos Aires, Argentina (2 votes). One hundred twelve nations attended with 5,555 athletes competing (4,771 men and 784 women).

In 1963, the IOC awarded the Olympics to Mexico, despite warnings about the effects of competing at the altitude (2,134 meters) of Mexico City. The warnings would prove prophetic, both for good and bad, but also prominent at Mexico City was the first large-scale incursion of politics into the Olympic scene since 1936.

Political problems first manifested themselves as protests by Mexican students before the Games. The students were upset that so much money was spent on the Olympics in the face of such widespread poverty in their own country. As the protest movement gathered momentum leading up to the Games, the Mexican army took charge on the night of 2 October. When 10,000 people demonstrated in the Square of the Three Cultures in Mexico City, the army surrounded the crowd and opened fire. More than 250 people were killed and over a thousand were injured.

In the United States, Harry Edwards, a professor at San Jose State University, urged American blacks to boycott the Olympics to protest the rampant racism of American society. The boycott never materialized. However, his efforts came to fruition in the victory ceremony of the 200 meters. The race was won by Tommie Smith (USA) with the bronze medal going to John Carlos (USA). On the victory platform, as

"The Star-Spangled Banner" played in the background, almost unheard, the two black Americans stood barefoot, heads bowed, and raised a singled black-gloved fist in their own form of protest. The IOC banned the two from future Olympic participation and ordered them to leave the Olympic Village immediately.

On a positive political note, the Federal Republic of Germany (West Germany) and the German Democratic Republic (East Germany) entered separate national teams for the first time, although they competed wearing the same emblems and flag, and using a joint anthem for medal ceremonies.

The altitude severely affected many track and field events. Bob Beamon used the lesser gravity to set a stunning world record in the long jump of 8.90 meters (29'2½"). It would not be broken for 23 years. In the 100, 200, 400, 400 meter hurdles, 4 × 100 relay, 4 × 400 relay, and the triple jump, all sprint events not requiring much oxygen, and aided by the lessened pull of gravity, new world records were set by the men. Many of these records would last for years. But the distance running events saw very slow times, as the runners gasped for the oxygen that was not there.

The 11th Olympic Winter Games (1972) The 11th Olympic Winter Games were held in Sapporo, Japan, from 3 through 13 February 1972. Thirty-five nations attended with 1,008 athletes competing (802 men and 206 women). At the 65th IOC session in Rome on 26 April 1966, Sapporo was chosen on the first ballot (32 votes) over Banff, Alberta, Canada (16 votes); Lahti, Finland (7 votes); and Salt Lake City, Utah, USA (7 votes).

The controversy that had started in Grenoble four years earlier continued and erupted at the beginning of the Games. Avery Brundage insisted on ending commercialization by skiers and singled out Austrian star Karl Schranz, who was expelled from the Games.

Another controversy occurred when Canada refused to send its ice hockey team, protesting professionalism by the Soviets. The USSR won that gold medal quite easily, though it is unlikely the Canadians would have made a difference, as by 1972, the Soviets were showing that they could now play well against the NHL (National Hockey League).

Ard Schenk (NED) was the best publicized athlete at these Olympics as he won three championships in speed skating. His triple was matched in women's cross-country skiing by Galina Kulakova (URS), though a bit more surreptitiously to the world's media. The Japanese, not usually a winter sports power, were exultant when three of their ski jumpers, led by Yukio Kasaya, swept the medals in the 70 meter ski jumping.

The Games of the XXth Olympiad (1972)   The Games of the XXth Olympiad were held in Munich, Germany (Federal Republic/West), from 26 August through 11 September 1972. At the 65th IOC session in Rome in 1966, Munich had been awarded the Games on the second ballot (31 votes) over Montreal, Quebec, Canada (15 votes); Madrid, Spain (13 votes); and Detroit, Michigan, USA (eliminated after round one). One hundred twenty-one nations attended with 7,116 athletes competing (6,057 men and 1,059 women).

The Munich Olympics began as the "Games of Joy," in which the West German government attempted to atone for the militaristic Nazi image so associated with the 1936 Berlin Games. They ended as the "Games of Terror and Tragedy."

The first 11 days of the 1972 Olympics were beautiful. But on the morning of 5 September, stark reality hit when the Games were interrupted by eight Arab terrorists, representing the militant Black September group. They entered the Olympic Village and took 11 members of the Israeli Olympic team as hostages. While the world watched on television and waited, the terrorists occupied the building of 31 Connollystraße and demanded freedom for several Arabs held in Israeli prisons. The Israeli government refused this as a day of tense negotiations ensued.

Late in the evening of 5 September, the terrorists took their hostages to Fürstenfeldbruck, an Army air base near Munich. There, in a few quick minutes of fighting as the Germans tried to save them, all the Israelis were murdered by a bomb the terrorists had set in the helicopter that was to take them to freedom. Several of the terrorists were killed, but most escaped. A few were later captured, but none ever came to trial.

The murdered Israeli athletes and coaches were David Marc Berger, Zeev Friedman, Yossef Gutfreund, Eliezer Halfin, Yossef Romano, Amitzur Shapira, Kehat Shorr, Mark Slavin, Andrei Spitzer, Yacov Springer, and Moshe Weinberg.

The day after the murders, a memorial service was held in the Olympic stadium, and the Olympic Games were halted for a single day. Many people called for the cancellation of the remainder of the Olympics in memoriam. At the memorial service, International Olympic Committee president Avery Brundage incensed many when he compared the Israeli murders to the political problems that the International Olympic Committee had had with the African nations who wished to expel Rhodesia prior to the Olympics. During the service, Brundage made the now famous statement, "The Games must go on."

There were some marvelous athletic performances at the 1972 Olympics, notably Mark Spitz winning seven gold medals, and setting seven world records, but they seemed of little consequence. The Olympic Games would never be the same again.

The 12th Olympic Winter Games (1976)   The 12th Olympic Winter Games were held in Innsbruck, Austria, from 4 through 15 February 1976. Thirty-seven nations attended with 1,129 athletes competing (898 men and 231 women). Innsbruck was not originally even a candidate city for the 1976 Olympic Winter Games. At the 70th IOC session in Amsterdam on 13 May 1970, the original choice of the IOC was Denver, Colorado, USA, which had won on the third ballot (39 votes) over Sion, Switzerland (30 votes in round three); Tampere, Finland (second round); and Vancouver, British Columbia, Canada (first round). In November 1972, the citizens of Colorado, in a referendum, indicated that they did not wish the Olympics to be held in Denver, fearing a negative impact on the environment. Denver officially withdrew as host on 12 November 1972. Innsbruck, which had held the Games so successfully in 1964, was able to step in on short notice, after being selected over hastily arranged bids from Lake Placid (USA), Chamonix (FRA), and Tampere. And once again Innsbruck demonstrated how well an Olympic Winter Games could be staged.

The competitions were well contested though no single athlete could be said to dominate, as in years past. Rosi Mittermaier (FRG) was perhaps the best publicized Olympian in 1976. She won the downhill and slalom early in the Games and had a chance to equal the feats of Toni Sailer and Jean-Claude Killy by winning the giant slalom. Older than many of the competitors, close to retirement, and born nearby, just across the German border at Reit im Winkl, she was a heavy sentimental favorite. But it was not to be. Canada's Kathy Kreiner defeated Mittermaier by 12/100ths of a second in the giant slalom. In men's skiing Austria's Franz Klammer electrified fans and the television audience with a spectacular run, in which he skied to the edge and was on the verge of falling several times, to win the downhill gold medal over Switzerland's Bernhard Russi.

In figure skating, Irina Rodnina (URS) again won a pairs gold medal, but with a different partner than in 1972. In men's figure skating Britain's John Curry and Canada's Toller Cranston introduced a more balletic style than in years past. Among the women, Dorothy Hamill of the United States became a media favorite with her ability and style, wholesome looks, and pixie-like hairdo.

The Games of the XXIst Olympiad (1976)   The Games of the XXIst Olympiad were held in Montreal, Quebec, Canada, from 17 July through 1 August 1976. At the 70th IOC session on 13 May 1970, Montreal had been awarded the Games in the second round of balloting (41 votes) by the IOC over Moscow, USSR (28 votes) and Los Angeles, California, USA (eliminated after round one). Ninety-two nations eventually competed in the Montreal Games, with 6,074 athletes participating (4,812 men and 1,262 women).

The city of Montreal spent extravagantly to host the Games, leaving the citizens of Canada and Quebec with a tax debt they would be repaying for years, and the Games were dubbed the billion-dollar circus by the Canadian press. In 1994, the debt still remaining to the Quebec citizenry was estimated at $304 million (US). Much of the debt, however, was incurred to finance infrastructure that Montreal would have needed to eventually build.

Shortly before the 1976 Olympics were to start they were marred by a boycott of 22 African countries, Guyana, and Chinese Taipei (then Taiwan). The African/Guyanan boycott was in protest of a recent tour of South Africa by the New Zealand national rugby team. As South Africa was ostracized from international sporting competition, the African nations demanded that New Zealand not be allowed to compete at Montreal. But the IOC had little control over this problem, as rugby had no current affiliation with the Olympic movement. New Zealand competed, but most of Africa did not.

The Taiwan boycott occurred when Canada at first considered refusing to allow the team to enter the country, as the Canadian government did not recognize the island nation. This was in direct violation of their agreement as host country to admit all eligible nations in honoring the Olympic Charter. The Canadians acquiesced and were going to allow the Taiwanese to compete, but they refused to allow them to do so under the title of the Republic of China, their official national name. Several other countries protested and threatened withdrawal, notably the

United States, if the Taiwan athletes were not allowed to compete. However, these protests were short-lived, and the IOC finally gave in to the Canadian government. Taiwan withdrew and did not compete.

Twenty-six nations eventually boycotted the Montreal Olympics. Twenty-two of these did not compete at all and are as follows: Algeria, Central African Republic, Chad, People's Republic of Congo, Ethiopia, The Gambia, Ghana, Guyana, Iraq, Kenya, Libya, Malawi, Mali, Niger, Nigeria, Sudan, Swaziland, Tanzania, Togo, Uganda, Upper Volta, and Zambia. In addition, Egypt, Cameroon, Morocco, and Tunisia also boycotted, although they are listed as competing nations, because some of their athletes competed on the first two days of the Olympics before they officially withdrew.

After all this the Olympics began. Despite the absence of some top African track athletes, they were well run, and the boycotts had minimal effect on competition. The fans thrilled to the exploits of Romania's Nadia Comăneci in gymnastics as she dominated the competition, scoring the first perfect 10s ever awarded at the Olympics. The major effect of the boycott on track and field athletics was in the 1,500 meters, in which John Walker (ironically of New Zealand) and Filbert Bayi (Tanzania) were to compete. They were the two best milers in the world by far, but in Bayi's absence, Walker had only himself to beat, and he managed a comfortable gold medal victory. The most spectacular athlete on the track was probably Cuba's Alberto Juantorena, who won the 400 and 800 meter runs.

The 13th Olympic Winter Games (1980)   The 13th Olympic Winter Games were held in Lake Placid, New York, USA, from 13 through 24 February 1980. Thirty-seven nations attended with 1,072 athletes competing (837 men and 235 women). Lake Placid was unopposed in its bid and was chosen by the IOC at its 75th session in Vienna on 23 October 1974.

Lake Placid, like St. Moritz and Innsbruck before it, was given a second chance to host the Olympic Winter Games. In the era of spiraling costs, Lake Placid promised a simpler Olympics. But the complexity of television and millions of spectators proved almost too much for the small upstate New York village. Transportation and communication were difficult, and the IOC vowed never to return the Games to such a small venue.

As if these were not enough problems, shortly before the Olympics, the Soviet Union invaded Afghanistan. President Jimmy Carter promptly called for a U.S.-led boycott of the Moscow Olympics. And he used Secretary of State Cyrus Vance to lecture the IOC at its session in Lake Placid days before the Games started, which greatly offended the International Olympic Committee.

But Lake Placid had two great redeeming features—Eric Heiden and the U.S. ice hockey team. In speed skating, Heiden was the greatest skater in the world, and pre-Games predictions had him possibly winning five gold medals, though few believed he could actually win all five. But he did. He ended his Olympic dominance with a gold medal in the 10,000 meters. Racing in the second pair with Viktor Lyoskin (URS), Heiden set a world record by six seconds and earned his fifth gold medal.

In ice hockey, the Soviet Union was by now conceded the gold medal at all Olympics. A week before the Olympics, the USA and the USSR played an exhibition game in Madison Square Garden, and the Soviets won, 10-3. But the U.S. team had more fortitude than anyone suspected and was led by a coach, Herb Brooks, who brought more out of them than they knew they had. The Americans could not, and would not, be intimidated.

In the semifinals they faced the Soviets. The score was tied in the third period when captain Mike Eruzione scored to put the U.S. ahead, 4-3. As time ran out with that same score, Al Michaels, ABC television announcer, echoed every American's thoughts when he asked, "Do you believe in miracles?" Two nights later, the Americans came from behind to defeat Finland and win the gold medal.

The Games of the XXIInd Olympiad (1980) The Games of the XXIInd Olympiad were held in Moscow, Russian Republic, USSR, from 19 July through 3 August 1980. At the 75th IOC session in Vienna on 22 October 1974, Moscow was awarded the Games by a vote of 39-20 over Los Angeles, the only other city that bid for the Olympics. Eighty countries eventually competed in Moscow, with 5,252 athletes competing (4,132 men and 1,120 women).

In late December 1979, Soviet tanks invaded Afghanistan. After the Soviet invasion of Afghanistan, U.S. president Jimmy Carter called for a boycott of the Moscow Olympics if the Soviets did not withdraw before 20 February 1980. They did not. Carter pressed his efforts, attempting to enlist other countries to join his boycott. But American allies Britain, Finland, France, Ireland, Italy, New Zealand, Spain, and Sweden all competed at Moscow. Carter made his announcement public to the IOC via Secretary of State Cyrus Vance, who rather rudely addressed the IOC at the Lake Placid Games in February.

Approximately 63 countries eventually boycotted the Moscow Olympics. Notable among these were the United States, Canada, West Germany, Japan, China, Kenya, and Norway (a full list follows at the end of this section). Several countries that did not boycott protested at the Olympic ceremonies in various ways. Ten countries elected not to march at the opening ceremonies, while six other nations marched behind flags of their National Olympic Committees, or the Olympic flag, rather than their national flags. Several countries chose not to have their national anthems played at victory ceremonies, substituting instead the Olympic hymn. Finally, at the closing ceremony, President Carter refused to allow the American flag to be raised as the host country of the next Olympics. The flag of Los Angeles was raised instead.

The Games suffered in level of competition, but they were marvelously run, although spectators spoke often of the military atmosphere as Soviet soldiers were on every street corner with automatic weapons. The most-awaited races matched two British athletes in the 800 and 1,500 meters in the track and the boycott had no effect on them. Sebastian Coe was favored in the 800 and Steve Ovett in the 1,500. They each won a gold medal, but in the "other man's" event. The athlete winning the most medals in Moscow was Soviet gymnast Aleksandr Dityatin, who won medals in all eight gymnastics events, three of them gold, setting a record for the most medals won at a single Olympics.

It is almost impossible to be certain how many nations boycotted or chose not to attend the 1980 Olympic Games in response to the Soviet invasion of Afghanistan. The U.S. government dogmatically stated numerous times that 65 nations joined the U.S.-led boycott, but that number is almost certainly wrong and too high. Because of political repercussions, many nations simply stated that they could not attend because of financial or other reasons, when in likelihood they were joining the boycott. On the other hand, among the nonparticipating nations, it is likely that a few were not boycotting, but did not compete for other reasons. No definitive further conclusions can be drawn concerning the number of boycotting nations.

For the record, the following 63 nations did not compete in Moscow but were IOC members, and eligible to compete in the Olympics, as of 27 May 1980, the due date for acceptance of invitations to the 1980 Olympic Games: Albania, Antigua, Argentina, Bahamas, Bahrain, Bangladesh, Barbados, Belize, Bermuda, Bolivia, Canada, Cayman Islands, Central African Republic, Chad, Chile, China, Egypt, El Salvador, Federal Republic of Germany, Fiji, Gabon, the Gambia, Ghana, Haiti, Honduras, Hong Kong, Indonesia, Israel, Ivory Coast, Japan, Kenya, Korea, Liberia, Liechtenstein, Malawi, Malaysia, Mauritania, Mauritius, Monaco, Morocco, Netherlands Antilles, Niger, Norway, Pakistan, Panama, Papua-New Guinea, Paraguay, the Philippines, Saudi Arabia, Singapore, Somalia, Sudan, Suriname, Swaziland, Thailand, Togo, Tunisia, Turkey, United States, U.S. Virgin Islands, Upper Volta, Uruguay, and Zaire.

As stated, the deadline for responding to the Moscow invitation to compete at the Olympic Games was 27 May 1980. The above nations can be separated into three categories based on this deadline: 1) declined the invitation, 2) did not respond to the invitation, and 3) accepted the invitation but eventually did not compete.

Twenty-eight nations declined the invitation to compete, as follows: Albania, Argentina, Bahrain, Bermuda, Canada, Cayman Islands, China, Federal Republic of Germany, the Gambia, Honduras, Hong Kong, Indonesia, Israel, Kenya, Liechtenstein, Malawi, Malaysia, Mauritania, Pakistan, Paraguay, the Philippines, Saudi Arabia, Singapore, Thailand, Tunisia, Turkey, United States, and Uruguay.

Twenty-nine nations did not respond to the invitation to compete by 27 May 1980, as follows: Antigua, Bahamas, Bangladesh, Barbados, Belize, Bolivia, Central African Republic, Chad, Chile, Egypt, El Salvador, Fiji, Ghana, Haiti, Ivory Coast, Japan, Korea, Liberia, Monaco, Morocco, Netherlands Antilles, Norway, Papua-New Guinea, Somalia, Sudan, Swaziland, Togo, U.S. Virgin Islands, and Zaire.

Six nations accepted the invitation to compete, but eventually chose not to, as follows: Gabon, Mauritius, Niger, Panama, Suriname, and Upper Volta. The reasons for these nations eventually choosing not to participate are not clear.

There were two further categories of "IOC-member" nations in 1980. Both Chinese Taipei and Iran had been member nations of the IOC, but at the time of the Moscow invitation they were in suspension and were not eligible to compete at the 1980 Olympic Games.

Finally, three nations were accepted into IOC membership at the IOC Executive Board Meeting in Lausanne on 9–10 June 1980, after the due date for acceptances to the Moscow invitation. These were Mozambique, Qatar, and the United Arab Emirates. These nations were, therefore, not technically eligible to compete at Moscow. However, Mozambique did compete, although Qatar and the United Arab Emirates did not. It is likely that, because of the boycott, late invitations were extended to these three nations to fill out the list of competing nations in Moscow, and Mozambique was able to field a team in time, and chose to do so.

The 14th Olympic Winter Games (1984) The 14th Olympic Winter Games were held in Sarajevo, Bosnia-Herzegovina Province, Yugoslavia, from 8 through 19 February 1984. Forty-nine nations attended with 1,273 athletes competing (996 men and 277 women). At the 80th IOC session in Athens on 18 May 1978, Sarajevo was chosen in the second round of balloting (39 votes) over Sapporo, Japan (36 votes); and Göteburg, Sweden (eliminated after round one).

After the controversy, problems, and excitement that were Lake Placid, Sarajevo's Winter Olympics were much quieter, in marked contrast to the Yugoslavian civil war that would come to Sarajevo within the next decade. The only difficulties were early weather problems. An initial concern about lack of snow was alleviated when a blizzard hit shortly after the opening ceremonies, forcing the men's downhill to be postponed twice.

In nordic skiing, Marja-Liisa Hämäläinen (FIN) won three cross-country skiing gold medals—but nordic skiing rarely captures the press notices of figure skating, alpine skiing, or ice hockey, and Hämäläinen's feat was noted with little fanfare outside Finland.

In ice hockey, the Soviets restored the status quo when they easily won the gold medal. The Canadians, having returned to Olympic ice hockey in 1980, were thought to have a chance as some professionals could now be used. But the USSR played seven games, won seven games, and won the gold medal.

In ice dancing, the British couple Jayne Torvill and Christopher Dean was heavily favored based on past performances. Their final program was quite controversial, however, as it probably violated ice dancing protocol by being based on a single piece of music, Ravel's "Bolero."

Their performance to "Bolero" was mesmerizing, building to an almost orgiastic finish that brought the crowd to a frenzy. The judges awarded the British pair the highest scores ever seen in figure skating, with 12 perfect 6.0s out of 18 marks.

In singles figure skating, Scott Hamilton (USA) and Katarina Witt (GDR) won gold medals. Hamilton was expected to win as he had been nonpareil since the 1980 Olympics. Witt was not as well known and was not favored, but her stunning beauty helped to make her a crowd favorite.

Sarajevo had been a beautiful Olympic city, but within a decade it would lie in ruins, as would many of the sports facilities, destroyed by the senseless war in the Balkans—victims, with so many innocent people, of ethnic cleansing.

The Games of the XXIIIrd Olympiad (1984)　The Games of the XXIIIrd Olympiad were held in Los Angeles, California, USA, from 2 July through 12 August 1984. Los Angeles was awarded the Olympics by acclamation at the 80th IOC session in Athens on 18 May 1978. No other candidate city bid for these Olympics. One hundred forty nations attended the Los Angeles Olympics with 6,799 athletes competing (5,224 men and 1,575 women).

In May 1984, the Soviet Union announced that it would not attend the Olympics in Los Angeles, citing concerns over the safety of its athletes because of the "anti-Soviet and anti-Communist activities" in the Los Angeles area. Most people considered the boycott one of retribution for the United States' refusal to compete in Moscow. Most of the Eastern European countries joined in the Soviet-bloc boycott, notably East Germany (GDR), and it was joined by Cuba. Although only 14 invited countries did not compete in Los Angeles, the absence of the USSR, Cuba, and the GDR made many of the events mere shadows of what was anticipated.

Still, more countries and athletes competed at Los Angeles than in any previous Olympics. However, what the 1984 boycott lacked in numbers relative to the 1980 boycott, it made up for in its impact on the competition. Boxing, weightlifting, wrestling, gymnastics, and, to a certain extent, track and field would have been dominated by the boycotting nations. The nations that did not compete were Afghanistan, Bulgaria, Cuba, Czechoslovakia, Ethiopia, German Democratic Republic, Hungary, Laos, Mongolia, North Korea, Poland, South Yemen, Vietnam, and the USSR. Bravely, Romania defied the boycott and competed at the Olympics, receiving an ovation at the opening ceremonies second only to that of the United States.

China also returned to the Olympic Games at Los Angeles in 1984, after an absence of 32 years (China had competed at the Olympic Games of 1932, 1936, 1948, and 1952). The country had competed at the 1980 Olympic Winter Games in Lake Placid. China's appearance at the opening ceremonies was greeted warmly by the American crowd, especially in light of the Soviet boycott. Yugoslavia, not Soviet dominated, was the only other country from Eastern Europe to compete.

After all that, the Olympics were very well run, although the Europeans had numerous complaints, mostly about customary American methods of doing business. American television concentrated on U.S. athletes, which infuriated the Europeans. For the first time ever, the Games were managed in an entrepreneurial fashion. Organizing committee president Peter Ueberroth insisted that the Olympics be designed to break even or even provide a profit. Again, the Europeans, used to the simon-pure idealistic image of the Olympics for the Olympics' sake, rebelled against this philosophy. But Ueberroth was determined that the Games would be financially independent and he succeeded admirably in that regard. Ueberroth's marketing methods, though initially vilified by the Europeans, have since been copied by all organizing committees and even the IOC itself.

As to the sports themselves, the competition was good, though diluted in many ways because of the boycott. Carl Lewis emerged as the American men's star, equaling Jesse Owens's 1936 feat of winning four gold medals in track and field. But Lewis did not have Owens's appeal to the American public and his image, almost obsequiously nurtured by his manager, failed to live up to his deeds on the track.

Failing Lewis, the American public reached instead to Mary Lou Retton, who became the first American gymnast to win the all-around individual gold. To win she needed a perfect 10 on her last event, the horse vault. Given two vaults, she achieved the 10, not once, but twice.

After the difficulties of Munich and Montreal, Los Angeles had been the only bidder for the Games of 1984. And Los Angeles, despite its problems, revitalized the Olympic movement to some degree. Having shown that the Olympics did not need to be a "loss-leader" and could, in fact, produce an operating profit, many cities now were interested in hosting the Olympics. Shortly after the 1984 Olympics, six cities would submit official bids to host the 1992 Games.

The 15th Olympic Winter Games (1988)   The 15th Olympic Winter Games were held in Calgary, Alberta, Canada, from 13 through 28 February 1988. Fifty-seven nations attended with 1,425 athletes competing (1,110 men and 315 women). At the 84th IOC session in Baden-Baden, Germany, on 30 September 1981, Calgary was chosen on the second round (48 votes) over Falun, Sweden (31 votes); and Cortina d'Ampezzo, Italy (eliminated after round one).

In ice hockey, the Soviets again were dominant. The speed skating hero was the unlikely Yvonne van Gennip of the Netherlands. All attention was focused on the GDR's quartet of Karin Kania, Andrea Ehrig, Christa Rothenburger, and Gabi Zange, and the United States' Bonnie Blair. They skated well, with Blair winning the 500 and Rothenburger the 1,000, and between them, those five won 12 of the available 15 medals. But the other three were won by van Gennip, who won the 1,500, 3,000, and 5,000 meters, defeating the favored Ehrig and Zange in the long-distance races.

One of the media heroes was Italian alpine skier Alberto Tomba, who won two gold medals, and delighted the press with his nightly antics. He attempted to date the GDR's Katarina Witt, who won her second consecutive figure skating gold medal, but he got nowhere, which further delighted the media. Witt's top competitor was the American, Debi Thomas, who had been World Champion in 1987, but Thomas skated relatively poorly and finished third. Her bronze medal was the first ever won by a black athlete at the Olympic Winter Games.

In men's speed skating, the real hero was probably a man who never finished a race at Calgary. Dan Jansen was a favorite in the 500 meters, and in the 1,000, he was thought to have a chance to win. But on the morning of the first race, the 500, he found out that his sister, who had been ill with leukemia, had died. He elected to skate that night but fell on the first turn. A few days later, he hoped to redeem himself in the 1,000 meters and through 600 meters, he had the fastest pace. But he fell again. The world watched and suffered with him, but Dan Jansen offered no excuses. He was gracious and magnanimous throughout. Years of effort were lost, certainly by the emotions of the moment, but he responded with the grace so often requested of our athletes, and yet so rarely offered.

The Games of the XXIVth Olympiad (1988)   The Games of the XXIVth Olympiad were held in Seoul, Republic of Korea, from 17 September through 5 October 1988. One hundred fifty-nine nations attended the Olympics with 8,447 athletes competing (6,251 men and 2,196 women).

On 30 September 1981, the IOC elected Seoul as the host city over Nagoya, Japan, by a vote of 52-27 at the 84th IOC session in Baden-Baden, Germany. The choice was highly controversial, as many prominent nations in the Olympic movement, notably the Soviet-bloc nations, did not have diplomatic relations with the Seoul government. There was widespread concern that another boycott would ensue because of this.

The problem became more complicated in July 1985 when North Korea demanded that it be allowed to cohost the Games with the Republic of Korea. Over the next three years the IOC negotiated with North Korea and offered to allow it to stage several events. However, no IOC concession was ever enough for the North, which wanted equal cohost status and an equal number of events. It demanded this despite the fact that the Games were close at hand and it had no possible hope of building the necessary facilities in time. When the IOC would not acquiesce further to the North's demands, North Korea announced that it would definitely boycott the Seoul Olympics.

By then, however, most of the Soviet-bloc countries had agreed to compete in Seoul, making 1988 the first Summer Olympic competition in 12 years between the United States, the Soviet Union, and the German Democratic Republic. After North Korea's official boycott announcement, Cuba and Ethiopia also made it official that they would not attend the Olympics, out of solidarity with North Korea. Nicaragua, Albania, and the Seychelles also did not attend the Olympics, although their reasons were less clear and may not have been directly related to any boycott.

Thus, although there was a boycott of the 1988 Olympics, it encompassed only six nations and had minimal effect on the Games themselves. The Seoul Games went on and saw the largest participation in Olympic history. There were more nations and athletes represented than ever before. The Games themselves were excellent and were very well run. Controversies and political intrusions, unlike the Games of the last 20 years, were relatively few and comparatively minor.

Three swimmers and one female track and field athlete dominated the sporting events. In the pool, the GDR's Kristin Otto broke all sorts of records by winning six gold medals, an unmatched performance by a woman at the Olympics. Her only rival for swimming supremacy was America's Janet Evans who won three distance swimming gold medals. On the men's side of the pool, Matt Biondi was attempting to equal Mark Spitz's record of seven gold medals. He failed in his first two events, taking a silver and a bronze, but won gold medals in his last five events.

On the track, the world was stunned by the performances of sprinter Florence Griffith Joyner. At the Olympics she won the 100 and 200, setting a world record in the 200 finals, and helped the American women win a gold medal in the 4 × 100 relay. She also ran anchor on the 4 × 400 relay team, adding a silver medal to her three golds, in the best race of the 1988 Olympics, as the Soviet Union narrowly defeated the American relay team.

The biggest media event of the 1988 Olympic Games was the disqualification of sprinter Ben Johnson, after he had won the 100 meters in a world-record time of 9.79 seconds, defeating Carl Lewis. Johnson tested positive for an anabolic steroid (stanazolol) and was disqualified, with Lewis receiving the gold medal. After the uproar of the scandal, the Canadians organized an investigation into drug use in international athletics, the Dubin Inquiry. At the inquiry, Johnson admitted that he had used steroids for several years.

The 16th Olympic Winter Games (1992)   The 16th Olympic Winter Games were held in Albertville, France, from 8 through 23 February 1992. Sixty-four nations attended with 1,801 athletes competing (1,313 men and 488 women). At the 91st IOC session in Lausanne on 17 October 1986, Albertville was chosen by the IOC on the fifth round of voting over a large field of candidate cities: Sofia, Bulgaria (fifth round); Falun, Sweden (fifth round); Lillehammer, Norway (fourth round); Cortina d'Ampezzo, Italy (third round); Anchorage, Alaska, USA (second round); and Berchtesgaden, Germany (first round).

This was the third Olympic Winter Games to be held in France, and the second to be held in the French Savoie, after the 1924 Games in Chamonix in the Haute-Savoie. The 1968 Games in Grenoble (Isère) were in the Dauphiné area of the French Alps. The Games were awarded to Albertville, but they were actually spread over several small towns and villages of the French Savoie in the French Alps. Expected problems with transportation between the villages did not materialize, and the Games were extremely well run.

Another innovation was the introduction of a number of new Olympic sports and events to the Winter Games. Women competed in biathlon for the first time. Men and women competed in short-track speed skating skated in a pack style. Freestyle skiing, which had been a demonstration sport in 1988, returned with moguls débuting as a full-medal sport. Speed skiing and the other two freestyle disciplines, ballet and aerials, were demonstration events.

The biggest news was the Olympic appearance of several new teams because of the political upheavals that had occurred in the past two years. Germany competed as a single team and independent nation for the first time since 1936. Because of the breakup of the Soviet Union, the Baltic States of Estonia and Latvia competed for the first time since 1936, and Lithuania for the first time since 1928. Two newly independent nations that had been former states of Yugoslavia, Croatia, and Slovenia, competed at the Olympics as independent nations. The Soviet Union, which no longer existed, was represented instead by the Unified Team (Équipe Unifée), representing a portion of the Commonwealth of Independent States. Russia, Belarus (formerly Byelorussia), the Ukraine, Kazakstan, and Uzbekistan made up the states of the Unified Team at Albertville.

Athletically the biggest winners were two male cross-country runners from Norway and two female cross-country runners from the Unified Team. Yelena Välbe and Lyubov Yegorova won five medals in the women's events while Vegard Ulvang and Bjørn Dæhlie won four medals in the men's events.

The Games of the XXVth Olympiad (1992) The Games of the XXVth Olympiad were held in Barcelona, Spain, from 25 July through 9 August 1992. At the 91st IOC session in Lausanne on 17 October 1986, Barcelona (47 votes) was awarded the Games on the third ballot over Paris, France (23 votes); Brisbane, Australia (10 votes); and Belgrade, Yugoslavia (5 votes). Other candidate cities that were eliminated earlier in the voting were Birmingham, England, Great Britain (second round); and Amsterdam, the Netherlands (first round). One hundred sixty-nine nations attended the Games with 9,386 athletes competing (6,663 men and 2,723 women).

The Barcelona Olympics were the Games of the New World Order. They were the most highly attended Olympics in history, both in terms of countries and athletes attending. After four consecutive Olympics with some form of protest or boycott, the Barcelona Olympics were boycott-free.

Since Seoul in 1988, the world had taken on a new face. The Soviet Union no longer existed, but the Commonwealth of Independent States did. Estonia, Latvia, and Lithuania were once again free countries. East and West Germany were no more, replaced again by a unified Germany; Yugoslavia was now split into several republics; and North and South Yemen had merged into one. All of these new national groupings appeared at Barcelona. South Africa had eliminated, at least constitutionally, apartheid, and competed at the Olympics for the first time since 1960. The Commonwealth of Independent States competed as a "Unified Team" for the last time, representing all the former republics of the Soviet Union, save for the Baltic States.

The Games were opened beautifully and dramatically as archer Antônio Rebollo lit the Olympic Flame via bow and arrow. The drama and beauty of Catalonia continued onstage throughout the 16 days of the Olympics. There was concern about terrorist activity because the area was home to some terrorist groups, but heightened security and vigilance helped avoid any problems.

The competition was excellent. For the first time since 1972, all the major nations of the world attended. The most publicized athletes were the American basketball players. The U.S. was allowed to use professional players from the NBA (National Basketball Association), since all the other nations were by now using professionals. The NBA All-Star team, nicknamed "The Dream Team," did not disappoint, putting on a clinic for all nations and winning the gold medal unchallenged. It was led by professional greats Magic Johnson, Michael Jordan, and Larry Bird.

Many East European countries and the former Soviets continued to dominate certain sports, such as gymnastics and weightlifting. There were many great athletic performances, but other than the Dream Team, no one athlete seemed to capture these Games like so many had in the past. It was probably fitting, for then no athlete seemed larger than the

Games themselves; fitting, because Barcelona was possibly the finest manifestation yet seen of the Olympic movement.

The 17th Olympic Winter Games (1994)   The 17th Olympic Winter Games were held in Lillehammer, Norway, from 12 through 27 February 1994. Sixty-seven nations attended with 1,738 athletes competing (1,216 men and 522 women). At the 94th IOC session in Seoul on 15 September 1988, Lillehammer was chosen on the third round (45 votes) over Östersund, Sweden (39 votes, third round); Anchorage, Alaska, USA (second round); and Sofia, Bulgaria (first round).

For the first time, the Olympic Winter Games were not scheduled for the same year as the Games of the Olympiad. The International Olympic Committee had decided to hold the Olympic Winter Games in the second year after the Olympic Games, thus shortening the cycle so that an Olympic Games or Olympic Winter Games would be held in a rotation every two years. The decision was ostensibly because this would result in greater advertising and sponsorship money.

Before the Lillehammer Olympics began, they were haunted by the Nancy Kerrigan–Tonya Harding story, in which Harding's bodyguard and ex-husband admitted to attacking Kerrigan prior to the U.S. Olympic trials, a story that was ubiquitous in the U.S. press and television. Eventually, both Kerrigan and Harding made the U.S. Olympic figure skating team. Kerrigan skated well, winning a silver medal behind the Ukraine's Oksana Bayul. Harding eventually pleaded to having knowledge of the attack on Kerrigan and her figure skating effectively ended after her eighth-place finish at Lillehammer.

But even the "Kardigan Saga" would not mar what was a fairy-tale–like two weeks, which ended all thoughts of the problems that had preceded them, and reminded us again of what the Olympics and sport can bring to the world. There were many great athletic feats at the Lillehammer Games. Manuela Di Centa won five medals in cross-country skiing. Norway's Johann Olav Koss won three speed skating gold medals in world record time. Dan Jansen won the hearts of sports fans everywhere when he finally won a gold medal in the 1,000 meter speed skating. But through it all, the champions seemed to be the small town of Lillehammer and the people of Norway itself.

There were also many poignant memories of Sarajevo, which had hosted the 1984 Olympic Winter Games, and which lay in ruins because of the war in the Balkans. Katarina Witt skated her long program to "Where Have All the Flowers Gone?" in memory of the citizens who had lost their lives in that war. On the next-to-last night, at the figure skating exhibition, Jayne Torvill and Christopher Dean skated "Bolero" as they had done so hauntingly in 1984 at Sarajevo. Koss donated a major portion of his Olympic bonus (about $33,000 [US]) to Olympic Aid for the citizens of Sarajevo. And during the Lillehammer Olympics, IOC president Juan Antonio Samaranch visited Sarajevo, seeing in person the stark contrast between the Olympic city and the Sarajevo of 1994. At the closing ceremonies, Samaranch also spoke movingly about the war-torn city.

It was said of the Lillehammer Olympics: "The XVII Winter Olympics did not exist. Norway did not exist. These were the fairy-tale Games, drawn from the imagination, staged in the pages of a children's book. They could not exist. Reality cannot be this good" (*Sports Illustrated* [March 7, 1994]: 90).

The Games of the XXVIth Olympiad (1996)   The Games of the XXVIth Olympiad were held in Atlanta, Georgia, USA, from 19 July through 4 August 1996. Atlanta won the IOC nomination at the 96th IOC session on 18 September 1990 in the fifth round (51 votes) over Athens, Greece (35 votes). Other candidate cities were Toronto, Ontario, Canada (fourth round); Melbourne, Australia (third round); Manchester, England, Great Britain (second round); and Belgrade, Yugoslavia (first round). For the first time ever, all IOC member nations competed at the Olympics, with 197 nations present, with 10,323 athletes competing (6,815 men and 3,508 women).

Atlanta was a highly controversial choice, as Athens was favored. Athens had not been an Olympic host since 1906, or officially 1896, and the Greeks seemed to feel that the 1996 Olympics belonged to them as a birthright. When they lost the bid, the Greeks were irate, feeling that the Games had been stolen from them.

The 1996 Olympics were a chance for Atlanta to demonstrate itself as a major international city. However, Atlanta had problems as the city was inundated with vendors and salespeople selling Olympic-related merchandise and attempting to make a fast buck off the Olympics. The atmosphere was unsavory and commercialized and not appreciated by many foreign visitors. The major problem that occurred at the 1996 Olympics came on Saturday, 27 July, shortly after midnight, when a bomb exploded in the Centennial Olympic Park, where many spectators and fans congregated and partied throughout the night. The bomb killed two people and injured several more. In late 2004, Eric Rudolph was caught and found in the mountains of North Carolina. He later admitted his guilt in the bombing, as well as in the bombings of several abortion clinics.

The biggest medal winner at Atlanta was American swimmer Amy Van Dyken, who won four gold medals. She was challenged in the pool by the Irish swimmer Michelle Smith, who won three gold medals. But Smith was dogged by doping rumors because her times had improved so dramatically. In track and field athletics, Michael Johnson was expected to be the most publicized athlete, and he did win the 200 meters in world record time, and added a second gold medal in the 400 meters. But he was overshadowed by Carl Lewis, competing in his fourth Olympics, who came through as had done so often, winning a fourth long jump gold medal in his last Olympics.

The 18th Olympic Winter Games (1998)   The 18th Olympic Winter Games were held in Nagano, Japan, from 7 through 22 February 1998. At the 97th IOC session in Birmingham, England, on 15 June 1991, Nagano won the nomination in the fourth round (46 votes) over Salt Lake City, Utah, USA (42 votes, fourth round); Östersund, Sweden (third round); Aosta, Italy (second round); and Jaca, Spain (first round). Nagano had been an "upset" choice over the more favored selections of Salt Lake City and Östersund.

A number of new events made their Olympic début in Nagano, probably foremost among these being women's ice hockey, which was won by the United States team in a mild upset over the favored Canadians. Snowboarding and curling also were new to the program. Snowboarding had four events—men's and women's halfpipe and giant slalom. There were 72 nations present at Nagano, a record for the Olympic Winter Games, with 2,180 athletes competing (1,391 men and 789 women).

In men's ice hockey, the big story was the presence of the top professional players in the world for the first time ever. The National Hockey League (NHL) closed down its midseason schedule for two weeks to allow all the pros to represent their countries, reminiscent of the "Dream Team" of NBA players at Barcelona. The difference in ice hockey, however, was that the top players were not solely from one nation, but were spread among several hockey powers—Canada, United

States, Russia, Sweden, Finland, and the Czech Republic. The two favorites, the United States and Canada, went out early, and neither won a medal. The final came down to Russia against the Czech Republic, and the Czechs won in a slight upset, aided by the superb goaltending of Dominik Hašek of the Buffalo Sabres of the NHL. The Czech team defeated successively the three greatest hockey nations in Olympic history—Canada, Russia, and the United States.

Norway's Bjørn Dæhlie added to his list of Olympic records by winning four medals and three golds, to bring his overall Olympic total to 12 medals and eight gold medals, all Olympic Winter Games' records. Russia's Larisa Lazutina won the most medals at Nagano, with five in women's nordic skiing. She and Dæhlie were the only athletes to win three gold medals at Nagano.

Also dominant at Nagano were the Dutch speed skaters, whose men won nine of 15 Olympic medals, and four of five events. Marianne Timmer also added two golds in the women's 1,000 and 1,500. Germany's Gunda Niemann won three medals in speed skating, bringing her Olympic career total to eight, equaling the Olympic speed skating record.

The Games of the XXVIIth Olympiad (2000)   The Games of the XXVIIth Olympiad were held in Sydney, New South Wales, Australia, from 16 September to 1 October 2000, with preliminary football (soccer) matches actually opening the Games on 14 September. In a closely fought contest, Sydney was awarded the 2000 Olympics during the 101st IOC session in Monte Carlo on 23 September 1993 over Beijing, China, by only two votes (45-43) in the fourth round. Other candidate cities participating in the voting were Manchester, England (third round); Berlin, Germany (second round); and Istanbul, Turkey (first round). Brasilia, Brazil; Milan, Italy; and Tashkent, Uzbekistan, also made bids to the IOC but withdrew before the final vote. At Sydney, 199 nations competed, along with East Timor, not yet an IOC member, but whose athletes (four men and one woman) competed at the invitation of the IOC as Independent Olympic Athletes (IOA). There were 10,647 competitors (6,579 men and 4,068 women).

The 2000 Olympic Games began on a Sydney evening in which the Olympic torch was lit by Australian 400 meter runner, Cathy Freeman. Freeman was a decidedly political choice, as she was of aboriginal origin, and the country had effectively adopted her in keeping with their recent policy of making amends to the aboriginal peoples, for years of mistreatment. If Freeman, who went on to win the 400 meters, could be considered a perfect choice for the final torchbearer, as many felt she was, it was only the beginning of many perfect choices made by the Australian hosts.

The venues were centered around Sydney Olympic Park, built on the site of an old cattleyard. This one relatively small region contained virtually all the major venues for the Olympic events. The park served as an international collegial meeting place, while providing easy access for all spectators to the venues. And the venues met with uniform raves from the athletes, fans, and media alike.

Strangely, no single athlete dominated the 2000 Olympic Games, though several tried. Marion Jones (USA) tried to win five gold medals in track and field. She won three, and added two bronzes but it seemed almost anticlimactic. Australia's Ian Thorpe was predicted to dominate the pool, but he won only one individual event, and added another gold in a relay. In cycling, Dutchwoman Leontien Zijlaard-van Moorsel won three gold medals and four medals in all. But no athlete seemed bigger than the host city itself. Sydney was the star of the 2000 Olympic Games.

Were the Sydney Olympic Games a perfect Olympics? No, because nothing of that sort could ever exist. But they came close, and at the closing ceremony, there were few who had attended who would not be willing to cede all future Olympic Games to the New South Wales capital. As he has done several times before, IOC president Juan Antonio Samaranch declared the Sydney Olympics "the best ever." This time, there were no dissenters.

The 19th Olympic Winter Games (2002) The 19th Olympic Winter Games were held in Salt Lake City, Utah, United States, from 8 through 24 February 2002. At the 104th IOC session in Budapest, Hungary, on 16 June 1995, Salt Lake City was chosen as the host city in round one over three other finalist cities, with 55 votes. The other finalist cities were Östersund, Sweden (14 votes); Sion, Switzerland (14 votes); and Quebec City, Quebec, Canada (7 votes). Ten cities made preliminary bids; the other six candidate cities were as follows: Almaty, Kazakstan; Graz, Austria; Jaca, Spain; Poprad-Tatry, Slovakia; Sochi, Russia; and Tarvisio, Italy. On 24 January 1995, the IOC Evaluation Commission eliminated all but four bidding cities in a new effort to decrease time, effort, and costs by so many bid candidates.

In late 1998–early 1999, the Salt Lake City bid was rocked by rumors of rampant bribery given to IOC members in an attempt to secure the bid. This led to the Olympic bribery scandal, and multiple investigations of the IOC, the Salt Lake City Bid Committee, and the Olympic movement in general. Full details of this can be found in the dictionary entry discussing the Olympic bribery scandal. With the withdrawal of several administrators who were implicated in the scandal, the Olympic Winter Games were only two years away and without leadership. Worse still was that several sponsors were making noises about withdrawing financial support, threatening a fiscal disaster. And as the stock market in 1999–2000 began to fall from its raging-bull status, new money to support the Salt Lake City Olympics could not be easily found. The Salt Lake Organizing Committee reached out to Mitt Romney as their new chief. Romney was the son of George Romney, a former U.S. presidential candidate, and he was a financial wizard, having made a fortune as the leader of Bain Capital, a venture capital firm. He quickly righted the ship, and all seemed well again on the banks of the Great Salt Lake.

Then, on 11 September 2001, a scant five months before the opening ceremony, Arab terrorists attacked American soil, hijacking four airplanes and crashing two of them into the twin towers of the World Trade Center, another into the Pentagon, and the fourth into a field in Pennsylvania. The United States responded by launching a war on terrorism and within weeks was waging war on Arab terrorists and the Al-Qaeda organization in Afghanistan. A larger war seemed imminent. Now the question was not if Salt Lake City could fund Olympic Games in February 2002, but whether there would be any Games at all. Security concerns would have to be ramped up an order of magnitude. But federal security forces, which were to be used at the Winter Olympics, might be diverted to fight the war, and it was not known if they would be available for the Olympics. And if the United States waged an all-out war, would other nations attend peaceful Olympic Games? Remember, the United States had boycotted the Moscow 1980 Olympics specifically because they thought it was wrong to attend Olympic Games while the host nation was fighting a war.

But somehow, the 2002 Olympic Winter Games were held, and they were Olympic Games to remember. Mitt Romney and the Salt Lake Organizing Committee (SLOC) overcame all the obstacles. Security was tight, but not much more intrusive than that which was seen at Sydney.

The American public embraced the Winter Olympics as "our" Games, a chance to heal the wounds from the assault on its shores. The Europeans, often critical of American Olympic Games, made a few by now standard grumblings about too much television coverage of American athletes, but much less so than at Los Angeles in 1984. And there were none of the organizational problems of the 1996 Atlanta Olympics. The weather cooperated as well, with plenty of snow before the Games, but clear, cold weather in the first week, and then almost springlike conditions in the second week. There were 77 nations competing at Salt Lake City, with 2,399 athletes (1,513 men and 886 women).

The biggest news of the 2002 Olympic Winter Games was the controversy surrounding the pairs figure skating event. On the night of the free skate, the leaders were the Russians, Yelena Berezhnaya and Anton Sikharulidze, with the Canadian pair, Jamie Salé and David Pelletier, close behind in second. Whoever won the free skate would win the gold medal, and to the audience, and many figure skating experts, that appeared to be the Canadians, who skated cleanly while the Russians had made several errors. But the judges voted 5-4 in favor of the Russians, giving them the gold medal. The audience and media howled in protest, and within 24 hours rumors of vote-fixing were rampant, focusing on the French skating judge, Marie Reine LeGougne. Eventually, IOC president Jacques Rogge ordered the International Skating Union (ISU) to hold emergency meetings to investigate the rumors. Within three days, the ISU and IOC announced that the two pairs would be considered cochampions and Salé and Pelletier were also given gold medals. The controversy reached even further, calling for a complete overhaul of figure skating judging.

The two biggest medal winners at Salt Lake City received them in seeming obscurity, as the American media focused on the figure skating furor. Ole Einar Bjørndalen of Norway won four gold medals in the four biathlon events, sweeping the competition. In women's alpine skiing, Croatia's Janica Kostelić won three gold medals and four medals in all. She became the first Olympic alpine skier to win four medals at one Games.

The Games of the XXVIIIth Olympiad (2004)   The Games of the XXVIIIth Olympiad were held in Athens, Greece, from 13 through 29 August 2004. Athens was awarded the 2004 Olympics during the 106th

IOC session in Lausanne on 5 September 1997 over Rome, Italy (fourth round); Cape Town, South Africa (third round); Stockholm, Sweden (second round); and Buenos Aires, Argentina (first round). There were originally 11 candidate cities. Because of the number of candidate cities, the IOC Evaluation Commission eliminated all but the above five cities prior to the voting. The other candidate cities, which did not advance to the voting round, were Istanbul, Turkey; Lille, France; Rio de Janeiro, Brazil; San Juan, Puerto Rico; Seville, Spain; and St. Petersburg, Russia. There were 10,560 competitors in Athens (6,255 men and 4,305 women), with 201 nations competing. (The press usually states that there were 202 nations, but Djibouti, which entered four athletes, two in track and field athletics and two in tennis, had no athletes actually compete.)

The Athens Olympic Games were a return of the Olympic movement to its roots, as the ancient Olympic Games were held in Greece, in ancient Olympia, on the Peloponnesus Peninsula. The first modern Olympic Games were held in Athens, and in 1906, Athens again hosted an Olympic Games. In 1990, Athens bid to host the 1996 Olympic Games, the centennial Olympics, but lost out to Atlanta. The Greeks and Athenians were bitter that they had not been awarded the right to host the 100th anniversary of the modern Olympics but regrouped to bid successfully for the 2004 Olympic Games, narrowly defeating the favorite, Rome.

But all would not be well with the Athens organization. In early 2001, IOC president Juan Antonio Samaranch visited Athens with the Coordination Commission for the Games of the XXVIIIth Olympiad and was alarmed that, only three years prior to the Olympics, construction had not been started on many of the venues and much of the infrastructure needed to host this huge international celebration was not to be found. Samaranch told the media that he was giving a yellow light to Athens, the smallest Olympic host city since Helsinki in 1952, and many people wondered if the Greeks could actually host a 21st-century Olympic Games. There was conjecture in the media that the IOC might try to move the site to another city at the figurative last minute.

Around the time of Samaranch's announcement, the Athens Organizing Committee (ATHOC) hired Gianna Angelopoulos-Daskalaki to return as president of the Organizing Committee. Mrs. Angelopoulos-Daskalaki had been the leader of the successful bid to host the 2004

Olympic Games but originally stepped down from leading ATHOC. Her return was heralded as the best chance the Greeks had to pull off what was becoming by early 2002 an organizational miracle.

Further complicating matters for the Greeks and the IOC was the international situation. After the Twin Towers attack of 11 September 2001, the United States waged war on Afghanistan and in late 2002, invaded Iraq. The Middle East, which sits geographically contiguous to the Greek peninsula, was a firecracker waiting to be lit. Security in Greece was considered to be almost impossibly difficult because of the geography. In addition to sitting next to the site of an ongoing war, Greece's northern border is mountainous, which made securing it difficult at best. And the Greek coastline is ragged and completely surrounds 80 percent of the nation. The cost of increasing security, in light of the world situation, became a major economic drag to ATHOC.

But in the end the Greeks did it. The venues were virtually all completed. The new airport and access roads to and from Athens were finished in plenty of time. Train routes around Athens and to the port city of Piraeus were upgraded and functioned well during the Olympics. There were almost no organizational difficulties once the Games began. The security worries never fully materialized. The only significant breach occurred during the men's marathon race, on the last day of the Olympics. The Brazilian, Vanderlei Lima, had a comfortable lead at 20 miles, when he was assaulted by a man who burst on the race course and knocked Lima into the crowd. Lima recovered but lost his rhythm and was eventually passed and finished third. The assailant was an Irish priest who had made similar disruptions at previous sporting events, notably a Formula One race.

The most publicized athlete in Greece was American swimmer Michael Phelps. Phelps was trying to better Mark Spitz's performance from 1972 by winning eight gold medals. He "failed" although he did win eight medals, but "only" six of them gold, missing the seven won by Spitz. Phelps won the 100 butterfly, the 200 butterfly, the 200 individual medley, the 400 individual medley, and relay gold medals in the 4×200 freestyle and 4×100 medley relay. In the 4×100 freestyle, the South Africans pulled off an improbable upset, and the favored United States team, led by Phelps, took only a bronze. In the 200 freestyle, Phelps finished third, with Australia's Ian Thorpe winning the race. Thorpe, the swimming star of the 2000 Olympics, also won the

400 freestyle, and added a silver in the 4 × 100 free relay, and a bronze in the 100 freestyle.

On the track, the biggest star was Britain's Kelly Holmes, who became only the third woman to win the Olympic 800 meter/1,500 meter double (also won in 1976 by Tatyana Kazankina [URS] and in 1996 by Svetlana Masterkova [RUS]). But the highlights of the track and field competition did not take place within the main Olympic stadium. The men's and women's marathons ran the original marathon course, beginning in the village of Marathon, and finished in the original Panathenaic Stadium, site of the 1896 and 1906 Olympics.

And for the first known time since the end of the ancient Olympic Games in 393 BCE, the Olympics returned to ancient Olympia. The men's and women's shot put competitions were held in the ancient Olympic stadium, with no seats. As in the ancient Games, the spectators sat on the side of a hill, with no cover from the brilliant Greek summer sun. The Olympic Games had come home.

The 20th Olympic Winter Games (2006)   The 20th Olympic Winter Games are scheduled to be held in Torino (Turin), Italy from 11 through 26 February 2006. At the 109th IOC session in Seoul, Korea, on 19 June 1999, Torino was chosen as the host city in round one with 53 votes, against 36 votes for Sion, Switzerland, the only other city that advanced to the voting round. There were other candidate cities, but the IOC Evaluation Commission eliminated all but Torino and Sion prior to the vote. The other candidate cities were Helsinki, Finland (with Lillehammer, Norway); Klagenfurt, Austria (with Cortina d'Ampezzo, Italy, and Ješnice, Slovenia); Poprad-Tatry, Slovakia; Zakopane, Poland.

The Games of the XXIXth Olympiad (2008)   The host city for the Games of the XXIXth Olympiad was chosen at the 112th IOC session in Moscow, Russia, in July 2001. Ten cities made application to the IOC to host the 2008 Olympic Games—Bangkok, Thailand; Beijing, China; Cairo, Egypt; Havana, Cuba; Istanbul, Turkey; Kuala Lumpur, Malaysia; Osaka, Japan; Paris, France; Seville, Spain; and Toronto, Ontario, Canada. At the first cut, Bangkok, Cairo, Havana, Kuala Lumpur, and Seville were eliminated. In the final voting, Beijing won in the second round with 56 votes to 22 for Toronto, 18 for Paris, and 9 for Istanbul. Osaka had been eliminated in the first round. The 2008 Olympic Games are scheduled to be held from 8 through 24 August 2008.

The 21st Olympic Winter Games (2010)   The 21st Olympic Winter Games are scheduled to be held in Vancouver, British Columbia, Canada, from 12 through 28 February 2010. There were eight cities that applied to host the 2010 Olympic Winter Games. One of these, Berne, Switzerland, withdrew shortly after the application, when the citizens of its canton voted in a referendum to withdraw the bid. This left Andorra la Vella, Andorra; Harbin, China; Jaca, Spain; Pyongchang, Korea; Salzburg, Austria; Sarajevo, Bosnia and Herzegovina; and Vancouver. The final cities that advanced to voting by the IOC were Vancouver, Salzburg, and Pyongchang, with Vancouver defeating Pyongchang 56-53 in the second round to win the right to host the 2010 Winter Olympics.

The Games of the XXXth Olympiad (2012)   The host city for the Games of the XXXth Olympiad was chosen at the 117th IOC session on 6 July 2005. The original nine candidate cities were Havana, Cuba; Istanbul, Turkey; Leipzig, Germany; London, Great Britain; Madrid, Spain; Moscow, Russia; New York, New York, United States; Paris, France; and Rio de Janeiro, Brazil. Four cities were eliminated, and the five remaining cities that advanced to the final vote were London, Madrid, Moscow, New York, and Paris. London was selected as the host city in the fourth round of voting over Paris 54-50.

The 22nd Olympic Winter Games (2014)   The 22nd Olympic Winter Games host city is yet to be selected. Initial applications to the IOC are due by 28 July 2005, with questionnaires required to be submitted to the IOC by 1 February 2006. The IOC will narrow the field in June 2006. The final candidate cities will file their bid books prior to 10 January 2007. The selection of the host city will occur at the IOC session in Guatemala City in July 2007. Preliminary inquiries for the 2014 Olympic Winter Games have been received from Salzburg, Austria; Pyongchang, Korea; and Östersund/Åre, Sweden.

Introduction

Nearly everyone has heard of the Olympic Games, as they are the most watched sporting event on the planet. But the term "Olympic movement" is foreign to all but devoted followers of the Olympic Games and Olympic movement. Basically, the Olympic movement is an attempt to bring all the nations of the world together in a series of multisport festivals—the Olympic Games—and seeks to use sport as a means to promote internationalism and peace. But in reality, it is much more complex than that, and one must examine its origins to fully understand the concept.

The Olympic movement began with the ancient Olympic Games that were held in Greece on the Peloponnesus Peninsula at Olympia, Greece. It is not clear why the Greeks instituted this quadrennial celebration in the form of an athletic festival. The recorded history of the ancient Olympic Games begins in 776 BCE, although it is suspected that the Games had been held for several centuries by that time. The Games were conducted as religious celebrations in honor of the god Zeus, and it is known that Olympia was a shrine to Zeus after about 1000 BCE. They were a simple event, especially in comparison to the modern Olympic Games. They lasted for five days, with only one day given to the competitions and the other four days devoted to the religious ceremonies. In the beginning, the ancient Olympic Games consisted of only one competition—a footrace of about 190 meters, termed the *stadion*.[1]

The origins of the ancient Olympic Games are also obscure. Some classicists state that they began to honor Hercules and he founded them after his victory over Augeas. Hercules declared the Games to be in honor of his father, Zeus. Another legend connects the Games to Pelops, a Phyrgian after whom the Peloponnesus was named. He defeated Oenomaus, King of Pisa, in a chariot race, which Oenomaus had ordered as a race in which Pelops could win the hand of his daughter,

Hippodameia. Oenomaus was thrown from his chariot and killed, and Pelops was worshipped as a hero. He took over the kingdom, and the Games were supposedly held at his tomb and in his honor.

Many legends surround the ancient Olympic Games, most of which are untrue. One concerns the Olympic truce. It is often stated that the ancient Greeks proclaimed a truce during the Olympic Games and all wars were stopped. In actuality, the Olympic truce only guaranteed safe passage for athletes and spectators traveling to and from Olympia to witness or participate in the Olympic Games. The ancient Olympic Games never stopped any wars. Another popular legend is that the ancient Greek athletes were simon-pure amateurs. But in truth, the term *amateur* did not even exist in the Greek language in that era. All of the greatest Greek Olympians were professionals, most of whom made their living by traveling from one athletic contest to the next, winning prizes at these events that provided their income.[2]

The ancient Olympic Games were contested through 393 CE, when they were stopped by imperial decree of the Roman emperor Theodosius I. By that time, they had degenerated into more of a circus atmosphere, popularized in the Roman Empire, but far from the original Olympic ideal that had inspired the Greeks.[3]

For almost 15 centuries, the world did not have Olympic Games, although they were not forgotten and were often mentioned in literature. The first attempts to restore the Olympic Games came in the 17th century with Robert Dover's Games, which were not much more than a series of country-fair athletic contests held in the Cotswolds of England. In the 19th century, a series of attempted revivals of the Olympic Games were held in various parts of the world. The most prominent of these were the Much Wenlock Olympian Games, held in Shropshire, England, beginning in 1850, and the Zappas Olympic Games, held in Athens, Greece, which were first conducted in 1859. The Zappas Olympic Games were held four times and were strictly Greek national sporting festivals. The Much Wenlock Olympian Games were the brainchild of Dr. William Penny Brookes. Modern scholars of the Olympic movement give much credit to Brookes as one of the men who originated the idea of reviving the ancient Olympic Games.[4]

However, full credit for the renovation of the Olympic Games is usually given to the Frenchman Baron Pierre de Coubertin. To Coubertin, in particular, should credit be given for instituting the modern Olympic movement, and for his efforts, Coubertin has been termed *le rénovateur*. Pierre de Coubertin was a French aristocrat born in 1863; in the 1880s, he became interested in education and the French educational system and sought ways to improve it. He traveled to Great Britain, the United States, and Canada to study their educational systems, and he became fascinated with the fact that their educational systems emphasized physical education as being an important part of their overall development. In England, he was especially entranced by the teachings of Thomas Arnold, the former headmaster at Rugby School, who developed the philosophy of "muscular Christianity," a concept by which athletic endeavors supposedly made one a better person spiritually.[5]

Coubertin's studies led him to the study of the ancient Greeks and the ancient Olympic Games. The ancient Greeks also believed in a philosophy similar to muscular Christianity, epitomized by the well-known saying "*Mens sana in corpore sano*," or in English, "A sound mind in a sound body." The Greek philosophy was actually called *kalokagathia*, or the harmonic combination of beauty and goodness. In concert with his study of the ancient Greek philosophy of *kalokagathia*, Coubertin became enamored by the idea of the ancient Olympic Games.

In Coubertin's mind, all of this seemed to fit together into one coherent goal. He would develop a movement that would emphasize international sports and athletics as a way of furthering the education of young men (but not women, as we will learn later). This movement would have as its finest hour an international gathering of these young men in a great sporting festival reminiscent of the ancient Olympics, the modern Olympic Games. What could be more perfect?

Coubertin first publicly suggested the idea of modern Olympic Games at a meeting of sports dignitaries at the Sorbonne in 1892, but nothing came of this. At this meeting, however, he first uttered his now famous plea,

> Let us export rowers, runners, and fencers; there is the free trade of the future, and on the day when it is introduced within the walls of old Europe the cause of peace will have received a new and mighty stay. This is enough to encourage your servant to dream now about the second part of his program; he hopes that you will help him as you have helped him hitherto, and that with you he will be able to continue and complete, on a basis suited to the conditions of modern life, this grandiose and salutary task, the restoration of the Olympic Games.

In 1894, he arranged another conference, entitled the Paris International Athletic Congress, which was held ostensibly to discuss amateurism. However, Coubertin had different ideas. He began with a seven-point program on amateurism but appended to it three further points, all to discuss the resurrection of the Olympic Games. His idea met with favor among the candidates, and the modern Olympic Games began two years later in Athens, Greece.[6]

The early years of the Olympic movement were difficult ones, and it was not certain that the idea would survive. In 1896, the Greeks actually resisted Coubertin's efforts and were not necessarily enthralled with the idea of holding modern Olympic Games. They were a poor country, and the effort was a difficult one for them financially. But Coubertin and the Greeks persisted and worked together, and the 1896 Olympic Games were successful, although they looked nothing like the more modern festivals. In both 1900 and 1904, the Olympic Games were held in conjunction with world's fairs, virtually as sideshows to the fairs. In 1900, the French concurrently held the Exposition Universelle in Paris, and the 1900 Olympic Games suffered for the lack of attention. A similar fate awaited the 1904 Olympic Games, held in concert with the Louisiana Purchase International Exposition.[7]

Although the Greeks had not been keen on holding the 1896 Olympics, they quickly warmed to the Olympic idea. In 1906, the Greeks held another Olympics, outside of the normal quadrennial cycle. Usually termed Intercalated or Interim Olympics, the IOC still does not recognize these Games, which is unfortunate, as, after the debacles of 1900 and 1904, the 1906 Olympic Games were the best held to date and probably saved the nascent Olympic movement. The Greeks actually planned to hold "Greek Olympic Games" every four years, spaced in between the "International" Olympic Games, but because of Greek political and financial troubles, it never came to be.[8]

In 1908, the Olympic Games were held in London, and all that could be heard was bickering between the British hosts and the American officials, who protested multiple events and acted every bit like the "ugly American." But the Games were actually the most international to date and were well run—even if the U.S. officials thought otherwise. In addition, the 1908 Olympics forced many sports to form International Federations to govern their sports on a worldwide basis and set up standard sets of rules in order to prevent future repeats of the many rules controversies from 1908.[9]

After 1908, the Olympic Games simply took off as the most successful sporting event in the world. Since 1896, the Olympic Games have been held every four years, with the exception of 1916, 1940, and 1944, when they were not held because of world wars. In 1924, the first Olympic Winter Games were held in Chamonix, France. These Winter Olympics have since been contested every four years, save 1940 and 1944 (see above), until 1992. In that year, the cycle for Olympic Winter Games changed, and the next ones were contested in 1994, with a new four-year cycle to ensue such that the next Winter Olympics would be held in 1998. This ensures that the Olympic Games and the Olympic Winter Games are not held in the same calendar year.

In 1894, Coubertin was responsible not simply for suggesting the revival of the Olympic Games but also for the formation of the International Olympic Committee (IOC). However, the first president of the IOC was Demetrios Vikelas, who was established in the office by Coubertin, who felt that the IOC president should come from the host of the first Olympic Games. But Coubertin took over as president in 1900 and held the post until 1924. The IOC has existed since 1894 as an international nongovernmental organization (NGO) whose responsibilities include the planning and staging of the Olympic Games, overseeing the Olympic movement, and spreading its philosophy, termed *Olympism*.

The IOC, and its responsibilities and philosophy, have evolved greatly since its first century of existence. Originally the IOC basically consisted of a group run by Coubertin. Although there were other members, he was in charge, and the ideas and plans he espoused were usually accepted without argument by the other members of the IOC. Coubertin initially ran the IOC out of his home in Paris at 20 rue Oudinot. In April 1915, he moved to Lausanne, Switzerland, and established the IOC headquarters in that city, where it has remained to this day.

Through World War II, and even until the early 1960s, the IOC, the Olympic Games, and the Olympic movement did not change a great deal, although they both became a bit larger and better known. However, the IOC was still run basically by its president and a small headquarters staff, and with relatively small financial backing. In fact, through the late 1950s the financial backing to run the IOC came from membership dues assessed to the IOC members.

In the 1960s, television began to realize the benefits they could receive by televising the Olympic Games, and since that time, things have changed greatly. Network telecasts of the Olympic Games eventually engendered huge fees paid by the networks for that right. The money generated would give the IOC and the Olympic movement significant financial freedom. This enabled the IOC to expand its horizons in an effort to spread its philosophy of Olympism and also to lend financial support to various structures within the Olympic movement via Olympic Solidarity.[10]

In the 1980s, the IOC began to seek other sources of financing its operations, via a commission of the IOC originally termed the Commission for New Sources of Financing and now called simply the Finance Commission. The purpose of this effort was to counteract the fact that by the 1980s the IOC, and even more so, the various organizing committees, had become completely dependent financially on the American television network televising the Olympic Games. Held somewhat hostage by this arrangement, the IOC realized it had to expand its financial sources and did so with the formation of TOP (The Olympic Programme), which is discussed in further detail below. This has only served to strengthen the financial situation of the IOC and allow it to pursue its purpose even more aggressively.

The increasing economic independence, however, also engendered great problems. The Olympic Games became so highly publicized that they became subject to political manipulation, ending in several boycotts. In 1968, when political activists in Mexico City protested the Mexican government's staging of the Olympic Games, the Mexican army and police intervened and killed several hundred protesters. In 1972, Arab terrorists kidnapped most of the Israeli Olympic team in the Olympic Village and, eventually, after hours of negotiations, savagely murdered 11 of the Israelis. Between 1968 and 1988, all the Olympic Games saw some form of protest or boycott.[11]

Coubertin hated politics, stating, "We have not worked, my friends and I, to restore the Olympic Games to have them made a museum piece or a movie, nor for commercial or political interests to take over."[12] And so, initially, the IOC attempted to remain nonpolitical. However, this has been difficult, probably not realistic, and is no longer accurate at all.

The IOC, via its seventh president, Juan Antonio Samaranch, was once quoted as saying that the mere act of declaring the group nonpolitical is, in itself, a political statement. The IOC realizes it cannot operate in a vacuum, attempting to divorce itself from all the political problems of a world that, superficially at least, appears to have no desire to pursue freedom for all people and more internationalism. Samaranch's philosophy of not allowing the IOC to be politically isolated is best exemplified by his negotiations with respect to the 1988 Seoul Olympics, in which he attempted to negotiate with DPR Korea (North) in an effort to allow it to host several Olympic events.[13] In fact, the IOC has now formed a Commission on International Relations, specifically to deal with the changing political world.

The purpose of the IOC may seem to the rest of the world to be to stage Olympic Games. But the IOC would state that its primary reason for existence is to spread the philosophy of Olympism via the Olympic movement. It is not easy to define either Olympism or the Olympic movement. Both are defined in the Olympic Charter, basically the constitution of the IOC, and fuller definitions are given within this dictionary.

The Olympic Charter has stated simply that "The Olympic Movement, led by the IOC, stems from modern Olympism."[14] The IOC has, however, defined the concept more fully in some of its press releases. It has stated that the Olympic movement encompasses the International Olympic Committee (IOC), the International Federations (IFs), and the National Olympic Committees (NOCs) and that the IOC is the supreme authority of the Olympic movement. The Olympic movement should also include the organizing committees of the Olympic Games (OCOGs or COJOs), which are groups formed in the host cities, whose only purpose is the staging of the Olympic Games, and which usually disband within the year after their Olympic Games close. The main criterion for belonging to the Olympic movement, per the Olympic Charter, is "Belonging to the Olympic Movement requires compliance with the *Olympic Charter* and recognition by the IOC."[15]

The International Federations are the international governing bodies of the individual sports on the Olympic program, and also of the IOC affiliated sports. The IOC gives the IFs almost complete autonomy in designing, organizing, and regulating the Olympic competitions under their aegis. The IFs have in the past defined amateurism for each sport and thus Olympic eligibility, although the concept of amateurism is fading. The IFs provide the international officials who conduct the Olympic events. The IFs also set qualifying regulations for the Olympic sports, as it would not be possible for all athletes who wish to compete at the Olympic Games to do so.

National Olympic Committees are the governing bodies of Olympic sports in their respective countries or regions. (This is an important distinction as not all NOCs represent autonomous nations, and the IOC recognizes this by their definition of NOCs.) The NOCs are responsible for fielding Olympic teams to represent their nation or NOC. The NOCs and IFs also work closely with groups termed *national governing bodies* (NGBs). NGBs are the national governing organizations for individual sports. They come under the umbrella both of their own NOC and their own IF. Thus, for example, USA Track and Field (USATF), which governs track and field in the United States, is a member of its NOC (the U.S. Olympic Committee) and its IF (the International Amateur Athletic Federation).

The philosophy of Olympism is quite difficult to define with precision, but certainly stems from the writings and philosophy of Coubertin. The official definition of Olympism, as given in the Olympic Charter, is "Olympism is a philosophy of life, exalting and combining in a balanced whole the qualities of body, will and mind. Blending sport with culture and education, Olympism seeks to create a way of life based on the joy of effort, the educational value of good example and respect for universal fundamental ethical principles."[16] It further states that, "The goal of Olympism is to place everywhere sport at the service of the harmonious development of man, with a view to promoting a peaceful society concerned with the preservation of human dignity."[17]

However, most scholars of the Olympic movement would tell you that Olympism is even more encompassing than the above rather broad definition. Coubertin considered sport a method of education and stated that "sport is not a luxury activity, or an activity for the idle, or even a physical compensation for cerebral work. It is, on the contrary, a possible source of inner improvement for everyone. Sport is part of every man and woman's heritage and its absence can never be compensated for."[18]

This basically outlined Coubertin's philosophy of "sport for all," a concept that is a cornerstone of the modern Olympic movement. In 1919, Coubertin defined this philosophy thusly: "All sports for all people. This motto will no doubt be criticized as utopian lunacy, but that doesn't worry me. I have given it considerable thought and I believe its realization is just and possible."[19] He also noted, "Class distinctions should have no place in sport."[20]

Coubertin defined Olympism as "not a system but a state of mind. It may be applied to the most diverse situations and is not the exclusive monopoly of any one race or time. The Olympic spirit is a state of mind created by the cultivation of both effort and eurhythmy . . . which in a paradoxical sense are the basis of all absolute virility."[21] Coubertin was not a great classics scholar, but he understood a great deal about the religious and philosophical aspects of the ancient Olympic Games.

To the bulk of the world, the Olympic movement is the Olympic Games, and nothing else. Certainly they are the best publicized aspect of the Olympic movement, and the Olympic Games themselves now see politicians, philosophers, and the IOC itself wrestling with several controversial issues pertaining to the Games.

One is the commercialization of the Olympic Games. While the IOC has become financially independent, this is not always considered a good thing, and as noted above, Coubertin himself never wanted this to occur. Many sports historians and philosophers of sport yearn for the days when Avery Brundage was IOC president and the IOC was run on a financial shoestring. Though it was less glamorous, Brundage simply did not allow commercialism and fought its encroachment into the Olympic Games to his dying day.

Commercialism has become a much bigger problem for the IOC now that financial riches have befallen the Olympic movement. In the 1980s, IOC president Juan Antonio Samaranch stated that one of his goals was to bring the IOC financial freedom. In the 1970s, although television rights' fees for the Olympic Games were increasing dramatically, bringing significant dollars to the IOC, the IOC was fully dependent on the largesse of the television networks, notably the American network hosting the Olympic Games. Samaranch was assisted by IOC member Dick Pound, a Canadian tax lawyer, and together they devised "The Olympic Programme," known as TOP. TOP enlists major international corporations to support the Olympic movement during each quadrennium. Membership in TOP is very expensive, with fees now more than $50 million/quadrennium, but it is also very exclusive. Pound and the IOC made the exclusivity important but demanded that the corporations pay dearly for it. Via TOP, and television rights' fees, which continued to increase dramatically through the 1980s, the IOC was awash with riches by the 1990s.

And at Atlanta in 1996, many people thought that these riches had gone overboard in an orgiastic display of commercialism. Downtown Atlanta was a city plastered with marketing and merchants, with every corporation, and seemingly everybody, trying to sell something related to the Olympic Games. Even the IOC was taken aback, stating that something would have to be done in the future to control this, and prevent such gross spectacles at future Olympic Games.[22]

Another debate that has enveloped the Olympic movement has been the concept of amateurism, a concept that has engendered multiple philosophical imbroglios since its inception in 19th-century England. English rowers of that era began to protest the inclusion of competitors who worked on the docks or rowed boats for a living, stating that it gave them an unfair advantage. Eventually, the concept was expanded by the British to exclude anybody who worked at manual labor, believing that the work strengthened them unfairly. Thus, an amateur was somebody who either worked a desk job or was a member of the leisure class.

In the 20th century, the arguments concerning amateurism became more complex. Athletes who were given paid time off from work to compete or train, termed "broken-time payments," were considered to be violating the rules of amateur status. But after World War II, when the Eastern-bloc nations began competing at the Olympics, it was known that most of their athletes were essentially state-supported amateurs, who had no other job except to train and compete in sports. Many of the countries placed these athletes in their military, although they were far from typical soldiers. This gave an unfair advantage to the Soviet-bloc athletes compared to Western athletes who were required to either work for a living or be declared a professional. But the IOC never drew the line against state-supported athletes, even while they were stringently opposed to any type of financial support for Western athletes.

Coubertin actually tired of debating the concepts of amateurism, finally declaring, "All I ask of the athlete . . . is loyalty to sport."[23] The ancient Olympic Games are considered by many journalists and the lay public to have been contested by "amateur" athletes, but that is almost certainly false. In fact, the ancient Greeks did not even have a word for the modern term "amateur," and all of the greatest Greek athletes were paid, and paid well, for their efforts.[24]

Amateurism with respect to the Olympic Games is dying out. Each International Federation is now responsible for providing its own definition of amateurism. The IOC leaves Olympic eligibility requirements to the International Federations, and this situation has allowed professionals to compete in the Olympic Games in many sports: track and field athletics, basketball, cycling, football (soccer), figure skating, and volleyball, among them.

Some sporting purists would demur, stating that the Olympics should remain an amateur festival, but they usually have only a neophyte's understanding of the original meaning of the Olympic Games and the Olympic movement. In today's world, many of the top international athletes are highly paid for their performances, and to exclude them would prevent the world's greatest athletes from competing in the world's greatest sporting event—the Olympic Games. It is very unlikely; however, that prize money will be given at the Olympic Games. It is offered at many of the International Federation's World Championships, but Samaranch once noted, "I think the Olympic Games are different."[25]

"Gigantism" is a term that deals with the increasing size of the Olympic Games and the commensurate increase in costs. This concept is interwoven with the commercialism of the Olympic Games, because as the Games increase in size and thus become more expensive, increased financial resources must be generated via commercialism to conduct the Olympic Games and run the Olympic movement.

Gigantism of the Olympic Games is a very difficult problem to solve. To make the Olympic Games smaller, only two real solutions exist: decrease the number of sports and events, or decrease the number of competitors in each sport. Decreasing the number of competitors also raises difficult philosophical questions. The simple solution would be to limit each event only to the top-rated athletes in the world in that event. But this would virtually eliminate many of the world's sporting nations. Of the 202 National Olympic Committees (NOCs) currently recognized by the IOC, only a few can be considered sporting powers. Sports facilities and training techniques are simply not available to many of the world's athletes. To limit events to only the top competitors would prevent many of the world's NOCs from competing in the Olympic Games. This completely violates the IOC's ideals of sport for all and of promoting internationalism and international good will by bringing together the youth of all nations in a great sporting festival.

Further, the IOC has now mandated that any sport wishing to be represented on the Olympic program must present an equal program for men and women. While this is certainly desirable, it adds twice the number of athletes in the Olympic Games every time a sport is added. But in a few cases, those women's sports may not be fully qualified according to the Olympic Charter. To be eligible for a spot in the Olympic Games, a sport is supposed to be practiced in 75 nations and four continents. At the Olympic Winter Games, the rule is 25 nations and three continents. Recently, women's bobsled and skeleton racing was added to the program of the 2002 Winter Olympics in Salt Lake City. But a few critics noted that there are not close to 25 nations in the world in which women compete in these two sports—at Salt Lake City, women from 11 nations competed in bobsledding and women from 10 nations in skeleton. Further, the same critics in the media have also questioned whether or not there are actually 25 nations that compete in skeleton racing for men—there were only 18 nations represented in the 2002 men's skeleton event.

But the IOC is fully committed to equalizing the Olympic program for men and women. To this end, it has sponsored conferences on Women and Sport, at which all aspects of women's sports participation has been discussed. More recent societal questions have arisen, however. When South Africa banned blacks from their Olympic teams, the IOC took action, banning the South African Olympic Committee, effectively kicking South Africa out of the Olympics until that ban was lifted and apartheid became only a memory. Many nations, notably the Muslim nations, and until the recent Afghan War, especially Afghanistan, have had prohibitions against women in sport, in part because the standard athletic uniforms are often far too revealing for the religious strictures mandated in those nations. A prohibition against women in sport is as wrong as was apartheid in South African sports. The IOC has been mostly silent on this issue, but women's groups are mobilizing against these restrictions, and the problem may become more prominent in the near future.

In addition to bringing in more women to the Olympic program, the IOC has other problems concerning gigantism at the Olympic Games. Mainly, there are multiple sports that want to be in the Olympics. In addition to the Olympic sport federations, whose sports are on the Olympic program, the IOC recognizes 28 other international sporting federations, among them dance sport (ballroom dancing), sumo wrestling, rugby football, water skiing, bowling, and netball. All of them want to be in the Olympic Games. Further, the General Association of International Sports Federations (GAISF) currently (2004) recognizes 75 sporting federations (and 16 other federations ancillary to sport). Twelve members of the GAISF are not even recognized by the IOC, but all of them would like to be. And if recognized, you can be certain that all of these sports will try to get on the Olympics program.

At the December 1999 IOC session in Lausanne, at which multiple changes to the Olympic Charter, and other rules, were made, one of these concerned the Olympic program. The IOC mandated a maximum of 280 events in future Olympic Games, even though the Sydney Olympic program for 2000 had 300 events, and there were 301 events at Athens in 2004. Further, with at least 14 IFs applying for admission to the Olympic program, many close observers of the Olympic movement feel this rule has no chance of ever being implemented at the level of 280 events.

The IOC also has an unwritten rule limiting the number of athletes at the Olympic Games to 10,000. There were 10,310 in Atlanta in 1996, but 10,647 at Sydney in 2000 and 10,560 at Athens in 2004.[26] So by adding more events, or more sports, the IOC will need to decrease the number of athletes per event and sport. But there is another problem. The IOC is fully committed to having all member nations compete in the Olympics. In fact, the IOC 2000 Commission passed another change to the Olympic Charter, stating basically that all NOCs are expected to compete in the Olympic Games—an antiboycott clause. So if there will be fewer athletes permitted per event, but all member NOCs are expected to compete, there may be less room for elite athletes in the Olympic Games. But the IOC does not want this either. Each year the IOC opens up the Olympic program to true professionals in more sports, and there are currently very few federations that limit who may compete in the Olympic Games in their sport.

None of these are easy problems concerning the Olympic program, and it is not certain how they will be resolved. In an ideal world, all the best athletes from all the nations would compete in all the world's sports. But that would probably allow 20,000 athletes to compete and push gigantism up another notch, perhaps exponentially so, and significantly increase the costs of the Olympic Games. Paying for these huge Games would be difficult, and the payment would likely be earned only by "selling the Olympic soul to the devil," or the television networks and other corporations.

Further, the world situation has made gigantism even more of an evil because security costs have skyrocketed in response to terrorism, and security costs will likely rise more than linearly with an increasing number of athletes. The 1972 Olympic Games was the first so afflicted when Arab terrorists raided the Olympic Village, kidnapping the entire Israeli team, and eventually cowardly murdering 11 of the team members.[27] With the World Trade Center attacks in September 2001, security at the 2004 Olympic Games was increased multifold, as the fear was exacerbated by the proximity of Greece to the Middle East, and its unique geography, surrounded totally by mountains and sea, which made protecting the border especially difficult. Prior to 1972, security was a relatively minor afterthought for organizing committees, but it is now foremost in their minds, and after the construction of new venues, it is probably the most expensive line item on their budgets.

The budgets have escalated in response to the growing size of the Olympic Games and the security costs. In 2004, the bottom line for the Athens Olympic Games was quoted in the press as over $11 billion (US), a figure dwarfing all previous Olympics. The previous "record holder" was Barcelona in 1992 with a quoted cost of $7 billion, although the 1964 Tokyo Olympics, costing about $2 billion, probably rivaled Athens as the most expensive Olympics ever, when corrected for inflation. (When corrected for inflation, and on a cost-per-athlete basis in real dollars, the 1964 Olympic Games remain, by far, the most expensive Olympic Games ever.)

The Athens $11 billion had to be raised among the smallest population of any Olympic nation since the Helsinki Olympics of 1952, when the budget was probably nearer $10 million (US), giving the Olympic movement a thousandfold absolute increase in costs in just over 50 years. And much of the cost was allocated to the construction of huge athletic venues, which often become white elephants to the host city after the Olympics are over, requiring millions of dollars yearly for upkeep but generating precious little income in the future. Even Sydney, in sports-mad Australia, has found the cost of maintaining the Olympic venues to be a problem. One has to wonder if these costs are worth it. Even Coubertin asked this question almost 100 years ago.

> It would be very unfortunate, if the often exaggerated expenses incurred for the most recent Olympiads, a sizeable part of which represented the construction of permanent buildings, which were moreover unnecessary—

temporary structures would fully suffice, and the only consequence is to then encourage use of these permanent buildings by increasing the number of occasions to draw in the crowds—it would be very unfortunate if these expenses were to deter [small] countries from putting themselves forward to host the Olympic Games in the future.[28]

Further, the entire question of Olympic finance is a very difficult one. What counts as an Olympic cost and what does not? In 1996, Atlanta significantly upgraded Hartsfield International Airport, which was badly needed. The renovation was done in response to the Olympics coming to Atlanta. But was it an Olympic cost or not to upgrade the city's airport? The same argument applies to Athens, which built an entirely new airport, multiple access roads around the city, and a new train line to and from the port city of Piraeus, all badly needed, and all of it was infrastructure that probably would not have been developed for decades had the Olympics not been coming to Greece. Is this an Olympic cost? If these infrastructure costs are added to Olympic bottom lines, then the costs would be far higher than even those quoted above. But is this a bad thing or a good thing? The host cities obtain much needed civic improvements and can excuse these costs as necessary to support the Olympic Games. The question is asked often but answered only poorly, if at all.

Further, are these costs justified to the host nation, even if they increase taxes to its citizens and further increase national debts? It is known that the citizens of Montreal and Quebec continue to pay taxes related to the financing of the 1976 Olympic Games—now 29 years past. Many city politicos, at least those pro-Olympic, argue that the Olympic Games are worth the cost by allowing them to place their city on an international stage unlike any other, burning brilliantly in the media sun for two full weeks, but rising and setting for months prior to and after the Olympic Games.

There is probably no other way for a city to obtain so much publicity, usually positive, for itself, and present itself in a better way to the world. Tokyo used the 1964 Olympic Games to signal to the world that it had recovered from the horrors of World War II. Munich tried a similar tack in 1972, though the Black September terrorist movement put paid to that idea. Seoul in 1988 proved to the world that its burgeoning Pacific Rim economy had made it a first-world nation. Atlanta, only a sleepy southern American city in the 19th and early 20th century, best known for being ravaged during the American Civil War, used the 1996 Olympic Games to proclaim itself a major international city.

Has all this worked? Have the positive exposures the cities received outweighed the huge debts incurred? Since 1984, most organizing committees, through accounting legerdemain, have made it look like the Olympic Games have actually made money. A few certainly have, notably Los Angeles in 1984, probably Sydney in 2000, and possibly Atlanta in 1996. But adding in the infrastructure the cities have built, the Olympic Games must be considered only a huge loss leader for the host cities. Has the loss leader brought the positive publicity, increased tourism, and additional business investment that the host cities and nations have sought? Most economic studies would suggest that they have not, and that the Olympic Games still remain a huge financial drain on the citizens of the host nation. But there is no way to put a dollar amount on the publicity brought to the host city and the host nation by the positive aspects of the Olympic Games, by aligning their city with the Olympic rings, and becoming an "Olympic City." No generally acceptable answer exists, although politicians and economists debate it.[29]

Many other problems are currently plaguing the IOC. Drug use in sports has become even more rampant in the past decade, but the problem goes back to at least the 1950s. The IOC set up a medical working group in 1961 and a Medical Commission in 1966, which was specifically charged with investigating the use of drugs in sport. Testing for drugs first occurred at the 1968 Olympic Games in Mexico City. But testing has not deterred many athletes from using performance-enhancing drugs (PED), and several scandals related to drug use in sports have occurred.

In the 1970s and 1980s it is quite certain that the athletes from the former East Germany (German Democratic Republic) were supplied with PED by their coaches and trainers. This was never proven during their competitive era, and no GDR athlete ever tested positive for drugs at the Olympic Games. But after the fall of the Berlin Wall, official East German documents of their secret police (the Stasi) documented rampant and organized drug use by the sporting authorities. No sanctions to their athletes were ever undertaken by the IOC.

In 1983, at the Pan-American Games in Caracas, Venezuela, the organizers had installed a new drug-testing lab that was much more sensitive and able to detect drug use at much lower levels. On the threshold of the Games, several athletes were found to be positive for PED. Further, when the results started leaking out to the athletes, numerous athletes withdrew and returned home from Venezuela to avoid the drug-testing procedure.

At the 1988 Olympic Games, Ben Johnson won the 100 meter dash, defeating his rival Carl Lewis, as he had at the 1987 World Championships. But Johnson tested positive for anabolic steroids shortly after the race, his title and gold medal were withdrawn, and Lewis was eventually declared the champion. It created a furor in the press at the Seoul Olympics and eventually led to the Canadian government setting up the Dubin Investigation to look into the systematic use of drugs among Canadian athletes. During that investigation, Johnson and his doctor, Dr. Jamie Astaphan, admitted to the use of PED for several years.

In the early 1990s, several track performances by female Chinese athletes shattered world records at their national championships. The records were literally off the bell curve and caused at least one Olympic distance-running medalist, Lynn Jennings, to sit down and cry when she heard of the times the Chinese women were running. It was also revealed that the Chinese were now being coached by former East German coaches, and it was strongly suspected that these off-the-chart records were the result of doping. Within a few years of those performances, over a dozen Chinese women runners and swimmers tested positive for drug use.

In 1998, the Tour de France was rocked by revelations of drug use among professional cyclists (who were by then eligible to compete in the Olympic Games, beginning in 1996). It was not unexpected, given the history of drug use in professional cycling, but it received major play in the media, both written and spoken, and it again cast international professional sport in a very bad light. The scandal focused on the Festina team, which eventually withdrew from the Tour. One of the Festina trainers, Willy Voet, eventually wrote a book, *Massacre à la Chaîne: Révélations sur 30 ans de tricheries* (Breaking the Chain: Drugs and Cycling—The True Story), that described the systematic use of drugs in cycling.

In 2004, a drug scandal involved an American drug and food supplement laboratory near the Bay Area of California, entitled BALCO (Bay Area Laboratory Co-operative). The head of BALCO was Victor Conte Jr. Many American professional athletes, including baseball stars Barry

Bonds and Jason Giambi, and 2000 Olympic star Marion Jones, were found to have worked with Conte and BALCO. The U.S. government began an investigation that included grand jury testimony. Unfortunately, much of the grand jury testimony was leaked to the media (which is illegal), but much of it indicted several athletes (notably Giambi and Bonds) as having used PED. In a televised interview, Conte also accused Jones of using human growth hormone, although she has denied that and the investigation is ongoing at this writing.

The IOC has responded to these many scandals by forming the World Anti-Doping Agency (WADA). Announced in 1999, WADA has been led since its inception by the prominent Canadian IOC member Dick Pound. In early 1999, the IOC held a conference on the problems of doping in sport, which included setting up the structure of WADA. The IOC has passed several rules to help, including adding an antidoping statement to the Olympic oath, and perhaps most importantly, requiring that Olympic sport federations follow the rules of WADA and the IOC on doping in sport. WADA has set up a uniform set of regulations, termed the World Anti-Doping Code, that describes in great detail the measures that sport federations and international Games should take against doping and the penalties to be involved. WADA has also taken over the responsibility for publishing the "Prohibited List of Drugs in Sport."

In addition to WADA, another international entity helps combat drugs in sports, the Court of Arbitration for Sport (CAS). The CAS was formed in the early 1980s and is based in Lausanne, Switzerland, to adjudicate any dispute related to sport and law. However, in the late 1990s, the IOC increased its importance by requiring Olympic athletes to allow any disputes during the Olympic Games to be settled by the CAS, rather than going to the judicial system. Thus, appeals for doping positives are usually not heard by a panel of arbitrators chosen by the Court of Arbitration for Sport.

The media response to drug use at the Olympics has been interesting. Much of the media has adopted a very politically correct response to this, especially in the United States, and rarely examines all the issues involved in a critical manner. The issue is far more complex than one would read in American newspapers. Notably, the IOC is usually condemned as allowing, and almost promoting, drug use in sport, because so many Olympic athletes have been caught testing positive for drugs.

But this argument fails to consider that the IOC was the first sports organization to test for drug use in sports (in 1968); was the first sports organization to set up a medical commission to examine the issues of doping (in 1966); and was the first to institute random, out-of-competition tests to catch drug cheaters; and the IOC penalties for doping are far more stringent than most professional sports federations. In comparison, the four American professional sports (baseball, football, basketball, ice hockey) test their athletes far less frequently than Olympic athletes, they test for far fewer drugs, and their penalties, if they exist at all, are relative slaps on the wrist compared to the IOC and WADA. (Further details and discussion are given in dictionary entries on Court of Arbitration for Sport, Doping and Drugs in Sport, World Anti-Doping Agency, and the biography of Dick Pound.)[30]

Of the many problems that have beset the Olympic movement, it was rocked by its greatest scandal ever in late 1998 and early 1999, and one that threatened its very existence. In November 1998, a Salt Lake City television station revealed that the Salt Lake City Bid Committee had paid the tuition for the daughter of an IOC member. It was not an isolated event. The ensuing scandal eventually saw 10 members of the IOC resign, and the scandal spread beyond the Salt Lake City Bid Committee, with bid and organizing committees in Atlanta, Nagano, and Sydney being implicated. Further, the Toronto Bid Committee for the 1996 Olympics had released a report in 1991 that told of IOC members requesting and being given gifts in exchange for votes to become the Olympic host city.

The Olympic bribery scandal forced the IOC to confront its problems. It was investigated on several fronts, and several investigative reports were issued concerning the scandal. The IOC formed a committee, headed by IOC vice president Dick Pound, and they released a report on the scandal in March 1999. Salt Lake City requested and received a similar report from its Board of Ethics. The U.S. Olympic Committee formed a commission, headed by former U.S. senator George Mitchell, and their report was released in early March 1999. The U.S. Federal Bureau of Investigation (FBI) has also been investigating the Olympic movement and the IOC, and that investigation continued through 2002, although it has now been basically settled.

In response to these reports, the IOC formed two important new commissions—the IOC Ethics Commission and the IOC 2000

Commission. The Ethics Commission set up guidelines for conduct by IOC members and bid committees. The IOC 2000 Commission made 50 recommendations to the IOC, several of them based on the earlier reports, and in December 1999, at the IOC session, the IOC enacted all 50 recommendations, in an effort to overcome the effects of the scandal.

It is sad that the public, especially the American public, via the media, often hears about the Olympic movement only during these times of controversy, for there is much good in the Olympic movement, and the IOC attempts to accomplish many admirable things. The Olympic movement is first and foremost a movement of internationalism, and the IOC wants to be known as a peace organization. To that end, it has recently reinstituted the Olympic truce, reminiscent of the truce of Ancient Greece, with the Olympic truce receiving the imprimatur of the United Nations. During the 1990s, the IOC began a closer alliance with the United Nations, and specifically UNESCO. Together, these two organizations promoted the passage of a modern version of the Olympic truce, calling for the cessation of international hostilities during the celebration of the Olympic Games and Olympic Winter Games. Regrettably, this did not occur during the 2002 Olympic Winter Games, nor the 2004 Olympic Games, with invasions of Afghanistan and Iraq by U.S.-led coalitions occurring concurrently with the sporting events.

Finally, the IOC has also become more concerned with the environment of late. It now promotes, and virtually demands, acceptance of the concept of "green" Olympic Games. This concept really began with the Lillehammer Winter Olympics of 1994. The Lillehammer Organizing Committee designed all of their sports stadia and settings with the intention of doing minimal harm to the environment. Later that summer, at the Centennial Olympic Congress, the topic of environmental concerns at the Olympic Games was discussed. The IOC has seized upon this idea as a good one, and is now requiring that future candidate cities give primary consideration to this concept.[31] The Olympic Charter has been changed to reflect this emphasis, with Rule 2.13 stating, "[The IOC's role is] to encourage and support a responsible concern for environmental issues, to promote sustainable development in sport and to require that the Olympic Games are held accordingly."[32]

Thus, there are many good things that the IOC does under the umbrella of the Olympic movement, even if many of them are transparent to the public. The IOC has been the recipient of a great deal of money since the early 1980s, and it is trying to use this money to accomplish what it considers necessary to promote international sport as a means to a more peaceful world. This would seem positive on the whole. Yet a few critics of the IOC have recently complained that it tries to do too much. These critics have insisted that the IOC should return to what is its primary mission—to hold international sporting events in the form of the Olympic Games and the Olympic Winter Games. It would seem difficult to criticize an organization for trying to do too many good things, although people who continually criticize the IOC add even that to their myriad polemics.

Thus, we have come full circle, from a small, simple religious festival in Ancient Greece, to a huge festival seen on television by billions of people that American sportscaster Jim McKay has termed "The largest peacetime gathering of humanity in the history of the world."[33] To the athletes, the Olympic Games are the supreme test of their abilities. But even to the athletes, the Olympic Games are special, witnessed by the statement of Al Oerter, an Olympic legend and four-time discus gold medalist: "There is no job, no amount of power, no money to approach the Olympic experience."[34]

Though "just" a big sporting event, even the politicians have realized that the Olympics are more than that. Former California governor Jerry Brown once commented, "These are just games and people should see them for fun; there shouldn't be any ulterior motives to the Olympics. They're just games, frivolous things. They're not really necessary. But don't forget some of the least necessary things in life are the most important. Art, religion, friendship, leisure time, games—they make life worth living."[35]

Besides Coubertin, there were others who realized, almost from the start of the Olympic movement, the good that the Olympic idea could accomplish. At the closing banquet after the 1908 Olympic Games, the Reverend Robert Stuart de Courcy Laffan, who was honorary secretary of the 1908 Olympic Games, noted,

> The Olympic Movement was one with great ideals—the perfect physical development of a new humanity, the spreading all over the world of the spirit of sport, which was the spirit of the truest chivalry, and the drawing together of all the nations of the earth in the bonds of peace and mutual amity. They were at the beginning of one of those great world movements which was going to develop long after all present had passed away.[36]

And the Olympic movement itself, as described above, encompasses much more than the Olympic Games. Via its philosophy of Olympism it attempts to bring together people of all nationalities in peaceful competition, creating an air of internationalism rarely seen in today's divisive world. This has perhaps been best summed up by the emotional speech of Lord Killanin, outgoing IOC president, at the closing ceremonies of the 1980 Lake Placid Winter Olympics. Referring specifically to the planned U.S.-driven boycott of the Moscow Olympics, Killanin stated, "Ladies and gentlemen, I feel these Games have proved that we do have something to contribute to the mutual understanding of the world, what we have in common and not what our differences are. If we can all come together it will be for a better world and we shall avoid the holocaust which may well be upon us if we are not careful."[37]

NOTES

1. From which the modern word *stadium* is derived.

2. See David C. Young, *The Olympic Myth of Greek Amateur Athletes* (Chicago: Ares, 1984).

3. Background books on the ancient Olympic Games are myriad. Please refer to the bibliography for a complete listing for further reference.

4. The most complete early description of the various attempts to revive the Olympic Games, though now somewhat dated, was given in Karl Lennartz, *Kenntnisse und Vorstellungen von Olympia und den Olympischen Spielen in der Zeit von 393-1896* (Schorndorf: Verlag Karl Hofmann, 1974). A more recent work focusing a bit more on the Greek efforts is by Konstantinos Georgiadis, *Olympic Revival: The Revival of the Olympic Games in Modern Times* (Athens: Ekdotike Athenon, 2003).

5. For information specifically concerning Coubertin's efforts to resuscitate the Olympic Games, see John J. MacAloon, *This Great Symbol: Pierre de Coubertin and the Origins of the Modern Olympic Games* (Chicago: Univ. of Chicago Press, 1981); and David C. Young, *The Modern Olympics: A Struggle for Revival* (Baltimore: Johns Hopkins Press, 1996). The approaches are different, with MacAloon emphazing Coubertin's contributions, while Young discusses the efforts of Panagiotis Soutsos, a Greek poet of the mid-19th century, and William Penny Brookes, but they complement each other in subject matter.

6. By far the best and most complete description of Coubertin's works is the encyclopaedic three-volume set, *Pierre de Coubertin: Textes Choisis*, ed. Norbert Müller, 3 vols. (Zürich: Weidmann, 1986).

7. There are many books on the 1896 Olympic Games, but the series by Mallon on the 1896–1920 Olympic Games gives background for the 1896, 1900, and 1904 Olympic Games, published by McFarland (Jefferson, N.C., 1997–1999). For 1900, see also *Les Jeux Olympiques Oubliés* by André Drevon (Paris: CNRS Editions, 2000).

8. The best short analysis of the 1906 Olympic Games and their status as Olympic Games is the monograph by Karl Lennartz, "The 2nd International Olympic Games in Athens 1906," published in a Special Commemorative Edition of the *Journal of Olympic History: The Official Publication of the International Society of Olympic Historians* 10 (December 2001–January 2002): 10–26.

9. Complete descriptions of all the controversies at the 1908 Olympics Games are given in Bill Mallon and Ian Buchanan, *The 1908 Olympic Games: Results for All Competitors in All Events, with Commentary* (Jefferson, N.C.: McFarland, 2000). The section describing the controversies and protests is found in pp. 313–406.

10. For a comprehensive reference, see Miguel de Moragas Spà, Nancy K. Rivenburgh, and James F. Larson, *Television in the Olympics* (London: John Libbey, 1995).

11. See either Allen Guttmann, *The Olympics: A History of the Modern Games* (Urbana: Univ. of Illinois Press, 1992); or Alfred E. Senn, *Power, Politics, and the Olympic Games: A History of the Power Brokers, Events, and Controversies That Shaped the Games* (Champaign, Ill.: Human Kinetics, 1999).

12. Speech to the sports youth of all nations at Olympia, Greece, 17 April 1927; quoted in the *International Pierre de Coubertin Committee* (Lausanne: International Pierre de Coubertin, 1983), 15.

13. Richard W. Pound, *Five Rings over Korea: The Secret Negotiations behind the 1988 Olympic Games in Seoul* (Boston: Little, Brown, 1994).

14. Olympic Charter, "Fundamental Principles," no. 4, p. 9 (Lausanne: International Olympic Committee, July 4, 2003). Please note that the new edition of the Olympic Charter, as of September 1, 2004, does not quite contain this same phrase.

15. Olympic Charter, "Fundamental Principles," no. 6, p. 9 (Lausanne: International Olympic Committee, September 1, 2004).

16. Olympic Charter, "Fundamental Principles," no. 1, p. 9 (Lausanne: International Olympic Committee, September 1, 2004).

17. Olympic Charter, "Fundamental Principles," no. 2, p. 9 (Lausanne: International Olympic Committee, July 4, 2003).

18. Conrado Durántez, *Pierre de Coubertin: The Olympic Humanist* (Lausanne: International Olympic Committee and International Pierre de Coubertin Committee, 1994), 27.

19. Durántez Corral, *Pierre de Coubertin*, 29.

20. Durántez Corral, *Pierre de Coubertin*, 29.

21. Durántez Corral, *Pierre de Coubertin*, 36.

22. A very solid analysis of the IOC's ventures into commercialism and the problems engendered therein is by Robert K. Barney, Stephen R. Wenn, and Scott G. Martyn, *Selling the Five Rings: The International Olympic Committee and the Rise of Commercialism* (Salt Lake City: University of Utah Press, 2002).

23. Barney, Wenn, and Martyn, *Selling the Five Rings*, 33.

24. See Young, *The Olympic Myth of Greek Amateur Athletes*.

25. *USA Today*, March 1995.

26. IOC president Rogge was recently quoted after the 2004 Olympic Games that the limit is 10,400 athletes. Until the most recent edition of the Olympic Charter (September 1, 2004), By-law 8 to Rule 49 actually limited the number of Olympic athletes at the Games of the Olympiad to 10,000, in compliance with the decision of the IOC 2000 Commission.

27. Further details of the Israeli massacres at the 1972 Olympics can be found in Serge Groussard, *The Blood of Israel: The Massacre of the Israeli Athletes, the Olympics 1972* (New York: Morrow, 1975); Simon Reeve, *One Day in September: The Full Story of the 1972 Munich Olympics Massacre and the Israeli Revenge Operation "Wrath of God"* (New York: Arcade, 2000); and Richard D. Mandell, *A Munich Diary: The Olympics of 1972* (Chapel Hill: University of North Carolina Press, 1991).

28. Pierre de Coubertin, *Olympic Review*, April 1911, 59–62.

29. The topic of the economics of the Olympic Games is a difficult one, but the first book-length analysis of the problem was done by Holger Preuss in *Economics of the Olympic Games: Hosting the Games 1972–2000* (Petersham, NSW, Australia: Walla Walla Press, 2000).

30. The fullest description of the problems of drug use in sport, and also addressing some of the controversies, can be found in Wayne Wilson and Edward Derse, *Doping in Elite Sport: The Politics of Drugs in the Olympic Movement* (Champaign, Ill.: Human Kinetics, 2000).

31. There is even now a Sport and Environment Commission.

32. Olympic Charter, "Fundamental Principles," Rule 2.13, p. 12 (Lausanne: International Olympic Committee, September 1, 2004).

33. Bill Mallon, *The Olympics: A Bibliography* (New York: Garland, 1984), ix.

34. Mallon, *The Olympics*, v.

35. *Los Angeles Times*, 1982.

36. Originally quoted in the *Times* (London), November 2, 1908, p. 17; see also Mallon and Buchanan, *The 1908 Olympic Games*, 17.

37. Lord Killanin, *My Olympic Years* (London: Secker & Wartburg, 1983), 187.

The Dictionary

– A –

AAMODT, KJETIL ANDRÉ (NOR–ASK). B. 2 September 1971. Kjetil André Aamodt's record of five Olympic medals (one gold, two silver, two bronze) in alpine skiing has only been matched by **Vreni Schneider** (SUI), **Alberto Tomba** (ITA), and **Katja Seizinger** (GER). Aamodt's only gold medal came in the super-giant (super-G) slalom in 1992 when he also took bronze in the giant slalom. In 1994, he won a silver in the downhill and alpine combined and a bronze in the super-giant slalom. Aamodt won 20 races in the World Cup (1 downhill, 1 slalom, 5 super-G, 6 giant slalom, 7 combined) and was overall World Cup champion in 1994. He won the World Championships in combined in 1997 and 1999.

ACROBATICS. Acrobatics has never been contested at the **Olympic Games**, even as a demonstration sport. However, the International Federation of Sports Acrobatics (IFSA) has previously been recognized by the **International Olympic Committee** (IOC), although it is not currently recognized as of 2005.

AERONAUTICS. Aeronautics is governed internationally by the Fédération Aéronautique Internationale (FAI), which was created in 1905 and is recognized by the **International Olympic Committee** (IOC). There are 95 affiliated nations as of late 2004. At the 1936 **Olympic Games** a gold medal for Merit for Aeronautics was presented to Hermann Schreiber (glider flight).

AFGHANISTAN (AFG). Afghanistan first competed at the 1936 Olympics in Berlin, the same year in which its **National Olympic**

1

Committee (NOC) was recognized by the **International Olympic Committee** (IOC). Since then the country has failed to be represented at the Olympic Games of 1952, 1976, 1984, 1992, and 2000. Afghanistan's National Olympic Committee was suspended by the IOC in 1999, and it was not eligible to compete at Sydney, presumably because of prohibitions against **women** in sport brought on by the ruling Taliban. After the Afghan War of 2001–2002, Afghanistan formed a new National Olympic Committee and competed in 2004 at Athens. Afghanistan has never competed at the **Olympic Winter Games**. No Afghan athlete has won a medal while representing Afghanistan, their best finish being fifth by Mohammed Ebrahimi in 1964 featherweight freestyle **wrestling**. But the most successful Afghani at the Olympic Games was Sayid M. Yusuf, who won a gold medal in 1928 as a member of the **Indian field hockey team**.

ALBANIA (ALB). Albania's **National Olympic Committee** (NOC) was founded in 1958 and recognized by the **International Olympic Committee** (IOC) in 1959, but Albania did not compete at the Olympics until 1972. Albania then did not compete again at the Olympics for 20 years, returning in 1992, 1996, 2000, and 2004. Albania has not won any medals and has never competed at the Olympic Winter Games. Albania has had fairly good **weightlifters**, and a few of their lifters have immigrated to **Greece** and competed for that nation at the Olympics.

ALEKSEYEV, VASILIY IVANOVICH (URS–WLT). B. 7 January 1942, Pokrovo-Shishkino, Ryazan Oblast. Unbeaten from 1970 to mid-1978, Vasiliy Alekseyev is the greatest super-heavyweight lifter in history. His feat of winning eight successive gold medals at the **Olympic Games** and World Championships (1970–1977) equaled the record of Americans **John Davis** and **Tommy Kono**. Alekseyev won the gold medal in the unlimited class at the 1972 and 1976 Olympics. He competed in 1980 at Moscow, although injured, but did not finish. Alekseyev also won eight European titles and set 79 world records. He was finally defeated at the 1978 World Championships when suffering from a damaged hip tendon.

ALGERIA (ALG). Algeria formed a **National Olympic Committee** (NOC) in 1963 that was recognized by the **International Olympic Committee** (IOC) in 1964, and Algeria first competed officially at the 1964 **Olympic Games**. It has since competed at the Olympic Games of 1968, 1972, and all Olympics since 1980. Algeria competed at the **Olympic Winter Games** for the only time to date in 1992. Through 2000, Algerians have won seven medals, five in **boxing** and two in track and field **athletics**. Prior to Algeria's independence in July 1962, several Algerian athletes competed for **France** at the Olympics. The first were four **gymnasts** from Oran who took part in the 1900 Olympic Games, and they had the distinction of being the first African Olympians. Two Olympic **marathon** winners, Mohammed Bouguerra El Ouafi (1928) and Alain Mimoun O'Kacha (1956), were both Algerians representing France.

ALI, MUHAMMAD (née Cassius Marcellus Clay) (USA–BOX). B. 17 January 1942, Louisville, Kentucky. Muhammad Ali first gained international prominence as Cassius Clay by winning the light-heavyweight gold medal at the 1960 Rome Olympics. In February 1964, he upset Sonny Liston to win the world heavyweight championship. Shortly after the fight he embraced the Muslim faith and took the name Muhammad Ali. No fighter defeated him for the rest of the 1960s. But Ali was defeated by the U.S. draft board when he refused induction to military service based on a conscientious objection, and he was subsequently stripped of his heavyweight title. Eventually, Ali won his battle against the draft board in the Supreme Court, but the best years of his career were lost. He returned to fighting in 1970 and the next year lost a much-ballyhooed fight against **Joe Frazier**. In 1974, Ali regained the heavyweight championship against **George Foreman**, and, after losing to Leon Spinks in 1978, he would become the only man to hold the title three times by defeating Spinks in a rematch. Ali's career professional record was 56 wins (37 by knockout) and 5 losses. At the 1996 **Olympic Games**, Ali was given the honor of lighting the **Olympic flame** at the opening ceremony. Sadly, he now suffers from a relatively advanced case of Parkinson's disease. After their final epic battle, "The Thrilla in Manila," his redoubtable opponent, Frazier, said of him, "Lawdy,

lawdy, he's a great champion. I hit him with punches that'd bring down the walls of a city and he took them."

ALPINE SKIING. Alpine ski racing is the newer form of ski racing, as **nordic** (or cross-country) competitions were held in the Scandinavian countries for many years before alpine racing was developed. The first known alpine skiing race was in 1911 at Montana, **Switzerland**, when the British organized a downhill race for a challenge cup given by Lord Roberts of Kandahar. The first slalom-style race was held in 1922 at Mürren, Switzerland.

Alpine skiing was first placed on the **Olympic program** in 1936 at Garmisch-Partenkirchen. The only event that year was a combined competition of both downhill and slalom. In 1948, this was held again along with separate downhill and slalom races. In 1952, the giant slalom was added as an event, and in 1988, the super-giant slalom became a fourth separate event. Alpine combination, a point-scored mix of downhill and slalom, returned to the **Olympic Winter Games** program in 1988, after not being contested from 1952 to 1984.

Events for both sexes were held in 1936 and have been at all Olympics since. Men and women contest alpine skiing separately, but interestingly, the program for men and women has been identical at all Olympics. The sport is governed by the Fédération Internationale de Ski (FIS), which was founded in 1924 and had 101 member nations as of December 2004.

The two greatest alpine skiers among the men have been **Toni Sailer** of **Austria** and **Jean-Claude Killy** of **France**, both of whom won all three gold medals available, in 1956 and 1968, respectively. **Kjetil André Aamodt** of Norway, **Alberto Tomba** of Italy, **Vreni Schneider** of Switzerland, and **Katja Seizinger** of **Germany** have won the most Olympic medals with five each. At Salt Lake City in 2002, **Croatia**'s **Janica Kostelić** won three gold medals (in five events) and became the first alpine skier to win four medals at a single Winter Olympics. Austria, Switzerland, and France have been the top nations in Olympic alpine skiing, with Italy and the United States not far behind.

ALPINISM. Alpinism (mountain climbing) is governed internationally by the Union Internationale des Associations d'Alpinisme (UIAA), also known by the name of the International Mountaineering and Climbing Federation. It was created in 1932 and is recognized by the **International Olympic Committee** (IOC), with 92 affiliated nations as of late 2004. Gold medals for Merit for Alpinism were presented at the 1924, 1932, and 1936 **Olympic Games**. In addition, **Coubertin** had plans for medals to be awarded for alpinism at the Olympic Games. It is mentioned in the original program for the first Olympic Games.

AMERICAN FOOTBALL. *See* FOOTBALL, AMERICAN.

AMERICAN SAMOA (ASA). American Samoa has competed at the 1988, 1992, 1996, 2000, and 2004 **Olympic Games** and the 1994 **Olympic Winter Games**. In 1992, Robert Peden won two matches in flyweight **boxing** to finish equal fifth of 30 in his class, the top finish to date from this small island country.

ANCIENT OLYMPIC GAMES. The ancient Olympic Games were one of the four great Panhellenic sporting festivals of ancient Greece, along with the **Isthmian**, **Nemean**, and **Pythian Games**. The Olympic Games were considered to be the greatest of the Panhellenic contests. The first recorded Olympics are known to have been held in 776 BCE, although it is probable that they began several centuries earlier. The Games lasted until 393 CE when they were banned by imperial decree of the Roman emperor Theodosius I. The ancient Olympic Games were held in Olympia, which was near the city-state of Elis on the Greek Peloponnesus. (They were *not* held on or near Mt. Olympus, as is often incorrectly written.) The ancient Olympic Games were held quadrennially. Winners at the ancient Olympic Games received crowns of wild olive.

The origins of the ancient Olympic Games are uncertain, but several traditional explanations exist. One connects the Games to Pelops, after whom the Peloponnesus was named. Pelops was a Phrygian who made his way to the peninsula that would later take his name. There he defeated Oenomaus, King of Pisa, in a **chariot race**, which Oenomaus had ordered as a race in which Pelops could win the hand of his daughter, Hippodameia. Oenomaus was thrown from his chariot and killed, and Pelops was worshipped as a hero. He took over the kingdom, and the Games were supposedly held at his tomb and in his honor. Later beliefs, popularized by **Pindar**, state that the Games originated to honor Hercules and that he founded them after his victory over Augeas. Hercules declared the Games to be in honor of his father, Zeus.

Originally, the ancient Olympic Games consisted of only a single footrace, one length of the ancient Olympic stadium of about 192 meters, and now termed the *stadion* race. Champions are recorded in this event from 776 BCE (**Coroebus of Elis**) until 269 CE. A second race of two laps of the stadium, termed the *diaulos,* was added in 724 BCE, followed in 720 BCE by the *dolikhos,* which was a long-distance race of about 20–25 laps of the stadium. **Wrestling** champions are recorded from 708 BCE, while **boxing** was added to the list of victors in 688 BCE. The **pentathlon**, an all-around championship of five events, was added at the Olympics of 708 BCE. The **pankration**, which was a brutal combination of wrestling and boxing, is known to have been contested at the ancient Olympics since 648 BCE.

In addition to the above, a number of horse races and chariot races were contested at the Olympic Games. There were events at Olympia for boys who were defined as being older than 12 but less than 18 years old. Competitions for heralds and lyre playing were also contested at the Ancient Olympics.

Athletes from the Peloponnesus dominated the earliest Olympics, winning the first 13 *stadion* events, but Greeks from other city-states later produced many Olympic champions. Elis produced the most known ancient Olympic champions with 110 recorded victories, followed by Sparta with 76 known victories. In the later years of the ancient Olympics, athletes from the Roman Empire began to compete at Olympia, winning many titles. The ancient Olympic Games reached their zenith in the Golden Age of Greece, dimming once the Roman Empire took over the celebrations.

ANDERSEN, HJALMAR JOHAN "HJALLIS" (NOR–SSK). B. 12 March 1923, Rødoy. Hjallis Andersen was the winner of three gold medals at the 1952 **Olympic Winter Games** (1,500 meters, 5,000 meters, 10,000 meters). His winning margin in the 5,000 meters was an astounding 11 seconds, and he also won the 10,000 meters by a substantial margin. Andersen retired after the 1952 Games but returned to competition in 1954 to win his fourth Norwegian title, having earlier won the World, European, and Norwegian all-around titles in 1950–1952. He set one world record at 5,000 meters and three at 10,000 meters.

ANDERSON, PAUL EDWARD (USA–WLT). B. 17 October 1932, Toccao, Georgia. D. 15 August 1994, Vidalia, Georgia. After winning the world heavyweight title by a record margin in 1955, Paul Anderson won the Olympic gold medal in Melbourne the following year. He was quite possibly the strongest man who ever lived. Anderson set hundreds of records as a powerlifter, including a bench press of 625 lbs. (284 kg.), a squat with 1,200 lbs. (545 kg.), a dead-lift of 820 lbs. (373 kg.), and three repetitions in the squat with 900 lbs. (409 kg.). In addition he performed a back-lift off trestles, supporting 6,270 lbs. (2,850 kg.)—the greatest weight ever lifted by a human.

ANDERSSON, AGNETA (SWE–CAN). B. 25 April 1961, Karlskoga. With seven Olympic medals and three gold medals, Sweden's Agneta Andersson trails only **Birgit Schmidt-Fischer** among female **canoeists** at the Olympics. Andersson began her Olympic career in 1984, winning gold in both the K-1 and K-2 events and silver in the K-4. She competed at the 1988 Olympics but failed to medal. In 1992 she won silver in the K-2 and bronze in the K-4, while in 1996 she ended her career with gold in the K-2 and bronze in the K-4 event. Andersson was less successful at the World Championships in terms of titles, claiming only the 1993 K-2 gold, but she won 11 medals at the Worlds in an international career that began in 1979.

ANDORRA (AND). At the end of 1967, an Andorran committee, which had been set up to form a **National Olympic Committee** (NOC), approached the **International Olympic Committee** (IOC) with a view to obtaining recognition in time to send a team of alpine skiers to the 1968 **Olympic Winter Games** in Grenoble. As the draft constitution submitted did not comply with the Olympic rules on many points, the application was rejected, and it was not until 1975 that the IOC approved a revised set of rules. This enabled Andorra to take part in the 1976 Olympic Winter Games in Innsbruck, and since then it has competed in every Olympics, both Winter and Summer. Andorra has not yet won a medal at the Olympics.

ANDRIANOV, NIKOLAY YEFIMOVICH (URS–GYM). B. 14 October 1952, Vladimir. Nikolay Andrianov was the most successful Olympic male **gymnast** of all time. Between 1972 and 1980 he won seven gold medals (six individual, one team), five silver, and three bronze for a total of 15 medals, an Olympic record for men in any sport. At the World Championships he won gold on the rings in 1974, the all-around and rings in 1978, and the team event in 1979. He also won seven silver medals at the World Championships. Andrianov's international career started at the 1971 European Championships where he was a late substitute, and he won six medals that year, including a bronze in the all-around. In individual European Championships he eventually won eight gold, six silver, and two bronze medals.

ANGOLA (ANG). Angola's first application for Olympic recognition was rejected at the 1975 **International Olympic Committee** (IOC) session in **Lausanne, Switzerland**, but after the formation of a **National Olympic Committee** (NOC) in 1979, recognition was granted in 1980. After first competing at the Olympics that year, Angola has also competed at the **Olympic Games** of 1988, 1992, 1996, 2000, and 2004, but has not yet competed at the **Olympic Winter Games**. The top Angolan Olympic performance likely occurred in 1992 at Barcelona when its **basketball** team qualified for the Olympics but drew the **United States "Dream Team"** as a first-round opponent. It eventually finished 10th of 12 teams. In 1996, Angola's women's **handball** team did qualify for the Olympic tournament, finishing eighth of eight teams.

ANTIGUA AND BARBUDA (ANT). Antigua and Barbuda formed a **National Olympic Committee** (NOC) in 1965 with the object of participating in the 1966 British Commonwealth Games that year. After being refused recognition in 1975, because its statutes did not conform to **International Olympic Committee** (IOC) requirements, recognition was granted in 1976, and Antigua and Barbuda competed at the 1976 **Olympic Games**. It has participated at all subsequent Summer Games except for 1980, but has not yet competed at the **Olympic Winter Games**. Antigua and Barbuda has not yet won a medal at the Olympics.

ANTILLES (WEST INDIES) (ANL). *See* WEST INDIES FEDERA-
TION.

APENE. Ancient Olympic sport. The apene race was a **chariot race** in
which two mules pulled the chariot. The first known winner was
Thersias of Thessaly in 500 BCE. The event was discontinued after
444 BCE.

AQUATICS. The **International Olympic Committee** (IOC) recognizes a sport termed "aquatics," which consists of four **disciplines** —
swimming, diving, synchronized swimming, and **water polo**. Many
people consider these to actually be separate sports, and we have
listed them as such. Aquatics is governed by the Fédération Internationale de Natation Amateur (FINA), which was formed in 1908 and
currently has 179 members.

ARCHERY. Archery is one of the oldest known sports. Use of the bow
and arrow for hunting can be traced back to the Aurignacians, a race
of people existing 15,000 years ago. By the 14th century, archers
were found to be valuable as soldiers and the English kings made
archery practice mandatory for the British soldiers. Archery as a sport
became popular in the 16th and 17th centuries. In 1676, the first organized group, the Royal Company of Archers, was formed in **England** for the purpose of advancing the sport. This was followed in
1781 by the Royal Toxophilite Society. The first British championships were conducted in 1844.

Archery is governed worldwide by the Fédération Internationale
de Tir à l'Arc (FITA), which was founded in 1931. Through 2004,
131 nations were members of FITA. Archery was first held as a sport
in the 1900 Paris Olympics and again in 1904, 1908, and 1920, but
then left the **Olympic program**. In those years it was possible for an
athlete to compete in multiple events and win several medals. The top
Olympic medal winner is **Hubert Van Innis** of **Belgium**, who competed in the 1900 and 1920 Olympics, winning 10 medals, six of
them gold.

When the sport was returned to the Olympics in 1972, there was
only one event for men and one for women. In 1988, team events
for men and women were added to the program. Also, in 1988, the

individual formats were changed. Previously (1972–1984), men and women shot a Double FITA Round (288 arrows at various distances). Now, qualifying is contested over 72 arrows, and the archers and teams then engage in single-elimination matches until a champion is crowned.

ARGENTINA (ARG). Argentina first competed officially at the 1924 Olympics in Paris. Prior to that, three Argentine athletes had competed at the Olympics—Eduardo Camet as a **fencer** in 1900, Henri Torromé in 1908 **figure skating**, and a **boxer**, Ángel Rodríguez, in 1920. Since 1924, Argentina has competed at every **Olympic Games** with the exception of 1980. Argentina has competed at the **Olympic Winter Games** of 1928, 1948, 1952, and all Winter Games since 1960. Through 2004, Argentine athletes have won 60 medals, 15 of them gold. Argentina has won more Olympic gold medals than any other South American country except for **Brazil**.

ARLEDGE, ROONE PINCKNEY (USA). B. 8 July 1931, Forest Hills, New York. D. 5 December 2002, New York, New York. Roone Arledge was a **television** producer who first popularized televising the **Olympic Games** to an American audience. After majoring in journalism at Columbia University, Arledge worked most of his career for ABC Television, initially leading the sports division, but later also named head of the news division. In 1961, he created and developed a sports anthology show entitled *ABC's Wide World of Sports*, which became hugely popular. He later produced telecasts of the Olympic Games of 1964, 1968, 1972, 1976, and 1984, and the **Olympic Winter Games** of 1964, 1968, 1976, 1980, 1984, and 1988. His innovative style focused on bringing profiles of the athletes to the public, rather than simply showing the competitions. The profiles were entitled, and coined the phrase, "Up Close and Personal." Arledge also started the American television phenomenon of *Monday Night Football* in 1970. Arledge won numerous awards for his work, including 37 Emmy awards, the Cannes Film Festival Grand Prize in 1965–1966, and three George Foster Peabody awards for promoting international understanding. In 1994, *Sports Illustrated* selected Arledge as the third most influential person in sports in the past four decades.

ARMENIA (ARM). Armenia's first connection with the modern Olympics can be traced to the 1912 Olympics when two Armenian **track and field** athletes represented **Turkey**. These two athletes, Mığır Mığıryan and Haret Papazyan, comprised the entire Turkish team in 1912, but they had, in fact, been sent to Stockholm by the Armenian General Sports Union. After 1918 Armenia enjoyed a brief period of independence and planned to take part in the 1920 Olympics, but their hopes were thwarted when the country was occupied by Russian forces in 1920. For many years the Russian **International Olympic Committee** (IOC) member, Prince Urosov, championed the cause of a group of émigrés known as the Young Armenian Emigrants Union, but he failed to gain Olympic recognition for them. In his *Olympic Memoirs*, **Coubertin** aptly wrote, "Armenia existed only as a hope and a memory in the hearts of its loyal subjects."

As part of the **Soviet Union**, Armenian athletes competed for the USSR Olympic team from 1952 to 1988, and in 1992 they formed part of the **Unified Team**. Having eventually obtained independence, a **National Olympic Committee** (NOC) was established in 1990, and IOC recognition was sought the following year. This was provisionally granted in 1992, and full IOC recognition was given in 1993, thereby enabling Armenia to compete as an independent nation at the Olympics. Armenia competed for the first time at the 1994 **Olympic Winter Games** in Lillehammer. At the Lillehammer opening ceremony, the Armenians wore replicas of the uniform that they had hoped to wear at the 1920 Olympics. Armenia first competed at the **Summer Olympic Games** in 1996. Armenia has won three Olympic medals, one of each color.

ART CONTESTS. Art contests were held at the Olympics of 1912, 1920, 1924, 1928, 1932, 1936, and 1948. The winners of the competitions were awarded gold, silver, and bronze medals, similar to the winners of the athletic competitions. The events were inspired by **Pierre de Coubertin**, who wished to combine the competitions in sports with competitions in the arts. The art competitions were dropped from the **Olympic program** because of the difficulty of determining the amateur status of the artists. Competitions were held in architectural designs; designs for town planning; sculpture, medals; sculpture, reliefs; sculpture, any kind; applied graphics; drawings and watercolors; other graphic arts; paintings; dramatic works; epic works; literature, all kinds; lyrics; musical compositions for one instrument; musical compositions for orchestra of all kinds; musical compositions of songs for soloist or choir, with or without instrumental accompaniment; music, all kinds; merit for **aeronautics**; and merit for **alpinism**. Two artists won three medals: Alex Walter Diggelmann of **Switzerland** (all in applied graphics) and Joseph Petersen of **Denmark** (one in epic works and two in literature, all kinds). Jean Jacoby of **Luxembourg** was the only artist to win two gold medals in the art competitions, one in drawings and watercolors and one in paintings. In 1912, Coubertin won a gold medal in the literature category. Coubertin's gold medal was for his work entitled "Ode to Sport," which he entered under the dual pseudonym of Georg Hohrod and Martin Eschbach. Two arts medalists also won medals in sports at the **Olympic Games**. Alfred Hajós of **Hungary** won two **swimming** gold medals in 1896 and a medal for designs for town planning in 1924; and Walter Winans won running deer **shooting** medals in 1908 and 1912 and also won an arts gold medal in sculpture in 1912.

ARUBA (ARU). Aruba's **National Olympic Committee** (NOC) was formed in 1985 and recognized by the **International Olympic Committee** (IOC) in 1986. Aruba competed in the **Olympic Games** for the first time in 1988 at Seoul and also competed in 1992, 1996, 2000, and 2004, but has not yet competed at the **Olympic Winter Games**.

ASSOCIATION DES COMITÉS NATIONAUX OLYMPIQUES (ACNO). The Association des Comités Nationaux Olympiques was formed in 1968 by Giulio Onesti, then the president of the Italian Olympic Committee, as a method of uniting the various **National Olympic Committees** (NOCs). Originally entitled the PGA, or Permanent General Assembly, of National Olympic Committees, this would allow them a more unified voice to present their concerns to the **International Olympic Committee** (IOC). This union of National Olympic Committees greatly displeased then IOC president Avery Brundage. The group was later renamed the Association of National Olympic Committees (ANOC), but is better known by the

French name given above. ACNO is currently based in Paris, and its president, as of 2004, is **Mexico**'s Mario Vázquez Raña. Formation of the ACNO has been responsible for the foundation of various continental and regional associations of National Olympic Committees. *See also* ASSOCIATION DES COMITÉS NATIONAUX OLYMPIQUES D'AFRIQUE (ACNOA); EUROPEAN OLYMPIC COMMITTEES (EOC); OCEANIA NATIONAL OLYMPIC COMMITTEES (ONOC); OLYMPIC COUNCIL OF ASIA (OCA); ORGANIZACIÓN DEPORTIVA CENTROAMERICANA Y DEL CARIBE (ODECABE); PAN AMERICAN SPORTS ORGANIZATION (PASO).

ASSOCIATION DES COMITÉS NATIONAUX OLYMPIQUES D'AFRIQUE (ACNOA). This group consists of the **National Olympic Committees** (NOCs) from the African nations. The association has its headquarters in Yaoundé, **Cameroon**. The president of ACNOA is Alpha Ibrahim Diallo of Cameroon, and the secretary-general is Raymond Ibata (both as of July 2005).

ASSOCIATION DES COMITÉS NATIONAUX OLYMPIQUES D'EUROPE (ACNOE). *See* EUROPEAN OLYMPIC COMMITTEES, THE (EOC).

ASSOCIATION GÉNÉRALE DES FÉDÉRATIONS INTERNATIONALES DE SPORTS (AGFIS). *See* GENERAL ASSOCIATION OF INTERNATIONAL SPORTS FEDERATIONS (GAISF).

ASSOCIATION OF SUMMER OLYMPIC INTERNATIONAL FEDERATIONS (ASOIF). On 20 May 1983, 21 **International Federations** governing sports on the program of the **Olympic Games** met in **Lausanne** and established the Association of Summer Olympic International Federations (ASOIF). The ASOIF constitution defines its purpose as "to coordinate and defend the common interests of its members to ensure close cooperation between them, the members of the Olympic Movement and those of other organizations, with the aim of preserving the unity of the Olympic Movement while maintaining the authority, independence and autonomy of the member International Federations." The ASOIF is currently based in Lausanne, **Switzerland**, and its president, as of July 2005, is Denis Oswald of Switzerland and the Fédération Internationale des Sociétés d'Aviron (FISA).

ASSOCIATION OF THE INTERNATIONAL OLYMPIC WINTER SPORTS FEDERATIONS (AIOWF). In 1982, led by Marc Hodler of **Switzerland** and the International Ski Federation, the Winter Sports Federations formed their own group, the Association of the International Olympic Winter Sports Federations. The AIOWF deals with specific questions concerning winter sports in general, and the **Olympic Winter Games** in particular. It is also responsible for choosing the delegations and appointments of the winter sports representative to **IOC** commissions. The group is based in Oberhofen, Switzerland. Hodler was the president until 2001, when he was replaced by René Fasel, the current president.

ASSOCIATION OF THE IOC-RECOGNIZED INTERNATIONAL SPORTS FEDERATIONS (ARISF). The **International Olympic Committee** (IOC) recognizes a number of international sports federations whose sports are not yet on the **Olympic program**. This recognition is important, for it is a first step toward getting a sport admitted to the Olympic program. As of July 2005, the IOC has recognized the **International Federations** (Ifs) for the following sports (in addition to those on the Olympic program): **aeronautics, alpinism, automobile racing, bandy, billiards, bowling, bowls, bridge, chess, dance sport, golf, karate, korfball,** life saving, **motorcycling, netball, orienteering, pelota basque, polo, racquetball, roller skating, rugby football, squash rackets, surfing, tug-of-war, underwater swimming, water skiing,** and **wushu**. These IOC-recognized international sports federations have grouped together to form the Association of the IOC-Recognized International Sports Federations. They are headquartered in Leidschendan, the **Netherlands**, and the ARISF currently has 31 member federations, as noted above. The current (2004) president is Ralf Froehling of the Union Internationale Motonautique. The statutes of the ARISF state that its aims are "to determine the consensus of the member federations on questions relating to the Olympic Movement . . . and to coordinate and defend the common interest of its members in [that] context."

ASTAKHOVA, POLINA GRIGORYEVNA (URS/UKR–GYM). B. 30 October 1936, Donetsk, Ukraine. Polina Astakhova won team gold medals at the 1956, 1960, and 1964 **Olympic Games**, a feat that she shares with **Larisa Latynina**, making them the only **gymnasts** to be members of three gold-medal winning teams. Astakhova also won gold on the uneven parallel bars and placed third in the individual all-around in both 1960 and 1964. She added silver medals in both 1960 and 1964 in the floor exercises, and her final Olympic tally included 10 medals, five gold, three silver, and two bronze. At the World Championships she was less successful, but was a member of the Soviet Union team that won the team title in both 1958 and 1962.

ATHLETES COMMISSION. The Athletes Commission was formed in 1981 as a solution to the complaint at the 1981 **Olympic Congress** that Olympic athletes had very little say in the workings of the **International Olympic Committee** (IOC) and the **Olympic movement**. It was felt that the IOC had too few former Olympic athletes among its members and that those athletes were too far removed from their competitive days. The chairman of the Athletes Commission from 1980 to 2000 was Peter Tallberg of **Finland**, an IOC member and a former yachtsman who competed in the **Olympic Games** in 1960, 1964, 1968, 1972, and 1980. Since 2000, the chairman has been Sergey Bubka of the **Ukraine**, the renowned pole vaulter and current IOC member. The current vice-chairman is Prince Albert of **Monaco**, an IOC member but also a competitor in the bobsled events at three **Olympic Winter Games**. The composition of the Athletes Commission is: 1) eight summer sports athletes elected during the Games of the Olympiad (four at each edition of the Games), 2) four winter sports athletes elected during the Olympic Winter Games (two at each edition of the Games), and 3) seven athletes appointed by the IOC president to ensure a fair balance in terms of gender, sport, and region. The 12 athletes elected during the Olympic Games and Olympic Winter Games serve an eight-year term and become IOC members during their term on the Athletes Commission. The Athletes Commission has been charged with three responsibilities: 1) discuss its views biannually with the IOC **Executive Board** and report to the IOC session, 2) delegate athlete representatives to other IOC commissions, and 3) establish working groups to act as liaison to the **Organizing Committees of the Olympic Games** (OCOGs).

ATHLETICS (TRACK AND FIELD). Athletics, or track and field, is the original Olympic sport. The first event contested in the **ancient Olympic Games** was the *stadion*, a sprint of about 190 meters. Recorded victors in this event are known as far back as 776 BCE. Other athletics events in the Ancient Olympics included longer races, races in armor, and a **pentathlon** consisting of the *stadion*, long jump, discus throw, javelin throw, and **wrestling**.

Throughout recorded sports history, athletics has always been practiced. Many of the **attempted revivals** of the Olympics in the 19th century consisted mostly of athletics events. Since the revival of the Olympics in 1896, athletics has been the most publicized sport on the **Olympic program**. Today, athletics is rivaled only by **football** (**soccer**) and **volleyball** as the sport practiced in the most countries in the world. The sport is governed internationally by the International Amateur Athletic Federation (IAAF), which was formed in 1912 and had 211 member nations as of 2004.

Athletics has been held at every Olympics. Women's athletics began at the 1928 Olympics and has been contested continually since. The program has varied but has been fairly standard since 1932. The current program includes sprint races (100, 200, and 400 meters), middle-distance races (800 and 1,500 meters), distance races (5,000 meters, 10,000 meters, and **marathon** [26+ miles]), hurdle races (110 meters for men, 100 meters for women, and 400 meters for both), steeplechase (3,000 meters for men only), walking events (20 km. for men and women, and 50 km. for men), flat jumping events (long jump and triple jump), vertical jumping events (high jump and pole vault), throwing events (shot put, discus throw, hammer throw, and javelin throw), and **multi-events** (decathlon for men and heptathlon for women).

Although **women** were first allowed to compete in only a few events, today they have a program with almost as many events as the men. The only current differences in the women's program is that they do not compete in a steeplechase event, they have only one walking event (20 km.), and they compete in the heptathlon, as opposed to the decathlon for men (this is likely to change in the very near future).

The **United States**' men have always been the top performers in the world in track and field athletics. Among the women, the **USSR** and the **GDR** were the top powers after their admission to the Olympics, and prior to their dissolution by the political events at the end of the 1980s.

ATTEMPTS AT REVIVAL. Prior to the 1896 **Olympic Games** in Athens, many efforts had been made at attempting to resurrect the **Ancient Olympic Games** and stage them with a program mainly containing contemporary events. These include **Robert Dover's Cotswold Olimpick Games,** the **Much Wenlock Olympian Games,** and the **Zappas Olympic Games** in Athens. Other attempts at Olympian-type festivals are known to have been held in Ramlösa, **Sweden** (near Helsingborg) in 1834 and 1836 under the initiative of Professor Gustav Johann Schartau of the University of Lund; in Montreal, Quebec, **Canada**, in the early 1830s and 1840s; in **England**, held by the National Olympian Association from 1866 to 1883, which was an offshoot of the Much Wenlock Olympian Games, as well as the Olympic Festivals of Liverpool (1862–1867); the Morpeth Olympic Games in Morpeth, England (1873–1958); and the Olympic Games at Lake Palić, held from 1880 to 1914 in Palić, a spa eight kilometers east of Subotica, then in **Hungary** and now in the Vojvodina province of **Serbia**. In addition, various Highland and Caledonian Games were held in the 19th century, which brought together various Celtic peoples in athletic competition. However, none of these events had the international flavor of **Pierre de Coubertin**'s revived Olympic Games.

Much of the impetus for revival in the 19th century was due to recent archaeological finds at Ancient Olympia and other classical sites in Greece. These digs were initiated by A. Blouet, a Frenchman, and continued by the Germans, notably Ernst Curtius. Curtius began his digs in 1875, and reports on his finds were issued between 1890 and 1897. However, the German government published yearly reports between 1875 and 1881.

The idea of revival was also in the air for at least a century prior to Coubertin. The terms *Olympic* and *Olympian* were apparently used frequently to refer to any athletic contest. Note Shakespeare's phrases from the late 1500s: "such rewards as victors weare at the Olympian

Games" *(Henry VI*, Act 2) and "Olympic wrestling" *(Troilus and Cressida*, Act 4). Milton discussed "As at th' Olympian Games or Pythian fields" in *Paradise Lost* in 1667.

Professor John Lucas of Penn State University discovered a letter from T. B. Hollis written in 1788 to Josiah Willard, president of Harvard University, in which Hollis states, "Our documents carry mention of an eventual rebirth of the Olympic Games in America. The friends of this latter [idea] want and pretend to be capable of it: after having acted according to Greek Principles, they must practice Greek exercises."

In 1793, Johannes C. F. Guts-Muths discussed the Ancient Olympics in his *Gymnastik für Jugend,* and by the second edition in 1804, he was considering a revival. In 1813, the philologist and historian Bartold Georg Niebuhr wrote of "a vast hall [in Rome] which, once properly decorated, could serve for the resumption of the Olympic Games."

Thus, Pierre de Coubertin did not come to his Olympic idea without help. However, a great deal of credit is due him as he was the visionary who, apart from **William Penny Brookes**, really envisioned the possibility of a great international festival bringing together the youth of all nations in peaceful competition. Without Coubertin's vision, it is almost certain that the Olympic Games would have been revived—but it is not as certain that they would be anything like the Olympic Games we know today. *See also* Appendix R ("Attempts at Olympic Revival Prior to 1896").

AUSSIE RULES. *See* FOOTBALL, AUSTRALIAN RULES.

AUSTRALIA (AUS). Australia, whose **National Olympic Committee** (NOC) was formed and recognized by the **International Olympic Committee** (IOC) in 1895, has competed at every **Summer Olympic Games**. In 1908 and 1912 it competed as Australasia in a combined team with **New Zealand**. Australia has also competed at the **Olympic Winter Games**—those of 1936 and continuously since 1952. Australia has been successful in many sports, but particularly so in **swimming** and **track and field**. As of 2004, Australia has won 401 medals, including three at the Olympic Winter Games, 121 of which were gold. Australia has also hosted the Games of the XVIth Olympiad in 1956 in Melbourne, and more recently, the sublime Games of the XXVIIth Olympiad in 2000 in Sydney.

AUSTRALIAN RULES FOOTBALL. *See* FOOTBALL, AUSTRALIAN RULES.

AUSTRIA (AUT). Austria competed at the first Olympics in 1896 and has missed only one Games since—those of 1920 when it was not invited as an aggressor nation in World War I. Austria has also competed at every **Olympic Winter Game**s, where it has often been the dominant nation in **alpine skiing**. It is one of only three countries (with **Norway** and **Liechtenstein**) to have won more medals at the Winter Olympics than at the **Summer Olympic Games**. Through 2004, Austrian athletes have won 163 medals (42 gold medals) at the Olympic Winter Games and 94 medals (22 gold medals) at the Summer Olympics. Austria has also twice hosted the Olympic Winter Games, those of 1964 and 1976, both times in Innsbruck.

AUTOMOBILE RACING. Automobile racing has never been contested at the **Olympic Games**, even as a demonstration sport. But in 1900 at Paris, auto racing was contested during the sporting events held in conjunction with the Exposition Universelle. As it is difficult to know which events were Olympic in that year, some historians list the auto racing events in their records. In 1908 at London, automobile racing was on the preliminary program, but the sport was not contested, and there have been no moves to include the sport in the Olympic Games since. Internationally, automobile racing is governed by the Fédération Internationale de l'Automobile (FIA), which was founded in 1904 and currently has 119 affiliated member nations. Automobile racing is actually precluded by the **Olympic Charter**, in which Rule 47.4.2 states, "Sports, disciplines or events in which performance depends essentially on mechanical propulsion are not acceptable."

AVEROF, GEORGIOS (GRE). B. 15 August 1818, Metsovo, Greece. D. 15 July 1899, Alexandria, Egypt. Georgios Averof was a Greek merchant in **Egypt**, who acquired enormous wealth as a trader in Alexandria. Averof's donation of almost one million drachma for the excavation and rebuilding of the Ancient Panathenaic stadium for the 1896 Games ensured that the first modern Olympics were staged in an appropriate setting. A dedicated patriot, he had already given several schools and a military academy to the nation, but as a man of a shy, retiring nature, he declined an invitation to be a guest at the **Olympic Games** that he had personally financed. His generosity was marked by the erection of a life-size statue that was unveiled shortly before the Games opened. His nephew was a member of the **International Olympic Committee** (IOC) from 1926 to 1930.

AZERBAIJAN (AZE). From 1952 to 1988 athletes from Azerbaijan formed part of the **Soviet Union** Olympic team, and at Barcelona in 1992, four Azerbaijani athletes were chosen for the **Unified Team**. After independence and formation of a **National Olympic Committee** (NOC), Azerbaijan was granted recognition by the **International Olympic Committee** (IOC) in 1992 and first competed as an independent nation at the 1996 **Olympic Games** and the 1998 **Olympic Winter Games**. Azerbaijani athletes have won eight Olympic medals, including three gold medals.

– B –

BABASHOFF, SHIRLEY FRANCES (USA–SWI). B. 31 January 1957, Whittier, California. Shirley Babashoff was the winner of a record eight Olympic medals, a total matched at the time among Olympic women **swimmers** by **Kornelia Ender** and **Dawn Fraser**. Her two gold medals both came in the 4 × 100 meter freestyle relay (1972, 1976), to which she added two silver medals in 1972 and four in 1976. Babashoff was the World Champion at 200 meters and 400 meters in 1975 and set many world records in individual and relay events between 1974 and 1976. Babashoff's performance at the 1976 Olympics, with one gold and four silvers, was considered somewhat disappointing, as she was favored in several events. At the time, she claimed she was beaten by East German females who were using illegal performance-enhancing drugs, claims that were later substantiated when files of the East German secret police, the Stasi, were reviewed after the fall of the Berlin Wall.

BADMINTON. Badminton was invented in **India**. It was adopted by English soldiers there in the 19th century, who brought the game to Britain and eventually to many other countries. The game was originally called "Poona." The new sport took hold in **England** when it was exhibited there in 1873 at a party given by the Duke of Beaufort at his country estate, "Badminton," in Gloucestershire.

Badminton was contested as a **demonstration sport** at the 1972 **Olympic Games** in Munich. It made its début as a full medal sport in 1992 at Barcelona. After 1972 it did not appear at the Olympics until its appearance at Barcelona on the medal program. This was then an unusual mode of entry into the Olympics. Men and women compete in singles and doubles, and there is a mixed doubles event at the Olympics. Badminton is governed by the International Badminton Federation (IBF), which was formed in 1934 and which had 145 members as of December 2004.

BAHAMAS, THE (BAH). As the Bahamas did not have a **National Olympic Committee** (NOC) at the time of the 1948 **Olympic Games**, their two leading yachtsmen chose to represent **Great Britain**, which was permitted under Olympic rules as the Bahamas was a British colony. In 1952 an NOC was established and recognized by the **International Olympic Committee** (IOC), and the Bahamas competed at the Olympic Games under its own name for the first time that year. Since then, it has failed to be represented only at the Moscow Games in 1980, and it has not yet competed in the **Olympic Winter Games**. Bahamian athletes have won eight medals.

BAHRAIN (BRN). The Bahrain **National Olympic Committee** (NOC) was organized in 1978 and recognized by the **International Olympic Committee** (IOC) in 1979. Bahrain has competed at all the **Olympic Games** since 1984. The top finish by a Bahraini athlete was 14th in the 1992 men's hammer throw by Reyadh Rasheed Saad Al-Ameeri. Bahrain has not yet competed at the **Olympic Winter Games**.

BAILLET-LATOUR, COUNT HENRI DE (BEL). B. 1 March 1876, Antwerp. D. 6 January 1942, Brussels. Henri de Baillet-Latour was a Belgian aristocrat who proved himself to be an able sports administrator at an early age. Elected to the **International Olympic Committee**

(IOC) in 1903 at the age of 27, he organized the **Olympic Congress** in Brussels two years later and, after playing a major role in securing the 1920 Games for Antwerp, became president of the Belgian Olympic Committee in 1923, serving until 1942. He was named to the IOC **Executive Board** in 1921 and remained in that capacity until he took over as IOC president in 1925, following **Coubertin**'s resignation. During his presidency, the IOC was concerned with the problems of the definition of an amateur and the program of the **Olympic Games**. Baillet-Latour remained president until his death in 1942.

BALCZÓ, ANDRÁS (HUN–MOP). B. 16 August 1938, Kondoros. András Balczó was the winner of a record six individual and seven team titles in the **modern pentathlon** at the World Championships. After placing fourth at the 1960 Olympics, he won team gold and individual silver medals in 1968 and then, in 1972, won the individual title and a silver medal in the team event for a total of six Olympic medals (three gold, three silver). Although the reigning World Champion, Balczó did not compete in the 1964 Games, but his overall record is the greatest of any modern pentathlete.

BALLANGRUD, IVAR (né Ivar Eriksen) (NOR–SSK). B. 7 March 1904, Lunner, Hadeland. D. 1 June 1969, Trondheim. Ivar Ballangrud's record of seven Olympic medals has only been matched by **Clas Thunberg** (FIN) among male speed skaters. In 1928, he won the 5,000 meters, and in 1936, he was the winner at 500 meters, 5,000 meters, and 10,000 meters. He also won two silver medals (1932, 1936) and a bronze (1928). Ballangrud's record at the World Championships has never been approached; he won the 5,000 meters seven times, the 1,500 meters and 10,000 meters four times each, and was a four-time winner of the overall title (1926, 1932, 1936, and 1938). He also set a total of five world records at 3,000 meters, 5,000 meters, and 10,000 meters.

BALLROOM DANCING. *See* DANCE SPORT.

BANDY. Bandy was contested as a **demonstration sport** at the 1952 **Olympic Winter Games**. It is an outdoor form of **ice hockey** played on a large rink with 11 players to a side, using a ball instead of a puck. The

International Bandy Federation (IBF) is a provisional member of the **General Association of International Sports Federations** (GAISF) and was recently given provisional recognition by the **International Olympic Committee** (IOC). It was founded in 1955 and currently has 13 affiliated nations.

BANGLADESH (BAN). The Bangladesh Olympic Association was formed in 1979 and recognized by the **International Olympic Committee** (IOC) in 1980. Bangladesh did not compete in Moscow in 1980 but has been represented at all the **Olympic Games** since 1984. Bangladesh athletes have never competed at the **Olympic Winter Games**, and the country has yet to win an Olympic medal.

BARBADOS (BAR). The Barbados Olympic Association was formed in 1955, but, as an independent country, Barbados did not compete in the Olympics until 1964. Barbados has since competed at every **Olympic Games** except for 1980. It has not won a medal in those years. Barbados has not yet competed at the **Olympic Winter Games**. In 1960, Barbados competed with **Jamaica** and **Trinidad** representing the **West Indies Federation**. One of the Barbadan runners, James Wedderburn, ran with three Jamaicans as a member of the 4 × 400 meter relay team and helped win a bronze medal.

BASEBALL. Baseball is an American sport, the game having been invented in the early 19th century. Popular lore attributes its discovery to Abner Doubleday in Cooperstown, New York, but research indicates that it is highly unlikely he actually discovered the game. Its exact origins are unclear, although it is probably based somewhat on the British games of **cricket** and rounders.

American baseball has been contested at the Olympics as a **demonstration sport** in 1912, 1936, 1956, 1964, 1984, and 1988. In 1952, Finnish baseball (*pesäpallo*) was demonstrated at the Helsinki Olympics. American baseball became a full medal sport at Barcelona in 1992. The Americans do not dominate the sport in international play, as the **Cubans** and several Central American countries produce excellent teams, although the **United States** upset the Cubans and won the gold medal at Sydney in 2000. Internationally, baseball is governed by the International Baseball Association (IBA), which was founded in 1938 and had 113 members at the end of 2004. At the 2005 IOC session in Singapore, baseball was eliminated from the Olympic program beginning in 2012.

BASKETBALL. Basketball is one of the few sports for which the precise origin is known. The game was invented in 1891 by James W. Naismith, an instructor at the International YMCA Training School in Springfield, Massachusetts, now Springfield College. The game was originally played with peach baskets, and an attendant on a ladder retrieved the ball after a made basket. Naismith formulated 13 rules of the game, of which 12 still form the basics of the modern game.

In 1936, basketball made its first appearance as a medal sport at the Olympics. In 1976, **women**'s basketball was added to the program. The **United States** has dominated international basketball until recently. The U.S. won all the Olympic titles until 1972 when it was upset by the **Soviet Union** in a very controversial game. The Soviet women were originally the top team on the female side, but the U.S. women have surpassed them, winning the gold medal in 1996, 2000, and 2004.

Today, basketball has become one of the most popular sports in the world. U.S. college basketball is wildly popular in the United States, and the National Basketball Association (NBA) has engendered international interest. In addition, numerous international leagues have added to the growth of the sport. In 1992, for the first time, the United States was allowed to use professional players from the NBA. This NBA All-Star Team, dubbed the "**Dream Team**" by the world's media, is certainly the greatest basketball team ever assembled, and it dominated the 1992 Olympic tournament. An NBA All-Star team also represented the United States in 1996 and 2000, winning those gold medals as well, though the margin between the NBA and the rest of the world is shrinking, and in 2004, despite using NBA players, the United States men won only a bronze medal. The sport is governed worldwide by the Fédération Internationale de Basketball Amateur (FIBA). As a measure of its popularity, FIBA currently (2004) has 212 member nations. *See also* DREAM TEAM, THE; UNITED STATES MEN'S BASKETBALL TEAM—1960; UNITED STATES MEN'S BASKETBALL TEAM—1984.

BASZANOWSKI, WALDEMAR (POL–WLT). B. 15 August 1935, Grudziadz. Never weighing more than 70 kg., Waldemar Baszanowski was one of the greatest lifters ever, pound-for-pound. He won gold medals in both 1964 and 1968 at the Olympics in the lightweight class and was also World Champion in 1961 and 1965. Baszanowski was a great technician who did very well in the quick lifts of snatch and clean and jerk. He was the first man to clean and jerk two-and-one-half times his bodyweight. He set 24 world records, capped by his greatest day, 26 June 1964, when he broke the world overall record three times in the same competition.

BAUMGARTNER, BRUCE ROBERT (USA–WRE). B. 2 November 1960, Haledon, New Jersey. Bruce Baumgartner is the greatest heavy **wrestler** ever produced in the **United States**. A freestyler, he competed four times at the **Olympic Games** (1984–1996) and won a medal at each Olympics, one of only four Olympic wrestlers to win medals at four Games. Baumgartner won the unlimited class freestyle gold medal in 1984 and 1992, won silver in 1988, and finished his career in Atlanta with a bronze. He was also World Champion in 1987, 1991, and 1995, and runner-up at the Worlds in 1989–1990 and 1994. He won the Pan-American Games gold medal three times consecutively—1987, 1991, and 1995. His record in the World Cup was particularly impressive, with seven titles—1984–1986, 1989–1991, and 1994.

BEACH VOLLEYBALL. Beach volleyball became popular in the 1980s, played originally on the beaches of Southern California. Unlike the indoor six-person game, beach volleyball is played usually by two-person teams, although events with four-person teams are also contested. The game is played on a sand-based surface. Beach volleyball was added to the **Olympic program** in 1996 and has been contested in 1996, 2000, and 2004 at the Olympics. It has been written of in the media as "Baywatch with a medal ceremony."

BEAMON, ROBERT "BOB" (USA–ATH). B. 29 August 1936, Jamaica, New York. With a single performance, lasting no more than a few seconds, Bob Beamon achieved sporting immortality at Mexico

City in October 1968. His long jump of 8.90 meters (29′2½″) gave him the Olympic gold medal and a new world record by a massive margin. Rated by many as the greatest performance in **track and field** history, his record was thought to be unbeatable. But like all records it was inevitably surpassed, and in 1991, the record fell to Mike Powell (USA). Beamon never again approached the form he showed at the 1968 Olympics, and he turned professional in 1972.

BECHUANALAND. *See* BOTSWANA.

BEHRENDT, JAN (GDR/GER–LUG) and KRAUSSE, STEFAN (GDR–LUG). Jan Behrendt (B. 29 November 1967, Ilmenau) and Stefan Krausse (B. 17 September 1967, Ilmenau) formed a redoubtable doubles luge team, competing first for the **German Democratic Republic** and after 1992 for **Germany**. At the Olympics, they won gold medals in 1992 and 1998, silver in 1988, and bronze in 1994. Behrendt and Krausse began to compete together internationally at the 1985 European Junior championships. Together, they won four World Championships: 1989, 1991, 1993, and 1995; and were runners-up in 1996–1997. They were also World Cup champions in 1994–1996 and European champions in 1996. They announced their retirement after the 1998 **Olympic Winter Games**.

BELARUS (BLR). The **National Olympic Committee** (NOC) of the Republic of Belarus was formed in 1991 after the breakup of the **Soviet Union**. Many Belarus (formerly Belorussia, or Byelorussia [White Russia]) athletes competed from 1952 to 1988 for the Soviet Union, and Belarus athletes were present at both Albertville and Barcelona in 1992 as members of the **Unified Team**. Belarus competed as an independent nation for the first time at the 1994 **Olympic Winter Games** in Lillehammer, with 33 athletes who won two medals. It first competed independently at the **Summer Olympic Games** in 1996, and through 2004, it has won six gold medals and 51 medals. Belarus has never hosted an Olympic Games, but in 1980, several preliminary football (soccer) matches were held in Minsk, the capital of Belarus.

BELGIUM (BEL). Belgium has competed at every **Olympic Games**, with the exception of 1896 and 1904. Belgium began competing at the **Olympic Winter Games** in 1924, and also competed in **figure skating** and **ice hockey** in 1920, but the country missed the 1960 and 1968 Olympic Winter Games. Belgium has won 144 medals (38 gold medals) in the Olympic Games, four medals in the Olympic Winter Games, and eight medals in the now defunct **Art Contests**. Belgium also hosted the Games of the VIIth Olympiad at Antwerp in 1920.

BELIZE (BIZ). As British Honduras, this country formed a **National Olympic Committee** (NOC) in 1967 and made three Olympic appearances in 1968, 1972, and 1976. As Belize it has been represented at all the **Olympic Games** beginning in 1984. Belize has never competed at the **Olympic Winter Games** and has never won an Olympic medal.

BELMONDO, STEFANIA (ITA–NSK). B. 13 January 1969. With nine Olympic medals, the Italian **cross-country skier** Stefania Belmondo trails only **Raisa Smetanina** among female athletes at the **Olympic Winter Games**. Belmondo first competed at the Winter Olympics in 1988. In 1992, she won three medals, including a gold medal in the 30 km. race. She failed to medal at the 1994 Lillehammer Olympics, but won four medals at Nagano in 1998, and in 2002 won two medals, including her second gold in the 15 km. race, after which she retired. The 15 km. gold medal was particularly dramatic as Belmondo broke a pole with 4.5 km. remaining and skied in with only one pole. Belmondo won the World Cup for cross-country skiing in 1999, and she finished second in that competition three times (1991, 1992, 1997) and third three times (1993, 1998, 2002). She also won the Sprint World Cup in 1997 and was a four-time World Champion. Nicknamed the "Tiny Tornado" for her relatively small size of 5'3" (160 cm.) and 100 lbs. (45 kg.), Belmondo was renowned for her huge training regimen, covering over 10,000 km. per year on skis.

BELOUSOVA, LYUDMILA (later Protopopov) (URS–FSK) and PROTOPOPOV, OLEG ALEKSEYEVICH (URS–FSK). The husband-and-wife team of Lyudmila Belousova (B. 22 November 1935, Ulyanovsk) and Oleg Protopopov (B. 16 July 1932, Moscow) won the Olympic pair skating title in 1964 and 1968. As the first Russian pair skaters to achieve international acclaim, they provided the stimulus that ultimately led to many successes by future generations of **Soviet** and **Russian** skaters. They began skating as a pair shortly before 1957 and were married that year. In addition to their two Olympic gold medals they were World Champions four times (1965–1968). After losing their world title in 1969, Soviet authorities turned their sights on younger skaters and refused to allow them to compete at the 1972 **Olympic Winter Games**. Belousova and Protopopov then emigrated to **Switzerland** and turned professional, touring in many different ice shows.

BELOV, SERGEY ALEKSANDROVICH (URS–BAS). B. 23 January 1944, Nashchekova, Tomsk Oblast. Sergey Belov played guard for the **Soviet** national **basketball** team from 1967 until 1980. He won four Olympic medals—bronzes in 1968, 1976, and 1980, and a gold medal in 1972. In addition, Belov played on teams that won the World Championships in 1967 and 1974 and European Championships in 1967, 1969, 1971, and 1979.

BENIN (BEN). Benin was originally part of French West Africa, but became independent from **France** under the name of Dahomey in 1960. Dahomey competed in the 1972 Olympics at Munich. The name was changed to Benin in 1975, and, after missing the 1976 Games, it has competed at every Olympics since 1980. Benin has never competed in the **Olympic Winter Games** and has not yet won an Olympic medal. Benin's best Olympic performance came in 1980 when featherweight **boxer** Barthelemy Adoukonou received a first-round bye, won one match, and then lost in the third round to place equal ninth of 35 boxers.

BERESFORD, JACK, JR. (GBR–ROW). B. 1 January 1899, Chiswick, Middlesex. D. 3 December 1977, Shiplake-on-Thames, Oxfordshire. With five medals Jack Beresford was the most successful Olympic oarsman of the pre-World War II era. To his gold medals in the single sculls (1924), coxless fours (1932), and double sculls (1936), he added silver in the single sculls (1920) and the eights (1928). Beresford's remarkable career spanned five **Olympic Games**, and it was almost certainly only the cancellation of the 1940 Games that prevented a sixth Olympic appearance. He was awarded the **Olympic Diploma** of Merit in 1949. At Henley, he won the Diamond

Sculls four times (1920 and 1924–1926), the Nickalls Challenge Cup in 1928 and 1929 (coxless pairs with Gordon Killick), and the Double Sculls Challenge Cup in 1939 with Dick Southwood. He also won the Wingfield Sculls for seven consecutive years from 1920. His father, Julius Beresford (né Wisniewski), won an Olympic silver medal in the eights in 1912.

BERLIOUX, MONIQUE LIBOTTE (FRA–SWI). B. 22 December 1925. Monique Berlioux was a French national **swim** champion, primarily in the backstroke, in the 1940s. During World War II she worked for the French underground, often swimming across the River Seine with messages detailing German intelligence gathering. She competed at the 1948 **Olympic Games**, finishing sixth in a semi-final of the 100m. backstroke. But her Olympic fame would come later. Berlioux was educated at the Sorbonne and then began a career in journalism. In the 1960s she took a job at the **International Olympic Committee** (IOC) and shortly thereafter was made the media chief by IOC president **Avery Brundage**. In 1971, she was appointed director of the IOC, the first female to be so named, and still remained through 2004, the highest ranked female in the world of sports administration. She worked under three IOC presidents, Brundage, **Lord Killanin**, and **Juan Antonio Samaranch**. But her relations with Samaranch were more difficult than with Brundage and Killanin, and in 1985, she "resigned" from her position as IOC director, a decision apparently made mutually after discussions with President Samaranch.

BERMUDA (BER). Bermuda first entered international competition in 1930 at the British Empire Games in Canada. Following this, a **National Olympic Committee** (NOC) was formed in 1935 and **International Olympic Committee** (IOC) recognition was granted in 1936. Bermuda has competed at the Olympics since 1936, failing to appear only in 1980. It has competed at the **Olympic Winter Games** of 1992, 1994, and 1998. Bermuda's athletes have won one medal, a bronze medal in **boxing** in 1976 by Clarence Hill.

BHUTAN (BHU). Bhutan established a **National Olympic Committee** (NOC) in February 1983. This was noted by the IOC **Executive**

Board later that year, and provisional **International Olympic Committee** (IOC) recognition was granted in April 1984. Bhutan took part in the 1984 Olympics, since which time it has been represented in their national sport by a total of 18 **archers** at six Olympics (1984–2004). Bhutan has not been represented in any other sport. It has won no medals and has not yet competed at the **Olympic Winter Games**.

BIATHLON. Attempts to introduce a winter **multi-event**, patterned after the **modern pentathlon**, began in 1948, when the **winter pentathlon** was contested at the St. Moritz Olympics as a **demonstration sport**. It consisted of **cross-country** and downhill skiing, and also **shooting**, **fencing**, and horse riding. Biathlon, which consists of cross-country skiing in which the runner stops at intervals to shoot a rifle at a target, was known in the 1920s but was not popular until the 1950s. The first World Championships were held in 1958 at Saalfelden, Austria. The sport quickly was placed on the **Olympic program**, showing up at Squaw Valley in 1960. Women's biathlon made its Olympic début in 1992 as a full medal sport at Albertville. In 1924, a military patrol race was a medal sport on the **Olympic Winter Games** program. **Military ski patrol** was similar to a team biathlon event, with team members skiing together.

Biathlon is currently governed by the International Biathlon Union (IBU), which had 62 member nations as of December 2004. Beginning in 1948, biathlon was governed by the Union Internationale de Pentathlon Moderne et Biathlon, which oversaw both sports, but the organization split into two governing bodies in 1993.

Biathlon events have consisted of a single men's race and a men's relay until 1980 when a second individual event was contested. The event is scored by time. In the longer individual race, a one-minute penalty is assessed for a missed shooting bull's-eye, and a two-minute penalty is assessed for missing a target. In the shorter individual race and the relay, missing a target is penalized by requiring the skier to ski a 150-meter penalty loop. **Women** currently also compete in the Olympics in both a short (7.5 km.) and a long (15 km.) individual race, and a relay race. In 2002, a new individual pursuit event for men (12 km.) and women (10 km.) was added to the Olympic Winter program.

BICYCLE POLO. First played in **Ireland** in 1891, the game's growing popularity led to a demonstration match between Ireland and **Germany** being included in the program at the 1908 **Olympic Games**. Although the sport has been included in the Asian Games, the chances of it becoming an Olympic sport are very remote.

BIKILA, ABEBE (ETH–ATH). B. 7 August 1932, Mout. D. 25 October 1973, Addis Ababa. Though his life came to a tragic early end, Abebe Bikila is usually considered the greatest marathoner ever. He was the first person to win the Olympic **marathon** consecutively, doing so in 1960 and 1964. His marathon career began only a few months before the Rome Olympics in 1960, when he won a trial race in the altitude of Addis Ababa. Between that race and a marathon he won in Seoul in October 1966, Bikila ran 15 marathons, winning 14, losing at the 1963 Boston Marathon, in which he finished fifth. He sustained an injury in 1967 and never fully recovered, which caused him to withdraw after starting the 1968 Olympic marathon in Mexico City. Late in 1969, Bikila was in a car accident, and the injuries he sustained rendered him a permanent quadriplegic. He lived only a few more years, dying in October 1973. His funeral in Addis Ababa was attended by thousands who came to mourn their nation's first great, and still greatest, runner.

BILLIARDS. Billiards, and the many pool variants, have never been on the **Olympic program**. But the World Confederation of Billiards Sports (WCBS) is currently recognized by the **International Olympic Committee** (IOC). Founded in 1992, the federation currently has 194 affiliated member nations.

BIONDI, MATTHEW NICHOLAS (USA–SWI). B. 8 October 1965, Moraga, California. Matt Biondi won 11 swimming medals at the 1984, 1988, and 1992 Olympics, matching the record of **Mark Spitz**. He was at his best at the 1988 Games, winning seven medals (five gold, one silver, one bronze), and, although essentially a freestyle swimmer, he won his silver medal in the 100 meter butterfly. Biondi set seven individual world records and won six gold medals at the World Championships (1986, 1991). In 1986, he won seven medals at the World Championships and added four more in 1991.

BJØRNDALEN, OLE EINAR (NOR–BIA). B. 27 January 1974, Drammen, Norway. Ole Einar Bjørndalen first competed at the **Olympic Winter Games** in 1994, but with only minimal success. In 1998 at Nagano, he won the 10 kilometer **biathlon** event and won silver with the Norwegian relay team. But prior to the 2001–2002 season he gave no indication of what he would do at the Salt Lake City Olympics. Earlier in the season he won two World Cup biathlon races, but at Salt Lake City he won gold medals in all four biathlon events— 10 kilometers, 20 kilometers, pursuit, and relay. No biathlete before him had won more than two gold medals at a single Winter Olympics. Bjørndalen also ran the 30 kilometer cross-country event in 2002, finishing sixth.

BLAIR, BONNIE KATHLEEN (USA–SSK). B. 18 March 1964, Cornwall, New York. With victories in the 500 meters in 1988, 1992 and 1994, Bonnie Blair is the only woman to have won an Olympic **speed skating** event at three successive Games. She also won the 1,000 meters in 1992 and 1994 after taking the bronze in 1988, and her total of five gold medals has only been bettered by the Russian **Lidiya Skoblikova**. Blair won four World Championships, those being the World Short-Track Championships in 1986 and the World Sprints in 1989 (at which meet she set a long-standing world record of 159.435 points for the sprint all-around), 1994, and 1995. During her career, she set four world records in the 500 meters.

BLANKERS-KOEN, FRANCINA ELSJE "FANNY" (née Koen) (NED–ATH). B. 26 April 1918, Baarn. Fanny Blankers-Koen was an outstanding all-around athlete who made her Olympic début as a high jumper in 1936. World War II deprived her of the opportunity of making further Olympic appearances until 1948 when, at the age of 30 and the mother of two, she was the star of the London Games. Blankers-Koen won the 100 meters, 200 meters, and 80 meters hurdles, and ran the anchor leg on the winning relay team. She would likely have won more medals in 1948 but women were then restricted to competing in three individual **track and field** events, although she was at the time world record holder in the high jump, long jump, and pentathlon. She set world records at eight different events, won five European titles (1946–1950), and a statue was erected in her honor in her native Amsterdam. She married her coach, Jan Blankers, a Dutch Olympic triple jumper in the 1928 Games.

BLEIBTREY, ETHELDA (later Macrobert, then Schlafke) (USA–SWI). B. 27 February 1902, Waterford, New York. D. 6 May 1978, Atlantis, Florida. Ethelda Bleibtrey was the first American female **swimmer** of international renown and the first female star of the Olympic pool. At the 1920 Games she won a gold medal in each of the three swimming events for women—100 meters and 300 meters freestyle and relay—and would almost certainly have won a fourth had a backstroke event been included, as she was, at the time, a world record holder in this style. Bleibtrey set seven world records before turning professional in 1922, after which she became a swimming instructor.

BLONAY, BARON GODEFROY DE (SUI). B. 25 July 1869, Wiederschöfal. D. 14 February 1937, Biskra, Algeria. Baron Godefory de Blonay was appointed as the first Swiss **International Olympic Committee** (IOC) member in 1899 and remained a member until his death in 1937. He was a founder of the Swiss Olympic Committee in 1912 and was its first president (1912–1915). During the latter part of World War I he served as provisional IOC president (1916–1919) when **Pierre de Coubertin,** who had enlisted in the French army, felt that it would not be appropriate for a military man to serve as head of the IOC. After Coubertin was discharged from the military because of his age, Blonay relinquished his presidential duties and Coubertin again took over the presidency. Blonay was a member of the IOC **Executive Board** from 1921 to 1937 and was president of the Executive Board from 1921 to 1925. He then was vice president of the IOC from 1925 until his death in 1937. Although Blonay was originally a close friend of Coubertin, severe tensions developed between them when Blonay attempted to obtain certain administrative functions for the Executive Board. A distinguished Egyptologist, Blonay lived in Paris for many years but eventually settled in **Switzerland** where he taught at the University of Neuchâtel.

BOBSLEDDING. Bobsledding as a sport originated in **Switzerland** in 1888 when an Englishman, Wilson Smith, connected two sleighs with a board to travel from St. Moritz to Celerina. Bobsledding was first practiced on the Cresta Run at St. Moritz, but the run was not suitable for the faster bobsleds, so a separate bob run—the world's first—was constructed there in 1904.

Bobsledding was on the program of the first **Olympic Winter Games** in 1924 with a single four-man event. In 1928, the event was one for sleds with either four or five men. In 1932, the present program of two events began, one for two-man sleds and one for four-man sleds. In 2002 at Salt Lake City, **women** competed in Olympic bobsledding for the first time, in a two-person event. The bobsledding federation currently also governs the sled sport of **skeleton**. Skeleton appeared on the **Olympic program** at the Cresta Run in St. Moritz in both 1928 and 1948. Skeleton was recently placed back on the Olympic program, and a skeleton event for men and women was held in 2002 at Salt Lake City.

Bobsledding has been contested at all Olympic Winter Games except in 1960 at Squaw Valley. Because of the distance to travel to California, only nine countries indicated that they would enter bobsled teams. The Squaw Valley organizers thus decided not to build a bob run and the sport was not held that year.

Bobsledding has been dominated by the Swiss, the Italians, and, until 1992, the **German Democratic Republic**. The sport is governed by the Fédération Internationale de Bobsleigh et de Tobogganing (FIBT), which was founded in 1923 and had 60 members as of December 2004. *See also* SKELETON.

BODY BUILDING. Body building has never been on the **Olympic program**, but the sport is governed by the International Federation of Body Builders (IFBB), which, until 2003, had achieved provisional recognition by the **International Olympic Committee** (IOC). It is not currently recognized by the IOC. Founded in 1946, the IFBB has 145 affiliated member nations.

BOHEMIA (BOH). Prior to becoming the largest province of **Czechoslovakia** in 1918, Bohemia appeared at the Olympics of 1900, 1906, 1908, and 1912. In those Olympics, Bohemian athletes won six Olympic medals.

BOLIVIA (BOL). Bolivia formed a **National Olympic Committee** (NOC) in 1932 and had a single **swimmer** at the 1936 Olympics in Berlin, but the nation did not compete at the Olympics again until 1964. It has since competed continuously with the exception of Moscow in 1980. Bolivian athletes have not yet won an Olympic medal. Bolivia has also competed five times at the **Olympic Winter Games**, sending **alpine** skiers in 1956, 1980, 1984, 1988, and 1992. Bolivia did not compete at the 1994, 1998, or 2002 Olympic Winter Games.

BOSNIA-HERZEGOVINA (BIH, formerly BSH). Until 1992, Bosnia-Herzegovina was a republic in the nation of **Yugoslavia**. In that year, Bosnia-Herzegovina, along with several other Yugoslav republics, declared independence, but unfortunately, the Serbians declared war on the republic. Still, Bosnia-Herzegovina quickly formed a **National Olympic Committee** (NOC) and, on the eve of the 1992 Olympics, was granted provisional recognition by the **International Olympic Committee** (IOC) and competed at Barcelona. Despite the civil war in the country, Bosnia-Herzegovina valiantly sent competitors to the 1994 **Olympic Winter Games** in Lillehammer. Bosnia-Herzegovina has also competed at the 1996, 2000, and 2004 **Olympic Games** and the 1998 and 2002 Olympic Winter Games. The 14th Olympic Winter Games were held in Sarajevo in 1984 in what was then part of Yugoslavia, but Sarajevo is presently the capital city of Bosnia-Herzegovina. With the conflicts in the Balkans there have been nationalistic uprisings that may cause Bosnia and Herzegovina to split into two nations. In early 2000, the IOC announced that it had brokered an agreement with Bosnia and Herzegovina so that they competed as one nation, with athletes from both ethnic groups, at the 2000 Olympic Games.

BOTSWANA (BOT). Botswana formed a **National Olympic Committee** (NOC) in 1978 and has competed at every Olympics since 1980. Formerly called Bechuanaland, the country never made an Olympic appearance under that name. Botswanan athletes have yet to win an Olympic medal, and the country has not yet competed at the **Olympic Winter Games**.

BOWLING. Ten-pin bowling (as opposed to lawn bowling or bowls) was a **demonstration sport** in Seoul at the 1988 **Olympic Games**. Its governing body, the Fédération Internationale de Quilleurs (FIQ), was founded in 1952 and is currently one of the **International Olympic Committee** (IOC)-recognized **International Federations** (IFs), with 126 national members.

BOWLS. Bowls has never been contested at the **Olympic Games**, even as a **demonstration sport**, but the Confédération Mondiale des Sports de Boules (CMSB) is currently one of the **International Olympic Committee** (IOC)-recognized **International Federations** (IFs). There were 94 affiliated nations in the CMSB as of 2004.

BOXING. Boxing was contested at the **Ancient Olympic Games** and many other sporting festivals in Ancient Greece. Boxing was then even a more brutal sport. The combatants wore leather thongs on their hands. Originally the thongs were simple straps of leather, but later they were reinforced with sharp pieces of metal, and the glove was called a *cestus*. The first known Ancient Olympic boxing champion was Onomastos of Smyrna, who won in 688 BCE. The last known was Varasdates of Armenia, in 369 CE, who is also the last known champion of the Ancient Olympic Games. Professional boxing has been around since the early 18th century, with a recognized list of professional champions dating from the late 1700s.

The United States has traditionally been the premier nation in Olympic boxing. However, it has been surpassed in the last 20 years first by the **Soviet Union** and, more recently, by **Cuba**. Three boxers have won three Olympic gold medals: **László Papp** of **Hungary**, **Teófilo Stevenson** of Cuba, and **Félix Savón** of Cuba. A number of Olympic boxers have gone on to become professional World Champions, notably Cassius Clay (**Muhammad Ali**), **George Foreman**,

Joe Frazier, **Sugar Ray Leonard**, Oscar de la Hoya, and Lennox Lewis.

Olympic boxing is contested in 12 weight classes. Amateur matches are currently four rounds of two minutes each with a one-minute rest between rounds, although until 2000 they were three rounds of three minutes each. There are five judges who score the match. Scoring is now done by a complicated system in which the judges register successful punches. If three of the five judges register a punch within one second, that scores one point for the boxer who lands the punch. Decisions are made only by the punches-landed point score. At the Olympics, all weight classes are conducted by single-elimination tournaments. There is currently no match for third place, with both losing semifinalists receiving bronze medals.

Amateur boxing is governed by the Association Internationale de Boxe Amateur (AIBA), which currently has 202 member nations and was founded in 1946.

BOYARSKIKH, KLAVDIYA (URS–NSK). B. 11 November 1939, Verkhnyaya Pyshma, Sverdlovsk. To three gold medals (5 km., 10 km., and relay) at the 1964 Olympics, Klavdiya Boyarskikh added two further golds at the 1966 World Championships to establish herself as the world's leading female **cross-country** skier of the 1960s.

BOYCOTTS AND POLITICS. The **Olympic Games** have rarely been able to escape the influence of politics since they became a major international event. The first significant intrusion of politics occurred in 1936 when several nations considered boycotting the Berlin Olympics to protest the policies of **Germany**'s Adolf Hitler. *See* "The Games of the XIth Olympiad" in the chronology.

Minimal political intrusions occurred in 1948 and 1952. The major disruption in 1952 occurred at the opening ceremony, when a fairly large woman in a flowing white robe interrupted the proceedings, strode to the podium, and began to read a peace message, before being escorted away—this was in the era of far less security, obviously. In 1956, however, a small boycott ensued because of the recent incursion of **Soviet** troops into **Hungary**, and because of an **Egyptian-Israeli** dispute over the Sinai peninsula. *See* "The Games of the XVIth Olympiad" in the chronology.

The Rome Olympics in 1960 were once again free of significant political conflicts. In 1964, a dispute arose concerning the eligibility of certain nations that had competed at the **Games of the New Emerging Forces (GANEFO)** in 1963. *See* "The Games of the XVIIIth Olympiad" in the chronology.

In 1968, the **Mexican** government faced numerous student protests over the presence of the **Olympic Games** in the Mexican capital despite the poverty and hunger of many of its citizens. As the protest movement gathered momentum leading up to the Games, the Mexican army took charge on the night of 2 October. As 10,000 people demonstrated in the Square of the Three Cultures in Mexico City, the army surrounded the crowd and opened fire. More than 250 people were killed and thousands were injured or imprisoned. *See* "The Games of the XIXth Olympiad" in the chronology.

The worst intrusion of politics into the Olympics occurred in 1972 when Arab terrorists representing the Black September movement entered the **Olympic Village** and took as hostage 11 Israeli competitors and coaches. The hostages were all eventually murdered. *See* "The Games of the XXth Olympiad" in the chronology.

Shortly before the 1976 Olympics were due to start, they were marred by a boycott of 22 African countries, **Guyana**, and Chinese Taipei (then **Taiwan**). This was in protest of a recent tour of **South Africa** by the **New Zealand** national **rugby** team. As South Africa was ostracized from international sporting competition, the African nations demanded that New Zealand not be allowed to compete at Montreal. However, as the **International Olympic Committee** (IOC) had no control of international rugby, New Zealand was properly allowed to start in the Olympics.

The Taiwan boycott occurred when the **Canadian** government did not allow the Taiwanese team to enter the country, as it did not recognize the island nation, in violation of its agreement as host country to admit all eligible nations in honoring the **Olympic Charter**. The Canadians eventually acquiesced and gave permission for the Taiwanese to compete, but refused to allow them to do so as the **Republic of China**, its official national name and the name by which it was then recognized by the IOC. Several other countries protested and threatened withdrawal, notably the **United States**. However, these protests were short-lived and the IOC finally gave in to the

Canadian government. Taiwan withdrew and did not compete. *See* "The Games of the XXIst Olympiad" in the chronology.

The largest-scale Olympic boycott occurred in 1980. The Games were held in Moscow in July 1980. In December 1979, Soviet troops entered **Afghanistan**. The United States led a vocal protest and eventually boycotted the 1980 Olympic Games. It was joined by approximately 60 other nations who also boycotted. *See* "The Games of the XXIInd Olympiad" in the chronology.

In 1984, the Soviet Union exacted its revenge on the United States when it boycotted the Los Angeles Olympic Games. This was officially because of concerns over security and the safety of its athletes, but there was little doubt as to the reason, which was revenge for the 1980 U.S.-led boycott. The Soviet Union boycott was joined, quite naturally, by other members of the Soviet bloc, including Eastern Europe and **Cuba**. Only **Romania**, among Soviet-bloc nations, defied the Soviet-led boycott. *See* "The Games of the XXIIIrd Olympiad" in the chronology.

The IOC awarded the 1988 Olympics to Seoul. This was a highly controversial decision, as many prominent nations in the Olympic movement did not have diplomatic relations with the Seoul government. The problem became more complicated in 1985 when **North Korea** demanded that it be allowed to cohost the Games with the **Republic of Korea**. Over the next three years the IOC negotiated with North Korea and offered to allow it to stage several events. When the IOC would not concede further to the North's demands, North Korea announced that it would boycott the Seoul Olympics.

By then, however, most of the Soviet-bloc countries had agreed to compete in Seoul, making 1988 the first **Summer Olympic Games** competition in 12 years between the United States, the Soviet Union, and the German Democratic Republic. After North Korea's official boycott announcement, Cuba and **Ethiopia** also announced that they would boycott the Olympics. **Nicaragua**, **Albania**, and the **Seychelles** also did not attend the Olympics, although their reasons may not have been directly related to any boycott. *See* "The Games of the XXIVth Olympiad" in the chronology.

In 1992, the Olympics were held in Barcelona. These Games were remarkably free of political protest and intrusions. They were the first Olympic Games since 1968 that saw no form of boycott.

In addition to boycotts of the Olympic Games, political problems have haunted the IOC since the end of World War II. This has mostly been in terms of the official recognition of certain nations. In many cases, the nations have not been on good political terms with other IOC members, and these IOC members have protested their official recognition.

In particular, the IOC has dealt with the problems of the "two" Germanys (*see* Germany and the **German Democratic Republic**); the "two" Chinas (*see* **China** and **Chinese Taipei**); the "two" Koreas (*see* Korea, Democratic People's Republic of, and Korea, Republic of); and the question of recognition of South Africa (*see* South Africa) despite its apartheid policies. Similar problems existed in the later 1960s and early 1970s concerning Rhodesia (see **Zimbabwe**).

BRAZIL (BRA). Brazil has competed at every Olympics since 1920, with the sole exception of 1928. It has competed at the **Olympic Winter Games** in 1992, 1994, and 1998. Brazil's successes have come in a variety of sports. It has won medals in several different sports, and it has always had one of the top **basketball** and **football (soccer)** teams. Brazilian athletes have won 76 Olympic medals, 16 of them gold medals, the most medals by any South American country.

BRIDGE. Bridge has never been contested at the Olympics, but the World Bridge Federation (WBF) was recognized by the **International Olympic Committee** (IOC) in 2000. Founded in 1958, the WBF currently has 159 national members.

BRITISH VIRGIN ISLANDS (IVB). The British Virgin Islands formed a **National Olympic Committee** (NOC) in 1980 that was recognized in 1982. The nation has competed at every **Olympic Games** since 1984, but it has not yet been represented at the **Olympic Winter Games**. No athlete from these islands has won an Olympic medal.

BROOKES, WILLIAM PENNY (GBR). B. 1809, Much Wenlock, England. D. 10 December 1895, Much Wenlock, England. William Penny Brookes was the founder of the **Much Wenlock Olympian**

Games, an early influence on the thinking of **Pierre de Coubertin** toward the revival of the Olympics. Brookes was a doctor who was educated at various schools in Shropshire and began his study of medicine at Guy's and St. Thomas's Hospitals in London in about 1827. He finished his studies in Paris and Padua, returning to Much Wenlock in 1831 to carry on the general practice of medicine that his father had started. He founded the National Olympian Association in 1865, the forerunner of the British Olympic Association. He was active in public affairs, serving as justice of the peace and commissioner for roads for the borough of Wenlock, and in 1841 he formed the Wenlock Agricultural Reading Society. He eventually became a licentiate of the Society of Apothecaries and, in 1881, a fellow of the Royal College of Surgeons.

Brookes was an invited dignitary to Coubertin's Sorbonne Congress of 1894 that founded the modern **Olympic Games,** but he was unable to attend because of illness. He and Coubertin corresponded frequently, and Brookes had Coubertin visit the Much Wenlock Olympian Games in October 1890. In 1881, Brookes was the first person who proposed that international Olympian Games be staged again, to be held in Athens. *See also* MUCH WENLOCK OLYMPIAN GAMES.

BRUNDAGE, AVERY (USA). B. 28 September 1887, Detroit, Michigan. D. 7 May 1975, Garmisch-Partenkirchen, Germany. Avery Brundage was an American who served as president of the **International Olympic Committee** (IOC) from 1952 to 1972, the longest reign ever, aside from **Pierre de Coubertin,** and equal to that of **Juan Antonio Samaranch.** As a participant in the **track and field** events in 1912 (**decathlon** and **pentathlon**), he was the first IOC president, and one of only two to date (also **Jacques Rogge**), to have actually competed in the Olympics (as of 2001). He enjoyed the financial freedom to devote his time to the administrative side of sport, having made a fortune in the construction business. Brundage served seven terms as president of the Amateur Athletic Union (AAU), was president of the U.S. Olympic Committee for 25 years, and, after becoming a member of the IOC in 1936, he was elected to the IOC **Executive Board** in 1937, and as IOC vice president in 1946, before becoming president six years later. His dedication to amateurism bordered on the fanatical and anachronistic, but he gradually lost his lifelong battle to the rising tide of commercialism in sport. Although never terribly popular, and undoubtedly the most controversial IOC president ever, Brundage traveled constantly in the cause of **Olympism** and did much to widen the international scope of the **Olympic movement**.

BRUNEI (BRU). The Brunei National Olympic Council was formed in 1984 and recognized by the **International Olympic Committee** (IOC) in that year. After sending an official as an observer to both Seoul (1988) and Barcelona (1992), Brunei first competed at the 1996 **Olympic Games**, where it was represented by a single competitor in the skeet shooting event. To date Brunei has been represented by four Olympic athletes—one in 1996, two in 2000, and one in 2004.

BUCHANAN, IAN (GBR). B. 28 January 1932, Sheffield, Yorkshire. Ian Buchanan was one of the founding members of the **International Society of Olympic Historians** (ISOH) and served as that organization's first president for two terms, from 1991 to 2000. He guided ISOH through its formative years and helped the group become internationally known and achieve official recognition by the **International Olympic Committee** (IOC). Buchanan was well known to the world of Olympic history, writing numerous books, including *British Olympians*, the definitive history of the British Olympic teams, and *Quest for Gold: The Encyclopaedia of American Olympians* (with Bill Mallon), a similar study of the **United States**' Olympic athletes. He also has published a number of other works on sports history, notably *All-Time Greats of British and Irish Sports* (with Peter Matthews) in 1995, and *The Guinness International Who's Who of Sport* (with Peter Matthews and Bill Mallon). Buchanan's business career was as a reinsurance agent, primarily based in Hong Kong, although in retirement he settled back in his native **England**. For his work in Olympic history, he was made an honorary member of ISOH after he stepped down as president in 2000, and was awarded the **Olympic Order** in silver in 1997 by the IOC.

BUDO. *Budo* is a general term referring to the many different forms of Japanese martial arts. In 1964, the Japanese gave exhibitions of

Japanese **archery** (*kyudo*), **fencing** (*kendo*), and **wrestling** (*sumo*), all of which are examples of *budo*, at the Tokyo Olympics.

BULGARIA (BUL). Five Bulgarian athletes went to Athens for the 1896 **Olympic Games**, but due to a misunderstanding over the use of the Gregorian and the Julian calendars, they arrived too late to compete. It was not until 1923 that a **National Olympic Committee** (NOC) was formed, and **International Olympic Committee** (IOC) recognition followed in the next year. Bulgaria first competed at the Olympic Games in 1924, and it has since missed only the Olympic Games of 1932, 1948, and 1984. Its first appearance in the **Olympic Winter Games** was in 1936, and it has competed at all celebrations since. Bulgaria has had its greatest successes in strength sports, mainly **weightlifting** and **wrestling**, and in the 1980s it was the premier nation in the world in weightlifting. Bulgarian athletes have won 212 Olympic medals, 51 of them gold.

BURGHLEY, LORD; DAVID GEORGE BROWNLOW CECIL (later the Sixth Marquess of Exeter) (GBR). B. 9 February 1905, Stamford, Lincolnshire. D. 22 October 1981, Stamford, Lincolnshire. Lord Burghley was the Olympic 400 meter hurdles champion in 1928 and later a distinguished sports administrator. In 1933, at the age of 28, he was elected a member of the **International Olympic Committee** (IOC), and three years later he became chairman of the British Olympic Association and president of the British Amateur Athletic Association. In 1946, Lord Burghley took over from J. Sigfrid Edström as president of the International Amateur Athletic Federation (IAAF) and was chairman of the organizing committee for the 1948 Olympic Games. He failed in a bid for the IOC presidency in 1952 and 1964, but from 1952 to 1966 he served as vice president of the IOC.

BURKINA FASO (BUR). Taka Gangua and Taki N'Dio competed in the javelin throw in 1924 for **France**, but were nationals of what was then called Upper Volta. Burkina Faso sent a single competitor to the 1972 Olympics, representing Upper Volta. The country changed its name to Burkina Faso in 1984, and as Burkina Faso, its first Olympic participation occurred in 1988 at Seoul, and it has also competed in

1992 and 1996. No athlete from this nation has won an Olympic medal.

BURMA (BIR). *See* MYANMAR.

BURUNDI (BDI). Burundi's **National Olympic Committee** (NOC) was founded in 1990 and given official recognition by the **International Olympic Committee** (IOC) in September 1993. Burundi first competed at the 1996 **Olympic Games**, but it has not yet competed at the **Olympic Winter Games**. In 1996, Burundi won one medal, a gold by Venuste Niyangabo in the men's 5,000 meters of track and field **athletics**. Burundi also competed at the 2000 and 2004 Olympic Games.

BUTTON, RICHARD TOTTEN "DICK" (USA–FSK). B. 18 July 1929, Englewood, New Jersey. Dick Button was noted for bringing a new dimension of athleticism to **figure skating**. Between 1943 and 1952, he was only defeated twice, and his many victories included the Olympics of 1948 and 1952. He was the World Champion for five consecutive years (1948–1952). Button was U.S. champion for seven consecutive years (1946–1952), won the North American title in 1947, 1949, and 1951, and in 1948 became the only American to win the European championships. After his European title, the event was closed to non-Europeans. Thus, in 1948, he uniquely held the championships of the **United States**, North America, Europe, the Olympics, and the World. Known for his innovative, dynamic freeskating, Button was undefeated to the end of his career in 1952, after having finished second at the 1947 World Championships. A Harvard-educated lawyer, Button later became an award-winning **television** commentator and sports-event producer.

– C –

CAMBODIA (CAM). Cambodia made its first Olympic appearance at the Equestrian Olympic Games of 1956 in Stockholm, although it did not compete at the Melbourne Olympics that year. It again participated in 1964 and 1972. It has yet to win a medal. Briefly known as

Kampuchea, the country has retaken the name Cambodia. With the frequent changes in government, the status and even the existence of a **National Olympic Committee** (NOC) has often been in doubt, but the latest body was recognized by the **International Olympic Committee** (IOC) in 1994, and Cambodia competed at Sydney in 2000 and Athens in 2004, represented in both years by four athletes, two men and two women.

CAMEROON (CMR). In 1959 Cameroon approached the **International Olympic Committee** (IOC) for advice concerning the establishment of a **National Olympic Committee** (NOC). It took four years for plans to reach fruition, with the NOC being formed in 1963 and receiving IOC recognition in the same year. Cameroon made its Olympic début in 1964 at Tokyo and has appeared at all Games since. It has not yet attended the **Olympic Winter Games**. Cameroon athletes have won four Olympic medals, two in **boxing**. But the highlight of their Olympic performances have been the gold medal won at Sydney in 2000 by their men's **football (soccer)** team and the gold won by Françoise Mbango Etone in the women's triple jump at Athens in 2004.

CANADA (CAN). Canada first appeared officially at the 1904 **Olympic Games** in St. Louis. However, in 1900, two Canadian citizens competed, both under U.S. colors (George Orton in steeplechase and Ronald MacDonald in the **marathon**). Since 1900, Canada has failed to be represented only at the 1980 Moscow Olympic Games. It has appeared at every **Olympic Winter Games** since their inception in 1924, and, in addition, the **Canadian ice hockey team** competed in the 1920 hockey tournament, winning decisively. This began a trend that continued until the **Soviet Union** entered the Olympic ice hockey tournaments, starting in 1956. Canada has won 338 Olympic medals (87 gold), 242 of them at the Olympic Games and 96 at the Olympic Winter Games. Canada has also hosted the Games of the XXIst Olympiad at Montreal in 1976 and the 15th Olympic Winter Games at Calgary in 1988.

CANADIAN ICE HOCKEY TEAMS (1920–1952). **Canada** dominated **ice hockey** at the Olympics from 1920 through 1952, winning all the Olympic tournaments during that time with the exception of the 1936 **Olympic Winter Games**, when it was upset by a British team that contained a number of Canadians who held dual British citizenship. Canada was always represented by a club team during their ice hockey reign. The teams were as follows: 1920—Winnipeg Falcons; 1924—Toronto Granites (with the addition of two players from the Winnipeg Falcons and Montreal Victorias); 1928—Toronto Varsity Graduate Team; 1932—Winnipeg Falcons (with the addition of two players from the Selkirk Fisherman); 1936—Port Arthur Bearcats (with the addition of several players from the Montreal Victorias); 1948—Royal Canadian Air Force Flyers; and 1952—Edmonton Mercurys. During this era of dominance, the Canadians posted a record of 35 wins, one loss, and three ties in Olympic competition. The loss was to **Great Britain**, 2-1, in 1936. The ties were in 1932 to the **United States** (2-2), in 1948 to **Czechoslovakia** (0-0), and in 1952 to the United States (3-3). In 1956, the Soviet Union entered the ice hockey tournament at the Olympic Winter Games and began its own period of dominance. In 2004, Canada saw both its men's and women's ice hockey teams win the gold medal at Salt Lake City, the first gold for the Canadian men in 52 years. *See also* SOVIET UNION ICE HOCKEY TEAMS (1956–1992).

CANOEING AND KAYAKING. Many years ago, canoeing began as a means of transportation. Competition in canoeing began in the mid-19th century. The Royal Canoe Club of London was formed in 1866 and was the first organization interested in developing the sport. In 1871, the New York Canoe Club was founded.

In 1924, canoeing was on the **Olympic program** as a **demonstration sport**. Canoeing became a full medal sport in 1936 with both canoe and kayak events. The program has varied a great deal over the years with many events now discontinued and several new ones added. **Women** began Olympic canoeing in 1948, competing only in kayaks, which is still the case. Whitewater canoeing, or slalom canoeing, was held at the 1972 Olympics in Munich and returned to the Olympic program in 1992 at Barcelona, and has also been on the Olympic program in both 1996 and 2000. The two types of canoe events are often called flatwater and whitewater, or sprint and slalom. The two types of canoes used are the kayak, in which the paddler sits inside a covered shell, and the Canadian, in which the paddler kneels with the top of the canoe open. The events are usually designated by codes, such as K1-500. The code indicates the type of canoe (K = kayak, C = Canadian), the number of canoeists (1, 2, or 4), followed by the distance (500 or 1,000 meters).

Canoeing is governed worldwide by the Fédération Internationale de Canoë (FIC), which was founded in 1924 and currently has 118 member nations. The top medal winners in Olympic canoeing history have been **Sweden**'s **Gert Fredriksson** and **Romania**'s **Ivan Patzaichin**. Among women, **Germany**'s **Birgit Schmidt-Fischer** and Sweden's **Agneta Andersson** have won the most canoeing medals.

CAPE VERDE (CPV). Cape Verde's **National Olympic Committee** (NOC) was formed in 1989 and given official recognition by the **International Olympic Committee** (IOC) in September 1993. Cape Verde made its Olympic début in 1996, and also competed in 2000 and 2004, but it has not yet competed at the **Olympic Winter Games**.

ČÁSLAVSKÁ, VĚRA (TCH–GYM). B. 3 May 1942, Prague. Attractive, vivacious, and talented, Věra Čáslavská was the outstanding **gymnast** at the 1964 and 1968 Games. In Tokyo she won three gold medals and one silver, and in **Mexico** she won four golds (one shared) and two silvers. Having earlier won a silver medal in 1960, Čáslavská's total of 11 Olympic medals has only ever been bettered by **Larisa Latynina** (URS) among female gymnasts. After winning her final gold medal in 1968, she married **Czech** Olympic silver medalist (1,500 meters in 1964) Josef Odložil (1938–1993), in Mexico. In 1989, she was appointed president of the Czech Olympic Committee, and in 1995 Věra Čáslavská was elected as a member of the **International Olympic Committee** (IOC).

CAYMAN ISLANDS (CAY). The Cayman Islands **National Olympic Committee** (NOC) was formed in 1973 and was recognized by the **International Olympic Committee** (IOC) in 1976. The Cayman Islands first competed at the 1976 **Olympic Games** and has been represented at every Olympics since, with the exception of 1980. It has not yet competed at the **Olympic Winter Games**, nor has it won an Olympic medal.

CENTRAL AFRICAN REPUBLIC (CAF). The Central African Republic **National Olympic Committee** (NOC) was formed in 1961, and, after lengthy negotiations over the suitability of the statutes of the NOC, the **International Olympic Committee** (IOC) granted full recognition in 1965. Since first competing at the 1968 **Olympic Games**, the Central African Republic has participated in all subsequent Olympics. The Central African Republic has not yet competed at the **Olympic Winter Games**, and it has not yet won a medal at the Olympics.

CENTRAL AMERICA. Central America is a region and, as such, has never had full recognition by the **International Olympic Committee** (IOC), nor has it ever competed at the **Olympic Games** as a region. But from 1918 to 1940, Pedro Jaime de Matheu was an IOC member to the Central American region. De Matheu was from the area that later became **El Salvador**.

CEYLON (CEY). *See* SRI LANKA.

CHAD (CHA). Chad's **National Olympic Committee** (NOC) was formed in 1963 and recognized by the **International Olympic Committee** (IOC) in 1964. Chad first competed at the **Olympic Games** in that year. With the exception of the Olympics of 1976 and 1980, Chad has taken part in every Games since making its début in 1964. Chad has not yet competed at the **Olympic Winter Games** and has never won an Olympic medal. The first Chadian athlete to compete at the Olympics was high jumper Mahamat Idriss, who represented **France** in 1960.

CHAND, DHYAN (IND–HOK). *See* DHYAN CHAND.

CHARIOT RACES. Ancient Olympic sport. Several different chariot races were contested at the **Ancient Olympic Games**. These include the **apene**, the synoris, a foals' synoris race, the tethrippon, a foals' tethrippon, a chariot race for foals, a chariot race for 10 horses, and an event listed simply as chariot race. The last three were contested only in 65 CE.

CHARPENTIER, ROBERT (FRA–CYC). B. 4 April 1916, Paris. D. 28 October 1966. Robert Charpentier was the winner of the individual road race at the 1936 Games when he also won gold medals in the team road race event and the 4,000 meter team pursuit. Charpentier got started in **cycling** when he was an apprentice to a butcher and made his deliveries on his bicycle. He was runner-up at the 1935 amateur World Championship road race. World War II prevented him from having any success after the 1936 Olympics as a professional.

CHESS. Chess has never been on the **Olympic program**, even as a **demonstration sport**. However, in 1999, the **International Olympic Committee** (IOC) recognized the world governing body of chess, the Fédération Internationale des Échecs (FIDE). Founded in 1924, the FIDE had 159 members at the end of 2004.

CHILE (CHI). Chile's initial Olympic appearance came in 1912. Since that time, however, it has missed only the Games of 1932 and 1980. Chile first competed at the **Olympic Winter Games** of 1948 and has competed 12 times in the winter celebrations, missing only 1972 and 1980. Chilean athletes have won 12 Olympic medals, two gold (both in 2004), six silver, and four bronze. Chile formed its **National Olympic Committee** (NOC) in 1934 and was recognized by the **International Olympic Committee** (IOC) in the same year.

CHINA, PEOPLE'S REPUBLIC OF (CHN). Although the current **National Olympic Committee** (NOC) was recognized by the **International Olympic Committee** (IOC) in 1979, the first Chinese Olympic Committee was formed in 1910 and recognized in 1922. China competed at the **Olympic Games** of 1932, 1936, and 1948. In September 1949, Chinese Communists assumed control of the government, and many of the former rulers escaped to the island province of **Taiwan**, including many former members of the Chinese Olympic Committee (possibly as many as 19 of 26). Athletes from the Chinese mainland did compete at the 1952 Olympic Games in Helsinki. Thus began a 40-year political problem for the IOC: the question of the "two Chinas."

In May 1954, at the 50th IOC session in Athens, the IOC voted by 23-21 to recognize both the Chinese Olympic Committee in Beijing (then Peking) (as the "Olympic Committee of the Chinese Republic," later [in 1957] as the "Olympic Committee of the People's Democratic Republic of China") and in Taipei (as the "Chinese Olympic Committee").

Both Chinas were invited to the 1956 Olympics in Melbourne. Beijing accepted the invitation on 20 November, which led Taipei to reject the invitation. However, Taipei changed its decision and elected to compete, which caused Beijing to withdraw in protest. At Melbourne, no athletes from mainland China competed, while 21 athletes from the island nation competed under the banner of the Republic of China. The Beijing committee withdrew from the IOC on 19 August 1958, in protest of the International Olympic Committee's continued recognition of Taiwan.

A request to be recognized again was submitted in 1975. The IOC requested the All-China Sports Federation to send its rules for inspection, a standard procedure. The All-China Sports Federation took two years to comply, but its application was eventually approved on 25 November 1979.

In the interim, the IOC sent a three-member contingent, led by **New Zealander** Lance Cross, to inspect sporting facilities in China. Cross reported to the IOC at its 81st session in Montevideo in April 1979. The IOC made the following recommendations at this session:

> In the Olympic spirit, and in accordance with the Olympic Charter, the IOC resolves: 1) to recognize the Chinese Olympic Committee located in Peking (Beijing), and 2) to maintain recognition of the Chinese Olympic Committee located in Taipei. All matters pertaining to names, anthems, flags and constitutions will be the subject of studies and agreements which will have to be completed as soon as possible.

The full session approved this motion by 36-30. The IOC **Executive Board** modified this slightly, changing part 2 to read "to maintain recognition of the Olympic Committee located in Taipei."

China returned to the Olympic fold in 1980 at Lake Placid. It did not compete in 1980 at Moscow, but China has competed at all other Olympic Games and **Olympic Winter Games** since 1984. Chinese athletes have won 308 Olympic medals, 114 of them gold, all since

1984. Chinese athletes excel in **gymnastics**, **table tennis**, **diving**, and **swimming**. *See also* CHINESE TAIPEI (AKA TAIWAN, FORMOSA, REPUBLIC OF CHINA).

CHINESE TAIPEI (AKA TAIWAN, FORMOSA, REPUBLIC OF CHINA) (TPE). The Chinese Taipei **National Olympic Committee** (NOC) was first formed in 1949 by members of the mainland Chinese committee who had fled to the island. The **International Olympic Committee** (IOC) official policy at this time was that the mainland Chinese Olympic Committee had simply changed its address and was now located on the island of Taiwan. For many years thereafter, the country was embroiled in a dispute with mainland China over recognition by the IOC.

In October 1959, the IOC **Executive Board** recommended that the Olympic Committee in Taiwan be recognized as the "Olympic Committee of the Republic of China," but it also insisted that, at the 1960 Olympic opening ceremonies, this team should march behind a banner reading "Formosa." The banner eventually read "Taiwan/Formosa," but the placard bearer also posted a sign of his own, reading "Under Protest."

The greatest controversy concerning the participation of the athletes from Chinese Taipei occurred in 1976 at Montreal. In 1970, Canada had given political recognition to mainland China. Only a few weeks before the Montreal Olympics, Canada's government announced that it would not allow Chinese Taipei athletes to compete under the name of the "Republic of China." This was in complete violation of the **Olympic Charter** and the contract Montreal had signed as host of the **Olympic Games**, in which it agreed to allow all eligible athletes to enter the nation with the use of the **Olympic identity card**. The **United States** government protested vociferously, even threatening a boycott. Eventually, however, the U.S. athletes competed, although Chinese Taipei refused to compete under any name other than the Republic of China. On 11 July, only six days before the start of the Olympics, the IOC Executive Board gave in and proposed to the full IOC that the island nation should compete at Montreal as Taiwan. The IOC approved this recommendation by 58-2, with six abstentions. Chinese Taipei/Taiwan/Republic of China withdrew in protest and did not compete at the 1976 Olympics.

After competing for several years under the banner "China" or "Republic of China," the IOC eventually banned the country from competing under this name. The current NOC was recognized in its present form on 26 November 1979, and on 23 March 1981 it signed an agreement with the IOC in which the NOC agreed to change its name to the Chinese Taipei Olympic Committee and compete under a new flag and emblem.

Taiwan/Chinese Taipei first competed at the Olympic Games in 1956, and since then has taken part at every Olympics with the exception of 1976 and 1980. It has competed in nine Olympic Games under various names—the Republic of China (1956), Taiwan (1960–1972), and Chinese Taipei (1984–1996). The nation has competed at nine **Olympic Winter Games**—as Taiwan from 1972 to 1976, and as Chinese Taipei from 1984 to 2002. The nation has won 15 Olympic medals, including its first two gold medals in 2004. *See also* CHINA, PEOPLE'S REPUBLIC OF.

CHUKARIN, VIKTOR IVANOVICH (URS/UKR–GYM). B. 9 November 1921, Mariupol (now Zdhanov). D. 26 August 1984, Lvov. A former World War II prisoner of war, Viktor Chukarin was 30 years old when the **USSR** first competed at the **Olympic Games** in 1952. Despite these handicaps, he dominated the **gymnastics** competition in Helsinki, winning the all-around title in addition to taking gold in the team event and two gold and two silver medals on the individual apparatus events. In 1956, Chukarin successfully defended his all-around title and added two more gold, a silver, and a bronze medal to bring his tally of Olympic medals to a then-record total of 11. He was also World All-Around Champion in 1954, and after retiring, he became head of gymnastics at the Lvov Institute of Physical Culture.

CHUN LEE-KYUNG (KOR–STK). B. 6 January 1976. In the relatively new Olympic sport of short-track **speed skating**, Chun Lee-Kyung has been the most successful Olympian to date. She competed in both 1994 and 1998, winning the 1,000 meters at both Olympics, and skating on the winning relay team both times, to earn her four gold medals. To that she added a bronze in the 500 meters in 1998. Chun was also a three-time World Champion, in 1995–1997.

CITIUS, ALTIUS, FORTIUS. See OLYMPIC MOTTO.

CLAUDIUS, LESLIE WALTER (IND–HOK). B. 25 March 1927, Bilaspur, Madhya Pradesh. Leslie Claudius shares with **Udham Singh** the distinction of being one of only two players to win four Olympic medals for field **hockey**. To his gold medals in 1948, 1952, and 1956, he added silver in 1960 when he captained the team. He was the first player ever to earn 100 caps, and competed for **India**, in addition to the Olympics, on their European tour of 1949, **Malaysian** tour of 1952, **Australian** and **New Zealand** tours of 1955, and at the Third Asian Games in 1958. After the 1960 Olympics, he continued to compete domestically, retiring after the 1965 season. In 1971, he became the sixth Indian hockey player to be given the prestigious Padamshree civil award by the Indian government.

CLAY, CASSIUS MARCELLUS (USA–BOX). *See* ALI, MUHAM-MAD.

COCHELEA-COGEANU, VERONICA (ROM–ROW). B. 15 November 1965. Among **women**, only her countrywoman **Elisabeta Lipa-Oleniuc** has won more Olympic **rowing** medals than the six won by Veronica Cochelea-Cogeanu. Lipa-Oleniuc and Cochelea-Cogeanu combined for five of these medals—1988 doubles sculls silver medal, 1988 quadruple sculls bronze medal, 1992 double sculls silver medal, and 1996 and 2000 coxed eights gold medals. Cochelea-Cogeanu also won a silver medal with the quad in 1992. She was less successful at the World Championships, winning only one gold. Her 1988 Olympic appearance was as Miss Cogeanu, but she competed as Veronica Cochelea after marrying.

COE, SEBASTIAN NEWBOLD (GBR–ATH). B. 29 September 1956, Chiswick, London. Sebastian Coe is considered by many track experts as the greatest 800 meter runner in history. His world record (1:41.73) for the distance, set in 1981, remained unbeaten for 16 years. Coe never won an Olympic title at this distance and had to settle for a silver medal in 1980 and 1984, but he won a gold medal in the 1,500 meters at both Games. A controversial omission from the 1988 British Olympic team denied him the opportunity of further honors. A prolific record breaker, he set nine outdoor and three indoor world records. After retirement, Coe continued to serve the sport as an administrator and, in 1992, was elected a member of the British Parliament, in which he served through 1997.

COLOMBIA (COL). Colombia first competed at the 1932 **Olympic Games**, represented by a lone athlete, **marathon** runner Jorgé Perry Villate. The country first formed a **National Olympic Committee** (NOC), however, only in 1936, and this National Olympic Committee was recognized by the **International Olympic Committee** (IOC) in 1939. Colombia has since competed at every Olympics with the exception of 1952. It has yet to compete in the **Olympic Winter Games**. Colombian athletes have won eight Olympic medals through 2004.

COMĂNECI, NADIA (ROM–GYM). B. 12 November 1961, Onesti, Moldavia. Nadia Comăneci was the first **gymnast** in Olympic history to be awarded a perfect score of 10.0. She achieved this landmark as a 14-year-old, first on the uneven parallel bars in 1976, and the judges awarded her maximum marks a further six times during the Games. In the 1976 and 1980 Games, Comăneci won a total of nine Olympic medals (five gold, three silver, one bronze). Following the 1980 Games, natural physical development began to inhibit her performance, and after a victory at the 1981 World Student Games she retired. In 1989, she defected from **Romania** and settled in North America. She has since married American Olympic gymnastic medalist Bart Conner.

COMITÉ INTERNATIONAL PIERRE DE COUBERTIN. *See* INTERNATIONAL PIERRE DE COUBERTIN COMMITTEE.

COMMISSION FOR THE OLYMPIC MOVEMENT. The Commission for the Olympic Movement was formed in 1982, but its forerunner was the Tripartite Commission, which existed from 1975 to 1981. The Tripartite Commission was formed in response to complaints from the **National Olympic Committees** (NOCs) and **International Federations** (IFs), who felt that they had little say in the **Olympic movement** and no process through which to voice their opinions officially. The Tripartite Commission consisted of members of the **International Olympic Committee** (IOC), the NOCs, and the

IFs. The Commission for the Olympic Movement has had a similar composition. The chairman of this commission was always the IOC president, originally **Lord Killanin** (Tripartite Commission), and since 1980, **Juan Antonio Samaranch**. The Olympic Movement Commission was disbanded in 2001. It has essentially been superseded by the **Olympic Games Study Commission** and the **Olympic Programme Commission**.

COMMISSIONS OF THE IOC. The **International Olympic Committee** (IOC) has created a number of commissions that deal with specific issues related to the **Olympic movement**. The currently recognized commissions (as of the end of 2004) are as follows: Athletes Commission; **Culture and Olympic Education Commission**; Coordination Commission for the XX Olympic Winter Games—Turin 2006; Coordination Commission for the XXIXth Olympiad—Beijing 2008; Coordination Commission for the XXI Olympic Winter Games—Vancouver 2010; IOC 2000 Commission (dissolved); **Ethics Commission; Finance Commission; International Relations Commission; Juridical Commission; Marketing Commission; Medical Commission; Nominations Commission; Olympic Games Study Commission; Olympic Philately, Numismatic, and Memorabilia Commission; Olympic Programme Commission; Olympic Solidarity Commission; Press Commission; Radio and Television Commission; Sport and Environment Commission; Sport and Law Commission; Sport for All Commission; Television and Internet Rights Commission**; and the **Women and Sport Commission**. Several of the IOC commissions have subcommissions, notably: Medical Commission—Subcommission on Doping and Biochemistry of Sport, Subcommission on Biomechanics and Physiology of Sport, Subcommission on Sports Medicine and Coordination with the **National Olympic Committees** (NOCs), Subcommission on Out of Competition Testing. In addition, the IOC also recognizes several working groups that often have the status of a commission, at least briefly. Currently, these include the Remuneration Working Group; and the Council of the Olympic Order. The IOC will also form *ad hoc* commissions to study certain problems, such as a Disciplinary Commission recently formed to look into certain **doping** allegations.

COMMONWEALTH OF INDEPENDENT STATES (CIS). In 1992, former republics of the **Union of Soviet Socialist Republics** (Soviet Union) competed at the **Olympic Games** in Barcelona and the **Olympic Winter Games** in Albertville. By then, the former republics had formed the Commonwealth of Independent States. Because of the short time after the breakup of the Soviet Union, it was agreed that the former republics would compete as one team, which was called the **Unified Team**, or L'Équipe Unifiée, and which, loosely, represented the Commonwealth of Independent States.

COMOROS ISLANDS (COM). The Comoros Islands **National Olympic Committee** (NOC) was founded in 1979 but was not recognized by the **International Olympic Committee** (IOC) until September 1993. The nation first competed at the **Olympic Games** in 1996, but it has not yet competed at the **Olympic Winter Games**. At Atlanta in 1996, the Comoros Islands were represented by one female and three male athletes. At Sydney in 2000, two athletes—one male and one female—competed for the Comoros Islands. In 2004, the Comoros Islands were represented by three athletes—one male and one female in track and field **athletics**, and one male **weightlifter**.

COMPETITION FOR HERALDS. Ancient Olympic sport. This event was held at the **Ancient Olympic Games** from at least 396 BCE to 261 CE. The last four known championships were won by Valerius Eclectus of Sinope.

COMPETITION FOR TRUMPETERS. Ancient Olympic sport. The competition for trumpeters was held from at least 396 BCE to 217 CE at the **Ancient Olympic Games**. The event was won consecutively from 328 BCE through 292 BCE by Herodoros of Megara.

CONGO, DEMOCRATIC REPUBLIC OF THE (COD). This nation was formerly known as the Belgian Congo, but changed its name to the Democratic Republic of the Congo in June 1960. In October 1971, the name was changed to Zaire, but in May 1997, the nation took back the name the Democratic Republic of the Congo. As the Democratic Republic of the Congo, Zaire was represented by five cyclists at the Mexico City Olympics in 1968. The nation's second

Olympic appearance came 16 years later in Los Angeles as Zaire, where it was represented by three **track and field** athletes—two men and a woman—and six **boxers**. Zaire also competed in 1988, 1992, and 1996. The country never competed in the Olympics as the Belgian Congo, and competed as the Democratic Republic of the Congo again in 2000 and 2004. No athlete from this variantly named nation has yet won an Olympic medal.

CONGO, PEOPLE'S REPUBLIC OF THE (CGO). Since making its Olympic début in 1964, the Congo has competed at every **Olympic Games** with the exception of 1968 and 1976. It has never competed at the **Olympic Winter Games**. Its best finish in the Olympics was sixth, albeit last, in **women's handball** in 1980.

CONNOLLY, JAMES BRENDAN BENNETT (USA–ATH). B. 28 November 1865, South Boston, Massachusetts. D. 20 January 1957, Boston, Massachusetts. James Connolly was the first champion at the modern **Olympic Games** and the first known Olympic champion since Varasdates in the fourth century CE. Connolly achieved this distinction by winning the hop, step, and jump (now known as the triple jump) on 6 April 1896. He also tied for second place in the high jump and placed third in the long jump in Athens, and in 1900, he narrowly failed to retain his hop, step, and jump title. Connolly did not take part in the 1904 Games and made his final Olympic appearance in 1906 when he failed to record a valid jump in either of the horizontal jumps. Unable to obtain a leave of absence from Harvard to travel to Greece for the first modern Games, he quit college, but his place in Olympic history no doubt provided ample compensation. James Connolly later became well known as a writer of seafaring novels.

COOK ISLANDS (COK). The Cook Islands Sports and Olympic Association was first organized and recognized by the **International Olympic Committee** (IOC) in 1986. The Cook Islands first competed at the 1988 Olympics in Seoul, and also competed in 1992 at Barcelona, 1996 in Atlanta, 2000 in Sydney, and 2004 in Athens. The nation has not yet competed at the **Olympic Winter Games** and has not won an Olympic medal.

COORDINATION COMMISSION FOR THE OLYMPIC GAMES. In 1985 the **International Olympic Committee** (IOC) formed the Study and Evaluation Commission for the Preparation of the Olympic Games. The name was changed to the Coordination Commission for the Olympic Games in 1986. The Coordination Commission consists of several subcommissions at any one time, as each **Olympic Games** in the planning stage has a subcommission of the Coordination Commission. For instance, there are current subcommissions for the 20th Olympic Winter Games (Turin 2006), the Games of the XXIXth Olympiad (Beijing 2008), and the 21st Olympic Winter Games (Vancouver 2010). Each subcommission has a separate chairman, with the members representing various entities—media, athletes, **television**, environment, as well as IOC members. The subcommissions work closely with their associated **Organizing Committee of the Olympic Games** (OCOG) to help them plan and organize the Olympic Games, and act as liaisons between the IOC, the OCOG, the **International Federations** (IFs), and the **national Olympic committees (NOCs)**. The current chairman of the Coordination Commissions are Turin 2006—**Jean-Claude Killy**; Beijing 2008—Hein Verbruggen; and Vancouver 2010—René Fasel.

COROEBUS OF ELIS (GRE–ATH). fl. ca. 800–750 BCE. Coroebus was a cook in the city-state of Elis in Ancient Greece. His Olympic fame rests on the fact that he is the first recorded champion in Olympic history, as in 776 BCE he won the *stadion* race. His feat was inscribed on his tomb.

COSTA RICA (CRC). Costa Rica has competed at eleven **Olympic Games**—1936, and continuously since 1964. Costa Rican athletes have won four medals, by the **swimming** sisters Silvia and Claudia Poll Ahrens. The nation has competed at four **Olympic Winter Games**—1980, 1984, 1988, and 1992.

COSTAS, ROBERT QUINLAN (USA). B. 22 March 1952, Queens, New York. Bob Costas has succeeded **Jim McKay** as the voice of the Olympics on American **television**. Costas has worked primarily for NBC Television, which has televised all **Olympic Games** to the American public since 1988, and more recently the 2002 **Olympic**

Winter Games. Costas has been the main studio host now for five Olympic Games or Olympic Winter Games, backing up Bryant Gumbel in 1988. He began his career in broadcasting after majoring in communications at Syracuse University, known for its broadcasting curriculum. Aged only 22, he was selected to broadcast **basketball** for the Spirits of St. Louis in the now defunct ABA. He then joined CBS Sports, covering regional **football** and basketball games. In 1980 he joined NBC, and has since handled lead broadcast duties for **baseball**, basketball, and football. He has branched out from sports and for a time hosted "Later with Bob Costas," a general interview show that aired after midnight on NBC. Costas has won numerous awards for his work, being named Sportscaster of the Year several times and winning six Emmy awards.

CÔTE D'IVOIRE (CIV). Formerly known as the Ivory Coast, Côte d'Ivoire formed a **National Olympic Committee** (NOC) in 1962, which was recognized by the **International Olympic Committee** (IOC) in 1963. Côte d'Ivoire has competed in the **Olympic Games** since 1964, missing only the 1980 Games. The country has not yet appeared at the **Olympic Winter Games**. Côte d'Ivoire can claim one Olympic medal, a silver won by Gabriel Tiacoh in the 400 meters (track and field **athletics**) in 1984.

COTSWOLD OLIMPICK GAMES. *See* ROBERT DOVER'S GAMES.

COUBERTIN, BARON PIERRE DE (née Pierre Frédy) (FRA). B. 1 January 1863, Paris. D. 2 September 1937, Geneva. Pierre de Coubertin is the founder of the **Olympic movement**. His inspirational idea to revive the Ancient Greek festivals grew out of his general interest in physical education, and, at the early age of 24, he began a campaign to restructure educational methods in **France** along the lines of the British public school system, of which he was a great admirer. His idea of reviving the **Olympic Games** grew more from his interest in sociology, history, and education than from any particular enthusiasm for competitive sports, but it was these sports that were to provide his lasting monument. In view of his aesthetic inclination, it must have been a source of satisfaction that he won the prize for literature in the **Art**

Contests in 1912. His entry, "Ode to Sport," was submitted under a pseudonym. Taking over as president of the **International Olympic Committee** (IOC) from **Demetrios Vikelas** in 1896, Coubertin faced many problems in the turbulent early years of the Olympic movement, and the current strength of the movement is a tribute to his dedication and diplomacy in the difficult pioneering days. From 1896 to 1924, he attended every celebration of the Games, except those of 1904 and 1906, but at the Paris Games of 1924 he resigned the presidency of the IOC at the age of 61 on the grounds that he was too old to continue in office. Surprisingly, his interest in Olympic matters seems to have declined rapidly, but he recorded a message that was replayed at the opening ceremony of the 1936 Olympic Games in Berlin. The following year Coubertin collapsed and died from a heart attack while walking in Lagrange Park in Geneva, and, although he is buried in Geneva, his heart is preserved in a marble stele at Ancient Olympia. Many other aspects of Coubertin's involvement with the Olympic movement are covered in the separate entries on various subjects in this volume. *See also* the bibliography for a list of some of his published works on the Olympic movement.

COUGHLIN, NATALIE (USA–SWI). B. 23 August 1982, Concord, California. Natalie Coughlin burst onto the international **swimming** scene at the 2001 World Championships, winning a gold medal in the 100 backstroke and a bronze in the 50 backstroke. In 2002 at the Pan-Pacifics, she was more dominant, winning six medals—four gold, with three individual championships in the 100 free, 100 fly, and 100 back. Coughlin was an early favorite for the 2004 Olympics, but her performance in 2003, and especially at the World Championships, was lackluster. There she won only two relay medals, although it was later revealed that she was quite sick and had considered not competing. Although somewhat overshadowed by the media attention given **Michael Phelps**, Coughlin was the top female swimmer at the 2004 **Olympic Games**, winning five medals, including two gold. Individually, she won the 100 meter backstroke and finished third in the 100 freestyle. She won her second gold medal in the 800 meter freestyle relay and added two silvers as a member of the **United States**' teams in the other relays.

COURT OF ARBITRATION FOR SPORT (CAS). At the end of the 20th century and the dawn of the new millennium, sport, like many other facets of society, has become beset by many legal challenges. Many of these deal with drug use in sport, or **doping**. When athletes are accused of doping, they usually challenge the legality of the testing system, ensuring a long, and often expensive, legal battle. The **International Olympic Committee** (IOC) attempted to solve some of these legal problems by forming the Court of Arbitration for Sport, based in **Lausanne, Switzerland**. The CAS was formed in 1983 by the IOC, but it was restructured in 1994 as an independent body after a legal decision made note that the IOC and the CAS were very closely aligned.

At major international sporting events, athletes must now sign an agreement that any legal problems that may ensue from their participation, including a doping disqualification, will be adjudicated by submitting the problem for arbitration to the CAS. Of minor importance in the first few years of its existence, the CAS has now assumed a prominent role at major international sporting events. Many of the **International Federations** (IFs) and other sport governing bodies have agreed to give the CAS binding authority to rule on disputes involving sports law.

When a dispute arises, the parties may choose one arbitrator from CAS's pool of 150 internationally recognized arbitration experts, or each party may choose one arbitrator with the CAS choosing a third arbitrator to serve as the president of the panel for that dispute. Costs of the arbitration process are paid by the loser in the dispute, as is common in European courts of law. During the **Olympic Games** a panel of CAS arbitrators is available for emergency decisions to be adjudicated within 24 hours.

CRICKET. Cricket was contested only at the 1900 Olympics, when a British squad beat a French team, which was actually made up of British residents of France. The International Cricket Council is not currently recognized by the **International Olympic Committee** (IOC). There is almost no chance it will return to the **Olympic program**.

CROATIA (CRO). Until the **Yugoslavian** civil war of 1991 Croatia had never competed at the Olympics as an independent nation. However, prior to 1991, many top Yugoslavian athletes were from Croatia, including several of the top Yugoslavian **basketball** players. Croatia made its Olympic début at the 1992 **Olympic Winter Games** in Albertville and has since competed in the 1994, 1998, and 2002 Winter Olympics. Croatia first competed at Barcelona in 1992 where its best finish was the silver medal its basketball team won, losing only to the "**Dream Team**." Through 2004, Croatian athletes have won 16 Olympic medals.

CROQUET (ROQUE). Croquet was contested at the 1900 Olympics in Paris, with three events. Two of the competitors were **women**, among the first women to compete in the modern **Olympic Games**. In 1904, roque, an American variant of croquet, was on the **Olympic program** as well. The sport has not been held at the Olympics since 1904. The name *roque* is derived by dropping the first and last letters from the name of its parent game of croquet. Croquet is not currently recognized by the **International Olympic Committee** (IOC), nor is it even a member of the **General Association of International Sports Federations**.

CROSS-COUNTRY SKIING. *See* NORDIC SKIING.

CUBA (CUB). In 1900, the **fencer** Ramón Fonst competed at the **Olympic Games** and actually won the first gold medal for the small Caribbean country. Fonst also competed in the 1904 Olympics along with a few other Cuban athletes. In 1924, Cuba was represented by nine competitors, while in 1928, the country had one competitor. In 1948, Cuba sent a full team to the London Olympic Games, and its participation was continuous until it elected to boycott the 1984 Olympic Games in Los Angeles. In support of the **North Korean** government, Cuba also elected not to compete in 1988 in Seoul. Cuba returned to the Olympics in 1992. Cuban athletes have not yet competed in the **Olympic Winter Games**. Cuba has been successful in several sports, winning 164 Olympic medals (64 gold), but by far its greatest success has come in **boxing**. Since the mid-1970s, Cuba has probably had the best amateur boxers in the world. Cuba is also the dominant nation internationally in **baseball** and won the gold medal in 1992, 1996, and 2004.

CULTURAL COMMISSION. The Cultural Commission of the **International Olympic Committee** (IOC) was created in 1969 with Polish IOC member Włodzimierz Reczek serving as the first chairman of the commission. The Cultural Commission consisted of six IOC members, two representatives of the **International Federations** (IFs) and **National Olympic Committees** (NOCs), one athlete representative, and several independent members. Based on recommendations of the **IOC 2000 Commission** and approved at the 110th IOC session in December 1999, the Cultural Commission and the Education/IOA Commission were merged into a single **Culture and Olympic Education Commission**. In 2000, the IOC also created a new Department of Culture and Education.

CULTURE AND OLYMPIC EDUCATION COMMISSION. The Commission for the **International Olympic Academy** (IOA) and Olympic Education was first formed in 1967, with Danish **International Olympic Committee** (IOC) member Ivar Emil Vind as the first chairman. This commission oversaw the IOA in Olympia, Greece, and the commission had as its mission following the activities of the IOA, contributing to the success of the IOA, receiving the periodical reports of IOA sessions, and keeping the IOC informed of the progress of the IOA. This commission also helped promote Olympic education by spreading the message of **Olympism**. In addition to IOC members, the IOA/Education Commission had representatives from the **National Olympic Committees** (NOCs), **International Federations** (IFs), and former Olympic athletes, as well as several academic scholars, usually sports historians or sociologists. The original name of this commission was the Commission for the International Olympic Academy, but the name was enlarged in 1993, reflecting the increased emphasis on Olympic education. Upon the recommendations of the **IOC 2000 Commission**, the Commission for the International Olympic Academy and Olympic Education was merged with the **Cultural Commission** in early 2000. The current charge for this commission is to develop links between sport and culture in all its forms, encourage cultural exchange, and promote the diversity of cultures. It helps organize special events and, with the National Olympic Committees, develops Olympic education programs. As of December 2004, the chairman of this commission is IOC member He Zhenliang (CHN).

CURLING. Curling was a **demonstration sport** at the 1932, 1988, and 1992 **Olympic Winter Games**. In 1924, it also appeared on the **Olympic program**, and recent evidence indicates that curling was a full medal sport that year. Previously it had been considered a demonstration sport in 1924. In addition, in 1936 and 1964, German curling (*Eisschießen*) was contested as a demonstration sport. Curling returned to the Olympic Winter program as a full medal sport at the 1998 Olympic Winter Games in Nagano. The sport is governed by the World Curling Federation (WCF), was founded in 1966, and had 45 member federations as of 2004.

CUTHBERT, ELIZABETH "BETTY" (AUS–ATH). B. 20 April 1938, Merrylands, Sydney. Betty Cuthbert won two gold medals in the individual track sprints and a third gold in the relay at the 1956 Olympics. The 18-year-old Australian was instantly acclaimed as a national heroine by the Australian crowd. Injury spoiled her chances at the 1960 Games, but she came back to win the 400 meters in 1964 and claim her fourth Olympic gold medal. Including relays, Cuthbert set 18 world records. Sadly for such a fine athlete, she now suffers from multiple sclerosis, although at the opening ceremony in 2000, she carried the **Olympic torch** into the stadium while in her wheelchair.

CYCLING. Bicycles were first developed in the late 18th century and have since been used as a form of transportation. Originally the front wheel was much larger than the rear wheel and the rider was elevated a great deal, making them difficult to control and very dangerous. In 1885, J. K. Starley of **England** devised the more modern bike with a chain and gearing to allow the wheels to be of equal size. Although bike races had been held on the old "penny farthings," the new bikes stimulated the growth of bicycle racing as a sport.

From 1880 to 1900, cycling became immensely popular both in Europe and the **United States**. The sport was primarily a professional one at that time. The sport continues its grip on the European continent to this day, but bike racing ceased to be a popular sport in the United States at about the time of the depression. Only the American

Olympic victories at Los Angeles in 1984 and the recent exploits of Greg LeMond and Lance Armstrong have again stimulated interest in bicycle racing in the United States.

Cycling is one of the few sports that have been on the program of every **Olympic Games**. The program has varied but now consists of an individual pack-style road race, individual time-trial road race, track races, and cross-country mountain biking. In 1984, **women** were admitted to Olympic cycling with a single road race. In 1988, a sprint race on the track for women was also held, and in 1992 the women contested an individual pursuit track race. In 2000 at Sydney, three new track events for men were added—the Olympic sprint, a three-man sprint contest; the Madison, a two-man sprint-type event; and the *keirin*, a paced, pack-style race. A track time trial over 500 meters was also added to the **Olympic program** for women.

The Europeans have dominated Olympic cycling, notably the French, Italians, and Germans. However, the East Europeans have also won many medals, especially on the track. Mountain biking has recently become a very popular sport, and in 1993 the **International Olympic Committee** (IOC) approved mountain biking as an Olympic event that appeared on the Olympic program for the first time at the 1996 Atlanta Olympics. Cycling is governed by the Union Cycliste Internationale (UCI), which was founded in 1900 and had 169 members as of December 2004.

CYPRUS (CYP). The Cyprus **National Olympic Committee** (NOC) was formed in 1974 and recognized by the **International Olympic Committee** (IOC) in 1978. Since making its official Olympic début in 1980, Cyprus has competed at the Olympics of 1984–1996. Its first Olympic participation, however, occurred at the **Olympic Winter Games** of 1980 in Lake Placid, and it has sent competitors to every Winter Olympics since. However, already in 1896, several athletes of Cypriot nationality competed, representing **Greece**. Cyprus has not yet won an Olympic medal.

CZECH REPUBLIC (CZE). Formerly a part of **Czechoslovakia**, the Czech Republic has been represented at the Olympics by many athletes. However, the Czech Republic did not compete officially at the Olympics as an independent nation until its appearance at Lillehammer for the 1994 **Olympic Winter Games**. The Czech Republic has since competed at the 1996, 2000, and 2004 **Olympic Games** and the 1998 and 2002 Olympic Winter Games. As an independent nation, the Czech Republic has won 33 medals, including nine gold medals.

CZECHOSLOVAKIA (TCH). Athletes from what later became Czechoslovakia first competed at the 1900 Olympics, representing **Bohemia**. In 1920, Czechoslovakia sent its first true Olympic team to Antwerp. From 1920 to 1992 the only **Olympic Games** not attended by Czechoslovakia, including the **Olympic Winter Games**, was the 1984 Los Angeles Olympics. Czechoslovakia excelled in many different sports at the Olympics. The country's most noteworthy athletes were distance runner **Emil Zátopek** and female **gymnast Věra Čáslavská**. Czechoslovakia split peacefully into the **Czech Republic** and **Slovakia** on 1 January 1993.

– D –

DÆHLIE, BJØRN (NOR–NSK). B. 19 June 1967, Råholt. With 12 medals and eight gold medals, Bjørn Dæhlie is the most successful male **nordic skier** in Olympic history, and is now considered the greatest cross-country skier of all time. In 1992, he won the combined pursuit, the 50 km. classical, and was a member of the winning relay team, while in 1994, he was the winner of the 10 km. classical and the combined pursuit. To these gold medals he added silver in the 30 km. in 1992 and 1994, and a third silver in the relay in 1994. In 1998 at Nagano, Dæhlie won four more medals—three gold in the 10 km., 50 km., and the relay, and a silver in the pursuit race. His records of 12 medals and eight gold are absolute records for the **Olympic Winter Games** in any sport. Dæhlie has won a further nine titles at the World Championships and was World Cup champion for cross-country in 1992–1993 and 1995–1997.

DAHOMEY. *See* BENIN.

DANCE SPORT. The International Dance Sport Federation (IDSF), which governs ballroom-type dancing competitions, was founded in

1957 and currently has 79 affiliated member nations. The IDSF was given **International Olympic Committee** (IOC) recognition in 1997.

DANIELS, CHARLES MELDRUM (USA–SWI). B. 24 March 1885, Dayton, Ohio. D. 9 August 1973, Carmel Valley, California. Charles Daniels's three Olympic gold medals for **swimming** in 1904 and one in 1906 were won against rather limited opposition, but he proved his true worth in 1908 by winning the 100 meter freestyle against a truly international field. Despite the increased number of swimming events on the **Olympic program**, Daniels's total of four individual gold medals in swimming has not yet been beaten by a man, although Hungary's **Krisztina Egerszegi** has won five individual gold medals. Daniels set seven world records over various distances between 1907 and 1911, but his most significant legacy to the sport was his development of the American crawl stroke. He was a fine all-round sportsman, excelling at **golf** and squash and also at **bridge**.

DAVIS, JOHN HENRY, JR. (USA–WLT). B. 12 January 1921, Smithtown, New York. D. 13 July 1984, New York. John Davis was six times a world **weightlifting** champion and twice an Olympic gold medalist. His Olympic gold medals came in the unlimited class in 1948 and 1952, and he would undoubtedly have been a medal contender in 1940 and 1944. Davis set 18 world records between 1946 and 1951. Never defeated between 1938 and 1953, his only defeat prior to his retirement was a second place at the 1954 World Championships to Doug Hepburn of **Canada**.

DEAN, CHRISTOPHER COLIN (GBR–FSK). *See* TORVILL, JAYNE.

DE BRUIJN, INGE (NED–SWI). B. 24 August 1973, Barendrecht. Inge de Bruijn competed at the 1991 World **Swimming** Championships and helped the Netherlands win a bronze medal in the 400 freestyle relay. She then competed at the 1992 Olympics, with minimal success, and her career when into hiding for several years. But she resurfaced in 1999, winning the 50 free and the 100 fly at the European Championships and the 50 free at the World Championships. She was named 1999 European Swimmer of the Year although it was but a prelude to 2000. At the Sydney **Olympic Games**, de Bruijn won three individual gold medals—50 free, 100 free, and 100 fly. She continued to compete after Sydney, and in 2001 won the 100 free and the 50 fly at the Worlds, and the 50 and 100 free at the Europeans. She was named World Swimmer of the Year in both 2000 and 2001. At the 2003 World Championships, de Bruijn won her third consecutive world title in the 50 free and also won the 50 butterfly. Although she was 31 years old in 2004, ancient for a world-class swimmer, Inge de Bruijn again won the 50 freestyle at the Athens Olympics.

DECUGIS, MAXIME OMER "MAX" (FRA–TEN). B. 24 September 1882, Paris. D. 6 September 1978, Biot. Max Decugis was the winner of a record six Olympic medals (four gold, one silver, one bronze) for lawn **tennis** between 1900 and 1920. His victories included the mixed doubles in 1906 when he was partnered by his wife. Although the Olympic tournaments during that era attracted many of the world's top players, Decugis's greatest non-Olympic achievement was to win the Wimbledon doubles with his countryman André Gobert in 1911 when they defeated the previously unbeaten holders, Tony Wilding (NZL) and Major Josiah Ritchie (GBR). He was also an eight-time French singles champion (1903–1904, 1907–1909, and 1912–1914), although the event was then closed to French players only.

DEMONSTRATION SPORTS. Numerous sports have been contested at the **Olympic Games** and **Olympic Winter Games** as **demonstration sports**. These have usually been sports that were being considered for the **Olympic program** or sports indigenous to the country hosting the Olympic Games. In 1992, the **International Olympic Committee** (IOC) announced that demonstration sports would no longer officially be contested at the Olympic Games. *See also* AMERICAN FOOTBALL; AUSSIE RULES FOOTBALL; BADMINTON; BANDY; BASKETBALL; BICYCLE POLO; BOWLING; BUDO; CANOEING AND KAYAKING; CURLING; DOGSLED RACING; FREESTYLE SKIING; GLIDING; ICE DANCING (IN FIGURE SKATING); JEU DE PAUME; JUDO (WOMEN); KORFBALL; LACROSSE; MILITARY PATROL; PELOTA BASQUE; ROLLER HOCKEY; SHORT-TRACK SPEED SKATING; SKIJÖRING;

SPEED SKATING (WOMEN); SPEED SKIING; TAEKWONDO; TENNIS; WATER SKIING; WINTER PENTATHLON.

DENMARK (DEN). Denmark's connection with the **Olympic movement** began in 1894 when Frederik Bajer, a member of the Danish parliament, was an honorary member of the International Congress in Paris at which the **Olympic Games** were revived. After Denmark had participated in the 1896 Olympics, the first Danish IOC member, Niels Holbeck, was co-opted in 1899, but it was not until 1905 that a Danish **National Olympic Committee** (NOC) was formed. Denmark has competed at every **Summer Olympic Games** except 1904, but its attendance at the **Olympic Winter Games** has been less consistent. Since making its Winter début in 1948, it has missed the Winter Olympics of 1956, 1972, 1976, 1980, and 1984, and in its nine appearances at the Olympic Winter Games, it has been represented by a total of only 25 athletes. Danish athletes have won 170 Olympic medals, 42 of them gold. Denmark has won one medal in the Olympic Winter Games, a silver in curling in 1998.

DHYAN CHAND (IND–HOK). B. 28 August 1905, Allahabad. D. 3 December 1979, Delhi. Dhyan Chand won three gold medals as a center-forward and is considered the greatest **field hockey** player ever. He learned the game from British army officers and had his first international competition in 1926 on a tour of Australia and New Zealand. He led **India** to gold medals in 1928, 1932, and 1936. In 1947–1948 Dhyan Chand was still the star of the Indian team but declined selection to the 1948 team, which prevented him from being the only hockey player to have won four gold medals. His younger brother, Roop Singh, played on the 1932 and 1936 Olympic teams, and his son, Ashok Kumar, won an Olympic bronze medal in 1972. He was honored in his native India by the issuance of a commemorative postage stamp, and he is the only Indian hockey player to be given the top civil award, the Padma Bhushan. In 1995, a statue of Dhyan Chand was erected in front of the National Stadium. The Indian Olympic Association named him the "Player of the Century."

DIAULOS RACE. Ancient Olympic sport. The *diaulos* race was one of the major running events of the **Ancient Olympic Games**. It consisted of a race of two laps of the stadium or about 385 meters. Champions are known from 724 BCE (Hypenos of Pisa) through 153 CE (Demetrios of Chios). The greatest champions of the diaulos were **Leonidas of Rhodes** (4 titles, 164–152 BCE), Chionis of Sparta (3 titles, 664–656 BCE), Hermogenes of Xanthos (3 titles, 81–89 CE), and Astylos of Kroton and Syracuse (3 titles, 488–480 BCE). An athlete from Argos also won the event four times, but his name is not known.

DIBIASI, KLAUS (ITA–DIV). B. 6 October 1947, Solbad Hall, Austria. After winning a silver medal in the platform **diving** at the 1964 Olympics, Klaus Dibiasi went on to win the gold on the platform at the next three Games (1968, 1972, 1976) and remains the only Olympic diver to have won three successive gold medals in the same event. A silver in the 1964 springboard gave him what was then a record total of five Olympic medals. He also won the world platform title (1973, 1975), the European platform (1966, 1974), and the European springboard championship (1974). Dibiasi was born in **Austria** of Italian parents who returned to **Italy** when he was a child. He was coached by his father, a former Italian champion and a 1936 Olympian.

DI CENTA, MANUELA (ITA–NSK). B. 31 January 1963. In her first three Olympic appearances Manuela Di Centa failed to win a single medal, but at Lillehammer in 1994 she uniquely won a medal in all five **nordic skiing** events. To her gold medals in the 15 km. and 30 km. she added silver in the 5 km. and combined pursuit, and a bronze in the relay. Di Centa also claimed relay medals at the 1992 and 1998 **Olympic Winter Games**, giving her seven Olympic medals in all, a total surpassed among **women** only by **Raisa Smetanina**, **Galina Kulakova**, and **Lyubov Yegorova** (all **Soviets**). In late 1999, Di Centa was named one of the new athlete members to the **International Olympic Committee** (IOC). On 23 May 2003, Di Centa achieved another athletic feat when she became the first Italian woman to reach the summit of Mt. Everest.

DIDRIKSON, MILDRED ELLA "BABE" (née Didriksen, later **Mrs. Zaharias**) **(USA–ATH).** B. 26 June 1911, Port Arthur, Texas. D. 27 September 1956, Galveston, Texas. Babe Didrikson is considered by many authorities to be the greatest all-round sportswoman in history. At the 1932 Olympics, she won gold medals in the 80 meter hurdles and the javelin and a silver in the high jump. She set new world records in each of these three disparate events. Didrikson was an All-American **basketball** player and held the world record for throwing a **baseball**, and she excelled as a **golfer** after giving up track and field **athletics**. She won the U.S. Women's Amateur title in 1946, the British Ladies' Amateur in 1947, and the U.S. Open in 1948, 1950, and 1954, her third victory being by a record margin of 12 strokes, and coming after surgery for colon cancer.

DIEM, CARL (GER). B. 24 June 1882, Wurzburg. D. 17 December 1962, Cologne. Carl Diem is one of the cofounders of the **International Olympic Academy** and is one of the most important writers and historians of the **Olympic movement**, authoring dozens of books and articles on **Olympism** and the Olympic movement. He studied at the University of Berlin, after which, from 1917 to 1933, he was secretary-general of the German Committee for Physical Education. He was secretary-general of the organizing committee of the 1936 **Olympic Games** and conceived the idea of the **Olympic torch relay**. From 1938 to 1944, at **Coubertin**'s request, he served as director of the International Olympic Institute in Berlin. After World War II, Diem was a sports consultant to the German government. A sports university was founded in his honor, the Carl-Diem-Sporthöchscule in Köln (Cologne).

DIETRICH, WILFRIED (FRG–WRE). B. 14 October 1933. D. 3 June 1992. A competitor at five **Olympic Games** (1956–1972), Wilfried Dietrich competed in seven Olympic tournaments (four freestyle and three Greco-Roman) and won five medals (one gold, two silver, two bronze), a record for an Olympic **wrestler**. All his medals came in the unlimited class and unusually included a gold in the freestyle and a silver in the Greco-Roman style in 1960. Dietrich was the World Champion in 1961 and he was unbeaten in the unlimited freestyle from 1955 to 1962. At the World Championships he also won two silver and two bronze medals between 1957 and 1969.

DIMAS, PYRROS (né Pirro Dhima) (GRE–WLT). B. 13 October 1971, Tirane, Albania. Although born in **Albania**, Pyrros Dimas always competed internationally for **Greece**. Though the weight classes changed several times in the 1990s, Dimas was World Champion between 80–85 kg. in 1993, 1995, and 1998. To those titles he added three consecutive Olympic gold medals in 1992, 1996, and 2000, one of only three weightlifters to have accomplished that feat. In 2004, he won a bronze medal at Athens, equaling the feat of **Norbert Schemansky** in winning Olympic **weightlifting** medals at four consecutive Olympics.

D'INZEO, PIERO and D'INZEO, RAIMONDO (ITA–EQU). Piero (B. 4 March 1923, Rome) and Raimondo (B. 2 February 1925, Poggio Mirteto, Rietil) were Italian brothers who both competed in the **equestrian events** at eight **Olympic Games** (1948–1976), a record bettered only by Austrian yachtsman Hubert Raudauschl, who competed at nine Olympics. They each won six Olympic medals (Raimondo—one gold, two silver, three bronze; Piero—two silver, four bronze), with their best collective performance coming in 1960 when they took the first two places in the individual show jumping—Raimondo winning the event. Raimondo was also the World Individual Champion in 1956 and 1960. Both brothers followed their father in making their career in the Italian cavalry.

DISCIPLINES. The **International Olympic Committee** (IOC) recognizes three levels of competition—sports, disciplines, and events. Sports are well known and relatively self-explanatory. Events are any competition at which final results occur and medals are awarded at the **Olympic Games**. Disciplines are considered a subcategory of sports. Rule 47.2 defines a discipline, which is essentially a branch of a sport. The standards of admission to the **Olympic program** are the same for a discipline as they are for a sport. Most sports, such as track and field **athletics** or **shooting**, do not have disciplines, but consider all events part of one sport. There are seven Summer Olympic sports that recognize disciplines: **Aquatics**—**diving**, **swimming**, **synchronized swimming**, and **water polo** (most people outside the IOC consider these four separate sports); **Canoeing and Kayaking**—sprint (flatwater) and slalom (whitewater); **Cycling**—track, road, and mountain biking; **Equestrian**—three-day event, dressage, jumping; **Gymnastics**—artistic, rhythmic, and **trampoline**; **Volleyball**—indoor volleyball and **beach volleyball**; and **Wrestling**—freestyle and Greco-Roman.

There are three Winter Olympic sports that recognize disciplines: **Bobsledding**—bobsled and **skeleton**; Skating—**figure skating, speed skating**, and short-track **speed skating**; and skiing—**alpine skiing, cross-country skiing**, freestyle skiing, nordic combined, **ski jumping**, and snowboarding.

DISL, URSULA "USCHI" (GER–BIA). B. 15 November 1970, Bad Tölz. Uschi Disl has been the most successful women's biathlete at the **Olympic Games**. She has had a very long career, starting **biathlon** in 1986, first competing internationally in 1990, and finishing fifth and eighth that year at the two World Championship events. **Women**'s biathlon became an Olympic sport in 1992. Disl has since won eight Olympic medals, including gold in the relay events of 1998 and 2002. She has not yet won an individual Olympic gold medal, with two silver and two bronze in the individual events since 1994. At the World Championships, she has won eleven medals, with four golds in the relay, but an individual championship has again eluded her. Disl has recorded 27 wins in World Cup events but has never ranked first in the World Cup standings for a full season.

DITYATIN, ALEKSANDR (URS/RUS–GYM). B. 7 August 1957, Leningrad. By winning a medal in all eight **gymnastics** events at Moscow in 1980, Aleksandr Dityatin established a record that has been equaled only by **Michael Phelps** in 2004. Dityatin's three gold medals came in the team and individual all-around and on the rings, to which he added four silver medals and one bronze medal. His finest performance was in the horse vault when he received the first perfect score (10) ever awarded to a male gymnast at the Olympics. Dityatin was equally dominant at the World Championships, winning 12 medals (seven gold, two silver, three bronze).

DIVING. Diving is not considered to be a separate sport by the Fédération Internationale de Natation Amateur (FINA), the organizing body of world **aquatics**. FINA contests four disciplines of aquatic competition—**swimming**, diving, **synchronized swimming**, and **water polo**. FINA was formed in 1908 and currently has 179 affiliated nations.

Diving contests are known to have been held in the 19th century, although the sport is relatively modern. It was held at the 1904

Olympics in St. Louis, and its appearance on the **Olympic program** has been continuous since 1904. Diving has been contested in two basic events at the Olympics—3-meter springboard and 10-meter platform, with both men and **women** contesting both events. Four new diving events were added to the Olympic program for 2000, the first change to the diving program since 1924. These were two-person synchronized diving competitions for men and women on both platform and springboard.

The **United States** has absolutely dominated the sport of diving, perhaps more than any sport has been dominated in the Olympics. In the late 1980s the Chinese entered diving competition and posed the first serious threat to this dominance. While the United States' **Greg Louganis**, considered the greatest diver ever, was still competing, the Chinese men posted few victories, but the Chinese women have been almost unbeatable of late.

DJIBOUTI (DJI). The Djibouti **National Olympic Committee** (NOC) was founded in 1983, and recognition by the **International Olympic Committee** (IOC) in 1984 enabled it to make its Olympic début at the Los Angeles Games that year. Since then, it has competed at every **Summer Olympic Games**, excluding 2004, but has not yet participated in the **Olympic Winter Games**. In 2004, Djibouti entered athletes in track and field **athletics** and **tennis**, but none of them competed, for unknown reasons. Their appearances have been highlighted by their excellent **marathon** runners, one of whom (Ahmed Salah) won a bronze medal in 1988 at Seoul.

DMITRIYEV, ARTUR (EUN/RUS–FSK). B. 21 January 1968. Artur Dmitriyev began his pairs **figure skating** career with Nataliya Mishkutyenok, and after placing third in 1990, they were World Champions in 1991–1992 and won the Olympic gold medal in 1992. At the 1994 Lillehammer Olympics, they placed second behind Sergey Grinkov and Ekaterina Gordeeva, who had been gold medalists in 1988, but Dmitriyev and Mishkutyenok recovered to win the 1994 World Championships. Dmitriyev then began competing with Oksana Kazakova, and together they won the gold medal at Nagano in 1998, after placing third at the 1997 World Championships. Dmitriyev competed for the **Soviet Union** early in his career, for the **Unified Team** at Albertville in 1992, and later, for **Russia**.

DOGSLED RACING. A dogsled race with seven dogs per team was held at the 1932 **Olympic Winter Games** as a **demonstration sport**. The race was run over 40.5 km. (25.1 miles), lasting two days. Twelve sled-dog teams from **Canada** and the **United States** took part, with Émile St. Goddard of Canada winning the event.

DOHERTY, REGINALD FRANK (GBR–TEN). B. 14 October 1872, Wimbledon, Surrey. D. 29 December 1910, Kensington, London. Reggie Doherty and his younger brother, Laurie, dominated world **tennis** at the turn of the century. As a doubles pairing they were virtually unbeatable, winning the Wimbledon title eight times, the U.S. title twice, and all five of their Davis Cup rubbers. Together they won the 1900 Olympic doubles title, and in 1908, Reggie won a second gold medal in doubles when he was partnered by George Hillyard. Reggie Doherty confirmed his status as the world's leading player of the era by winning the Wimbledon singles title four years in succession (1897–1900).

DOLIKHOS RACE. Ancient Olympic sport. The *dolikhos* race was the long-distance running race of the **Ancient Olympic Games**, consisting of a running event of 20–25 laps (*circa* 4,000–5,000 meters). Champions are known from 720 BCE (Akanthos of Sparta) through 221 CE. The last known champion, Graos of Bithynia, is the only runner known to have won the race three times at Olympia.

DOMINICA (DMA). Founded in 1987, the Dominica **National Olympic Committee** (NOC) was recognized by the **International Olympic Committee** (IOC) in 1993, and the country made its Olympic début in 1996 when five **track and field** athletes and one **swimmer** competed at the Atlanta Olympics. Dominica competed at Sydney represented by four athletes, and at Athens represented by two athletes. Dominica has not yet competed at the **Olympic Winter Games**.

DOMINICAN REPUBLIC (DOM). The first Dominican Republic **National Olympic Committee** (NOC) was established in 1946 as a prerequisite to allow the Dominican Republic to participate in the Central American and Caribbean Games to be held that year. In 1953 the Olympic Sports Commission took control of participation in

Olympic and Regional Games, and in 1962 the NOC was reestablished in its present form. This body was recognized by the **International Olympic Committee** (IOC) in 1962. Albert Torres was the first Dominican Republic athlete to make an Olympic appearance, competing in the 1964 100 meter dash. The Dominican Republic has competed 11 times since, never failing to appear since its début. It has not yet competed in the **Olympic Winter Games**. Through 2004, the Dominican Republic has won two Olympic medals, a bronze by Pedro Nolasco in 1984 bantamweight **boxing** and a gold in men's 400 meter hurdles by Félix Sánchez in 2004.

DOPING. Doping refers to the illegal use of drugs to enhance performance in sport and is considered illegal by the **International Olympic Committee** (IOC) and the **International Federations** (IFs). The IOC rules against doping are contained in Rule 44 of the **Olympic Charter**. Basically the IOC has a proscribed list of medications that are considered to be illegal for use by athletes taking part in its competitions. After each **Olympic Games**, all medalists, and certain other randomly selected athletes, are chosen to submit a urine sample that is then tested for these drugs. If any of the proscribed drugs are present in the athlete's urine in sufficient quantities, he or she may be disqualified from competition, pending further urine studies and, usually, legal hearings. In recent years, when these penalties have been handed out, they have virtually always been contested by the athletes and their lawyers.

In addition, it is considered unlikely that previous IOC methods of testing for illegal drugs were sufficient to prevent athletes from using drugs. This is because athletes, coaches, and their doctors were able to learn enough about the drugs in order to know how long they had to be withdrawn from the athlete before a competition. This would enable the athlete to pass frequent drug tests despite being habitual users of the drugs. This is now being circumvented by IFs, **National Olympic Committee**s (NOCs), and national governing bodies performing random, out-of-competition tests of athletes at all times of the year.

Doping is not new. In the **Ancient Olympics**, trainers gave athletes various concoctions that they felt would improve their performance. The first physician to be considered a specialist in sports medicine was Galen, who prescribed as follows: "The rear hooves of an Abyssinian ass, ground up, boiled in oil, and flavored with rose hips and rose petals, was the prescription favored to improve performance." The name *doping* itself comes from the 19th century, when the Dutch term "dop" was used to describe a South African drink which was an extract of cola nuts to which was added xanthines (found in caffeine) and alcohol. The drink was intended to improve endurance, and the term *doping* was derived from it.

Numerous doping scandals have existed in sports. The most famous occurred at the 1988 Seoul Olympics when the original 100 meter champion, **Ben Johnson**, tested positive for stanazolol, an anabolic steroid, and was disqualified. At the 1960 Rome Olympics, Danish cyclist Knut Enemark Jensen collapsed and died during the cycling road race. He was later found to have been given amphetamines (Ronital) and nicotinyl tartrate (a nicotine-type of stimulant). In the 1967 Tour de France, the great British cyclist Tommy Simpson collapsed and died while ascending Mont Ventoux. He was found to have been heavily dosed with stimulants. In 1998, a major doping scandal enveloped the Tour de France, and many of the professional cyclists and their team trainers, notably the Festina team, were charged with legal action by the French authorities.

The deaths of Jensen and Simpson alerted the sporting authorities to the dangers inherent in drug use in sports. At the 1968 **Olympic Winter Games**, the IOC tested for drugs for the first time. The first athlete to be disqualified in the Olympics for drug use was **Sweden**'s Hans-Gunnar Liljenvall at the 1968 Olympic Games. Liljenvall was a modern pentathlete who had helped his team win a bronze medal. Prior to the **shooting** event he drank a few beers to help steady his nerves. This was commonplace among modern pentathletes in those days, but it cost him and his teammates a bronze medal.

In the 1970s and 1980s, the athletes of the **German Democratic Republic** (GDR–East Germany) were suspected of doping violations that were never detected. No GDR athlete ever failed a doping test at the Olympics. After the fall of the Berlin Wall and the reunification of the two Germanys, former German athletes and coaches revealed that much of the success of the great GDR athletic machine was due to the systematic use of illegal drugs. In the 1990s, the Chinese women **swimmers** and runners were suspected of using similar

practices to make great strides in their sports. Adding to this suspi-
cion was the fact that several of the former GDR coaches were then
coaching in **China**.

More recently, in the **United States**, a number of drug accusations
have centered on an enterprise called BALCO (Bay Area Laboratory
Co-operative), based in the Bay Area of California. BALCO is led by
a former musician, Victor Conte, who has impugned many well-
known American athletes, including **baseball** players Barry Bonds
and Jason Giambi and Olympic athletes **Marion Jones** and Tim
Montgomery, as users of performance-enhancing medications provided by BALCO.

In 1999, the International Olympic Committee was instrumental in
pushing the fight against drugs to a new level, by forming the **World
Anti-Doping Agency** (WADA). Headed since its inception by Canadian IOC member **Dick Pound**, WADA's task is to oversee and monitor the use of drugs in international sports and find better methods of
prevention and detection, as well as educating athletes to the danger
and impropriety of drug use in sports.

The issue of drug use in sports is complicated, and there are many
people who write of and speak about the fact that this stringent testing may not always be in sports' and the athletes' best interests. It is
not politically correct to be on this side of the argument, as politicians, sports administrators, and the media have come down strongly
against drugs, but there are a number of issues that are discussed in
this regard, and should at least be presented.

The list of prohibited substances is quite long, numbering well
over 100. In medical trials of drugs, the gold standard is termed an
RCT—an acronym referring to a **R**andomized, **C**ontrolled, prospective, double-blind **T**rial, in which the drug is compared on this basis
to a placebo. Proof of improvement in athletic performance via RCTs
is certainly lacking for most of the drugs on the prohibited lists. The
drugs that have been best studied—anabolic steroids—have had
varying results when subjected to true RCTs, and even then, few of
the gold standard-type studies have been done. Proponents of strict
drug testing will demur, stating that it is "obvious" that these drugs
enhance performance and this can be seen by looking at the improved
performances. But that reasoning neglects the strength of the placebo
effect and that its psychological effects may mimic the physiologic

effects of performance-enhancing drugs. Further, because of the op-
probrium that now surrounds many of these substances, even performing an RCT may border on being unethical and be difficult to get
through an Institutional Review Board (IRB). In fact, WADA regulations now recommend that prohibited drugs not be given to athletes
for medical studies. Thus, the political correctness of drug testing and
the WADA regulations prevent the authorities from being able to con-
clusively prove that they are testing for substances that enhance athletic performance.

Other opponents of drug testing decry the lack of the athletes'
rights to privacy. Currently, world-class athletes in Olympic sports
can be tested at any time of the year, at any time of the day. They are
required to inform sports administrators of their whereabouts at all
times. Failure to do so constitutes a "positive test in absentia." In
some countries, there are even moral and religious objections to providing urine or blood samples, but the athlete must still do so, or be
considered in violation.

Furthermore, some authors have written that the current status of
drug testing denies athletes due process, their right to be considered
innocent until proven guilty. In fact, currently, if a positive drug test
occurs, the athlete is considered guilty, and the onus is on the athlete
to then prove his/her innocence. While this may be acceptable in
some nations, in the United States it is not, and American athletes
have fought the results many times using this argument. In addition,
the publicity that ensues effectively convicts the athlete in the press,
even if he or she is later exonerated. Paraphrasing the words of U.S.
secretary of labor Ray Donovan in the early 1980s, after he was
found innocent of charges made against him, "Where do [the ath-
letes] go to get their reputation back?"

Finally, some argue that the fight against doping artificially draws
a line against certain performance-enhancing techniques, while allowing others. Certainly, world-class athletes do many things in training and in their lives that are designed to make them better athletes.
Not all of these are actually good for their health. While running and
aerobic exercise enhance one's health, nobody would argue that running 150 miles/week is good for one's general health. In fact, modern athletic training is designed to push the body to the brink of
breakdown, but never pass that line.

As an example of non-drug methods that enhance performance, consider the use of altitude sleep chambers. Many distance runners and professional cyclists sleep in these chambers, which lower the oxygen content and mimic training at altitude, usually increasing the blood count, or hematocrit. This is legal. But it is not legal to take erythropoietin (EPO), a drug that stimulates red blood cell production, and increases one's hematocrit. Both methods have the same result, but arbitrarily, one is legal, while one is not.

Still, even when viewing the arguments of those who oppose drug testing, it must be remembered that these world-class athletes are often role models to children and adolescents. More and more studies have now shown that drug use has infiltrated high schools and even lower levels of school, where preadolescent athletes use the drugs, emulating their athletic idols, in an attempt to enhance their own athletic abilities. There are no voices who consider this to be a positive result of using drugs in sports.

Concerning drug use in sports, one approach that is usually used by the media is to simply say the Olympics are the "dirtiest" of all sporting events, because more Olympic athletes are caught for doping than athletes in most of the professional sports. But what this argument fails to consider is that the International Olympic Committee (IOC) was the first sports organization in the world to test for drugs in sport; it was the first to institute random, out-of-competition testing; and it still imposes the strictest penalties for anyone caught using drugs. By comparison, for four American professional sports (**baseball**, **football**, **basketball**, **ice hockey**) drug testing procedures are far less frequent, test for fewer drugs, and their penalties are relative slaps on the wrist compared to the IOC and WADA penalties.

As an example, under the IOC and WADA rules, Olympic athletes are subject to random, out-of-competition testing at any time of the year. The penalty for a positive doping test is a two-year suspension, and a lifetime ban ensues for a second positive test. In major league baseball, until January 2005, the athletes were subject to one announced test set for a specified time each year. The penalty for a positive test was probation and counseling, but no expulsion from the sport. The bans increased, but a lifetime ban did not occur until the athlete tested positive five times. However, there is one rather famous case in which an athlete was in legal problems for drug use at least seven times and continued to play major league baseball. (In January 2005, major league baseball passed stricter doping regulations, but they are still far short of those enacted by the IOC and IFs.) In the NFL, a first positive test results in only a two-game suspension, while a second positive test results in a four-game suspension—hardly punitive compared to the IOC penalties.

At the dawn of a new century, there are far more problems on the horizon. With the recent scientific analysis of the human genome, gene therapy and genetic manipulation of the human body is close to becoming a reality. Some of the gene therapies that are being studied concern building muscle to help people overcome diseases such as muscular dystrophy, multiple sclerosis, cerebral palsy, and other neuromuscular illnesses. But the gene therapies that would build muscle in these patients would likely also build super-muscular humans, who may well be tempted to try the therapies as methods to enhance athletic performance. The therapies do not exist yet, but already this nightmare scenario is envisioned and is being discussed by the doping authorities.

The controversy concerning drug use in sport is not going away. It will continue to be fought at the highest levels of sports administration, in the media, by the athletes, by the lawyers, and by the scientists. The scientists, who should properly be at the forefront in this argument, will probably take up the rear in this fight, shunted aside by lawyers, by the media, and by sports administrators. The final word is far from being written. *See also* SHIRLEY BABASHOFF; Appendix Q ("List of All Positive Drug Tests at the Olympic Games").

DREAM TEAM, THE—1992 USA BASKETBALL. The Dream Team was the **basketball** team that represented the **United States** at the 1992 Olympics. For the first time, all basketball professionals were declared eligible to compete at the Olympics, including members of the National Basketball Association (NBA), the United States' major professional league. This allowed the U.S. to field a team of professional all-stars, which was certainly the greatest basketball team ever assembled. The team gained incredible attention from the media and fans, both in the United States and **Spain**, as well as throughout the world, and easily won the gold medal. The team members were Charles Barkley, Larry Bird, Clyde Drexler, Patrick Ewing, Earvin "Magic" Johnson, **Michael Jordan**, Christian Laettner, Karl Malone, Chris Mullin, Scottie Pippen, David Robinson, and John Stockton. Subsequent U.S. teams, made up of NBA players, have been labeled Dream Team II and Dream Team III, but the 1992 team is considered by far the most outstanding.

DRESDEN FOUR, THE—GDR COXLESS FOUR ROWING TEAM (1968–1972). Also known as the Einheit Dresden Four, this coxless four rowing team won Olympic gold medals in 1968 and 1972 and was never beaten in international competition. Representing the GDR, they were World Champions in 1966 and 1970 and European Champions in 1967 and 1971. The team members were Frank Forberger, Dieter Grahn, Frank Rühle, and Dieter Schubert.

– E –

EAGAN, EDWARD PATRICK FRANCIS "EDDIE" (USA–BOX/BOB). B. 26 April 1898, Denver, Colorado. D. 14 June 1967, New York. Eddie Eagan was the Olympic light-heavyweight **boxing** champion in 1920 and a member of the winning four-man **bobsled** crew in 1932. He is the only man to have won an Olympic gold medal at both the **Olympic Winter Games** and **Summer Olympic Games**. While a Rhodes Scholar at Oxford University, Eagan made a second appearance at the Summer Games in 1924 when he was eliminated in the semifinals of the heavyweight boxing.

EAST TIMOR (TLS). Timor is an island in the Lesser Sunda Islands, a portion of the Indonesian archipelago, south of Sulawesi. The island was controlled by the Portuguese for 400 years, but in the 20th century it was divided into a Portuguese half (East) and an Indonesian half (West). In 1975, **Indonesia** invaded East Timor and seized it, but a separatist movement developed almost immediately. On 30 August 1999, East Timor was allowed to vote in a referendum, and 79 percent of the population opted to secede from Indonesia. Rioting and violence ensued when Indonesia refused to allow this, and United Nations' forces entered East Timor on 12 September 1999. In early 2000, East Timor was granted provisional independence by Indonesia. East Timor first competed at the **Olympic Games** in 2000 at Sydney, although not under that name. The **International Olympic Committee** (IOC) allowed athletes from East Timor to compete under the designation of **Independent Olympic Athletes** (IOA). Four athletes represented East Timor at Sydney—three men (one each in track and field **athletics, boxing**, and **weightlifting**) and one woman (in track and field athletics). East Timor was recognized by the IOC at the 115th session in Prague on 3 July 2003. At Athens in 2004, East Timor was represented by two athletes, one man and one woman in track and field athletics.

EBERSOL, RICHARD (USA). B. 28 July 1947. Dick Ebersol has succeeded **Roone Arledge** as the producer of Olympic **television** in the **United States**. Ebersol earned his college degree from Yale in 1971 and then began working under Arledge at ABC Sports. He was the first person to be an Olympic researcher, producing reams of Olympic minutiae to be used by the ABC sportscasters during the Olympic broadcasts. In 1974, Ebersol was hired away from ABC and joined NBC. There he first worked in programming and developed the still-running late night hit, *Saturday Night Live*, with Lorne Michaels. In 1989, Ebersol became head of the NBC Sports Division. His primary influence on the Olympics has actually been in finance. In 1996, working in concert with **Dick Pound**, Ebersol negotiated a long-term contract between NBC and the **International Olympic Committee** (IOC) that gave NBC the broadcast rights to the 2000, 2004, and 2008 **Olympic Games** and the 2002 and 2006 **Olympic Winter Games**. The contract guaranteed income to the **organizing committees** of future Olympic Games and put the **Olympic movement** on much stronger financial footing. The long-term contracts have been extended, and NBC has garnered broadcast rights through 2012.

ECUADOR (ECU). Ecuador sent three **track and field** competitors to the 1924 **Olympic Games**—Alberto Jurado Gonzales, Luis Jarrin, and Belisario Villacis—prior to the Ecuadorean **National Olympic Committee** (NOC) being formed in 1925. A gap of 44 years then occurred before it returned to the Olympics at Mexico City, and it has competed continuously since. It has never appeared at the **Olympic Winter Games**. Ecuador has won one medal at the Olympics, a gold in 20 km. race walking at the 1996 Olympics by Jefferson Perez.

EDSTRÖM, JOHANNES SIGFRID (SWE). B. 21 November 1870, Morlanda. D. 18 March 1964, Stockholm. As president of the **International Olympic Committee** (IOC) and the International Amateur Athletic Federation (IAAF), Sigfrid Edström was a man of immense sporting influence. Born in **Sweden** and educated partly there and in the **United States** and **Switzerland** (1891–1893), he was one of the organizers of the 1912 **Olympic Games** in Stockholm. During those Olympic Games he took the initiative of founding the IAAF, for which he served as the first president, remaining in that office from 1913 until 1946. Edström founded the Federation of Swedish Industries in 1910 (chairman, 1928–1929), was chairman of the Swedish Employers' Confederation (1931–1942), and founded the International Chamber of Commerce in 1918 (president, 1939–1945). His main business career was as managing director (1903–1933) and chairman of the board (1934–1949) for Allmåna Svenska Elektriska Aktiebolagel (ASEA), a world leader in the high-tension current industry. Edström was elected an IOC member in 1921 and became a member of the IOC **Executive Board** when it was created in the same year. He chaired the **Olympic Congresses** in 1921 and 1925 and was appointed vice president of the IOC in 1937. Following the death of IOC president **Henri de Baillet-Latour** in 1942, Edström was, as a neutral, well placed to keep the **Olympic movement** alive during the war years as a de facto president. In 1946, at the first postwar IOC session in **Lausanne**, he was elected president by acclamation. On his retirement in 1952, at the age of 81, he was given the title of honorary president of the IOC. In 1947, he was awarded the **Olympic Cup** for his contributions to the Olympic movement.

EDWARDS, TERESA (USA–BAS). B. 19 July 1964, Cairo, Georgia. One of the greatest female guards to ever play **basketball**, Teresa Edwards played collegiately at the University of Georgia, where she was a consensus All-American in 1984 and 1985. Her record is unmatched by **women** in international competition. She won gold medals at the 1984, 1988, 1996, and 2000 Olympics, and a bronze medal at the 1992 Olympics. She set two Olympic basketball records and was the play-making leader of championship teams at the 1986 and 1990 World Championships, the 1986 and 1990 Goodwill Games, and the 1987 Pan-American Games. In 1991, she played on the U.S. team that won a bronze at the Pan-American Games. She was the USA basketball player of the year in both 1987 and 1991.

EGERSZEGI, KRISZTINA (HUN–SWI). B. 16 August 1974, Budapest, Hungary. Krisztina Egerszegi established herself as one of the greatest backstrokers in **swimming** history. She won a gold and silver in the two backstroke events at the 1988 Olympics when only 14 years old. In 1992, she returned to win three individual gold medals, in the 100 meter backstroke, the 200 meter backstroke, and the 400 meter individual medley. In 1996 at Atlanta, Egerszegi won her third consecutive gold medal in the 200 backstroke, making her only the second swimmer, after **Dawn Fraser** in the 100 free, to win the same event at three straight Olympics. She is the only Olympic swimmer to have won five individual gold medals. At the European Championships she won three silver medals in 1989 and three gold medals in 1991 and 1993. At the 1991 World Championships, she won both backstroke events. She set two world records during her career, one each in the 100 meter and 200 meter backstroke.

EGYPT (EGY). Egypt first competed at the 1896 **Olympic Games**, and after missing the Olympics of 1900 and 1904, it was again represented at the Intercalated Games of 1906. The country was not present at the 1908 Olympics, but after forming a **National Olympic Committee** (NOC) in 1910, it was more formally represented at the 1912 Stockholm Olympics. Since then, it has been absent only from the Olympics of 1932, 1956 (missing Melbourne, but not Stockholm), and 1980. Egypt's absence from the 1932 Olympics was the result of political turmoil that resulted in the NOC being disbanded in 1929, but it was reestablished in time for a large team (53 athletes) to be sent to the Berlin Olympics in 1936. From 1960 through 1968, Egypt competed as the United Arab Republic (UAR), joining in a union in 1960 with **Syria**, although all but three of the 74 UAR athletes were Egyptian. Egypt also boycotted the Olympic Games of 1956, 1976, and 1980, making it one of three nations to have boycotted three Olympics. Egypt's greatest Olympic successes have come in the strength sports of **weightlifting** and **wrestling**. Egypt has competed at the **Olympic Winter Games** only in 1984 at Sarajevo. *See also* ETHIOPIA; KOREA, PEOPLE'S DEMOCRATIC REPUBLIC.

EHRIG-SCHÖNE-MITSCHERLICH, ANDREA (GDR–SSK). B. 1 December 1960, Dresden. Andrea Ehrig won seven Olympic **speed skating** medals—one gold, five silver, one bronze. After starting with a silver in 1976, she failed to win a medal in 1980 but won her only gold in 1984 at her favorite distance of 3,000 meters. She ended her Olympic career in 1988 with silvers in the 3,000 and 5,000 meters and a bronze in the 1,500 meters. Primarily a distance skater, Ehrig set world records over the three distances at which she won Olympic medals. Her first Olympic appearance, when only 15 years old, was under her maiden name of Mitscherlich. She later competed under her married name of Schöne, and following her second marriage in 1985 to fellow Olympic speed skater Andreas Ehrig, she made her final Olympic appearance under that name.

EL SALVADOR (ESA). El Salvador's **National Olympic Committee** (NOC) was formed in 1949, but it was not recognized by the **International Olympic Committee** (IOC) until 1962. Six years then passed before El Salvador competed at the **Olympic Games** in 1968, since when it has been absent only from the Olympics of 1976 and 1980. It has won no Olympic medals to date and has not yet competed at the **Olympic Winter Games**. Its best Olympic performance was a fifth-place finish by Maureen Kaila Vergana in the 1996 women's points race **cycling**.

ELVSTRØM, PAUL BERT (DEN–YAC). B. 25 February 1928, Gentofte (Hellerup), Copenhagen. Paul Elvstrøm competed as a yachtsman in eight Games over a 40-year period. Although three other competitors have had similarly lengthy Olympic careers, none of them could match Elvstrøm's record of successes. He won the Firefly class in 1948 and the Finn class in 1952, 1956, and 1960, and was the first competitor in any sport to win individual gold medals at four successive Games. After being a reserve on the Danish team in 1964,

Elvstrøm then competed in 1968 and 1972 without winning a medal. He also competed in 1984 and 1988 when his daughter, Trine, crewed for him.

ENDER, KORNELIA (later Matthes, then Grummt) (GDR–SWI). B. 25 October 1958, Plauen. Kornelia Ender won a total of eight Olympic medals, including four gold medals in 1976 in the 100 and 200 meter freestyle, the 100 meter butterfly, and the 400 meter medley relay. The most prolific record breaker of modern times, she set 23 world records (1973–1976) in currently recognized events, and her total of 10 medals (eight gold, two silver) at the World Championships is also a record. She married first Roland Matthes and then Olympic decathlete Steffen Grummt.

ENDO, YUKIO (JPN–GYM). B. 18 January 1937, Akita. Yukio Endo won seven Olympic medals and five gold medals in **gymnastics**. He helped Japan to the all-around team championship in 1960, 1964, and 1968. In 1964 he was the individual all-around champion and added a gold medal on the parallel bars. His other two individual medals were silver in the 1964 floor exercises and the 1968 horse vault. Endo won only one individual title at the World Championships—the 1962 floor exercise title. In 1962 he won seven medals at the Worlds, and he followed that with three more in 1966. In both years, he won golds with the Japanese team.

ENGEL-GULBIN-KRÄMER, INGRID (GDR–DIV). B. 29 July 1943, Dresden. Ingrid Krämer won gold in both platform and springboard **diving** in 1960, making her the first non-American female to achieve this feat. After repeating this double at the 1963 European Championships, Engel-Krämer was a strong favorite to retain both titles in 1964, but she was successful only in the springboard, narrowly losing her platform crown. At her third Olympics in Mexico in 1968, she competed only in the springboard where she finished fifth. She competed under three different names at the Olympics. She appeared under her maiden name of Krämer in 1960, while in 1964 she used the name of her first husband (Engel) and in 1968 that of her second husband (Gulbin).

ENGLAND. *See* GREAT BRITAIN.

EQUATORIAL GUINEA (GEQ). Equatorial Guinea's **National Olympic Committee** (NOC) was formed in 1980 and recognized by the **International Olympic Committee** (IOC) in 1984, which enabled the nation to make its Olympic début at the Los Angeles Games that year. Since then it has been represented at every **Olympic Games** but only had athletes in the **track and field** events until 2000 at Sydney, when two **swimmers** (one male and one female) and two track and field athletes represented the nation at the Olympics. At Athens, Equatorial Guinea was represented by one male and one female track and field athlete.

EQUESTRIAN EVENTS. Equestrian events have been on the **Olympic program** since 1900 when jumping events were held at the Olympics in Paris. However, equestrian events were not held again until 1912 in Stockholm. Since that year, the sport has always been on the Olympic program.

There are three equestrian disciplines contested, with an individual and team event in each, making six events on the Olympic program. These are jumping (or show jumping, or Grand Prix de Nations as a team event), dressage, and the three-day event. Jumping consists of jumping over a series of obstacles in an attempt to not disturb the fences. Dressage is a sort of ballet on horseback in which the rider has the horse perform certain intricate maneuvers of stepping. The scoring is done by judges who evaluate how well the horse executes the moves. The three-day event combines the above two disciplines and adds a third competition of riding a cross-country course. Scoring is by a series of tables evaluating each day's performance. It actually occurs now over four days at the Olympics, as two days are devoted to the dressage. Equestrian sports are governed by the Fédération Équestre Internationale (FEI), which was formed in 1921 and had 131 member nations at the end of 2004. The top nations at the Olympics in equestrian events have been **Germany**, **Sweden**, the **United States**, and **France**.

ERITREA (ERI). The **International Olympic Committee** (IOC) granted provisional recognition to the **National Olympic Commit-**

tee (NOC) for Eritrea in 1998, and full recognition followed in 1999. Eritrea was the northernmost province of **Ethiopia** until it became independent in May 1993. Prior to Eritrean independence, several of their athletes competed for Ethiopia at the Olympics. Eritrea first competed at the Olympics in 2000 at Sydney, represented by one female and two male runners in track and field **athletics**. In 2004, Zersenay Tadesse won a bronze medal for Eritrea in the men's 10,000 meter run.

ESTONIA (EST). Three Estonian athletes were members of the Russian team at the 1912 **Olympic Games**, and, as a separate nation, Estonia competed at the Olympic Games continuously from 1920 to 1936. At the 1924 **Olympic Winter Games**, **speed skater** Christfried Burmeister participated in the opening ceremony but he did not take part in the competitions that followed, and Estonia first competed at the Olympic Winter Games of 1928 and also competed in 1932 and 1936. From 1952 to 1988, Estonia was a republic of the **USSR** and thus did not compete as an independent nation, but many Estonian athletes competed for the **Soviet Union**. After the Soviet Revolution of 1991, Estonia declared and was granted its independence. The nation returned to the Olympic fold by competing in 1992 in both Albertville and Barcelona, and it has competed at every Olympic Games and Olympic Winter Games since. Estonia has won 29 Olympic medals, 21 from 1920 to 1936, two in Barcelona, three in Sydney, and three at Athens. Eight of these were gold medals, including an emotional victory for **Erika Salumäe** in women's match sprint **cycling** in 1992. Estonia has never hosted an Olympic Games, but in 1980, all of the sailing events of the Moscow Olympics were actually held in the Gulf of Finland off Tallinn, the capital of Estonia.

ETHICS COMMISSION. The Ethics Commission was formed in 1999 in response to the **Olympic bribery scandal**. The Ethics Commission's primary focus was to address the responsibilities of the **International Olympic Committee** (IOC), to oversee the selection process of host cities, and to investigate any allegations of breaches of conduct by IOC members or Olympic candidate or host cities. The Ethics Commission currently consists of eight members—three IOC members (Chairman Judge **Kéba Mbaye**, Pernilla Wiberg, and Chiharu

Igaya), and five independent members, as follows: Javier Perez de Cuellar (PER), former United Nations secretary-general; Robert Badinter (FRA), former president of the French Constitutional Court; Kurt Fürgler (SUI), former president of the Swiss Confederation; Right Honorable Sir Ninian Stephan (AUS), former governor-general of Australia; and Andrew Young (USA), former mayor of Atlanta, Georgia, USA. In the summer of 1999, the Ethics Commission produced an IOC Code of Ethics.

ETHIOPIA (ETH). Ethiopia made its first Olympic appearance in 1956. It has since missed the 1976, 1984, and 1988 Olympics, all due to political boycotts, making Ethiopia one of only three nations—with **Egypt** and **Korea (North)**—to have boycotted three **Olympic Games**. The country has made no appearances at the **Olympic Winter Games**. Ethiopia's top athletes have been distance runners. Heading this list is **Abebe Bikila**, Olympic **marathon** champion in 1960 and 1964, generally considered the greatest marathoner of all time. Ethiopia has won 31 Olympic medals, 14 of them gold, all in track and field **athletics**.

EUROPEAN OLYMPIC COMMITTEES, THE (EOC). The **National Olympic Committees** (NOCs) from Europe have formed this group to further their interests with the **International Olympic Committee** (IOC). The EOC is headquartered in Rome, **Italy**. The president as of 2004 was Mario Pescante of Italy. The group's name was changed to the European Olympic Committees (EOC) in November 1994 at its meeting in Atlanta. Prior to that time it was known as the **Association des Comités Nationaux Olympiques d'Europe** (ACNOE).

EVANS, JANET ELIZABETH (USA–SWI). B. 28 August 1971, Fullerton, California. Janet Evans is considered to be the greatest female long-distance **swimmer** of all time. She entered the 1988 Olympics as the world record holder in the 400 meters, 800 meters, and 1,500 meters and improved her own world record in winning the 400 meters, in addition to taking gold medals in the 800 meters and the 400 meter individual medley. At her second Olympic appearance in 1992 Evans successfully defended her 800 meters title but suffered her first defeat in the 400 meters since 1986, when she placed second to Dagmar Hase (GER). She won a host of medals at the World Championships, the Goodwill Games, and other major championships and brought a new dimension to long-distance swimming for women. Evans finished her career at the 1996 **Olympics Games** where, by then past her prime, she finished sixth in the 800 meter freestyle. Through 2004, she still holds the world records for 400, 800, and 1,500 meters.

EWRY, RAYMOND CLARENCE "R. C." (USA–ATH). B. 14 October 1873, Lafayette, Indiana. D. 29 September 1937, Queens, New York. R. C. Ewry was a victim of polio as a child, but remedial leg-strengthening exercises resulted in his becoming the greatest exponent of the now defunct standing jumps. He was unbeaten in 10 Olympic competitions, winning the standing high jump and standing long jump four times each (1900, 1904, 1906, 1908) and the standing triple jump twice (1900, 1904). His 10 individual gold medals remain an Olympic record for any sport. Ewry retired shortly after the 1908 Games having won 15 AAU (Amateur Athletic Union [USA]) titles and setting world records in each of his three specialty events.

EXECUTIVE BOARD OF THE IOC. The Executive Board of the **International Olympic Committee** (IOC) manages the affairs of the IOC. It functions by making its recommendations to the IOC sessions. These recommendations are rarely overturned, thus the Executive Board effectively runs the IOC. As of 2001, it consists of the president of the IOC, four vice presidents, and 10 additional members, for a total of 15 members. Prior to 2000, the Executive Board consisted of 11 members—the president, four vice presidents, and six other members, but the size of the board was increased based on the recommendations of the **IOC 2000 Commission**. The commission also mandated that future Executive Boards should have representative members from the various classes of IOC members: independent members, **National Olympic Committee** (NOC) members, **International Federation** (IF) members, and athletes. Executive Board members are elected by the **IOC sessions**. The vice presidents and board members are elected for four-year periods. Founded in 1921, it was known as the Executive Committee until 1955.

– F –

FEDERAL REPUBLIC OF GERMANY (FRG). *See* GERMANY.

FENCING. Fencing began as a form of combat and is known to have been practiced well before the birth of Christ. As a sport, fencing began in either the 14th or 15th century, and both **Italy** and **Germany** lay claims to the origins of the sport. In 1570, Henri Saint-Didier of **France** gave names to fencing's major movements, and most of that nomenclature remains.

Until the 17th century the fencing weapons were large and unwieldy, like the combat weapons. However, the combat sword evolved into the épée and, somewhat, into the saber. The foil was originally a practice weapon for combat and became popular as a sporting event in the late 19th century.

The foil is a light, quadrangular tapering blade in which only hits made with the blade point on the opponent's torso count. The épée, developed from the dueling weapons of European noblemen, is the same length as the foil, but is heavier and has a larger handguard. Hits must also be made with the tip of the blade but can be scored over the opponent's entire body. The saber owes its origins to the Middle Eastern scimitar and the 18th-century cavalry saber. Hits may be scored with the tip of the blade, with its front edge, or with the last one-third of its back edge. The target area is from the bend of the hips up, including the head and arms.

Fencing was first contested at the 1896 Olympics and is one of the few sports to have been contested at every **Olympic Games**. **Women**'s fencing first appeared in the Olympics in 1924. Today, men compete in the Olympics with three types of swords—the foil, the épée, and the saber—in both team and individual events, thus six events in all. Women have competed in the Olympics in the foil and épée, with both a team and an individual event, épée having been added to the **Olympic program** at the 1996 Olympics in Atlanta. Women's saber events were added to the Olympic program in 2000 at Sydney. Electronic scoring has been used for the foil and épée for decades now, while electronic scoring for the saber made its Olympic début at Barcelona.

Fencing is governed worldwide by the Fédération Internationale d'Éscrime (FIE), which was formed in 1913 and had 108 member nations affiliated as of 2004. Fencing has been dominated at the Olympics by France and Italy in the foil and épée, and **Hungary** in the saber.

FERGUSON, IAN GORDON (NZL–CAN). B. 20 July 1952. After an undistinguished Olympic début in 1980, Ian Ferguson retired from **canoeing** and went into business. After a two-year hiatus, Ferguson came back in 1983 and won a silver medal at the 500 meters at the World Championships. Then in 1984, at the age of 32, he won three gold medals at the Los Angeles Olympics in the K1-500, K2-500, and the K4 event. Paul McDonald joined Ferguson in the last two events, and at the 1988 Olympics, they retained the Olympic K2-500 title as well as winning a silver in the K2-1,000.

FIGURE SKATING. Figure skating began in the mid- to late-19th century almost concurrently in Europe and North America, but two Americans are responsible for major developments in its history. In 1850, Edward Bushnell of Philadelphia revolutionized skating technology when he refined the use of steel-bladed skates. This allowed the creation of fancy twists and turns on the ice. Another American, Jackson Haines, a ballet master, visited Vienna in the 1860s and added the elements of music and dance to figure skating. Originally, free skating was subordinate to school figures, or the tracing of pretty patterns on the ice.

International figure skating competitions were held in Europe in the 1880s, and the International Skating Union (ISU) was formed in 1892 as the first true international governing body of any winter sport (now with 77 members, but representing only 60 nations). Originally men and women competed together, with the first World Championship being held in what was then and is now St. Petersburg, **Russia** (formerly Leningrad) in 1896. The first **women**'s championship was held in 1906.

Figure skating is the oldest sport on the **Olympic Winter Games** program. It was contested at the London Olympics of 1908 and again in 1920 at Antwerp. Events for men, women, and pairs were contested through 1972. In 1976, **ice dancing**, long a popular event, was added to the program as a fourth event, although it had been held as a **demonstration sport** in 1968.

Scoring has evolved during the century also, as the former predominance of compulsory figures in the scoring gave way in the early 1970s. A short program of free skating was added, primarily to equalize results among skaters who were excellent at compulsories but lesser free skaters, to those who were poor compulsory skaters but top-notch free skaters. This was exemplified in that era by Beatrix "Trixi" Schuba (AUT), who was an excellent skater in compulsories, but was a relatively poor free skater, and Janet Lynn (USA), who was a superb free skater but was usually beaten by Schuba because of her lesser skill in the compulsories. This gave impetus to the movement to decrease the importance of compulsory figures. At the end of the 1980s, the International Skating Union ruled that compulsory figures would no longer be held at international competitions. They were last contested at the 1990 World Championships, and they have not been a part of the Olympic figure skating program since 1988.

Since World War II, figure skating has been dominated in the men's and women's singles by the **United States**, which has won six men's gold medals and seven women's gold medals. In pairs and ice dancing, by far the dominant nation has been the **Soviet Union** and its former republics. Since 1964, the Soviet Union (or its former republics) has won every pairs and dance gold medal available, with the exception of the 1984 ice dancing gold medal that went to **Great Britain**'s **Jayne Torvill** and **Christopher Dean**, and the 2002 ice dancing gold medal, won by **France**'s Marina Anissina and Gwendal Peizerat.

FIJI (FIJ). Fiji formed a **National Olympic Committee** (NOC) in 1949 and first competed at the Olympics in 1956. Fiji has since competed at all the Olympics with the exception of 1964 and 1980. It has competed at the **Olympic Winter Games** in both 1988 and 1994, their sole representative on each occasion being **nordic skier** Ruscale Rogoyawa. It has won no medals. Its best Olympic performance to date occurred in 1992, when Anthony Philip finished 10th of 44 sailors in the Lechner boardsailing class.

FINANCE COMMISSION. The Finance Commission is one of the most important commissions since the **Olympic movement**, like all organizations, depends on finances to remain solvent. The Finance

Commission was formed in 1967 at a time when the **International Olympic Committee** (IOC) was almost bankrupt. The original chairman was Lord Luke of **Great Britain**. Currently, the Finance Commission is chaired by Richard L. Carrión of **Puerto Rico**. The previous chairman was Marc Hodler (SUI), who in late 1998 spoke to the media after the IOC session and discussed the problems in the bidding process, which led to the Olympic scandal of 1999. With the exception of a financial advisor, all members of the Finance Commission are IOC members. On its website, the IOC lists the following as the mandates of the Finance Commission: 1) to ensure that the accounting records of the IOC and its subsidiaries are maintained according to International Accounting Standards. That an external audit be performed on an annual basis by a recognized and independent accounting firm for the IOC and all its subsidiaries; 2) to ensure that the IOC and its subsidiaries have an efficient and transparent budgeting and financial control process and that the Financial Policies and Procedures approved by the IOC **Executive Board** are respected; and 3) to make recommendations to the IOC Executive Board on the strategy to be followed for its financial investments and then to monitor on a monthly basis through the Finance Management Committee that such strategy is followed or updated based on changing conditions in the financial markets.

FINLAND (FIN). Finland first competed at the 1906 Intercalated Games in Athens and also appeared two years later at the 1908 London Olympics. Its first **Olympic Winter Games** appearance was in 1924 at Chamonix, although it had two skaters entered in the **figure skating** events in 1920. Since those dates Finland's participation has been continuous, never missing an **Olympic Games** or an Olympic Winter Games. Finland's greatest successes have come in the distance running events in the Summer Games. In those events, led by **Hannes Kolehmainen**, **Paavo Nurmi**, and **Lasse Virén**, Finland has been the preeminent nation, until the recent advent of the African distance runners. Prior to World War II, Finland was also the dominant nation in **wrestling**. In the Winter Games, Finland has excelled at **nordic skiing** and, in the early Games, at **speed skating**. Finland hosted the Games of the XVth Olympiad in Helsinki in 1952. Through 2004, Finland has won 441 Olympic medals, 143 of them gold. Of these, 143 medals, and 42 gold, were won at the Olympic Winter Games.

FLANAGAN, JOHN JESUS (USA/IRL–ATH). B. 9 January 1873, Kilbreedy, County Limerick, Ireland. D. 4 June 1938, Kilmallack, County Limerick, Ireland. John Flanagan's three successive victories in the hammer throw (1900, 1904, 1908) remained an Olympic record for any **track and field** event until **Al Oerter** won his fourth consecutive gold medal in the discus in 1968. Flanagan would almost certainly have won four Olympic titles had the hammer been included in the program at the 1896 Games. Between 1896 and 1909 he improved the world best for the hammer no fewer than 18 times, his first record coming when he won the British title in 1896 shortly before he emigrated to the **United States**. He competed for the United States at all three of his **Olympic Games**.

FLESSEL-COLOVIC, LAURA (FRA–FEN). B. 6 November 1971, Pointe-a-Pitre, Guadeloupe. Laura Flessel-Colovic has become the top women's épée **fencer** at the **Olympic Games**. This discipline is relatively new for **women**, first appearing on the **Olympic program** in 1996. But since that time, Flessel-Colovic, known as "The Wasp," has won five Olympic medals, including gold in both the individual and team events in 1996. She added an individual bronze in 2000 and an individual silver and team bronze in 2004. Born on the island of Guadeloupe, she began fencing at age seven. Seeking stronger competition, Laura Flessel emigrated to **France** in 1990, and in her first year of competition there, she became French junior champion. In addition to her Olympic successes, Flessel-Colovic was individual épée World Champion in 1998 and 1999, and she has been ranked first in the World Cup standings since the épée was first contested in 2001.

FOOTBALL, AMERICAN. American football was a **demonstration sport** at the 1932 Olympics. It is not a recognized sport by the **International Olympic Committee** (IOC), and it will not become a part of the **Olympic program** at any time in the near future.

FOOTBALL, ASSOCIATION (SOCCER). Football (soccer) is the world's most popular sport, played in more countries than any other.

The World Cup of football, the quadrennial competition played in the even year between Olympics (last in 2002), is considered by some as the most watched single sporting event on the planet, possibly surpassing even the **Olympic Games**. The sport is governed internationally by the Fédération Internationale de Football Association (FIFA), which was formed in 1904 and had 204 members as of December 2004.

The origins of football are vague. The Greeks played a game that loosely resembled its modern counterpart, as did the Romans. By the 14th century it was so popular in **England** that King Edward II issued a proclamation on 13 April 1314, forbidding the game "forasmuch as there is great noise in the city caused by hustling over large balls from which many evils might arise which God forbid; we commend and forbid, on behalf of the King, on pain of imprisonment, such game to be used in the city of the future." In 1349, Edward III objected to the game because it prevented the practice of **archery**, necessary for the military strength of the country. Banning the game had little effect, however, as similar edicts had to be issued in 1389 (Richard II), 1401 (Henry IV), 1436 (Henry VIII), 1457 (James II), and again in 1491.

Gradually, despite attempts to ban it, football spread throughout the world, becoming popular almost everywhere, with the **United States** being a notable exception. Football was first contested at the 1900 and 1904 Olympics. The sport has been played at every Olympics since, with the exception of 1932 in Los Angeles.

The World Cup began in 1930 and brings together the world's top professional players. In recent years, Olympic eligibility has become a problem. Eastern European countries stated that they had no true professionals, although their players were state supported. Thus they often entered similar teams in both the World Cup and the Olympics, and the Eastern Europeans have been dominant in Olympic football since the 1950s. Recently, however, eligibility rules have changed as other countries may be allowed to use some of their professional players who have competed in the World Cup. The problem is not yet fully resolved. Currently, professional players may compete at the Olympics providing they are not more than 23 years old, although each team is allowed three exceptions to the age rule. There is some sentiment among **International Olympic Committee** (IOC) officials to change this and allow all professionals to compete.

Football (soccer) for **women** is now becoming more popular, with the first women's World Cup being contested in 1991. Women's football appeared on the **Olympic program** for the first time in 1996. *See also* URUGUAY FOOTBALL TEAMS (1924 AND 1928).

FOOTBALL, AUSTRALIAN RULES (AUSSIE RULES). Australian Rules Football was a **demonstration sport** at the 1956 Olympics in Melbourne. It is not a recognized sport by the **International Olympic Committee** (IOC) and is basically played only in Australia.

FOREMAN, GEORGE (USA–BOX). B. 22 January 1948, Marshall, Texas. George Foreman won the 1968 Olympic heavyweight **boxing** championship. After the Olympics, Foreman quickly turned professional and began knocking out fighters left and right with his powerful punching ability. In 1973, he fought **Joe Frazier** for the heavyweight title, winning easily. Foreman defended the title twice, but on 30 October 1974 in Zaire, **Muhammad Ali** stopped him in eight rounds in "The Rumble in the Jungle." Foreman was never a championship factor again in his "first" career, and he retired after a 1977 loss to Jimmy Young. However, in 1987, George Foreman, by then weighing close to 300 pounds, began a comeback. Through 1990 he was not defeated in that comeback. In April 1991, he fought for the heavyweight title again and lost a 12-round decision to Evander Holyfield. In 1994, however, he defeated Michael Moorer to claim the World Boxing Association (WBA) and International Boxing Federation (IBF) world heavyweight championships at the age of 46 years. Foreman lost those titles in 1995 when he refused to fight certain opponents, as mandated by those governing bodies, and has since retired.

FORMOSA. *See* CHINESE TAIPEI.

FRANCE (FRA). France can be said to be the home of the modern **Olympic Games**, being the home of **Pierre de Coubertin**, their founder. Not unexpectedly, it has competed at every celebration of the Olympic Games and at every **Olympic Winter Games**. In addition to appearing at all the Olympic Games, France has hosted five

Olympic Games, second only to the **United States**. These were the Games of the IInd Olympiad in Paris in 1900, the Games of the VIIIth Olympiad in Paris in 1924, the 1st Olympic Winter Games in Chamonix in 1924, the 10th Olympic Winter Games in Grenoble in 1968, and the 16th Olympic Winter Games in Albertville in 1992. France's greatest athletic successes have come in the sports of **cycling** and **fencing**, sports at which it has often been the dominant nation. France has won 719 Olympic medals (223 gold) with 74 having been won at the Olympic Winter Games, of which 22 have been gold medals.

FRASER, DAWN LORRAINE (AUS–SWI). B. 4 September 1937, Balmain, Sydney. The greatest female sprint **swimmer** ever, Dawn Fraser was the first woman swimmer to win eight Olympic medals, a record since surpassed by several swimmers. She won four gold and four silver medals at the Games of 1956, 1960, and 1964, including three successive golds in the 100 meter freestyle, a record for any Olympic swimming event equaled only by **Krisztina Egerszegi** (HUN) in the 200 backstroke in 1988–1996. Fraser was denied the opportunity of adding to her medal total when she received a lengthy suspension following misbehavior at the 1964 Games. Dawn Fraser set 27 individual and 12 relay world records. During her career, she won 30 Australian championships (23 individual and 7 team), and at the British Empire and Commonwealth Games, she won eight medals—six gold and two silver. She represented Balmain in the New South Wales Parliament from 1988 to 1991.

FRAZIER, JOSEPH WILLIAM "SMOKIN' JOE" (USA–BOX). B. 12 January 1944, Beaufort, South Carolina. Joe Frazier won a gold medal as a heavyweight **boxer** at the 1964 Olympics. Frazier first won the heavyweight World Championship in 1970 by stopping Jimmy Ellis in five rounds. He defended the title four times before being knocked out by **George Foreman**. Frazier later fought three tremendous battles with **Muhammad Ali**. The first, in 1971, was the fight of the century, a battle of undefeated heavyweight champions, and Frazier won by a decision in 15 rounds. Frazier was on the losing end in the next two fights, but all three were great spectacles. After losing his heavyweight title, he continued to fight for a few years before retiring in the mid-1970s. Despite the acclaim accorded

Muhammad Ali, which somewhat diminished Frazier's appeal, his opponent knew of his greatness, describing him as follows, "Fighting Joe Frazier is the closest thing to death that I know of. Of all the men I fought in boxing, including Sonny Liston and George Foreman, the roughest and toughest was Joe Frazier. . . . If God ever calls me to a Holy War, I want Joe Frazier fighting beside me."

FREDRIKSSON, GERT FRIDOLF (SWE–CAN). B. 21 November 1919, Nyköping. With eight medals (six gold, one silver, one bronze) between 1948 and 1960, Gert Fredriksson is the most successful male canoeist in Olympic history. He was at his best in the K1-1,000 meters, winning a gold medal at three successive Games (1948–1956), and in the K1-10,000 meters, in which he won two gold medals (1948, 1956) and a silver (1952). He is one of only 21 Olympians to have won gold medals at four or more consecutive **Olympic Games**. At the World Championships he won four individual titles and a further three in the relay. In 1956, Fredriksson was awarded the Mohammed Taher Trophy by the **International Olympic Committee** (IOC). *See also* Appendix E ("Awards of the International Olympic Committee").

FRÉDY, PIERRE. *See* COUBERTIN, BARON PIERRE DE.

FREESTYLE SKIING. Freestyle skiing was held at the 1988 **Olympic Winter Games** as a **demonstration sport**. In 1992, moguls was contested as a full-medal sport in Albertville. In Lillehammer in 1994, both moguls and aerials were full-medal events. The moguls event consists of a timed race down a short course made up entirely of small hills or bumps termed moguls. The skier receives a point score for style that is added to a point score for the time to derive an overall score. Aeriels is a jumping event in which skiers take off from an elevated platform after a short run and then execute intricate gymnastics-like maneuvers in the air. The contest is decided by point scores awarded by judges. The third event of freestyle skiing is ballet, but that event has not yet appeared on the **Olympic program**, although it was demonstrated in 1988. Freestyle is considered a **discipline** of the sport of skiing by the **International Olympic Committee** (IOC), and, as such, it is governed by the Fédération Internationale de Ski (FIS).

FU MINGXIA (CHN–DIV). B. 16 August 1978. China's Fu Mingxia was the top female **diver** of the 1990s. She has been at her best on the platform, winning the Olympic gold medal in that event in 1992 and 1996, and was World Champion in 1991 and 1994. In 1996, Fu won both the springboard and platform at the Olympics, duplicating the feats of Vicky Draves (1948), **Pat McCormick** (1952–1956) and **Ingrid Engel-Krämer** (1960), who also won both events at the same Olympics. Fu retired briefly after the 1996 Olympics, but she returned to compete in the 2000 Olympics, defending her springboard gold medal and winning a silver medal in the new synchronized springboard event.

– G –

GABON (GAB). Gabon formed a **National Olympic Committee** (NOC) in 1965 but did not compete at the Olympics until 1972. Gabon has competed at seven **Olympic Games**, those of 1972, 1984, 1988, 1992, 1996, 2000, and 2004. It has never had an athlete compete at the **Olympic Winter Games**, and no athlete from Gabon has won an Olympic medal.

GAMBIA, THE (GAM). The Gambia's **National Olympic Committee** (NOC) was formed in 1972 and recognized by the **International Olympic Committee** (IOC) in 1976. The Gambia has competed at the **Olympic Games** of 1984, 1988, 1992, 1996, 2000, and 2004, but has never competed at the **Olympic Winter Games**. The Gambia has yet to win an Olympic medal.

GAMES OF THE NEW EMERGING FORCES (GANEFO). These were very controversial **Regional International Games**. In the summer of 1962, Jakarta hosted the Asian Games, but it refused to issue visas to athletes from **Taiwan** and **Israel**. For this, the **International Olympic Committee** (IOC) suspended the Indonesian **National Olympic Committee** (NOC). Unfortunately for the IOC, similar rulings had recently been made by **France** and the **United States**, which refused to issue visas to East German athletes competing in those countries. Those nations were not suspended. In response to the IOC actions, Indonesian president Sukarno proposed the Games of the New Emerging Forces in early 1963 to "promote the development of sports in new emerging nations so as to cement friendly relations among them." The original conference on these Games occurred in April 1963, with the following nations present: **Cambodia**, **China**, **Guinea**, **Indonesia**, **Iraq**, **Mali**, North **Vietnam**, **Pakistan**, the **United Arab Republic**, and the **Soviet Union**. But Sukarno denounced the IOC in his opening speech and also noted, "Let us frankly declare that sport has something to do with politics. And Indonesia now proposes to mix sport with politics." GANEFO was an obvious attempt to compete against the **Olympic Games**. GANEFO I was held in November 1963 in Jakarta, Indonesia, with 50 nations present. The problem was that China, **DPR Korea (North)**, and North Vietnam were present, none of which were recognized by several of the **International Federations** (IFs) organizing sports at GANEFO, notably the IAAF (track and field **athletics**) and FINA (**swimming**). Indonesian athletes also competed, quite naturally, since they hosted the Games. In response, the IOC banned the athletes from Indonesia and DPR Korea who had competed at GANEFO from participating at the 1964 Tokyo Olympics. (China and North Vietnam could not compete at Tokyo as they did not have recognized National Olympic Committees.) Indonesia and DPR Korea responded by demanding that their athletes be reinstated or their entire teams would boycott the Tokyo Olympics. The athletes were not reinstated, and the two nations did not compete at Tokyo. One athlete, North Korean runner Sin Kim-Dan, was sorely missed, as she was the world record holder in the 800 meters for **women** and would have been favored at Tokyo. Sukarno was ousted from power in 1965, and the IOC rescinded its suspension of Indonesia. GANEFO II went on, however, in Phnom Penh, Cambodia, in 1966, and again North Korea competed. For this, North Korea was also suspended from the 1968 Olympic Games at Mexico City. By then, however, the idea of the Games of the New Emerging Forces had lost favor. They were not held again.

GAMES OF THE OLYMPIAD. *See* OLYMPIC GAMES; OLYMPIC WINTER GAMES.

GEESINK, ANTONIUS JOHANNES "ANTON" (NED–JUD). B. 6 April 1934, Utrecht. With the introduction of **judo** to the **Olympic**

program in 1964, Anton Geesink provided one of the surprises of the Games by winning the open class. He had, however, earlier destroyed the myth of Japanese invincibility by becoming the first non-Japanese *judoka* to win a world title in 1961. Between 1953 and 1967, Geesink won 13 European titles in the open and unlimited classes. He later became a member of the **International Olympic Committee** (IOC).

GENDER VERIFICATION. Men and **women** compete in most Olympic events separately. The exceptions are few, but they have competed against each other in certain **shooting** events, **equestrian events**, and **sailing** and also compete concurrently in **figure skating** (pair and dance). They have previously competed concurrently in mixed doubles in **tennis** and currently do so in mixed doubles **badminton**.

The two sexes compete separately in most events because of the physical advantage claimed by men. Men posing as women would have a significant competitive advantage over natural women. At the 1936 Olympics, Dora Ratjen of Germany finished fourth in the women's high jump, but was later found (1938) to be a hermaphrodite. There were several other similar examples in the 1930s, notably Czechoslovakia's Ždenka Koubková, who competed in **track and field** events internationally, but never competed at the Olympics. The 1932 women's 100 meter Olympic champion was Stanisława Walasiewiczówna of Poland. At her death in 1980, her autopsy revealed she had mixed sexual characteristics. Her original birth certificate was later examined, and "she" was found to have been christened Stefania Walasiewiczówna.

In the 1960s, concern about this problem of men posing as women to gain a competitive advantage led to the introduction of gender verification, at the time called sex testing. At that time, several of the women track and field athletes were suspected of being genetically male. Sex testing began at the 1966 European Athletics Championships and was first used at the Olympics in 1968. At the 1966 European Athletics Championships, Ewa Kłobukowska of Poland was disqualified from further international competition. Kłobukowska had won a gold and bronze medal at the 1964 **Olympic Games**. Because of the obvious emotional and psychological trauma engendered by such an announcement, all subsequent sex testing results have not been released publicly.

From 1968 to 1988, all women wishing to compete in the Olympics were required to undergo sex testing. (With one exception, that being Princess Anne of **Great Britain**, who competed in the 1976 Olympics in the equestrian events.) Testing was initially done by obtaining a buccal smear, or a scraping of the cells of the inner wall of the mouth. The cells were examined for the presence of a Barr body, which occurs almost exclusively in females. Females are genetically labeled as XX, while men are labeled as XY, those being the classifications of the respective sex chromosomes. The second X chromosome possessed by women contains a structure termed the Barr body.

Though some men did attempt to breach the rules and compete as women, the entire subject of mixed sexual characteristics is a highly complex and emotional one. A number of people with mixed sexual identity may have elected to compete as women for psychological reasons. In addition, doctors typically label babies with indeterminate genitalia as women. And in certain cases of mixed sex classification, some people who would be considered women lack a Barr body, and would thus have been disqualified. Because of these problems, the test was later changed and the buccal smear no longer used. Women were then cleared for international competition by doctors after simply undergoing a physical examination. In the late 1980s, this method was replaced by a polymerase chain reaction evaluation, looking for the Y-linked SRY gene (sex-determining region Y), and this method was used at both the 1992 and 1996 Olympics.

But problems still existed. It has been noted that the tests fail to exclude all potential impostors, are discriminatory against women with disorders of sexual development, and can be psychologically devastating for a female athlete failing such a test. Thus, during the 1996 IOC World Conference on Women and Health, the **International Olympic Committee** (IOC) passed a resolution "to discontinue the current process of gender verification during the Olympic Games." The IOC **Athletes Commission** recommended to the IOC **Executive Board** in January 1999 that gender identification should be eliminated, and this decision was ratified by the IOC Executive Board in June 1999.

GENERAL ASSOCIATION OF INTERNATIONAL SPORTS FEDERATIONS (GAISF). In the early 1960s, many sports federations were unhappy that they had so little influence with the **International Olympic Committee** (IOC). Led by the Frenchman Roger Coulon, president of the Fédération Internationale des Luttes Associées (FILA) (wrestling), the **International Federations** (IFs) banded together in 1967 to form the General Assembly of International Federations (GAIF), later the General Association of International Sports Federations (GAISF), or Association Générale des Fédérations Internationales de Sports (AGFIS). The headquarters is currently in Monte Carlo, and the president as of 2005 is Dr. Kim Un-Yong (KOR), although because of his legal problems, the current acting president is Hein Verbruggen (NED). As of 2004 there were 75 sports member federations and 16 affiliated federations. Many of these federations govern Olympic sports (35), several are IOC-recognized federations (30), but as of 2004, 10 of them were not directly affiliated with the IOC, and the GAISF gives them a small voice within the **Olympic movement**. The aims of the GAISF are "to act as a forum for the exchange of ideas and for discussion on common problems in sport; to collect, collate, and circulate information; to provide members with secretarial and translating services, the organization of meetings, technical documentation and consultancy; to collect news bulletins, technical rules and regulations from members; to assemble and coordinate the dates of main international competitions; and to publish a half-yearly calendar."

GEORGIA (GEO). Many Georgian athletes competed from 1952 to 1988 for the **Soviet Union**. Its top sports were **judo** and **wrestling**, and, in fact, Georgian *judoka* won more medals for the Soviet Union than any other republic, including **Russia**. The most famous Georgian Olympic athletes were wrestlers David Gobedzhishvili and Levan Tediashvili and **track and field** athletes Viktor Saneyev and Robert Shavlakadze. Georgian athletes were present at Barcelona in 1992 as members of the **Unified Team**. Georgia's first Olympic appearance as an independent nation occurred in 1994 at Lillehammer, where it was represented by five athletes who competed in **luge**, **alpine skiing**, and **ski jumping**. Georgia has since competed at all

Olympic Games and **Olympic Winter Games**. Georgia has won 12 Olympic medals, including two gold, all at the Summer Olympics.

GEREVICH, ALADÁR (HUN–FEN). B. 16 May 1910, Jászbéreny. D. 14 May 1991, Budapest. Aladár Gerevich was one of the greatest of Olympic **fencers**. His six successive gold medals in the saber team event at every Games from 1932 to 1960 stands as a record for any Olympic sport. In the saber, he also won individual gold in 1948, silver in 1952, and bronze in 1936, and a further bronze in the foil team event in 1952. Gerevich confirmed his reputation as the world's greatest saberur with three individual titles at the World Championships (1935, 1951, 1955). His wife, son, and father-in-law were also Olympic medalists.

GERMAN DEMOCRATIC REPUBLIC (GDR). The German Democratic Republic (frequently termed East Germany) was formed on 7 October 1949 after the division of Germany into two countries following World War II. The problem of the "two Germanys" perplexed the **International Olympic Committee** (IOC) for two decades. From 1952 until 1964, the two nations purportedly competed at the Olympics as a single combined team. However, it should be noted that in 1952, a combined German team was planned and envisioned by the IOC, but the GDR refused to start in an all-German team, and no East German athletes competed on the 1952 "combined" team. In 1968 at Mexico City and Grenoble, the two Germanys competed as separate teams, but under the same banner, and using the same anthem and flag. The German Democratic Republic, however, was forced to use the name East Germany in 1968, a name that it detested. At the IOC session in 1968, full recognition came to the German Democratic Republic when it was allowed to compete at the Olympics, beginning in 1972, using its correct name, with its own anthem, emblems, and uniforms.

Between 1956 and 1988, the GDR developed into a true Olympic powerhouse. Beginning with the 1968 Olympics, it was one of the three most powerful sporting nations in the world, with the **United States** and the **Soviet Union**. The German Democratic Republic, competing as an independent nation, won 563 Olympic medals, 445 at the **Olympic Games** and 118 at the **Olympic Winter Games**. Of these, 202 were gold medals, 43 of which were won at the Olympic

Winter Games. The sporting leviathan was fully state supported, with the help of a highly advanced sports medicine program, and the athletes were treated royally in their country. After the reunification of Germany, it was revealed that the GDR's sports medical program had helped develop many of its athletes by the use of drugs. *See also* DOPING; GERMANY.

GERMAN FEDERAL REPUBLIC (FRG). *See* GERMANY.

GERMANY (GER/FRG). Prior to World War II, Germany appeared at all Olympics (Winter and Summer) with the exception of 1920 and 1924, when, as an aggressor nation in World War I, it was not invited. Because of its actions in World War II, and because no true German state existed at the time, Germany was again not allowed to compete in 1948. After World War II, Germany split into two nations. The Federal Republic of Germany (FRG) (West) was proclaimed in Bonn on 23 May 1949 from the former United States, British, and French Zones of Occupation. The occupying powers restored civil status on 21 September 1949. The **German Democratic Republic** (GDR) (East) was formed on 7 October 1949 from the former Soviet Zone of Occupation. As well, the province of **the Saar** formed an independent country until 1956. The Saar competed independently in 1952, its only Olympic appearance.

From 1952 to 1968, the problem of the "two Germanys" was a major political problem for the **International Olympic Committee** (IOC). The FRG **National Olympic Committee** (NOC) was formed on 24 September 1949 and requested IOC recognition immediately. On 29 August 1950, the IOC **Executive Board** gave provisional recognition to the FRG Olympic Committee. Full recognition came in May 1951 at the 46th IOC session in Vienna. The GDR formed an Olympic Committee on 22 April 1951 and also asked for recognition. In 1952, a German team was entered at Oslo and Helsinki. Although titularly a combined German team, it was made up entirely of athletes from the Federal Republic of Germany.

At the 51st IOC session in Paris in 1955, the GDR was granted recognition by the IOC by a vote of 27-7. However, the proviso to this recognition was that both Germanys would compete at the Olympics with a combined team. IOC president **Avery Brundage** boasted, "We have obtained in the field of sports what politicians have failed to achieve so far."

In 1956, 1960, and 1964, a combined East and West German team competed under one flag. On 6 October 1965, at the 64th IOC session in Madrid, the IOC gave the GDR the right to enter a separate team at the 1968 Olympic Games. However, the decision mandated that both Germanys compete with the same uniforms, using the same flag adorned with the Olympic symbol, and using the same anthem, the choral theme from Beethoven's Ninth Symphony. In addition, the GDR agreed to compete as East Germany, a name it did not recognize.

At the 68th IOC session at Mexico City in 1968, the IOC voted 44-4 that, beginning in 1972, both the FRG and the GDR could compete separately at the Olympic Games, wearing their own uniforms, and using their own flag and anthem, and with the correct names of their nations.

On 3 October 1990, the GDR and the FRG dissolved their separate governments to once again form a single united German state. Competing in Albertville and Barcelona in 1992 was a single team representing a unified Germany.

Germany, wholly or separately, has always been one of the most powerful nations at the Olympics. Germany has also hosted three **Olympic Games**: the Games of the XIth Olympiad in Berlin in 1936, the 4th **Olympic Winter Games** in Garmisch-Partenkirchen, also in 1936, and the Games of the XXth Olympiad in Munich in 1972. In addition, the 1916 Olympic Games were originally planned for Berlin, and the 1940 Olympic Winter Games were rescheduled for Garmisch-Partenkirchen after Sapporo and then St. Moritz withdrew as hosts.

GERMESHAUSEN, BERNHARD (GDR–BOB). B. 28 August 1951, Heiligenstadt. Bernhard Germeshausen won the two-man bob in 1976 with his compatriot **Meinhard Nehmer**, and they were both members of the winning four-man crew in 1976 and 1980. The three Olympic gold medals they each won stand as the current Olympic record for bobsledding. Germeshausen also won the silver in the two-man event at the 1980 Olympics (partnering Hans-Jürgen Gerhardt), and he was the winner at the World Championships in the two-man in 1981 (with Gerhardt) and in the four-man in 1977 and 1981.

GHANA (GHA). Ghana first appeared at the Olympics in 1952, as the Gold Coast. It did not attend the 1956 Olympics, but competed from 1960 through 1972. After boycotting the 1976 and 1980 Olympics, Ghana has attended the **Olympic Games** from 1984 through 2004, but has never competed at the **Olympic Winter Games**. Ghanian athletes have won four medals at the Olympic Games.

GIBRALTAR. The application of the Gibraltarian **National Olympic Committee** (NOC) for **International Olympic Committee** (IOC) recognition was on the agenda for discussion at the San Francisco IOC session in 1960, and on numerous subsequent occasions. Each time Gibraltar's application was denied, and it became increasingly apparent that **Spain** was making territorial claims on the British colony and was actively opposing Gibraltar's recognition. Although the **Olympic Charter** prohibits any political interference, the Spanish Ministry of Foreign Affairs chose to blatantly ignore these provisions and issued a directive on 5 September 1985 banning Gibraltarians from competing in championships held on Spanish soil even though Gibraltar was a member of several **International Federations** (IFs). After 40 years, Gibraltar remains excluded from the **Olympic movement** and has never been permitted to compete at the Olympics. Yet as of December 2004, Gibraltar is a member of 10 International Federations.

GLIDING. A gliding exhibition was held at the 1936 Olympics in Berlin. The sport is not recognized by the **International Olympic Committee** (IOC) or by the **General Association of International Sports Federations** (GAISF).

GOLD COAST. *See* Ghana.

GOLF. Golf was on the program of the 1900 and 1904 Olympics. In 1900, men and women competed in separate individual events. In 1904, a men's individual match-play event and a team stroke-play event were contested. Golf was on the Olympic schedule in both 1908 and 1920 but was not contested in either year. The International Golf Federation (formerly the World Amateur Golf Council) is recognized by the **International Olympic Committee** (IOC), headed by the executive directors of the U.S. Golf Association and the Royal and Ancient Golf Club of St. Andrews (Scotland). There has been recent discussion of golf becoming an Olympic sport again in the near future. It was approved for addition to the **Olympic program** at a meeting of the Executive Board in 2001, but the proposal was tabled, and at the 2005 IOC session in Singapore, golf was not voted back onto the Olympic program for 2012.

GOODWILL GAMES. The Goodwill Games were held for the first time in 1986 in Moscow. They were the brainchild of Ted Turner of Atlanta, Georgia, the head of Turner Broadcasting and the Cable News Network. Turner was upset about the boycotts of the Olympics in both 1980 and 1984 and saw the need to hold a "peaceful" sporting festival outside of the **Olympic movement**. They were held in 1990 in Seattle, Washington, in 1994 in St. Petersburg, Russia (the former Leningrad and Petrograd), and in 1998 in New York City. In 2000, the 1st Winter Goodwill Games were contested in Lake Placid, New York, USA. The 2001 Goodwill Games were planned for Brisbane, Australia, but with the breakup of the Soviet Union, the need for a Goodwill Games was far from clear. In addition, all of the Goodwill Games hemorrhaged money. The Goodwill Games were discontinued in 2000.

GOROKHOVSKAYA, MARIYA KONDRATYEVNA (URS-GYM). B. 17 October 1921. Mariya Gorokhovskaya's Olympic fame rests on one Olympics, the 1952 Helsinki Games. As a member of the Soviet **gymnastics** team, she won seven medals, which remains the record for the most medals at one Olympic Games by a woman. That mark has been equaled by seven men, and bettered by two men — **Aleksandr Dityatin** and **Michael Phelps**, both with eight. In 1952, Gorokhovskaya won gold medals in the individual and team all-around, silver medals on all four apparatuses, and a silver medal in the team portable apparatus event. She never won an individual championship at the World Championships, and her competitive career predated the European Championships.

GOULD, SHANE ELIZABETH (AUS–SWI). B. 23 November 1956, Brisbane. Shane Gould was a swimmer of phenomenal talent who became the first woman to hold the world freestyle record at every distance from 100 meters to 1,500 meters. She achieved this remarkable feat in December 1971, just three weeks after her 15th birthday. At the Olympic Games the following year she won the 200 and 400 meter freestyles and 200 meter individual medley, each in a new world record time, and, in addition to her three gold medals, she took the silver in the 800 meters and the bronze in the 100 meter freestyle. In 1973, still aged only 16, she retired, but during her brief career she had become one of the legends of the sport.

GRAFSTRÖM, GILLIS EMANUEL (SWE–FSK). B. 7 June 1893, Stockholm. D. 14 April 1938, Potsdam, Germany. Gillis Grafström was the supreme figure skater in the years following World War I. He won a record three Olympic gold medals (1920, 1924, 1928) and, in 1932, earned a silver medal in Lake Placid. He was also a three-time World Champion (1922, 1924, 1929). A noted amateur painter and sculptor, he skated more for aesthetic pleasure than for the competitive challenge. Grafström was a professional architect who worked mainly in Germany and spent little time in his native Sweden.

GREAT BRITAIN (GBR). Great Britain is the only nation that has never failed to be represented at the **Olympic Games**, including all the usual exceptions. It competed at the 1906 Intercalated Games in Athens, the 1908 **figure skating** events in London, the 1920 figure skating events in Antwerp, and the 1956 Equestrian Olympics in Stockholm. Through 1920, Great Britain competed as a combined team with **Ireland**, which was still not an independent nation, and its 1904 participation is due only to three Irish athletes. Great Britain has won 688 Olympic medals, 198 of them gold, most of them at the Summer Olympics. Great Britain has twice hosted the Olympic Games, the Games of the IVth Olympiad in London in 1908, and the Games of the XIVth Olympiad in London in 1948.

GREECE (GRE). Greece is the home of the Olympics, the **Ancient Olympic Games** having been held there from at least 776 BCE through 393 CE. The modern **Olympic Games** were revived and first held in Athens in 1896. Prior to 1896, several attempts at revival of the Olympics were contested in Greece, notably the **Zappas Olympic**

Games of 1859, 1870, 1875, and 1889. Since 1896, Greek participation has been continuous at all Games of the Olympiad. Greece has also competed at the **Olympic Winter Games**, first appearing in 1936 and missing only the 1960 Squaw Valley Olympics. Greece hosted the Games of the Ist Olympiad in Athens in 1896, the Intercalated Olympic Games of 1906 in Athens, and Athens hosted the Games of the XXVIIIth Olympiad in 2004. Greek athletes have won 136 medals in the Olympics (38 gold), with 83 of those occurring in 1896 and 1906, and 16 medals (six gold) won in 2004.

GREENLAND. Traditionally, Greenland's Olympic affairs have been overseen by **Denmark**, but in 1996 they started to make efforts to establish their own Olympic identity. So far, they have not been successful, although at the 1998 **Olympic Winter Games** three Greenlandic **nordic skiers** competed as part of the Danish team. As of 2004, Greenland is a member of four **International Federations** (IFs).

GRENADA (GRN). The Grenada Olympic Association was founded in 1982 and, after provisional **International Olympic Committee** (IOC) recognition was granted that year, full recognition was accorded in 1984. This enabled Grenada to make its Olympic début at the 1984 **Olympic Games**, and it has competed at each of the Olympics since. It has not yet competed at the **Olympic Winter Games**.

GRIFFITH JOYNER, DELOREZ FLORENCE (née Griffith) (USA–ATH). B. 21 December 1959, Los Angeles, California. D. 21 September 1998, Los Angeles, California. Florence Griffith Joyner was a superb sprinter who completely dominated the women's track season in 1988. After setting a world record for 100 meters at the 1988 U.S. Olympic Trials, she won three gold and one silver medal at the Seoul Games. Victories in the 100 meters and 200 meters, in which she twice broke the world record, were followed by a third gold in the sprint relay and a silver in the 4 × 400 meters relay. She had previously won a silver medal in the 200 meters in 1984. The flamboyant outfits she wore on the track made her a darling of the media who gave her the name "Flo-Jo" after her marriage in 1987 to the 1984 Olympic triple jump gold medalist, Al Joyner. She tragically died very young from a seizure disorder.

GRISHIN, YEVGENY ROMANOVICH (URS–SSK). B. 23 March 1931, Tula. Yevgeny Grishin was the winner of gold medals for **speed skating** in the 500 meters and 1,500 meters at both the 1956 and 1960 **Olympic Winter Games**. He set world records at both distances but was at his best at 500 meters, winning six world titles and achieving the distinction of being the first skater to break the 40 second barrier. Grishin became a coach with the national speed skating squad after he retired from competition. He was European All-Around Champion in 1956. In his era, there were no Sprint World Championships, and he never won a World All-Around title, as he could not skate distances well, but seven times he won the 500 meters at the World All-Around. He set seven world records, four over 500 meters, one at 1,000 meters, and two at 1,500 meters.

GROß, MICHAEL (FRG–SWI). B. 17 June 1964, Frankfurt. Michael Groß won six Olympic medals, three gold, mostly in the butterfly and sprint freestyle **swimming** events. He was known as "The Albatross" because of his enormous arm span of over seven feet (2.14 meters). At the World Championships he won a record 13 medals (five gold, five silver, three bronze), and he also won a record 18 medals at four European Championships (13 gold, four silver, one bronze). During his career Groß set ten world records in individual events. His top Olympics was 1984 when he won the 200 meter freestyle and the 100 meter butterfly, and took silver at the 200 meter butterfly and in anchoring the 4 × 200 meter freestyle relay.

GRØTTUMSBRÅTEN, JOHAN (NOR–NSK). B. 24 February 1899, Sørkedalen, Oslo. D. 21 January 1983. Together with fellow Norwegian, **Thorleif Haug**, Johan Grøttumsbråten dominated the **nordic skiing** events at the early editions of the **Olympic Winter Games**. In 1924, he won silver at 18 km. and bronze in the 50 km. and the nordic combined event, and then in 1928 he won the 18 km. and the nordic combined. Grøttumsbråten won his third gold and sixth medal overall in 1932 when he successfully defended his title in the nordic combined event.

GUAM (GUM). Guam formed a **National Olympic Committee** (NOC) in 1976, but it was not recognized by the **International Olympic**

Committee (IOC) until 1986. Guam's initial Olympic appearance came at the 1988 **Olympic Winter Games**, but it has not taken part in the Olympic Winter Games since. Guam has participated in the **Olympic Games** of 1988, 1992, 1996, 2000, and 2004.

GUATEMALA (GUA). Guatemala first competed in the 1952 Olympics. It did not appear again until 1968 but has not missed an **Olympic Games** since. Guatemala appeared at its only **Olympic Winter Games** in 1988 at Calgary. Its top performances have been a tie for fifth (quarterfinals) by Carlos Mo Ha-Taracena in 1984 light-flyweight **boxing** and a sixth-place finish by Edgardo Zachrisson in skeet shooting at Montreal in 1976.

GUIANA, BRITISH. *See* GUYANA.

GUINEA (GUI). Guinea formed a **National Olympic Committee** (NOC) in 1964, which was recognized by the **International Olympic Committee** (IOC) in 1965. Since making its Olympic début in 1968 Guinea has competed at eight **Olympic Games**, missing only 1972 and 1976. It has never competed at the **Olympic Winter Games**, nor has any Guinean athlete won a medal.

GUINEA-BISSAU (GBS). The Olympic Committee of Guinea-Bissau was given official recognition by the **International Olympic Committee** (IOC) in June 1995 at the 104th IOC session in Budapest. The nation made its Olympic début at the 1996 **Olympic Games** in Atlanta and also competed in 2000 at Sydney and 2004 in Athens. Guinea-Bissau has not competed at the **Olympic Winter Games**.

GUYANA (GUY). Guyana has competed at 14 **Olympic Games** since 1948, missing only 1976. It competed from 1948 to 1964 as British Guiana, competing first as Guyana in 1968. Guyana has never competed at the **Olympic Winter Games**. Guyana has won one Olympic medal, a bronze medal in 1980 bantamweight **boxing** by Michael Anthony.

GYARMATI, DEZSÖ (HUN–WAP). B. 23 October 1927, Miskolc. Dezső Gyarmati is considered the greatest of all Olympic **water polo** players. His feat of winning medals at five successive **Olympic Games** (gold, 1952, 1956, 1964; silver, 1948; bronze, 1960) has never been matched. A national hero, he coached the Hungarian team that won the Olympic title in 1976 and later became a member of parliament. Gyarmati married the 1952 Olympic 200 meter breaststroke champion Eva Székely. Their daughter, Andrea, was an Olympic silver medalist in the 100 meter backstroke in 1972, and she later married Mihály Hesz, a 1968 Olympic **canoeing** champion.

GYMNASTICS. Gymnastics is an ancient sport, having been practiced in various forms in Ancient Greece and Rome. However, gymnastics competitions are relatively modern. The modern development of gymnastics began in the mid-19th century in Europe. Gymnastics societies were formed in **Germany** (Turnvereins) and **Bohemia** of the Austro-Hungarian Empire (Sokols). Similar societies were formed in **France** and **Switzerland** and then spread generally throughout Europe. The sport is governed worldwide by the Fédération Internationale de Gymnastique (FIG), which was founded in 1881 and currently has 126 member federations.

Modern competitive gymnastics has developed from two systems—the German Turnverein system emphasizing apparatus work of a formal nature and stressing muscular development, and the Swedish system of free exercises concerned with developing rhythmic movements.

Gymnastics has been contested at every **Olympic Games**. The program has varied widely, but since World War II it has been fairly constant. Men compete in teams on six apparatuses—still rings, floor exercises, horizontal bar, parallel bars, pommel horse, and horse vault. The top competitors in the team event are eligible for the individual all-around event (maximum of three per nation). This is conducted again on all six apparatuses. The top performers in each apparatus are then advanced to the individual apparatus finals, now with a maximum of two performers from any nation per event.

Women's competition is similar, except that they compete in only four events—uneven parallel bars, floor exercises, horse vault, and balance beam. In 1984, rhythmic gymnastics for women was added to the **Olympic program**. **Trampoline** events for men and women were added to the gymnastics program at Sydney in 2000.

At the Olympics, the **Soviet Union** and its republics have been dominant in the **women**'s events. **Romania** has also had superb female gymnasts, notably the remarkable **Nadia Comăneci**. Men's gymnastics has been divided almost evenly since World War II by the **Japanese** and Soviet Union. The **Chinese** men are also now of top caliber.

– H –

HACKETT, GRANT (AUS–SWI). B. 9 May 1980, Gold Coast, Queensland. Grant Hackett succeeded his countryman, **Kieren Perkins**, as the top distance **swimmer** in the world, and his overall record rivals that of Perkins and **Vladimir Salnikov** as the greatest distance freestyler ever. Hackett has been undefeated at his best distance, 1,500 meters, since 1997, winning the Olympic gold medal in that event in both 2000 and 2004. His record at major meets is remarkable, winning the 1,500 at the Commonwealth Games in 1997 and 2002, and the 1,500 at the World Championships in 1998, 2001, and 2003. At the Pan-Pacific Meet, Hackett won the 400, 800, and 1,500 in 1997, the 1,500 in 1999, and the 800 and 1,500 in 2002. He has also frequently won medals at international meets on the 4×200 meter freestyle relay team for Australia. Hackett has set one world record at 1,500 meters, 14:34.56, in winning the 2001 World Championship in Fukuoka, **Japan**.

HACKL, GEORG (FRG/GER–LUG). B. 9 September 1966, Berchtesgarden. Georg Hackl is the only lugist to have won medals at three consecutive Olympics in singles. After a silver medal in 1988 at Calgary, Hackl also became the first man to defend the Olympic **luge** singles title, winning in both 1992 and 1994. In 1998, Hackl won the Olympic singles luge for the third consecutive time, while in Salt Lake City in 2002, he earned an individual silver medal. In addition to his Olympic successes, Hackl was singles World Champion in 1989 and 1990, and also won the luge World Cup in those years. In 1993, he was second in the World Championships and the World Cup, after having placed third in the World Cup in the Olympic year of 1992.

HAITI (HAI). Haiti formed a **National Olympic Committee** (NOC) in 1956 that was recognized by the **International Olympic Com-**

mittee (IOC) in the same year. Haiti has a curious Olympic history. A **fencer** named Léon Thiercelin represented it at the 1900 Olympics in Paris. Its next appearances were in 1924, 1928, and 1932, followed by a long gap before its return to the Olympic fold in 1960. Haiti did not attend the 1964 or 1968 Olympics. Despite having appeared in five Olympics through 1960, it had a total Olympic representation of only 12 men to that date. Haiti has since appeared at each Olympics since 1972, except for 1980. It has not yet competed in the **Olympic Winter Games**. Haiti has won two medals in the **Olympic Games** through 2004.

HAKULINEN, VEIKKO JOHANNES (FIN–NSK). B. 4 January 1925, Kurkijoki. Veikko Hakulinen won seven medals (three gold, three silver, one bronze) in **cross-country skiing** at four **Olympic Winter Games**. His first gold came in the 50 kilometer event in 1952, the second in the 30 kilometers in 1956, and the last in the 1960 cross-country relay. His last gold medal, at the age of 35 years, 51 days, makes him the oldest male gold medalist in cross-country skiing at the Olympics. Hakulinen competed at the Olympics for a fourth time in 1964 in the **biathlon**, having previously won a world team silver at his new sport in 1963. He was also world cross-country skiing champion in 1954 and 1958 over 15 kilometers and in the relay in 1954 and 1968. Hakulinen was the outstanding **nordic skier** of his generation, and he continued competing well into his sixties, by which time he had also become proficient at ski orienteering.

HALL, LARS (SWE–MOP). B. 30 April 1927, Karlskrona. D. 26 April 1991, Täby. After winning the Modern **Pentathlon** World Championships in 1950 and 1951, Lars Hall won individual gold medals at the 1952 and 1956 **Olympic Games**. He is the only modern pentathlete in history to win two Olympic titles, and in 1952, he became the first non-military winner of the event. Hall also won an Olympic team silver in 1952 and was a member of the winning team at the World Championships four times (1949–1951 and 1953).

HÄMÄLÄINEN-KIRVESNIEMI, MARJA-LIISA (née Hämäläinen) (FIN–NSK). B. 10 September 1955, Simpele, Finnish South Karelia. After competing without distinction in the 1976 and 1980

Olympic Winter Games, Marja-Liisa Hämäläinen achieved unprecedented success at the 1984 Games. With victories in the 5 km., 10 km., and 20 km. she became the first woman to win three individual gold medals for **nordic skiing** at one Games. She also won a bronze medal in the relay and won a second relay bronze in 1988, but illness prevented her from adding to her medal tally at her fifth Olympics in 1992. At the 1994 Olympic Winter Games, she finished her Olympic career with bronze medals in the 5 km. and 30 km. races, giving her a total of seven Olympic medals. After her triple victory in 1984 she married Harri Kirvesniemi, himself an Olympic nordic skiing bronze medalist. Hämäläinen-Kirvesniemi is one of only two women to compete in six Olympic Winter Games.

HANDBALL (TEAM HANDBALL). Handball is a team sport that combines aspects of **basketball**, **soccer**, and **water polo**. It is played on a basketball-sized court by teams of seven players who attempt to score goals by throwing a ball slightly smaller than a volleyball into a goal on the ground that is about the size of a lacrosse goal.

The game was invented in **Germany** in the early 20th century and became very popular in Europe. At the 1936 Olympics, the Germans added it to the program, but it was contested outdoors on a large field with 11 men to a side. It was not again on the **Olympic program** until 1972 when it was added to the Olympics at Munich. This time the sport was contested as described above with seven men to a side and indoors. In 1976, women's handball became an Olympic sport.

Handball is immensely popular in Europe, surpassed by only **football (soccer)**, **cycling**, **athletics** (track and field), and, perhaps recently, **basketball** and **volleyball**. The same popularity has not extended to other areas of the world, notably the **United States**; thus the sport has been dominated by the Europeans. The sport is governed worldwide by the International Handball Federation (IHF), which was founded in 1946 and currently has 150 members.

HAUG, THORLEIF (NOR–NSK). B. 28 September 1894, Lier. D. 12 December 1934, Drammen. Thorleif Haug was the winner of all three **nordic skiing** events (18 km., 50 km., and nordic combination) at the 1st **Olympic Winter Games** in 1924, and the 29-year-old Norwegian was considered the star of the Games. Although his feat has been equaled on many occasions, no nordic skier has yet succeeded in winning more than three gold medals at one Games. In 1924, he was also awarded the bronze medal in the ski jump, but 50 years later it was discovered that the scores had been incorrectly calculated and that Anders Haugen (USA) had finished third, with Haug in fourth place. Haug's daughter later presented her father's bronze medal to the rightful owner.

HEIDEN, ERIC ARTHUR (USA–SSK). B. 14 June 1958, Madison, Wisconsin. Eric Heiden is recognized as the greatest **speed skater** of all time. He completely dominated the 1980 **Olympic Winter Games** speed skating, winning the gold medal at all five distances. He set new Olympic records in every event, adding a world record in the 10,000 meters. At the World Championships following the 1980 Olympics he suffered his first defeat since 1977, after which he retired. Heiden then turned to **cycling**, and, after coming close to making the U.S. Olympic team in a second sport, he had a brief career as a professional cyclist, once winning the United States' professional championship and competing in one Tour de France. His sister, Beth, was also an outstanding speed skater and cyclist, winning World Championships in both sports. Eric Heiden later attended medical school and now practices as an orthopedic surgeon, specializing in sports medicine.

HENIE, SONJA (later Topping, Gardiner, and Onstad) (NOR–FSK). B. 8 April 1912, Oslo. D. 12 October 1969, in flight, Paris-Oslo. Sonja Henie was a triple Olympic gold medalist (1928, 1932, 1936) who did more to popularize **figure skating** than any other individual. After winning 10 world and three Olympic titles she turned professional in 1936 and soon amassed a fortune. Her flair for showmanship ensured the success of the 10 feature films she made in Hollywood and accelerated the public awareness of ice skating as a sport. Henie toured the world with spectacular ice reviews, achieving great popularity, particularly in the **United States**. She was initially idolized in her native **Norway**, but had some image problems after World War II when she was perceived to be a Nazi sympathizer who failed to support war relief efforts in Norway. Henie later suffered from leukemia and died during a flight from Paris to Oslo where she was to visit a medical specialist.

HILDGARTNER, PAUL (ITA–LUG). B. 8 June 1952, Kienz. One of the few lugers to win three Olympic medals and two gold medals, Paul Hildgartner uniquely won his gold medals 12 years apart. In 1972, Hildgartner joined Walter Plaikner to win the Olympic doubles **luge** gold medal. He then turned to singles luge exclusively, earning a silver medal in 1980 and winning the Olympic title in 1984 at Sarajevo. Hildgartner was also World Champion in singles in 1978, and in doubles in 1971 (with Plaikner). Hildgartner was the singles World Cup leader in both 1981 and 1983.

HOCKEY (FIELD). Hockey is the oldest known ball and stick game. Records exist of it having been played in Persia in 2000 BCE. It became so popular by the Middle Ages that it was banned in **England** for a time because it interfered with the practice of archery, which was the basis for national defense.

The modern game of hockey, however, was developed in England in the late 19th century. It spread throughout the British Empire, as a result, and most of the dominant nations in the sport have been nations that are, or were, members of that Empire. This includes **India**, **Pakistan**, **Australia**, **New Zealand**, and the United Kingdom. India's dominance in this team sport is matched only by the **United States**' dominance of basketball, **Hungary**'s dominance of water polo, and **Canadian** and **Soviet** dominance of ice hockey. Between 1928 and 1956, India won six gold medals and 30 consecutive games.

Hockey appeared on the **Olympic program** in 1908 and 1920. In 1928, it was held at Amsterdam and has been an Olympic sport since. In 1980, hockey for **women** was first introduced as an Olympic sport. Hockey is governed internationally by the Fédération Internationale de Hockey (FIH), which was formed in 1924 and had 118 member nations at the end of 2004. *See also* INDIA FIELD HOCKEY TEAMS (1928–1964).

HOLMES, KELLY (GBR–ATH). B. 19 April 1970, Pembury, Kent. Kelly Holmes's career as a middle-distance runner has been a testament to her perseverance. Frequently hampered by injuries, she starred as a runner while an English schoolgirl but joined the army at 18, where she played on the **volleyball** and **judo** teams, and she did not break through to world class until 1993. She won the Commonwealth Games 1,500 meters in 1994 and 2002, which were her major international achievements until the 2004 **Olympic Games**. But at Athens she became only the third female runner to win the 800 and 1,500 meters at the same Olympics, despite not being favored in either event. At the end of 2004, Lady Kelly Holmes was made a dame for her efforts.

HONDURAS (HON). Honduras has competed at the **Olympics Games** of 1968, 1976, 1984, 1988, 1992, 1996, 2000, and 2004. In 1992, Honduras competed at Albertville in its only appearance at the **Olympic Winter Games** to date. No Honduran athlete has won an Olympic medal.

HONG KONG, CHINA (HKG). Hong Kong first competed at the 1952 **Olympic Games** and has since missed only the 1980 Moscow Olympics. Hong Kong first competed at the **Olympic Winter Games** in 2002, represented by two female short-track **speed skaters**. Despite this long Olympic history, prior to 1992, no Hong Kong athlete had ever finished in the top 10. In 1996, Lee Lai-Shan won Hong Kong's first Olympic medal, a gold in boardsailing. On 1 July 1997, **China** regained sovereignty over Hong Kong, but it was agreed that the territory would retain a separate Olympic identity as Hong Kong, China.

HONORARY IOC MEMBERS. The matter of honorary **International Olympic Committee** (IOC) membership was first raised in 1948. Following a proposal by Lord Arthur Porritt (NZL), it was agreed that those IOC members who has passed the age limit of 70 would be eligible to become honorary members and would be entitled to attend future IOC sessions. They would be permitted to take part in the discussions but would not be accorded a vote. The first honorary member to be appointed was the 86-year-old Riccardo Aldão (ARG). The age at which IOC members may advance to honorary membership has varied. Currently, an IOC member may become an honorary member at the age of 70, if he or she has served on the IOC for 10 years and is nominated by the **Executive Board**. Honorary IOC members may attend the **Olympic Games**, Olympic Congresses, and IOC sessions, but they no longer retain voting rights.

HOPLITE RACE. *See* RACE IN ARMOR.

HOPPE, WOLFGANG (GDR/GER–BOB). B. 14 November 1957, Apolda. Wolfgang Hoppe started his sports career in track and field **athletics** and won the GDR junior decathlon championship in 1976. He later turned his talents to **bobsledding** and became the world's top driver in the 1980s. In the two-man event, Hoppe won Olympic gold in 1984 and a silver in 1988 and was three times the World Champion. He was equally accomplished in the four-man event, winning an Olympic gold in 1984, a silver in 1988 and 1992, and ending his Olympic career with a four-man bronze in 1994. Hoppe won the World Championship in the four-man event in 1991, and at the European Championships he won the two-man title in 1986–1987 and the four-man event in 1987.

HUNGARY (HUN). Hungary was one of the countries that attended the first **Olympic Games** in 1896 in Athens. A **National Olympic Committee** (NOC) was formed in Hungary in 1895 by Dr. Ferenc Kémény, who was one of the founding members of the **International Olympic Committee** (IOC). Hungary has missed only two Olympics, including the **Olympic Winter Games**, at which it has appeared at all celebrations. Hungary was not invited to the 1920 Olympics in Antwerp, having been an aggressor nation in World War I, and Hungary chose not to attend the 1984 Los Angeles Olympics.

Hungary has been very successful in a variety of sports, but by far its greatest honors have come in **fencing**. In one fencing discipline, the saber, it has been the dominant nation, and in fact, between 1908 and 1960 Hungary won 9 of 11 team titles and 10 of 11 individual titles in this event. Through 2000, Hungary has won 464 Olympic medals, including 158 gold. All but six of these came at the **Summer Olympic Games**.

HURLEY, MARCUS LATIMER (USA–CYC). B. 22 December 1883, New York, NY. D. 28 March 1941, New York, NY. With four gold medals in the 1904 Olympic **cycling** events, Marcus Hurley tied a record for individual golds at one Games that stood until **Eric Heiden**'s domination of the 1980 **speed skating** events. Hurley was the greatest American amateur cyclist of his era. He won the U.S. amateur sprint championship from 1901 until 1904 and was world amateur sprint champion in 1904, as well. Hurley was also an excellent basketball player at Columbia University, captaining that team in 1908 and earning All-American honors from 1905 to 1908. He also captained the New York basketball team that won the Metropolitan Championship in 1905. Hurley was later enshrined in the College Basketball Hall of Fame.

– I –

ICE DANCING. *See* DEMONSTRATION SPORTS; FIGURE SKATING.

ICE HOCKEY. Ice hockey is a Canadian sport that began in the early 19th century. Around 1860, a puck was substituted for a ball, and in 1879, two McGill University students, W. F. Robertson and R. F. Smith, devised the first rules, combining **field hockey** and **rugby** regulations. Originally the game was played nine to a side. The sport became the Canadian national sport with leagues everywhere. In 1894, Lord Stanley of Preston, governor-general of **Canada**, donated the Stanley Cup that was first won in 1894 by a team representing the Montreal Amateur Athletic Association.

Ice hockey was contested at the 1920 **Summer Olympic Games** at Antwerp, held in early April. These were also the first World Championships and were played by seven-man sides, the only time seven-man teams played in the Olympics. In 1924, the Olympics began using the current standard of six men per side on the ice at a time.

Ice hockey has been held at every **Olympic Winter Games**. Canada dominated early Olympic ice hockey tournaments as might be expected. In 1956, the **Soviet Union** first entered the Olympic Winter Games and won the ice hockey tournament quite handily. It was the preeminent country until its political division, its dominance interrupted only by major upset victories by the **United States** in 1960 and 1980.

Women's ice hockey appeared for the first time on the **Olympic program** in 1998 at Nagano. The sport is governed by the International Ice Hockey Federation (IIHF), which was founded in 1908, and had 63 affiliated nations at the end of 2004. *See also* CANA-DIAN ICE HOCKEY TEAMS (1920–1952); SOVIET UNION ICE HOCKEY TEAMS (1956–1992).

ICE SKATING. *See* FIGURE SKATING; ICE HOCKEY; SPEED SKATING.

ICELAND (ISL). Iceland sent one athlete to the 1908 Olympics, Johannes Jósepsson, a **wrestler**. The country also sent two athletes to the 1912 Olympics, but did not again appear until 1936. Since that time it has never failed to be present at an **Olympic Games**. It has competed at all the **Olympic Winter Games** since 1948, except for 1972. Iceland has won three medals in the Olympic Games, a silver in triple jump (track and field **athletics**) by Vilhjálmur Einarsson in 1956, a bronze in half-heavyweight **judo** by Bjarni Fridriksson in 1984, and a bronze by Vala Flosadóttir in women's pole vault in 2000. It could be argued that Icelanders have won a gold medal. In 1920, **Canada** won a gold medal in **ice hockey** at Antwerp, represented by the club team, the Winnipeg Falcons. Of the eight Canadians on that team, seven were of Icelandic origin and had dual citizenship.

INDEPENDENT OLYMPIC ATHLETES (IOA). At Sydney in 2000, the **International Olympic Committee** (IOC) allowed athletes from the disputed nation of **East Timor** to compete under the designation of Independent Olympic Athletes (IOA). This was despite the fact that the nation did not yet have a **National Olympic Committee** (NOC) recognized by the IOC. East Timor was represented in 2000 by four athletes—three men and one woman, who competed in track and field **athletics**, **boxing**, and **weightlifting**.

INDEPENDENT OLYMPIC PARTICIPANTS (IOP). In 1992, at Barcelona, 58 athletes (39 men and 19 women) from **Yugoslavia** were allowed to compete as Independent Olympic Participants. The United Nations Security Council Resolution No. 757 had placed a ban on Yugoslav teams competing internationally because of the war in **Bosnia-Herzegovina**. However, the **International Olympic Committee** (IOC) made arrangements allowing individual athletes to compete, providing they did not officially represent Yugoslavia.

INDIA (IND). India's first Olympic appearance can be traced to 1900 when Norman Pritchard, a British resident of Calcutta, competed in the sprints at Paris, representing the London Athletic Club and **Great Britain**. India's next Olympic appearance occurred in 1920, although India's **National Olympic Committee** (NOC) was not formed until 1927. India has competed at all the **Olympic Games** since 1920. In 1928, India entered its first **field hockey** team and won the gold medal. This was the first of six consecutive gold medals won by India in men's field hockey. Twelve of India's 17 medals in the Olympics have been won by its field hockey team. India has competed at the 1964, 1968, 1988, 1992, 1998, and 2002 **Olympic Winter Games**.

INDIA FIELD HOCKEY TEAMS (1928–1964). India dominated Olympic **hockey (field hockey)** from its first appearance in 1928 through 1964. During that time, India won 30 consecutive games (1928–1960), the streak being broken, 1-0, in the 1960 finals by **Pakistan**. India won the gold medal in seven of the eight Olympics between 1928 and 1964, inclusive, losing only in 1960 to Pakistan, but still taking a silver medal. India continued to be one of the top nations in Olympic hockey through the 1970s, winning a bronze medal in 1968 and 1972, and another gold medal in 1980. Since that time, India's best finish has been fifth in 1984. Overall, India has an Olympic hockey record of 73 wins, 23 losses, and 11 ties. It has outscored its opponents 402 goals to 120 goals. India's **women** have competed in Olympic hockey since 1980 but with less success, not having won any medals to date.

INDONESIA (INA). Indonesia formed a **National Olympic Committee** (NOC) in 1946 but did not compete at the Olympics until 1952. Indonesia missed the 1964 **Olympic Games** when it withdrew after several of its athletes were banned for their participation at the 1963 **Games of the New Emerging Forces** (GANEFO). Indonesia also boycotted the 1980 Olympics. The country has never competed at the **Olympic Winter Games**. Indonesia's national sport is **badminton**, at which it is one of the dominant countries in the world and in the Olympics. Through 2004, Indonesia has won 20 Olympics medals, 15 of them in badminton, four in **weightlifting**, and one in **archery**. *See* KOREA, DEMOCRATIC PEOPLE'S REPUBLIC OF. *See also* "The Games of the XVIIIth Olympiad" in the chronology.

INTERNATIONAL COMMITTEE FOR FAIR PLAY (ICFP). The International Committee for Fair Play was founded in 1963 to promote the principles of fair play. Each year, the ICFP awards International Fair Play Prizes after receiving nominations from various groups. The athletes may be neophytes or Olympic champions and are chosen for their commitment to fair play.

INTERNATIONAL FEDERATIONS (IFs). International Federations are nongovernmental organizations that administer sports on an international level. The IFs' role is to establish and enforce the rules governing the practice of their sport, promote development of their sport internationally, and assume responsibility for the technical control of their sport at the **Olympic Games**. The sports governed by the IFs may be admitted to the **Olympic program** if they satisfy the following requirements: Games of the Olympiad—the sports must be widely practiced by men in at least 75 countries and four continents, and by women in at least 40 countries and three continents. **Olympic Winter Games**—the sports must be widely practiced in at least 25 countries and three continents. There are two categories of International Federations affiliated with the **International Olympic Committee** (IOC). One is the International Olympic Federations, which govern sports currently on the Olympic program. There are 35 such IFs. A second category relates to IOC-recognized International Federations, of which there are currently 30. These federations are not yet on the Olympic program, but IOC recognition is a necessary first step to that end. (See the individual sports of the Olympics, which give the names, dates of foundation, and number of member nations for the various International Federations.)

INTERNATIONAL OLYMPIC ACADEMY (IOA). The idea of an International Olympic Academy was first conceived in the 1930s by **Ioannis Ketseas,** an **International Olympic Committee** (IOC) member in **Greece,** and **Carl Diem**. The idea never died, but it took many years of informal discussions before the foundation of an academy, to be located at Olympia, Greece, was unanimously approved by the IOC during a session in Rome in 1949. Of the 80 invitations sent to **National Olympic Committees** (NOCs) or the first preliminary session, only four replies were received, and all of these were in the negative. Ketseas, who was working closely with Diem, a German professor with a passionate interest in Olympic matters, persisted with his goal, and with the assistance of Olympic and archaeological bodies from **Germany** and Greece, the academy eventually came into being and has subsequently prospered. The first session was held from 16 to 23 June 1961. A plot of some 150 acres of land bordering the ancient Olympic stadium was acquired by the IOA, buildings were erected, and the complex, which now provides accommodations, a library, and several sports facilities, is a popular center for students of the **Olympic movement**. The IOA holds an annual session each summer during which students of the Olympic movement gather for several days to hear speeches and discussions on Olympic subjects. In addition, many other international symposia are held at the IOA each year. The idea of Olympic Academies has now spread and, as of the late 1990s, there were also 72 National Olympic Academies, helping to spread the message of Olympism and the Olympic movement.

INTERNATIONAL OLYMPIC COMMITTEE (IOC). The International Olympic Committee is the international governing organization of the **Olympic movement** and the **Olympic Games**. It is a nongovernmental, nonprofit organization of unlimited duration, in the form of an association with the status of a legal person, recognized by decree of the Swiss Federal Council of 17 September 1981. The International Olympic Committee was founded by **Pierre de Coubertin** in 1894, at the **Olympic Congress** that reestablished the Olympic Games. The IOC is currently based in **Lausanne**, Switzerland, and has been since Coubertin moved there during World War I. The mission of the IOC is to lead the Olympic movement in accordance with the **Olympic Charter**.

The IOC consists of members who are chosen and co-opted to membership. IOC member nations may have one member on the IOC, although not all do. However, until recently any nation that had hosted the Olympic Games or **Olympic Winter Games** was entitled to a second member on the IOC. IOC members are not considered to be members from their respective nations. Rather, they are considered to be IOC ambassadors to, or in, their respective nations. The **IOC 2000 Commission** helped change the structure of the IOC in late 1999. There are now four classes of IOC members: independent members, co-opted as they have always been; athlete members, who have competed in the most recent Olympic Games; **International Federation** (IF) president members; and **National Olympic Committee** (NOC) president members. The eventual size of the IOC was also restricted to 115 members, as follows: 70 independent members, 15 athlete members, 15 IF president members, and 15 NOC president members. Previously, IOC members were elected for life, but the new changes to the Olympic Charter call for reelection every eight years, with athlete members restricted to one term.

The IOC is led by a president, four vice presidents, and an executive board. The president is elected initially for a term of eight years but may be reelected for one further term of four years. Prior to 1999, presidents could be reelected with no term limits, but this was changed based on the recommendations of the IOC 2000 Commission. Vice presidents and executive board members are elected for a term of four years. They may not be reelected to the same position for consecutive terms, although they may return to that position on the executive board after a period of four more years.

IOC sessions consist of meetings of the entire membership and are required to be held at least once a year. The IOC session is considered to be the supreme organ of the IOC but may delegate its powers to the executive board. The executive board meets more frequently and works by making recommendations to the IOC session, which is then responsible for enacting or denying its recommendations. Day-to-day decisions are delegated to the IOC president.

The Olympic Charter is the document that specifies the principles, rules, and bylaws of the IOC. Only IOC sessions have the power to modify and interpret the Olympic Charter. *See also* Appendix A ("Presidents of the International Olympic Committee"); Appendix D ("Members of the International Olympic Committee"). *See also* the separate biographies of IOC presidents: VIKELAS, DEMETRIOS; COUBERTIN, BARON PIERRE DE; BAILLET-LATOUR, COUNT HENRI DE; EDSTRÖM, J. SIGFRID; BRUNDAGE, AVERY; KILLANIN, LORD; SAMARANCH, JUAN ANTONIO; ROGGE, JACQUES.

INTERNATIONAL PIERRE DE COUBERTIN COMMITTEE. The International Pierre de Coubertin Committee was founded in

1976. It is committed to the dissemination and study of **Coubertin**'s works and his humanitarianism. The first president of the International Pierre de Coubertin Committee was Dr. Paul Martin (SUI), followed in 1977 by Geoffroy de Navacelle (FRA), Coubertin's grand-nephew, and later by Conrado Durántez Corral (ESP). The current president is Dr. Norbert Müller (GER). There was previously an independent **International Olympic Committee** (IOC) Commission, the Pierre de Coubertin Commission, although several executives served on both boards, but this commission has been disbanded.

INTERNATIONAL RELATIONS COMMISSION. The International Relations Commission was formed in 2002, with a mandate to facilitate and promote relations between the **Olympic movement**, particularly the **International Olympic Committee** (IOC), the **National Olympic Committees** (NOCs), and governments and public authorities. It prepares position papers on specific political issues related to sport and advises the IOC president and the executive board accordingly. The commission is composed of 12 IOC members, with the current chairman being Guy Drut (FRA).

INTERNATIONAL SOCIETY OF OLYMPIC HISTORIANS (ISOH). The International Society of Olympic Historians was founded in 1991 to promote and study the history of the **Olympic movement** and the **Olympic Games**. The immediate worldwide response from Olympic historians provided a clear indication of the need for such an organization, with over 350 members from 50 nations at the end of 2004. A journal of the group, *Journal of Olympic History*, is published three times per year, and the website is accessible via www.isoh.org. The first president was **Ian Buchanan** (GBR), who served two terms (1991–2000). Buchanan was followed as president by Bill Mallon (USA), who served through 2004. The officers elected in 2004 were President Karl Lennartz (GER); Vice President David Wallechinsky (USA); Secretary-General Tony Bijkerk (NED); and Treasurer John Grasso (USA). In November 2004, the **IOC Executive Board** gave official recognition to ISOH.

IOC PARTNERS. The **International Olympic Committee** (IOC) works with several organizations, which it considers partners, in assistance projects for human development, via sport and physical activity. The

IOC notes on its website, "It is a matter of using sport as a means for a positive change. Although these projects are specific and merely symbolic, the Olympic Movement's contribution is intended to complement the efforts of the governments and inter- and non-governmental organizations to meet the challenges of our society. The IOC's commitment in this area is based on the need to place sport, which has become a real social force within society, at the service of human development." The IOC lists its partners as the following: the United Nations Education, Scientific and Cultural Organization (UNESCO), the World Health Organisation (WHO), the Office of the United Nations High Commissioner for Refugees (UNHCR), the United Nations Development Programme (UNDP), the United Nations Office for Drug Control and Crime Prevention (UNODCCP), the Office of the High Commissioner for Human Rights (OHCHR), the Food and Agriculture Organisation of the United Nations (FAO), the United Nations Environment Programme (UNEP), and the International Labour Organisation (ILO).

IOC 2000 COMMISSION. The IOC 2000 Commission was another commission formed in response to the **Olympic bribery scandal**. The purpose of the IOC 2000 Commission was to study the structure of the **International Olympic Committee** (IOC) and the candidate city bidding process and make recommendations to update these entities to prevent many of the problems that were occurring. The IOC 2000 Commission was made up of 82 members, with fewer than half of them IOC members, and with an executive board of 26 members, of whom 13 were IOC members. The commission produced an intermediary report in June 1999, and its final report was released in November 1999. The IOC 2000 Commission made 50 recommendations to the IOC in its final report, with recommendations made by each of the working groups. At the IOC session in December 1999, the IOC approved all 50 of the recommendations, which has led to a major rewriting of the **Olympic Charter**. A summary of the recommendations is as follows:

1. Members: The maximum IOC membership should be 115, with 15 active athletes (defined as having taken part in the **Olympic Games** or **Olympic Winter Games** within four years of their membership), 15 **International Federation** (IF) presidents, 15 presidents of **National Olympic Committees**

(NOCs) or Continental Associations, and 70 members elected on an individual basis.

2. Procedure for Selecting Candidates and Electing Members: Proposed forming a Nomination Committee. Each of the above four classes of IOC members may propose candidate members. The Nomination Committee consists of seven members, including at least one athlete, elected for a four-year period, three members elected by the IOC, three by the **IOC Ethics Commission**, and one by the **Athletes Commission**. The Nomination Committee will evaluate prospective members who will be voted upon by the full IOC session.

3. Nationality: One member per nation for members chosen on an individual basis; one member per nation among the athletes; one member per nation among NOC presidents; no restrictions on nationality among IF presidents.

4. Terms of Office: Term limit of eight years, renewable, with re-election to follow the same procedure as election.

5. Age Limit: 70 years of age for all members and all functions. However, current members will be "grandfathered" to follow the limit of 80 that existed prior to this vote.

6. Rights and Responsibilities of Members: When a vote concerns a country of a member, the member may not take part in the vote.

7. Honorary Members: Awarded to members of 10 years' standing and for exceptional services. The previous rule remained in force through 31 December 2001.

8. Executive Board: Increase number of members to 15, with four vice presidents. Four-year terms limits on the board.

9. President: Elected for an eight-year term; may be reelected one time for a four-year second term of office.

10. Current Members: Current members will be "grandfathered" in place for eight years, at which time they will be subject to reelection as will all new members.

11. Transition Period: During the transition period, to conclude 1 January 2001, the number of IOC members may be greater than the recommended 115 (currently set at 130).

12. Entry into Force: The new rules will come into force on 1 January 2000, with an implementation period of one year allowed.

13. Program and Participation:

    13.1 The obligation of each NOC to participate in the games of the Olympiad will be added to the Olympic Charter—somewhat of an "antiboycott" clause. All NOCs will be allowed to enter six athletes in the Games of the Olympiad, even if they do not meet the minimum qualification standards.

    13.2 Sports Program: A maximum of 280 events is recommended for future Games of the Olympiad. Events included in World Championships programs do not necessarily need to be included in the Olympic Games. Significant discussion followed this vote, as there will be 300 events at Sydney in 2000 and 14 sports are currently applying for admission to the **Olympic program**. President **Juan Antonio Samaranch** suggested that the IOC Sports Commission study this proposal and make recommendations to the next IOC session.

14. Finance: The IOC will transfer knowledge concerning licensing programs to future **Organizing Committees of the Olympic Games** (OCOGs). The IOC will also provide guidelines and recommendations concerning ticketing and pricing to the OCOGs.

15. Paralympics: The **Paralympics** must be held in the same city as the Olympics, following the Games. The IOC will formalize its relationship with the International Paralympic Committee.

16. Management of the Olympic Games: The IOC established an operational structure to transfer knowledge and expertise from one edition of Olympic Games and Olympic Winter Games to the next.

17. Athletes (1): Defined an active Olympic athlete as one who is still competing or has participated in the most recent edition of the Olympic Games.

18. Athletes (2): Athletes should be represented at all levels of the Olympic movement.

19. Athletes (3): The Athletes Commission should be represented on the IOC Executive Board, and recommends the same for IFs, NOCs, and **National Governing Bodies** (NGBs).

20. Athletes (4): Organizing Committees of the Olympic Games (OCOGs) must include an athlete on their boards.
21. Athletes (5): The IOC Athletes Commission must be allocated a budget for its operation.
22. Athletes (6): During the closing ceremony of the Olympic Games and Olympic Winter Games, the elected athletes will be recognized by their peers and the **Olympic family**.
23. Role of **Olympic Solidarity**: Olympic Solidarity should act as the coordinator of development programs for all members of the Olympic movement.
24. Decentralized Programs: Olympic Solidarity must provide support to Continental/Regional Games under IOC patronage and will also help develop Regional and Subregional Sports Training Centers.
25. Humanitarian Projects: These will be pursued and reinforced if they relate to members of the Olympic movement and the development and practice of sport.
26. Information Transfer: Olympic Solidarity will ensure that all NOCs have access to the technology necessary for information transfer between sectors of the Olympic movement.
27. Education: Proposed that NOCs include a session in all Olympic Solidarity–funded programs to educate the participants concerning the Olympic movement.
28. Regional Information Centers: Proposed that Olympic Solidarity set up Regional and Subregional Sports Information Centers to help disseminate information on the Olympic movement and sports administration.
29. Evaluation/Accountability: Better coordination between the IOC departments and an improved auditing procedure of Olympic Solidarity to be implemented.
30. Education and Culture (1): Merge the **Cultural Commission** and IOA/Education Commission into a single Commission on Education and Culture. Create a new department of Education and Culture within the IOC. Hire additional professional staff for the **Olympic Studies Centre** at the **Olympic Museum**.
31. Education and Culture (2): Several recommendations to spread the message of **Olympism** to appropriate regional

structures, including publishing the *Olympic Review* and the official reports of the Olympic Games on the Internet.

32. Education and Culture (3): Creation of a traveling exhibit of the Olympic movement and Olympic history to be set up in host cities, with a clause added to the host city contract.

33. Education and Culture (4): Greater recognition of the IOC on the educational importance of the **Olympic flame** relay and participation by the IOC Executive Board in the flame-lighting ceremonies at Olympia.

34. **Doping** (1): The Athletes' Oath will be amended to include a statement concerning drug-free sport.

35. Doping (2): Implementation by the **World Anti-Doping Agency** (WADA) of an athletic passport concerning the athlete's health, allowing doping controls to be carried out and to monitor the participant's health.

36. Doping (3): The IOC will conduct out-of-competition drug tests beginning at the time of accreditation of athletes at the Olympic Games and Olympic Winter Games.

37. Doping (4): In the event of an appeal against sanctions, the "B" sample should be tested by a different laboratory than the one that tested the "A" sample.

38. Doping (5): Sports not conforming to the Olympic movement anti-doping code and that do not perform out-of-competition drug testing will be dropped from the Olympic program. IOC-recognized sports not conforming to this code will lose their recognition.

39. Relations with Governments and Non-Governmental Organizations (NGO) (1): The IOC will provide more assistance to the NOCs to develop closer relationships with their respective local governments.

40. Relations with Governments and Non-Governmental Organizations (NGO) (2): The passage of the United Nations' **Olympic truce** could be supplemented by similar declarations from world leaders and other NGOs to support the Olympic truce.

41. Relations with Governments and Non-Governmental Organizations (NGO) (3): The Olympic truce will be given greater prominence. Six months prior to the Olympic Games or Olympic Winter Games, the IOC president will contact the

protagonist nations in major internal and international conflicts and ask them to observe the Olympic truce for the duration of the Games. During the opening ceremony, the IOC president will refer to the Olympic truce and will note that it is a first step toward lasting peace.

42. Internal Communications: Internal communications within the Olympic movement must be open, substantive, two-way, and timely.

43. External Communications: An IOC spokesperson will be appointed to support the IOC president and other IOC executives. The Communications Department of the IOC will develop a proactive approach to media relations. IOC sessions will be open to the media on closed-circuit television.

44. Transparency (1): The flow of IOC funds for each Olympiad will be disclosed beginning with the current Olympiad, via independent, external auditors.

45. Transparency (2): The IOC will disclose the allocation of funds to each NOC and IF, and each entity of the Olympic movement will submit to the IOC an accounting of its expenditure of funds provided by the IOC.

46. Transparency (3): The IOC will seek a more transparent disclosure of fund distribution to be phased in over future Olympiads.

47. Transparency (4): Each bid city must disclose the source of funding for bid expenditures, which will be audited at the conclusion of the bid process.

48. Transparency (5): The IOC will encourage NOCs and IFs to disclose their sources and uses of funds.

49. Role of the NOCs in the Bid Process: The NOC should be involved in any Olympic candidature as a full partner with the bid committee and should take responsibility for the Olympic bid to the IOC.

50. New Candidature Procedure: A new bid acceptance phase will be instituted, with a series of recommendations as follows:

    50.1 Strict minimum technical requirements applied to the selection of a bid city.

    50.2 In the new bid acceptance process, representatives of the IOC, IFs, NOCs, athletes, and external experts examine the proposed bids and recommend to the IOC Executive Board which cities should be accepted as candidate cities.

50.3 The IOC will enter into a contractual agreement with the NOC and the Bid Committee.

50.4 The IOC will issue candidate city manuals and prepare candidature files.

50.5 An Evaluation Commission will be formed to visit each of the candidate cities.

50.6 Selection of final candidate cities, if necessary. The Executive Board may reduce the number of candidates by selecting a limited number of cities.

50.7 It is not considered necessary for IOC members to visit the candidate cities nor for the representatives or candidate cities, or third parties acting on their behalf ("agents"), to visit IOC members.

In the end, all 50 recommendations of the IOC 2000 Commission were approved, most of them unanimously. The main points of contention were the age limit, which had eight dissenting votes, and Recommendation 50.7, which eliminated IOC members' visits to candidate cities, but even those passed with over 90 percent of the vote.

IRAN (IRI, formerly IRN). Although Iran was represented in 1900 by a **fencer**, Prince Freydoun Malkom, it was only in 1947 that Iran formed a **National Olympic Committee** (NOC). Iran was granted **International Olympic Committee** (IOC) recognition in the same year. Apart from boycotting the Olympics of 1980 and 1984, Iran has competed at every **Olympic Games** since it made its Olympic début as a team in 1948. It has competed at the **Olympic Winter Games** of 1956, 1964, 1968, 1972, 1976, 1998, and 2002. All of Iran's success has come in the strength or combative sports of **weightlifting**, **wrestling**, and **taekwondo**. Through 2004, it has won 46 Olympic medals (10 gold medals) with 31 medals won in wrestling, 12 won in weightlifting, and 3 in taekwondo.

IRAQ (IRQ). Iraq formed its **National Olympic Committee** (NOC) in 1948 and made its first Olympic appearance in that year. Iraq then did not compete until the Rome Olympics of 1960. Iraq missed the 1972 and 1976 Olympics but has competed continuously since, including the 1984 **Olympic Games**. Iraq has never competed at the **Olympic Winter Games**. One Iraqi athlete has won an Olympic medal, that being a bronze medal by Abdul Wahid Aziz in lightweight **weightlifting** in 1960. Perhaps the greatest performance by Iraqi Olympic athletes occurred at the 2004 Olympic Games. Shortly after Iraq was invaded and fought a war, resulting in the ousting of President Saddam Hussein, it qualified a **football (soccer)** team for Athens. The team was known to have suffered torture in recent years at the orders of Uday Hussein, president of the Iraqi NOC and son of Saddam, whenever its players did not perform well. But at Athens, the Iraqi football team went to the semifinals and narrowly lost out on a medal, finishing fourth.

IRELAND (IRL). Ireland formed a **National Olympic Committee** (NOC) in 1922, shortly after it became independent of **Great Britain** in December 1921. Ireland first competed as a separate state in the 1924 **Olympic Games** at Paris. Prior to that time, however, many Irish athletes had competed—mostly for Great Britain. In addition, many of the great American weight-throwers had been recent Irish emigrants. Ireland also entered separate teams in 1908 **field hockey** and the 1912 **cycling** road race, although the 1912 cycling team technically was a second team representing Great Britain. Since 1924, Ireland has competed at every Olympic Games except those of 1936. Ireland has competed at the **Olympic Winter Games** in 1992, 1998, and 2002. Through 2004, Ireland has won 21 Olympic medals: nine gold, six silver, and six bronze.

ISRAEL (ISR). The formation of the state of Israel as an independent Jewish state occurred on 15 May 1948. Israel dates its **National Olympic Committee** (NOC) to 1933, but that was a **Palestine** organization, and not truly a precursor of the current NOC. The original Palestine Olympic Committee was recognized by the **International Olympic Committee** (IOC) in 1934, and was to represent Jews, Muslims, and Christians from the Palestine region. However, the rules of the original Palestine NOC stated, "Palestine is the National Home of the Jews, and so the Palestine NOC represents the Jewish National Home." Given that manifesto, the Palestine NOC refused to compete at the 1936 **Olympic Games** in Berlin, in protest of

Adolf Hitler's policies. After World War II, the 1948 London Organizing Committee originally invited the Palestine NOC but later withdrew the invitation. The problem of the status of the Palestine Olympic Committee was solved in 1951 when the Israel Olympic Committee was formed.

Israel competed at its first Olympics in 1952 at Helsinki, the same year in which its NOC was formally recognized by the IOC. Israel has missed only the 1980 Moscow Olympics since 1952. Israel made its first **Olympic Winter Games** appearance in 1994 at Lillehammer and also participated in 1998 at Nagano. The zenith of Israel participation came in 1992 when two Israeli *judoka* won the nation's first medals. The nadir occurred at Munich on 5 September 1972 when Arab terrorists savagely and cowardly murdered 11 Israeli athletes and officials. Through 2004, Israel has won six Olympic medals—three in **judo**, two in **sailing**, and one in **canoeing**. *See also* "The Games of the XXth Olympiad (1972)" in the chronology.

ISTHMIAN GAMES. The Isthmian Games were ancient sporting festivals that were held biennially. With the **Olympic Games**, **Nemean Games**, and **Pythian Games**, they were one of the four great sporting festivals of ancient Greece. The Isthmian Games were contested at the sanctuary of Poseidon at the Isthmus of Corinth. They are first known to have been held in 582 BCE and lasted through the fourth century CE. Their origin is attributed to Sisyphus, King of Corinth. Champions at the Isthmian Games originally received crowns of dry wild celery, which was later changed to a crown of pine wreath during Roman times. One report suggests that the Isthmian Games were highly commercialized.

ITALY (ITA). Italy has never missed an **Olympic Winter Games** and has missed only the **Olympic Games** of 1904. Although it is usually considered not to have competed in 1896, recent research has discovered that an Italian shooter named Rivabella did compete in 1896. But Italy did not form a **National Olympic Committee** (NOC) until 1908, and it was not until 1915 that this committee was recognized by the **International Olympic Committee** (IOC). Italy has had success in many different sports. Italy has often been the dominant country in **cy-**

cling and fencing. Italy has won 603 Olympic medals, 221 of them gold. Of these, 90 medals and 31 gold have been won at the Olympic Winter Games. Italy also hosted the Games of the XVIIth Olympiad at Rome in 1960 and the 7th Olympic Winter Games at Cortina d'Ampezzo in 1956. Italy is also scheduled to host the 20th Olympic Winter Games in Torino (Turin) in 2006.

IVORY COAST (CIV). *See* CÔTE D'IVOIRE.

– J –

JAGER, THOMAS MICHAEL (USA–SWI). B. 6 October 1964, East St. Louis, Illinois. Tom Jager won seven Olympic swimming medals and five gold medals. All of his golds came in relays. His individual medals were a silver in the 1988 50 meter freestyle and bronze in the 1992 50 meter freestyle. Jager was a pure sprinter, specializing in the 50 free, at which he set six world records. He won the first two World Championships at that event in 1986 and 1991. His other major international titles came in the 50 free at the 1989 and 1991 Pan-Pacific Championships. His great sprint rivals were **Matt Biondi**, who beat him at the Olympics in 1988, and **Aleksandr Popov** (RUS), who won the 50 freestyle in 1992 and 1996.

JAMAICA (JAM). Jamaica has sent athletes to all the **Olympic Games** since 1948. In 1960, Jamaica, Barbados, and Trinidad combined to form the **West Indies Federation** team. That team won two medals, one of which was won by George Kerr, a Jamaican, in the 800 meters, while the other was a bronze in the 4 × 400 meter relay. Three members of that team were Jamaican while one was from Barbados. In 1988, Jamaica competed at its first **Olympic Winter Games**, represented by the now famous Jamaican **bobsled** team, which also represented the nation at Albertville in 1992 and Lillehammer in 1994. Two members of the bobsled team, the brothers Dudley and Christian Stokes, also competed in 1998, their fourth appearance. A movie, *Cool Runnings,* was later made about the Jamaican bobsled team. Jamaica has won 35 Olympic medals through 2004, 34 of them in track and field **athletics**, led by its outstanding sprinters. The other medal was a bronze in **cycling** won by David Weller in the 1,000 meter time trial.

JAPAN (JPN). Japan first competed at the 1912 **Olympic Games**, its delegation and Olympic committee led by Dr. Jigoro Kano, the founder of **judo**. Japan has since failed to compete only at the Games of 1948, when, as an aggressor nation in World War II, it was not invited, and 1980, when it chose to **boycott** the Moscow Olympics. At the **Olympic Winter Games**, Japan first competed in 1928 and has since missed only 1948 when it also was not invited. Japan was the dominant country in men's **gymnastics** from 1956 until the mid-1980s. In addition, at times it has been the top country in **swimming** and one of the top in **wrestling** and **weightlifting**. Japan has won 364 Olympic medals (121 gold medals), of which 31 (eight gold) have come at the Olympic Winter Games. Japan hosted the Games of the XVIIIth Olympiad in Tokyo in 1964, the 11th Olympic Winter Games in Sapporo in 1972, and the 18th Olympic Winter Games in Nagano in 1998. Prior to the outbreak of hostilities, Japan was also scheduled to host both editions of the 1940 Olympics; the Olympic Winter Games were scheduled for Sapporo, and the Games of the XIIth Olympiad were scheduled for Tokyo.

JERNBERG, SIXTEN (SWE–NSK). B. 6 February 1929, Lima, Dalarria (Dalecarlia). Sixten Jernberg is one of the most successful male Olympic **nordic skiers** and set records that have only been broken recently by **Bjørn Dæhlie** (NOR). Between 1956 and 1964, Jernberg won four gold, three silver, and two bronze for a record total, at the time, of nine Winter Olympic medals. He added three gold and two bronze medals at the 1954, 1958, and 1962 World Championships, including four medals in the 50 km. Between 1952 and 1964 he took part in 363 ski races, winning 134. In his prime years of 1955–1960, Jernberg won 86 of 161 races. Initially a blacksmith and then a lumberjack, his daily work provided the essential stamina for the rigors of long distance cross-country skiing. In 1965, the **International Olympic Committee** (IOC) awarded him the Mohammed Taher Trophy.

JEU DE PAUME **(Court Tennis or Real Tennis).** *Jeu de paume*, or game of the hand, the original version of **tennis**, has been contested

Spyridon Louis of Greece, winner of the first Olympic marathon. Courtesy of Erich Kamper

Martin Sheridan, considered the best discus thrower, prior to Al Oerter, and the top all-around track and field athlete in the world during the first decade of the 20th century. Courtesy of Erich Kamper

A young French boy (middle) pulled from the crowd to serve as a coxswain for the Dutch team in the pairs with cox during the 1900 Olympics. He has never been identified, however, he is considered the youngest Olympic competitor, somewhere between seven and eleven years old. Courtesy of Erich Kamper

After collapsing multiple times on the stadium track, Italy's Dorando Pietri is helped over the finish line at the 1908 Olympic marathon. He was later disqualified. Courtesy of Erich Kamper

Jim Thorpe, the greatest all-around athlete of all time and winner of the pentathlon and decathlon at the 1912 Olympic Games. Courtesy of Erich Kamper

Nedo Nadi of Italy, winner of five gold medals in fencing at the 1920 Olympic Games. Courtesy of Erich Kamper

Paavo Nurmi of Finland leads his countryman, Ville Ritola, at the 1924 Olympic Games. Together, they won nine gold medals in distance running. Courtesy of Erich Kamper

Babe Didrikson, considered the best all-around woman athlete ever, winning the javelin throw at the 1932 Olympics. Courtesy of Erich Kamper

Fanny Blankers-Koen, the Dutch mother and housewife who won four gold medals in track and field athletics at the 1948 Olympics. Courtesy of Erich Kamper

Dezsö Gyarmati of Hungary, won three gold medals and five medals in water polo between 1948 and 1964. Courtesy of Erich Kamper

Paul Elvstrøm, the Danish winner of four consecutive individual sailing gold medals from 1948–1960. Courtesy of Erich Kamper

Viktor Chukarin of the Soviet Union, winner of the all-around men's gymnastics title in 1952 and 1956. Courtesy of Erich Kamper

Murray Rose of Australia, considered the dominant Olympic distance swimmer from 1956–1964. Courtesy of Erich Kamper

Al Oerter of the United States, considered the finest discus thrower ever, won the gold medal at four consecutive Olympic Games from 1956–1968. Courtesy of Erich Kamper

Carol Heiss (left), gold medalist in 1960 women's figure skating, with her future husband, Hayes Alan Jenkins (right), winner of the 1956 men's figure skating gold medal. Courtesy of Erich Kamper

Wilma Rudolph wins her fourth gold medal at the 1960 Rome Olympics, leading the United States team to victory in the 4 x 100 meter relay. Courtesy of Erich Kamper

American swimmer Don Schollander (right), is congratulated by Scotland's Robby McGregor (left), after winning the 100 metre freestyle, one of his four gold medals at the 1964 Olympics. Courtesy of Erich Kamper

Věra Čáslavská (TCH), dominated women's gymnastics at the 1964 and 1968 Olympic Games. Courtesy of Erich Kamper

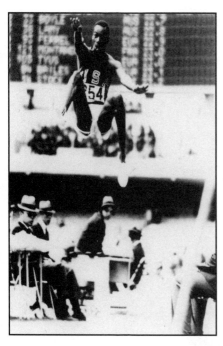

Bob Beamon in-flight, which led to the greatest single track and field performance ever, when he obliterated the long jump world record at the 1968 Olympic Games. Courtesy of Erich Kamper

Gert Frederikson of Sweden (left), considered the greatest male canoeist in Olympic history. Courtesy of Erich Kamper

Princess Ann, an equestrian competitor at the 1976 Montreal Olympic Games. Courtesy of Erich Kamper

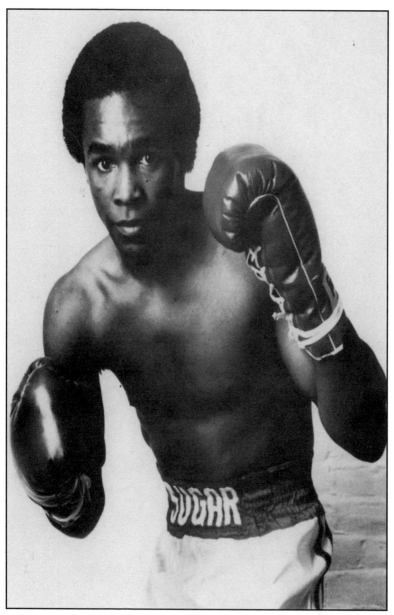

Sugar Ray Leonard, one of the most popular boxers ever, shortly after winning a boxing gold medal in 1976. Courtesy of Erich Kamper

The 1980 USA Ice Hockey team, also known as "The Miracle on Ice Team," defeated the Soviet Union and captured the gold medal. Courtesy of Erich Kamper

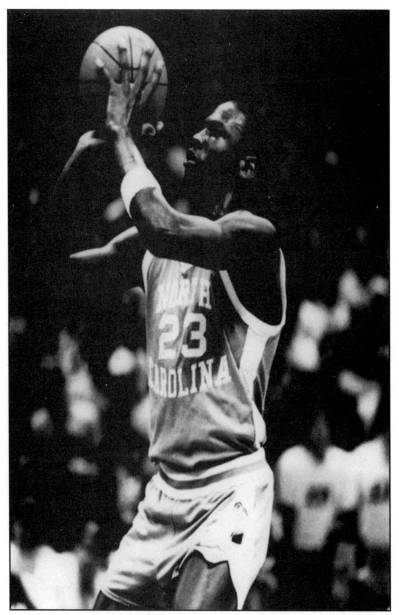

Michael Jordan of the United States, considered the greatest basketball player ever and winner of two Olympic gold medals in 1984 and 1992. Courtesy of Erich Kamper

Daniel Morelon compiled the finest Olympic record of any track cyclist ever, mostly in the match sprint. *Courtesy of Erich Kamper*

in the Olympics only in 1908, when the gold medal was won by American Jay Gould. In 1928, the sport was a **demonstration** event in Amsterdam. The sport is variously also called court tennis, real tennis, and royal tennis.

JOHANSSON, IVAR (SWE–WRE). B. 31 January 1903, Kuddby, Ostergötland. D. 4 August 1979. Ivar Johansson is one of only three men to have won Olympic gold medals in both styles of **wrestling** and also one of four wrestlers to have won a total of three Olympic gold medals. In 1932, he won the freestyle middleweight and the Greco-Roman welterweight titles, and in 1936, he won the Greco-Roman middleweight. Johansson won nine European Championships between 1931 and 1939, six at Græco and three at freestyle. He was a 22-time Swedish champion, winning 13 at Græco and nine at freestyle. His last Swedish title came in 1943 at the age of 40.

JOHNSON, MICHAEL DUANE (USA–ATH). B. 13 September 1967, Dallas, Texas. Michael Johnson is acknowledged as the greatest long sprinter in the history of **track and field**, specializing in the 200 and 400 meters. Johnson made his Olympic début in 1992, but was ill at the time, and his only medal, a gold, came in the 4 × 400 meter relay. At Atlanta in 1996, he won both the 200 and 400 meters, the first man to accomplish that feat at the Olympics, with his 200 meter victory achieved in the stunning world record time of 19.32. Johnson's Olympic career ended at Sydney, where he defended his 400 meter title and added a third gold in the 4 × 400 relay, giving him six gold medals in all. At the World Championships, Johnson was even more dominant, winning the 200 meters in 1991 and 1995 and the 400 meters in 1993, 1995, 1997, and 1999. He added the 400 meter world record in August 1999, when he ran 43.18 in Seville, Spain. With his upright style and short, rapid strides, he was an unmistakable figure on the track and is universally recognized as being the greatest one-lap runner ever.

JONES, MARION LOIS (USA–ATH). B. 12 October 1975, Los Angeles, California. Marion Jones first came to prominence as a high school sprint star in the early 90s. She narrowly missed making the 1992 U.S. Olympic team in the individual sprints as a high school senior, and she declined a place on the relay team. She then attended the University of North Carolina, where she starred as a point guard on the basketball team, and she led the team to the NCAA Women's Championship in 1994. She ran no international track while in college but returned to star at the 1997 World Championships when she won gold medals in the 100 meters and 4 × 100 meter relay. In 1998, she won 34 individual events, losing only a late season long jump competition. At the 1999 World Championships, she defended her title at 100 meters, but was injured in attempting to win the 200. Jones set herself the goal of winning five gold medals at the 2000 Olympic Games. She succeeded in winning five medals, three of them gold. The golds came in the 100, 200, and 4 × 400 meter relay, while she earned bronze medals in the long jump and 4 × 100 relay. She was later married to C. J. Hunter, who was 1999 World Champion in the shot put, although they eventually divorced. Jones competed at Athens in 2004, but under rumors and suspicions of **doping** at previous competitions, and failed to win a medal.

JORDAN (JOR). Jordan formed a **National Olympic Committee** (NOC) in 1957 that was recognized by the **International Olympic Committee** (IOC) in 1963. However, it was not until 1980 that Jordan's athletes competed on Olympian fields, since which time they have participated at every **Olympic Games**. Jordan has not yet appeared in the **Olympic Winter Games**. In 2000, Mohammad Al-Fararjeh finished equal seventh in light-heavyweight **taekwondo**, the best ever finish by a Jordanian Olympian.

JORDAN, MICHAEL JEFFREY (USA–BAS). B. 17 February 1963, Brooklyn, New York. Michael Jordan is considered by most experts to be the greatest **basketball** player of all time. He played collegiately at the University of North Carolina, where he helped it win an NCAA (National Collegiate Athletic Association) championship in 1983. In 1984, Jordan led the **United States** to an Olympic gold medal. Turning to professional basketball after his junior year in college, he became the greatest scorer in the National Basketball Association (NBA), leading the league in scoring every year except one in which he sat out most of the season with an injury. In 1991, Jordan finally achieved his greatest thrill, leading the Chicago Bulls to an

NBA Championship, and completing his Triple Crown of titles. Jordan eventually led the Bulls to six NBA titles (1991–1993, 1996–1998). In 1992, Jordan also played on the **Dream Team** that won the basketball gold medal at Barcelona. Jordan did not play in the NBA in 1994 and for most of the 1995 season, as he attempted a career in professional baseball, playing in the minor leagues. Since his retirement from the NBA after the 1998 season, Jordan has become an owner of the NBA's Washington Wizards, and he briefly returned to playing for that team as well, but with less success than in his younger days. *See also* UNITED STATES MEN'S BASKETBALL TEAM—1984.

JUDO. The founder of judo, Dr. Jigaro Kano, was a longtime member of the **International Olympic Committee** (IOC). Judo is a form of **wrestling** that was developed by Dr. Kano from the ancient Japanese schools of *yawara* and *jujitsu*. He founded his first *dojo* (judo school) in 1882, termed the *Kodokan.* The contestants are termed *judoka* and are classified into grades consisting of pupils (*Kyu*) and degrees (*Dan*). There are five classes of *Kyu*, advancing to first *Kyu*, and wearing a brown belt. Thereafter, the *judoka* achieve a *Dan*, beginning with first *Dan* (black belt) and advancing theoretically to 12th *Dan* (white belt). Fighting ability and technical knowledge advance a *judoka* to fifth *Dan*, after which advancement depends on service to the sport. Leading international *judoka* are usually fourth or fifth *Dan*. The 11th and 12th *Dan* have never been awarded.

Judo made its first Olympic appearance in 1964, but was not included on the program of the 1968 **Olympic Games**. Judo returned to the Olympic fold in 1972, and the 1992 Olympics included judo events for **women** for the first time. The sport, not surprisingly, has been dominated by the **Japanese**, followed by the **Soviet Union**, with the **Koreans** also winning many medals. The sport is governed internationally by the International Judo Federation (IJF), which was formed in 1951 and had 187 members as of December 2004.

JURIDICAL COMMISSION. Originally called the Legal Commission, the Juridical Commission was formed in 1974 with Marc Hodler as the original chairman. The current chairman is the German Thomas Bach. There are five other members of the commission, all

International Olympic Committee (IOC) members, and all either lawyers in their day job, or who are legally trained. Its charge by the IOC is listed as follows: 1) providing legal opinions to the IOC president, the IOC Executive Board, and the IOC session, upon their request, on issues relating to the exercise of their respective competences; 2) providing preliminary opinions concerning draft amendments to the **Olympic Charter**; 3) considering actions or defenses concerning the IOC; 4) carrying out studies of a legal nature on issues which may affect the interests of the IOC; and 5) performing any other tasks of a legal nature entrusted to it by the IOC president, the IOC Executive Board, or the IOC session.

– K –

KAKHIASHVILI, AKAKIOS (né Kakhi Kakhiashvili) (GRE/ EUN–WLT). B. 13 July 1969, Tbilisi, Georgia. Akakios Kakhiashvili was born in **Soviet** Georgia and first competed at the **Olympic Games** in 1992, representing the **Unified Team (Équipe Unifié)** and earning a gold medal in the 90 kg. class. Kakhiasvili then emigrated to **Greece**, for whom he has competed internationally since 1995. Representing Greece, he was World Champion in 1995, 1998, and 1999, and won further Olympic gold medals in both 1996 and 2000, one of only three **weightlifters** to win three gold medals. Kakhiashvili was also European Champion in 1992, 1993, 1995, and 1996, and has won seven medals at the European Championships. He competed in 2004 at Athens, but failed to complete a successful lift in the clean and jerk, and did not officially finish.

KALPE. Ancient Olympic sport. The *kalpe,* or race for mares, was a truly curious event. It is not known how many laps of the hippodrome were contested, but, on the last lap, the rider dismounted and ran alongside the mare to the finish. The race was first contested in 496 BCE and was dropped in 444 BCE, although only one winner is known, that being Pataikos of Dymai in 496 BCE.

KAMPUCHEA. *See* CAMBODIA.

KANIA-BUSCH-ENKE, KARIN (GDR–SSK). B. 20 June 1961, Dresden. Initially a leading **figure skater**, Karin Kania later became a champion **speed skater** and is one of the very few athletes to have reached world class in both disciplines. As she felt that chances for improvement on her ninth place in the 1977 European Figure Skating Championships were limited, she turned to speed skating with considerable success. Her total of eight medals (three gold, four silver, one bronze) between 1980 and 1988 remains an Olympic record for speed skating, and her record at the World Championships was even more impressive. She won the sprint title a record six times (1980, 1981, 1983, 1984, 1986, 1987), and her five victories in the overall event were also a record for the Championships even though she missed the 1985 Championships because of pregnancy.

KARATE. Karate has never been on the **Olympic program**. But the Fédération Mondiale de Karaté (FMK) is recognized by the **International Olympic Committee** (IOC). Founded in 1992, the FMK had 150 affiliated member nations as of 2000.

KARELIN, ALEKSANDR (URS/EUN/RUS–WRE). B. 19 September 1967. Aleksandr Karelin is one of only four men to have won three Olympic gold medals in **wrestling,** the others being **Ivar Johansson** (SWE), **Aleksandr Medved** (URS/UKR), and **Carl Westergren** (SWE). Known for his strength, Karelin won his first gold medal in 1988 in the super-heavyweight Greco-Roman event, competing for the **Soviet Union**. He defended that title in 1992, competing for the **Unified Team**, and in 1996, competing for **Russia**. He was also World Champion in the class nine times—1989–1991, 1993–1995, and 1998–1999—being undefeated in international competition between 1988 and 1996. Karelin's 12 World and Olympic championships is an all-time best. Karelin competed at Sydney in 2000, attempting to win his fourth consecutive Olympic gold medal, for which he was the heavy favorite. In perhaps the biggest upset of the Olympics, he lost, 1-0, in the final to the unheralded American, Rulon Gardner. Karelin retired after the Sydney Olympics.

KÁRPÁTI, GYÖRGY (HUN–WAP). B. 23 June 1935, Budapest. György Kárpáti played at outside forward and used his great swimming speed to great effect. In his prime, he was considered the fastest **water poloist** in the world. When only 17 years old, he won his first Olympic gold medal in 1952, and this was followed by another gold in 1956, a bronze in 1960, and a third gold in 1964. Kárpáti was a member of the **Hungarian** water polo team that won the European Championships in 1954 and 1962.

KÁRPÁTI, RUDOLF (HUN–FEN). B. 17 July 1920, Budapest. D. 1 February 1999. Rudolf Kárpáti was a member of the noted Hungarian **fencing** teams that dominated saber competition for more than three decades. In team saber, he won Olympic gold medals at four successive Olympics (1948–1960), and he was a member of the winning team at five World Championships (1953–1955, 1957–1958). Individually, Kárpáti was twice Olympic saber champion (1956 and 1960) and twice world saber champion (1954 and 1959). After his retirement, Rudolf Kárpáti became president of the Hungarian Fencing Federation and an administrator with the Fédération Internationale d'Éscrime (FIE). He was also a talented musician and was the leader of the People's Army Central Artistic Ensemble.

KATO, SAWAO (JPN–GYM). B. 11 October 1946, Sugadaira, Niigata Prefecture. Sawao Kato was the winner of a record (for men) eight gold medals for **gymnastics**. He was a member of the winning all-around team in 1968, 1972, and 1976, and also took the individual title on the first two occasions, but had to settle for a silver medal in 1976. Kato's other gold medals came in the individual floor exercises (1968) and the individual parallel bars (1972, 1976).

KAYAKING. See CANOEING AND KAYAKING.

KAZAKSTAN (formerly Kazakhstan) (KAZ, formerly KZK). Kazakstan's **National Olympic Committee** (NOC) was recognized by the **International Olympic Committee** (IOC) in 1992 shortly after the breakup of the **Soviet Union (USSR).** Many Kazakstani athletes competed from 1952 to 1988 for the Soviet Union, and Kazakstani athletes were present at Barcelona and Albertville in 1992 as members of the **Unified Team**. Kazakstan first competed at the Olympics as an independent nation in 1994 at Lillehammer, where its great **cross-country skier** Vladimir Smirnov won three medals, one gold and two silver. Kazakstan made its summer début at the 1996 **Olympic Games** in Atlanta, and it also competed in 1998 at Nagano. Through 2004, Kazakstani athletes have won 31 medals, eight gold, five of the medals at the **Olympic Winter Games**.

KELES. Ancient Olympic sport. In the *keles*, or horse race, the horse with a rider covered six full laps of the hippodrome. The first known champion was in 648 BCE (Krauxidas of Krannon), with champions known through 193 CE (Theopropos of Rhodes). Hieron, Tyrant of Syracuse, is the only known two-time champion — 476 and 472 BCE.

KELETI, ÁGNES (HUN–GYM). B. 9 January 1921, Budapest. Ágnes Keleti won 10 Olympic **gymnastic** medals (five gold, three silver, two bronze) in 1952 and 1956, making her **Hungary**'s most successful female Olympian. Keleti won her first gold in 1952 and then dominated the gymnastics competition at the 1956 Olympics, winning four gold medals. She was originally a fur worker and later a professional cellist. After the 1956 Melbourne Olympics, she defected to **Australia**, but she eventually settled in **Israel** where she became the national women's gymnastics coach.

KELLY, JOHN BRENDEN "JACK" (USA–ROW). B. 4 October 1889, Philadelphia, Pennsylvania. D. 26 June 1960, Philadelphia, Pennsylvania. Jack Kelly is the greatest sculler the **United States** has ever produced. Kelly joined the Vesper Boat Club in 1909. Between 1909 and his competitive retirement after the 1924 Olympics, Kelly won every sculling title available to him, including the World Championship in both singles and doubles, the Olympics in singles and doubles, and many national titles in both boats. Kelly never won the Diamond Sculls at the Henley Regatta because he was denied entry as the Vesper Boat Club was banned for, in the view of the British rowing officials, earlier professional activities. Kelly fathered two very famous children — John Kelly Jr., another Olympic rower who was later U.S. Olympic Committee president, and the late Grace Kelly, the American movie star who later became Princess Grace of **Monaco**.

KENDO (JAPANESE FENCING). *See* BUDO.

KENYA (KEN). The Kenyan **National Olympic Committee** (NOC) was founded in 1955 and recognized by the **International Olympic Committee** (IOC) in the same year. In 1956 it made its Olympic début, and since then it has been absent only from the Olympics of 1976 and 1980, both of which it **boycotted**. Kenya has won 61 Olympic medals through 2004, with 17 gold. Kenya has won seven medals in **boxing**, but all of its other medals are due to its excellent runners, the most outstanding of these having been Kipchoge Keino. Kenya first competed at the **Olympic Winter Games** in 1998, when their sole representative, Paul Boit, finished in 92nd and last place in the 10 km. **cross-country skiing** event. Boit is the nephew of former Kenyan middle-distance Olympian Mike Boit.

KETSEAS, IOANNIS (GRE). B. 16 September 1887, Athens. D. 6 April 1965, Athens. Ioannis Ketseas was the cofounder of the **International Olympic Academy** (IOA) with **Carl Diem**. His lifelong interest in sports led to his becoming president of the Hellenic AAU (SEGAS) in 1929 and president of the Greek Federation of Lawn Tennis in 1939. From 1946 to his death in 1965, he was an **International Olympic Committee** (IOC) member in Greece. His business was as general director of the National Bank of Greece from 1906 to 1928, and he also served the Greek government as Minister of Foreign Affairs from 1921 to 1922. He and Diem founded the IOA officially in 1961, although they had promulgated the idea for almost 30 years. Ketseas served as the first chairman of the Ephoria of the IOA, its ruling council, from 1961 to 1965.

KILLANIN, LORD, OF DUBLIN AND SPIDDAL; SIR MICHAEL MORRIS (IRL). B. 30 July 1914, London, England. D. 25 April 1999, Dublin. Lord Killanin was elected as president of the Olympic Council of Ireland in 1950. He became an **International Olympic Committee** (IOC) member two years later. In 1967, he was elected to the IOC **Executive Board**. In 1968, he ascended to third vice president of the IOC, and in 1970 he was named first vice president. Lord Killanin was elected as president of the IOC in 1972 and held that office until his retirement in 1980, when he was awarded the **Olympic Order** in

Gold. He was also elected Honorary President for Life of the IOC. A noted journalist, author, and film producer, Lord Killanin also served as a director of many leading Irish business companies.

KILLY, JEAN-CLAUDE (FRA–ASK). B. 30 August 1943, Saint-Cloud, Seine-et-Oise. At his Olympic début in 1964, Jean-Claude Killy placed fifth in the giant slalom, but four years later he matched **Toni Sailer**'s 1956 record by winning Olympic gold in all three **alpine skiing** events. Unlike Sailer, who won his events by substantial margins, all Killy's victories were narrow ones, and he only won the slalom after the controversial disqualification of the Austrian, Karl Schranz. Killy was also World Champion in the alpine combination (1966, 1968) and downhill (1966) and was a convincing winner of the first two World Cup competitions (1967, 1968). Following his retirement at the end of the 1968 season, he amassed a fortune from endorsements, and he also became involved in motor racing, films, and professional ski racing. Killy was copresident of the **organizing committee** for the 1992 **Olympic Winter Games** in Albertville. He then became president of the Amaury Group, which controls the Tour de France, the Paris-Dakar auto rally, and *L'Équipe,* the French sporting daily newspaper. Killy is the only person to have won an Olympic gold medal and been awarded the **Olympic Order** in Gold. In addition, in 1995 Killy was elected as a member of the **International Olympic Committee** (IOC).

KIM, NELLI VLADIMIROVNA (URS–GYM). B. 29 July 1957, Surab, Leninabad. Nelli Kim was born of a Korean father and a Russian mother. Blessed with striking good looks, she was the darling of the media who also recognized her exceptional talent as a **gymnast**. She débuted at the World Championships in 1974 as a 17-year-old, finishing third on the balance beam. At the 1976 Montreal Olympics, Kim won three gold medals, but is best remembered for scoring a perfect 10 in the vault and floor exercise. At the 1980 Olympics she helped the **Soviet Union** retain the team championship and shared first place in the floor exercises. Kim was also impressive at the World Championships, at which she won 11 medals between 1974 and 1979. She married international gymnast Vladimir Akhasov.

KIM SOO-NYUNG (KOR–ARC). B. 5 April 1971, Choong Chung Book Province. In only a few short years, Kim Soo-Nyung established herself as the greatest woman **archer** of the modern era. In 1988, Kim won an individual and team gold medal in archery at the Olympics. Nicknamed "Viper," she was women's individual and team World Champion in both 1989 and 1991. Through 1990, she held every women's world record at all distances, and overall as well. At the Barcelona Olympics she again helped **Korea** to the team gold but finished second in the individual event. Kim also competed at Sydney in 2000, winning a bronze medal in the individual event and helping Korea win another team gold medal.

KIRALY, CHARLES FREDERICK "KARCH" (USA–VOL). B. 3 November 1960, Jackson, Michigan. Karch Kiraly is regarded by many as the greatest **volleyballer** ever. In 1986, the Fédération Internationale de Volleyball (FIVB) declared him the top player in the world, the first time that distinction had been given. He won gold medals at the 1984 and 1988 Olympics, 1985 World Cup, 1986 World Championships, 1987 Pan-American Games, and in **beach volleyball** at the 1996 Olympics. Kiraly played at UCLA (University of California at Los Angeles) in college, where he led them to three NCAA (National Collegiate Athletic Association) championships and was twice named most valuable player of the NCAA Tournament. Playing professionally in **Italy**, he helped Il Messaggero win the 1991 World Club Championship. Later a star at beach volleyball, he was the leading professional money winner at that sport from 1991 to 1994, and when that sport débuted at the 1996 **Olympic Games**, Kiraly won the gold medal, partnered by Kent Steffes.

KIRIBATI (KIR). Kiribati is an archipelago nation in the South Pacific Ocean that was formerly known as the Gilbert Islands, and was part of the Gilbert and Ellice Islands. It was a British colony from 1892 but achieved independence in 1979 as two states: Kiribati (Gilbert Islands) and Tuvalu (Ellice Islands). The name is pronounced "Kiribass." Kiribati formed a **National Olympic Committee** (NOC) in 2002 and held its inaugural meeting in November 2002. Kiribati was recognized by the **International Olympic Committee** (IOC) at the 115th session in

Prague on 3 July 2003. At Athens in 2004, Kiribati was represented by three athletes—one female and one male in **track and field**, and one male **weightlifter**.

KIRK, OLIVER (USA–BOX). Oliver Kirk is the only **boxer** to win two gold medals in separate weight classes at the same Olympics, a feat he accomplished at the 1904 St. Louis Olympics and that will surely never again be equaled. Kirk first won the bantamweight division, knocking out George Finnegan, the only other competitor. He was not entered in the featherweight class, but after only two boxers entered, the crowd wanted to see Kirk fight the winner, Frank Haller. Kirk, from the Business Men's Gym in St. Louis, did so and won by decision, and was awarded the gold medal. Kirk is a mystery to Olympic historians as we know nothing else of his athletic career or his life.

KLIMKE, REINER (FRG/GER–EQU). B. 14 January 1936, Münster. Reiner Klimke's six gold and two bronze medals in dressage events stand as the Olympic record for any of the **equestrian** disciplines. He won team gold in 1964, 1968, 1976, 1984, and 1988 and the individual gold in 1984. Klimke's two bronze medals came in the individual event in 1968 and 1976. He also had a fine record at the World Championships, winning six gold medals (two individual [1974, 1982] and four team [1966, 1974, 1982, 1986]).

KOLEHMAINEN, JOHAN PIETARI "HANNES" (FIN–ATH). B. 9 December 1889, Kuopio. D. 11 January 1966, Helsinki. Hannes Kolehmainen was the first of the great Finnish distance runners. At the 1912 Olympics, he won the 5,000 meters with a new world record, the 10,000 meters, and the individual cross-country race, in which he also won a silver medal in the team event. Kolehmainen also set a world record for 3,000 meters in a heat of the team event. The cancellation of the 1916 Games undoubtedly prevented him from winning further Olympic honors, but he returned in 1920 and won the gold medal in the **marathon**. Kolehmainen set eight world records or bests, at distances varying from 3,000 meters to the marathon. In 1952, he lit the **Olympic flame**, after receiving the torch from **Paavo Nurmi**, who had brought it into the Olympic stadium.

KONO, TOMMY TAMIO (USA–WLT). B. 27 June 1930, Sacramento, California. Between 1953 and 1959 Tommy Kono was undefeated as a **weightlifter** in world and Olympic competition, adding six straight world titles to his two Olympic gold medals in the 1952 lightweight class and 1956 light-heavyweight class. He also won three straight gold medals in the Pan-American Games, in 1955, 1959, and 1963. Kono is the only man to ever set world records in four distinct classes, and he won 11 Amateur Athletic Union (AAU) championships—in three different weight classes.

KORBUT, OLGA VALENTINOVNA (URS/BLR–GYM). B. 16 May 1955, Grodno, Belarus, USSR. Olga Korbut burst onto the world's **gymnastics** scene at the 1972 Olympics in Munich, amazing experts with her flexibility and daring moves. A fall on the uneven parallel bars dropped her to seventh overall in the all-around individual. However, she won three gold medals: two individual in the apparatus finals (balance beam and floor exercises) and one with the **Soviet** all-around team. Korbut never defeated her teammate, **Lyudmila Turishcheva**, but she was the darling of the fans and the media for her courage to try new moves, and for her willing smile. She later won the 1973 World University Games all-around title and was second at the 1973 Europeans and 1974 World Championships in all-around. She competed at the 1976 Olympics, winning a gold medal in the team event and a silver on the balance beam. Korbut retired from competition in 1977 and has now settled in Atlanta, Georgia.

KOREA, DEMOCRATIC PEOPLE'S REPUBLIC OF (NORTH) (PRK). The Democratic People's Republic (DPR) of Korea (often termed North Korea) proclaimed its establishment on 9 September 1948. DPR Korea applied to the **International Olympic Committee** (IOC) for recognition in June 1956 and received provisional IOC recognition in 1957, on the understanding that it would only be allowed to compete at Rome in 1960 as a combined team with the **Republic of Korea** (often termed South Korea).

Originally, the IOC policy was for both Koreas to form a combined team, similar to **Germany** in 1956–1964. DPR Korea agreed to this, but South Korea said it was impossible. DPR Korea received full

IOC recognition for its Olympic committee in March 1962. DPR Korea then competed at the Innsbruck **Olympic Winter Games** in 1964, but with a flag that did not conform to the IOC decision made at the 1963 session in Baden-Baden.

DPR Korea was to make its début at the **Olympic Games** in 1964 in Tokyo but withdrew. This was because in November 1963, DPR Korea had competed at the **Games of the New Emerging Forces** (GANEFO). These were highly controversial games that were not recognized by the IOC because GANEFO organizers refused admission to **Israel** and **Taiwan**. All athletes competing in **shooting, swimming,** and **athletics** at GANEFO were banned by their **International Federations** (IFs) from competing at Tokyo in 1964. This included several athletes from DPR Korea, including its greatest athlete, 800 meter world-record holding runner Dan Sin-Kim. When these athletes were not allowed to compete, DPR Korea withdrew in protest.

GANEFO II was held from 25 November to 6 December 1966, and DPR Korea again competed at these games. Because of this, the track and field athletes from DPR Korea who had competed at GANEFO II were subsequently barred from the 1968 Mexico City Olympics, and the nation withdrew again, choosing not to send any athletes.

The 1968 withdrawal was also partly motivated by anger over a recent IOC decision. At the 68th session in Mexico City shortly before the Olympics, the IOC decided that, after 1 November 1968, the nation would be referred to as the Democratic People's Republic of Korea, but that at Mexico City, the nation would compete under its geographic name of North Korea. Precisely similar decisions were made with respect to East Germany and Taiwan, who were forced by the IOC to compete at Mexico City under names they did not recognize, rather than their proper names of the **German Democratic Republic** and Republic of China.

DPR Korea made its first Olympic appearance at the Olympic Winter Games in Innsbruck in 1964. The nation has also competed at the Winter Games of 1972, 1984, 1988, 1992, and 1998. DPR Korea has competed at the Olympic Games of 1972, 1976, 1980, 1992, 1996, 2000, and 2004, also skipping the 1984 Los Angeles Olympics and the 1988 Seoul Olympics. DPR Korea has won 37 Olympic medals through 2004, including eight gold medals, which includes one silver and one bronze medal won at the Winter Games.

DPR Korea withdrew from the 1984 Olympics in obvious sympathy with the Soviet **boycott** of the Los Angeles Olympics. DPR Korea withdrew from the 1988 Olympics in protest of the hosting of the Games by the rival government of the Republic of (South) Korea. Long political discussions were held from 1985 to 1988 between representatives of the **National Olympic Committees** (NOCs) of the two countries. These dealt with demands by the North Koreans to co-host the 1988 Olympics or at least host several of the events. The Korean Olympic Organizing Committee and the IOC were never able to satisfy the demands of the North Koreans, and talks eventually broke off, resulting in the North Korean boycott.

At the 2000 opening ceremony in Sydney, a historic event occurred when the teams from the Democratic People's Republic of Korea and the Republic of Korea marched into the stadium together, led by one flagbearer from each nation at the head of the combined contingent. This "athletic peace" was brokered by the IOC, and it occurred at a time when the two Koreas were also beginning to have some political exchanges for the first time in decades. The flagbearer for DPR Korea at Sydney was the official, Pak Jang-Chul, while the Republic of Korea was led by **basketball** player Chung Eun-Song. *See also* KOREA, REPUBLIC OF.

KOREA, REPUBLIC OF (SOUTH) (KOR). The Republic of Korea, as we know it today, was created on 15 August 1948, after the end of World War II. Korea first officially competed at the 1948 **Olympic Games** in London. However, in both 1932 and 1936, during the occupation of the country by the Japanese (1910–1945), several Korean athletes competed at the Olympic Games wearing the colors of **Japan**. Korea has competed at all Olympics since 1948 with the exception of 1980, when it **boycotted** the Moscow Olympics. Korea also made its first **Olympic Winter Games** appearance in 1948 and has since missed only the Winter celebration of 1952.

Since 1948, Korea has done well in combative sports, winning virtually all of its medals in **boxing, wrestling, judo**, and **weightlifting**. The **women** have also medaled in **volleyball, basketball, field hockey, table tennis**, and **archery**. Korea has won 204 medals through 2004, 66 of them gold. Twenty of these were won at the

Olympic Winter Games. Korea ably hosted the Games of the XXIVth Olympiad in Seoul in 1988. See also KOREA, DEMOCRATIC PEO-PLE'S REPUBLIC OF (NORTH).

KORFBALL. Korfball was contested as a **demonstration sport** at the Olympics of 1920 and 1928. The International Korfball Federation (IKF) is a recognized federation by the **International Olympic Committee** (IOC). Founded in 1933, the IKF had 34 affiliated member nations as of December 2004.

KOSS, JOHANN OLAV (NOR–SSK). B. 29 October 1968, Drammen. Johann Olav Koss was the winner of the 1,500 meters, 5,000 meters, and 10,000 meters **speed skating** events at the 1994 **Olympic Winter Games**, setting a world record in each event. He had earlier won Olympic gold in the 1,500 meters and silver in the 10,000 meters in 1992. In 1994, he donated his first gold medal cash bonus to Olympic Aid for Sarejevo and retired shortly after the Lillehammer Games to pursue a career in medicine. Koss was world all-around champion in 1990, 1991, and 1994, and was also World Cup champion at the distance events in 1991. In 1999, he was named one of the new athlete members to the **International Olympic Committee** (IOC).

KOSTELIĆ, JANICA (CRO–ASK). B. 5 January 1982, Zagreb, Croatia. When only 16 years old, Janica Kostelić competed at the 1998 **Olympic Winter Games**, with a best finish of 8th place in the **alpine** combined. Her skiing improved dramatically as she grew older, and in 2000–2001 she won the overall World Cup title, which stamped her as a favorite going into the Salt Lake City Winter Olympics. She was then made the first athlete to be featured on a Croatian postage stamp. Although much was expected of her in 2002, she exceeded expectations at Salt Lake City by winning three gold medals and adding a silver for her fourth medal. Her golds were in the slalom, giant slalom, and alpine combined, and she finished second in the super-G. Kostelić became the first alpine skier, male or female, to win four medals at one Olympics, and the first woman to win three gold medals at the same Olympic Winter Games. She again dominated the World Cup technical events in the winters of 2002–2003, but then missed the 2003–2004 season due to an injury. She is primarily a technical skier, although she does compete in some downhill races as well as the combined.

KOVÁCS, PÁL (HUN–FEN). B. 17 July 1912. D. 8 July 1995, Debrecen. Pál Kovács began his sports career as a promising hurdler, but he later turned to **fencing** and was a member of the winning **Hungarian** saber team at five successive Olympics (1936–1960). In the individual saber he was Olympic champion in 1953 after winning a bronze in 1948. Kovács was also world saber champion in 1937 and 1953. In 1980, he became vice president of the Fédération Internationale d'Éscrime (FIE).

KRAENZLEIN, ALVIN CHRISTIAN (USA–ATH). B. 12 December 1876, Milwaukee, Wisconsin. D. 6 January 1928, Wilkes Barre, Pennsylvania. At the 1900 Games Alvin Kraenzlein won the 60 meters, the 110 and 200 meter hurdles, and the long jump, and his four individual gold medals remain the unmatched record for a **track and field** athlete at one Games. His pioneering technique of straight-leg hurdling brought him two world hurdle records in addition to his five world records in the long jump. Although a qualified dentist, Kraenzlein never practiced, preferring to become a track coach, notably of the **German** and **Cuban** national teams and at the University of Michigan.

KRAUSSE, STEFAN. *See* BEHRENDT, JAN.

KULAKOVA, GALINA ALEKSEYEVNA (URS–NSK). B. 29 April 1942, Logachi, Udmurtya. Galina Kulakova was the greatest **cross-country skier** of the 1970s, setting records for Olympic medals that would stand until the program was expanded for **women** in late 1980s. Her finest Olympics came in 1972 at Sapporo when she won both individual events for women—5 and 10 km.—and helped the **Soviet Union** to a relay gold medal. She repeated this triple at the 1974 World Championships. In all she won eight Olympic medals and four gold at four Olympics, those of 1968 through 1980. She earned five golds at the World Championships, with a 5 km. individual and relay gold in 1970 added to her feats of 1974. Her career was marred somewhat by a **doping** positive for ephedrine at the 1976 Olympics. In an unusual ruling, the **International Olympic Committee** (IOC) gave her a warning, but no suspension, and allowed her to enter the remaining races.

KURLAND, ROBERT ALBERT (USA–BAS). B. 23 December 1924, St. Louis, Missouri. Bob "Foothills" Kurland was the first dominating seven-footer to play college **basketball**; so dominant, in fact, that he caused the rules-makers to outlaw goaltending, because he could block almost every shot from going into the basket. In 1945 and 1946, he led his Oklahoma A&M team to the NCAA (National Collegiate Athletic Association) championship and then went on to play for six years with the Phillips 66ers, being named Amateur Athletic Union (AAU) All-American every year he played. While playing with Phillips, Kurland became the first man to play on two Olympic championship teams (1948 and 1952).

KUWAIT (KUW). Kuwait's **National Olympic Committee** (NOC) was formed in 1957 and recognized by the **International Olympic Committee** (IOC) in 1966. Kuwait has competed continuously at the **Olympic Games** since 1968. It has yet to win a medal, and it has never competed at the **Olympic Winter Games**. Kuwait's best Olympic finish was equal fifth in 1980 **football** (soccer).

KWAN, MICHELLE WING (USA–FSK). B. 7 July 1980, Torrance, California. Michelle Kwan has been the best **figure skater** of the postschool figure era, but one who has been unable to win an elusive Olympic gold medal. She first competed at the World Championships in 1994, finishing eighth. Her first big season was 1996, when she won the **United States'** and World Championships. She was favored at the 1998 **Olympic Winter Games** in Nagano, but she skated poorly in the free skate and lost out to Tara Lipinski (USA), Kwan earning a silver medal. Michelle Kwan took the rare defeat with magnanimity and came back later in the year to win the World Championships and Goodwill Games. She was also favored at Salt Lake City in 2002, but again had difficulties in the free skate and finished third, with her teammate Sarah Hughes winning the gold medal. Through

2005, Kwan has been U.S. champion nine times and World Champion five times. She continues to skate competitively and likely will compete in 2006 at Torino, trying to shed the title of greatest figure skater without an Olympic gold medal.

KYRGYZSTAN (KGZ). Kyrgyzstan's **National Olympic Committee** (NOC) was recognized by the **International Olympic Committee** (IOC) in 1992 shortly after the breakup of the **Soviet Union**. Several Kyrgyzstani athletes competed from 1952 to 1988 for the Soviet Union, and Kyrgyzstani athletes were present at Barcelona in 1992 as members of the **Unified Team**. Kyrgyzstan's first Olympic appearance as an independent nation occurred in 1994 at Lillehammer, represented by Yevgeniya Roppel. It was also represented by a lone **biathlete** at the 1998 Nagano Winter Olympics and two male skiers at the 2002 **Olympic Winter Games**. Kyrgyzstan made its **Olympic Games** début in 1996 at Atlanta.

KYUDO (JAPANESE ARCHERY). *See* BUDO.

– L –

LACROSSE. Lacrosse was twice on the Olympic program as a full-medal sport, in 1904 and 1908. Lacrosse has also been contested as a **demonstration sport** at the Olympics, in 1928, 1932, and 1948. Strangely, lacrosse does not have an IF that is a member of the **General Association of International Sports Federations** (GAISF).

LAGUTIN, BORIS NIKOLAYEVICH (URS/RUS–BOX). B. 24 June 1938, Moscow. Boris Lagutin began his **boxing** career in 1955. He won his first international title in 1960 and won a bronze medal in the light-middleweight class at the Rome Olympics that year. In 1964 and 1968, Lagutin won the gold medal in the light-middleweight class, making him the second Olympic boxer to win three Olympic medals, after **László Papp** (HUN), and only the second to defend his Olympic title in the same class—after **Great Britain's Harry Mallin**. Lagutin was also European champion in 1961 and 1963.

LAOS (LAO). Laos formed a **National Olympic Committee** (NOC) in 1975 and saw it recognized by the **International Olympic Committee** (IOC) in 1979. Laos's first Olympic appearance was in 1980 at Moscow. The country competed again in 1988, 1992, 1996, 2000, and 2004. It has not competed at the **Olympic Winter Games** and has never won a medal.

LATVIA (LAT). Prior to its annexation by the **Soviet Union** in 1940, Latvia competed at the Olympics of 1924, 1928, 1932, and 1936, winning three medals. Latvia also competed at the **Olympic Winter Games** of 1924, 1928, and 1936. From 1952 to 1988, many Letts (preferred to Latvians) competed for the USSR. After the Soviet revolution of 1991, Latvia declared and was granted its independence, and its **National Olympic Committee** (NOC) was recognized by the **International Olympic Committee** (IOC) in 1991. Latvia returned to the Olympic fold in 1992 by competing at both Albertville and Barcelona and has also competed at Lillehammer in 1994, Atlanta in 1996, Nagano in 1998, Sydney in 2000, and Athens in 2004. Through 2004, Latvia has won 14 medals, one gold, 10 silver, and three bronze.

LATYNINA, LARISA SEMYONOVA (née Diriy) (URS–GYM). B. 27 December 1934, Kherson. Larisa Latynina was a Russian **gymnast** whose total of 18 Olympic medals is an absolute Olympic record. Between 1956 and 1964 she won nine gold, five silver, and four bronze medals with individual gold coming in the floor exercises (1956, 1960, 1964). She dominated other major championships to a similar extent and at the Olympic, World, and European Championships, Latynina won 24 gold, 15 silver, and five bronze for a total of 44 medals. This phenomenal record was achieved despite the fact that her career was interrupted when she gave birth to two children.

LAUSANNE, SWITZERLAND. Lausanne, Switzerland, bills itself as the Olympic City, serving as the headquarters of the **International Olympic Committee** (IOC). The city is located in southwestern Switzerland, on the banks of Lake Geneva (Lake Léman to the Swiss). Lausanne is the capital of the French-speaking canton of Vaud and has a population of approximately 600,000. It rivals

Geneva as the intellectual and cultural center of French Switzerland, with several European writers having lived there, including Voltaire, Rousseau, Charles Dickens, Victor Hugo, Shelley, and Lord Byron. It is home to the Federal Court of Justice and is known as a center for international fairs and conferences. Lausanne was the site of the 1922–1923 peace conference at the end of World War I, at which the Treaty of Lausanne was created, between the Allies and the Ottoman Empire. In 1932, representatives from **Great Britain, Belgium, Italy,** and **France** met in Lausanne and agreed that the Great Depression made the continued payment of **German** war reparations impossible, and the Lausanne Protocol of 1932 ended those payments.

During World War I, **Pierre de Coubertin** felt that the International Olympic Committee (IOC) should be based in a neutral country and chose Switzerland, which he had frequently visited. He moved to Lausanne in 1915, and on 10 April 1915, in the Lausanne Town Hall, he signed an agreement to transfer the base of operations of the IOC to Lausanne, despite objections from other IOC members. But because of the war, the move officially occurred only in 1922, when the IOC headquarters was moved to de Coubertin's home, Mon Repos. The IOC moved its headquarters in 1968 to Château de Vidy, an older building on the banks of Lake Geneva that has since been enlarged several times to house the significantly expanded administrative staff of the IOC. In addition, the **Olympic Museum** is based in Lausanne, in the Ouchy section, about 4 miles (7 km.) from the IOC headquarters, on a hill overlooking Lake Geneva. Because of the presence of the IOC, several **International Federations** (IFs) and the **Court of Arbitration for Sport** (CAS) have established their headquarters in Lausanne as well.

LAZUTINA, LARISA (EUN/RUS–NSK). B. 1 July 1965. Larisa Lazutina followed in the steps of **Galina Kulakova, Yelena Välbe,** and **Raisa Smetanina** as the greatest Russian female **cross-country skier**. She won 11 championships at the Olympics and World Championships, trailing only the 16 won by Välbe. These include six relay titles—Olympics in 1992, 1994, and 1998, and Worlds in 1993, 1995, and 1997. In 1998 at Nagano, she put on her greatest performance, winning medals in all five events open to **women**, with three gold (5 km., pursuit, relay), a silver in the 15 km., and a bronze in the 30 km.

Her individual World Championships came in the 1993 and 1995 5 km., the 1995 15 km., and the 1995 pursuit.

LEBANON (LIB). After the establishment of a **National Olympic Committee** (NOC) in 1947, Lebanon was awarded **International Olympic Committee** (IOC) recognition in 1948 and made its Olympic début that year. Since then Lebanon has competed at every **Olympic Games** with the exception of 1956 when it **boycotted** in protest against the **Israeli** occupation of the Sinai Peninsula. Lebanon competed at every **Olympic Winter Games** from 1948 to 1992, but was not present at the Winter Olympics of 1994 or 1998. Through 2004, Lebanon has won four Olympic medals.

LEDNEV, PAVEL SERAFIMOVICH (URS/UKR–MOP). B. 25 March 1943, Gorky. Although Pavel Lednev never won the Olympic individual modern **pentathlon** title, he won a record seven Olympic medals. In the team event, he took gold in 1972 and 1980 and silver in 1976, and in the individual event he won silver in 1976 and bronze in 1968, 1972, and 1980. In contrast to his Olympic record, Lednev was the individual winner at the World Championships four times (1973, 1974, 1975, 1978) and was twice a member of the winning team at the World Championships (1973, 1974).

LEE, WILLIS AUGUSTUS, JR. (USA–SHO). B. 11 May 1888, Natlee, Kentucky. D. 25 August 1945, Portland, Maine. Willis Lee is the only man to win five gold medals for **shooting** at one Games. He achieved this feat in 1920 when he also won a silver and a bronze. All seven medals were won in team events. A U.S. Naval Academy graduate, he enjoyed a highly successful naval career and commanded the U.S. Pacific fleet during World War II, eventually rising to the rank of vice-admiral. Lee was a member of champion Navy rifle teams in 1908, 1909, 1913, 1919, and 1930. He was a distant relative of Robert E. Lee.

LEINO, EINO AUKUSTI (FIN–WRE). B. 7 April 1891, Kuopio. D. 30 November 1986, Tampere. Eino Leino had a very unusual **wrestling** career. He won medals in freestyle at four consecutive Olympics, making him one of only four wrestlers to win medals at four Games. In 1920, he won the gold medal in the middleweight division, his only Olympic title. He followed this with a welterweight silver in 1924, a lightweight bronze in 1928, and a welterweight bronze in 1932. Strangely, Leino never competed at the European or World Championships. After 1920 he lived in the **United States**, competing mostly there, and winning Amateur Athletic Union (AAU) Championships in 1920 and 1923.

LEMMING, ERIC OTTO VALDEMAR (SWE–ATH). B. 22 February 1880, Göteborg. D. 5 June 1930, Göteborg. Eric Lemming was the first of the great modern javelin throwers. He was Olympic javelin champion in 1906, 1908, and 1912, winning both the orthodox and freestyle event in 1908. He would almost certainly have been the champion in 1900 had the javelin been on the program, but, in the absence of his specialty event, he competed in six other field events, placing fourth in the pole vault and the hammer. In 1906, he also won bronze medals in the shot, **pentathlon**, and **tug-of-war**. As a 19-year-old, Lemming set a world javelin best of 49.32 meters (161′10″) in 1899 and made 13 further improvements to the record, culminating with a mark of 62.32 meters (204′5″) in 1912, which was later accepted as the first official International Amateur Athletic Foundation (IAAF) record.

LEONARD, RAY CHARLES "SUGAR RAY" (USA–BOX). B. 17 May 1956, Wilmington, North Carolina. Sugar Ray Leonard won a gold medal at the 1976 Olympics in Montreal rather easily. After the Olympics, Leonard immediately became one of the top professional welterweight **boxers**. In 1979, he won his first world title by defeating Wilfred Benitez for the WBC version of the welterweight championship. Leonard eventually won world titles in five different weight classes, from welterweight to light-heavyweight. One of the fastest boxers ever, his skills were virtually unmatched, and he deserves comparison as a fighter to his namesake, Sugar Ray Robinson. His popularity also enabled him to command ring fees that made him one of the wealthiest athletes of his time.

LEONIDAS OF RHODES (GRE–ATH). fl. ca. 180–130 BCE. Leonidas of Rhodes was the greatest runner and sprinter of the **an-**

cient **Olympic Games**. He won 12 Olympic titles, the most by any athlete, ancient or modern. In 164, 160, 156, and 152 BCE, he was proclaimed *triastes* or Olympic champion in three events, the *stadion, diaulos*, and **race in armor** (*hoplite*).

LESOTHO (LES). Lesotho formed a **National Olympic Committee** (NOC) in 1971, which was recognized by the **International Olympic Committee** (IOC) in 1972. Lesotho made its Olympic début that year and has since competed at every **Olympic Games** except for those of 1976 when it joined the African **boycott**. Lesotho has never competed at the **Olympic Winter Games** and has never won an Olympic medal.

LEWIS, FREDERICK CARLTON "CARL" (USA–ATH). B. 1 July 1961, Birmingham, Alabama. Carl Lewis is considered by many to be the greatest **track and field** athlete of all time, and, with nine Olympic gold medals, 11 Olympic medals, and seven golds at the World Championships, it is a justifiable claim. His Olympic gold medals came in 1984 (100 meters, 200 meters, 4 × 100 meters relay, long jump), 1988 (100 meters, long jump), 1992 (4 × 100 meters relay, long jump), and 1996 (long jump). His four victories in 1984 matched the record set by **Jesse Owens** at the 1936 Games. He twice set individual world records at 100 meters (1988, 1991), and in the relays he was a member of teams that posted world records at 4 × 100 meters six times and 4 × 200 meters three times. In 1996 at Atlanta, Lewis ended his Olympic career by equaling **Al Oerter**'s record of winning the same Olympic event four times consecutively, with Lewis's feat occurring in the long jump.

LIBERIA (LBR). Liberia first competed at the Olympics in Melbourne in 1956. It has since missed the **Olympic Games** of 1968, 1976, 1980, and 1992. Liberia has not competed at the **Olympic Winter Games** and has not won an Olympic medal.

LIBYA (LBA). Libya formed a **National Olympic Committee** (NOC) in 1962, and although it was recognized by the **International Olympic Committee** (IOC) in 1963, Libya did not take part in the 1964 **Olympic Games**. Libya's first appearance was in 1968, since which time it has competed in the 1980, 1988, 1992, 1996, 2000, and 2004 Olympics. Libya has not competed at the **Olympic Winter Games** and has not won an Olympic medal.

LIECHTENSTEIN (LIE). Liechtenstein made its first Olympic appearances at the Games of 1936, both Winter and Summer. Since that time it has failed to appear only at the 1952 Oslo Winter Olympics, the 1956 Melbourne Olympics, and the 1980 Moscow Olympics. Liechtenstein has the rare distinction of having won medals at the **Olympic Winter Games** (nine, two gold) but not at the Games of the Olympiad. This is because of the country's outstanding **alpine skiers**, and especially two families, the Frommelts and the **Wenzels**.

LIPA-OLENIUC, ELISABETA (née Oleniuc) (ROM–ROW). B. 26 October 1964. Elisabeta Lipa-Oleniuc is the only **rower** to have won eight Olympic medals and the only women rower to win five gold medals. In 1984, as Miss Oleniuc, she won the double sculls (with Marioara Popescu), and after her marriage she took the silver medal in this event in 1988 and 1992 (with **Veronica Cochelea-Cogeanu**). She also won a second gold in the single sculls in 1992 and a bronze in the quadruple sculls in 1988. Lipa-Oleniuc was also World Champion in 1989 in single sculls. Her Olympic career continued with golds in the Romanian eight in 1996, 2000, and 2004.

LITHUANIA (LTU, formerly LIT). Prior to its annexation by the **Soviet Union** in 1940, Lithuania competed at the **Olympic Games** of 1924 and 1928, but failed to win any medals. Lithuania also competed at the 1928 **Olympic Winter Games**. From 1952 to 1988, many Lithuanians competed for the USSR. After the Soviet revolution of 1991, Lithuania declared and was granted its independence, and its **National Olympic Committee** (NOC) was recognized by the **International Olympic Committee** (IOC) in 1991. Lithuania returned to the Olympic fold in 1992 by competing at both Albertville and Barcelona. Subsequently, the nation has competed at the Olympics in Atlanta in 1996, Sydney in 2000, and Athens in 2004, and the Olympic Winter Games of 1992, 1994, 1998, and 2002. Through 2000, Lithuanians have won 11 Olympic medals, four of them gold.

LOUGANIS, GREGORY EFTHIMIOS (USA–DIV). B. 29 January 1960, San Diego, California. Greg Louganis is considered the greatest **diver** of all time. After winning Olympic silver on the platform in 1976, he missed the 1980 Games because of the **boycott**, when he would have been favored to win both diving events. But Louganis returned to win the springboard-platform double in both 1984 and 1988. His 1988 springboard gold was the stuff of high drama when he struck his head on the board during qualifying. He required stitches to continue competing but managed to qualify and won the gold medal the next day. Louganis also took both titles at the World Championships of 1982 and 1986, having earlier won the platform in 1978. Of Samoan and European descent, he studied classical dance for many years, and this training provided the basis for the elegance and artistry of his performances. Louganis's superiority over his contemporaries was considerable, and he held many records for the highest marks ever achieved in competition. After his career ended, it was revealed that he had been HIV-positive at the time of the 1988 Olympics when he sustained his head wound during qualifying.

LOUIS, SPYRIDON (GRE–ATH). B. 12 January 1873, Amarousi. D. 26 March 1940. As the winner of the first Olympic **marathon** at Athens in 1896, Spyridon Louis's place in sporting history is assured. Having placed only fifth in one of the Greek trial races, he was not favored to win the Olympic title, but his unexpected triumph gave **Greece** its only victory in a track and field **athletics** event at the 1896 **Olympics Games**, and Louis was accorded the status of a national hero. Despite the acclaim, Louis returned to his village of Amarousi, where he worked as a shepherd, and he never raced again. He remained an Olympic legend and was a guest of the **organizing committee** at the 1936 Games in Berlin.

LUDING-ROTHENBURGER, CHRISTA (née Rothenburger) (GDR–SSK/CYC). B. 4 December 1959, Weißwasser. Christa Luding-Rothenburger is the only woman to win medals at both the Winter and Summer Games. A **speed-skating** gold medalist at 500 meters (1984) and 1,000 meters (1988), she also won a silver in the **cycling** match sprint in 1988. Luding-Rothenburger also earned a speed-skating silver medal in 1988 and bronze medal in 1992 in the 500 meters. She was a World Champion at both sports, winning the speed-skating sprint title in 1985 and 1988 and the cycling sprint championship in 1986. Although many athletes have demonstrated proficiency in both cycling and speed skating, few have competed at the top level in both sports at the same time, and only Sheila Young (USA) and Beth Heiden (USA) have approached Luding-Rothenburger's success at both.

LUGE. Tobogganing is one of the oldest winter sports. Descriptions of it in the 16th century are found in literature. As a racing sport, it can be traced to the mid-19th century when British tourists started sledding on the snowbound roads of the Alps. The original form of the sport was the **skeleton** sleds that were used on the Cresta Run at St. Moritz. Twice this sport was contested in the Olympics, in 1928 and 1948, both times when the **Olympic Winter Games** were held at St. Moritz.

Luge spread to Switzerland in the 1890s as a variant of the skeleton race. The first recorded competitions took place in 1890 at the Innsbruck-based Academic Alpine Club. An International Tobogganing Association was formed in 1913, and the first European Championships were held in 1914 at Reichenfeld, **Austria**.

At the **International Olympic Committee** (IOC) meeting in Athens in 1954, luge tobogganing was recognized as an official Olympic sport, but luge events were not contested in the Olympics until 1964. The first world luge championships were contested in Oslo in 1955. It was planned to introduce the sport at the 1960 Olympic Winter Games, but the Squaw Valley organizers had decided not to build a bob run and not to hold **bobsled** events, and they likewise opposed building a luge run for the participation of only a few countries. Thus, luge's Olympic début was delayed until 1964. Since that time luge has been contested at all Olympic Winter Games, with a singles and doubles event for men, and a singles event for **women**.

The sport has been dominated by the **Germans**, Austrians, and **Italians**. Luge is now governed by the Fédération Internationale de Luge de Course (FIL), which was formed in 1957 and currently has 48 members.

LUXEMBOURG (LUX). Luxembourg is usually considered to have first competed at the 1912 **Olympic Games**, the same year in which it formed its **National Olympic Committee** (NOC). However, it was recently discovered by French athletics historian Alain Bouillé that Michel Theato, the winner of the 1900 **marathon**, was from Luxembourg, not **France**, as previously believed. Luxembourg has competed at a total of 20 celebrations of the Olympiad since 1912, missing only the 1932 Los Angeles Games. It has also competed at the **Olympic Winter Games** of 1928, 1936, 1988, 1992, 1994, and 1998. Luxembourg has won five Olympic medals (two gold) in sporting events (two at the Olympic Winter Games), and three Olympic medals in the now-defunct **Art Contests**.

– M –

MACEDONIA, FORMER YUGOSLAV REPUBLIC OF (FYROM) (MKD, formerly MCD). This former Yugoslav republic declared its independence from **Yugoslavia** on 8 September 1991. The Olympic Committee of the Former Yugoslav Republic of Macedonia was formed in 1992 and recognized by the **International Olympic Committee** (IOC) in 1993. The republic first competed at the **Olympic Games** as an independent nation in 1996 and at the **Olympic Winter Games** in 1998. The name of the nation, since its independence from Yugoslavia, is very controversial. **Greece**, **Bulgaria**, **Serbia**, and **Albania** all lay claim to regions of Macedonia, and the name. The European Community recognizes Macedonia's independence, but only under the name "Former Yugoslav Republic of Macedonia (FYROM)." In late 2004, the **United States** controversially recognized Macedonia under the name "Republic of Macedonia."

From 1924 to 1988 a few Yugoslav Olympians were from Macedonia. The best-represented sport at the Olympics among Macedonians has been **wrestling**. Both Šaban Trstena and Šaban Šejdi from Skopje won two wrestling medals at the Olympics between 1980 and 1988. At the 2000 Olympics, Macedonia won its first Olympic medal as an independent nation, with a bronze by Mogomed Ibragimov in light-heavyweight freestyle wrestling.

In the Ancient Olympics, it is known that Macedonians, then part of Ancient Greece, won nine championships, including four in the ***stadion*** (sprint) event. Two of these were consecutive by Antigonos in 292–288 BCE. The greatest Olympic champion of ancient Macedonia was Philip II, the father of Alexander the Great, who won three Olympic titles.

MADAGASCAR (MAD). Madagascar formed a **National Olympic Committee** (NOC) in 1964, which was recognized by the **International Olympic Committee** (IOC) that year. Madagascar made its Olympic début in the same year and has since missed only the Games of 1976 and 1988. Madagascar has never competed at the **Olympic Winter Games**, and no Madagascan athlete has won an Olympic medal through 2004. Its top athlete has been the sprinter, Jean-Louis Ravelomanantsoa, who finished eighth in the 100 meters in 1968, the country's best finish ever.

MALAWI (MAW). Founded in 1968, Malawi's **National Olympic Committee** (NOC) was initially granted only provisional recognition by the **International Olympic Committee** (IOC), and full recognition did not follow until 1971. Malawi has competed at the 1972, 1984, 1988, 1992, 1996, and 2000 Olympics. Malawi has never competed at the **Olympic Winter Games**, and through 2004, it has never won an Olympic medal. In 1984, Peter Ayesu, a flyweight **boxer**, won two matches and lost one to finish equal fifth of 32 competitors, the best finish ever by a Malawian Olympian.

MALAYA. *See* MALAYSIA.

MALAYSIA (MAS, formerly MAL). Malaysia has competed in the Olympics since 1956, missing only the 1980 Moscow Olympics. Its **National Olympic Committee** (NOC) was formed in 1953 and recognized by the **International Olympic Committee** (IOC) in 1954. In 1956 and 1960, the country competed as Malaya. In 1963, Malaya joined with **Singapore**, **North Borneo** (now Sabah), and Sarawak to form the Federation of Malaysia. In 1964, Singapore competed as a part of the Malaysian team, but Singapore separated from Malaysia in 1965, and since then Singapore has competed on its own. Malaysia has never competed in the **Olympic Winter Games**. It won its first Olympic medal, a bronze in men's **badminton**, its national sport, in 1992, and has won three Olympic medals, one silver and two bronzes, all in badminton.

MALDIVES (MDV). The Maldives **National Olympic Committee** (NOC) was founded in 1985 and recognized by the **International Olympic Committee** (IOC) that same year. The Maldives has competed at the 1988, 1992, 1996, 2000, and 2004 **Olympic Games**. The nation has not yet competed at the **Olympic Winter Games** and has never won an Olympic medal.

MALI (MLI). Mali formed a **National Olympic Committee** (NOC) in 1962, which was recognized by the **International Olympic Committee** (IOC) in 1963. In 1964 Mali made its first appearance at the **Olympic Games** and has since missed only the 1976 Olympics. It has never won a medal, and it has not competed at the **Olympic Winter Games**. Its best Olympic performance came in 1972 when discus thrower Namakoro Niaré finished 13th of 29 men.

MALLIN, HARRY WILLIAM (GBR–BOX). B. 1 June 1892, Shoreditch, London. D. 8 November 1969, Lewisham, London. With victories in the middleweight division at the 1920 and 1924 Games, Harry Mallin became the first man to successfully defend an Olympic **boxing** title. Even in those days the competence and partiality of the judges posed problems, and Mallin only won his second gold medal after the decision giving the quarterfinal bout to French hometown hero Roger Brousse had been overturned. Mallin's record was incomparable; he was unbeaten in more than 300 fights and won five British amateur titles.

MALTA (MLT). Malta first competed at the Olympics in 1928. It has participated rather sporadically since then, missing the **Olympic Games** of 1932, 1952, 1956, 1964, and 1976. It has never competed at the **Olympic Winter Games**. Malta's top Olympic moment occurred in 1928 when its **water polo** team won one match, defeating Luxembourg 3-1, before losing to France in the second round. This placed it equal fifth, of a starting field of 14 teams.

MANGIAROTTI, EDOARDO (ITA–FEN). B. 7 April 1919, Renate Veduggio, Milan. Edoardo Mangiarotti was the winner of a record 13 Olympic medals (six gold, five silver, two bronze) for **fencing** from 1936 to 1960. He was most successful in the épée team event, winning four gold medals (1936, 1952, 1956, 1960) and a silver (1948).

His other gold medals came in the épée individual (1952) and the foil team (1960). At the World Championships he won two individual épée titles and was a member of 13 winning teams in the épée and foil. Mangiarotti later became secretary-general of the Fédération Internationale d'Éscrime (FIE). His brother, Dario, was also a member of the **Italian** medal-winning Olympic épée teams in 1948 and 1952.

MÄNTYRANTA, EERO ANTERO (FIN–NSK). B. 20 November 1937, Pello, Lapland. Eero Mäntyranta competed at four **Olympic Games** (1960–1972), winning **cross-country skiing** medals at three of them. A member of the **Finnish** 4 × 10 km. relay team from 1960 to 1968, he won gold in 1960, silver in 1964, and a bronze in 1968. At his peak in 1964, Mäntyranta won both the 15 km. and the 30 km. and added a silver and a bronze in these two events in 1968 to bring his total medal haul to seven. He was also World Champion at 30 kilometers in 1962 and 1966. By the time of his fourth Olympic appearance in 1972, he was past his prime and was selected only for the 30 km., in which he finished 19th. He career ended soon afterwards when he had a **doping** positive at the Finnish trials.

MARATHON. The marathon is the longest running event conducted on the track and field **athletics** program at the **Olympic Games**. The marathon standard distance is 42,195 meters (26 miles, 385 yards), although in the early years of the Olympics, it varied from 25 miles to just under 27 miles. The standard distance was first used at the 1908 Olympic Games in London, when the race started by the gardens of Windsor Castle, so the Queen's children could watch the start. The distance from Windsor Castle to the finish line at the White City Stadium was 42,195 meters. This was adopted as the standard in the 1920s. Two marathoners have won the Olympic race twice—**Abebe Bikila** (ETH) in 1960 and 1964, and Waldemar Cierpinski (GDR) in 1976 and 1980. Although it was not always so, the men's marathon now is usually the last event on the last day of the Olympics. **Women** began competing in the Olympic marathon in 1984.

MARKETING COMMISSION. The Marketing Commission, formerly called the New Sources of Financing Commission, was formed in 1983. The most notable chairman of this commission was **Richard Pound**, the Canadian **International Olympic Committee** (IOC) member who has become well known for his negotiating skills with **television** networks and with prospective sponsors of the **Olympic movement**. It was Pound and this commission that were responsible in 1984–1985 for forming **The Olympic Programme** (TOP), which recruits a small number of major corporations to be supporting sponsors of the Olympic movement for each Olympiad. The current commission has 19 IOC members and is headed by the **Norwegian** Gerhard Heiberg. The IOC lists the mandate to this commission as 1) to review and study possible sources of financing and revenue for the IOC and the Olympic movement, whilst ensuring that control of sport rests with sports authorities; 2) to make recommendations to the IOC **Executive Board** regarding marketing and related programs; 3) to monitor the implementation of the IOC's marketing and related programs, and report thereon to the IOC Executive Board; and 4) to seek means of maximizing the potential benefits to the Olympic movement available through association with marketing partners.

MARSHALL ISLANDS. The application by the Marshall Islands, which is a member of the United Nations, to become an IOC member has, to date, not been successful. In 1993 their case was taken up by Paul Wallwork, formerly the IOC member to Samoa, but the IOC's response was that, as citizens of the Marshall Islands carry U.S. passports, the **United States** could, in effect, send a second team to the Olympics. This unusual reply completely overlooked the fact that other territories (e.g., **Guam**, **Puerto Rico**, **British Virgin Islands**, **Netherlands Antilles**, and **American Samoa**) were in a similar situation but had already been accorded membership in the IOC.

MASSON, PAUL (FRA–CYC). B. 1874. D. 1945. At the first modern Olympics in 1896, Paul Masson won three **cycling** events—the match sprint, the one-lap time trial, and the 10,000 meter track event. The three cycling golds at one Games has been bettered among men only by **Marcus Hurley** (USA) in 1904 and equaled only by **Robert Charpentier** (FRA) in 1936. Masson had no significant international record prior to the 1896 Olympics. After the Olympics he turned professional, adopting the name Paul Nossam (Masson spelled backwards). His only significant performance as Paul Nossam was third in the world professional sprint championship in 1897. Paul Masson was not related to the namesake of the famous wine company.

MATHIAS, ROBERT BRUCE "BOB" (USA–ATH). B. 19 November 1930, Tulare, California. Bob Mathias was the first of only two men to win successive Olympic decathlon titles. His first gold medal came in 1948 when, as a 17-year-old, he became the youngest-ever winner of an Olympic **track and field** event. Mathias set his third world record in defending his title in 1952, but the following year he forfeited his amateur status by starring in a film of his life. Although a professional, he was, as a Marine officer, eligible to compete in the 1956 Inter-Services championships when he won his 11th and final decathlon competition to maintain his unbeaten record in the event. A politician later in life, Mathias was first elected as a Republican congressman for California in 1966. He served four terms in the House of Representatives before losing out in the Democratic landslide of 1974. In 1973, he introduced legislation to amend the U.S. **Olympic Charter** that effectively created a Bill of Rights for amateur athletes. *See also* THOMPSON, FRANCIS MORGAN.

MATTHES, ROLAND (GDR–SWI). B. 17 November 1950, Pössneck. With victories in the 100 meter and 200 meter backstrokes at both the 1968 and 1972 Games, Roland Matthes is the most successful male backstroke **swimmer** of the Olympics. He also won two silver and one bronze medal in the relays and added his eighth Olympic medal (a bronze) in the 1976 100 meter backstroke. Matthes set 16 world backstroke records (eight at each distance) but was also a world-class performer in other events, winning silver medals at the European Championships in the freestyle and butterfly and setting three European butterfly records. He was briefly married to **Kornelia Ender**.

MAURITANIA (MTN). Mauritania formed a provisional **National Olympic Committee** (NOC) in 1962, but in 1977 a more formal body was constituted. After the **International Olympic Committee** (IOC) granted provisional recognition in 1979, full recognition followed in

1980. Mauritania first competed at the **Olympic Games** in 1984 and has been present at each of the subsequent Olympics. It has never competed at the **Olympic Winter Games** and has never won an Olympic medal.

MAURITIUS (MRI). Mauritius formed a **National Olympic Committee** (NOC) in 1971 but did not compete at the Olympics until 1984 in Los Angeles. Mauritius has also competed at the **Olympic Games** of 1988, 1992, 1996, 2000, and 2004. Mauritius has never competed at the **Olympic Winter Games** and has never won an Olympic medal.

MBAYE, KÉBA (SEN). Over the last 20 years, Kéba Mbaye has been one of the more influential **International Olympic Committee** (IOC) members, probably serving on more commissions than any nonpresidential IOC member, with the exception of **Dick Pound**. Mbaye's background is as a lawyer. He served as a vice president of the International Court of Justice and as honorary chief justice of the Supreme Court of Senegal. He has served as chairman of the **Court of Arbitration for Sport** (CAS) since 1983. First elected to the IOC in 1973, he served on the IOC **Executive Board** from 1984 to 1988 and 1993 to 1998, and as an IOC vice president from 1988 to 1992 and 1998 to 2002. He became an **honorary IOC member** in 2002. He served as chairman of the following IOC commissions: Apartheid and Olympism (1989–1992), Information on the Olympic Movement in the Baltic States (1990–1991), **Sport and Law** (1995–2002), **Juridical** (1993–2002), Study of the Centennial Olympic Congress, Congress of Unity (1994–1996), **Ethics** (1999–), and **Nominations** (2000–2002).

McCORMICK, PATRICIA JOAN KELLER (née Keller) (USA–DIV). B. 12 May 1930, Seal Beach, California. With victories in both the springboard and platform at the 1952 and 1956 Olympics, Pat McCormick became the first **diver** in history to win four Olympic gold medals. Her second double victory at Melbourne came only five months after the birth of her son. Pat McCormick won 17 Amateur Athletic Union (AAU) titles at the outdoor championships, at all three levels— one-meter and three-meter springboard, and the one-meter platform— and nine indoor AAU championships. McCormick's husband was the

AAU champion at both springboard and platform, and her daughter, Kelly, was on the U.S. diving team at the 1983 Pan-American Games. Kelly also competed for the **United States** at the 1984 and 1988 Olympics, winning a silver in 1984 and a bronze in 1988, both on the springboard.

McGEE, BRADLEY JOHN (AUS–CYC). B. 24 February 1976, Sydney, New South Wales. With five Olympic medals, Brad McGee has equaled the modern mark for most medals among Olympic **cyclists**, originally set by **Daniel Morelon**. McGee first competed at the Olympics in 1996, winning bronze medals in both the individual and team pursuit events. At Sydney in 2000, he again finished third in the individual pursuit. In 2004, McGee improved to a silver in the individual pursuit and helped Australia to a gold medal in the team pursuit. He also rode on the World Championship–winning Australian pursuit team in 1995. In 1998, McGee won gold medals in the individual and team pursuit at the Commonwealth Games. Brad McGee has since joined the professional *péloton*, where he is known primarily as a sprinter. In 2003 he held the *maillot jaune* at the Tour de France for four days, and in 2004, wore the *maglia rosa* at the Giro d'Italia for three days. This makes him the only **Australian** to earn the leader's jerseys at the two most prestigious cycling tours. He has twice won stages at the Tour de France and in 2002, won the points classification at the Dauphiné-Libere.

McKAY, JAMES KENNETH "JIM" (née James Kenneth Mc-Manus) (USA). B. 24 September 1921, Philadelphia, Pennsylvania. In the **United States**, Jim McKay achieved fame as the "Voice of the Olympics." He was host or cohost on the U.S. **television** network televising the Olympics an unprecedented seven times: six times for ABC Sports—1976 and 1984 for the **Olympic Games**, and for the **Olympic Winter Games** consecutively from 1976 through 1988—and for CBS in 1960. McKay was not the main studio host in 1972 at Munich, but it was there that he achieved his greatest fame as an Olympics host. He was called on to broadcast the news reports of the horrific **Israeli** hostage massacre, and he was on the air in the United States for over 15 consecutive hours. He was the one who eventually told the world, in his own poignant words, "They're all gone." He was awarded an Emmy for that broadcast, one of ten individual Emmys won by McKay, nine for sportscaster of the year, and one for lifetime achievement.

MEAGHER, MARY TERSTEGGE (USA–SWI). B. 27 October 1964, Louisville, Kentucky. Mary T. Meagher is the greatest female butterfly **swimmer** ever, and for her feats she earned the nickname of "Madame Butterfly." Meagher won three gold medals at the 1984 Olympics, in both butterfly events, and on the 4 × 100 meter medley relay. In 1988, by then past her prime, she earned a bronze in the 200 meter butterfly and a silver with the medley relay. Meagher would likely have won both butterfly events in 1980 had the **United States** not **boycotted** the Moscow Olympics. She was World Champion in 1982 over 100 meters and in 1986 over 200 meters. She set two world butterfly records over 100 meters, and five over 200 meters, beginning in 1979. Her performance at the 1981 U.S. Nationals remains her greatest effort when she set world records of 57.93 for 100 meters and 2:05.96 for 200 meters, both of which lasted until the late 1990s.

MEDICAL COMMISSION. The Medical Commission is the oldest permanent **International Olympic Committee** (IOC) commission, having been officially formed in 1966, and actually starting as a working group in 1961. The current chairman is Arne Ljungqvist, a **Swedish** IOC member. The longest-serving chairman was the **Belgian** IOC member, Prince Alexandre de Merode, now deceased. The commission has several consultant members, along with members from the **NOCs, IFs**, and the **OCOGs**. The Medical Commission's primary responsibility is the fight against **doping** and writing and rewriting the medical bylaws to the **Olympic Charter**. This commission has also dealt with the question of determining female identity, originally called sex testing, but now known by the politically correct name of **gender identification**. The IOC notes that the Medical Commission is charged with 1) protection of the health of athletes; 2) respect for both medical and sport ethics; and 3) equality for all competing athletes. It also describes the work of the Medical Commission as having included 1) establishing the Olympic Movement Anti-Doping Code, which is applicable to all constituents of the

Olympic movement; 2) the IOC World Congress on Sport Sciences, the main forum for all the scientists working close to the athlete, held every two years; and 3) the IOC Olympic Prize on Sport Sciences, which is awarded to researchers who have excelled in the field of science applied to human movement, physical activity, and sports. Some of its work on doping control has now been ceded to the **World Anti-Doping Agency**.

MEDVED, ALEKSANDR VASILYEVICH (née) Oleksander Medvid (URS/UKR–WRE). B. 16 September 1937, Belaya Tserkov, Kiev Oblast, Ukraine. With victories in the freestyle light-heavyweight (1964), heavyweight (1968), and super-heavyweight (1972) divisions, Aleksandr Medved was the first **wrestler** to win gold medals at three successive **Olympic Games**. He also won seven world titles. Medved's record was remarkable for the fact that his physique seldom matched that of his opponents; on his way to the Olympic super-heavyweight title in 1972 he overcame the giant American bronze medalist Chris Taylor, who enjoyed an incredible weight advantage of almost 100 pounds (45 kg). His World Championships came at light-heavyweight (1962, 1963, and 1966) and at super-heavyweight (1967, 1969, 1970, and 1971). Medved was European champion in 1966, 1968, and 1972, competing less often at that meet.

MEXICO (MEX). Mexican athletes first competed at the 1900 **Olympic Games** when several **polo** players of mixed Mexican/Spanish ancestry played at Paris. Mexico did not compete again at the Olympics until 1924, but it has competed since without fail. Mexico sent five **bobsled** competitors to the 1928 **Olympic Winter Games**, and in 1932 it entered another bobsled team but it did not compete. Its other Winter Olympic appearances have come in 1984, 1988, 1992, and 1994. Mexico has won 52 Olympic medals, 11 of them gold, all at the Games of the Olympiad. Mexico also hosted the Games of the XIXth Olympiad at Mexico City in 1968.

MEYER, DEBORAH "DEBBIE" (later Reyes) (USA–SWI). B. 14 August 1952, Haddonfield, New Jersey. With victories in the 200 meter, 400 meter, and 800 meter freestyles in 1968, Debbie Meyer became the first woman **swimmer** to win three individual gold medals at one **Olympic Games**. She won each event by a large margin and achieved her unique Olympic treble despite the fact that she was handicapped by a severe upset stomach in Mexico City. Between 1967 and 1970 Meyer set 15 world records and retired before her abilities had been fully extended.

MICRONESIA, FEDERATED STATES OF (FSM). After becoming a member of the United Nations in 1991, the Federated States of Micronesia formed a **National Olympic Committee** (NOC) in 1995. The **International Olympic Committee** (IOC) recognized Micronesia in 1997. Micronesia first competed at the 2000 Olympic Games in Sydney, represented by five athletes—two in **track and field** (one man/one woman), two in **swimming** (one man/one woman), and one in **weightlifting** (one man). Micronesia also competed in 2004 at Athens, represented by an exactly similar roster.

MILITARY SKI PATROL. A military ski patrol event was held at the **Olympic Winter Games** in 1928, 1936, and 1948 as a **demonstration sport**. The event was also contested at the 1924 Olympic Winter Games in Chamonix and, until recently, has always been considered a demonstration event. But more recent evidence makes it clear that this was a full-medal event in 1924 and not a demonstration. Military ski patrol is an event similar to team **biathlon**, in which all the team members ski together over a course, stopping periodically to shoot at targets.

MILON OF KROTON (GRE–WRE). fl. ca. 540–508 BCE. The son of the well-known athlete Diotimos, Milon of Kroton was the greatest **wrestler** of Ancient Greece and the **Ancient Olympic Games**. He was champion six times at the Olympic Games (540 BCE in boys' wrestling and 532–516 BCE in wrestling), seven times at the **Pythian Games**, 10 times at the **Isthmian Games**, and nine times at the **Nemean Games**. In four Olympiads, he was *periodonikes*, meaning he won all of the four major festival titles. The base of his statue at Ancient Olympia reads, "he had never been brought to his knees." Milon's strength was supposedly developed when he was a young boy and began carrying a wild heifer on his shoulders. As the heifer grew, Milon continued to carry it for exercise and his strength became legendary, but it eventually killed him. One day in a forest, he saw a tree that had been cut open with wedges in it. He decided to pull open the trunk with his massive hands, but when he did this the wedges flew out and the trunk trapped his hands. He was caught in the tree and wild beasts tore him to pieces that night.

MITCHELL REPORT. *See* OLYMPIC BRIBERY SCANDAL.

MITTERMAIER, ROSI (later Neurather) (FRG–ASK). B. 5 August 1930, Reit-im-Winkel. Rosi Mittermaier had a long career in international **skiing**, winning 10 individual World Cup races between 1969 and 1976. In 1976, she was the World Champion in **alpine** combined and led the overall World Cup, although she did not lead in any of the individual disciplines. Mittermaier's greatest fame came at the 1976 **Olympic Winter Games** when she won the slalom and downhill. With the giant slalom still to come, she had a chance to equal the feats of **Toni Sailer** and **Jean-Claude Killy** by winning all three available alpine ski events. However, in the giant slalom, she finished second, losing out by 12/100th's of a second to **Canada**'s Kathy Kreiner. Mittermaier later married Christian Neurather, another **German** Olympic skier.

MIYAKE, YOSHINOBU (JPN–WLT). B. 24 November 1939. Yoshinobu Miyake was **Japan**'s greatest **weightlifter** ever. He finished second in the 1960 Olympic bantamweight class but won gold medals at the 1964 and 1968 Olympics as a featherweight. He also won World Championships in 1962–1963 and 1965–1966. Miyake set 25 world records, including 10 consecutive records in the snatch and nine consecutive total records in the 60 kg. class.

MODERN PENTATHLON. Modern pentathlon is a sport invented by the founder of the **Olympic Games**, the **Baron Pierre de Coubertin**. It is better termed the "military pentathlon," as it supposedly mimics the skills needed by a soldier. He must first ride a horse and then fight off an enemy with a sword. He must then swim a river to escape, then fight off more enemies with a pistol, and finally, effect the final escape by running a cross-country course.

Coubertin was able to get the sport on the **Olympic program** in 1912. The order of the events has varied, but the current order is as in the soldier's trial—riding, **fencing**, **swimming**, **shooting**, and cross-country running. The riding is a cross-country steeplechase course. Fencing is a series of one-touch bouts done with épée swords. Shooting is done with an air pistol from 10 meters, but was formerly performed with a rapid-fire pistol. The swim is now a 200 meter freestyle (formerly 300 meters) and the run is a 3,000 meter cross-country event (formerly 4,000 meters). The final event is now arranged such that the runners leave the start in the order of their positions after four events. Further, the starts are arranged such that the time intervals correspond to the number of points separating the competitors. Thus, the finishing order in the run now corresponds exactly to the finishing order of the entire pentathlon, adding to the drama of the event. Beginning at the 1995 World Championships and the 1996 Olympics, the modern pentathlon was changed so that all the events are now contested in one day.

Modern pentathlon was originally dominated by the Swedes. After World War II, the Hungarians and the Soviets became the top countries. Scoring was originally on a points-for-place system with the lowest score winning, but the competition is now scored using tables for each of the five events.

Modern pentathlon is governed by the Union Internationale de Pentathlon Moderne (UIPM), which was founded in 1948 and currently has 94 members. Originally, **biathlon** and modern pentathlon were governed together, by the Union Internationale de Pentathlon Moderne et Biathlon (UIPMB), but the federation split into two separate groups in 1993, with the International Biathlon Union governing that sport. A modern pentathlon event for **women** débuted on the Olympic program at Sydney in 2000. Within the **International Olympic Committee** (IOC), there has been some discussion recently about removing modern pentathlon from the Olympic program.

MOLDOVA (MLD). Moldova was formerly the Soviet Republic of Moldavia, which achieved independence after the **Soviet** breakup of 1991. Its **National Olympic Committee** (NOC) was formed shortly thereafter and recognized by the **International Olympic Committee** (IOC) in 1993. Though the smallest of the former Soviet Republics, a few Moldavan athletes competed from 1952 to 1988 for the Soviet Union, and Moldavan athletes were present at Barcelona in 1992 as members of the **Unified Team**. Moldova first competed at the Olympics as an independent nation in 1994 at Lillehammer, represented by one male and one female biathlete. It first competed at the **Summer Olympic Games** in Atlanta in 1996, and also competed in 1998 at Nagano, the 2000 Olympics in Sydney, the 2002 Salt Lake **Olympic Winter Games**, and the 2004 Olympics in Athens. To date, Moldova has won four Olympic medals.

MONACO (MON). Monaco competed at the 1920 **Olympic Games** and has since missed only the Games of 1932, 1956, and 1980. Since first competing at the **Olympic Winter Games** in 1984, it has been represented at each of the subsequent Winter Olympics. The country has been represented in the **bobsled** events by Albert Grimaldi, Prince of Monaco, an **International Olympic Committee** (IOC) member and the son of Prince Rainier and Princess Grace. No Monegasque athlete has won a medal in a sporting event, but in 1924 Julien Médecin won a bronze medal in the architecture portion of the now-defunct **Art Contests**.

MONGOLIA (MGL). Mongolia has competed at the **Olympic Games** since 1964, its only absence being the 1984 Los Angeles Olympics, which it **boycotted**. Its first Olympic appearance was at the 1964 Winter Olympics, and it has since missed only the 1976 **Olympic Winter Games**. Mongolia claims the unusual distinction of having won the most Olympic medals of any country that has not yet won a gold medal (15 through 2004, all in the Olympic Games).

MONTI, EUGENIO (ITA–BOB). B. 23 January 1928, Dobbiaco, Bolzano. Eugenio Monti is considered the greatest **bobsled** driver in history. After winning two Olympic silver medals in 1956 he was deprived of the opportunity of further honors in 1960 as the bobsled was not included in the program at Squaw Valley. At his second Olympics in 1964 he won two bronze medals, and in 1968, Monti took the gold medals in both events. The bobsled events at the 1968 **Olympic Winter Games** also carried the status of the World Championships, and, including his Olympic victories, Monti won the world title in the two-man event eight times and was the world four-man champion three times. He retired after the 1968 Olympics and became the Italian team manager. In addition to his championships he is known for his sportsmanship at the 1964 Innsbruck Winter Olympics. Trailing the British team of Anthony Nash and Robin Dixon going into the final run, he lent them a bolt off his own sled when theirs failed. Nash and Dixon won the gold medal, but for this magnanimous action, Monti was awarded the International Fair Play Award. At the victory ceremony, Nash and Dixon pulled Monti up to the top step of the podium, to join in their victory.

MORELON, DANIEL (FRA–CYC). B. 24 July 1944, Bourg-en-Bresse. Between 1966 and 1975, Daniel Morelon won a record nine world amateur sprint titles and three Olympic gold medals. He won the Olympic match sprint in 1968 and 1972 to become the first of only two men to claim a repeat victory in the event. In 1968 he also won the tandem match sprint partnered by Pierre Trentin. Together they had also won the world title in 1966. Morelon won a total of 14 French titles and set a world indoor record for 500 meters in 1976. He was essentially a track sprinter and saw no need to turn professional. After retirement he became the French sprint cycling coach.

MOROCCO (MAR). Morocco has competed at eleven **Olympic Games**. First appearing in 1960, it has since missed only the 1980 Games. Morocco has sent athletes to the **Olympic Winter Games** in 1968, 1984, 1988, and 1992. Through 2004, Moroccan athletes have won 19 Olympic medals, 16 in track and field **athletics** and three in **boxing**.

MORROW, BOBBY JOE (USA–ATH). B. 15 October 1935, Harlingen, Texas. Bobby Joe Morrow was the winner of gold medals in the 100 meters, 200 meters, and the 4 × 100 meter relay at the 1956 Games. In winning the 200 meters he became the first man to set an official world record for this distance at the **Olympic Games**. He also equaled the world record for 100 meters three times during the Olympic year, equaled the world 100 yards record in 1957, and was a member of six world record–breaking teams in the sprint relays (4 × 100 and 4 × 200, or the imperial equivalents). Morrow won four Amateur Athletic Union (AAU) titles between 1955 and 1958, but he failed to make the 1960 U.S. Olympic team.

MOSES, EDWIN CORLEY (USA–ATH). B. 31 August 1955, Dayton, Ohio. Edwin Moses dominated the 400 meter hurdles like few athletes have ever dominated an event. He won the Olympic gold medal in 1976 and 1984, and only the American boycott of the Moscow Olympics in 1980 prevented him winning a third gold medal. In 1988, he competed again, but past his prime, he won a bronze medal. Moses set the first of his four world records in the event in the 1976 Olympic final, and at one stage of his career, he won 122 successive races, including the first World Championships in 1983. Moses took the **Olympic oath** on behalf of the competitors at the opening ceremony of the 1984 **Olympic Games**. He was also briefly a member of the U.S. World Cup **bobsled** team in 1990–1991.

MOTORBOATING. Motorboating was contested at the Olympics only in 1908. Motorboating will not be appearing on the **Olympic program** in the near future and, in fact, the **Olympic Charter** precludes the sport, as Rule 47.4.2 states, "Sports, disciplines or events in which performance depends essentially on mechanical propulsion are not acceptable." However, the Union International Motonautique (UIM) does have provisional **International Olympic Committee** (IOC) recognition, although it is not clear why, since the rules do not allow motorboating on the Olympic program. It should be noted, however, that aeronautics, automobile racing, and motorcycling also have **International Federations** (IFs) that have been granted provisional IOC recognition. Founded in 1922, the UIM currently has 60 members.

MOTORCYCLING. Motorcycling has never been contested at the Olympics, even as a **demonstration sport**. It is highly unlikely that motorcycling will be on the **Olympic program** at any time in the foreseeable future as the **Olympic Charter** actually precludes the sport. Rule 47.4.2 states, "Sports, disciplines or events in which performance depends essentially on mechanical propulsion are not acceptable." However, the Fédération Internationale de Motocyclisme (FIM) does have provisional **International Olympic Committee**

(IOC) recognition, although it is not clear why, since the Olympic Charter would preclude motorcycling from appearing on the Olympic program. It should be noted, however, that aeronautics, automobile racing, and motorcycling also have **International Federations** (IFs) that have been granted provisional IOC recognition. Founded in 1904, the FIM currently has 88 members.

MOZAMBIQUE (MOZ). Since making its Olympic début in 1980, Mozambique has competed at each of the subsequent **Olympic Games**. Mozambique has not yet competed at the **Olympic Winter Games**. Their only medal winner has been middle-distance running phenomenon Maria Lurdes Mutola, who won bronze in the women's 800 meters in 1996 and succeeded to the gold medal in that event in 2000.

MUCH WENLOCK OLYMPIAN GAMES. The Much Wenlock Olympian Games were one of the various attempts at revival of the **Ancient Olympic Games** that preceded **Pierre de Coubertin**'s successful attempt. Much Wenlock is a small town in Shropshire, England, 12 miles south of Shrewsbury and 40 miles west of Birmingham. On 22 October 1850, these games were held for the first time. They were the brainchild of British sports enthusiast **Dr. William Penny Brookes** (1809–1895).

The games were only national in nature, and the events were those of a British medieval country fair enriched by modern athletic sports disciplines. The original events in 1850 consisted of cricket, 14-a-side football, high and long jumping, quoits, a hopping race, and a running race. However, several athletic events were added in the next few editions. But, in 1855, a popular event was the blindfolded wheelbarrow race, and in 1858 a pig race was contested in which the pig "led its pursuers over hedge and ditch right into the town where it took ground in the cellar of Mr. Blakeway's house; and where it was captured by a man called William Hill." The most popular event became tilting-at-the-ring, which was first held in 1858. The competitors, compulsorily dressed in medieval costume, rode down a straight course and used their lances to spear a small ring, suspended from a bar over the course.

The Much Wenlock Olympian Games, altogether 45 in number up to 1895, achieved their high point in the 1860s and 1870s. In those years, representatives of the **German** Gymnastic Society (which was based in London) competed regularly. In 1859, Brookes contacted the **Greeks** and donated a £10 prize to the **Zappas Olympic Games**. The winner of the long footrace at the 1859 Zappas Olympics, Petros Velissariou, was made an honorary member of the Much Wenlock Olympian Society.

In 1860, 1861, 1862, and 1864, Brookes also organized the Shropshire Olympian Games on a regional level in, respectively, Much Wenlock, Wellington, Much Wenlock, and Shrewsbury. These were followed by the games organized by the National Olympic Association: 1866 (London), 1867 (Birmingham), 1868 (Wellington), 1874 (Much Wenlock), 1877 (Shrewsbury), and 1883 (Hadley).

The Much Wenlock Olympian Games were held more sporadically after Brookes's death in 1895, but they are actually still held today, sponsored by the Much Wenlock Olympian Society, which celebrated the 100th Much Wenlock Olympian Games in 1986. The Much Wenlock Olympian Games are important in the history of Olympic revivals because of their influence on Pierre de Coubertin. Coubertin knew of Brookes's efforts and visited the Much Wenlock Olympian Games as a guest of honor in October 1890. In 1891, he donated a gold medal that was given to the winner of tilting-at-the-ring. However, as early as 1881, William Penny Brookes was the first person ever to propose that an international Olympic festival be staged in Athens. *See also* ATTEMPTS AT REVIVAL.

MULTI-EVENTS (DECATHLON, HEPTATHLON, PENTATHLON). Since the late 19th century, there have always been multi-events contested in track and field **athletics**, in an attempt to determine the greatest all-around athlete. The first of these was the all-around event, which was contested at the 1904 **Olympics Games** for the only time. In 1906, a **pentathlon** event similar to the Ancient pentathlon was contested at Athens. In 1912, men began competing in the 10-event decathlon. The decathlon is considered the truest test of all-around athletic ability. A portion of the track and field athletics program, it consists of 10 events conducted over two days: Day One—100 meters, long jump, shot put, high jump, and 400 meters; Day Two—110 meter hurdles, discus throw, pole vault, javelin throw, and 1,500 meters. The winner of the Olympic decathlon is usually accorded the title of the "World's Greatest Athlete." Two decathletes have won the Olympic decathlon twice—**Bob Mathias** (USA) and **Daley Thompson** (GBR).

Women first began competing in athletics multi-events in 1964 with the addition of a pentathlon to the program, consisting of the 200 meters, high jump, long jump, shot put, and originally the 80 meter hurdles. The 200 meters was later replaced by the 800 meters, and the hurdle event lengthened to 100 meters. In 1984, the women's multi-event was changed to a seven-event heptathlon over two days, consisting of the following events: Day One—100 meter hurdles, high jump, shot put, and 200 meters; Day Two—long jump, javelin throw, and 800 meters. It is planned that women will soon move up to the decathlon, contesting the same events as men, although the field events will be held on opposite days to the men's. The best known female heptathlete has been Jackie Joyner-Kersee (USA), who won the gold medal in the event in 1988 and 1992 and was the first woman to better 7,000 points.

MUSIOL, BOGDAN (GDR/GER–BOB). B. 25 July 1957, Swielochowice, Poland. Bogdan Musiol was the winner of an Olympic gold medal with the GDR four-man **bobsled** team in 1980, when he also won a bronze medal in the two-man. He went on to win silver medals in 1984 and 1988 at both the two-man and four-man, and in 1992, he won his silver medal in the two-man. In 1989, Musiol won the world two-man title as the brakeman for **Wolfgang Hoppe**, with whom he won an Olympic silver in 1988.

MYANMAR (MYA). As Burma (name change in May 1989), Myanmar competed at all Olympics from 1948 through 1988, with the exception of the 1976 Olympics. As Myanmar, the nation has also competed at the 1992, 1996, 2000, and 2004 **Olympic Games**. It has never attended the **Olympic Winter Games** nor has it won a medal. Its best finishes by men at the Olympics have been fifth in 1972 flyweight **weightlifting** by Gyi Aung and equal fifth in 1964 by featherweight **boxer** Tun Tim. But in 2000 at Sydney, Win Kay Thi finished fourth in women's 48 kg. class weightlifting.

– N –

NABER, JOHN PHILLIPS (USA–SWI). B. 20 January 1956, Evanston, Illinois. At the 1976 Games John Naber won four gold medals, each in world record time, and his records in the 100 and 200 meter backstrokes remained unbeaten for seven years. He also won gold in the 4 × 100 meter freestyle relay and the medley relay and won a silver in the 200 meter freestyle. Perhaps the greatest of these performances came in the 200 meter backstroke when Naber became the first man to break two minutes for the distance. After winning three gold medals at the 1977 Pan-American Games, he retired from international competition.

NADI, NEDO (ITA–FEN). B. 9 June 1894, Livorno. D. 29 January 1940, Rome. Nedo Nadi was the most versatile **fencer** in history, and he uniquely won an Olympic title with each of the three weapons at the same Games. In 1912, he won the individual foil title, and then, in 1920, he produced one of the greatest of all Olympic performances. He won the individual foil and saber titles and led the **Italians** to victory in all three team events. His brother, Aldo, also won a gold medal in each of the three team events. After the 1920 Olympics, Nedo Nadi taught as a professional in South America, but on his return he was reinstated as an amateur and served as president of the Italian Fencing Federation.

NAMIBIA (NAM). Namibia's **National Olympic Committee** (NOC) was recognized by the **International Olympic Committee** (IOC) at its summer session in 1991. It competed at the 1992 and 1996 Olympics where sprinter Frank Fredericks won two silver medals at each **Olympic Games**, earning all of Namibia's four Olympic medals. Namibia has not yet competed at the **Olympic Winter Games**. Namibia also competed in 2000 at Sydney and at Athens in 2004.

NATIONAL GOVERNING BODIES (NGBs). Each sport on the **Olympic program** is governed by an **International Federation** (IF). Each nation competing at the **Olympic Games** must have a properly formed **National Olympic Committees** (NOCs). In each nation, the various sports have National Governing Bodies (NGBs) that are responsible for the administration of that sport in that nation. The NGBs are invariably members of both their own NOC and the respective IF. As an example, the governing body of track and field **athletics** in the United States is USA Track and Field (USATF), which is a member of the United States Olympic Committee (USOC) and the International Amateur Athletic Federation (IAAF).

NATIONAL OLYMPIAN ASSOCIATIONS (NOAs). *See* WORLD OLYMPIANS ASSOCIATION (WOA).

NATIONAL OLYMPIC ACADEMIES (NOAs). *See* INTERNATIONAL OLYMPIC ACADEMY (IOA).

NATIONAL OLYMPIC COMMITTEES (NOCs). National Olympic Committees (NOCs) are the bodies responsible for the **Olympic movement** in their respective countries. The **Olympic Charter** states that their mission "is to develop and protect the Olympic Movement in their respective countries, in accordance with the *Olympic Charter*." National Olympic Committees have not always been representative of autonomous national regions. Currently, **Puerto Rico**, which is a Commonwealth of the United States, has its own NOC. In the early part of this century, Bohemia was represented on the **International Olympic Committee** (IOC), even though it was only a part of the Austro-Hungarian Empire. For the most part, however, NOCs represent independent nations. They are recognized by the IOC at the IOC sessions. There are currently 202 National Olympic Committees recognized by the IOC.

NOCs are very important to the athletes competing in the **Olympic Games**. Specifically, athletes may not enter the Olympic Games independently or as individual competitors, but may only represent an NOC, and they must be entered by their NOC. In addition, NOCs often provide financial assistance for training and allow athletes to compete internationally.

NOCs are supposed to be autonomous and resist political pressures and influences of any kind, but that principle has been recognized more in word than deed. Notably, prior to the fall of the Soviet bloc, all the Eastern European Communist nations had NOCs that basically were puppets of their governments. And, in 1980, the **United States**

Olympic Committee (USOC) was coerced into **boycotting** the Moscow Olympics (against its wishes) by the U.S. president and government to protest the Soviet invasion of Afghanistan.

NAURU (NRU). Nauru's **National Olympic Committee** (NOC) was recognized by the **International Olympic Committee** (IOC) at the 1994 **Olympic Congress** after having been given provisional recognition earlier in 1994. Nauru first competed in the Olympics in 1996. It has since competed in 2000 and 2004, represented to date in only one sport at the **Olympic Games**, **weightlifting**, with both men and women competing in 2000 and 2004.

NECKERMANN, JOSEF (FRG–EQU). B. 5 June 1912, Würzburg. D. 13 January 1992, Dreieich. Josef Neckermann was an extremely wealthy man who earned his money from his mail-order and department store businesses. His wealth allowed him and his family to pursue their passion for **equestrian** sports. Neckermann competed in the dressage at four **Olympic Games** (1960–1972) and won a medal on each occasion. To his gold medals in the team event in 1964 and 1968, he added two silver and two bronze medals. His daughter, Eva-Maria Pracht, won a team bronze representing **Canada** in 1988, and her daughter, Martina—Neckermann's granddaughter—also represented Canada at the 1992 Olympics.

NEHMER, MEINHARD (GDR–BOB). B. 13 January 1941, Boblin. Meinhard Nehmer only took up **bobsledding** after retiring from **athletics**, in which he was a nationally ranked javelin thrower. Although well past the age of 30, he formed a formidable partnership with **Bernhard Germeshausen**, and they won the 1976 Olympic two-man and were both members of the winning four-man crew in 1976 and 1980. Nehmer and Germeshausen share the record for the most gold medals won by bobsledders. Nehmer also won an Olympic bronze medal in the two-man in 1980 with Bogdan Musiol, and he was coach of the U.S. bobsled team for the 1992 Olympics.

NEMEAN GAMES. The Nemean Games were one of the four great Panhellenic sporting festivals, along with the **Olympic Games, Isthmian Games**, and **Pythian Games**. They were held biennially, with the first known Nemean Games being contested in 573 BCE. The Nemean Games were held in honor of Zeus. They were held in July in the Nemean sanctuary in Argolis. The Nemean sanctuary was near the site on the Peloponnesus where Hercules killed and skinned the Nemean lion, the first of his famed twelve labors. Winners in the Nemean Games were crowned with a wreath of fresh wild celery.

NEMOV, ALEKSEY (RUS–GYM). B. 28 May 1976, Barashevo, Soviet Union. Aleksey Nemov has won 12 Olympic medals in **gymnastics**, the most by any gymnast since the breakup of the **Soviet** juggernaut gymnastic teams of the 1960s and 1970s. He starred at the 1996 and 2000 **Olympic Games**, unusually winning two gold, one silver, and three bronze medals both times. He has won three individual Olympic gold medals—1996 horse vault, and 2000 all-around and horizontal bar. Nemov also competed in 2004, but well past his prime, his top performance was a fifth on the horizontal bar, his best event. Nemov won 11 medals at the World Championships between 1993 and 2002, including five individual gold medals. He also won eight medals at the European Championships, with four gold medals, three in individual events.

NEPAL (NEP). The Nepalese **National Olympic Committee** (NOC) was founded in 1962 and recognized by the **International Olympic Committee** (IOC) in the following year. Nepal first competed at the **Olympic Games** in 1964, and since then it has missed only the 1968 Olympics. This Himalayan country first competed at the **Olympic Winter Games** in 2002 at Salt Lake City.

NETBALL. Netball has never been contested at the **Olympic Games**, even as a **demonstration sport**. However, its governing body, the International Federation of Netball Associations (IFNA), is recognized by the **International Olympic Committee** (IOC). Founded in 1960, it currently has 38 affiliated nations.

NETHERLANDS ANTILLES (AHO). Known as Curaçao, the name of the capital city, until 1948, the Netherlands Antilles formed a **National Olympic Committee** (NOC) in 1931 with a view to participating in the 1932 Los Angeles Olympics. Although recognized by the **International**

Olympic Committee (IOC) in 1931, representation at the 1932 **Olympic Games** did not materialize, and there was little Olympic activity in the nation for many years. IOC recognition was reconfirmed in 1950, and the Netherlands Antilles first competed at the Olympics in 1952 when they were represented by a **football (soccer)** team. The nation did not travel to Melbourne in 1956, and it **boycotted** the 1980 Olympics, but it has otherwise competed at every Olympic Games since 1952. The Netherlands Antilles made its **Olympic Winter Games** début in 1988 at Calgary and also competed in 1992 at Albertville. The Netherlands Antilles has won one Olympic medal, a silver by Jan Boersma in boardsailing in 1988.

NETHERLANDS, THE (NED, formerly HOL). The Netherlands sent 27 athletes to the 1900 Paris Olympics. After missing the 1904 St. Louis Olympics, the Netherlands has never missed another **Olympic Games**, although in 1956 it competed only at the Equestrian Games in Stockholm, **boycotting** the 1956 Olympic Games in protest of the **Soviet** invasion of **Hungary**. At the **Olympic Winter Games**, the Netherlands appeared first in 1928, missed the 1932 Lake Placid Games, but has appeared continuously since. In the Summer Games, the Netherlands has had a variety of successes in different sports but has never dominated any sport. In the Winter Olympics, however, the Netherlands has always been one of the very top nations in **speed skating**. The Netherlands has won 304 Olympic medals, 87 of them gold. Of these, 69 medals and 22 gold medals were won at the Olympic Winter Games. The Netherlands hosted the Games of the IXth Olympiad in Amsterdam in 1928.

NEW ZEALAND (NZL). New Zealand was first represented at the 1908 Olympic Games. In that year it formed a combined team with **Australia** as Australasia. One New Zealander competitor, Harry Kerr, a walker, won a bronze in the 3,500 meter walk. In 1912, three New Zealanders competed with Australasia. Finally, in 1920 at Antwerp, New Zealand took part in the **Olympic Games** as a separate nation, and it has never missed an Olympic Games since. New Zealand competed at its first **Olympic Winter Games** in 1952 at Oslo. It missed the Winter Games of 1956 and 1964 but has competed at all the others since 1952. New Zealand has had its greatest success in **track and field** with several of its middle-distance runners being Olympic champions. New Zealand has won 80 Olympic medals, 33 of them gold.

NI XIONG (CHN–DIV). B. 6 January 1974, Hu Nan. With five Olympic medals, Ni Xiong trails only **Dmitry Sautin** among Olympic **divers**. In 1988, Ni won his first Olympic medal, a silver behind **Greg Louganis** on the platform. In 1992, Ni finished third in the Olympic platform event. Turning his emphasis to the springboard, he won the gold medal in 1996 and 2000, and in 2000, he added a gold medal in the new event of synchronized springboard diving, partnered by Xiao Hailiang. In 2000, Ni and Xiao also won the World Cup and the Grand Prix Super Final in synchronized springboard.

NICARAGUA (NCA). Although the **International Olympic Committee** (IOC) recognized their **National Olympic Committee** (NOC) in 1959, Nicaragua did not compete at the 1960 or 1964 Olympics, and it was not until 1968 that it first competed at the **Olympic Games**. Apart from missing the 1988 Olympics in Seoul, Nicaragua's Olympic participation has been continuous since 1968. The country has never competed in the **Olympic Winter Games**. Its best Olympic performance occurred in 1992 when flyweight **weightlifter** Alvaro Marenco Ramos finished 11th of 17 lifters in his class.

NIEMANN-STIRNEMANN-KLEEMANN, GUNDA (née Gunda Kleemann) (GER–SSK). B. 7 September 1966, Sondershausen. Gunda Niemann-Stirnemann has won eight Olympic medals and three golds at the **Olympics Winter Games** of 1992, 1994, and 1998, equaling the marks of fellow **German Karin Kania-Enke**. Primarily a distance skater, her golds came at 3,000 meters in 1992 and 1998 and at 5,000 meters in 1992. At the World All-Around championships, Niemann-Stirnemann has won seven championships—1991–1993 and 1995–1998, breaking Kania-Enke's record of five titles. She also won the World Cup title at 1,500 meters in 1991–1993 and 1995–1998, and at distances (3K and 5K) in 1992–1996 and 1998. She has set 14 world records (through February 2000)—six at 3,000 meters, four at 5,000 meters, and four in the combined all-around.

NIGER (NIG). After recognition by the **International Olympic Committee** (IOC) early in 1964, Niger made its Olympic début in Tokyo later that year when it was represented by one **boxer**. Niger did not take part in the 1976 or 1980 **Olympic Games** but has competed at all the other Olympics since 1964. Niger has never competed at the **Olympic Winter Games**. To date, Issaka Daborg has won the only Olympic medal for this country in 1972 when he finished third in light-welterweight boxing.

NIGERIA (NGR). The Nigerian **National Olympic Committee** (NOC) was formed in 1951 and recognized by the **International Olympic Committee** (IOC) in the same year. Nigeria first competed in the Olympics in 1952. It has since missed only the 1976 **Olympic Games**, owing to the African **boycott**. Nigeria has not yet competed at the **Olympic Winter Games**. Nigerians have won 19 Olympic medals, including two golds. Six of these have come in **boxing**, 11 in track and field **athletics**, one in **weightlifting**, and one from their 1996 **soccer (football)** team.

NOMINATIONS COMMISSION. The Nominations Commission was formed at the 110th **International Olympic Committee** (IOC) session in 1999 in order to institute a procedure for electing and re-electing IOC Members. The commission's charge is to prepare a report on each prospective IOC candidate and present it to the IOC **Executive Board**. The Nominations Commission is composed of seven members, three chosen by the **IOC Ethics Commission**, three chosen by the IOC session, and one chosen by the IOC **Athletes Commission**. The members serve a four-year term and may be reelected. The current (2005) chairman is Francisco Elizalde (PHI).

NORDIC GAMES. The **Olympic Winter Games** formally began in 1924 at Chamonix, although they were originally known as the *Semaine internationale des sports d'hiver* (International Winter Sports Week). Prior to that time, winter sports events had been held during the Summer Games of 1908 (**figure skating**) and 1920 (figure skating and **ice hockey**). But there existed an earlier international winter sports festival, the Nordic Games, which began in 1901. Suggested by **Sweden**'s Professor E. Johan Widmark, the initiative to hold

Nordic Games was taken in 1899, the first ones being arranged in 1901. After this inaugural event in Stockholm, Sweden, Nordic Games were held in 1905, 1909, 1913, 1917, 1922, and 1926, always during February, mostly in Stockholm. They began, and were perpetuated, largely by the work of the influential Swedish sports administrator Viktor Gustaf Balck. The Nordic Games were not without political problems, nor were they originally planned as precursors to the Olympic Winter Games, as often stated. In fact, despite Balck's influential status on the **International Olympic Committee** (IOC), he and other Swedish and **Norwegian** sporting leaders opposed early suggestions to start Olympic Winter Games. The Olympic Winter Games themselves began only after several heated IOC debates concerning their merits. The Nordic Games ended after 1926, partly because of the growth of the Olympic Winter Games, partly because of Balck's death and the loss of his leadership, and partly because of the growth of the Fédération Internationale de Ski.

NORDIC SKIING. Nordic skiing has been practiced in the Scandinavian countries since the 18th century, and competitions are known from the early 19th century. The sport has been on the **Olympic program** since the Chamonix Games of 1924. The international governing body is the Fédération Internationale de Ski (FIS), which was founded in 1924 and has 101 members (2004).

Nordic skiing consists of three major disciplines: **cross-country skiing**, **ski jumping**, and nordic combined, combining elements of both cross-country and ski jumping. All three disciplines have been contested at all Winter Olympics. **Women** compete only in cross-country skiing and first began to do so in 1952. Nordic skiing has been dominated, not surprisingly, by the Scandinavian countries and the **Soviet Union** and **Russia**.

Cross-country skiing consists of races varying from 10 to 50 kilometers for men, and from 5 to 20 kilometers for women, as well as relay races. The skiers race in time-trial fashion, starting at intervals. Match sprint racing over 1,500 meters will be added to the Olympic program in 2002. Ski jumping is contested on two hills, a 90 meter and a 120 meter hill, called the normal hill and the large hill. The size of the hill is not necessarily 90 or 120 meters, but those figures refer to the expected length of the jumps measured to the "norm" point of the hill. Nordic combined consists of a cross-country ski race and ski jumping with the results determined by a points table. In 1988, team events for men in both nordic combined and ski jumping were added to the Olympic program.

In the 1980s, cross-country skiing underwent a revolution that was started by Bill Koch, the first American to be a top international skier. He changed from the classic cross-country of alternating legs and arms with the stride being pushed straight backwards, remaining in the ski track, to a style similar to skating on skis. The FIS was pushed to ban this style by the north Europeans, but it was decided instead to allow two styles. However, races are now designated as either "classic" or "freestyle," with skating being allowed in freestyle races. Men's 50 km. and women's 20 km. racers were permitted to use any style. In the relays, the classical style must be used for the first 100 meters, for safety reasons as the relays are a mass start, but after that the racers may use the skating technique.

NORELIUS, MARTHA (USA–SWI). B. 20 January 1908, Stockholm, Sweden. D. 23 September 1955. Martha Norelius was America's first great female **swimmer**. She was originally coached by her father, Charles Norelius, who swam for **Sweden** at the 1906 Olympics. She was the top U.S. swimmer from 1924 to 1929 with her fame resting primarily on her Olympic accomplishments. In 1924 at Paris, she won the 400 meter freestyle event, and in 1928 she defended that championship, winning the final with a world record of 5:42.8. She is the only woman to have defended the 400 meter event at the Olympics. At the 1928 Olympics, Norelius won her third gold medal when she swam on the 4 × 100 meter freestyle relay team.

Norelius won 11 individual Amateur Athletic Union (AAU) titles between 1925 and 1929, and between 1925 and 1928 she set 19 world records and 30 American records. In 1929 Norelius was suspended by the AAU for giving an exhibition in the same pool as some professionals. She therefore decided to turn professional herself and won the $10,000 Wrigley Marathon in Toronto. While there she met Joe Wright, one of **Canada**'s greatest **rowers**. Wright had won an Olympic silver medal for Canada in the 1928 double sculls, and also played professional football with the Toronto Argonauts of the Canadian Football League. Norelius and Wright were subsequently married on 15 March 1930.

NORTH BORNEO. Borneo is one of the world's largest islands, bordering the South China Sea. The northern section of the island was formerly an independent state called North Borneo. North Borneo competed at the **Olympic Games** one time only, at Melbourne in 1956. The northern part of the island is now divided into two states of **Malaysia**—Sabah and Sarawak and the independent sultanate of **Brunei.** The southern part of the island is ruled by **Indonesia** and is known as Kalimantan.

NORTHERN RHODESIA. *See* ZAMBIA.

NORWAY (NOR). Norway competed at the Olympics of 1900 and has since missed only the 1904 and the 1980 **Olympic Games.** Norway has competed at every **Olympic Winter Games.** Until 1984, Norway could claim to be the top nation at the Olympic Winter Games in terms of medals and gold medals won. In that year, however, the **Soviet Union** surpassed Norway in both categories. With the demise of the Soviet Union, Norway again tops the list of most medals won by a single country at the Olympic Winter Games with 264, 96 of them gold medals. Norway shares with **Liechtenstein** and **Austria** the unusual distinction of having won more medals in the Winter Games than in the Summer Olympics. Norway has twice hosted the Olympic Winter Games, in 1952 in Oslo and in 1994 in Lillehammer.

NOVIKOV, IGOR ALEKSANDROVICH (URS/ARM–MOP). B. 19 October 1929, Drezna, Moscow Oblast. Igor Novikov was one of the most consistent performers in the modern **pentathlon.** At the 1952–1964 Olympics, he finished fourth, fourth, fifth, and second in the individual event. In the team event, Novikov won two gold medals (1956 and 1964) and a silver (1960). He was heavily favored to win the individual gold medal in 1960, based on his string of world titles (1957–1959 and later in 1961), but he finished fifth because of difficulty in the riding sequence. Strong at all five disciplines, Novikov set a world pentathlon best for the **fencing** section when he won the 1957 World Championship. Novikov became a coach and held several administrative positions in sports.

NURMI, PAAVO JOHANNES (FIN–ATH). B. 13 June 1897, Turku. D. 2 October 1973, Helsinki. Paavo Nurmi was an Olympic legend whose dedication to a rigorous training schedule and mastery of pace judgment brought a new dimension to distance running. Between 1920 and 1928 he won a record nine Olympic gold medals (seven individual, two team) and three individual silver medals. His medals came in a wide range of events: 1,500 meters, 3,000 meters (team), 5,000 meters, 10,000 meters, steeplechase, and cross-country. In 1932, Nurmi was banned for alleged professionalism and missed the chance to add the 1932 **marathon**, for which he was one of the favorites, to his list of Olympic successes. Although subsequently reinstated as an amateur for domestic races, he continued to be excluded from international competition, a decision that left him embittered for the rest of his life. However, Nurmi returned to the Olympic arena in 1952 when he carried the torch at the opening ceremony. The incomparable "Flying Finn" set 22 official and 13 unofficial world records, and statues (done by Waino Aaltonen in 1925) honoring his feats stand in his hometown of Turku, outside the Olympic stadium in Helsinki, and in the park of the **Olympic Museum** in **Lausanne**.

NYKÄNEN, MATTI ENSIO (FIN–NSK). B. 17 July 1963, Jyvaskyla. Matti Nykänen was the winner of a record four Olympic gold medals for **ski jumping**. At the 1984 **Olympic Winter Games** Matti Nykänen won on the large hill and placed second on the normal hill before winning both events in 1988 when he won a further gold medal in the newly introduced team event. He was also the World Champion on the large hill in 1982 and won four World Cup titles between 1983 and 1988. A controversial and often ill-tempered individual, Nykänen earned considerable respect for his sporting talents but little for his general behavior. In 1991 he launched a career as a pop singer. In late 2004, he was arrested and was to be imprisoned after being found guilty of assault and battery.

– O –

OCEANIA NATIONAL OLYMPIC COMMITTEES (ONOC). The Oceania National Olympic Committees, headquartered in **Fiji**, is a confederation of 14 **National Olympic Committees** (NOC) from Oceania and is one of the recognized organizations of the **International**

Olympic Committee (IOC). It was created on 25 September 1981 to promote the **Olympic movement** and its ideals in Oceania and to encourage and assist in the promotion and development of Olympic sports in Oceania. The presidents of ONOC have been Harold Austad (NZL) (1981–1983), Sir Lance Cross (NZL) (1983–1989), and currently, IOC member Kevan Gosper of **Australia** (1989 to date).

OERTER, ALFRED ADOLPH (USA–ATH). B. 19 September 1936, Astoria, New York. Al Oerter, a discus thrower, was the first **track and field** athlete to win four successive Olympic titles, a feat since equaled by **Carl Lewis** in the long jump. Oerter won the gold medal in the discus in 1956, 1960, 1964, and 1968, setting a new Olympic record on each occasion, although he was never the favorite to win the event. His third victory in 1964 was remarkable for the fact that he overcame the handicap of neck and rib injuries but still managed to set a career best. He also won the Pan-American title in 1959 and set four world records, the first of which in 1962 gave him the distinction of being the first man to record a legal throw of over 200 feet (60.96 meters). In 1979, Oerter came out of retirement with the goal of earning a fifth gold medal. He threw well in 1980, finishing fourth at the U.S. Olympic trials, but his chances were lost earlier than that by the 1980 U.S. **boycott**.

OFFICIAL REPORTS. At the end of every **Olympic Games** and **Olympic Winter Games**, the organizing committee of the Games is required to compile a comprehensive report of the organization, planning, finances, and results of the Olympic Games. The **Olympic Charter** requires that the official report be published in at least French and English. It is now common that the report is published in French, English, and the language of the host nation, and often in Spanish and German as well. Some of the reports are compiled as one book, with parallel texts in differing languages, but the more recent ones, which are larger, tend to be published as separate editions by language. There have only been a few instances in which an official report was not issued. In 1900, the report consisted of the report of the Physical Culture section of the Exposition Universalle. In 1904, there were two reports, neither of which would be considered comprehensive by today's standards. In 1924, the report of the Olympic

Winter Games was not issued separately but published at the end of the report of the 1924 Paris Olympic Games. There were reports issued by the scheduled host cities for the 1916 Olympic Games and the 1940 Olympic Games and Olympic Winter Games. No reports were ever issued for the scheduled 1944 Olympics.

OLYMPIAD. An Olympiad is a measure of time, designating a period of four consecutive years. Until the most recent edition of the **Olympic Charter**, the definition of an Olympiad has been that it begins with the opening of one edition of the Games of the Olympiad and ends with the opening of the following edition. However, in the current edition of the Olympic Charter, as of 1 September 2004, the rule has been changed and an Olympiad is now defined as a period of four consecutive calendar years, beginning on the first of January of the first year and ending on the thirty-first of December of the fourth year. Unfortunately, the current rule does not actually define the "first year of," nor the "fourth year of," but based on a later rule an Olympiad now appears to begin on 1 January of the year in which the Games of the Olympiad are held. The term is based on the Greeks, who used the term *Olympiad* to measure the time between **Olympic Games**. Olympiad may be the term associated with the Olympics that is most often misused by the public, the media, and broadcasters. Specifically, the Olympic Games are not an "Olympiad." They are correctly termed the "Games of the Olympiad."

OLYMPIC ANTHEM. An Olympic anthem, also called the Olympic hymn, was composed for the 1896 Olympic Games by Greek composer Spyros Samaras (1863–1917), with words added by his colleague Kostis Palamas. The Olympic anthem was first played at the 1896 Olympic opening ceremonies, performed by nine bands and a chorus. It was used again in 1906. Thereafter, a variety of musical offerings provided the background to the opening ceremonies until 1960. In 1954, the **International Olympic Committee** (IOC) launched a worldwide competition for a new version of an Olympic anthem. From the 392 scores presented, the first prize went to Michael Spisak for his ultramodern atonal work, with lyrics extracted from **Pindar**'s odes. It was never terribly popular, and Spisak's demands for excessive royalties led it not to be chosen as the official

Olympic anthem. It was elected to return to the Samaras/Palamas composition as the official Olympic anthem.

The Samaras/Palamas anthem was played and sung at the 55th IOC session in 1958 in Tokyo. It was such an impressive demonstration that IOC member Prince Axel (DEN) suggested that it should be adopted as the official anthem. This was unanimously approved, although two years of legal work then took place dealing with the heirs of Samaras and Palamas.

The Olympic anthem was first used in that regard at the opening ceremonies in Rome three years later, since which time it has become an established part of the Olympic ceremonies. The **Olympic Charter** terms this the Olympic anthem, although it is often referred to as the Olympic hymn.

In English, the lyrics to the Olympic anthem are as follows:

> Immortal spirit of antiquity,
> Father of the true, beautiful and good,
> Descend, appear, shed over us thy light
> Upon this ground and under this sky
> Which has first witnessed thy unperishable fame
> Give life and animation to those noble games!
> Throw wreaths of fadeless flowers to the victors
> In the race and in the strife!
> Create in our breasts, hearts of steel!
> In thy light, plains, mountains and seas
> Shine in a roseate hue and form a vast temple
> To which all nations throng to adore thee,
> Oh immortal spirit of antiquity!

OLYMPIC BRIBERY SCANDAL. On 24 November 1998, the Salt Lake City (Utah) television station KTVX reported that the Salt Lake Organizing Committee for the **Olympic Winter Games** of 2002 (SLOC) had been paying for Sonia Essomba to attend American University in Washington. Sonia Essomba was the daughter of René Essomba, the late **International Olympic Committee** (IOC) member (1978–1998) to **Cameroon**. The payments, it would be revealed, were part of a larger scheme set up by the SLOC to award scholarships to the family members and friends of IOC members in an effort to win their votes to become the host city. Within a few days after the revelation of the Essomba "scholarship," the media reported that, beginning in 1991, shortly after Salt Lake City had lost the 1998 Winter Olympic bid to Nagano, 13 individuals had received scholarship assistance worth almost $400,000 from the Salt Lake Organizing Committee or SLOC. Of these 13 individuals, at least six were close relatives of IOC members.

Shortly thereafter, at the close of the IOC **Executive Board,** on 12 December 1998, Swiss IOC member Marc Hodler spoke openly to the press, stating that at least 5–7 percent of IOC members had taken or solicited bribes by bid cities. Within a few days, all manner of revelations were published by the media, which descended like sharks on a feeding frenzy. Shortly before Hodler's interview, upon the recommendation of the **Juridical Commission**, President **Juan Antonio Samaranch** had already formed an ad hoc commission to look into the allegations and accusations made against the host cities and bid cities. Canada's **Dick Pound** was named to head the inquiry, usually called the Pound Commission.

At the beginning of 1999, investigating the IOC and the bid city process seemed to be all the rage. In addition to the Pound Commission, the SLOC formed its own Board of Ethics to investigate its own practices. The U.S. Olympic Committee (USOC) also formed an investigative panel, headed by the former U.S. senator from Maine, George Mitchell. Concurrently, the Federal Bureau of Investigation (FBI) began its own inquiry into the SLOC to determine if any federal laws were violated relating to bribery and the Foreign Corrupt Practices Act. Of note, only the Pound Commission actually interviewed the IOC members under investigation, allowing them a chance to answer the charges before them.

New announcements from Salt Lake City appeared in the press almost daily in January 1999. On 7 January the Associated Press reported that IOC member Jean-Claude Ganga of the Republic of Congo had earned a $60,000 profit on a land deal arranged by a member of the SLOC. On 8 January 1999, the president and CEO of the SLOC, G. Frank Joklik, resigned, as did his senior vice president, Dave Johnson. At his press conference, Joklik described some of the transgressions of the bid committee and the SLOC, and said,

> Therefore, I have today obtained the resignation of David Johnson, who was a vice president of the Bid Committee, and has been acting as

senior vice president of the organizing committee until today. I have recommended the appointment of a new chief operating officer. The other two principal members of the Bid Committee, Tom Welch, who was chief executive officer and Craig Peterson, who was the chief administrative officer, are no longer employees of the corporation. . . . Finally, to ensure that the Games go immediately forward, I must take steps of my own. Although I had no knowledge of these improper payments during my tenure as the volunteer chairman of the Board of Trustees of the Bid Committee, in order to assure the people of Salt Lake City, the state of Utah, and the world that the organizing committee is distinct from the Bid Committee and is off to a fresh start, I have tendered my resignation today.

Tom Welch was the main impetus behind the Salt Lake City bid to host the 2002 Winter Olympics. Though no longer in an administrative position with the SLOC, he was on their payroll as a consultant when the scandal hit. Joklik stated that Welch's consulting agreement was terminated as of his announcement. Over the next few months, Welch was a marked man, and a reclusive one, who made no public statements but spoke only through his lawyers.

On 15 January 1999, Samaranch called for an extraordinary IOC session to be held in **Lausanne, Switzerland**, on 17–18 March, but he also stated that he would not resign, despite frequent calls in the media for him to do so. On 19 January, Finnish IOC member Pirjo Häggmann resigned. She was one of the first two female members of the IOC, having served since 1981. But her "crime" was that her ex-husband had worked for the Salt Lake City Bid Committee and had also worked for the Toronto Bid Committee when that city bid to host the 1996 Olympics. The second IOC member to resign was the Libyan, Bashir Mohamed Attarabulsi, who did so on 22 January. It was revealed that his son had attended an English-language center at Brigham Young University in Salt Lake City, with tuition paid by the SLOC and the son was provided with $700/month by the organizing committee. The Sydney bid for the 2000 Olympics, to date, had been relatively unscathed. But on the same day that Attarabulsi resigned, John Coates, who had headed the Sydney bid, admitted that he had made last-minute offers of $70,000 to two African IOC officials, but he said the action was legitimate.

On 23 January, the IOC Executive Board met in Lausanne to discuss the preliminary findings of the Pound Commission and make some early decisions. At the end of the meeting, Samaranch announced that the IOC had made mistakes, that they were responsible, and that it must never happen again. Six IOC members were suspended, pending the final Pound Report, with a vote to be taken on their possible expulsion at the special IOC session in March.

The six IOC members suspended (and eventually expelled) were Lamine Keita of **Mali**, Agustin Arroyo of **Ecuador**, Charles Mukora of **Kenya**, Zein El-Abdin Mohamed Ahmed Abdel Gadir of **Sudan**, Sergio Santander Fantini of **Chile**, and the aforementioned Jean-Claude Ganga. A third member resigned voluntarily, David Sibandze of **Swaziland**, while investigations continued into the status of other members.

On 8 February 1999, the Board of Ethics of the Salt Lake Organizing Committee for the Olympic Winter Games of 2002 was released. It described a litany of indiscretions by the bid committee and the SLOC. These included payment of hundreds of thousands of dollars to IOC members and their families, usually in the form of "scholarship assistance." As an example, the revelations that began the scandal, the payments to Sonia Essomba, were noted to total $108,350. The Board of Ethics Report also revealed direct monetary payments to IOC members, often in the form of sports assistance programs for their **National Olympic Committees** (NOCs).

The Board of Ethics did not stop with the above, and it noted that "Many witnesses before the Board of Ethics described Mr. [Jean-Claude] Ganga as the IOC member who most took advantage of the Bid Committee's and the community's generosity." The report then gave details of a litany of indiscretions concerning Ganga and the Salt Lake City Bid Committee.

On 1 March 1999 the Mitchell Commission released its report. The Mitchell Report was more encompassing, dealing with several arms of the **Olympic movement**. It looked at the bidding process, the IOC structure, and the USOC itself. Its 50 pages of documentation ended with seven pages of conclusions and recommendations, aimed both at revamping the structure of the IOC and the bid-city selection process.

The IOC extraordinary session was planned for 17–18 March. Before this meeting the IOC Executive Board met again and the final Pound Commission report was released. The Pound Report began with a short description of the conclusions of the Board of Ethics Report and the Mitchell Report. It then made its final recommendations near the beginning of the document, although these recommendations were supported by almost 50 pages of documentation describing the transgressions of certain IOC members. The report recommended expelling six IOC members: Agustin Arroyo, Zein El-Abdin Mohamed Ahmed Abdel Gadir, Jean-Claude Ganga, Lamine Keita, Sergio Santander Fantini, and Paul Wallwork of **Samoa**. Charles Mukora, whose expulsion had been recommended earlier, had since resigned. Nine other IOC members had been investigated but were given only warnings with no recommendations of expulsion.

After describing its recommendations concerning the IOC members, the Pound Report made several conclusions. It noted that the IOC must take action to correct the problems within its membership, and it must implement reforms to be certain these problems could never occur again. The Commission also noted that the IOC should have done more to avoid the problems concerning Salt Lake City's candidacy. The Pound Report then recommended changes in the host city selection process, limitations on travel by IOC members to bid cities, and creation of an IOC **Ethics Commission**.

The IOC met in full session a few days later. It voted to expel the members as recommended by the Pound Report, meaning that fully 10 members of the IOC lost their positions in the scandal. But more importantly, the IOC voted to form two new commissions to help reform the structure of the IOC and the Olympic movement and to ensure that such problems would never happen again.

The two commissions were the Ethics Commission and the **IOC 2000 Commission**. The IOC 2000 Commission was charged with reforming the entire structure of the Olympic movement into the next millennium to help prevent such ethical breaches in the future. The IOC 2000 Commission was made up of 82 members, with less than half of them IOC members, and with an executive board of 26 members, of whom 13 were IOC members. The Commission produced an intermediary report in June 1999, and its final report was released in November 1999, although early leaks of information were available. Altogether the IOC 2000 Commission studied more than 100 possible ideas concerning reform of the Olympic movement and eventually made 50 separate recommendations to the IOC.

The Ethics Commission's primary focus was to address the responsibilities of the IOC, oversee the selection process of host cities, and set guidelines for future conduct by members of the Olympic movement. The Ethics Commission produced an IOC Code of Ethics, in the spring of 1999, which addressed many of the concerns voiced by the public and in the media relating to the recent actions of several IOC members and the organizing committees.

During 1999, the U.S. Congress also began hearings into the conduct of the IOC. The House Commerce Subcommittee on Oversight and Investigation also requested an investigation into the Atlanta bid for the 1996 Olympic Games. This was assigned to the Atlanta law firm of King and Spaulding and was headed by former U.S. Attorney General Griffin B. Bell. Its final document, termed the Bell Report, was released on 15 September 1999.

The IOC met in an extraordinary session in Lausanne on 11–12 December to vote on the recommendations made by the IOC 2000 Commission. At this historic session, the IOC voted to enact all the recommendations made by the Commission. The most important changes implemented were 1) an age limit of 70 for IOC members; 2) term limits of eight years for most IOC members; 3) creation of four categories of IOC members—a) athletes, b) National Olympic Committee (NOC) presidents, c) **International Federation** (IF) presidents, and d) individual members; 4) eliminating visits by IOC members to the bid cities; 5) a complete change in the process of selecting host cities; 6) opening IOC sessions to the media via closed-circuit television; and 7) much more transparency in the financial transactions of the IOC, the bid cities, and the **Organizing Committees of the Olympic Games** (OCOGs). In the end, all 50 recommendations of the IOC 2000 Commission were approved, most of them unanimously. (These are listed in the IOC 2000 Commission entry.)

After the implementation of the numerous IOC reforms, IOC president Juan Antonio Samaranch testified before the House Commerce Subcommittee on Oversight and Investigations on 15 December 1999. It was a somewhat contentious appearance, as the members of the subcommittee were underwhelmed by the IOC's reform process. Rep. Joe Barton (R-Texas) asked him to resign on the spot. However, Samaranch was supported by former senators Howard Baker and George Mitchell, who had been involved in the reform process, as noted above. Both stated that the IOC was cleaning house, and Mitchell noted that the IOC had even gone beyond the recommendations made by his commission.

Why did the Olympic scandal occur, and why did these problems seemingly hit all at once? As has been well documented elsewhere, the IOC was once in dire financial straits, and it was only in the 1980s that it began to achieve financial independence. But all this happened quickly, too quickly for the IOC to adjust. And it is unlikely that the problems described here began only with the Salt Lake City bid. There were similar allegations going back to the mid-1980s. During his testimony before the U.S. House of Representatives on 14 October 1999, the IOC director-general, François Carrard, said, "Unfortunately, while the Games evolved, our organizational structure did not keep up with the pace of change. In effect, we did not realize we were going through a growth crisis. The result of an old-fashioned structure managing modern Games was not corruption, but a situation in which some of the less responsible members—a small minority—showed poor judgment and abused the system. Our problems were caused by weak people, structures, and procedures."

Were the new reforms undertaken by the IOC at its December 1999 session adequate to address the problems? The media were critical of these reforms and skeptical that they would truly solve these problems. Some of the criticisms were valid, but as George Mitchell noted, in many ways the IOC either enacted all of his commission's recommendations, and in some cases, went even further than they recommended.

OLYMPIC CEREMONIES. A number of ceremonies accompany the Olympic Games, notably the opening ceremonies, the closing ceremonies, and the victory, medals, and diplomas ceremonies. These ceremonies are conducted according to strict protocols defined in Rule 69 of the **Olympic Charter** (opening and closing ceremonies) and Rule 70 of the Olympic Charter (victory, medals, and diplomas ceremonies).

The opening ceremonies begin with the head of state of the host country (normally) entering the stadium, accompanied by the president of the **International Olympic Committee** (IOC) and the president of the **organizing committee** of the Games. The parade of nations then follows, with the nations of all participating countries entering the stadium. The nations march in alphabetical order, using the alphabetical designation of the language of the host country. However, Greece always enters the stadium first, as the founding nation of the **Ancient Olympic Games**, and the last nation to enter is always the host country. (In 2004, the Greek flag entered first, while the Greek team came in last.) Each nation is led by a flag bearer carrying the flag of the nation or the **National Olympic Committee** (NOC).

The president of the organizing committee then speaks for no more than three minutes. The IOC president then speaks briefly and ends by inviting the head of state of the host country to open the **Olympic Games**. He or she gives no speech but opens the Games by stating "I declare open the Games of [name of city] celebrating the [. . .] Olympiad of the Modern Era (or the [. . .] **Olympic Winter Games**)."

The Olympic torch is then brought into the stadium and the **Olympic flame** is lit by the final runner, followed by a symbolic release of pigeons, signifying peace. The flag bearers then form a semicircle around the main rostrum, and a competitor and an official of the host country take the **Olympic oath** on behalf of all competitors and officials. The national anthem of the host country is then played, after which an artistic program entertaining the spectators is held. This program is usually designed to have some symbolic nature, representing both the **Olympic movement** and the national features of the host country.

The closing ceremonies end the Olympic Games. The flag bearers of each nation first march into the stadium, followed by the athletes of all nations. The athletes march in no order and typically intermingle, signifying the friendships developed during the Olympic Games. (This change to the closing ceremony was suggested by John Ian Wing, a young British boy of Chinese origin, to the organizers of the 1956 Olympic Games in Melbourne.)

The presidents of the IOC and the organizing committee mount the rostrum in the center of the stadium. Three flags are then raised in the following order: the Greek flag on the right flagpole, the flag of the host country on the center flagpole, and the flag of the host country of the next Olympic Games (or Olympic Winter Games) on the left flagpole. All are raised to the playing of their respective national anthems.

The mayor of the host city then hands the official **Olympic flag** to the IOC president, who in turn hands it to the mayor of the host city of the next Olympic Games. The president of the organizing committee gives a brief speech. The IOC president then speaks briefly and ends the Olympic Games by stating, "I declare the Games of the [. . .] Olympiad (or the [. . .] Olympic Winter Games) closed and, in accordance with tradition, I call upon the youth of the world to assemble four years from now at [next host city] to celebrate with us there the Games of the [. . .] Olympiad (or the [. . .] Olympic Winter Games)." A fanfare then sounds, the Olympic flame is extinguished, and while the **Olympic anthem** is played, the Olympic flag is lowered from the flagpole.

The victory, medals, and diplomas ceremonies consist of the awarding of these respective items. The medals are to be presented by the IOC president or an IOC member designated by him. (In reality, the IOC president now awards only a very few medals.) The three place winners mount the victory platform, the winner on the highest step. Their names are announced and the medals are awarded to them. The national flags of the three medal winners are raised, the national flag of the winner on the central flagpole. While the flags are raised, the national anthem of the champion is played, usually in a shortened version.

OLYMPIC CHARTER. The *Olympic Charter* is, effectively, the constitution of the **International Olympic Committee** (IOC) and the **Olympic movement**. It sets out, basically in an outline form, the principles, rules, and bylaws that govern the workings of both the IOC and the Olympic movement and stipulates the conditions for the celebration of the **Olympic Games**. The *Olympic Charter* was first adopted in 1908, based on a handwritten set of rules created by **Pierre de Coubertin** shortly after the formation of the IOC. The 1908 list of rules was not called the *Olympic Charter* but rather Comité International Olympique: Annuaire (in French only). Since that time, the IOC's governing rules have been published under several different names, including *Olympic Rules*, *Protocol*, *Olympic Statutes*, and *Rules*, being first published officially as the *Olympic Charter* only in 1978.

Though the *Olympic Charter* is often held to be inviolate, it is, in fact, fairly easily modified and has been changed many times since its inception. Modifications, or amendments, can be made according to Rule 18.4 governing the sessions, which states, "The Session is the supreme organ of the IOC. It adopts, modifies, and interprets the *Olympic Charter*."

The *Olympic Charter* underwent major changes at the end of 1999, based on recommendations made by the **IOC 2000 Commission** in response to the **Olympic bribery scandal**. The changes were sweeping and made significant structural changes to the Olympic movement, many of which are discussed in various entries in this dictionary. Details of these recommendations can be found in the entry for the IOC 2000 Commission.

OLYMPIC CODE. *See* OLYMPIC CREED.

OLYMPIC COLLECTORS COMMISSION. The Olympic Collectors Commission was formed on 14 June 1993 by combining three associations that were recognized by the **International Olympic Committee** (IOC)—the Fédération Internationale de Philately Olympique (FIPO), the Fédération Internationale de Numismatic Olympique (FINO), and the Association of Collectors of Olympic Memorabilia (ACOM). President **Juan Antonio Samaranch**, an avid stamp collector, chairs this commission. The Olympic Collectors Commission now sponsors an annual Olympic Collectors World Fair and an Olympic stamp show, Olymphilex.

OLYMPIC CONGRESSES. Olympic congresses are gatherings of all the various bodies and individuals involved in the **Olympic movement**. The **Olympic Charter** now states that they are to be held, in principle, every eight years at a place and date determined by the **International Olympic Committee** (IOC). It should be noted that this has not always been the case. **Baron Pierre de Coubertin** intended Olympic congresses to be held from "time-to-time" to discuss the Olympic movement. However, a gap of 43 years occurred from the 9th Olympic Congress until the 10th Olympic Congress in 1973. The Olympic congress has no official power to make rules concerning the **Olympic Games** or to modify the Olympic Charter but only acts as a consultant to the Olympic movement.

To date, 12 Olympic congresses have been held. They have been as follows, with their themes following the name of the host city:

1st	16–24 June 1894—Paris—Reestablishment of the Olympic Games
2nd	23–31 July 1897—Le Havre—Sports hygiene and pedagogy
3rd	9–14 June 1905—Brussels—Sport and physical education
4th	23–25 May 1906—Paris—Art, literature, and sport
5th	7–11 May 1913—Lausanne—Sports psychology and physiology
6th	15–23 June 1914—Paris—Olympic regulations
7th	2–7 June 1921—Lausanne—Olympic regulations
8th	29 May–4 June 1925—Prague—Sports pedagogy and Olympic regulations
9th	25–30 May 1930—Berlin—Olympic regulations
10th	30 September–4 October 1973—Varna—Sport for a world of peace; the Olympic movement and its future
11th	23–28 September 1981—Baden-Baden—1. The future of the Olympics Games; 2. International cooperation; 3. The future of the Olympic movement
12th	29 August–3 September 1994—Paris—1. The Olympic movement's contribution to modern society; 2. The contemporary athlete; 3. Sport in its social context; 4. Sport and the media

As of early 2004, there are no current plans for the next Olympic congress. As it would take at least one to two years to organize a comprehensive congress, the IOC will be violating the receoommendation of the Olympic Charter that such a congress occur every eight years, although this has not been strictly observed since 1930.

OLYMPIC COUNCIL OF ASIA (OCA). The Olympic Council of Asia is a confederation of the **National Olympic Committees** (NOCs) from Asia formed in November 1982. The OCA is in overall charge of sports in Asia, coordinates the activities of Asian countries in sports at the regional and international level, and conducts the Asian Games every four years. It is headquartered in **Kuwait**, and as of

2004, its president is Sheikh Ahmad Al-Fahad Al-Sabah of Kuwait. There are currently 43 affiliated nations.

OLYMPIC CREDO. *See* OLYMPIC CREED.

OLYMPIC CREED. "The most important thing in the **Olympic Games** is not to win but to take part, just as the most important thing in life is not the triumph, but the struggle. The essential thing is not to have conquered but to have fought well."

This is the current form of the Olympic creed (also termed the Olympic code, the Olympic credo, an alternative **Olympic motto** or the Olympic competition motto) as it appears on the scoreboard at the opening ceremony of the Olympic Games, although many permutations of this basic message have been seen. The exact origin of this phrase is not clear, but it is possible that **Pierre de Coubertin** adopted this creed after hearing Ethelbert Talbot, the bishop of Central Pennsylvania, speak at St. Paul's Cathedral on 19 July 1908, during the London Olympics. The service was given for the Olympic athletes, who were all invited.

Talbot was in London for the fifth Conference of Anglican Bishops. During the conference, many of the visiting bishops spoke in various churches. Talbot actually did not say anything close to the above exact words during his speech, stating instead, "The only safety after all lies in the lesson of the real Olympia—that the Games themselves are better than the race and the prize. St. Paul tells us how insignificant is the prize. Our prize is not corruptible, but incorruptible, and though only one may wear the laurel wreath, all may share the equal joy of the contest."

However, Coubertin heard Talbot speak, and at a banquet at the Grafton Galleries on 24 July 1908, he echoed Bishop Talbot's words as follows, "*L'important dans ces Olympiades, c'est moins d'y gagner que d'y prendre part.*" ("The important thing at these Olympiads is not so much to win as to take part.") He then went on to say that these very words were the foundation of a clear and sound philosophy: "*L'important dans la vie ce n'est point le triomphe mais le combat. L'essentiel ce n'est pas d'avoir vaincu mais de s'être bien battu.*" ("The important thing in life is not the triumph but the struggle. The essential thing is not to have won but to have fought well.")

More recent research by David C. Young indicates that Coubertin probably had this thought in mind prior to hearing the speech of the bishop of Central Pennsylvania. Young attributes the phrase to Ovid's *Metamorphoses,* which Coubertin had read in school. A sentence in that work reads, "*Nec tam turpe fuit vinci quam contendisse decorum est,*" which can be translated as, "It was not so shameful to be beaten as it is honorable to have contended." Coubertin's knowledge of this statement is supplemented by a speech he gave in November 1894 to the Parnassus Literary Society in Athens, in which he said, "*Le déshonneur ne consisterait pas ici à être battu: il consisterait à ne pas se battre.*" This is literally translated as, "The dishonor here would consist not of being beaten, it would consist of not contending."

In connection with the Olympic Games in Stockholm in 1912 and in Antwerp in 1920, Coubertin again spoke of the words of the bishop of Central Pennsylvania, but it did not attract any notice. At the Olympic Games in 1924 and 1928 no reference was made to Bishop Talbot's sermon in St. Paul's Cathedral in 1908. However, at the Olympic Games in Los Angeles (1932) the message appeared during the opening ceremonies on the great scoreboard of the Los Angeles Memorial Coliseum. It was finally established at the 1936 Olympic Games in Berlin when, at the opening ceremony, Pierre de Coubertin's voice was heard over the loudspeaker, in a recording, delivering his message, "*Important aux Jeux Olympiques, ce n'est pas tant d'y gagner que d'y avoir pris part; car l'essentiel dans la vie, ce n'est pas tant de conquérir que d'avoir bien lutté.*" ("Important in the Olympic Games is not winning but taking part; for the essential thing in life is not conquering but fighting well.")

OLYMPIC CUP. The Olympic Cup was instituted by **Baron Pierre de Coubertin** in 1906. It is awarded to an institution or association with a general reputation for merit and integrity that has been active and efficient in the service of sport and has contributed substantially to the development of the **Olympic movement**. The Olympic Cup is one of the two awards currently given by the **International Olympic Committee** (IOC) outside of the **Olympic Games**. *See also* OLYMPIC ORDER; Appendix E ("Awards of the International Olympic Committee").

OLYMPIC DIPLOMAS. Diplomas are given to the first eight finishers of all events at an **Olympic Games**. It is not well known that the first three finishers receive, in addition to their medals, these diplomas. In team events, the members of the first eight teams also all receive diplomas.

OLYMPIC FAMILY. The Olympic family is a term used by the **International Olympic Committee** (IOC) that describes people considered to have certain privileges during the **Olympic Games** and **Olympic Winter Games**. The Olympic family consists of athletes, officials, media representatives, sponsors and their guests, and invited guests from the IOC, **National Olympic Committees** (NOCs), **International Federations** (IFs), and **Organizing Committees of the Olympic Games** (OCOGs). At the Olympic Games and Olympic Winter Games, members of the Olympic family are given access to preferred lodging, private transportation, and privileged seating at the Olympic sporting events. These privileges and access are prioritized with IOC members given the highest consideration.

OLYMPIC FILMS. Numerous Olympic films and movies have been produced. The **organizing committee** of each **Olympic Games** now produces its own official Olympic film celebrating in motion pictures "its" Olympics. This began with the 1936 Olympic Games in Berlin when German film producer Leni Riefenstahl, at the behest of Adolf Hitler, produced the most famous and haunting of all Olympic films, *Olympia*. Prior to that, the filmed record of the Olympics came from cinema newsreels. Other well-known official Olympic films have been *Tokyo Olympiad*, celebrating the 1964 Olympic Games in Tokyo, and *Visions of Eight*, celebrating the 1972 Olympic Games in Munich.

In addition to official Olympic films, many independent producers produce Olympic movies. The American television network that televises the Olympics now usually produces a cinematic summary of the Olympics, and their coverage is often available to be bought and viewed on VCRs or DVD players.

The most prominent producer of Olympic films has been the American Bud Greenspan, who was initially assisted by his late wife, Cappy Greenspan. Greenspan has produced a remarkable series of

Olympic movies termed "The Olympiad Series." In addition, he has been the producer of the official Olympic film five times: in 1984 (Los Angeles), 1988 (Calgary and Seoul), 1992 (Barcelona), and 1994 (Lillehammer).

OLYMPIC FLAG. The Olympic flag has a plain white background with no border. In the center is the **Olympic symbol**, which consists of five interconnected rings. They form two rows of three rings above, and two below. The rings of the upper row are, from left to right, blue, black, and red. The rings of the lower row are yellow and green. The rings are thought to symbolize the five continents—Europe, Asia, Africa, Australia, and America. The colors of the rings are thought to have been chosen because at least one of these colors can be found in the flag of every nation.

The origin of the flag's design is in some dispute. It is thought to be **Baron Pierre de Coubertin** who designed the symbol to honor and represent the 1914 **Olympic Congress** in Paris. Some sources state that de Coubertin saw the rings at Delphi in 1913, but classics scholars believe this is highly unlikely and that they are of his own modern invention. The idea of a flag was raised by the **International Olympic Committee** (IOC) in 1910, and a special committee worked to plan it. Several suggestions were made, notably by Theodore Cook (GBR) and Clarence von Rosen (SWE), but little progress was made until de Coubertin came up with his design. He commented in the August 1913 edition of *Revue Olympique*, "These five rings represent the five parts of the world from this point on won over to **Olympism** and given to accepting fruitful rivalry. Furthermore, the six colors (including the white background) thus combined reproduce the colors of all the nations, with no exception." The flag was first flown at Chatsby Stadium in Alexandria, Egypt, for the Pan-Egyptian Games on 5 April 1914. It was presented to the IOC by de Coubertin at the Olympic congress in 1914 at the Sorbonne in Paris, where it was officially approved on 15 June 1914. The flag was also flown in 1915 at the San Francisco Exhibition and at the 1919 IOC session in **Lausanne**, before it made its début at the **Olympic Games** in 1920 at Antwerp, Belgium. The "primary" Olympic flag was thus known as "the Antwerp flag" and has been the main Olympic flag flown at the stadium at all Olympic Games through 1984. In 1984, Seoul presented a new Olympic flag to the IOC, made of fine Korean silk, which was first flown at the 1988 Olympics. A second "primary" Olympic flag, donated in 1952 by the host city of Oslo, Norway, is used for the **Olympic Winter Games**.

The Olympic flag, donated in 1952 by the host city of Oslo, Norway, is raised at the opening ceremonies and flies over the main stadium throughout the Olympic Games. It is lowered at the closing ceremonies of the Olympic Games. The mayor of the Olympic host city then presents the Olympic flag to the mayor of the next Olympic host city. The flag is to be kept in the town hall of the host city until the next Olympic Games. *See also* OLYMPIC CEREMONIES.

OLYMPIC FLAME, OLYMPIC TORCH, AND TORCH RELAY.
The Olympic flame is a symbol reminiscent of the **Ancient Olympic Games**, in which a sacred flame burned at the altar of Zeus throughout the **Olympic Games**. The flame was first used at the modern Olympics in Amsterdam in 1928 and was lit again throughout the 1932 Los Angeles Olympics, but this marked the last time the flame was kindled at the site of the Games.

In 1936, **Carl Diem**, chairman of the **organizing committee** for the Berlin Olympics, proposed the idea of lighting the flame at Ancient Olympia and transporting it to Berlin via a torch relay. This was done and has been repeated at every Olympics since.

The flame for the Olympic Games is lit in the altis of the Ancient Olympic stadium at Ancient Olympia, on the Greek Peloponnesus. The flame is lit during a ceremony by women dressed in robes similar to those worn by the Ancient Greeks. The flame is lit naturally by the rays of the sun at Olympia, reflected off a curved mirror, and the high priestess then presents the torch to the first relay runner.

The flame for the **Olympic Winter Games** has not always been lit in Olympia. In 1952 and 1960 the flame for the Olympic Winter Games was lit at the hearth of Sondre Nordheim, the father of modern **skiing**, at his ancient home in Morgedal, Norway. In 1956 it was lit at the Temple of Jupiter in Rome for the Games in Cortina d'Ampezzo, Italy. Since 1964, the flame for the Olympic Winter Games has also been lit in Ancient Olympia. In 1994, a second, unofficial flame was lit in Morgedal for the Lillehammer Olympics, which greatly upset the Greeks, who claim proprietary rights to the Olympic flame.

OLYMPIC GAMES. The Olympic Games refer to the sporting festival that is held in the summer months and is often referred to as the Summer Olympics. The proper name of the sporting celebration is the "Games of the [. . .] Olympiad." The Games of the Olympiad are always held during the first year of the **Olympiad** that they celebrate. The Olympic Games are entrusted to a single host city, which is now elected seven years in advance of the scheduled Olympic Games. See discussions of the various Olympic Games in the chronology.

OLYMPIC GAMES KNOWLEDGE SERVICES (OGKS). For each **Olympic Games**, an **organizing committee** (OCOG) is formed to manage the affairs and organize the forthcoming Games. In the late 1990s it became apparent to the **International Olympic Committee** (IOC) that each of these OCOGs was forced to reinvent the wheel and essentially start from scratch. Knowledge, documents, and other material accumulated by each OCOG was rarely being passed along to the next OCOG. In response to this obvious lack of coordination of the OCOGs, in February 2002 the IOC formed the Olympic Games Knowledge Services as the exclusive knowledge management services company of the IOC. The role of OGKS is to pass information and know-how from one OCOG to the next and to assist the OCOGs in beginning their organization of the next Olympic Games.

OLYMPIC GAMES STUDY COMMISSION. The Olympic Games Study Commission was formed in 2002 to study all aspects of the **Olympic Games**, primarily looking at ways to reduce the size, cost, and complexity of organizing the Olympic Games. The commission prepared a report focusing on five areas of the organization of the Olympic Games: 1) Games format; 2) venues and facilities; 3) Games management; 4) number of accredited persons; and 5) service levels. The commission was chaired by **International Olympic Committee** (IOC) member **Richard Pound** (CAN) and presented its report to the 115th IOC session in Prague. After the report was presented, the commission was dissolved by IOC president **Jacques Rogge**.

OLYMPIC HYMN. *See* OLYMPIC ANTHEM.

OLYMPIC IDENTITY CARD. The Olympic identity card is an important political document. It is given to all members of the Olympic family, i.e., athletes, officials, **International Olympic Committee** (IOC) members and delegates, **National Olympic Committee** (NOC) members and delegates, and **International Federation** (IF) members and delegates. The importance of the Olympic identity card is that it establishes the identity of the holder and, with an appropriate national passport, is supposed to allow free passage into the country in which the host Olympic city is situated. Thus the card serves as, and supplants, a travel visa. Host cities are required agree to recognize the right of all members of the Olympic family to enter the country of the host city, based on a valid passport and the Olympic identity card, and not require a further visa.

OLYMPIC LITERATURE. The literature surrounding the **Olympic Games** is voluminous. The **International Olympic Committee** (IOC) now publishes various magazines, journals, press releases, and books. Each **National Olympic Committee** (NOC) and **International Federation** (IF) also may publish literature concerning the Olympic Games and often does so. The **organizing committees** publish a great deal of official information in addition to press releases and packets.

Private authors have also developed an enormous amount of Olympic literature. Books on the Olympics are now produced prior to and after each Olympic Games, in most of the major languages of the world. With the advent of advanced technology, some are now being produced on CD-ROMs to be read via computers.

No current up-to-date bibliography of Olympic literature exists. The two most complete and most recent are currently over 20 years old. They are *The Olympics: A Bibliography,* compiled by Bill Mallon (New York: Garland Press, 1984) and *Bibliography: Geschichte der Leibesübungen, Band 5, Olympische Spiele* (second edition), compiled by Karl Lennartz (Bonn: Verlag Karl Hofmann, 1983).

However, because of computer technology and Internet capabilities, it is unlikely that a full-scale book-type bibliography will be produced again. Probably the most complete and up-to-date Olympic bibliography can be found by searching the SPORTDiscus site, which is the sport bibliography of the Canadian literary resource,

SIRC (Sport Information Resource Centre), which is updated quarterly. The URL for this site is www.sirc.ca/products/, although a subscription is required to use the database. *See also* OLYMPIC MESSAGE; OLYMPIC REVIEW.

OLYMPIC MEDALS. Olympic medals are given as awards for finishing in the first three places in the events of the **Olympic Games**. The champion receives a gold medal, the runner-up a silver medal, and the third-place finisher a bronze medal. At the 1896 Olympics, the winner received only a silver medal and the runner-up a bronze medal.

The medals must be at least 60 mm. in diameter and three mm. thick. They are designed by the **Organizing Committee of the Olympic Games** (OCOG), upon approval by the IOC **Executive Board**. The "gold" medal is actually silver gilt which must be gilded with at least six grams of pure gold. It was only in 1908 and 1912 that the gold medalists received medals of pure gold. The metal for the first- and second-place medals must be silver of at least 925/1000 grade.

Olympic medals are given to the medalists at ceremonies at the conclusion of their events. The medals are draped around the athlete's necks, hung from a ribbon or other decorative necklace. This custom did not begin, however, until 1960 in Rome. Prior to that time, the medals were handed to the athletes in specially designed boxes.

OLYMPIC MESSAGE. The *Olympic Message* was a publication of the **International Olympic Committee** (IOC). It was first published in May 1982 and was published three or four times per year. Its publication was discontinued as of the December 1994 issue (Volume 40). The *Olympic Message* was different from the *Olympic Review* in that each issue usually studied in detail a single theme of the **Olympic movement**.

OLYMPIC MOTTO. The official Olympic motto is "*Citius, Altius, Fortius,*" a Latin phrase meaning swifter, higher, stronger. The Olympic motto was adopted by **Baron Pierre de Coubertin** for the **International Olympic Committee** (IOC) after hearing of its use by Reverend Father Henri Martin Didon of Paris, a Dominican friar and teacher. Didon, head master of Arcueil College, used the phrase while describing the athletic accomplishments of his students at that school. He had previously been at the school Albert Le Grand, where the Latin words were carved in stone above the main entrance. Coubertin used the motto in the very first issue of *Revue Olympique*. *See also* OLYMPIC CREED.

OLYMPIC MOVEMENT. The Olympic movement is a phrase often used by the **International Olympic Committee** (IOC) and practitioners and administrators of international sport. However, it is not well defined. The **Olympic Charter** states simply that "The Olympic Movement, led by the IOC, stems from modern **Olympism**." The IOC has, however, defined the phrase more fully in some of its press releases. It has stated that the Olympic movement encompasses the IOC, the **International Federations** (IFs), and the **National Olympic Committees** (NOCs) and that the IOC is the supreme authority of the Olympic movement. In addition, the IOC has stated its purpose and its fundamental principles as "to contribute to building a peaceful and better world by educating youth through sport practiced without discrimination of any kind and in the Olympic spirit, which requires mutual understanding with a spirit of friendship, solidarity, and fair play. The activity of the Olympic Movement is permanent and universal. It reaches its peak with the bringing together of the athletes of the world at the great sport festival, the **Olympic Games**." The Olympic movement is discussed in much more detail in the introduction.

OLYMPIC MUSEUM. An Olympic museum had been a dream of the **International Olympic Committee** (IOC) for many years. In 1915, **Pierre de Coubertin** announced his intention to set up an Olympic museum in **Lausanne** to store the archives of the IOC and to become a public information center on the **Olympic movement**. IOC president **Juan Antonio Samaranch** made the dream a reality. He began his plans for an Olympic museum in 1981, shortly after his election as IOC president, when the IOC bought a building at 18 avenue Ruchonnet in Lausanne and established a provisional museum. In 1984, the IOC acquired two plots of land in the Ouchy section of Lausanne, overlooking Lake Geneva (Lake Léman). Construction on the permanent Olympic Museum began on this land in 1988. On 23 June 1993, the Olympic Museum was inaugurated on the 99th anniversary of the creation of the IOC. The Olympic Museum is intended to be the universal depository of the written, visual, and graphic memory of the **Olympic Games**. Samaranch has stated that "the Olympic Museum will be a global source of information on the impact of the Olympic tradition on art, culture, the economy and world peace. The focal point of the meaning of the Olympic Games and their role in modern society, the Olympic Museum will be both a witness and a center for reflection."

OLYMPIC OATH. The Olympic oath is a pledge to uphold the spirit of sportsmanship and is spoken at the opening ceremonies by representatives of the host country on behalf of all competitors and officials. In the July 1906 edition of the *Revue Olympique*, **Pierre de Coubertin** referred to the urgent need to introduce into the few but very important **Olympic ceremonies** an athletes' oath of fairness and impartiality. The protocol was first introduced at Antwerp in 1920 when the noted Belgian **fencer**, Victor Boin, performed the ceremony. A similar ceremony was conducted at the first **Olympic Winter Games** at Chamonix in 1924 when all competitors took the oath collectively, although they were led by France's Camille Mandrillon. The first **woman** to take the oath was the Italian skier Giuliana Chenal-Minuzzo at the 1956 Olympic Winter Games in Cortina d'Ampezzo. The first woman to take the oath at the **Olympic Games** was German **track and field** athlete Heidi Schüller at the 1972 Olympic Games in Munich.

Boin initially recited the following words: "We swear that we will take part in the Olympic Games in a spirit of chivalry, for the honor of our country and for the glory of sport." This oath was modified slightly in 1961, when the term "swear" was replaced by "promise," and "the honor of our country" by "the honor of our teams," in an obvious desire to eliminate nationalism from the Games.

In 1999, the **IOC 2000 Commission** recommended a change to the Olympic oath, which was enacted by the IOC session. This change added a statement to the oath in which the Olympic athletes would renounce the use of drugs in sport. The current edition of the **Olympic Charter** establishes the following text for the athletes' oath: "In the name of all the competitors I promise that we shall take part in these Olympic Games, respecting and abiding by the rules which govern them, committing ourselves to a sport without **doping** and without drugs, in the true spirit of sportsmanship, for the glory of sport and the honor of our teams." Since 1972, the judges have also sworn an oath, the text of which, in conformity with the current Olympic Charter, is as follows: "In the name of all the judges and officials, I promise that we shall officiate in these Olympic Games with complete impartiality, respecting and abiding by the rules which govern them, in the true spirit of sportsmanship." *See also* OLYMPIC REVIEW; Appendix G ("Speakers of the Olympic Oath").

OLYMPIC ORDER. The Olympic Order is the supreme individual honor accorded by the **International Olympic Committee** (IOC). It was created in 1974 and is to be awarded to "Any person who has illustrated the Olympic Ideal through his/her action, has achieved remarkable merit in the sporting world, or has rendered outstanding services to the Olympic cause, either through his/her own personal achievement(s) or his/her contribution to the development of sport." Originally, the Olympic Order was separated into three categories—gold, silver, and bronze. Currently, there are only gold and silver categories. *See also* Appendix E ("Awards of the International Olympic Committee").

OLYMPIC PHILATELY, NUMISMATIC, AND MEMORABILIA COMMISSION. The Olympic Philately, Numismatic, and Memorabilia Commission (OPNMC) is composed of the International Federation of Olympic Philately (FIPO), the International Federation of Olympic Numismatic (FINO), and the International Olympic Memorabilia Federation (FIMO). The current chairman is former **International Olympic Committee** (IOC) president **Juan Antonio Samaranch**. The commission is led, however, by its coordinator, Manfred Bergman.

OLYMPIC PROGRAM. Rule 48 of the **Olympic Charter** concerns the "Program of the Olympic Games," and reads,

> 48.1 The Program of the Games of the Olympiad must include at least 15 Olympic sports. Such required minimum does not exist for the Program of the Olympic Winter Games.

48.2 After each Olympic Games, the International Olympic Committee (IOC) reviews the Program of the Olympic Games.

48.3 On the occasion of each review, the standards for the admission of sports, disciplines or events may be reviewed and the admission or exclusion of sports, disciplines or events determined by the competent IOC organs.

This is the official definition. In reality, no **Olympic Games** have had less than 15 sports since the 1912 Olympic Games.

The Olympic program is not immutable. In fact, the Olympic program changes for virtually every Olympic Games and **Olympic Winter Games** when the IOC reviews the program. These changes are usually considered and developed by the **Olympic Programme Commission**, working in concert with the various **International Federations** (IFs). The changes are then presented to the IOC **Executive Board**, which votes on their approval. If approved by the Executive Board, the program changes are then presented to the IOC session for a final vote and approval.

The Olympic program has changed greatly since the first modern Olympic Games in 1896, when there were nine sports on the program, with 43 events. **Women** need not have applied—there were no sports or events for women. Between 1900 and 1920 there was absolutely no consensus about which sports and events should be on the Olympic program. The choice of events was almost entirely up to the **Organizing Committees of the Olympic Games** (OCOGs), with some input from the International Federations (IFs), if they even existed at all. Several of the IFs were only formed in response to problems governing their sports at the Olympics, notably the track and field **athletics** federation, the International Amateur Athletic Federation (IAAF).

But the IOC knew that the idea of no organization or design behind the program was not acceptable. The 7th **Olympic Congress** was held in **Lausanne** from 2–7 June 1921. Its subject was "The Modification of the Olympic Program and Conditions of Participation." It was the first major attempt by the IOC to formalize the Olympic program, but it would not be the last. However, the congress did not achieve its aims, because the IFs would not relinquish their control over the program of their sports. Norbert Müller notes in his book

One Hundred Years of Olympic Congresses 1894–1994, "The Congress could not bring about a more concise Program of competition. The federations present referred to their right to determine the Program of competition themselves. The IOC had to realize that it had underestimated the self-confidence of the federations and the result(ant) resistance against cancellations."

In addition to the question of admitting new sports and events, the Olympic Programme Commission must address the problem of "gigantism" of the Olympic Games. The size of the Olympic Games has increased dramatically over the last 50 years. Note that in 1948 at London, 59 nations sent 4,099 competitors to the Olympics, while in 2000 at Sydney, there were 200 nations represented by 10,650 athletes. With this increase in size comes commensurate increase in cost. The cost increases at more than a linear rate relative to the athletes, because of the increased security and complexity of the competitions and venues. With these increased costs, ways must be found to pay for the Olympic Games, and some of these options, notably increasing marketing and commercialization, are not really palatable to the Olympic movement.

The main option remaining would seem to be to limit the number of events. With new sports clamoring to be included on the Olympic program, this seems almost impossible. One way is to limit the number of events in the sports already on the Olympic program. The **IOC 2000 Commission** recommended that no more than 280 events be contested at the Olympics Games, beginning in 2004, and this was passed by the IOC in 1999. But the question is which events should be eliminated. Do there need to be 15 swimming events for men and for women? Does boxing need 12 different weight classes? The IOC has also tacitly seemed to realize that 280 events is not currently possible, and has now stated that the Olympic program will not contain more than 300 events, although there were 301 in Athens in 2004.

These questions are asked all the time by the IOC and the Olympic Programme Commission, but, in fact, it is very rare that events on the Olympic program are dropped from it. If they are, they are usually replaced by another event in the same sport. Shortly after taking office as IOC president, **Jacques Rogge** formed the **Olympic Games Study Commission** to look into decreasing the size and cost of the Olympic Games. This ad hoc commission made several recommendations to the Executive Board, which adopted them. These included eliminating **baseball**, **softball**, and modern **pentathlon** and replacing them with **golf** and **rugby** sevens (seven-a-side rugby). Further recommendations including eliminating events within the sports, such as the three-day event in **equestrian** sport and the walks on the **athletics** program, and eliminating Greco-Roman wrestling. But at the IOC session in December 2002, the IOC voted to table these issues and bring them to a vote at the IOC session in July 2005.

One program item that definitely has increased the tendency toward gigantism and enlarging the Olympic program at the last few Olympics is women's sports and events. But this is accepted, and warranted, and the IOC is committed to increasing the number of sports and events for women. At almost every Olympics, new sports and events for women are added to the program.

The evolution has come a long way. At Athens in 2004, there were 301 events in 28 sports (by IOC definitions, see below), of which 26 sports were open to women. Of these 301 events, there were 166 events for men only, 125 for women only, and 10 mixed events. At Salt Lake City in 2002, there were 78 events in six sports (by IOC definitions, see below), of which all six sports were open to women. Of these 78 events, there were 42 events for men only, 34 for women only, and two mixed events.

What seems like a sport to most people may not actually be a sport in the world of the Olympic Games and the International Federations. In the Olympic Charter, the Olympic movement defines Olympic sports, disciplines, and events. A sport is not specifically defined in the Olympic Charter. Rule 47 does define an Olympic sport, effectively stating that it is a sport defined by IOC-recognized IFs. There are 28 summer Olympic sports listed, and seven winter Olympic sports listed. All of them were included on the Olympic program for Sydney and Salt Lake City.

Rule 47 details how sports may be included on the Olympic program. To be considered, summer Olympic sports must be practiced by men in at least 75 nations and four continents, and by women in at least 40 nations and three continents, while winter Olympic sports must be practiced in at least 25 nations on three continents. Rule 47.1.4 further states that "sports are admitted to the Program of the Olympic Games at least seven years before specific Olympic Games in respect of which no change shall thereafter be permitted." Although this is the rule, it can be broken and has been many times. Most recently, it was only in October 1999 that **skeleton** racing, effectively a new winter sport, was officially admitted to the Olympic program for Salt Lake City in 2002. But the IOC has an out allowing this, Rule 47.6: "Exceptional Admission of a Discipline or Event," which basically allows the IOC to break Rule 47.1.4 (and Rules 47.2.3 and 47.3.4, see below) whenever it so desires, as long as the IF involved and the OCOG agree.

Rule 47.2 defines a discipline, which is essentially a branch of a sport. The standards of admission to the Olympic program are the same for a discipline as they are for a sport. Most sports, such as track and field athletics, or **shooting**, do not have disciplines, but consider all events part of one sport. There are seven summer Olympic sports that recognize disciplines, as follows: aquatics—**diving, swimming, synchronized swimming**, and **water polo**; **canoeing** and **kayaking**—sprint (flatwater) and slalom (whitewater); **cycling**—track, road, and mountain biking; **equestrian**—three-day event, dressage, jumping; **gymnastics**—artistic, rhythmic, and trampoline; volleyball—volleyball and beach volleyball; and **wrestling**—freestyle and Greco-Roman. There are three winter Olympic sports that recognize disciplines, as follows: **bobsledding**—bobsled and skeleton; skating—**figure skating, speed skating**, and short-track speed skating; and skiing—**alpine skiing**, cross-country skiing, **freestyle skiing, nordic skiing, ski jumping**, and snowboarding.

An event is defined by Rule 47.3.1 as "a competition in an Olympic sport or in one of its disciplines and resulting in a ranking, (which) gives rise to the award of medals and diplomas." The rules for admission of an event are slightly different. The next rule (47.3.2) notes that "events must have a recognized international standing both numerically and geographically, and have been included at least twice in world or continental championships."

For summer Olympic sports, events must be practiced by men in at least 50 nations and on three continents and by women in at least 35 nations on three continents. The Olympic Charter does not make a similar restriction on events at the Olympic Winter Games. The rule for admission of events is less restrictive in terms of advance notice, as events may be admitted to the Olympic Games up to four years prior to the Olympics.

Not all sports or events can even warrant consideration to be on the Olympic program. Specifically, the IOC prohibits sports, disciplines, or events in which performance depends essentially on mechanical propulsion. Sorry, NASCAR and Jeff Gordon fans. (Strangely, there is a second category of IOC recognition of IFs, and several of them are federations of motorsports—automobile racing, motorcycle racing, and powerboat racing. It is not certain why they are recognized if they cannot be Olympic sports.)

For new events, the IOC has also decided that a single event may no longer be used to compile both an individual and team ranking, termed a "passive" team sport. By passive team sports, the IOC means any team event in which the result is not determined by team members participating together, but one in which the team members compete on their own and the team score is determined simply by adding together individual scores. Examples are the all-around team gymnastics event and the team modern pentathlon event. In response to this current philosophy, the team modern pentathlon event was deleted from the Olympic program in 1996 at Atlanta. This is also why shooting, which has multiple team events at its World Championships, has no team events on the Olympic program.

Other than satisfying the requirements of Rule 47, the Olympic Charter does not really say what an International Federation, and its sport, must do to become an Olympic sport, or achieve IOC recognition. Rule 26 simply states, "the IOC may recognize as IF's international non-governmental organizations administering one or several sports at world level and encompassing organizations administering such sports at national level." The IOC then defines the role of IFs, basically to govern the sport, promote the Olympic movement and **Olympism**, set the eligibility requirements for the Olympic athletes in their sport, and assume responsibility for the technical control and direction of the sport at the Olympic Games.

OLYMPIC PROGRAMME COMMISSION. The Olympic Programme Commission reviews and analyzes the program sports, disciplines, and events for each sport at the Games of the Olympiad and the **Olympic Winter Games**. It also develops recommendations on the principles and structure of the **Olympic program**. The commission makes recommendations to the IOC **Executive Board** and presents reports to the IOC session. The commission is composed of IOC members and representatives from the **National Olympic Committees** (NOCs) and the **International Federations** (IFs). The current chairman is Franco Carraro (ITA).

OLYMPIC PROGRAMME, THE. The Olympic Programme (TOP) is a fund-raising program administered by the **International Olympic Committee** (IOC) that began in the early 1980s. It is used to generate revenue for the IOC and has been very successful. TOP works by soliciting only a few sponsors, no more than 12 at a time to date, guaranteeing them exclusive marketing rights to the **Olympic symbol** within their market niche, and providing that guarantee for a complete **Olympiad**. Each TOP edition thus lasts for four years. To date, there have been TOP I, TOP II, TOP III, TOP IV, and TOP V. Because of the exclusivity of the program, the IOC has been able to command very large revenues from the sponsors, which has guaranteed the success of TOP.

OLYMPIC REVIEW. The *Olympic Review* is the official journal of the **International Olympic Committee** (IOC). It has been published under various titles relatively continuously since 1894. Originally published by **Pierre de Coubertin**, its first title was *Bulletin du Comité International des Jeux Olympiques*. From 1901 to 1914, it first took its current name in French, *Revue Olympique*. From 1938 to 1944, it was published in Berlin with the German title *Olympische Rundschau*, although French and English editions were also available. Other titles used during its publishing history include *Bulletin du Comité International Olympique*, *Bulletin Officiel du Comité International Olympique*, *Pages de critique et d'histoire*, and *Lettre d'information/Newsletter/Carta información*. It is now published monthly in English, French, German, and Spanish. Since 1970, the official title has remained *Olympic Review*, *Revue Olympique*, *Olympische Rundschau*, and *Revista Olimpica*.

OLYMPIC SOLIDARITY. Olympic Solidarity is a program in which the **International Olympic Committee** (IOC) helps the sporting development of underprivileged nations. Certain IOC fund-raising is distributed via Olympic Solidarity to the **National Olympic Committees** (NOCs) that the IOC recognizes to be in the greatest need. This has taken the form of coaching assistance, technical assistance, and funds to help athletes travel to the **Olympic Games** and other international sporting events. The goals of Olympic Solidarity are quoted in the **Olympic Charter** to be "promoting the fundamental principles of the Olympic Movement; developing the technical sports knowledge of athletes and coaches; improving the technical level of athletes and coaches; training sports administrators; and collaborating with the various IOC commissions."

Olympic Solidarity began in 1961 as the International Olympic Aid Committee at the suggestion of Jean, Count de Beaumont (FRA). In 1968, this committee became a commission of the IOC while retaining the same name. In 1971, Adriaan van Karnebeek (NED) took the initiative for further developments by setting up an Olympic Solidarity Commission through the Permanent General Assembly of National Olympic Committees. In 1972, the two groups merged to become what is now known as Olympic Solidarity. It was originally headquartered in Rome, but in 1979, at the 81st IOC session, Olympic Solidarity was moved to its present headquarters in **Lausanne**. In 1982, Anselmo López became its first full-time director, a position he held through 1995. He remains the honorary director, with the post of director being held since 1995 by Pere Miró. The chairman of the Olympic Solidarity Commission is IOC member Mario Vázquez Raña (MEX). *See also* ASSOCIATION DES COMITÉS NATIONAUX OLYMPIQUES.

OLYMPIC SOLIDARITY COMMISSION. *See* OLYMPIC SOLIDARITY.

OLYMPIC STUDIES CENTRE. The Olympic Studies Centre is located in the lowest level of the **Olympic Museum** in **Lausanne**, Switzerland. It was created by the **International Olympic Committee** (IOC) in order to preserve and disseminate information about the **Olympic movement** and to coordinate and promote research. The center contains a large library that is open to the public, as well as the IOC Historical Archives, parts of which can be examined by scholars with prior written approval. The Olympic Studies Centre also conducts conferences and symposia to spread the message of **Olympism**.

OLYMPIC SYMBOL. *See* OLYMPIC FLAG.

OLYMPIC TORCH AND TORCH RELAY. *See* OLYMPIC FLAME, OLYMPIC TORCH, AND TORCH RELAY.

OLYMPIC TRUCE. It is often stated that in Ancient Greece, a sacred Olympic truce, or *ekecheiria*, existed such that all wars ceased during the **Olympic Games**. In addition, all persons traveling to or from the Olympic Games were guaranteed free passage to Olympia, in the city-state of Elis, even if passing through lands or city-states that were at war. It is quite certain that the Olympic truce never existed fully in this form, and recent research by classical scholars indicates that this is an oversimplification of the facts. It has been noted that the Olympic truce "never stopped a war, nor indeed were the Eleans so foolishly utopian as to imagine they could achieve that" (Finley and Pleket 1976, 98). Apparently the Olympic law only forbade open warfare against the Eleans, and the truce was specifically meant only not to disrupt the Olympic Games, allowing safe passage for all athletes, artists, and spectators traveling to and from Olympia.

In 1992, the **International Olympic Committee** (IOC) made steps to reinstitute this important part of Olympic lore by creating the Olympic Truce Project. Contact was made by IOC president **Juan Antonio Samaranch** with all of the **National Olympic Committees** (NOCs), many nongovernmental organizations, and the United Nations General Assembly, in which he proposed an Olympic truce to take place during the period of and surrounding the Olympic Games. This was eventually approved by the United Nations General Assembly in Resolution A/Res/48/11 on 25 October 1993 at their 36th Plenary Meeting. This has been renewed by the United Nations every two years, one year before each edition of the Olympic Games or **Olympic Winter Games**. The sixth resolution on the Olympic truce was approved in November 2003 by the 58th session of the United Nations General Assembly.

Samaranch's appeal for the Olympic truce, released from Barcelona on 21 July 1992, read as follows:

> The International Olympic Committee,
> Considering the frequency of conflicts which seriously affect the lives and future of the youth of the world;
> Faithful to the mission which it has assigned itself, namely to contribute to peace;
> Anxious in this respect to restore the Ancient Greek tradition of *Ekecheiria* or "Olympic Truce Pledge";

Calls on
—all States (their heads, governments and assemblies);
—all international and national organizations;
to decide that:

1. During the period from the 7th day before the opening of the Olympic Games until the 7 th day after the end of these Games, the "Olympic Truce" shall be observed;
2. During the Olympic Truce dedicated, as in Ancient Greece, to the spirit of brotherhood and understanding between peoples, all initiatives shall be taken and all group or individual efforts made to begin and continue to achieve by peaceful means the settlement of conflicts, whether or not of an international nature, with a view to establish peace;
3. During this period, all armed conflicts, and any acts related to, inspired by or akin to such conflicts, shall cease, whatever the reason, cause or means of perpetration thereof.

The United Nations Resolution A/Res/48/11 reads as follows:

The General Assembly,

Considering the appeal launched by the International Olympic Committee for an Olympic Truce, which was endorsed by 184 Olympic Committees and presented to the Secretary General,

Recognizing that the goal of the Olympic Movement is to build a peaceful and better world by educating the youth of the world through sport, practiced without discrimination of any kind and in the Olympic spirit, which requires mutual understanding, promoted by friendship, solidarity and fair-play,

Recognizing also the efforts of the International Olympic Committee to restore the Ancient Greek tradition of the Ekecheiria, or "Olympic Truce," in the interest of contributing to international understanding and the maintenance of peace,

Recalling resolution CM/Res. 1472 (LVIII), which supports the appeal for an Olympic Truce, adopted by the Council of Ministers of the Organization of African Unity at its 58th Ordinary session, held in Cairo from 21 to 26 June 1993, and endorsed by the Assembly of Heads of State and government of that organisation,

Recognizing further the valuable contribution that the appeal launched by the International Olympic Committee for an Olympic Truce could make towards advancing the purposes and principles of the Charter of the United Nations,

1. Commends the International Olympic Committee, the International Sports Federations and the National Olympic Committees

for their efforts to mobilize the youth of the world in the cause of peace;

2. Urges Member States to observe the Olympic Truce from the seventh day before the opening until the seventh day following the closing of each of the Olympic Games, in accordance with the appeal launched by the International Olympic Committee.

3. Notes the idea of the Olympic Truce, as dedicated in Ancient Greece to the spirit of fraternity and understanding between peoples, and urges Member States to take the initiative to abide by the Truce, individually and collectively, and to pursue in conformity with the purposes and principles of the Charter of the United Nations the peaceful settlement of all international conflicts;

4. Calls upon all Member States to cooperate with the International Olympic Committee in its efforts to promote the Olympic Truce;

5. Requests the Secretary General to promote the observance of the Olympic Truce among Member States, drawing the attention of world public opinion to the contribution such a truce would make to the promotion of international understanding and the maintenance of peace and goodwill, and to cooperate with the International Olympic Committee in the realization of this objective.

In July 2000, the IOC established an International Olympic Truce Foundation (IOTF), headquartered in **Lausanne, Switzerland**, with a symbolic office in Olympia, with a foundation board chaired by IOC president **Jacques Rogge**. It has listed its objectives as 1) to promote the Olympic ideals to serve peace, friendship, and understanding in the world, and in particular, to promote the Ancient Greek tradition of the Olympic truce; and 2) to initiate conflict prevention and resolution through sport, culture, and the Olympic ideals, by cooperating with all inter- and nongovernmental organizations specialized in this field, by developing educational and research programs, and by launching communications campaigns to promote the Olympic Truce. The IOTF has established the International Olympic Truce Centre (IOTC), headquartered in Athens, with a liaison office in Lausanne, and a symbolic office in Olympia. It is responsible for the implementation of projects related to the worldwide promotion of a culture of peace through sport and the Olympic Ideal.

OLYMPIC VILLAGE. At each Olympics since 1924, the **organizing committees** have provided an Olympic Village that houses the athletes. In recent years with the spread of the Games over very large areas, many organizing committees have provided several Olympic Villages. Recently, the host cities to the **Olympic Games** have used the Olympic Villages to provide low-cost housing to their citizens at the end of the Olympics.

OLYMPIC WINTER GAMES. The Olympic Winter Games are held every four years. Originally they were held in the same year as the **Games of the Olympiad**. Currently, they are contested every four years, but during the second calendar year following the beginning of the **Olympiad**. This ruling was made at the 91st IOC session in 1986 in **Lausanne**, by a vote of 78-2, specifically to take advantage of the better use of advertising and television dollars to fund the **Olympic movement**. *See also* the chronology of the Olympic Games and Olympic Winter Games.

OLYMPISM. Olympism is a philosophy that is felt to be the cornerstone of the **Olympic movement**. It is not easily defined and probably means different things to different people. The **International Olympic Committee** (IOC) defines Olympism in the **Olympic Charter** as follows:

> Olympism is a philosophy of life, exalting and combining in a balanced whole the qualities of body, will and mind. Blending sport with culture and education, Olympism seeks to create a way of life based on the joy found in effort, the educational value of good example, and respect for universal fundamental ethical principles. The goal of Olympism is to place everywhere sport at the service of the harmonious development of man, with a view to encouraging the establishment of a peaceful society concerned with the preservation of human dignity.

Dr. John Powell, an eminent lecturer and author on Olympic ideals, has proposed another definition, which in 1986 was adopted by the executive committee of the Canadian Olympic Association: "Olympism is a harmony of ideas and ideals that affirm the value of Olympic sport in promoting and developing sound physical and moral qualities in individuals, and in contributing to a better and more peaceful world by enabling representatives of nations to meet in an atmosphere of mutual respect and international amity."

OMAN (OMA). Oman formed a National Olympic Committee (NOC) in 1982, which the **International Olympic Committee** (IOC) recognized in the same year. Oman made its Olympic début in 1984 at Los Angeles, where it was represented in **shooting**, track and field **athletics**, and **yachting**. Oman has also competed in 1988, 1992, 1996, 2000, and 2004. Its best Olympic finish came in 1988 when Mohammad Al-Malky finished eighth in the 400 meters in track and field athletics. Oman has never competed at the **Olympic Winter Games**.

O'NEILL, SUSAN (AUS–SWI). B. 2 August 1973, Mackay, Queensland. Susie O'Neill's record approaches that of **Dawn Fraser** among **Australian** distance swimmers. O'Neill competed at the 1992, 1996, and 2000 **Olympic Games**, winning eight medals, including individual gold medals in the 200 butterfly in 1996 and the 200 freestyle in 2000. Her top career performance may have come at the 1999 World Championships when she won the 200 fly, breaking the 19-year-old world record that had been set by **Mary T. Meagher**. O'Neill was remarkably consistent. Between 1990 and 2000, she never failed to win a medal at an international competition. She won 10 gold medals at the Commonwealth Games, the most by any Australian in any sport. O'Neill was named Australian Female Athlete of the Year in 1996 and 1998, and in 1997, she was given the Order of Australia. Shortly after the Sydney Olympics, O'Neill was elected by her peers as an athlete member of the **International Olympic Committee** (IOC). She resigned from this membership in January 2005, citing family commitments.

ONO, TAKASHI (JPN–GYM). B. 26 July 1931, Noshiro, Akita Prefecture. Takashi Ono was the first Japanese to win an individual Olympic gold medal for **gymnastics**. He won the horizontal bar in 1956 and 1960, shared first place in the horse vault in 1960, and won team gold in 1956 and 1960. To his five gold medals he added four silver and four bronze medals, highlighted by silver medals in the all-around in both 1956 and 1960. At the World Championships, Ono won four silver medals and a bronze in 1958 and won the World Championships on the horizontal bar in 1962.

ORGANIZACIÓN DEPORTIVA CENTROAMERICANA Y DEL CARIBE (ODECABE). The Organización Deportiva Centroamericana y del Caribe is a confederation of **National Olympic Committees** (NOCs) of the Central American and Caribbean region. It is the oldest association of NOCs, having been founded on 4 July 1924 as the Central American and Caribbean Sports Association (CACSO). They contest the Central American and Caribbean Games, which are the oldest **Regional International Games**, having first been held in 1926. The organization is headquartered in Mexico City and its president is José Joaquin Puello of the **Dominican Republic**.

ORGANIZACIÓN DEPORTIVA PANAMERICANA (ODEPA). *See* PAN AMERICAN SPORTS ORGANIZATION (PASO).

ORGANIZACIÓN DEPORTIVA SUDAMERICANA (ODESUR). All of the South American **National Olympic Committees** (NOCs) are members of the **Pan American Sports Organization** (PASO). But that group is somewhat dominated by the North American nations of the **United States** and **Canada**, so in 1976, the president of the Bolivian Olympic Committee, José Gamarra Zorrilla, began the process of forming an organization devoted to promoting the interests of the South American National Olympic Committees. ODESUR was formed on 26 March 1976, and also began contesting a **Regional International Games**, the South American Games, in 1978. The 15 NOCs that comprise ODESUR are **Argentina, Aruba, Bolivia, Brazil, Chile, Colombia, Ecuador, Guyana, Netherlands Antilles, Panama, Paraguay, Peru, Surinam, Uruguay**, and **Venezuela**.

ORGANIZING COMMITTEES OF THE OLYMPIC GAMES (OCOGs/COJOs). The organization of each **Olympic Games** or **Olympic Winter Games** is entrusted by the **International Olympic Committee** (IOC) to an **organizing committee**, which is then in charge of producing the Olympic Games or Olympic Winter Games. The committees are formed exclusively for the purpose of putting on the Olympics and, as such, dissolve shortly after the Olympics are held. The French acronym stands for Comité d'Organisateur des Jeux Olympiques.

ORIENTEERING. Orienteering has never been contested at the **Olympic Games**, even as a **demonstration sport**. However, the

International Orienteering Federation (IOF) is recognized by the **International Olympic Committee** (IOC). The IOF was founded in 1961 and currently has 63 affiliated member nations.

OSBURN, CARL TOWNSEND (USA–SHO). B. 5 May 1884, Jacksontown, Ohio. D. 28 December 1966, Helena, California. Carl Osburn was the most successful Olympic marksman in history. At the Games of 1912, 1920, and 1924 he won five gold, four silver, and two bronze medals for a record total of 11 medals. Three of his five gold medals came in 1920. He was a career naval officer who graduated from Annapolis in 1906 and rose to the rank of commander. Besides his Olympic **shooting** success, Osburn competed internationally for the **United States** at the World Championships of 1921, 1922, 1923, and 1924, and at the Pan-American Matches of 1913.

OTTEY, MERLENE JOYCE (JAM/SLO–ATH). B. 10 May 1960, Cold Spring. Merlene Ottey is one of only two women to compete in seven **Olympic Games**, and her eight medals won in **athletics** (track and field) equals the best mark for women. A sprinter who competes in the 100, 200, and the 4 × 100 relay, she has competed at the Olympics of 1980, 1984, 1988, 1992, 1996, 2000, and 2004, changing her allegiance to Slovenia in 2004. She has never won an Olympic gold medal, winning three silver medals and five bronze medals. At the World Championships, she has won 10 medals, including the gold medal over 200 meters in both 1993 and 1995. She won gold medals at the Commonwealth Games in the 100 meters in 1990 and the 200 meters in 1982 and 1990. Ottey won a silver medal in 2000 as a member of the Jamaican 4 × 100 relay team, when she was over 40 years old, making her the oldest female athletics medalist at the Olympic Games.

OTTO, KRISTIN (GDR–SWI). B. 7 February 1966, Leipzig. Kristin Otto's six gold medals at one Games (1988) is a women's record for any sport. In Seoul Otto uniquely won gold medals in three different strokes, freestyle, backstroke, and butterfly, and her overall performance at the 1988 Games ranks as one of history's greatest sporting achievements. At the World Championships (1982, 1986) she won seven gold medals. Otto set two individual world records and contributed to four relay world records in her career.

OWENS, JAMES CLEVELAND "JESSE" (USA–ATH). B. 12 September 1913, Decatur, Alabama. D. 31 March 1980, Tucson, Arizona. Jesse Owens is an Olympic legend whose four gold medals at the 1936 Games (100 meters, 200 meters, 4 × 100 meters relay, and long jump) did much to undermine Hitler's myth of Aryan superiority. His place in sporting history had already been assured when he set six world records in one day (25 May 1935), and his long jump record of 26′8½″ (8.13 meters), set that day, remained a world best for more than 25 years. At the end of the 1936 season, Owens turned professional, and in his later years he traveled extensively as a speaker promoting the cause of **Olympism** and related philosophies.

– P –

PAKISTAN (PAK). Pakistan first competed at the **Olympic Games** in 1948. It did not attend the 1980 Moscow Olympics but has attended all Games since. It has never competed at the **Olympic Winter Games**. Pakistan owes almost its entire Olympic success to one sport—**field hockey**. It won a medal in this sport at every celebration from 1956 through 1984, finished fourth in 1948 and 1952, fifth in 1988, third in 1992, sixth in 1996, fourth in 2000, and fifth in 2004. In 1960, it won the gold medal, defeating **India** in the final and ending its 32-year Olympic winning streak, a feat it repeated in both 1968 and 1984.

PALAU (PLW). The Palau **National Olympic Committee** (NOC) was granted provisional recognition by the **International Olympic Committee** (IOC) in 1998, and full recognition followed in 1999. Palau made its Olympic début in 2000 at Sydney, represented by five athletes, and also competed in 2004 at Athens, represented by four athletes.

PALESTINE (PLE). A Palestine Olympic Committee existed prior to World War II, formed in 1933. Palestine was ruled under a British mandate from 1921 through 1948. During those years, Palestine had a **National Olympic Committee** (NOC) that was recognized by the **International Olympic Committee** (IOC), although it never competed at the **Olympic Games**. The Palestine Olympic Committee was titularly to represent Jews, Muslims, and Christians from the region of Palestine, but the rules of the original Palestine NOC stated that they "represent the Jewish National Home." Thus, that olympic committeee was more a precursor of the **Israel** Olympic Committee than of the current Palestine Olympic Committee.

Palestine currently has no exact geographic boundaries, but its NOC was given provisional recognition by the IOC at its annual meeting in Monte Carlo in September 1993. This occurred shortly after the historic agreement signed between the Palestine Liberation Organization (PLO) and the state of Israel in that same month. Palestine first competed at the Olympic Games in 1996 when it was represented by a single athlete, who finished last in his heat of the 10,000 meters. Palestine was represented at Sydney in 2000 by one female swimmer and one male runner, and in 2004 by one male and one female runner and one male swimmer.

PAN AMERICAN SPORTS ORGANIZATION (PASO). The Pan American Sports Organization (PASO) is a confederation of **National Olympic Committees** (NOCs) in the Americas. It was founded on 8 August 1948, and in 1955, the current structure was put in place and the current name of the group was adopted. The official languages of the group are English and Spanish, and its name is listed as both the Pan American Sports Organization (PASO) and the Organización Deportiva Panamericana (ODEPA). The group's goals, as listed in its charter, are "to strengthen and tighten the bonds of friendship and solidarity among the peoples of America; to further the development and growth of the Olympic Ideal; to cooperate with the NOCs of the Americas; to ensure the periodic celebration of the Pan-American Games; and to coordinate the Olympic and Pan-American Solidarity Programs." The organization is headquartered in Mexico City, and the current president (2004) is Mario Vázquez Raña of Mexico. As of 2004 there were 42 member nations.

PANAMA (PAN). Panama was represented at the Olympics in 1928, 1948, and 1952 by a single athlete. It has sent larger contingents since 1960, although the country did not attend the 1980 Moscow Olympics. It has never competed in the **Olympic Winter Games**. Its lone competitor in 1948 did quite well, as Lloyd LaBeach won

Panama's only two Olympic medals to date, finishing third in both the 100 and 200 meter dashes.

PANKRATION. Ancient Olympic sport. The pankration was a violent sport with virtually no holds barred, in which kicking played an important part. It was a very popular sport with the fans, and it was actually less brutal than **boxing**, as the pankratiasts wore no gloves that inflicted so much harm on the boxers. Plato described it as "a contest combining incomplete wrestling with incomplete boxing." The first recorded champion was Lygdamis of Syracuse in 648 BCE, and champions are recorded through Aurelius Phoibammon of Egypt in 221 CE. Five separate athletes won at least three championships at Olympia in the pankration. A boys' pankration was held from 200 BCE through 117 CE. One of the most famous pankration champions, Arrikion of Figaleia, was killed while successfully defending his title in this sport. He was awarded the title posthumously when his opponent was disqualified.

PAPP, LÁSZLÓ (HUN–BOX). B. 25 March 1926, Budapest. After winning the Olympic middleweight title in 1948, László Papp won the light-middleweight crown in 1952 and 1956 to become the first **boxer** to win three Olympic gold medals. Possibly his finest victory in the Olympic ring came in the 1956 final when he beat José Torres (USA), a future world professional champion. A skillful, hard-punching southpaw, Papp was the first fighter from the **Soviet** bloc to turn professional, and he won the European middleweight title in 1962. However, in 1965, the **Hungarian** authorities withdrew their permission for him to fight professionally, and the chance of a world title bout was denied him.

PAPUA-NEW GUINEA (PNG, formerly NGU). Papua-New Guinea has competed at every **Olympic Games** since it made its début in 1976, with the exception of 1980. In 1992, Henry Kungsi posted its best Olympic performance yet. A lightweight **boxer**, he won one match to finish equal ninth of 29 competitors in his class. No athletes from Papua-New Guinea have competed in the **Olympic Winter Games**.

PARAGUAY (PAR). Paraguay has competed at every **Olympic Games** since its début in 1968, with the exception of 1980. Paraguay has not yet competed at the **Olympic Winter Games**. Paraguay has won one medal at the Olympic Games. In 2004, their **football (soccer)** team finished second, earning a silver medal.

PARALYMPIC GAMES. The Paralympic Games are an international sporting event, specifially for athletes with disabilities. They typically follow the **Olympic Games**, now usually in the same city that hosts the Olympic Games. Recent rules changes mandated by the **IOC 2000 Commission** have made it mandatory that the Paralympics be held just after the Olympic Games in the same city as the Olympics. The Paralympic Games are organized by the International Paralympic Committee, which is an organization recognized by the **International Olympic Committee** (IOC). The Paralympics trace their beginnings to shortly after World War II and the Stoke Mandeville Games. The Stoke Mandeville Hospital in England is a well-known spinal cord injury research and treatment center. The hospital began sponsoring a series of Games in 1948, called the Stoke Mandeville Games. The Games were originally for athletes with paralysis and were started by Dr. Ludwig Guttman.

The Paralympics first began in 1960 at Rome and have expanded on the Stoke Mandeville concept to include many other disabilities, including amputees and blind athletes. The International Paralympic Committee (IPC) has its headquarters in Bonn, **Germany**. In addition to the IPC, the International Olympic Committee (IOC) recognizes several other organizations for athletes with disabilities. These include the Cerebral Palsy International Sports and Recreation Association (CP-ISRA), the International Blind Sports Federation (IBSA), the International Sports Federation for Persons with an Intellectual Disability (INAS-FID), the International Sports Organization of the Disabled (ISOD), the Comité International des Sports des Sourds (CISS—Deaf Athletes), and the forerunner of them all, the International Stoke Mandeville Wheelchair Sports Federation (ISMWSF).

The Stoke Mandeville Wheelchair Games continue to be held annually in Buckinghamshire, England. The Paralympics have been expanded to include a winter version, conducted since 1976. Like the Summer Paralympics, they are usually held in the same city as the **Olympic Winter Games**, with the following exceptions: 1976—

Ornskoldsvik, Sweden (not Innsbruck); 1980—Geilo, Norway (not Lake Placid), and 1984—Innsbruck, Austria (not Sarajevo).

The IOC also recognizes Special Olympics International, which is an American group that organizes sporting events for athletes with disabilities. Originally, Special Olympics began as an American sports festival, but it has expanded and now includes international events as well, highlighted by the Special Olympic World Games, which are also held in both Summer and Winter Versions. The Special Olympic World Games began in 1968 in Chicago, while the Special Olympics World Winter Games began in 1977 in Steamboat Springs, Colorado.

PARISI, ANGELO (GBR/FRA–JUD). B. 3 January 1953, Italy. With four Olympic medals (one gold, two silver, one bronze) Angelo Parisi is the most successful *judoka* in Olympic history. Italian born, he won a bronze in the open class in 1972 representing **Great Britain**, and then he represented **France** in 1980 and 1984, following his marriage to a Frenchwoman. In 1980, Parisi won the unlimited class title and placed second in the open class, and in 1984 he won his fourth medal with a silver in the unlimited class. Parisi never managed to win at the World Championships.

PATZAICHIN, IVAN (ROM–CAN). B. 26 November 1949, Tulcea. Ivan Patzaichin won 13 **canoeing** titles at the **Olympic Games** and World Championships, equaling the record for men set by **Gert Fredriksson** (SWE) and Rüdiger Helm (GDR). His Olympic record included seven medals, of which four were gold and three silver. Patzaichin competed at five Olympic Games, from 1968 through 1984, representing the Dinamo Bucharest club for **Romania**. His Olympic titles were the C2-1000 in 1968, the C1-1000 in 1972, the C2-1000 in 1980, and the C2-1000 in 1984. His World Championships were at C2-500 in 1979, C2-1000 in 1970, 1973, and 1981, the C1-1000 in 1977, and the C1-10K in 1978.

PELOTA BASQUE. Pelota is a generic name for various hand-and-ball or racquet-and-ball games derived from the ancient French racquet sport of *jeu de paume*. It has similarities to the American pari-mutuel betting sport of jai alai. Pelota basque, the Spanish variant played in the Basque regions and contiguous provinces of **France** and **Spain**, has thrice been an Olympic **demonstration sport** in 1924, 1968, and 1992. In addition, at the unusual **Olympic Games** of 1900, a version of pelota can be considered to have been an Olympic sport. The Fédération Internationale de Pelote Basque (FIPV) was founded in 1929 and is recognized by the **International Olympic Committee** (IOC), with 25 affiliated national members as of 2004.

PENTATHLON. Ancient Olympic sport. The five events of the ancient pentathlon were jumping, a *stadion* race (sprint of about 190 meters), the discus throw, the javelin throw, and **wrestling**. The origin of the event is attributed to Jason (of Argonaut fame). According to mythology, Jason was to award the prizes at an ancient Games, and his friend Peleus was second in all the contests. So Jason combined the events out of a desire to honor his friend, and thus created the pentathlon.

It is unclear how the winner of the pentathlon was decided. The precise order of the events is also unclear. It is only known with certainty that the last event was wrestling. If any athlete won any three events, he was immediately declared the winner, and the ancient term *triakter* is often seen, meaning the winner of three events. However, classics and Olympics scholars have not agreed on how the victor was determined in other circumstances. In 1906, at the Intercalated Olympic Games, a pentathlon was held consisting of the same five events as the ancient pentathlon.

PENTATHLON, MODERN. *See* MODERN PENTATHLON.

PEOPLE'S DEMOCRATIC REPUBLIC OF YEMEN (YMD). *See* YEMEN.

PERKINS, KIEREN JOHN (AUS–SWI). B. 14 July 1973, Brisbane, Queensland. Kieren Perkins is considered by many as the best distance freestyler ever, rivaling **Vladimir Salnikov** and his countryman, **Grant Hackett**. Perkins burst onto the international scene in 1991, winning the 400, 800, and 1,500 meters at the Pan-Pacific meet, setting a world record of 7:47.85 in the 800. At the 1992 Australian Olympic trials, he won the 400 and 1,500 in world record times. Later that year, Perkins won the 1,500 Olympic gold medal in a world record 14:43.48. In the 400 at the 1992 Olympics, he bettered his 400 world record by over a second, recording 3:45.16, but was touched out for the gold by the **Unified Team**'s Yevgeny Sadovyi. Perkins's performance at the 1994 Commonwealth Games may be his finest ever, winning the 200, 400, 1,500, **swimming** on the winning 800 freestyle relay, and breaking his own world record in the 1,500 meters. In addition, his interval split during the 1,500 also broke his 800 meter world record. In 1996, Perkins defended his Olympic title in the 1,500 meters. After 1996, his performances dropped off and he was surpassed in the distances by Hackett. It was not certain he would even make the 2000 Australian team, but he reached back, recalling past glories, and followed Hackett to the wall for a silver medal in the 1,500 freestyle. During his career, Perkins set three world records over 800 meters, three at 1,500 meters, and two at 400 meters.

PERSIA. Although Persia had two early members of the **International Olympic Committee** (IOC), Mizzam Eddin Khoi (1921–1923) and Prince Samad Khan Momtazos Saltaneh (1923–1927), interest in Olympic matters was virtually nonexistent in the country. The fact that both of these IOC members were resident in Europe did nothing to improve matters, and it was not until the 1930s, when a program of modernization began and Persia became known as Iran, that a degree of Olympic interest developed. *See also* IRAN.

PERU (PER). After **International Olympic Committee** (IOC) member Carlos de Candamo competed as a **fencer** in the 1900 Olympics, Peru's next Olympic appearance was in 1936. It has since missed only the 1952 Games in Helsinki. The country has not competed at the **Olympic Winter Games**. Peru has won four Olympic medals, with one gold medal. Three of these were won in **shooting** and one in women's **volleyball**. The nation has won one medal each in 1948, 1984, 1988, and 1992.

PHELPS, MICHAEL, II (USA–SWI). B. 30 June 1985, Baltimore, Maryland. Michael Phelps was the single biggest star of the 2004 Athens **Olympic Games**. When only 15 years old, Phelps swam at the Sydney Olympics in the 200 butterfly but failed to win a medal. But starting in 2001 he began to dominate international **swimming**, when he won the World Championships and broke the world record in the 200 fly. From 2001–2004, he set 13 world records, swimming several different events, and won 20 national titles. He has been World Champion in the 200 fly in 2001, and in 2003 he won the the world title in the 200 fly, 200 individual medley (IM), 400 IM, and swam on the winning 4 × 100 medley relay. He had a chance at Athens to win gold medals in eight events, eventually winning six gold medals and eight medals in all, tying the record of eight medals at a single Olympics set in 1980 by the **Soviet gymnast Aleksandr Dityatin**. Media fanfare was rampant for Phelps after the 2004 Olympics, but it dimmed somewhat when he was arrested for drunken driving in October 2004. He continues to swim competitively and expects to compete through the 2008 Olympic Games.

PHILIPPINES, THE (PHI). The Philippines first competed at the Olympics in 1924 and has since missed only the 1980 Moscow Olympics. The Philippines has competed at the **Olympic Winter Games** of 1972, 1988, and 1992. The Philippines has won nine Olympic medals in **boxing**, **swimming**, and track and field **athletics**. Though the country has not yet won a gold medal in an official sport, Arianne Cerdena won the **women**'s **bowling** event in that exhibition sport in 1988.

PIERRE DE COUBERTIN COMMISSION. The Pierre de Coubertin Commission was created in 1975 and worked to promulgate the teachings of Baron **Pierre de Coubertin** and his philosophy. It worked very closely with the **International Pierre de Coubertin Committee** in this regard, but is no longer recognized by the **International Olympic Committee** (IOC).

PIETRI, DORANDO (ITA–ATH). B. 16 October 1885, Mandrio, Reggio Emilia. D. 7 February 1942. Dorando Pietri is the most famous loser in Olympic history. Entering the stadium at the end of the 1908 Olympic **marathon** he held a comfortable lead over Johnny Hayes (USA), but he then collapsed five times and had to be helped across the finishing line. This assistance from well-meaning officials resulted in his disqualification, but, in defeat, Pietri's fame far exceeded that of the winner. Queen Alexandra presented him with a large gold cup, which was an exact replica of the one awarded to the Olympic champion, and Irving Berlin wrote the popular song "Dorando" in his honor. Pietri turned professional shortly after the 1908 Olympics and enjoyed a successful career in America and Europe.

PINDAR (GRE). fl. ca. 520-440 B.C. Pindar was a Greek lyric poet, considered the greatest of the Greek choral lyricists. Few details remain of his life, but he was known to have been an aristocrat from Thebes who studied in Athens. Pindar is best known for his *epinicia,* which were odes celebrating athletic victories. Forty-four of these have survived, most celebrating victories in the **Olympic, Isthmian, Nemean**, and **Pythian Games**. The odes were usually commissioned by the victor or his family.

PINSENT, MATTHEW CLIVE (GBR–ROW). B. 10 October 1970, Holt, Norfolk. Matthew Pinsent graduated from St. Catherine's College at Oxford, where he captained the Oxford Rowing Club and led the Oxford eight to victories in 1990 and 1991 over Cambridge. Since that time, he has not failed to be at the top stage of international **rowing**, partnering **Stephen Redgrave** through much of his career, primarily in the coxless pairs, though later in the coxless fours. Beginning in 1991, Pinsent and Redgrave won an Olympic gold medal or a World Championships gold medal at every edition through Redgrave's retirement after the 2000 **Olympic Games**. Pinsent then began rowing with James Cracknell. Pinsent and Cracknell formed an unbeatable pair winning the world title in 2001 and 2002 in coxless pairs and in 2001 in the coxed pairs. Pinsent has won Olympic gold medals at the 1992, 1996, 2000, and 2004 Olympics—coxless pairs in 1992 and 1996 with Redgrave, and coxless fours in 2000 and 2004, with Redgrave and Cracknell. (Tim Foster in 2000 and Ed Goode in 2004 rounded out the four.) His record of four Olympic rowing gold medals is surpassed only by Redgrave and **Elisabeta Lipa-Oleniuc**, both with five. Pinsent also claims 14 championships at the Henley Royal Regatta, all in the coxless pairs or fours, failing to win since 1990 only in 1992. Pinsent retired from competitive rowing after the 2004 season, and Sir Matthew Pinsent was knighted shortly thereafter.

POLAND (POL). Poland competed continuously at the **Olympic Games** from 1924 through 1980, and after **boycotting** Los Angeles in 1984, it returned to the Olympic fold in 1988 at Seoul. Prior to 1924, several Poles probably competed for other countries. In 1908, Jerzy Gajdzyk, his name Americanized to George Gaidzik, won a **diving** bronze medal for the **United States**, and in 1912 the Polish-born Julius Beresford (né Wisniewski) won a silver medal with the British eight-oared crew. The 1912 Russian Olympic team included eight Poles. Poland has also competed at all the **Olympic Winter Games** since 1924. Through 2004, Poland has won 257 Olympic medals, 61 of them gold, with all but six of the medals coming at the Olympic Games.

POLO. Polo has been contested at the Olympics in 1900, 1908, 1920, 1924, and 1936. The Fédération Internationale de Polo (FIP) was founded in 1985 and is an **International Olympic Committee** (IOC)-recognized federation, currently with 75 national members.

POPOV, ALEKSANDR (EUN/RUS–SWI). B. 16 November 1971, Volgograd, Soviet Union. Known by a variety of nicknames—"Sasha," "The Russian Rocket," "Ice Man," and "Big Dog"—Aleksander Popov is considered the greatest sprint freestyle **swimmer** ever. In both 1992 and 1996, Popov won gold medals in the 50 and 100 meter freestyle sprint events. He competed at the Sydney Olympics in 2000 but was touched out in the 100 by Pieter van den Hoogenband, winning a silver medal. Popov also competed in 2004, without winning a medal, and retired shortly after the Athens **Olympic Games**. At the World Championships, he won the 50 meter freestyle in 1994 and 2003, and the 100 meter freestyle in 1994, 1998, and 2003. His comeback to world-class swimming after the Atlanta Olympics was the stuff of legend. During an altercation on a Moscow street with an Azeri watermelon vendor, he was stabbed in the abdomen, with the knife grazing his lung and an artery to his kidney. He required emergency surgery and spent three months in rehabilitation. He returned in 1997 to defend his European titles in both the 50 and 100 meter freestyle events. Popov set one world record at both of the two sprint distances.

PORTUGAL (POR). Portugal has competed at the **Olympic Games** continuously since 1912. Through 1984, Portugal had appeared at the **Olympic Winter Games** once with only one competitor. That was Duarte Espirito Santo Silva who competed in **alpine skiing** events in 1952 at Oslo. However, Portugal also competed at the Olympic Winter Games in 1988, 1994, and 1998. Portugal has won 20 Olympic medals through 2000, three of them gold. It has yet to win a medal at the Olympic Winter Games.

POUND REPORT. *See* OLYMPIC BRIBERY SCANDAL.

POUND, RICHARD WILLIAM DUNCAN "DICK," Q. C. (CAN–SWI). B. 22 March 1942, St. Catharines, Ontario. Dick Pound was a **swimming** finalist (sixth in the 100 meter freestyle) at the 1960 **Olympic Games** who became president of the Canadian Olympic Association in 1977 and a member of the **International Olympic Committee** (IOC), the following year. In 1987, he was appointed a vice president of the IOC, and throughout the 1980s and 1990s he exerted considerable influence in the financial sphere, particularly in negotiations with sponsors, setting up **The Olympic Programme** (TOP), and in the sale of TV rights. A Montreal-based lawyer specializing in tax law, Pound earned his undergraduate and law degrees at McGill University in Montreal. His legal skills provided invaluable support to President **Juan Antonio Samaranch** in the negotiations with **North Korea** over the 1988 Games. Pound was one of the prime candidates to succeed Samaranch as president of the IOC in 2001 but failed in his bid to win the IOC presidency. Pound was chairman of the IOC **Finance Commission** from its inception, until he resigned in 2001 after the election. He was also the chairman of the IOC commission that oversaw the **Olympic bribery scandal** in 1999 and was named the first chairman of the **World Anti-Doping Agency** (WADA), a post to which he was reelected in 2004. From 2002–2004, Pound also chaired the **Olympic Games Study Commission**, which prepared a report on ways to streamline the costs of the Olympic Games and **Olympic Winter Games**. Dick Pound is likely the most influential IOC member who has never succeeded to the IOC presidency.

PRESS COMMISSION. The Press Commission was originally called the Press and Public Relations Commission, which was formed in 1967 and lasted until 1972. A separate Press Commission was formed in 1973. The current chairman is Australian **International Olympic Committee** (IOC) member R. Kevan Gosper, a former Olympic 400 meter runner. There are three other IOC members on the commission along with representatives of the world's sporting press. Prior to becoming IOC presidents, both **Lord Killanin** and **Juan Antonio Samaranch** served as chairmen of this commission.

PROTOPOPOV, OLEG ALEKSEYEVICH (URS–FSK). *See* BELOUSOVA, LYUDMILA.

PUERTO RICO (PUR). Puerto Rico first competed at the 1948 Olympics in London and has not failed to compete at the **Olympic Games** since then. Puerto Rico also competed at the **Olympic Winter Games** of 1984, 1988, 1992, 1994, and 1998, but did not compete in 2002. Puerto Rican athletes have won one silver and five bronze medals at the Olympic Games.

PYTHIAN GAMES. The Pythian Games were one of the four great Panhellenic sporting festivals, along with the **Olympic Games, Isthmian Games**, and **Nemean Games**. They were held in honor of Apollo at Delphi. They were the only one of the four main Greek festivals that also featured musical contests. The Pythian Games were first recorded in 582 BCE and continued until the fourth century CE. The Pythian Games were held quadrennially, in the third year of each Olympiad. The victors at the Pythian Games were awarded laurel crowns.

– Q –

QATAR (QAT). Qatar made its initial Olympic appearance in Los Angeles in 1984 with a team of eight **track and field** athletes, a **football (soccer)** team, and four **shooters**. Qatar also competed in 1988, 1992, 1996, 2000, and 2004. Qatar won its first Olympic medal in 1992 when Mohamed Sulaiman finished third in the men's 1,500 meters in track and field athletics. In 2000, Said Asaad added another bronze, won in the 105 kg. class **weightlifting**. Qatar has never competed at the **Olympic Winter Games**.

– R –

RACE IN ARMOR. Ancient Olympic sport. The race in armor was contested at Olympia from 520 BCE through at least 185 CE. It was also known as the *hoplite* event. The event was held over two laps of the stadium, or about 385 meters. **Leonidas of Rhodes** won four championships consecutively, from 164 to 152 BCE.

RACQUETBALL. Racquetball is decidedly different from racquets and is a very modern sport. It has not been contested at the **Olympic Games**, but the International Racquetball Federation (IRF) is recognized by the **International Olympic Committee** (IOC). It was founded in 1968 and currently has 90 affiliated member nations.

RACQUETS. Racquets has been contested as an Olympic sport only in 1908, when a men's singles and doubles event was held in London.

RADIO AND TELEVISION COMMISSION. The Radio and Television Commission (RTV Commission) has been known by various names. The first "media" commission was the Press and Public Relations Commission, which was formed in 1967 and lasted until 1972. At that time, two separate commissions, the **Press Commission** and the Television Commission, were created. A Radio Commission existed briefly in 1984. In 1985, this was merged with the Television Commission to form the Radio and Television Commission. The current chairman of the commission is **International Olympic Committee** (IOC) president **Jacques Rogge**. There are eight IOC members on the commission, but the bulk of this commission is made up of representatives of the television and radio networks worldwide, as well as representatives of the **Organizing Committee(s) of the Olympics Games** (OCOGs) who deal with the electronic media.

RADMILOVIC, PAOLO FRANCESCO "PAUL" (GBR–WAP). B. 5 March 1886, Cardiff, Glamorgan, Wales. D. 29 September 1968, Weston-Super-Mare, Somerset. Paul Radmilovic won **water polo** gold medals at three successive **Olympic Games** (1908, 1912, 1920) and also swam on the British 4 × 200 freestyle relay team that won in 1908. Radmilovic competed in Olympic water polo again in 1924 and 1928. His career was marked by its extraordinary length and by the range of distances over which he excelled. He won his first national **swimming** title in 1901 and the last in 1929, and he won championships at distances from 100 yards to 5 miles. Radmilovic had a Yugoslavian father and an Irish mother. In 1967 he was the first Briton to be inducted into the International Swimming Hall of Fame.

REAL TENNIS. *See* JEU DE PAUME.

REDGRAVE, STEPHEN GEOFFREY (GBR–ROW). B. 23 March 1962, Amersham. With five Olympic gold medals and one bronze, Steve Redgrave is the most successful Olympic oarsman of all time. After winning the coxed fours in 1984, he won the coxless pairs at the next three Games (1988, 1992, 1996) and added a bronze in the coxed pairs in 1988. At Sydney in 2000, he added his fifth gold medal, in the coxless fours, at which he had also been World Champion in 1999. Redgrave won gold medals at the World Championships in coxless pairs in 1991, 1993, 1994, and 1995, and in the coxless fours in 1997 and 1999. In 1986 he became the first rower to win three gold medals at the Commonwealth Games. At Henley, he was also Diamond Sculls champion in both 1983 and 1985. In 1989, Redgrave was also a member of the crew that won the British four-man **bobsled** title.

REGIONAL INTERNATIONAL GAMES. In addition to the **Olympic Games**, numerous international sporting events are held throughout the world each year. Many of these are simply international championships in the various sports, such as the World Gymnastics Championships or the World Athletics Championships. But in addition, since the 1910s, the nations of the world have gathered together to compete in regional international multisport competitions. The **International Olympic Committee** (IOC) has encouraged this because it follows some of the principles of **Olympism** and the **Olympic movement**—bringing together the various peoples of the world in peaceful sporting competition. In addition, as the Olympic Games grow and grow, the Regional International Games often now serve as qualifying events for the Olympic Games. Thus they have become even more important. In addition, two of the regional games have had definite importance to the various political battles afflicting the Olympic movement. These are the **Games of the New Emerging Forces (GANEFO)** and the **Goodwill Games**.

The various regional games probably number over 100, but the most important of them may be listed as follows: African Games, Arab Games, Arctic Winter Games, Asian Games, Asian Winter Games, Baltic Sea Games, Black Sea Games, Bolivarian Games, Central American and Caribbean Games, Central American Games, Central Asian Games, Commonwealth Games (formerly the British Empire Games), East Asian Games, Far East Championships, Games of the Small Countries of Europe, Games of the New Emerging Forces, Goodwill Games, Goodwill Winter Games, Indian Ocean Islands Games, Inter-Allied Games, Island Games, Mediterranean Games, Micronesian Games, **Nordic Games**, Pacific Ocean Games, Pan-American Games, South American Games, South Asian Federation Games, South East Asian Games, South Pacific Games, South Pacific Mini Games, and the West Asian Games.

REVIVAL OF THE OLYMPIC GAMES. *See* ATTEMPTS AT REVIVAL.

REVUE OLYMPIQUE. *See* OLYMPIC REVIEW.

RHODESIA (RHO). *See* ZIMBABWE.

RITOLA, VILJO EINO "VILLE" (FIN–ATH). B. 18 January 1896, Peräseinäjoki. D. 24 April 1982, Helsinki. Ville Ritola was an outstanding distance runner who rivaled his legendary countryman, **Paavo Nurmi**. At the 1924 **Olympic Games**, Ritola won the steeplechase in his first attempt at the race and improved his own 10,000 meter world record to win that event. He also won two further gold medals in the 3,000 meter team event and the team cross-country event. Ritola and

Nurmi met on the track for the first time at these Olympics with Nurmi claiming the honors by winning the 5,000 meters and defeating Ritola in the cross-country and 3,000 meters. At the 1928 Amsterdam Olympics, the matchup was in the 5,000 meters with Ritola defeating Nurmi to win the gold medal. The 14th of 20 children, Ritola left home in 1913 to emigrate to the **United States** and eventually won 14 Amateur Athletic Union (AAU) titles, returning home in the Olympic years. He never competed in the Finnish national championships.

ROBERT DOVER'S GAMES (COTSWOLD OLIMPICK GAMES). Robert Dover's Games, or Cotswold Olimpick Games, were probably first contested in 1612, during Whitsun (Pentecostal) Week upon the Cotswold Hills. The Games were started by Robert Dover, a local lawyer who lived nearby in the Cotswold Hills. The Games were basically a medieval country fair type of festival, but they achieved great fame. They were held from about 1612 to 1642 and were immortalized in a collection of 30 laudatory poems, entitled *Annalia Dubrensia* and published about Robert Dover's Olimpick Games in 1636. Four of the poems were composed by great poets of the era: Ben Jonson, Michael Drayton, Thomas Heywood, and Sir William Davenant. It is slightly conjectural, but apparently even Shakespeare knew of these Games, possibly mentioning them in *Sir John Falstaff and the Merry Wives of Windsor.* "Slender: '. . . How does your fallow greyhound, sir? I heard say he was outrun on Cotsall.'"

The Cotswold Olimpicks did not end after 1642 but were simply stopped during the civil war in England. They were revived in the 1660s and were then held at unknown intervals for two centuries. In 1851, they were revived but were shortly thereafter suspended again. After another century, the Cotswold Olimpicks were revived in 1951, were briefly suspended, and then resumed in 1963 to continue to this day.

Though they were quite famous in their era, and though they have been contested for many centuries, the only justification to call them "Olympic" Games rests on the fact that they adopted that name and that they had been brought into contact with the **Olympic, Pythian, Nemean**, and **Isthmian Games** via the *Annalia Dubrensia.* They had no significant influence on **Pierre de Coubertin** or others who attempted to revive the Olympic Games.

RODNINA, IRINA KONSTANTINOVA (later Zaytsev) (URS–FSK). B. 12 September 1949, Moscow. Irina Rodnina was the most successful pair skater in history. Olympic victories in 1972 with Aleksey Ulanov and in 1976 and 1980 with Aleksandr Zaytsev gave her a record total of three gold medals. Her record at the World Championships was even more impressive. Rodnina won the title for 10 successive years (1969–1978), the first four with Ulanov and the next six with Zaytsev. She married Zaytsev in 1973, and their successes in the latter part of their partnership were as husband and wife. Rodnina is now a **figure skating** coach.

ROGGE, CHEVALIER DR. JACQUES (BEL). B. 2 May 1942, Ghent. On 16 July 2001, Jacques Rogge was elected to succeed **Juan Antonio Samaranch** and become the eighth president of the **International Olympic Committee** (IOC). Rogge was an accomplished sailor, competing in three **Olympic Games** (1968, 1972, 1976) with his best finish in that sport being 14th in the Finn Monotype Class in 1972 at Munich. He also competed on one World Championship team in **sailing** and was 16 times Belgian champion. In addition, he competed internationally for **Belgium** in **rugby football**, at which he was selected 10 times for the national team. Rogge is the former chairman of the International Sailing Federation (ISAF) Medical Commission, serving in his capacity as an orthopaedic surgeon, specializing in sports medicine. He was formerly chief of the Orthopaedic Surgery Department at Ghent Hospital, although he has stopped practicing medicine since his election as IOC president. As a sports administrator he became head of the Comité Olympique et Interfédéral Belge in 1989 and in 1990 became president of the European Olympic Committees (EOC). He was elected a member of the IOC in 1991 and was appointed to the **Executive Board** in 1998. Although it is early in his term as president, he has worked to further the fight against **doping**, streamline the **Olympic program**, and also try to control some of the costs of both the Olympic Games and running the IOC itself.

ROLLER HOCKEY. In 1992, roller hockey was contested as a **demonstration sport** at the Barcelona Olympics. Roller hockey has never been contested at the Olympics at any other time. Roller hockey is governed by the Fédération Internationale de Roller Sports (FIRS). *See also* ROLLER SKATING.

ROLLER SKATING. Roller skating has never been contested at the **Olympic Games**, although it is contested at many of the regional games, including the Pan-American Games. Roller skating is governed by the Fédération Internationale de Roller Sports (FIRS), which was founded in 1924 and is recognized by the **International Olympic Committee** (IOC). The FIRS currently has 114 affiliated member nations. *See also* ROLLER HOCKEY.

ROMANIA (ROM). Romania's first Olympic participant was future **International Olympic Committee** (IOC) member Gheorghe Plagino, who competed in the clay trap **shooting** event in 1900. The nation next competed at the 1924 **Olympic Games** and have since missed only the 1932 and 1948 Olympics. Romania defied pressure from its neighbors and valiantly was the only Warsaw Pact country to compete at the 1984 Olympics in Los Angeles. Romania has competed at the **Olympic Winter Games** since their inception in 1924, missing only 1960. It is best known for its outstanding **women gymnasts**, and has also produced excellent **canoeists**. Romania has won 285 Olympic medals: 140 by its men, 140 by its women, and five in mixed events, with 82 gold medals.

ROQUE. *See* CROQUET.

ROSE, IAIN MURRAY (AUS–SWI). B. 6 January 1939, Nairn, Scotland. Murray Rose was a triple gold medalist at the 1956 Games; he won the 400 and 1,500 meter freestyle and was a member of the world record–breaking team in the 4 × 200 meter freestyle relay. After the Melbourne Games, Rose enrolled at the University of Southern California, and at the 1960 Olympics, he retained his 400 meters title, won silver in the 1,500 meters, and won a bronze in the relay. His total of six Olympic medals would surely have been greater but for the fact that he was not selected for the 1964 Games as he refused to return from California for the Australian Championships, the qualifying meet. Earlier in the year Rose had set world records for 880 yards and 1,500 meters and would certainly have been a medal contender in

Tokyo. Rose continued to enjoy competitive **swimming** long after his Olympic career was over, and in 1981 he won the World Masters title in faster times than he recorded at the 1956 Games.

ROSE, RALPH (USA–ATH). B. 17 March 1885, Louisville, Kentucky. D. 16 October 1913, San Francisco, California. In 1904, 19-year-old Ralph Rose, a 6'6" (1.98 m.), 235 lb. (107 kg.) giant, won three Olympic medals. His best performance in St. Louis came in the shot put when, after trailing Wesley Coe in the early rounds, he came back to win the Olympic title with a new world record. Rose lost his world record to the Irishman, Denis Horgan, later in the season, and Coe made a further improvement in 1905, but Rose recaptured the record in 1907 and beat both Horgan and Coe at the 1908 Olympics. Rose also won the both-hands shot put gold medal in 1912, a silver in the 1904 discus throw (losing in a throw-off to **Martin Sheridan**) and 1912 shot put, and a bronze in the 1904 hammer throw.

By 1909, Rose's weight had risen to a massive (for the era) 286 lbs. (130 kg.), and, in winning his third straight AAU (Amateur Athletic Union) title, he became the first man to break the 50-foot barrier. Rose eventually won four AAU shot titles, won the discus twice, and was the inaugural AAU javelin champion in 1909. Rose attended the University of Michigan and later studied law at Chicago. He was the flag-bearer in 1908 who refused to dip the flag as he walked past the English king, leading to the American tradition that survives to this day. Rose was prevented from adding to his six Olympic medals when he died very young from pneumonia in 1913.

ROWING AND SCULLING. Rowing was first known as a means of transportation in the ancient cultures of **Egypt**, **Greece**, and Rome. Rowing as a sport probably began in England in the 17th and early 18th centuries. By the 19th century, rowing was popular in Europe and had been brought to America. Early races were usually contested by professionals, with heavy betting on races common. Competitive rowing precedes most of the other Olympic sports in its recorded modern history. The first Oxford-Cambridge race took place in 1828, and Yale and Harvard first rowed against each other in 1852.

Only in 1896 has rowing not been contested in the Olympics. It was actually on the program that year, but rough seas forced cancellation of the events. There have been several events for men in both sweep events (single oar used by alternate oarsmen) and sculling events (two oars used by a single sculler or by two or more scullers). Through 1992, these included races for single, double, and quadruple sculls, and in sweep events, races for two and four oarsmen/women, with and without coxswain, and the large boats with eight oarsmen/women and a coxswain. **Women** were admitted to the Olympic rowing program in 1976. They compete in a streamlined program, with only one sweep event for four oarswomen, but they also compete in single, double, and quad sculls and the eight-oar sweep event. The rowing program for the 1996 Olympics underwent a drastic change, with the introduction of lightweight events. The men's coxed pairs and coxed fours was discontinued, replaced by the lightweight double sculls and lightweight coxless fours. The women's coxless pairs was also discontinued, replaced by lightweight double sculls.

The **United States** was the dominant nation in Olympic rowing until about 1960. The **Soviet Union** quickly became a power in the sport, but during its existence the **German Democratic Republic** (East Germany) (GDR) in the 1970s and 1980s was by far the pre-eminent nation.

The world governing body of rowing is the Fédération Internationale des Sociétés d'Aviron (FISA), which was formed in 1892 and had 118 member nations as of 2000. *See also* DRESDEN FOUR, THE.

RUDOLPH, WILMA GLODEAN (USA–ATH). B. 23 June 1940, St. Bethlehem, Tennessee. D. 12 November 1994, Brentwood, Tennessee. Although born with polio and contracting scarlet fever and double pneumonia at the age of four, Wilma Rudolph overcame all these handicaps to become one the greatest women sprinters of all time. As a 16-year-old, she won a bronze medal in the relay at the 1956 Olympics, and four years later she was the heroine of the 1960 Games. After setting a world 200 meter record (22.9) at the 1960 U.S. Championships she was a triple gold medalist at the Rome Olympics, winning the 100 meters, 200 meters, and relay. A following wind deprived her of a world record in the 100 meters, but she anchored the U.S. team to a world record in the heats of the relay. The following year Rudolph equaled the world 100 meter record (11.3), and four days later, she posted a new record of 11.2, in addition to leading the

U.S. to another world relay record. Her brilliant career ended with her retirement in 1962 after which she devoted herself to coaching and worked extensively with underprivileged children. She died fairly young from a brain tumor.

RUGBY (UNION) FOOTBALL. Rugby (union) football has been contested at the Olympics in 1900, 1908, 1920, and 1924. Amazingly, the defending Olympic champion is the **United States**, who won the gold medals in both 1920 and 1924. The International Rugby Board (IRB) governs the sport worldwide and is recognized by the **International Olympic Committee** (IOC). Founded in 1886, it currently has 95 member nations. Rugby Sevens, or seven-a-side rugby football, was approved for inclusion to the **Olympic program** by the IOC **Executive Board** in 2001. This proposal was tabled by the IOC session; however, at the 2005 IOC session in Singapore, rugby was not voted back onto the Olympic program for 2012.

RUIZ-CONFORTO, TRACIE (USA–SYF). B. 4 February 1963, Honolulu, Hawaii. Tracie Ruiz-Conforto was the first Olympic star in the relatively new sport of **synchronized swimming**. In 1984, as Tracie Ruiz, she won gold medals in both the solo event and, with Candie Costie, the duet. She then retired and married a former Penn State football player. Ruiz-Conforto took up bodybuilding and competed briefly in that sport, but she returned to synchronized competition in 1987. At the 1988 Olympics, she competed only in the solo event, earning a silver medal. At the Pan-American Games she won a team gold in 1979, solo and duet golds in 1983, and a solo gold in 1987. She was 1982 World Champion in solo, and she also won six U.S. Championships in the solo and four in the duet.

RUSKA, WILLEM "WIM" (NED–JUD). B. 29 August 1940, Amsterdam. Willem Ruska is the only *judoka* to have won two gold medals at the same Olympics. In 1972 he was the Olympic champion in the heavyweight and the open class. Ruska was also heavyweight World Champion in 1967 and 1971. To this he added seven European titles and 10 Dutch championships during his career. He was not particularly large for the unlimited or open class (110 kg. at only 1.89 meters), but was extremely muscular and cut a striking figure with his light blond hair. Ruska began his judo career at age 20 and traveled to **Japan** to train and learn from the Japanese masters. He retired after the 1972 Olympics.

RUSSIA (RUS). Prior to the Bolshevik Revolution, Russia competed at the Olympics of 1900, 1908, and 1912. Although at the first two celebrations its representation was only four and six athletes, respectively, in 1912 it sent a large team of 169 athletes. At those Olympics, Russia won one gold medal, four silver medals, and three bronze medals. After the Bolshevik Revolution, Russia became the largest republic of the **Soviet Union** (USSR). The Soviet Union did not compete in the Olympics from 1920 to 1948, but returned to the **Olympic Games** at Helsinki in 1952 and competed in the Olympics through 1988. With the political events of 1991, Russia again became eligible to compete as an individual nation. At Albertville and Barcelona, Russia joined with other former Soviet republics to compete as the "**Unified Team**," representing the **Commonwealth of Independent States**. Russia returned to the Olympic fold after an absence of 82 years in 1994 at Lillehammer. Russia has also competed at the 1996, 2000, and 2004 Olympic Games and the 1998 and 2002 **Olympic Winter Games**. Through 2004, Russian athletes have won 303 medals at the Olympics, with 111 gold. Of these medals, 248 came in the Summer Olympics and 55 at the Winter Olympics.

RWANDA (RWA). Rwanda first competed in the Olympics in 1984 and has since participated in 1988, 1992, 1996, 2000, and 2004. Apart from 1992, when the Rwandan team included three **cyclists**, and 2000, when it had one male and one female **swimmer**, their representation has been exclusively in track and field **athletics**. Rwanda has not yet competed in the **Olympic Winter Games**, and no Rwandan athlete has won an Olympic medal.

RYSKAL, INNA VALERYEVNA (URS/AZB–VOL). B. 15 June 1944, Baku. Inna Ryskal won four consecutive Olympic medals playing for the Soviet **volleyball** team from 1964 to 1976. In 1972 and 1976 she helped the Soviets to gold medals, and she won silver medals in 1964 and 1976. She also played on a World Championship team in 1970 and European Championship teams in 1963, 1967, and 1971.

– S –

SAAR, THE. In 1952, the Saar was recognized as a separate **National Olympic Committee** (NOC) by the **International Olympic Committee** (IOC) and competed at the Helsinki Olympics, represented by 31 athletes but winning no medals. The Saar was reunited with the **Federal Republic of Germany** in 1956. Its athletes were absorbed by the combined German teams, and the Saar Olympic Committee was dissolved on 20 September 1956. Its best finishes in 1952 were equal eighth by Erich Schmidt in lightweight Greco-Roman **wrestling** and ninth by Therese Zenz in women's kayak singles **canoeing.**

SÁGINÉ-UJLAKINÉ-REJTÖ, ILDIKÖ (HUN–FEN). B. 11 May 1937. Ildikö Ságiné-Ujlakiné-Rejtö has the unusual distinction of winning Olympic medals under three different names—as Miss Rejtö in 1960, as Mrs. Ujlakiné-Rejtö in 1964 and 1968, and as Mrs. Ságiné-Ujlakiné-Rejtö in 1972 and 1976. She shares this distinction with German **speed skater Andrea Ehrig-Schöne-Mitscherlich.** Ildikö won seven Olympic medals, including gold in the individual and team foil in 1964. At the World Championships, she won four titles—individual foil in 1963 and team foil in 1962, 1967, and 1973.

SAILER, ANTON "TONI" (AUT–ASK). B. 17 November 1935, Kitzbühel. Toni Sailer, known as "The Blitz from Kitz" because of his hometown, was the greatest **alpine skier** in Olympic history. Although his feat of winning all three alpine events at the 1956 **Olympic Winter Games** was matched by **Jean-Claude Killy** 12 years later, Sailer's overall performance was far more impressive. He won the downhill by 3.5 seconds, the slalom by 4.0 seconds, and the giant slalom by a remarkable 6.2 seconds, whereas Killy's margins of victory were far narrower. Sailer was also World Champion at alpine combination (1956, 1958) and the downhill and slalom (1958). His career at the international level lasted only four seasons before he retired to become a hotelier and an occasional film actor and singer. A national hero, he was appointed technical director of the Austrian alpine team in 1972.

SAILING. Sailing as a competitive sport was called yachting until recently. The **International Federation** (IF) changed the sport's competitive name in an attempt to limit the elitist connotation associated with the term "yachting." The sport has been termed yachting at the Olympics through 1996, and sailing, in effect, made its Olympic début in 2000 at Sydney.

Yachting actually began as a form of sailing, which has been practiced since antiquity as a means of transport. In the modern sense, yachting probably originated in the Netherlands, and the word seems to come from the Dutch "jaght" or "jaght schip," probably a light, fast naval craft.

Sailing sport was brought to England by King Charles II about 1660 after his exile to Holland. International yacht racing began in 1851 when a syndicate of members of the New York Yacht Club built a 101-foot schooner named *America*. The yacht was sailed to England where it won a trophy called the Hundred Guineas Cup in a race around the Isle of Wight under the auspices of the Royal Yacht Squadron. The trophy was renamed the America's Cup, after the yacht, not after the United States, as is commonly thought. Sailing is now governed worldwide by the International Sailing Federation (ISAF), formerly the International Yacht Racing Union (IYRU), which was formed in 1907 and currently has 121 nations.

Sailing was first contested at the 1900 Olympics. It made its next Olympic appearance in 1908 and has been on every **Olympic program** since that year. Sailing has had a very varied program that is usually changed every few Olympiads as the popularity of various boats waxes and wanes. **Women** have always been allowed to compete in Olympic sailing with men. In 1988, separate sailing events exclusively for women were introduced. In 1984, the popular sport of boardsailing was also added to the Olympic program, and a separate boardsailing event for women was placed on the program for the first time in 1992.

The current trend is toward smaller boats with crews of only one to three people aboard. At Athens in 2004, there were four events open only to men: Mistral boardsailing (one-person windsurfing),

Finn Monotype (one-person dinghy), 470 Class (two-person dinghy), and Star Class (two-person keelboat); four events open only to women: Mistral boardsailing (one-person windsurfing), European Monotype (one-person dinghy), 470 Class (two-person dinghy), and Yngling Class (keelboat); and three mixed events: Laser Class (one-person dinghy), 49er Class (two-person dinghy), Tornado Class (two-person keelboat). Sailing is contested at the Olympics in a series of fleet races, with points awarded for the placement in each race. The only exception, through 2000, was the Soling Class. In Soling, a short series of fleet races qualified boats for a match racing elimination tournament, but this class was eliminated and not contested at the 2004 Olympics.

SAINT CYR, HENRI JULIUS RÉVÉRENOY (SWE–EQU). B. 15 March 1902, Stockholm. D. 27 July 1979. Henri Saint Cyr began his Olympic career in 1936 with the Swedish three-day team. In 1960 he ended his Olympic career, having appeared in five different Olympics with five different horses. He was the first rider to win two individual Olympic gold medals in dressage, 1952 and 1956, and he led **Sweden** to team gold medals at both Olympics. In 1956 he took the Oath of the Athletes at the opening ceremony on behalf of the competitors at the Olympic Equestrian Games in Stockholm.

SAINT KITTS AND NEVIS (SKN). *See* ST. KITTS AND NEVIS.

SAINT LUCIA (LCA). Saint Lucia was given official recognition by the **International Olympic Committee** (IOC) in September 1993, and the country first competed at the Atlanta **Olympic Games** in 1996. It has not yet competed in the **Olympic Winter Games**.

SAINT VINCENT AND THE GRENADINES (VIN). *See* ST. VINCENT AND THE GRENADINES.

SALNIKOV, VLADIMIR VALERYEVICH (URS–SWI). B. 21 May 1960, Leningrad. At the 1980 Games Vladimir Salnikov won gold medals in the 400 meters, the 1,500 meters (with the first ever sub-15-minute time), and the 4 × 200 meter freestyle relay. He remained the world's greatest long distance **swimmer** although the

Soviet boycott of the 1984 Games denied him the opportunity of Olympic honors in that year. But he returned from near retirement to win a somewhat surprising victory in the 1,500 freestyle at the 1988 Seoul Olympics. Salnikov set six world records at 400 meters (1979–1983), four at 800 meters (1979–1986), and three at 1,500 meters (1980–1983), and at the World Championships he won the 400 meters and 1,500 meters in both 1978 and 1982.

SALUMÄE, ERIKA (URS/EST–CYC). B. 11 June 1962. Erika Salumäe came to sports late; she took up **cycling** in 1981 and made the **Soviet** national team in 1984. She won the 1987 and 1989 world sprint championship and in 1988 and 1992 was Olympic match sprint champion. Her victory in 1992 at the Olympics was poignant as it was the first victory for **Estonia** at the **Olympic Games** after its independence from the Soviet Union. Salumäe also set several world records for the 200 meters (flying start) and 1,000 meters time trial from a standing start.

SAMARANCH (TORRELO), JUAN ANTONIO, MARQUIS DE SAMARANCH (ESP). B. 17 July 1920, Barcelona. Juan Antonio Samaranch served as the seventh president of the **International Olympic Committee** (IOC). First appointed to the IOC in 1966, he became a vice president in 1974 before succeeding **Lord Killanin** as president in 1980. During this period he was also appointed as Spanish ambassador to the **Soviet Union** in 1977. His period of office as president of the IOC was marked by the transformation of the **Olympic movement** into a vast businesslike organization, although not all the changes met with the approval of the traditionalists. Ably supported by a dedicated group of vice presidents, he took the Olympic movement into the modern era. Although not unique among IOC presidents in having to face situations that threatened the fabric of the Olympic movement, his diplomatic skills were invaluable in such matters as containing the **boycotts** of the 1984 and 1988 Games. In 1991, he was ennobled by the king of **Spain** for his services to **Olympism**. Samaranch's reign was marred by the **Olympic bribery scandal** that erupted in 1998–1999, the events of which occurred during his term of office. In mid-1999, the IOC supported Samaranch by giving him an almost unanimous vote of confidence. Samaranch stepped down as president after the IOC session in 2001 and was then given the **Olympic Order** in gold by his successor, **Jacques Rogge**, and made honorary president for life.

SAMOA, AMERICAN. *See* AMERICAN SAMOA.

SAMOA (SAM). Formerly called Western Samoa, Samoa has competed at the **Olympic Games** of 1984, 1988, 1992, 1996, 2000, and 2004. Marcus Stephan, a 1992 featherweight **weightlifter**, finished ninth of 31 in his class, this being the best finish by a Samoan in the Olympics. Samoa has not yet competed at the **Olympic Winter Games**.

SAN MARINO (SMR). San Marino has competed at eleven **Summer Olympic Games**—those of 1960 and all those from 1968 to 2004. It has competed at the **Olympic Winter Games** of 1976, 1984, 1988, 1992, 1994, and 2002, but missed 1998. The best finish by an athlete from San Marino was fifth in small-bore rifle (prone) **shooting** in 1984 by Francesco Nanni.

SÃO TOMÉ AND PRÍNCIPE (STP). São Tomé and Príncipe was given official recognition by the **International Olympic Committee** (IOC) in September 1993, and the country first competed at the **Olympic Games** in Atlanta in 1996. It has not yet competed in the **Olympic Winter Games**.

SAUDI ARABIA (KSA, formerly SAU). Recognized by the **International Olympic Committee** (IOC) in 1965, Saudi Arabia has competed at every Olympics since 1972, with the exception of 1980. It has never competed in the **Olympic Winter Games**. Saudi Arabia won its first Olympic medals at Sydney in 2000. Hadj Souan Somayli won a silver in the men's 400 meter intermediate hurdles, and Khaled Al-Eid won an **equestrian** bronze in individual show jumping.

SAUTIN, DMITRY (RUS/EUN–DIV). B. 12 June 1982, Voronege. With seven Olympic medals, Dmitry Sautin has won more Olympic medals than any other **diver**. Representing the **Unified Team** (Équipe Unifié) in 1992, he earned a bronze on the springboard. In

1996, he was the gold medalist on the platform, representing **Russia**. The addition of synchronized events in 2000 allowed Sautin to enter four diving events in Sydney, and he won medals in all four events, topped by a gold medal in the synchronized platform event. Sautin won his seventh Olympic medal, a bronze, in 2004 on the springboard. Sautin was also World Champion on the springboard in 1998 and the platform in 1994 and 1998, and he was European Champion on the springboard in 1995 and 1997 and the platform in 1993.

SAVÓN FABRÉ, FÉLIX (CUB–BOX). B. 22 September 1967. Félix Savón has likely been the greatest heavyweight **boxer** of the later 1980s and early 1990s, amateur or pro included. He began his international career winning the 1986 World Championship in the heavyweight class and later won that title six times consecutively—1986, 1989, 1991, 1993, 1995, and 1997. Cuba **boycotted** the 1988 **Olympic Games** in Seoul, which prevented Savón from a certain gold medal. But in 1992, 1996, and 2000 he easily won the Olympic gold medal in the heavyweight division. Savón also won Pan-American Games gold medals in 1987, 1991, and 1995 and won the AIBA World Challenge Matches for his weight class in 1989–1990, 1992, and 1994. He never turned professional because of Cuba's insistence on keeping their athletes amateur only, but he would certainly have been a leading contender to become professional heavyweight World Champion.

SCHEMANSKY, NORBERT (USA–WLT). B. 30 May 1924, Detroit, Michigan. Norbert Schemansky was the first man in history to win four medals in Olympic **weightlifting**, a feat since equaled only by **Pyrros Dimas**. After placing second to John Davis in the heavyweight division at the 1947 World Championships, he again finished as runner-up to Davis at the 1948 Olympics. Schemansky then won a gold medal at the 1952 Games and two bronzes in 1960 and 1964. When Schemansky won his fourth medal (1964), he had passed his 40th birthday, and he is the oldest man ever to win a medal in Olympic weightlifting.

SCHENK, ADRIANUS "ARD" (NED–SSK). B. 16 September 1944. In his 1968 Olympic début Ard Schenk tied for second place in the 1,500 meters **speed skating**, but four years later he won three gold medals (1,500 meters, 5,000 meters, and 10,000 meters). Each victory was by a wide margin, and he posted new Olympic records in the 5,000 meters and 10,000 meters. Schenk emphasized his superiority over his rivals two weeks later when he became one of only four men to win all four events at the World Championships. He set 18 world records at distances from 1,000 meters to 10,000 meters between 1966 and 1972, including four world records for the All-Around. He was European champion in 1966, 1970, 1972, and 1973 and World Champion for four consecutive years—1970–1973.

SCHMIDT, OSCAR DANIEL BECERRA "MÃO SANTO" (BRA–BAS). B. 16 February 1958, Rio Grande del Norte, RN. Although not as well known as some of the American **basketball** players, Oscar Schmidt has been the finest offensive performer at the **Olympic Games**. He competed for Brazil in 1980, 1984, 1988, 1992, and 1996, was the leading scorer at the 1988, 1992, and 1996 Olympics, and is the all-time leading scorer in Olympic history. He never won an Olympic medal, as Brazil's best finish from 1980 to 1996 was fifth (three times). His individual performance in 1988 was especially remarkable, averaging 42.3 points per game—only one other Olympic basketball player has averaged over 30 for an Olympic tournament (Edward Palubinskas of **Australia** in 1976). When considering the highest scoring individual games at the Olympics, Schmidt has seven of the top 10, and five of the top six, led by his 55-point explosion against **Spain** in 1988. Schmidt was a 6'8" (2.02 m.), 235 lb. (107 kg.) forward who played little defense and was known for his outside shooting, with an almost unlimited range. He never played in the National Basketball Association (NBA) but remained a legend in his home country, where he was known simply as Oscar.

SCHMIDT-FISCHER, BIRGIT (née Fischer) (GDR/GER–CAN). B. 25 February 1962, Brandenburg. Birgit Schmidt-Fischer is considered the greatest woman **canoeist** of all time. Her total of 26 gold medals (1977–1997) at the World Championships has never been approached, and her ten (seven gold) Olympic medals is also a record for women. Representing **East Germany** (GDR) she won the Olympic K1 title in 1980 (as Miss Fischer) and the K2 and K4 in 1988. After a three-year break from competition, during which she gave birth to her second child, she won the K1 in 1992 as a member of the unified **German** team. Her fifth Olympic gold medal came in 1996 as a member of the German K4 team. At Sydney in 2000, Schmidt-Fischer won gold medals in both the K2 and K4 events, while in Athens in 2004, she won her eighth gold in the K4. In addition to her eight Olympic gold medals, Schmidt-Fischer also won silver medals in the 1988 K1, the 1992 K4, the 1996 and 2004 K2. Her husband, Jörg, was a World Champion and Olympic silver medalist in canoeing.

SCHNEIDER, VRENI (SUI–ASK). B. 26 November 1964, Elm. With five medals, Vreni Schneider has won the most **alpine skiing** Olympic medals of any female, a number matched among men only by **Kjetil André Aamodt** (NOR) and **Alberto Tomba** (ITA), and among women only by **Katja Seizinger** (GER). Schneider won both the slalom and giant slalom at the 1992 **Olympic Winter Games**. In 1994 at Lillehammer, she won three more medals, repeating as champion in the slalom while earning a silver in the alpine combined and a bronze in the giant slalom. At the World Championships Schneider won the giant slalom in 1987 and 1989 and the slalom in 1991. She was overall World Cup champion in 1989 winning the following event championships: 1986, 1987, 1989, and 1991 giant slalom; and the 1989, 1990, 1992, and 1993 slalom. Among women, Schneider's 55 victories trails only **Austria**'s Annemarie Moser-Proll in overall World Cup race wins.

SCHOLLANDER, DONALD ARTHUR (USA–SWI). B. 30 April 1946, Charlotte, North Carolina. In 1964, Don Schollander became the first **swimmer** to win four gold medals at one **Olympic Games**. His victories came in the 100 and 400 meter freestyles and in both relays, and in all but the 100 meters he set a world record. He was unfortunate that the 200 meters was not on the program at the Tokyo Games, as he would set nine world records at this, his best, distance (1963–1968). He also posted three world records at 400 meters and shared in eight world records in the freestyle relays. At the 1968 Games he was unable to defend his 100 and 400 meter Olympic titles as he failed to make the U.S. team at these distances, but Schollander won his fifth gold in the 4 × 200 meter freestyle relay and took the silver in the 200 meter freestyle.

SCOTLAND (SCO). Scotland competed as a separate country in 1908 **field hockey**, finishing third, and with a separate team in the 1912 **cycling** road race. In all other Olympics, and in all the other sports at the 1908 and 1912 Olympics, Scotland has competed as a member of the United Kingdom of **Great Britain** and Northern Ireland. Scotland has also hosted one Olympic event, as in 1908 the 12 meters **yachting** was held on the River Clyde in Glasgow.

SEIZINGER, KATJA (GER–ASK). B. 10 May 1972. Katja Seizinger was the top female power skier of the 1990s, setting records at the Olympics by winning five medals, including three gold medals, matched only by **Vreni Schneider** (SUI) among **women**. Seizinger won the downhill in 1994 and 1998, becoming the first person, man or woman, to defend the Olympic downhill title. She added a third gold in the **alpine** combined in the 1998 **Olympic Winter Games**. Her other Olympic medals were bronze in the super-G in 1992 and in the giant slalom in 1998. Seizinger was less successful in the World Championships, winning only the 1993 super-G. However, she posted a remarkable record in the World Cup events, winning 36 times and reaching the podium 76 times. She was overall World Cup champion in 1996 and 1998 and won the following individual World Cup titles: super-G—1993–1996 and 1998, and downhill—1992–1994 and 1998.

SENEGAL (SEN). Senegal first competed at the 1964 **Olympic Games** and has competed at every Olympics since. It has competed at the **Olympic Winter Games** in 1984, 1992, and 1994. Amadou Dia Bâ won the nation's only medal to date, a silver in the 400 meter hurdles in track and field **athletics** in 1988. Prior to Dia Bâ's medal in 1988, it can be argued that Senegal had won a medal in 1960. In that year, Abdoulaye Seye won a bronze in the 200 meters while representing **France**. Seye was a Senegalese national, but the country was still a French territory, so he had to compete under the French flag. The first Senegalese national to compete in the Olympics was probably Cire Samba, who competed for France in the javelin throw in 1924.

SERBIA. Serbia competed at the 1912 Olympics, the only time Serbia has been represented at the Olympics as an independent nation. In that year, Serbia, later the largest province in **Yugoslavia**, sent two athletes to the **Olympic Games**. Dragutin Tomašević did not finish the **marathon** race, and Dušan Milošević finished third in his heat of the 100 meters. However, it is likely that Momcilo Tapavica, who competed in 1896 in **wrestling** and **tennis** and is usually listed as representing **Hungary**, was actually a Serbian student from Belgrade studying in Budapest. On 4 December 1918, Serbia became part of the country that was then termed the Kingdom of Serbs, Croats, and Slovenes and would later become Yugoslavia. Serbian athletes competed under that banner through 1988. With the breakup of Yugoslavia in 1991, Yugoslavia now consists solely of the former provinces of **Serbia and Montenegro** and is now recognized by that name both internationally and by the **International Olympic Committee** (IOC).

SERBIA AND MONTENEGRO (SCG). Although its official name at the time was the Kingdom of Serbs, Croats, and Slovenes, Yugoslavia first competed at the Olympics in 1920, although **Serbia** was represented by two athletes in 1912 at Stockholm. From 1920 to 1992, Yugoslavia appeared at every Summer Olympic celebration, but in 1932 it was represented by a lone **track and field** athlete. It first appeared at the **Olympic Winter Games** at their inception in 1924 and has returned every four years with the exception of 1932, 1960, and 1994. Recent civil unrest in Yugoslavia caused the secession of many of the individual republics. Both **Croatia** and **Slovenia** competed at the **Olympic Games** from 1992 to 2004 and the Olympic Winter Games from 1992 to 2002. **Bosnia-Herzegovina** was also present at Barcelona in 1992, Atlanta in 1996, Sydney in 2000, and Athens in 2004, and first competed at the Olympic Winter Games in 1994. The **Former Yugoslav Republic of Macedonia** (FYROM) competed at the Olympic Games in 1996, 2000, and 2004 and the Olympic Winter Games in 1998 and 2002. Yugoslavia now consists of only the former republics of Serbia and Montenegro, with Serbia consisting of two autonomous regions of Vojvodina and Kosovo, the latter under United Nations control and threatening to seek independence. Since 1996, the nation has technically competed as Serbia and Montenegro. Yugoslavia/Serbia and Montenegro has won 99 Olympic medals, 28 of them gold. In 1984, Yugoslavia hosted the 14th Olympic Winter Games in Sarajevo, which is presently the capital of Bosnia-Herzegovina.

SESSIONS OF THE IOC. The main decision making body of the **International Olympic Committee** (IOC) is the annual session of the IOC. Currently, these are held once a year, although special sessions may be called by the IOC president. Every other year, one session is held immediately before either the **Olympic Games** or the **Olympic Winter Games**, at the site of those Games. Formerly, when the Olympic Games and Olympic Winter Games were held in the same year, two sessions were held in the Olympic year, one at the site of the Olympic Games and one at the site of the Olympic Winter Games, immediately preceding those events. The session is a plenary meeting of the IOC and is considered its main rules-making body. In reality, the session is usually presented with a list of decisions made by the IOC **Executive Board**, and these are almost universally approved; thus the Executive Board really has the authoritative power. The session also votes on the approval of prospective IOC members, but the choices of the IOC president are usually approved without dissension. The session also has the power to modify the **Olympic Charter**.

SEX TESTING. *See* GENDER VERIFICATION.

SEYCHELLES (SEY). The Seychelles has competed at six **Olympic Games**, those of 1980, 1984, 1992, 1996, 2000, and 2004. For reasons not precisely clear, the Seychelles did not compete in 1988 at Seoul. Its best Olympic performance came in 1992 when light-heavyweight **boxer** Roland Raforme won two matches to finish equal fifth of 27 in his class, and in 1996 when another boxer, Rival Cadeau, finished equal fifth in the light-middleweight class. The Seychelles has never competed at the **Olympic Winter Games**. A Seychelles national, Henri Dauban de Silhouette, represented **Great Britain** in the javelin throw at the 1924 Olympic Games.

SHAKHLIN, BORIS (URS/UKR–GYM). B. 27 January 1932, Ishim, Tyumen Region. Boris Shakhlin won six gold medals in individual **gymnastic** events, which remains an Olympic best for men, bettered among **women** only by **Věra Čáslavská**. Between 1956 and 1964, he won a total of 13 Olympic medals (seven gold, four silver, two bronze) with his strongest individual event being the pommel horse, in which he won gold in 1956 and 1960. Shakhlin also won a total of 14 medals at the World Championships. Unusually tall for a gymnast, Shakhlin's height and reach were a distinct advantage on the horizontal bar, but he was weak at the floor exercise.

SHCHERBO, VITALY (URS/EUN/BLR–GYM). B. 13 January 1972, Minsk. Vitaly Shcherbo was the most successful **gymnast** at the 1992 **Olympic Games**, when he won six gold medals, adding four individual apparatus championships to the individual and team allaround titles. Shcherbo's record at the World Championships was also excellent. He won the all-around in 1993, the floor exercises in 1994–1995, the horizontal bar in 1994, the parallel bars in 1993 and 1995, and the horse vault in 1993–1994. Shcherbo competed again at the Olympics in 1996. He won four medals, again all of the same color, this time bronze.

SHERIDAN, MARTIN JOSEPH (USA–ATH). B. 28 March 1881, Bohola, County Mayo, Ireland. D. 27 March 1918, New York. Martin Sheridan was the world's finest all-round athlete until the arrival of **Jim Thorpe**, and the greatest discus thrower until **Al Oerter**. In addition to winning the discus at the 1904, 1906, and 1908 **Olympic Games**, Sheridan won the shot in 1906 and the Greek-style discus in 1908. To these five gold medals he added three silver medals in 1906 in the stone throw and the standing jumps and a bronze medal in the standing long jump in 1908. Between 1904 and 1911, Sheridan won 11 Amateur Athletic Union (AAU) titles at a variety of events, including three in the All-Around Championship. He was at his best before world records were officially recognized, but from 1902 to 1911 he set no less than 15 new "World Bests" in the discus, although irregularities in the specification of the throwing circle would have precluded some of these performances from being officially recognized under more stringent modern conditions. Irish-born, Sheridan emigrated to the U.S. at the age of 16 and died during the 1918 pneumonia pandemic, on the eve of his 37th birthday, while serving with the New York Police Department.

SHOOTING. Shooting originated as a means of survival, as shooting was practiced to hunt game for food. In the 19th century, as the industrial revolution occurred and hunting for food became less necessary for more people, shooting as a sport evolved. The sport was first popular in English-speaking countries, notably England and the **United States**, but also in **Ireland** and **South Africa**. The National Rifle Association (NRA) was formed in 1871 and provided the impetus for the development of organized shooting sport in the United States. The world governing body is the International Shooting Sport Federation (ISSF), formerly the Union Internationale de Tir (UIT), which was formed in 1907 and had 157 member nations in 2000.

Shooting has been contested at most of the **Olympic Games**. **Baron Pierre de Coubertin** was an avid pistol shot so he saw to it that the sport was included on the program in 1896. There were also events in 1900, but none were contested in 1904 at St. Louis. In 1928 at Amsterdam, shooting events were also not on the program.

The program has varied as much as any sport (with the possible exception of **yachting**). In 1908, 1912, 1920, and 1924, there were dozens of events, including numerous team events, and it was possible for shooters to win several medals at each Olympics. After the sport's hiatus in 1928, it returned to the Olympics in 1932 with only two events—one for pistols and one for rifles.

Women were first allowed to compete in Olympic shooting in 1968, and in that year, **Mexico**, **Peru**, and **Poland** each entered one female contestant. In 1976, Margaret Murdock (USA) won a silver medal in the small-bore rifle (three positions) event. In 1984, the UIT introduced separate events for women. Since 1984, the women's shooting program has been expanded at each Olympics, and the number of mixed events decreased. Beginning in 2000 at Sydney, men and women competed in fully separate shooting programs, with 10 events for men and 7 for women.

Shooting events at the Olympics have been held in several types of events: long-distance rifle, small-bore rifle, air pistol and rifle shooting, pistol shooting, skeet and trap shooting, and running target events. Team shooting events were discontinued after the 1924 Olympics.

SHORT-TRACK SPEED SKATING. *See* SPEED SKATING.

SIERRA LEONE (SLE). In 1960, a Sierra Leone athlete, Albert Massquoi, represented Liberia in the Olympic **marathon**, finishing 62nd. But as an independent nation, Sierra Leone made its Olympic début in 1968, after having been recognized by the **International Olympic Committee** (IOC) in 1964. It has since missed only the 1972 and 1976 **Olympic Games**, but has never competed at the **Olympic Winter Games**. Its best Olympic performance came in 1996 when Eunice Barber finished fifth in the women's heptathlon.

SINGAPORE (SIN). Singapore has competed independently at 12 **Olympic Games** since 1948, missing only 1964 and 1980. In 1964, Singaporean athletes also competed at the Olympic Games, but under the banner of **Malaysia** in a combined team with Malaya and **North Borneo**. Singapore left the Malaysian Federation in 1965. Singapore has not competed at the **Olympic Winter Games**. In 1960, Tan Howe-Liang won Singapore's only Olympic medal to date, a silver in lightweight **weightlifting**.

SINGH, UDHAM KULLAR (IND–HOK). B. 4 August 1928. Of the seven Indian players to win three Olympic gold medals for **hockey (field)**, only Udham Singh and **Leslie Claudius** also won a silver medal. Singh won gold in 1952, 1956, and 1964 and a silver in 1960. Singh was a center-forward who was the leading scorer at the 1956 Olympics with 14 goals.

SKATING. *See* FIGURE SKATING; ICE HOCKEY; SPEED SKATING.

SKELETON. Skeleton is a sledding sport founded on the famed Cresta Run at St. Moritz, Switzerland. In skeleton, the sliders lie prone on their sleds, face-down. Skeleton was contested at the **Olympic Winter Games** in 1928 and 1948, when they were held in St. Moritz. Skeleton was added to the **Olympic program** with events for men and women held at the 2002 Olympic Winter Games in Salt Lake City. *See also* BOBSLEDDING.

SKI JUMPING. *See* NORDIC SKIING.

SKIING. *See* ALPINE SKIING; BIATHLON; FREESTYLE SKIING; MILITARY SKI PATROL; NORDIC SKIING; SKIJÖRING; SPEED SKIING.

SKIJÖRING. Skijöring, originally called skid-körning, was held as a **demonstration sport** at the 1928 Winter Olympics in St. Moritz. Skijöring is a sport in which skiers are towed behind horses. It was considered a military competition in **Norway** and **Sweden** and was part of the **Nordic Games** in 1901, 1905, and 1909. It is today contested primarily in **Switzerland** and Sweden.

SKOBLIKOVA, LIDIYA PAVLOVNA (URS–SSK). B. 8 March 1939, Zlatoust, Chelyabinsk. Lidiya Skoblikova holds the record for **speed skating** with six Olympic gold medals. She was a world-class performer before speed skating for **women** was added to the **Olympic program** in 1960 at the Squaw Valley Games. In 1960, Skoblikova won gold medals in the 1,500 meters, with a new world record, and the 3,000 meters. At the 1964 **Olympic Winter Games**, she became the first woman to win all four speed-skating events at one Games, setting new Olympic records in the 500 meters, 1,000 meters, and 1,500 meters, and was only deprived of a fourth record by adverse ice conditions in the 3,000 meters. After these successes, her third Olympic appearance in 1968 was a disappointment when she finished 11th in the 1,500 meters. A teacher from Siberia, Skoblikova set world records at 1,000 meters and 3,000 meters and was the world overall champion in 1963 and 1964, winning all four events in both years.

SLEDDING. *See* BOBSLEDDING; LUGE; SKELETON.

SLOANE, WILLIAM MILLIGAN (USA). B. 12 November 1850, Richmond, Ohio. D. 11 September 1928, Princeton, New Jersey. William Milligan Sloane was the pioneer of the **Olympic movement** in America and a founding member of the **International Olympic Committee** (IOC). A close friend and supporter of **Pierre de Coubertin**, he was the driving force behind the establishment, maintenance, and development of the strong links between the Olympic movement and the **United States**. A professor of history at Princeton University and a distinguished academician, he later held the Roosevelt Chair at Berlin University but gave up most of his appointments after becoming ill in 1921, although it was not until 1924 that he resigned from the IOC. His best known academic work was his four-volume *Life of Napoleon Bonaparte*.

SLOVAKIA (SVK). Slovakia, which split from **Czechoslovakia** on 1 January 1993 along with the **Czech Republic**, competed in the **Olympic Games** as an independent nation for the first time at Lillehammer in 1994. Prior to the division, many Czechoslovakian athletes were actually from Slovakia. A Slovakian **National Olympic Committee** (NOC) was actually first formed in June 1939, and it attempted to revive its activities after World War II in 1945. However, in June 1947, it was co-opted into the Czechoslovak Olympic Committee. The Slovakian Olympic Committee was re-created in October 1990 and was then formed officially on 19 December 1992, before the nation's split from the Czech Republic on 1 January 1993. It received provisional recognition by the **International Olympic Committee** (IOC) on 16 March 1993 and official recognition at the 101st IOC session in Monaco in September 1993. Since 1994, Slovakia has competed at all Olympic Games and **Olympic Winter Games**.

SLOVENIA (SLO). Prior to 1992, Slovenia had never competed at the Olympics as a sovereign nation. However, many Yugoslav athletes were natives of Slovenia, notably Leon Štukelj (from Maribor) who won, between 1924 and 1936, more medals (six) and gold medals (three) than any other Yugoslav Olympian. Slovenia was also responsible for all of **Yugoslavia**'s medals in the **Olympic Winter Games** between 1984 and 1988. Slovenia made its Olympic début at both Albertville and Barcelona in 1992 after the Yugoslavian civil war. It has since competed at the 1996, 2000, and 2004 **Olympic Games** and the Olympic Winter Games of 1994, 1998, and 2002.

SMETANINA, RAISA PETROVNA (URS–NSK). B. 29 February 1952, Mokhcha, Komi. Over a long career that encompassed five Olympics, Raisa Smetanina compiled one of the greatest records of any female **cross-country skier**. Smetanina first came to international attention at the 1974 World Championships, where she helped the **Soviet Union** relay team to the championship. This led to her greatest Olympic performance at Innsbruck in 1976. She competed in three events, medaling in all three, with a silver at 5 km. and golds in the 10 km. and relay. Smetanina competed at the **Olympic Winter Games** in 1976, 1980, 1984, 1988, and 1992, retiring after the Albertville Olympics. During that time, she won 10 Olympic medals, including four gold. Two of the gold medals came in 1976, and she added another individual gold in the 1980 5 km. Smetanina's Olympic career ended after she helped the Soviet women's relay team to a gold medal at the 1992 Winter Olympics. Raisa Smetanina also won 13 medals at the World Championships. In addition to her international triumphs, she was 21 times champion of the Soviet Union and was named an Emeritus Master of Sport of the USSR.

SMITH, JOHN WILLIAM (USA–WRE). B. 9 August 1965, Del City, Oklahoma. John Smith is the most titled American **wrestler** ever. A freestyler, he won two National Collegiate Athletic Association (NCAA) championships while at Oklahoma State. His first major international victory was the **Goodwill Games** title in 1986. In 1987, he won the Pan-American Championship and the World Championship. In 1988 and 1992, he was Olympic champion, and from 1989 to 1991 he won the World Championship. In 1990 he also defended his Goodwill Games gold medal. From 1986 through 1990, Smith's international record was 150-3. He also received the Sullivan Award in 1990 to become the only American wrestler ever so honored. He retired from competition and became coach at his alma mater where his team won the NCAA Championship in his first year of formal coaching.

SMYRNA. At the 1906 Intercalated Olympics, an international team represented Smyrna in the **football (soccer)** tournament and won a silver medal. The athletes were actually all from **Armenia**, **France**, and **Great Britain**.

SOCCER (ASSOCIATION FOOTBALL). *See* FOOTBALL, ASSOCIATION (SOCCER).

SOFTBALL. Softball began in the 1890s as a variant of **baseball**, usually played by **women**. It was originally called mushball, kittenball, or indoor baseball, but acquired the name softball by the 1920s. In the **United States** the sport became organized with the formation of the Amateur Softball Association in 1933. Several variants of the sport exist in the United States, including fast-pitch, modified fast-pitch, and slow-pitch. The international organization is the International Softball Federation (ISF), which was formed in 1952 and had 125 member nations as of December 2004. Softball (fast-pitch) made its début as a full-medal sport for **women** at the 1996 Olympics in Atlanta. It is the only sport on the **Olympic program** open only to women and not men, although two disciplines also fall into this category—**synchronized swimming** and rhythmic gymnastics. At the 2005 IOC session in Singapore, softball was eliminated from the Olympic program beginning in 2012.

SOLOMON ISLANDS (SOL). The Solomon Islands **National Olympic Committee** (NOC) was recognized by the **International Olympic Committee** (IOC) in 1983, and it made its Olympic début in 1984. It has since competed at the 1988, 1992, 1996, 2000, and 2004 **Olympic Games**. The Solomon Islands has never competed at the **Olympic Winter Games**, and its athletes have yet to win a medal.

SOMALIA (SOM). Somalia has competed at six **Olympic Games**—those of 1972, 1984, 1988, 1996, 2000, and 2004. Somalia entered the 1992 Olympics but did not compete, probably because of the famine in the country. It has competed only in **track and field** with 15 men competitors, and two women, one each in 2000 and 2004. Somalia has not competed in the **Olympic Winter Games** and has not yet won an Olympic medal.

SOUTH AFRICA (RSA, formerly SAF). With the exception of the Intercalated Games of 1906, South Africa's participation at the **Olympic Games** was continuous from 1904 through 1960. From 1964 to 1988, however, it was not allowed to compete at the Olympics. This was due to the country's policy of apartheid and, in particular, its use of the policy in choosing its athletic teams, which is forbidden by **International Olympic Committee** (IOC) policy. It is ironic that the first South African Olympians were two Tsuana tribesmen who ran in the 1904 **marathon**; Len Tau and Jan Mashiani were both black men.

The story of South Africa's banishment from the Olympics is one of the most complex issues that has ever faced the IOC. South Africa did not always practice apartheid as a sporting policy. In the 1930s, there was frequent interracial competition, but in June 1956, a South African law was passed requiring an end to interracial sport. In 1958, IOC member Olav Ditlef-Simonsen of **Norway** informed IOC president **Avery Brundage** that his country would exclude an all-white South African team if his nation were awarded the Olympics. In 1959, the Indians, Egyptians, and Soviets pressed the IOC for South Africa's ouster from the Olympics, but the IOC was content with the promise that its 1960 Olympic team would be a multiracial one. It was not.

In 1962, South Africa Interior Minister Jan de Klerk commented publicly that "Government policy is that no mixed teams should take part in sports inside or outside the country." The IOC could scarcely ignore this message. At the 60th IOC session in Moscow in 1962, the IOC voted to suspend the South African National Olympic Committee (SANOC) "if the policy of racial discrimination practiced by the government . . . does not change before our Session in Nairobi which takes place in October 1963." SANOC was eventually suspended at the 62nd IOC session in Innsbruck in January 1964.

Further problems arose in December 1966 in Bamako, Mali, when 32 African nations formed the Supreme Council for Sport in Africa (SCSA). The SCSA's stated purpose was to coordinate and promote sport, but its true objective was to attack South Africa's apartheid policies in sport. At its founding conference, the SCSA resolved "to use every means to obtain the expulsion of South African sports organizations from the **Olympic movement** and from **International Federations** (IFs) should South Africa fail to comply fully with the IOC rules."

In mid-September 1967, an IOC commission visited South Africa to inspect the sporting facilities and see if the South Africa sporting groups were in violation of Olympic principles. The commission consisted of three IOC members: future IOC president **Lord Killanin**

(**Ireland**), Reginald Alexander (**Kenya**, a white man), and Sir Adetokunbo Ademola (**Nigeria**, a black man). They presented their report to the IOC on 30 January 1968, and it was felt to be generally positive. By a mail ballot, the IOC voted to restore recognition to SANOC, allowing a multiracial South African team to compete at the 1968 Olympics.

This prompted mass **boycott** demands from the African nations, which vehemently opposed this decision. The IOC **Executive Board** subsequently met in **Lausanne, Switzerland**, on 20 April 1968 and decided to poll the IOC members. By a postal ballot of 47-17 (with eight abstentions), the IOC reversed its course and withdrew its recognition of SANOC, preventing a huge boycott of the 1968 Olympics. In May 1970, at the 70th IOC session in Amsterdam, the South African Olympic Committee was expelled from the IOC by a vote of 35-28, with three abstentions.

In 1976, the South African question again became prominent when several African nations boycotted in protest of a **New Zealand** rugby team's having played several games on tour in South Africa. Ironically, **rugby** has not been an Olympic sport since 1924, and the New Zealand rugby team was named the All-Blacks.

In 1990, South Africa began to take steps to eliminate apartheid. In April 1991, the IOC, anticipating apartheid's elimination, gave provisional recognition to the South African Olympic Committee. On 9 July 1991, the IOC granted full recognition to the South African Olympic Committee and lifted its 21-year ban on its participation in the Olympics. In 1992 at Barcelona, South Africa competed on the Olympic stage for the first time in 32 years, and the nation competed again in 1996 at Atlanta, at Sydney in 2000, and at Athens in 2004.

South Africa has also competed at the **Olympic Winter Games** in 1960, 1994, 1998, and 2002. South Africa has won 69 Olympic medals, 20 of them gold, none of them at the Olympic Winter Games. Of these, two silver medals came at South Africa's return to the Olympic stage in 1992, and it also won five medals in both 1996 and 2000 and six in 2004.

SOVIET UNION (URS). *See* UNION OF SOVIET SOCIALIST REPUBLICS.

SOVIET UNION (USSR) ICE HOCKEY TEAMS (1956–1992). The **Soviet Union** first entered the **Olympic Winter Games** in 1956 and immediately established itself as a dominant force in most winter sports. However, it was in **ice hockey** that the Soviet Union would be most dominant over the next 36 years. From 1956 through 1992, the Soviet Union won all but two of the Olympic gold medals in ice hockey (eight in all), losing only in 1960 and 1980 to the "hometown" **United States'** teams. Its last gold medal in 1992 was won as the **Unified Team**, after the dissolution of the Soviet Union. During this time, Soviet and Unified ice hockey teams posted a record of 61 wins, 6 losses, and 2 ties.

SOVIET UNION (USSR) WOMEN'S GYMNASTICS TEAMS (1952–1992). The **Soviet Union**'s women's **gymnastics** teams produced a nonpareil record at the **Olympic Games**; they never lost. From 1952 to 1988, and as the **Unified Team** in 1992, the Soviet Union won every women's team all-around title in gymnastics (eight consecutive and nine titles), with the lone exception of 1984, when it did not compete because of the **boycott**.

SPAIN (ESP). In 1900, Spain was represented by 14 athletes at the Paris Olympics. A Spanish **National Olympic Committee** (NOC) was formed in 1905, at the urging of the Greeks, and 20 Spanish athletes competed at Athens in 1906. Spain next appeared on the Olympic stage in 1920 and has since missed only the 1936 Berlin Olympics. In addition, Spain did not compete at Melbourne in 1956, although Spanish riders did compete in the Olympic **Equestrian** Games at Stockholm in 1956. Spain's first winter appearance was in 1936 at Garmisch-Partenkirchen, and it has never failed to compete in the **Olympic Winter Games** since. Spain has won 97 Olympic medals, 30 of them gold, with two medals having been won at the Olympic Winter Games. In 1992, Barcelona hosted the Games of the XXVth Olympiad.

SPECIAL OLYMPICS. *See* PARALYMPIC GAMES.

SPEED SKATING. Speed skating emerged on the canals of Holland as early as the 13th century. Competition has been held in the Netherlands since 1676. The sport spread throughout Europe, and national competitions were held in the 1870s. The first World Championships were contested in 1889, although the International Skating Union (ISU) held its first championships in 1893, one year after its formation.

Speed skating was contested at the 1924 **Olympic Winter Games** and has been on the **Olympic program** since. **Women** first competed at the Olympics in 1932 when it was a **demonstration sport**. Women's speed skating as a full-medal Olympics sport began in 1960. The sport is governed by the International Skating Union, which also governs **figure skating**. The ISU was formed in 1892 and had 77 members (representing 60 nations) at the end of 1994.

Olympic speed skating has almost always been contested in the European system of skating time trials in two-man pairs. In 1932 at Lake Placid, the Americans convinced the ISU to hold the events in the North American style of pack racing. Many Europeans **boycotted** the events as a result, and the Americans won all four gold medals.

Short-track speed skating, racing in a pack indoors over a smaller rink, was contested as a **demonstration sport** in 1988 at Calgary. It became a full-medal sport for both men and women in 1992 at Albertville and continues on the Olympic program.

Speed skating has been dominated by the Norwegians, the Dutch, and the former **Soviet Union** and its republics. In addition, the women of the former **German Democratic Republic** were outstanding speed skaters. The **United States** has produced excellent sprinters, winning many medals and gold medals by both men and women. In addition, in 1980, the United States' **Eric Heiden** won all five available gold medals, a dominance in speed skating matched only by the USSR's **Lidiya Skoblikova**, who won all four women's events in 1964.

SPEED SKIING. Speed skiing was a **demonstration sport** at the 1992 **Olympic Winter Games** in Albertville. The event was marred by the death of one of the course officials who was struck by a skier during a training run.

SPITZ, MARK ANDREW (USA–SWI). B. 10 February 1950, Modesto, California. Usually considered the greatest **swimmer** ever, Mark Spitz remains an Olympic legend who won seven gold medals (four individual, three relay) for swimming, each in a new world record time, at the 1972 Olympics. At the 1968 Games he had won four medals (two gold, one silver, one bronze), and his overall total of 11 Olympic medals has only been matched by **Matt Biondi** among male swimmers. Spitz set 26 individual world records and six in the relays. He returned to competition in 1991 with the aim of making the 1992 Olympic team, but, as he was over 40 years of age, it was a forlorn hope and an unfortunate end to a career of unrivaled achievements.

SPORT AND ENVIRONMENT COMMISSION. The Sport and Environment Commission was formed after the 1994 Lillehammer **Olympic Winter Games**, in response to the Norwegian policy of conducting a "green" Olympics—quite a feat at the Olympic Winter Games. But the **International Olympic Committee** (IOC) thought the Lillehammer policies toward the environment were important and formed the commission to help institute similar policies in international sport. The chairman is Pál Schmitt of **Hungary**. The commission has seven IOC members, members from the **National Olympic Committees** (NOCs), the **International Federations** (IFs), and the athletes, and 14 independent members who act as consultants on the environment. The commission succeeded in having the following section added to the **Olympic Charter**, Rule 2.14, "[For that purpose the IOC] sees to it that the **Olympic Games** are held in conditions which demonstrate a responsible concern for environmental issues and encourages the **Olympic Movement** to demonstrate a responsible concern for environmental issues, takes measures to reflect such concern in its activities and educates all those connected with the Olympic Movement as to the importance of sustainable development."

SPORT AND LAW COMMISSION. The Sport and Law Commission was formed in 1996 with Judge **Kéba Mbaye** as its first chairman. The current chairman (2004) is Thomas Bach (GER). It consists of one other **International Olympic Committee** (IOC) member, Anita DeFrantz (USA), along with representatives of the **National Olympic Committees** (NOCs) and **International Federations** (IFs), three athletes, and several independent members who act as legal consultants.

SPORT FOR ALL COMMISSION. The **International Olympic Committee** (IOC) formed a Sport for All Working Group in 1983, and in 1985 the IOC formed the Mass Sport Commission, which was renamed the Sport for All Commission in 1986. The concept of the availability of Sport for All was a basic tenet of **Baron Pierre de Coubertin**'s philosophy of **Olympism**. The concept attempts to provide sport as a human right for all individuals regardless of race, social class, and sex and encourages the practice of sport by people of all ages, sexes, and social and economic conditions. The current chairman is Walther Tröger of Germany. The commission consists of 13 IOC members, members from both the **National Olympic Committees** (NOCs) and **International Federations** (IFs), and five independent members. In 1987 the Sport for All Commission developed the concept of an Olympic Day Run, held on 23 June each year (the anniversary of the founding of the IOC at the 1894 Sorbonne Congress).

SQUASH RACKETS. This sport is different from both **racquets** and **racquetball**, but it has never been contested at the **Olympic Games**, even as a **demonstration sport**. However, the World Squash Federation (WSF) is recognized by the **International Olympic Committee** (IOC), with 122 affiliated members as of 2004.

SRI LANKA (SRI). Sri Lanka, as Ceylon, competed at the **Olympic Games** from 1948 through 1968. Since its name change to Sri Lanka (on 22 May 1972), it has competed at the Olympics of 1972, 1980, 1984, 1988, 1992, 1996, 2000, and 2004. Sri Lanka has yet to compete in the **Olympic Winter Games**. The first Ceylonese national to compete at the Olympics was Carl Van Geyzel, who competed for **Great Britain** in the 1928 high jump. In 1948, Duncan White won a silver medal in the 400 meter hurdles in track and field **athletics** for Ceylon. The other medal for this nation was a bronze in the women's 200 meters in 2000 by Susanthika Jayasinghe.

ST. KITTS AND NEVIS (SKN). St. Kitts and Nevis was given official recognition by the **International Olympic Committee** (IOC) in September 1993 and competed at the **Olympic Games** in 1996, 2000, and 2004, represented on all occasions by two **track and field** athletes —

one female and one male. The country has not yet competed at the **Olympic Winter Games**.

ST. VINCENT AND THE GRENADINES (VIN). St. Vincent and the Grenadines first competed in the **Olympic Games** in 1988 at Seoul, when it was represented by six **track and field** athletes—five male and one female. The nation also competed in 1992, 1996, 2000, and 2004, but has not yet competed at the **Olympic Winter Games**. The nation has not yet won any Olympic medals.

STADION RACE. Ancient Olympic sport. The *stadion* race was the original Olympic event. It is a simple sprint of one length of the Ancient Olympic stadium of approximately 192 meters. From this event, our modern word for stadium is derived. The first known champion was **Coroebus of Elis** in 776 BCE. The last known champion of the *stadion* was Dionysios of Alexandria in 269 CE. In the earliest **Ancient Olympic Games**, the *stadion* was the only event contested. **Leonidas of Rhodes** won four consecutive titles in this event from 164 to 152 BCE. Five other athletes are known to have won at least three titles.

STEVENSON LORENZO, TEÓFILO (CUB–BOX). B. 29 March 1952, Dcilias. Teófilo Stevenson is one of only three men to win three Olympic gold medals for **boxing**. On his way to winning the heavyweight title in 1972, 1976, and 1980, he had 12 scheduled bouts; one of his opponents withdrew, and he won nine of his 11 Olympic fights by a knock-out. His devastating punching power resulted in all four of his bouts at the 1976 Games ending in a knockout. At his peak he was undoubtedly the best heavyweight in the world, but he resisted many lucrative offers to fight professionally. Had he done so there is little doubt that he would have been the World Champion. And had **Cuba** not **boycotted** the 1984 **Olympic Games**, Stevenson would have been the favorite to win his fourth gold medal. He was world amateur champion in 1974, 1978, and 1986. *See also* PAPP, LÁSZLÓ; SAVÓN FABRÉ, FÉLIX.

STRICKLAND DE LA HUNTY, SHIRLEY BARBARA (née Strickland) (AUS–ATH). B. 18 July 1925, Guildford, Western Australia.

With seven Olympic medals Shirley Strickland de la Hunty set a record for **women's track and field** that was subsequently equaled by **Irena Szewińska** and later bettered by **Merlene Ottey** (JAM/SLO). The Australian sprinter-hurdler won three gold medals in the 80 meters hurdles (1952, 1956) and the 4 × 100 meters relay (1956). Strickland de la Hunty also won one silver and three bronze medals in three Olympic appearances (1948–1956). She also competed in the 1950 British Empire Games, winning silver medals in both the 100 and 200 meters.

SUDAN (SUD). Sudan formed a **National Olympic Committee** (NOC) in 1956, which was recognized by the **International Olympic Committee** (IOC) in 1959. Since making its Olympic début in 1960, Sudan has missed only the **Olympic Games** of 1964, 1976, and 1980. It has never competed at the **Olympic Winter Games**. Its best Olympic performance came in 1984 when Omar Khalifa finished eighth in the men's 1,500 meters in track and field **athletics**.

SÜLEYMANOĞLU, NAIM (née Naim Suleimanov, aka Naum Shalamanov) (BUL/TUR–WLT). B. 23 January 1967, Ptichar, Bulgaria. It is likely that Naim Süleymanoğlu is the strongest man who has ever lived, pound for pound. He set his first world record at age 15, and at the 1984 European Championships he became the second man to lift three times his bodyweight overhead. Süleymanoğlu was also the first man to snatch two-and-a-half times his own bodyweight (27 April 1988). He was born in **Bulgaria** but defected to **Turkey** at the 1986 World Cup finals. Born Naim Suleimanov and of Bulgarian Turkish descent, he was quite upset when the Bulgarians changed his name to Naum Shalamanov in 1985, to remove vestiges of its Turkish origins. Once in Turkey, he changed the name again to a more Turkish one, and at the 1988 Olympics, Süleymanoğlu was absolutely dominant. He was World Champion at 60 kg. in 1985, 1986, 1989, and 1991, and at 64 kg. in 1993–1995. He did not compete in 1987 because of his defection. Süleymanoğlu also did not compete in 1990, retiring briefly before making a successful comeback. In 1992 at Barcelona, he defended his Olympic championship and he won again in 1996 at Atlanta. His 10 championships at the Olympics and World Championships is an all-time best, as are his three Olympic gold medals. Süleymanoğlu retired after Atlanta, but he returned to compete in Sydney, although he failed to make a successful lift at the 2000 Olympics.

SUMMER OLYMPIC GAMES. *See* OLYMPIC GAMES.

SUMO WRESTLING (JAPANESE WRESTLING). Sumo, the Japanese traditional form of **wrestling**, was contested as a **demonstration sport** at the 1964 **Olympic Games** in Tokyo, as part of the *budo* demonstration, along with *kendo* **(fencing)** and *kyudo* **(archery)**. Sumo wrestling is governed internationally by the International Sumo Federation (ISF), which was founded in 1946 and is recognized by the **International Olympic Committee** (IOC). The IFS currently has 81 affiliated member nations.

SURFING. Surfing has never been on the **Olympic program**, and it is unlikely that it will be, as surfing can only be contested at oceanside locations. However, the International Surfing Association (ISA) was founded in 1976 and is recognized by the **International Olympic Committee** (IOC), with 49 affiliated member nations as of early 2000.

SURINAME (SUR). Suriname has competed at eight **Olympic Games** since its début in 1968, missing only the 1980 Moscow Olympics. In 1960, Suriname sent one athlete to the Olympics, Wym Essajas. Essajas was entered in the 800 meters but, after being told the heats were in the afternoon, slept through the heats that were held that morning. One Suriname athlete, Anthony Nesty, is responsible for both medals won at the Olympics by Suriname. A **swimmer**, Nesty won a gold medal in the 1988 100 meter butterfly and a bronze medal in the same event in 1992.

SVAN, GUNDE ANDERS (SWE–NSK). B. 12 January 1962, Skamhed, Vansbro. Prior to the advent of **Norway**'s **Bjørn Dæhlie** in the 1990s, Gunde Anders Svan was the most bemedaled international **cross-country skier** ever. Svan began his Olympic career in 1984, winning gold in the 15 km. and relay, silver at 50 km., and bronze in the 30 km. He returned to the Olympics to win gold in 1988 at 50 km. and in the relay, giving him four gold and six Olympic medals. Svan was World Cup champion five times—1984–1986 and 1988–1989, placing in the top three for eight consecutive years—1983–1990. He won five individual World Championships: 1989, 15 km.; 1985 and 1991, 30 km.; and 1985 and 1989, 50 km. Overall he won 372 of 615 races at the national and international level from 1965 to 1991, won 30 World Cup races, and was Swedish national champion 16 times.

SWAHN, ALFRED GOMER ALBERT "ALF" (SWE–SHO). B. 20 August 1879, Uddevalla. D. 16 March 1931, Stockholm. Alfred Swahn was the son of Oscar Swahn, who holds the record as the oldest medalist and gold medalist in Olympic history. Together, father and son competed for Sweden at the 1908, 1912, and 1920 **Olympic Games**. Alfred Swahn also competed again in 1924. Alfred won nine Olympic medals, with three golds. He specialized in the running deer events and was certainly helped by the proliferation of **shooting** events on the **Olympic program**, especially team events, in the era in which he competed. His Olympic medals were as follows: 1908: Running deer shooting (single shot team) (1); 1912: Running deer shooting (single shot) (1); Running deer shooting (single shot team) (1); 1920: Running deer shooting (single shot) (2); Running deer shooting (double shot team) (2); Trap shooting (team) (3); 1924: Running deer shooting (single shot team) (2); Running deer shooting (double shot) (3); Running deer shooting (double shot team) (3).

SWAZILAND (SWZ). Swaziland has competed at seven **Olympic Games**—those of 1972, 1984, 1988, 1992, 1996, 2000, and 2004, and one **Olympic Winter Games**—1992. Swaziland has not yet won an Olympic medal.

SWEDEN (SWE). With the exception of the 1904 St. Louis Olympics, Sweden has competed at every **Olympic Games** and every **Olympic Winter Games**. In addition to having been one of the top countries in the Winter Games, it has also been outstanding in **equestrian** sport, **sailing**, **shooting**, and **wrestling** at the Summer Olympics. Sweden has won 586 Olympic medals, 179 of them gold medals. Stockholm, Sweden hosted the Games of the Vth Olympiad in 1912.

Stockholm also hosted the Equestrian Games of the XVIth Olympiad in 1956 when **Australia** was unable to hold the equestrian events in Melbourne because of the country's strict quarantine laws.

SWIMMING. Swimming is an ancient practice, as prehistoric man had to learn to swim in order to cross rivers and lakes. There are numerous references in Greek mythology to swimming, the most notable being that of Leander swimming the Hellespont (now the Dardenelle Straits) nightly to see his beloved Hero.

Swimming as a sport probably was not practiced widely until the early 19th century. The National Swimming Society of **Great Britain** was formed in 1837 and began to conduct competitions. Most early swimmers used the breaststroke or a form of it. In the 1870s, a British swimming instructor named J. Arthur Trudgeon traveled to South America where he saw natives there using an alternate arm overhand stroke. He brought it back to England as the famous trudgeon stroke—a crawl variant with a scissors kick.

In the late 1880s, an Englishman named Frederick Cavill traveled to the South Seas where he saw the natives there performing a crawl with a flutter kick. Cavill settled in **Australia** where he taught the stroke that was to become the famous Australian crawl.

Swimming has been held at every **Olympic Games**. The early events were usually only conducted in freestyle (crawl) or breaststroke. Backstroke was added later. In the 1940s, breaststrokers discovered they could go much faster by bringing both arms overhead together. This was banned in the breaststroke shortly thereafter but became the butterfly stroke, which is now the fourth stroke used in competitive swimming. **Women**'s swimming was first held at the 1912 Olympics. It has since been conducted at all the Olympics.

The current program has events for men and women in freestyle, backstroke, breaststroke, butterfly, individual medley, and relays. Both men and women compete in freestyle over 50, 100, 200, and 400 meters. The long-distance event for women is 800 meters and for men is 1,500 meters. Backstroke, breaststroke, and butterfly events are contested over both 100 and 200 meters. Individual medley is held at 200 and 400 meters. Men and women now compete in the same three relays: 4 × 100 meter freestyle relay, 4 × 100 meter medley relay, and 4 × 200 meter freestyle relay.

The **United States** has been by far the dominant nation in this sport at the Olympics. At various times, Australia, **Japan**, and previously the **German Democratic Republic** women (GDR—East Germany), have made inroads into that dominance. The governing body is the Fédération Internationale de Natation Amateur (FINA), which was formed in 1908 and had 179 member nations as of December 2000.

SWIMMING, UNDERWATER. *See* UNDERWATER SWIMMING.

SWITZERLAND (SUI). Switzerland first competed at the 1896 **Olympic Games** when it was represented by Louis Zutter, a gymnast from Neuchâtel. Switzerland also competed at the first **Olympic Winter Games** in 1924 and was represented before that in 1920 at Antwerp in both the **figure skating** and **ice hockey** events. It has been represented at every Olympic Games and every Olympic Winter Games, one of only three countries to make this claim (**Great Britain** and **France** are the others). Switzerland has really never been the dominant country in any sport. In the early Games it had top-notch **gymnasts**. Until the GDR became dominant it was the top nation in **bobsledding** in the Winter Games. Switzerland has won 286 medals, 80 gold, with 104 medals and 33 gold at the Olympic Winter Games. St. Moritz, Switzerland, hosted the 2nd Olympic Winter Games in 1928 and the 5th Olympic Winter Games in 1948.

SYNCHRONIZED SWIMMING. Synchronized swimming is one of the few sports or disciplines that are contested only by **women** (rhythmic **gymnastics** and **softball** are the others). It is not considered a separate sport but rather a discipline of **swimming**, or technically **aquatics**, and as such is governed by the Fédération Internationale de Natation Amateur (FINA).

Synchronized swimming is a relatively new sport with its origins dating to the beginning of the 20th century. Water show activities first received notice in the **United States** when Annette Kellerman (1886–1975), an **Australian** swimmer who toured the United States, performed her water acrobatics in a glass tank. Katherine Curtis was responsible for developing the sport in the United States, when she began to experiment around 1915 with water figures and had the figures perform to musical accompaniment. Her students performed at the 1933–1934 Chicago "Century of Progress" Fair, where the announcer, former Olympic swimming gold medalist Norman Ross, coined the term "synchronized swimming."

American film star Esther Williams later popularized synchronized swimming when she performed water ballet in several American movies. The competitive aspect was developed about the same time when Frank Havlicek, one of Curtis's students, drew up a set of rules.

Synchronized swimming was recognized as a separate discipline of swimming by FINA in 1952. World Championships in synchronized swimming have been held since 1973, when FINA first established swimming World Championships. Synchronized swimmers compete at the World Championships in solo, duet, and team competition.

At the Olympics, synchronized swimming was first held in 1984 with solo and duet events, and these events were also contested in 1988 and 1992. However, both events were discontinued in 1996 at Atlanta, replaced by an eight-person team event. In 2000 and 2004, the program consisted of a duet and team event.

SYNORIS. Ancient Olympic sport. The *synoris* was a two-horse **chariot race**, lasting for eight circuits of the hippodrome (circa 9,000 meters). Champions are known from 408 BCE (Euagoras of Elis) through 60 BCE (Menedernos of Elis).

SYRIA (SYR). Syria sent one athlete to the 1948 **Olympic Games**. In 1960, the United Arab Republic (**Egypt** and Syria) (UAR) competed at Rome with 74 athletes. Syria was a member of the UAR at that time, but only three of the 74 athletes were Syrian. Syria and Egypt split their political alliance in 1961, and Syria did not compete in the 1964 Olympic Games. It returned to the Olympic fold in 1968 and has since missed only 1976. It has yet to compete at an **Olympic Winter Games**. In 1984, Joseph Atiyeh won Syria's first Olympic medal, a silver in heavyweight freestyle **wrestling**. In 1996, Ghada Shouaa won Syria's first gold medal in the **women**'s heptathlon event.

SZEWIŃSKA-KIRSZENSTEIN, IRENA (née Kirszenstein) (POL–ATH). B. 24 May 1946, Leningrad, USSR. With a total of seven

Olympic medals in **track and field**, Irena Szewińska-Kirszenstein equaled the record of Australian **Shirley Strickland**, a record since broken only by Jamaica's **Merlene Ottey**. She won gold medals in the 4 × 100 meter relay (1964), the 200 meters (1968) and the 400 meters (1976), and she also won two silver and two bronze medals. Her Olympic career ended in 1980 when, in her fifth Games, she pulled up with a muscle strain in the semifinals of the 400 meters. Szewińska-Kirszenstein's tally of 13 world records included her Olympic victories of 1968 (200 meters) and 1976 (400 meters), and at the European Championships she won ten medals (five gold, one silver, four bronze). Born to Polish parents in the **Soviet** city of Leningrad she returned to **Poland** at an early age and during an outstanding career set 38 Polish records. In 1967 she married her coach, Janusz Szewińska. In 1998, Irena Szewińska was co-opted as a member of the **International Olympic Committee** (IOC).

– T –

TABLE TENNIS. Table tennis was developed in the late 19th century, though its origins are not well documented. Several different sources for its invention are credited, but the modern game is said to have started with the introduction of the celluloid ball circa 1891. This development can be attributed to the Englishman James Gibb, a world-record–holding distance runner who discovered the celluloid ball during a visit to America. This ensured the success of the game as a domestic pastime from which a competitive game emerged.

The sport is widely practiced throughout the world. However, it made an unusual entry into the **Olympic program**. Table tennis made its Olympic début as a full-medal sport in 1988 at Seoul. It was never contested at the Olympics as a **demonstration sport**, which the **International Olympic Committee** (IOC) then usually required of new sports. Men and **women** compete in four Olympic events, singles and doubles for men and women. Since the late 1950s, the Chinese have been by far the dominant factor in table tennis, although they are closely pushed by the Koreans. The governing body of the sport is the International Table Tennis Federation (ITTF), which was formed in 1926 and had 195 nations at the end of 2004.

TAEKWONDO. Taekwondo was contested as a **demonstration sport** at the 1988 and 1992 Olympics. The World Taekwondo Federation (WTF) was recognized by the **International Olympic Committee** (IOC) in 1973 and currently has 175 members. The sport made its Olympic début in 2000 at Sydney, with four weight classes for men and four for **women**.

TAIWAN. *See* CHINESE TAIPEI.

TAJIKISTAN (TJK). As a former member of the **Soviet Union**, a few Tajikistani athletes competed from 1952 to 1988 for the Soviet Union. Tajikistani athletes were also present at Barcelona in 1992 as members of the **Unified Team**. Tajikistan made its Olympic début as an independent nation in 1996 and first competed at the **Olympic Winter Games** in 2002.

TANGANYIKA. *See* TANZANIA.

TANZANIA (TAN). Tanganyika sent three athletes to the 1964 **Olympic Games**. In late 1964, the former nations of Tanganyika and **Zanzibar** merged to form Tanzania. Tanzania has competed at every Olympic Games since 1968, except for those of 1976. It has never competed at the **Olympic Winter Games**. In 1980 at Moscow, Filbert Bayi won a silver medal in the steeplechase. In 1976, Bayi had been a co-favorite with **New Zealand**'s John Walker in the 1,500 meters, and the battle between them was anticipated to be one of the great races in track history. It never occurred, as Tanzania joined the 1976 African **boycott** in protest of a New Zealand rugby team playing in **South Africa**. Tanzania's other Olympic medal occurred in 1980 when Suleiman Nyambui finished second in the 5,000 meters in track and field **athletics**.

TEAM HANDBALL. *See* HANDBALL (TEAM HANDBALL).

TELEVISION. Television is the method by which most of the world watches the **Olympic Games**. The rights fees paid by television are also critically important to the continued success of the **Olympic movement** as they are the primary method of financing the Olympic

Games and the activities of the **International Olympic Committee** (IOC). The Olympic Games were televised for the first time in 1936 but with only a few viewers in **Germany**. The next few Olympiads also saw Olympic Games telecast within the host country but with no significant rights fees. Television first began worldwide broadcasts in 1960 at Rome, with most of Europe seeing the Games live, and the **United States** viewing them on tape delay. The rights fee paid by the U.S. host television network, CBS (Columbia Broadcasting System), was $395,000. By contrast, NBC (National Broadcasting Company), which televised the 2004 Athens Olympic Games in the United States, paid $793,000,000 for the rights to the Games. The rights fees for recent Games were as follows: 2000 Sydney—U.S. $715 million, and worldwide $1.338 billion; 2002 Salt Lake City—U.S. $545 million, and worldwide $738 million; 2004 Athens—U.S. $793 million, and $1.498 worldwide billion; 2006 Torino—U.S. $613 million, and worldwide $832 million; and 2008 Beijing—U.S. $894 million, and worldwide $1.715 billion.

While only one country was able to watch the Olympic Games of 1936, 1948, and 1956 on television, 21 nations watched the 1960 Olympics on television, and that number increased to over 200 for the 2004 Olympics. It was estimated that the gross cumulative television audience for the 1992 Olympics was 24.6 billion people, and that 2.3 billion people (85% of all those with televisions) watched the 1992 Olympics at some time.

TENNIS (LAWN TENNIS). Tennis, originally lawn tennis, was invented by Major Walter Wingfield, a British army officer, in 1873. The original name was "sphairistike." However, tennis variants are much older than that. Court tennis, or royal tennis, real tennis, or **jeu de paume**, was known to have been played in the Middle Ages.

Tennis was contested at every **Olympic Games** from 1896 through 1924 as a regular medal sport. It was then discontinued, although it was on the schedule as a **demonstration sport** in 1968 and 1994. The reasons for dropping tennis as an Olympic sport probably were two: the **International Olympic Committee** (IOC) was upset that many of the top tennis players, though considered amateurs, infringed upon its strict definition of amateurism; and the tennis establishment, especially in Britain, was concerned that the Olympic events might become more important than Wimbledon, and did not wish that to occur.

Tennis returned to the Olympics as a full-medal sport in 1989 and almost certainly will remain on the **Olympic program**. Full-scale professionals now compete in the Olympics, with no other restrictions. There are four Olympic events, singles and doubles for both men and **women**. Mixed doubles is not currently contested on the Olympic program. The governing body of the sport is the International Tennis Federation (ITF), which was founded in 1913 and had 191 members at the end of 2000.

TETHRIPPON. Ancient Olympic sport. The *tethrippon* was a four-horse **chariot race** that was contested over 12 laps of the hippodrome (circa 14,000 meters). Champions are known from 680 BCE (Pagondas of Thebes) through 241 CE (Titus Domitius Prometheus of Athens). Euagoras of Sparta was the only three-time champion in this event (548–540 BCE).

THAILAND (THA). Competing in the Olympics since 1952, Thailand has missed only the 1980 Moscow Olympics. It has never competed in the **Olympic Winter Games**. Thai athletes have won nine Olympic medals, two gold, one silver, and six bronze. Eight of the medals have been won in **boxing** and one in **weightlifting**.

THEAGENES OF THASOS (GRE–BOX/WRE). fl. ca. 480–460 BCE. Theagenes is credited with over 1,400 victories in various sporting festivals in Ancient Greece. Theagenes won at Olympia in 480 BCE in **boxing** and in 476 BCE in the **pankration**. He and Kleitomachos of Thebes are the only two athletes to have won the boxing and pankration at Olympia.

The Thasians erected a statue to Theagenes in the town. A former athlete, who hated Theagenes, attacked the statue one night, and it fell on him and killed him. The Thasians followed Draconian law and threw the statue into the sea. A great drought fell upon the island of Thasos, and crops suffered, with many animals dying as a result. The oracle at Delphi told them this could be corrected by bringing back to the country all their exiles. They did this, but the drought and famine continued. They then consulted the wise Pythia at Delphi, who told them, "You have forgotten your great Theagenes, whom you threw in the sand, where he now lies, though before he won a thousand prizes." Several Thasian fishermen hauled the statue back in their nets, it was re-erected in its former position, and the drought ended. Later the Thasians sacrificed to Theagenes as a hero of healing.

THESSALONIKA (THESSALONIKÍ) (TSL). At the 1906 Intercalated Olympics, a **football (soccer)** team represented Thessalonika and won a bronze medal. This is the only independent Olympic appearance by this province and city of Greece, which was then under control of the Turkish Ottoman Empire. However, many of the athletes representing Thessalonika were actually **Greek** nationals.

THOMAS, PETRIA ANN (AUS–SWI). B. 25 August 1975, Lismore. Primarily a butterfly **swimmer**, Petria Thomas has overcome major shoulder injuries to become one of the top butterflyers ever. Thomas first competed at the Olympics in 1996, winning a silver medal in the 200 fly. At Sydney in 2000 she won three medals, bronze in the 200 fly and silvers in two relays. Her best Olympic performance came in Athens when she won four medals, with three gold medals. She also won her first individual gold medal in the 100 fly, adding gold in the 400 free relay and the medley relay. But Thomas's best meet may have been the 2001 World Championships when she won three gold medals, including both the 100 and 200 fly and the medley relay. In 2002, she became the first swimmer to win the same event at three consecutive Commonwealth Games, when she won the 200 fly in Manchester, England. Thomas has accomplished this despite having sustained numerous shoulder dislocations, which have required surgery on both shoulders.

THOMPSON, FRANCIS MORGAN "DALEY" (GBR–ATH). B. 30 July 1958, Notting Hill, London. Daley Thompson shares with **Bob Mathias** the distinction of successfully defending an Olympic decathlon title. Thompson won his Olympic gold medals in 1980 and 1984, setting his fourth and final world record at the Los Angeles Games. He also competed in the 1976 and 1988 Olympics and is one of only two decathletes to have taken part in four Games. Thompson was also the World (1983), European (1982, 1986), and British Commonwealth (1978, 1982, 1986) champion. He set four world records in the decathlon.

THOMPSON, JENNIFER BETH (USA–SWI). B. 26 February 1973, Danvers, Massachusetts. With 12 medals and eight gold medals, Jenny Thompson has won more **swimming** medals and gold medals than any woman in Olympic history. But all eight of her gold medals came in relays, and this immensely talented swimmer has been frustrated in her attempt to win an individual Olympic gold medal. Her only individual medals were a silver in the 1992 100 freestyle and a bronze in the same event in 2000. Twenty-three times a national champion, she was more successful individually at the World Championships, winning the 100 free and 100 fly at the 1998 Worlds. At the other major international event, the Pan-Pacifics, Thompson also won the 50 free four times (1989, 1991, 1993, 1999), the 100 free four times (1993–1999), and the 100 fly three times (1993, 1997–1999). Among all female Olympians, Thompson's eight gold medals is surpassed only by **Larisa Latynina**'s nine. Thompson seemingly retired after the 2000 Olympics and attended medical school at Columbia University, but she returned to competition and won two silver medals in relays at Athens in 2004.

THORPE, JAMES FRANCIS (née Wa-tho-huck) (USA–ATH). B. 28 May 1888, Bellemont, Oklahoma. D. 28 March 1953, Lomita, California. Jim Thorpe (whose Sac-and-Fox Indian name means "Bright Path") is often described as the greatest all-round athlete in history. The accolade is well merited when judged by his superiority over his contemporaries. At the 1912 Olympics, he won the **pentathlon** and decathlon by huge margins, setting world records in both events. The following year, his name was struck from the roll of Olympic champions after it was revealed that he had earlier been paid for playing minor league **baseball**. The amount involved was minuscule ($15 [US] per week) but it was not until 1982 that the **International Olympic Committee** (IOC) reversed its decision, and, after an interval of 70 years, the medals were returned, posthumously, to the family of their rightful owner. Part French and Irish, and part Sac-and-Fox Indian, he attended Carlisle Indian School where he established an awesome reputation as a football player, being voted All-American in 1911 and

1912. Thorpe later played professionally for the Canton Bulldogs and played major league baseball for the New York Giants, Boston Braves, and Cincinnati Reds.

THUNBERG, CLAS ARNOLD ROBERT (FIN–SSK). B. 5 April 1893, Helsinki. D. 28 April 1973, Helsinki. Clas Thunberg's record of five Olympic gold medals for **speed skating** was equaled by **Eric Heiden** in 1980 but has never been bettered. In 1924 he won the 1,500 meters, 5,000 meters, and the combined event and placed second in the 10,000 meters and third in the 500 meters. Four years later, he won the 500 meters and successfully defended his 1,500 meters crown. Further Olympic honors seemed likely at the 1932 Games, but, like many leading European skaters, Thunberg refused to compete at Lake Placid as a protest against the mass-start style of racing. An unusual character, he made his World Championship début in 1922 at the age of 28, and his final appearance was in 1935, when he was 42. During this period he missed three Championships (1926, 1930, 1935) but still won 14 individual titles and was the overall champion five times. Thunberg set five world records, the last in 1931 at the age of 38. He later became a Member of the Finnish parliament.

TIKHONOV, ALEKSANDR IVANOVICH (URS/RUS–BIA). B. 2 January 1947, Chelyabinsk Oblast. During his Olympic **biathlon** career, which ran from 1968 to 1980, Aleksandr Tikhonov won five medals, of which four were gold medals. All of his gold medals, however, came as a member of the winning **Soviet** relay teams, winning that event four times consecutively. He is the only athlete to have won a gold medal in the same event at four consecutive **Winter Olympics**. To his team gold medals, Tikhonov added a silver medal in the 1968 individual event over 20 kilometers. He also finished fourth in that event in 1972 and fifth in 1976. At the World Championships he won individual titles in 1969–1970 and 1973 over 20 kilometers and over 10 kilometers in 1977. Tikhanov won a further six relay gold medals at the World Championships, giving him a total of 13 biathlon gold medals at the Olympic and World Championships.

TIMMONS, STEPHEN DENNIS (USA–VOL). B. 29 November 1958, Newport Beach, California. With three Olympic medals, two of them gold, Steve Timmons shares the record for Olympic **volleyball** medals won by a man. Timmons led the U.S. to Olympic gold medals in both 1984 and 1988, being named most valuable player of the 1984 Olympic team. Between Olympics, he helped the U.S. win the 1986 World Championship and the 1985 World Cup. Timmons left the national team in 1989 to play professional volleyball for Il Messaggero in Rome. Timmons and **Karch Kiraly** led Il Messaggero to the 1991 World Club Championship. He then returned to the national team to help the U.S. win a bronze medal at the 1992 Olympics. Timmons owns a beach sportswear company, and he was briefly married to the former Jeanne Buss, the daughter of the owner of the Los Angeles Lakers.

TOGO (TOG). Togo has competed at seven **Olympic Games**—those of 1972, 1984, 1988, 1992, 1996, 2000, and 2004. The nation's best Olympic performance came in 1988 when welterweight **boxer** Abdoukerim Hamidou won one match to place equal ninth of 44 in his class. Togo has never competed at the **Olympic Winter Games**.

TOMBA, ALBERTO (ITA–ASK). B. 19 December 1966, San Lazzaro di Savena, Bologna. An Olympic gold medalist in the slalom and giant slalom in 1988, Alberto Tomba successfully defended his giant slalom title in 1992 when he also took the silver medal in the slalom. At his third **Winter Games** in 1994 he placed second in the slalom giving him a total of five Olympic medals: a record for alpine skiing that he shares with **Kjetil André Aamodt, Vreni Schneider**, and **Katja Seizinger**. Had Tomba chosen to compete regularly in the downhill and supergiant slalom events he would surely have won even more medals. Surprisingly, in view of his Olympic successes, he had a poor record at the World Championships where he won a solitary bronze medal in 1987. In contrast, he enjoyed a superb record in the World Cup, winning the slalom in 1988, 1992, and 1994–1995; the giant slalom in 1988, 1991–1992, and 1995; and the overall title in 1995. A flamboyant, dashing character, both on and off the slopes, he was the idol of the Italian sporting public, to whom he was known as "La Bomba."

TONGA (TGA). Tonga has competed at the 1984, 1988, 1992, 1996, 2000, and 2004 Olympics. Tonga has never competed at the **Olympic Winter Games**. Tonga's one Olympic medal to date came in 1996 when **boxer** Paea Wolfgram finished second in the unlimited class.

TOP (THE OLYMPIC PROGRAMME). *See* OLYMPIC PROGRAMME, THE.

TORRES, DARA GRACE (USA–SWI). B. 15 April 1967, Beverly Hills, California. Dara Torres has had the longest successful career of any Olympic **swimmer**, one that has seen her win nine Olympic medals and four gold medals. Torres began her career in 1984, winning a gold medal in the 4 × 100 freestyle relay. She added a silver and bronze in relays in 1988 and seemingly ended her swimming career with another gold in the 4 × 100 free relay in 1992. Tall and strikingly attractive, Torres then began a career as a model, becoming the first athlete to appear in *Sports Illustrated*'s swimsuit issue. She also achieved notice as a commercial spokeswoman on an infomercial for a fitness training method. But in late 1998, she elected to return to competitive swimming. With seemingly little time to prepare, she returned to the Olympic pool at Sydney and won five medals, including two golds in relays. She won three individual bronze medals at Sydney—in the 50 free, the 100 free, and the 100 fly.

TORVILL, JAYNE (later Mrs. Christensen), B. 7 October 1957, Nottingham; and **DEAN, CHRISTOPHER COLIN,** B. 27 July 1958, Nottingham **(GBR–FSK).** The ice dance partnership of Jayne Torvill and Christopher Dean produced one of the legendary performances in Olympic history. Their interpretation of Ravel's "Bolero" at the 1984 **Winter Games** in Sarajevo drew the maximum score of 6.0 for artistic impression on all nine judges' scorecards. They were clear winners of the Olympic gold medal and set a new standard against which ice dancing was to be judged in the future. Only four weeks later they repeated their own superlative Olympic performance to win their fourth consecutive world title. A successful and lucrative professional career followed, but, after Olympic eligibility had been restored, they took the bronze medal at the 1994 Olympic Winter Games, having earlier won the 1994 European title. Dean has twice been married to **figure skating** World Champions: first to Isabelle Duchesnay, French pair World Champion (1991), and later to the 1990 world ladies' champion, Jill Trenary (USA).

TRACK AND FIELD. *See* ATHLETICS (TRACK AND FIELD).

TRAMPOLINE. Trampolining was never contested at the **Olympic Games** as a **demonstration sport**. However, the Fédération Internationale de Trampoline (FIT) is recognized by the **International Olympic Committee** (IOC). Trampoline made its Olympic début on the 2000 **Olympic program** as a discipline within the **gymnastics** program, with one event for men and one for **women**.

TRETYAK, VLADISLAV ALEKSANDROVICH (URS–ICH). B. 25 April 1952, Moscow Oblast. Of the six **ice hockey** players to have won three Olympic gold medals, Vladislav Tretyak is the only one to have added a silver medal to his collection. Recognized as one of the greatest goalkeepers of all time, he won Olympic gold in 1972, 1976, and 1984 and silver in 1980 when the Americans defeated the **Soviets** in a major upset. Tretyak was also on the winning team at nine World Championships, and his talents attracted the attention of many National Hockey League (NHL) clubs. The Montreal Canadiens drafted him, but the authorities in the USSR refused to let him play abroad, although he later coached the Chicago Black Hawks goaltenders. Tretyak enjoyed the distinction of being the first Soviet player in the Hockey Hall of Fame.

TRIATHLON. Triathlon is a relatively new sport that consists of running, **swimming**, and **cycling**. Its origins date to the 1970s when the first major triathlon, the Ironman Race, was first held in Hawaii. Triathlon is governed by the International Triathlon Union (ITU) which was recognized by the **International Olympic Committee** (IOC) in 1989, currently with 94 member nations. Triathlon appeared on the **Olympic program** at the 2000 and 2004 **Olympic Games**, with two events—one for men and one for **women**. The Olympic triathletes race over what is termed the "Olympic distance"—1,500 meter swim, 40 km. cycling, and 10 km. running.

TRINIDAD AND TOBAGO (TRI). Trinidad and Tobago has competed continuously at the Olympics since its début in 1948, competing only as Trinidad through 1956 and in 1964. In 1960, it had one **cyclist** and one **track and field** athlete competing in a combined team with **Jamaica** and **Barbados** under the name of the **West Indies Federation**, termed the Antilles by the Rome **Organizing**

Committee. Though the West Indies Federation won two medals, no Trinidad athlete was a medal winner in 1960. Trinidad and Tobago competed in the **Olympic Winter Games** for the first time in 1994 at Lillehammer and competed again in 1998 and 2002. Trinidad and Tobago has won 12 Olympic medals, eight in track and field athletics, three in **weightlifting**, and one in **swimming**. Its only gold medal occurred in 1976 when Hasely Crawford won the men's 100 meters in track and field athletics.

TUG-OF-WAR. In 1900, 1904, 1906, 1908, 1912, and 1920, tug-of-war was contested as a part of the track and field **athletics** program. The sport has not returned to the Olympics since. Three British athletes, Frederick Humphreys, Edwin Mills, and James Shephard, won three tug-of-war medals, two of them gold. The sport is governed internationally by the Tug-of-War International Federation (TWIF), which is provisionally recognized by the **International Olympic Committee** (IOC).

TUNISIA (TUN). Tunisia has competed at the **Olympic Games** since 1960, missing only the 1980 Olympic Games. It has never competed at the **Olympic Winter Games**. Tunisia has won six Olympic medals, four of them by Mohamed Gammoudi, a distance runner, and two in **boxing**.

TURISHCHEVA, LYUDMILA IVANOVNA (later Borzova) (URS–GYM). B. 7 October 1952, Grozny, Checheno-Ingushskaya. Lyudmila Turishcheva ranks with **Larisa Latynina** as one of the two greatest Soviet female **gymnasts** ever. But Turishcheva never won the fans' affections that were often reserved during her career for her teammates Olga Korbut and **Nelli Kim**. Turishcheva won nine Olympic medals, four of them gold. She was all-around champion at the 1972 Olympics, 1970 and 1974 World Championships, 1971 and 1973 European Championships, and at the first World Cup in 1975, when she uniquely won all five individual events. She later married **Soviet** sprint great Valery Borzov and became coach of the Soviet gymnastics teams.

TURKEY (TUR). Turkey was first represented at the **Olympic Games** of 1906 when an Armenian student at Robert College in Constantinople (now Istanbul) competed in the 800 and 1,500 meter track events. It is often claimed that during a visit to Turkey in 1907, **Pierre de Coubertin** invited his guide, Aleko Mulas, to take part in the **gymnastic** events at the 1908 Olympics, but there is no evidence that Mulas competed—or was even officially entered. The two Turkish entrants at the 1912 Olympics were again Armenians, and Turkey could be said to have really made its Olympic début in 1924 when they sent a 21-man team to the Paris Olympics. Since then it has missed only the Games of 1932 and 1980. Turkey first competed at the **Olympic Winter Games** in 1936 and has since missed only the Winter Games of 1952, 1972, and 1980. Turkey has won 74 Olympic medals. Turkish **wrestlers** account for an outstanding 55 of these, with 27 wrestling gold medals.

TURKMENISTAN (TKM). As a former member of the **Soviet Union**, Turkmenistani athletes competed from 1952 to 1988 on the former Soviet Union teams, and their athletes were present at Barcelona in 1992 as members of the **Unified Team**. Turkmenistan first competed independently at the 1996 **Olympic Games**, but it has not yet participated in the **Olympic Winter Games**.

TURNER, CATHY ANN (USA–STK). B. 10 April 1962, Rochester, New York. Cathy Turner began her **speed skating** career in the 1970s, winning the 1979 U.S. short-track title. But she retired in 1980 to pursue a singing and songwriting career. When short-track speed skating became an Olympic sport in 1992, she came out of retirement and won the only individual event on the program, the 500 meters. She defended that title in 1994 at Lillehammer and added relay medals (silver in 1992 and bronze in 1994) to give her four short-track medals in all. She was one of the few speed skaters to appear in Ice Capades, which she did in 1992, skating and singing. She also appeared on **television** as one of the American Gladiators.

TELEVISION AND INTERNET RIGHTS COMMISSION. The Television and Internet Rights Commission was formed in 2002 in response to the concern about streaming images of Olympic events being sent out over the Internet. The commission is responsible for preparing and implementing the overall **International Olympic**

Committee (IOC) strategy for future broadcast rights negotiations. The commission is composed of six IOC members and is chaired by IOC president **Jacques Rogge**.

– U –

UEBERROTH, PETER VICTOR (USA). B. 2 September 1937, Evanston, Illinois. After the financial disaster of the 1976 Games and the **boycott** in 1980, there was no longer any great enthusiasm among cities to host the **Olympic Games**. Los Angeles was the only city to apply to stage the 1984 Games, and under Peter Ueberroth's able direction as president of the **organizing committee** they proved a great success. Although the Games had no public funding, a successful drive for corporate sponsorship and the sale of TV rights resulted in a surplus of over $220 million. This resulted in a worldwide revival of interest in hosting future editions of the Games. Although the European press initially vilified Ueberroth's methods, his marketing ideas have been adopted by the **International Olympic Committee** (IOC) and subsequent organizing committees and are now considered de rigueur. Ueberroth later served as commissioner of **baseball** in the **United States**, but after he lost the support of the owners he did not seek reelection for a second term. He also ran unsuccessfully for governor of California in 2004, losing to Arnold Schwarzenegger.

UGANDA (UGA). Uganda competed at the Olympics for the first time in 1956. Its participation was continuous through 1972—the highlight that year being John Akii-Bua winning the first Ugandan gold medal with his world record performance in the 400 meter hurdles. In 1976, after the overthrow of Idi Amin, and joining in the African **boycott**, Uganda did not participate at Montreal. It did compete, however, in both 1980 and 1984. Uganda has never competed at the **Olympic Winter Games**. Ugandan athletes have won six Olympic medals, two in track and field **athletics** and four in **boxing**.

UKRAINE (UKR). As a separate nation Ukraine had never competed at the Olympics until its début in 1994 at Lillehammer at the **Olympic Winter Games** and in 1996 at the **Olympic Games** in Atlanta. This is due mostly to the fact that until the **Soviet** revolution of 1991 the Ukraine had only been truly independent in the 20th century for a brief period around the time of the Bolshevik Revolution (and was at civil war for most of that time). Many Ukrainians have competed for the Soviet Union at the Olympic Games, however. The Ukraine was second only to Russia among Soviet republics in terms of medals won. Ukrainian athletes were present at Albertville and Barcelona in 1992 as members of the **Unified Team**. At Lillehammer, the Ukraine accounted for two Olympic medals, highlighted by the gold-medal-winning performance of Oksana Baiul in **women**'s **figure skating**. The Ukraine has never hosted an Olympic Games, but in 1980 several preliminary **football (soccer)** matches were held in Kiev. Through 2004, the Ukraine has won 72 Olympic medals, 22 of them gold.

ULVANG, VEGARD (NOR–NSK). B. 10 October 1963, Kirkenes. After achieving only modest success at the 1988 **Winter Games**, Vegard Ulvang dominated **cross-country skiing** at the 1992 Games. At Calgary in 1988, he won a bronze medal in the 30 km., and four years later at Albertville he won three golds (10 km., 30 km., and relay) and a silver (combined pursuit). In 1994, he was no longer a major contender for individual honors but won his sixth Olympic medal with a silver in the relay. He competed injured in 1994, shortly after the trauma of his younger brother's being lost and dying while running in the woods in the autumn of 1993. Ulvang spent one summer training by skiing across Greenland.

UNDERWATER SWIMMING. Underwater swimming has never been contested as a separate sport at the **Olympic Games**, even as a **demonstration sport**. However, the Confédération Mondiale des Activités Subaquatiques (CMAS) is recognized by the **International Olympic Committee** (IOC). Founded in 1959, it currently has 104 affiliated member nations. In 1900 at Paris, the **swimming** program did include an underwater swimming event, and the 1904 Olympic swimming program included a plunge for distance event.

UNIFIED TEAM (ÉQUIPE UNIFIÉ) (CIS) (EUN). Because of the **Soviet** revolution of 1991, the Unified Team represented the

Commonwealth of Independent States at the 1992 Olympics in both Albertville and Barcelona. At Albertville, the Unified Team was a loose confederation of five former Soviet republics—**Russia**, **Belarus** (formerly Byelorussia), the **Ukraine**, **Kazakstan**, and **Uzbekistan**. At Barcelona, the Unified Team had representatives from all the former Soviet republics, save for the Baltic states of **Estonia**, **Latvia**, and **Lithuania**, which competed independently. The Unified Team at Barcelona also included athletes from **Georgia**, which had not joined the Commonwealth of Independent States. In 1994 the republics began to compete independently.

UNION OF SOVIET SOCIALIST REPUBLICS (USSR) (URS). The **Soviet Union** has had two distinct periods of Olympic participation. From 1900 through 1912 it competed at the Olympics as **Russia**. However, after the Bolshevik Revolution the Soviet Union withdrew from international sport until the late 1940s. After World War II it competed in the European Championships in track and field **athletics** in 1946, but it did not return to the Olympics until 1952 at Helsinki. It made its inaugural **Olympic Winter Games** appearance in 1956 at Cortina. It competed at every Olympics from 1956 to 1988 with the exception of the 1984 Los Angeles Olympics, and in 1992 its constituent republics competed as the **Unified Team** (EUN). After returning to the Olympics, the Soviet Union was a dominant force in almost all Olympic sports. The Soviet Union was disbanded in late 1991 after the August revolution. It no longer competes as a single nation at the Olympics, as its 15 former republics now compete as independent nations. The Soviet Union hosted the Games of the XXIInd Olympiad in Moscow in 1980.

UNITED ARAB EMIRATES (UAE). The United Arab Emirates has competed at the Olympics in 1984, 1988, 1992, 1996, 2000, and 2004. It is no surprise that the United Arab Emirates, a desert nation, has never competed at the **Olympic Winter Games**. In 2004, Ahmed Al-Maktoum won a gold medal in double trap **shooting**, the first medal by an athlete from the UAE.

UNITED ARAB REPUBLIC (UAR). *See* EGYPT; SYRIA.

UNITED STATES MEN'S BASKETBALL TEAM—1960. The **United States** 1960 Olympic **basketball** team was one of the greatest basketball teams ever assembled. It is almost certainly the greatest amateur team ever, and its lineup would match up well with almost any professional team ever. The team easily won the gold medal at Rome in 1960. The team members were Burdette Haldorson, Jay Arnette, Walter Bellamy, Robert Boozer, Terry Dischinger, Darrall Imhoff, Allen Kelley, Lester Lane, Jerry Lucas, Oscar Robertson, Adrian Smith, and Jerry West. The starting lineup usually consisted of Robertson and West at guard, and as professionals, they would later be considered the two finest guards of their era.

UNITED STATES MEN'S BASKETBALL TEAM—1984. The **United States** 1984 Olympic **basketball** team rivaled the United States' 1960 team as a great amateur unit. The team was coached by Bob Knight of Indiana University and was never challenged in winning the gold medal. It was led by **Michael Jordan** of the University of North Carolina, who would later be considered the greatest professional player ever. The team members were Steve Alford, Leon Wood, Patrick Ewing, Vern Fleming, Alvin Robertson, Michael Jordan, Joseph Kleine, Jon Koncak, Wayman Tisdale, Chris Mullin, Samuel Perkins, and Jeffrey Turner. Ewing, Jordan, and Mullin would also later play on the 1992 **Dream Team**.

UNITED STATES OF AMERICA (USA). The United States has competed at every **Olympic Games**, with the exception of the 1980 Moscow Games, and has never failed to be represented at the **Olympic Winter Games**. In addition, it had skaters present in both 1908 and 1920 when those events were held with the summer celebration. It has been the dominant country in terms of medals won since the inception of the Games. However, in the era from 1952 to 1988, the **Soviet Union** won slightly more medals, and the **German Democratic Republic** threatened this dominance prior to its merger with West Germany in October 1990. The United States has also been host to the Olympic Games more than any other country. Four times the Games of the Olympiad have been held in the United States: 1904 in St. Louis, 1932 in Los Angeles, 1984 in Los Angeles, and 1996 in

Atlanta. The Olympic Winter Games have also been held in the United States four times: 1932 in Lake Placid, 1960 in Squaw Valley, 1980 in Lake Placid, and 2002 in Salt Lake City.

UNITED STATES' VIRGIN ISLANDS (ISV). Since making its Olympic début in 1968, the U.S. Virgin Islands has only missed the **Olympics Games** of 1980. It has competed at every **Olympic Winter Games** since 1984. Peter Holmberg won a silver medal in 1988 Finn monotype **yachting**, the only medal yet won by an athlete from the U.S. Virgin Islands.

UNITED STATES WOMEN'S BASKETBALL (1976–2004). In 1976, the **Soviet Union** won the gold medal in **women**'s **basketball**, with the **United States**' team finishing second. The USSR won again in 1980, although the United States did not compete because of the USA-led **boycott**. But from 1984 to 2004, the United States women's basketball team won the gold medal five times—1984, 1988, 1996, 2000, and 2004—failing only in 1992, when it earned a bronze medal behind the **Unified Team**. The United States has been led during this period by several star players who later played in the WNBA (Women's National Basketball Association). Notably, **Teresa Edwards** is the only player, man or woman, to win five medals in Olympic basketball, with gold medals in 1984, 1988, 1996, and 2000, and a bronze in 1992. Three players played in 1996, 2000, and 2004, all winning three gold medals—Dawn Staley, Lisa Leslie, and Sheryl Swoopes. Katrina McClain also won three medals, playing on the 1992, 1996, and 2000 teams. During this period of Olympic dominance, the United States' women have won the World Championships in 1979, 1986, 1990, 1998, and 2002, losing only in 1983 (USSR) and 1994 (**Brazil**).

UNITED STATES WOMEN'S FOOTBALL (SOCCER) (1996–2004). Women's **football (soccer)** was added to the **Olympic program** in 1996 at Atlanta. The **United States**' women have been the dominant team at the Olympics and internationally. They won the first Olympic tournament in 1996. In 2000 at Sydney, the U.S. women lost in the final match to **Norway**, 3-2, earning a silver medal. In 2004, the United States defeated **Brazil** after extra time in the final match to win a second gold medal. The United States has also dominated at the Women's World Cup, winning that title in both 1991 and 1999, losing in the final game in 1995 and finishing third in 2003. The 1999 World Cup victory was memorable with the championship in the final game against **China** earned on penalty kicks. On the final kick, Brandi Chastain scored the winning goal and yanked off her jersey, exposing her sports bra, for the start of an exultant victory celebration. It became one of the best known sports' photographs of the year. The United States' women's football team has been led by several players who competed from 1991 through 2000 and 2004. These include Mia Hamm, often considered the best women's player of the 1990s, Chastain, Julie Foudy, Michelle Akers, and Kristine Lilly.

UNITED STATES WOMEN'S SOFTBALL (1996–2004). Softball was admitted to the **Olympic program** in 1996, and the **United States' women** have won all three Olympic tournaments. In 1996 and 2004, the U.S. team was unchallenged, going undefeated at both tournaments. The 2004 team was particularly dominant, winning nine games and outscoring their opponents 51-1; **Australia** managed the only run in the final round loss, 5-1. The 2000 victory was a bit unusual. The team was highly favored, coming into the Olympics with an international win streak of 110 games. But at Sydney, the U.S. lost three games in the round-robin tournament and barely qualified for the four-team playoff. Two of those losses were consecutive, which was the first time that had happened to the U.S. softball team since 1983. However, it then won three consecutive games in the medal round to win the gold medal, defeating Australia, 1-0, in the final game. Four American women have played in three Olympics, winning three gold medals—Leah O'Brien-Amico (1st base and rightfield), Laura Berg (centerfielder), Lisa Fernandez (pitcher), and Lori Harrigan (pitcher). The United States' softball team has also won all the World Championships contested since 1982.

UPHOFF, NICOLE (FRG/GER–EQU). B. 25 January 1967, Duisburg. A dressage rider, Nicole Uphoff won her first international event in 1987 aboard Rembrandt. It presaged her dominance of dressage for the coming years. In both 1992 and 1996 she won the individual dressage gold medal and helped **Germany** to the team title at the Olympics. She repeated her double victories at the 1989 Europeans and 1990 World Championships. She retired after the 1996 Olympic Games, marrying German Olympic show jumper Otto Becker.

UPPER VOLTA (VOL). *See* BURKINA FASO.

URUGUAY (URU). Uruguay first competed at the 1924 Olympics in Paris and has competed at every **Olympic Games** since, with the exception of the 1980 Games in Moscow. It had only one competitor in 1932 but he did quite well; Douglas Guillermo won a silver medal in the single sculls rowing. Uruguay competed at the **Olympic Winter Games** for the first time in 1998. Uruguay first competed in the Olympic Winter Games in 1988 when it was represented by one **alpine skier**. Uruguay has won 10 Olympic medals. Two of these were gold, the outstanding victories by the Uruguayan **football (soccer)** teams in 1924 and 1928.

URUGUAY FOOTBALL TEAMS (1924 AND 1928). In both 1924 and 1928 **Uruguay** won the gold medal in the Olympic **football (soccer)** tournament. This was considered a major upset in 1924, as Uruguay had never before even entered the Olympic football (soccer) tournament. In fact, since 1928 Uruguay has not again competed in the Olympic football tournament. In 1930, the Uruguay team revealed its greatness when several of its Olympic players helped Uruguay to win the inaugural World Cup in football. The players who played on both the World Cup team and at least one of Uruguay's gold medal teams were Héctor Castro (1924, 1928 Olympic, 1930 World Cup); Pedro Cea (1928 Olympic, 1930 World Cup); José Nasazzi (1924, 1928 Olympic, 1930 World Cup); José Andrade (1924, 1928 Olympic, 1930 World Cup); Lorenzo Fernández (1928 Olympic, 1930 World Cup); Alvaro Gestido (1928 Olympic, 1930 World Cup); and Hector Scarone (1924, 1928 Olympic, 1930 World Cup).

UZBEKISTAN (UZB). Many Uzbeki athletes competed from 1952 to 1988 for the **Soviet Union**, and Uzbeki athletes were present at Barcelona and Albertville in 1992 as members of the **Unified Team**.

As an independent nation, Uzbekistan has competed at the **Olympic Winter Games** of 1994 and 1998 and the 1996 and 2000 **Olympic Games**. Lina Cheryazova won a gold medal in 1994 freestyle skiing aerials, the only medal won by Uzbekistan to date at the Olympic Winter Games. Uzbekistan has won 12 Olympic medals, four gold.

– V –

VAL BARKER AWARD. The Val Barker Award is given at each **Olympic Games** to the **boxer** who is judged to be the best overall technical boxer. It is named in honor of Val Barker of **Great Britain**, a former president of the Association Internationale de Boxe Amateur (AIBA), and was first awarded in 1936. Though typically it is given to one of the boxing gold medalists, three times it has been awarded to a nonchampion, as follows: 1936 flyweight bronze medalist Louis Lauria (USA); 1968 featherweight bronze medalist Philip Waruinge (KEN); and 1988 light-middleweight silver medalist Roy Jones (USA).

VÄLBE, YELENA (née Trubizina) (EUN/RUS–NSK). B. 24 April 1968, Magadan, Siberia. With 16 victories at the **Olympic Games** and World Championships, Yelena Välbe has won more major championships than any other female **cross-country skier**. She was World Cup champion in 1989 and 1991–1992 and was favored to win several medals at the 1992 **Olympic Winter Games**. She succeeded in earning a medal in every event, but in the four individual events, she won four bronze medals. She has three Olympic gold medals in the 1992, 1994, and 1998 relay. Her greatest performance came at the 1997 Worlds when she won a gold medal in all five cross-country events for **women**. At the World Championships, she has won the following titles: 1989—10 km. and 30 km.; 1991—10 km. and 15 km.; 1993—15 km. and relay; 1995—30 km. and relay; and 1997—5 km., 15 km., 30 km., pursuit, and relay.

VAN ALMSICK, FRANZISKA (GER–SWI). B. 5 April 1978, East Berlin. With 10 medals, Franziska Van Almsick trails only **Jenny Thompson** (12) among female Olympic **swimmers**, and she is one of only eight women to have won 10 or more Olympic medals. Van Almsick first competed at the **Olympic Games** in 1992, when she was only 14. She won four medals, including a silver in the 200 free and a bronze in the 100 free. Favored in 1996 at her best distance, the 200 freestyle, she finished second again. She also added two relay medals in 1996. In 2000, her only medal was a bronze in the 800 freestyle relay. At Athens in 2004, she won two more relay medals. Most of Van Almsick's Olympic success has been in relays, and she has not yet won an Olympic gold medal. Van Almsick was World Champion in the 200 free in 1994. Most of her success has come at the European Championships, in which she has won 17 gold medals, with five each in 1993, 1995, and 2002. She has set two world records in the 200 meter freestyle.

VAN INNIS, HUBERT (BEL–ARC). B. 24 February 1866, Elewyt. D. 25 November 1961, Zemst. Hubert Van Innis must be considered the supreme Olympic **archer**, with his record six gold medals and 10 medals at the Games of 1900 and 1920. Although the exceptional number of archery events at these Games clearly helped him toward his record medal total, this advantage was countered by his absence from the 1904 and 1908 Games and by the fact that archery events were not held at the 1912 Games. After his successes in 1920, archery was never again an Olympic sport during his lifetime, but, in 1933, at the age of 67, Van Innis won a team gold medal at the World Championships and in all probability would have won further Olympic medals had he been given the opportunity. Van Innis was an architect by profession.

VANUATU (VAN). Vanuatu made its Olympic début in 1988 at Seoul and also competed in 1992, 1996, 2000, and 2004. Vanuatu has not yet competed at the **Olympic Winter Games**, and its athletes have not yet won a medal.

VENEZUELA (VEN). Venezuela formed a **National Olympic Committee** (NOC) in 1935 and achieved **International Olympic Committee** (IOC) recognition in the same year. However, it was not until 1948 that Venezuelans competed at the Olympics. The Venezuelans have been represented at the **Olympic Games** without fail since

1948. It first competed in the **Olympic Winter Games** in 1998 when it was represented by a single **lugeist**. Venezuela has won 10 Olympics medals, five in **boxing**, and one each in men's track and field **athletics**, men's **shooting**, men's **swimming**, men's **taekwondo**, and men's **weightlifting**.

VIETNAM (VIE). The original **National Olympic Committee** (NOC) for Vietnam was founded on 25 November 1951 and was recognized by the **International Olympic Committee** (IOC) in 1952. After the Vietnam War, the committee was restructured on 20 December 1976 and waited four years for IOC recognition. Since making its Olympic début in 1952, Vietnam has only missed the **Olympic Games** of 1976 and 1984. It has never competed at the **Olympic Winter Games**. Vietnam won its first Olympic medal in 2000 at Sydney, when Trần Hiếu Ngân finished second in women's 57 kg. class **taekwondo**.

VIKELAS, DEMETRIOS (GRE). B. 6 June 1835, Syra. D. 7 July 1908, Athens. Demetrios Vikelas was the first **International Olympic Committee** (IOC) president (1894–1896). Vikelas was better known as a writer and for his interest in literature and the arts than for his sporting inclinations. But because he lived in Paris and was well acquainted with **Pierre de Coubertin**, he represented **Greece** and the Pan-Hellenic Gymnastic Club at the 1894 Olympic Congress in Paris. It was felt that the IOC president should come from the country hosting the next Games, and with Athens being awarded the 1896 Games, Vikelas was appointed president. Despite his lack of experience in sports administration, he proved an able and enthusiastic president before handing the office over to Coubertin at the successful conclusion of the 1896 Games.

VIRÉN, LASSE ARTTURI (ATH–FIN). B. 27 July 1949, Myrsklä. At Munich in 1972, Lasse Virén became, after **Emil Zátopek**, **Hannes Kolehmainen**, and Vladimir Kuts, only the fourth man to win the Olympic 5,000 and 10,000 meters at the same Games. Virén repeated this feat in 1976, a unique double-double. Despite falling early in the 1972 10,000 meters, his time was a new world record. Attempting to emulate Zátopek's 1952 triple that included a **marathon** victory, Virén entered the 1976 marathon as well, finishing fifth.

Virén also competed at the 1980 **Olympic Games**, finishing fifth in the 10,000 and failing to finish the marathon. Virén was less successful at other major meets, with his best efforts at the European Championships being a fourth in the 5,000 meters and third in the 10,000 meters in 1974.

VIRGIN ISLANDS, BRITISH (IVB). *See* BRITISH VIRGIN ISLANDS.

VIRGIN ISLANDS, UNITED STATES (ISV). *See* UNITED STATES' VIRGIN ISLANDS.

VOLLEYBALL. Volleyball, like **basketball**, is a sport whose origin is known almost to the day. Oddly, both sports were invented at the same college and within a few years of one another. Volleyball was invented in 1895 by William G. Morgan, a student at Springfield College and a director of the YMCA at Holyoke, Massachusetts. The game was originally called "minionette."

Volleyball quickly spread around the world and became more popular in other countries than in the **United States**. The sport was introduced in the Olympics in 1964 by the Japanese, although it was never contested as a **demonstration sport** at the Olympics. No country has been truly dominant in volleyball, although the **Soviet Union** has won the most medals. Originally the Japanese had the world's best women's players while the United States had the best men's team in the world for most of the 1980s.

Volleyball has now reached great heights of popularity in the United States, spurred on by **beach volleyball**, a two-man outdoor sport played by the ocean or on any sand-covered court. In 1993, the **International Olympic Committee** (IOC) approved beach volleyball as an Olympic sport that was contested at the 1996 Atlanta Olympics.

The international governing body of volleyball is the Fédération Internationale de Volleyball (FIVB), which was formed in 1947 and had 218 member nations as of December 2004. This makes volleyball the **International Federation** (IF) with the most affiliated nations worldwide.

VOLLEYBALL, BEACH. *See* BEACH VOLLEYBALL.

VON HALMAY, ZOLTÁN (HUN–SWI). B. 18 June 1881. D. 20 May 1956. Zoltán von Halmay was the first great **swimmer** from Continental Europe, winning nine Olympic medals (three gold, five silver, one bronze) between 1900 and 1908 at distances ranging from 50 yards to 4,000 meters. His gold medals came in the 50 and 100 yard freestyle in 1904 and the 4 × 250 meter relay in 1906. His 1904 50 yard freestyle victory came in a second race after the judges declared a dead heat in the first race between von Halmay and J. Scott Leary of the **United States**. Von Halmay swam mostly with his arms, without any leg movements, but in 1905 he set what is considered the inaugural record for 100 meters. The record remained unbeaten for more than four years, a remarkable length of time during a period of rapid development in the sport.

– W –

WALDO, CAROLYN (CAN–SYF). B. 11 December 1964, Montreal, Quebec. At the 1984 Olympics, Carolyn Waldo finished second in the solo **synchronized swimming** event behind **Tracie Ruiz** (USA). But Waldo then displaced her as the top synchronized performer, winning the 1986 World Championships in solo and duet, partnered by Michelle Cameron, and competing on the winning team. She had also earned a team gold at the 1982 Worlds. At the 1988 **Olympic Games** in Seoul, Waldo won the solo gold medal and, together with Cameron, added the duet gold medal as well. Waldo won "triples," the solo, duet, and team championships, at the 1985 FINA Cup, 1986 World Championships, and the 1987 Pan-Pacific Meet. She also competed on winning teams at the 1981 Pan-Pacifics and the 1983 Pan-American Games.

WALES. Wales competed as a separate country in 1908 **field hockey**, finishing third. In all other Olympics, and in all the other sports at the 1908 Olympics, Wales has competed as a member of the United Kingdom of **Great Britain** and Northern Ireland.

WALTER-MARTIN, STEFFI (née Martin) (GDR–LUG). B. 17 September 1962, Schlema. Steffi Walter-Martin is the only woman to win two Olympic gold medals for **luge**. She took the title in 1984 and 1988 and on each occasion led the East Germans to a clean sweep of the medals. She was also the World Champion in 1983 and 1985, and she won the World Cup in 1984.

WATANABE, OSAMU (JPN–WRE). B. 21 October 1940. It is possible that Osamu Watanabe is the greatest **wrestler** ever, pound for pound. He had a very short career, but he was never beaten. It is known that he won at least 187 consecutive matches until his victory in the 1964 Olympics at Tokyo when he won the featherweight freestyle gold medal. In that tournament, Watanabe won all of his matches without sacrificing a single point. This followed Watanabe's victories in the 1962 and 1963 World Championships. He was not immensely strong, but very quick, and his technical skills were unmatched in his era.

WATER POLO. Water polo was developed in Europe and the **United States** as two separate sports. In the United States it was termed softball water polo, as the ball was an unfilled bladder, and the sport was very rough, often degenerating into numerous fights. In 1897, Harold Reeder of New York formulated the first rules for that sport, which were intended to decrease the excessive roughness of the game. The European style of water polo predominated and today is the form of the game practiced universally. It is more scientific, faster, and less dangerous than the American game.

Water polo was played at the Olympics of both 1900 and 1904. It was not on the 1906 **Olympic program** but has been contested at all Games since. **Great Britain** won four of the first five Olympic tournaments, but by far the greatest exponents of water polo have been the Hungarians. Between 1928 and 1980, **Hungary** never failed to medal in the sport at the Olympics.

Women's World Championships are held in water polo, and **women** competed in water polo at the 2000 Olympic Games for the first time. Water polo, like **swimming** and **diving**, is governed by the Fédération Internationale de Natation Amateur (FINA), which was formed in 1908 and has 179 affiliated nations.

WATER SKIING. Water skiing was a **demonstration sport** at the 1972 Olympics. The sport is governed by the International Water Ski Federation (IWSF), which was formed in 1946 and is recognized by the **International Olympic Committee** (IOC). There are currently 85 affiliated member nations. It was thought that water skiing might possibly be added to the **Olympic program** for the 2004 Olympic Games in Athens, but that was voted down by the IOC **Executive Board** in December 2000.

WEIGHTLIFTING. Weightlifting in various forms has been popular for centuries. Strongmen of all types often performed at various fairs in the Middle Ages. In the 19th century, professional strongmen often toured with carnivals or vaudeville shows. However, weightlifting as a sport became organized only in the late 19th century. The governing body is the International Weightlifting Federation (IWF), which had 167 member nations in late 2004. The first governing body of weightlifting was founded in 1905 as the Amateur Athleten Weltunion. The current Federation was founded in 1920 as the Fédération Internationale Haltérophile and adopted the current name in 1972.

Weightlifting has been on the program of the Olympics except in the years of 1900, 1908, and 1912. The program has varied little except for the addition of more and more weight classes in recent years. Originally there were no weight classes, only an open competition, and in 1920 and 1924 there were also one-handed lifts. Beginning in 1928, the three Olympic lifts were standardized as the military press, the snatch, and the clean and jerk. Because of difficulties judging the press, and because there was some concern that the lift was biomechanically dangerous to lifters' backs, it was eliminated from international competition after the 1972 Olympics. Today lifters compete only in the snatch and the clean and jerk at the Olympics. **Women** made their Olympic début in weightlifting at the 2000 Olympic Games in Sydney, with seven weight classes.

Weightlifting has been dominated by the **Soviet Union** and its republics since its entry to the Olympics in 1952. In the 1970s and 1980s, **Bulgaria** challenged that dominance, although a number of its lifters ran afoul of drug testing, notably in 1992. The **United States** was once a weightlifting power but has won only one Olympic medal since 1968 (and none since 1976), with the exception of the 1984 Olympics, which were not attended by the East European nations.

Beginning in 1993, the weight classes in international weightlifting have been changed, with a completely new set of world records. This is to eliminate the possibility of earlier records having been set by drug users prior to stricter drug controls.

WEISSMULLER, JOHNNY (née Petr János Weiszmüller) (USA–SWI/WAP). B. 2 June 1904, Freidorf, then Hungary. D. 20 January 1984, Acapulco, Mexico. Johnny Weissmuller was the winner of the 100 meter freestyle in 1924 and 1928 and the 400 meter freestyle in 1928 and was a member of the winning relay team both years. He set 28 world records, and such was his margin of superiority over his contemporaries that some authorities still rate him ahead of **Mark Spitz** as the greatest **swimmer** of all time. Because of the limited number of events available to Weissmuller, his Olympic record cannot be fairly compared with that of Spitz, but the longevity of his records is testament to his greatness. His 1927 world record for the 100 yard freestyle was unbeaten for 17 years, a remarkable length of time. Much of his success was due to his revolutionary high-riding stroke, flutter kick, and head-turning breathing. Invited for a screen test for the role of Tarzan, Weissmuller was preferred to 150 other applicants and went on to become the most famous screen Tarzan of all, playing the role in 19 movies between 1934 and 1948.

WENZEL, HANNI (LIE–ASK). B. 14 December 1956, Staubirnen, Germany. With a total of four medals, Hanni Wenzel trails only **Vreni Schneider** and **Katja Seizinger** as the most successful of all women Olympic **alpine skiers**. After winning a bronze medal in the slalom in 1976, Wenzel won gold in the slalom and giant slalom and a silver in the giant slalom in 1980. Born in **Germany**, Wenzel moved to **Liechtenstein** as an infant and was granted citizenship after winning the slalom at the 1974 World Championships. Both her brother and sister were Olympic alpine skiers.

WEST INDIES FEDERATION. In 1960, **Jamaica**, **Barbados**, and **Trinidad** competed as a combined team, representing the West Indies Federation. The Rome **Organizing Committee** called the "nation" the Antilles, a term that has, unfortunately, been often copied in many books. The West Indies team consisted of 12 athletes in 1960, one from Barbados, four from Trinidad, and seven from Jamaica, who competed in track and field **athletics**, **cycling**, **sailing**, **shooting**, and **weightlifting**. Since 1960, the three constitutent nations have competed independently as separate nations.

WESTERGREN, CARL OSCAR "CALLE" (SWE–WRE). B. 13 October 1895, Malmö. D. 5 August 1958. Prior to the 1990s, Carl Westergren was the most successful Olympic **wrestler** in the Greco-Roman style, and his Olympic records in that discipline have been equaled only by **Russia**'s **Aleksandr Karelin**. A four-time Olympian he won gold in 1920 (middleweight), 1924 (light-heavyweight), and 1932 (unlimited), but in 1928, when he was defending his light-heavyweight title, he was surprisingly defeated in the first round by Onni Pellinen of **Finland** and withdrew from the competition. His total of three Olympic gold medals is a record shared with **Ivar Johansson** (SWE), **Aleksandr Medved** (URS), and Karelin. Westergren was a three-time European champion and was the world middleweight champion in 1922.

WESTERN SAMOA (SAM). *See* SAMOA.

WINKLER, HANS GÜNTER (FRG–EQU). B. 24 July 1926, Wuppertal-Barmen. Hans Günter Winkler has the finest record ever of any German show jumper, and his overall record internationally is rivaled only by **France**'s Pierre Jonquères d'Oriola and **Italy**'s **Raimondo D'Inzeo**. Winkler won seven Olympic medals (five gold, one silver, one bronze), but only one in the individual event. That individual medal, a gold, came in 1956 when Winkler won the show jumping at the Melbourne Olympics. He led **Germany** to team golds in 1956, 1960, 1964, and 1972, a bronze in 1968, and a silver in 1976. Winkler's 1956 championship was his third consecutive internationally, as in 1954 and 1955 he won the first two World Championships in show jumping.

WINTER PENTATHLON. In 1948 at St. Moritz, a winter **pentathlon** event was held as a **demonstration sport**. The events of the winter pentathlon were **cross-country skiing**, **shooting**, downhill skiing, **fencing**, and horse riding.

WITT, KATARINA (GDR/GER–FSK). B. 3 December 1965, Karl-Marx-Stadt (now Chemnitz). As a gold medalist in 1984 and 1988 Katarina Witt became the first woman **figure skater** to retain an Olympic title since **Sonja Henie**. She was also a four-time World Champion (1984–1985, 1987–1988), and after taking the Olympic and world titles in 1988 she turned professional. With the return to Olympic eligibility of certain professionals, Witt took part in the **Olympic Winter Games** for a third time in 1994, but some of the magic of the earlier days had gone and she finished in seventh place. Witt became enormously wealthy because of her talent, but also because of her beauty, which attracted many commercial endorsements.

WOMEN AND SPORT COMMISSION. In 1995, a Women and Sport Working Group was formed by the **International Olympic Committee** (IOC) to advise the IOC president on suitable policies to be developed in this field. The working group became a formal IOC commission in 2004. The commission has a consultative purpose and meets once a year, forwarding its policies to the IOC **Executive Board**. The commission consists of members from the IOC, the **National Olympic Committees** (NOCs), and the **International Federations** (IFs), as well as athletes' representatives and members from the **Paralympic** movement. The current chairperson is Anita DeFrantz (USA). *See also* WOMEN AT THE OLYMPICS.

WOMEN AT THE OLYMPICS. The first connection between women and the **Olympic Games** can be traced back to the 10th century BCE when the Herean Games, a sporting and religious festival exclusively for women, were held at Olympia, although not as part of the **Ancient Olympic Games**. The Herean Games were held quadrennially in honor of Hera, the wife of Zeus. There was only one event, a footrace of about 160 meters, but it was divided into three age categories, allowing young girls to compete. The women were given crowns of olive, similar to the Olympic prizes, and they also received a portion of a heifer that was sacrificed to Hera.

The first recorded Ancient Olympic Games occurred in 776 BCE, although it is considered that their origins date to the 12th century

BCE. Discrimination against women in sport is as old as these Games themselves, as women could not take part in the Ancient Olympic Games. In fact, with few exceptions, they were not even allowed as spectators. Strangely, young girls could watch, although the athletes were competing nude. Pausanias noted, "They do not prevent virgins from watching." Only one adult woman was allowed to witness the Games, that being the Priestess of Demeter Chamyne, who was awarded this honorary office every four years from the Eleans. The penalty for women watching the Olympic Games was severe. Any woman caught watching the Games, or even crossing the River Alpheios on the days the Olympics were held, would be put to death by being tossed from the cliffs of Mount Typaion.

The Olympic **boxing** crown in 404 BCE was won by Eukles, who was the son of Akousilaos and the grandson of Diagoras, who won the Olympic boxing championships in 464 and 448 BCE. To this time, legend has it that women were put to death if they were discovered watching the events. However, Eukles' mother, Kallipateira, attended his matches, disguised as a trainer. When he won, she leaped over the barrier behind the trainer's station and exposed herself as a woman. The judges withheld the death penalty "out of respect for her father and her brothers and son" (Finley and Pleket 1976, 45–46). A rule was then enacted requiring all trainers to thereafter attend all Olympic contests fully naked, like the athletes.

In 396 BCE the first female Olympic champion was crowned when Princess Kyniska of Sparta, the daughter of Sparta's King Archidamos, won the tethrippon, a four-horse **chariot race**. But it should be mentioned that in the Ancient Olympics, the winners of the chariot races were considered to be the owners of the chariots and horses, not the drivers.

No females officially competed in the first modern Olympics in 1896. There is fairly good evidence, however, that a woman ran the **marathon** course near the time of the Olympic race after she was not allowed to compete in the actual race. The Greek woman runner's name was Stamata Revithi, but this has only recently been discovered. For years, she has been known as Melpomene, a name chosen by the Greek media to honor the Greek muse of tragedy.

The 1900 Olympic Games were very odd, as they were held in conjunction with a large world's fair, the Paris International Exposition. It is not precisely certain which events conducted at the fair should be considered "Olympic," and years later, many athletes did not even know that they had competed in the 1900 Olympic Games. But the Games of 1900 are important for they saw the first official female Olympic participants when a total of 19 competitors from **Bohemia**, **France**, **Great Britain**, **Switzerland**, and the **United States** took part in **croquet**, **equestrian events**, **golf**, **sailing**, and **tennis**. The first known woman to compete in the Olympics was a Swiss yachtswoman, Helen de Pourtalès, who crewed on her husband's yacht in the 1-2 ton class. By winning the tennis singles and mixed doubles on 11 July 1900, Charlotte Cooper of Great Britain became the first individual female champion at the modern Olympic Games. There was a women's golf competition, won by Margaret Abbott of the United States, although in later life, Ms. Abbott did not even know she had competed at the Olympic Games. Women also competed in ballooning competition at the fair, although again, it is uncertain if this was an Olympic event. It is interesting to note that at the 1900 Paris Exposition, there was also a Feminist Congress held within the walls of the Exposition.

Over the next few Olympics, women gradually were allowed to compete in a few Olympic sports. A detailed list of how women's sports have been added to the **Olympic program** is given below. Briefly, in 1904 at St. Louis, there was a women's **archery** event. In 1908, women competed at London in **figure skating** and **motorboating**. A big step forward occurred in 1912 when women competed in **swimming** and **diving** at the Olympic Games, the first true "athletic" events at the summer Olympics.

Through the 1924 Olympics, women were not allowed to compete in track and field **athletics**, the most well publicized sport at the Olympic Games. In response, women formed their own organization, the Fédération Sportive Feminine Internationale (FSFI), which sponsored the "Women's Olympics" in Paris in 1922 and the "Second International Ladies' Games" in Göteborg, Sweden, in 1926. Only after these events proved that women could turn in credible athletic performances did the International Amateur Athletic Federation (IAAF) agree to allow them to compete in the 1928 Games, albeit only in five events.

All went well except in the 800 meters, when Lina Radke, the **German** winner, left a field of exhausted runners sprawled in various stages of collapse behind her. The **International Olympic Committee** (IOC) then banned women from any events beyond 200 meters, on the grounds that they were not physically equipped to run long distances. The ban remained in effect for 32 years, until the 1960 Olympics, when the 800 meters women's event was reinstated, with longer races to follow, beginning in 1972.

Why was there so much resistance to allowing women to compete at the Olympic Games? Much of the problem can be traced to the founder of the modern Olympic Games, **Baron Pierre de Coubertin**. He did not want women to compete on Olympian fields, and his philosophy toward woman and sports is the greatest stain on his remarkable achievement. Although Coubertin has been deified by some followers of the **Olympic movement**, others have not treated him so kindly, because of his views on women in sports. Jean-Marie Brohm wrote of him, "It is indeed confusion to declare Coubertin a great humanist when his written texts or his quoted remarks are clearly those of a blind reactionary for anyone who knows how to read them, [consisting of] elitism and sexism."

Coubertin wrote a great deal during his life, and his writings on women in sports, when read in the 21st century, do not reflect well on him. Note the following, "With regard to boys . . . sporting competition . . . is vital with all its consequences and all its risks. Feminized it becomes something monstrous." And, "I still . . . think that . . . feminine athletics . . . are bad and that these athletics should be excluded from the Olympic programme—that the Olympiads have been restored for the rare and solemn glorification of the [male adult]."

Since 1928, women have seen their presence in the Olympic stadium increase almost at every Olympic Games, although they do not yet have an equal role with men. Since 1900, it is only in 1920, 1932, 1956, and 1972 that the women's program at the Olympics has not been enlarged in some way. It is instructive to look at some of the numbers regarding women's participation at the Olympics. In 1912 there were 15 sports open exclusively to men, three for women, and two mixed sports. Men could compete in 143 events, while women only in 21, 14 of those mixed events. At Athens in 2004, there were 301 events in 31 sports, with 29 sports open to women, and only 28 open to men. Of these 301 events, there were 166 events for men only, 125 for women only, and 10 mixed events. Women now actually compete at the Olympics in three sports or disciplines not open to men—rhythmic **gymnastics**, **synchronized swimming**, and **softball**.

The **Olympic Winter Games** are even better for women, and near equality is upon us on the snow and ice. At Salt Lake City in 2002, there were 78 events in 6 sports and 14 disciplines, of which all sports and disciplines were open to women. Of these 78 events, there were 42 events for men only, 34 for women only, and 2 mixed events in figure skating. Women and men have equal programs in **alpine skiing**, **biathlon**, figure skating, freestyle skiing, **ice hockey**, short-track speed skating, snowboarding, and **speed skating**. Women still lag slightly with fewer events than men in **bobsledding** (1 vs. 2), **luge** (1 vs. 2), and, primarily, **nordic skiing**, in which the men have 12 events and the women, six. This discrepancy exists because women do not yet compete at the Olympics in the nordic disciplines of ski jumping and nordic combined.

As noted, the list of sports, disciplines, and events in which women compete at the Olympic Games has increased almost at every Olympics. See Table W.1 for the list of sports that have been added to the Olympic program for women and the years in which they have been added.

There are other roles women may play in the Olympic movement. In 1956 at Cortina, Italian skier Giuliana Chenal Minuzzo was the first woman to take the athletes' oath on behalf of the competitors. At Mexico City in 1968, Enriqueta Basilio de Sotelo became the first woman to light the main **Olympic torch** in the stadium, although Sweden's Karin Lindberg had lit one of the torches in 1956 at the Equestrian Olympic Games. Heidi Schüller (FRG) was the first woman to take the athletes' oath at the Summer Olympics in 1972 at Munich.

The IOC resisted female membership for a long time, and it was not until 1981 that the first women became members of the IOC. Two were elected in that year—Flor Isava-Fonseca (VEN) and Pirjo Vilmi-Häggman (FIN). Three women to date have served on the IOC **Executive Board**, which really has the power within the IOC. One is Anita DeFrantz of the United States, who was elected as a vice president in 1997 and in 2000 advanced to first vice president. Ms. DeFrantz was also an Olympic medalist, winning a bronze medal in **rowing** eights in 1976. The first female Executive Board member was Ms. Isava-Fonseca, serving from 1990 to 1994. They were joined in 2000 by Sweden's Gunilla Lindberg, who was elected to the Executive Board.

The IOC has publicly stated that it is committed to bringing more and more women into the highest levels of sports administration. In

Table W.1. Sports Added to the Olympic Program for Women

	Olympic Games	Winter Games/Sports
1900	Croquet, Golf, Tennis, Sailing	—
1904	Archery	—
1908	Motorboating	Figure Skating
1912	Diving, Swimming	—
1924	Fencing	—
1928	Gymnastics, Track and Field	—
1936	—	Alpine Skiing
1948	Canoeing and Kayaking	—
1952	Equestrian Events	Nordic Skiing
1960	—	Speed Skating
1964	Volleyball	Luge
1968	Shooting*	—
1976	Basketball, Handball, Rowing	—
1980	Hockey (Field)	—
1984	Cycling, Shooting†	—
1988	Table Tennis, Sailing‡	—
1992	Badminton, Judo	Biathlon
1994	***	—
1996	Football (Soccer), Softball	***
1998	***	Curling, Ice Hockey
2000	Modern Pentathlon, Taekwondo Triathlon, Weightlifting	***
2002	***	Bobsled, Skeleton
2004	Wrestling (Freestyle)	***

*Women were admitted to shooting in 1968 as mixed events.
†Separate shooting events for women began in 1984.
‡Separate sailing events for women began in 1988.
***Games not held in that year.

1996, the IOC mandated that **National Olympic Committees** (NOCs), **International Federations** (IFs), and other members of the Olympic movement should reach a goal of 10 percent of women in administrative positions by the year 2000, with that percentage increasing to 20 percent by 2005. Through 2004, the full list of women elected to the IOC is shown in Table W.2.

WORLD ANTI-DOPING AGENCY (WADA). In February 1999, the **International Olympic Committee** (IOC) convened the World Conference on Doping in Sport. The conference proposed the formation of an organization to police **doping** violations, and in November

Table W.2. Women Elected to the International Olympic Committee

Dates of Service	Name (Nation)
1981–1999	Pirjo Vilmi–Häggman (FIN)
1981–2002	Flor Isava–Fonseca (VEN)
1982–1993	Dame Mary Alison Glen Haig (GBR)
1984–	Her Royal Highness Princess Nora (LIE)
1986–	Anita Luceete DeFrantz (USA)
1988–	Princess Anne, Her Royal Highness the Princess Royal (GBR)
1990–2001	Carol Anne Letheren (CAN)
1995–2001	Věra Čáslavská (CZE)
1996–	Gunilla Lindberg (SWE)
1996–	Princess Doña Pilar de Borbon (ESP/FEI)
1996–2001	Lu Shengrong (CHN)
1998–	Irena Szewińska-Kirszenstein (POL)
1998–	Nawal El-Moutawakel Bennis (MAR)
1999–2000	Hassiba Boulmerka (ALG/Athlete)
1999–2004	Charmaine Crooks (CAN/Athlete)
1999–	Manuela Di Centa (ITA/Athlete)
2000–	Susan O'Neill (AUS/Athlete)
2001–	Els van Breda-Vriesman (NED/FIH)
2002–	Pernilla Wiberg (SWE/Athlete)
2002–2003	Sandra Baldwin (USA/United States OC)
2004–	Rania Elwani (EGY/Athlete)

1999, the World Anti-Doping Agency was established in **Lausanne**, Switzerland. WADA was formed in response to the proliferation of doping, or drug use in sports. Its express purpose is to oversee drug testing in sports, educate athletes against the use of drugs, and to eventually eliminate doping. The president of WADA since its inception has been the Canadian IOC member **Dick Pound**. WADA is composed of a foundation board, an executive committee, a board of directors, and several working committees. The foundation board is the decision-making body of WADA, but it delegates management of the agency to the executive committee. WADA has published a uniform list of prohibited substances, the World Anti-Doping Code of antidoping principles, has established and recognized specific drug-testing laboratories, and has been responsible for getting virtually all sports federations to be cognizant of the need to eliminate drugs in sport, and to that end, to test diligently for doping by athletes, both in and out of competition, by accepting the uniform code.

WORLD OLYMPIANS ASSOCIATION (WOA). The World Olympians Association was established on 21 November 1995 during a meeting at the **Olympic Museum** in **Lausanne**, Switzerland, with 25 founding members present. The group is essentially an alumni association of former Olympic athletes. Several nations have also formed **national Olympian associations** (NOAs). The WOA has several objectives as listed on their website. These include: 1) furthering the growth of the membership; 2) interacting with the national Olympian associations; 3) actively supporting the **International Olympic Committee** (IOC); 4) initiating discussions with the IOC in regards to special interests of former Olympians; 5) hosting an Olympians Center at the site of **Olympic Games**; 6) assisting NOAs with the development of an Olympian affinity card providing member benefits; 7) providing for a global Olympic Job Opportunity Program; 8) providing fraternal functions among members of the **Olympic family**; 9) forming an alliance with the ethical enforcement bodies of the IOC; and 10) working with youth and community programs as role models of excellence.

WRESTLING. Wrestling is the most ancient known competitive sport. Wrestling was introduced into the **Ancient Olympic Games** in 708 BCE, shortly after the Games' recorded history begins in 776 BCE. Ancient Olympic champions are recorded from Eurybatos of Sparta (708 BCE) through Aurelius Aelix of Phoenicia (213 CE). The most titled champions at Olympia were **Milon of Kroton**, who won five titles in wrestling (532–516 BCE) and one in boys' wrestling (540 BCE), and Hipposthenes of Sparta, who also won five wrestling titles (624–608 BCE) and one boys' wrestling title (632 BCE) at Ancient Olympia.

Only in 1900 has wrestling not been on the **Olympic program**. There are four main forms of amateur competitive wrestling practiced in the world—Greco-Roman wrestling, freestyle wrestling, judo wrestling, and sombo wrestling. **Judo** is considered a separate sport at the Olympics. Sombo is a combination of freestyle and judo and is most popular in the Asian republics of the former **Soviet Union**, but it has not yet been contested in the Olympics. Currently, both freestyle and Greco-Roman wrestling are contested at the Olympics, and both have been held since 1920. Prior to that (except in 1908), only one form was used, usually Greco-Roman. Freestyle wrestling is similar to American collegiate style, or folkstyle wrestling. Holds are relatively unlimited, provided they are not dangerous, and can be applied to any part of the body. Greco-Roman wrestling limits holds to the upper body. **Women**'s freestyle wrestling was added to the Olympic program in 2004 at Athens.

The dominant country in wrestling has been the Soviet Union and its former republics, especially in Greco-Roman style. The **United States** is close to the Soviets in freestyle, however. Other nations that produce good wrestlers include **Iran**, **Turkey**, and **Mongolia**. The wrestling **International Federation** (IF) is the Fédération Internationale de Luttes Associées (FILA), which was formed in 1912 and had 144 affiliated nations as of December 2004.

WUSHU. Wushu is a Chinese martial art. "Wu" in Chinese refers to the military or warfare, while "shu" refers to the method of performing an activity. Wushu has never been on the **Olympic program**, but the International Wushu Federation (IWUF) was recognized by the **International Olympic Committee** (IOC) in 1999. As of 2004, the IWUF had 97 member nations.

– Y –

YACHTING. *See* SAILING.

YEGOROVA, LYUBOV (EUN/RUS–NSK). B. 5 May 1966. Lyubov Yegorova was the winner of a female record six gold medals for **nordic skiing**. She won three golds in 1992 (15 km., combined pursuit, and relay) and a further three in 1994 (5 km., combined pursuit, and relay). Additionally she won two silver medals in 1992 (5 km. and 30 km.) and one in 1994 (15 km.). Yegorova was less successful in the World Championships, winning only one individual title, the 30 km. freestyle event in 1991.

YEMEN (YEM). Yemen was formed on 22 May 1990 by combining the nations of the People's Democratic Republic of Yemen and the Yemen Arab Republic. It was shortly thereafter recognized by the **In-**

ternational **Olympic Committee** (IOC). Yemen has since competed at the **Olympic Games** of 1992, 1996, 2000, and 2004, and prior to the merger, the People's Democratic Republic of Yemen competed in 1988 at Seoul, while the Yemen Arab Republic competed at both the 1984 Los Angeles Olympics and the 1988 Seoul Olympics.

YEMEN ARAB REPUBLIC (NORTH) (YAR). *See* YEMEN.

YEMEN DEMOCRATIC REPUBLIC (SOUTH) (YMD). *See* YEMEN.

YUGOSLAVIA (YUG). *See* SERBIA AND MONTEGRO.

– Z –

ZAIRE (ZAI). *See* CONGO, DEMOCRATIC REPUBLIC OF THE.

ZAMBIA (ZAM). Formerly Northern Rhodesia, this nation took the name Zambia on 24 October 1964. Zambia has competed at the **Olympic Games** of 1968–1972 and 1980–2004. In addition, the country competed at Tokyo in 1964 as Northern Rhodesia. Zambia has never competed at the **Olympic Winter Games**. In 1984, Keith Mwila won a bronze medal in light-flyweight **boxing**, the first medal won by a Zambian athlete at the Olympics. The nation's second Olympic medal came in 1996, when Samuel Matete finished second in the men's 400 meter intermediate hurdles.

ZANZIBAR. In 1964 Zanzibar united with Tanganyika to form the United Republic of **Tanzania**. Zanzibar never competed at the **Olympic Games** under its own name, but since the 1964 Olympic Games its athletes have been eligible to represent Tanzania.

ZAPPAS, EVANGELOS (GRE). B. 1800, present-day Albania. D. 1865. Evangelos Zappas was a wealthy landowner and businessman of Greek background, but he never set foot in Athens, where he would become famous for sponsoring an early effort at Olympic revival. He lived most of his life in **Romania**, settling there after fighting for

Greece in the Greek War of Independence. In early 1856, Zappas proposed to the Greek government a permanent revival of the Olympic Games and offered to finance the project. The first of the **Zappas Olympic Games** was held in 1859. Zappas had earmarked funds for restoration of the ancient Panathenaic Stadium, but this was not done for the 1859 Games. After his death, his will provided ample money to support a permanent revival of the Ancient Olympic Games and for restoration of the stadium. Prior to the 1870 Zappas Olympics, the Panathenaic Stadium was restored, thanks to Zappas's largesse.

ZAPPAS OLYMPIC GAMES. Numerous **attempts at revival** of the **Olympic Games** occurred prior to the successful efforts of **Baron Pierre de Coubertin**. Perhaps the most significant of these were the Zappas Olympic Games. They are today usually called by this name, although in the 19th century the Greeks termed them "Olympic Games for Greece."

The Zappas Olympic Games were conducted four times, in 1859, 1870, 1875, and 1889. They were held in Athens. The Games were the brainchild of Panagiotis Soutsos but were sponsored by **Evangelos Zappas**, a wealthy Greek who then lived in **Romania**. In 1856, he wrote to King Otto and offered to fund the entire Olympic revival himself. In early November 1859, a series of three festivals was conducted. The first was a series of agri-industrial contests. One week later, **chariot races** were conducted for professionals and laymen (the word "amateur" in reference to sports had not yet been invented).

On 15 November 1859, the athletic Games were conducted at Plateia Loudovikou, a city square on the edge of town. There were sprint races, a 1,500 meter race, two javelin throws (one for distance, the other for accuracy), and two discus throws (one for distance and one for accuracy). The winner of the 1,500 meters was Petros Velissariou, who came from Smyrna and won a first prize of 280 drachmas, the largest prize of the first Zappas Olympics because **William Penny Brookes**'s Much Wenlock prize of £10 was included.

In 1870, the Zappas Olympics were moved to the Ancient Panathenaic Stadium in the center of Athens. The stadium had been restored at Zappas's expense, although he had died in 1865. These Games, held on 15 November 1870, were the most successful of the

Zappas Olympics, with the newspapers calling them a resounding success. Over 30,000 spectators attended these Games.

The 1875 Zappas Olympics are termed by classics scholar David Young a "disaster." In 1870, the winner of the 400 meters had been Evangelis Skordaras, a butcher, and the **wrestling** winner was Kardamylakes, a manual laborer. Several of Athens' elite then suggested that the Games be restricted only to athletes from the upper class and that the general public be banned. This early attempt at elitism and using the early British concepts of amateurism proved highly detrimental to the Zappas Olympics. Only 24 athletes took part in 1875, with a small crowd that left large sections of the stadium empty.

The 1889 Zappas Olympics took place in May in a small gym, rather than in the stadium, and were not well organized. In fact, they were scheduled, begun, canceled, and then conducted again a few days later. Again, only a few privileged, upper-class athletes competed, and the crowd was much smaller. In 1891 and 1893, Panhellenic Gymnastic Society Games were contested, which were not organized by the Zappas Committee. Interestingly, several Greek athletes who competed in 1893 also competed at the 1896 Olympics.

The Zappas Olympic Games rank with the **Much Wenlock Olympian Games** as the most significant attempts to revive the Ancient Olympic idea. They probably surpass the Much Wenlock Games because they were national sporting contests. Though he later denied any knowledge of them, Coubertin was keenly aware of the efforts of the Zappas Committee to hold Olympic Games, having been told of them by **Demetrios Vikelas**, who would later be the first **International Olympic Committee** (IOC) president.

The Games themselves were fairly successful in 1859, and especially in 1870, but were "ruined" by elitism, anti-athleticism, bigotry, and attempts to apply an amateur-type code imposed on the athletes. The Zappas Olympics never had the international flavor that Coubertin would instill in the modern Olympic Games, but they were the closest attempt yet to a true Olympic revival. *See also* MUCH WENLOCK OLYMPIAN GAMES.

ZÁTOPEK, EMIL (TCH–ATH). B. 19 September 1922, Koprivnice, Moravia. D. 22 November 2000, Prague. Emil Zátopek was a supreme distance runner whose rugged training regimen was rewarded with unprecedented success. At the 1948 Olympics he won the gold medal in the 10,000 meters and finished second in the 5,000 meters. Then at Helsinki in 1952 he produced one of the greatest performances in distance running history. He won the 5,000 meters, successfully defended his 10,000 meters title, and then took his third gold medal in his first-ever **marathon** race to complete a "triple," which remains unique in Olympic history. Zátopek closed his Olympic career four years later when he placed sixth in the marathon in Melbourne. Between 1949 and 1954, he set 18 world records at every distance from 5,000 meters to 30,000 meters, a remarkable display of versatility at the very highest level. His wife, Dana (née Ingrova), was the Olympic gold medalist in the javelin in 1952.

Zátopek's was a remarkable life. Under the **Soviet** régime, his athletic feats earned him and his wife many perquisites not available to other Czech citizens. But despite that, after the Soviet tanks attacked Prague in 1968, he spoke out against the Soviet invasion, for which he paid dearly. For that he lost most of the favors bestowed upon him, and he spent much of the rest of his life as a trash collector, his status only restored after the fall of the Iron Curtain.

ŽELEZNÝ, JAN (CZE/TCH–ATH). B. 16 June 1966, Mladá Bolaslav. Jan Železný is considered the greatest javelin thrower in **track and field** history. At the 1988 **Olympic Games**, he narrowly missed winning the gold medal, settling for silver. But he has since won the gold medal at the 1992, 1996, and 2000 Olympic Games. He was also World Champion with the javelin in both 1993 and 1995. Although the javelin specifications have changed twice during his career, he can claim six world records with the various spears. In December 1999, Železný was elected a member of the **International Olympic Committee** (IOC) as an athlete member, having previously been a member of the **Athletes Commission**.

ZIJLAARD-VAN MOORSEL, LEONTINE MARTHA HENRICA PETRONELLA "LEONTIEN" (NED–CYC). B. 22 March 1970, Boekel. Leontien Zijlaard first competed at the **Olympic Games** in 1992, as Leontien van Moorsel, finishing 8th in individual pursuit and 23rd in the road race. This was somewhat disappointing, considering her record to that time at the World Championships. Van Moorsel was world road champion in 1991 and 1993 and won the individual pursuit in 1990. But van Moorsel was tortured by other demons, suffering from anorexia and bulimia, eating disorders, and shortly thereafter lost 20 kg. (44 lbs.) from a frame not considered obese. Her **cycling** career suffered, but she returned to prominence in the late 1990s, winning the individual time trial World Championship in 1998 and 1999 and the World Pursuit title again in 2001–2003. At the Sydney Olympics in 2000, she had the most successful Olympics ever by a woman cyclist. She won the individual pursuit in world record time, won the road race and the individual time trial, and added a silver medal on the track in points race. Van Moorsel continued competing and at Athens in 2004 won a gold medal in the individual time trial and a bronze medal in the individual pursuit. She was also a two-time winner of the Tour de France Féminin (1992, 1993) and in 2003, set the World Hour Record with 46.06511 km.

ZIMBABWE (ZIM). Zimbabwe was formerly Rhodesia, a British colony that was self-governing from 1923, and as Rhodesia, competed at three **Olympic Games**—those of 1928, 1960, and 1964. On 11 November 1965, Rhodesian prime minister Ian D. Smith announced his nation's unilateral declaration of independence from **Great Britain**. Britain termed the act illegal and demanded that Rhodesia broaden voting rights to provide for eventual rule by majority Africans. In May 1968, the United Nations Security Council condemned the white-dominated Rhodesian government, asking that Rhodesian passports not be accepted for international travel. Rhodesia did not compete at the 1968 Olympics, one reason being that the **International Olympic Committee** (IOC) did not recognize its independent status, another being that **Mexico** honored the U.N. Security Council ruling.

At the 71st IOC session in Luxembourg in 1971, the IOC ruled that Rhodesian athletes could compete at the 1972 Olympics under the same conditions as in 1968—using British uniforms, the Union Jack as a flag, and "God Save the Queen" as an anthem. Initially, this placated the African nations. However, shortly before the 1972 Munich Olympics, the African nations threatened a mass **boycott** if Rhodesia was allowed to compete. The petition stated that the Rhodesians had entered

Germany not on British passports, as still required by the U.N. Security Council, but using the **Olympic identity card**. Two days before the 1972 opening ceremonies, the IOC voted narrowly (36-31, with three abstentions) to withdraw the invitation to Rhodesia for the 1972 Olympics.

In 1975, the IOC sent a three-member contingent to visit Rhodesia to inspect the sporting facilities and groups. Led by Major Sylvio Magalhães de Padilha of **Brazil**, this commission of inquiry was not kind to Rhodesian sports, and the IOC expelled the Rhodesian Olympic Committee, by a 41-26 vote.

After changing its constitution to allow black rule and after normalizing relations with Great Britain, Rhodesia became Zimbabwe on 18 April 1980. Zimbabwe first appeared at the Olympics in 1980 at Moscow, and the highlight of its appearance was the gold medal performance of its women's **hockey (field)** team. Zimbabwe also competed at the 1984, 1988, 1992, 1996, 2000, and 2004 **Olympic Games**, but has not competed at the **Olympic Winter Games**. In 2004, Zimbabwean **swimmer** Kirsty Coventry won one medal of each color, including a gold in the 200 meter backstroke.

ZIMYATOV, NIKOLAY (URS/RUS–NSK). B. 28 June 1955, Rumyantsevo, Moscow Oblast. Nikolay Zimyatov is the greatest **Soviet** or **Russian** male **cross-country skier**. His fame rests primarily on his performance at the 1980 Olympics in Lake Placid, when he won three gold medals in the 30 km., 50 km., and on the Soviet relay team. He added two further Olympic medals in 1984, defending his 30 km. title and helping the Soviets win a silver in the relay. At other championships he was much less successful, winning only one World Championship, and that in the 1982 relay event. His best individual finish at a World Championship was second in the 1978 30 km. at Lahti.

Appendix A: Presidents of the International Olympic Committee

1894–1896	Demetrios Vikelas (Greece)
1896–1924*	Pierre Frédy, Baron de Coubertin (France)
1925–1942§	Count Henri de Baillet-Latour (Belgium)
1946–1952	J(ohannes) Sigfrid Edström (Sweden)
1952–1972	Avery Brundage (United States)
1972–1980	Sir Michael Morris, the Lord Killanin of Dublin and Spiddal (Ireland)
1980–2001	Juan Antonio Samaranch Torello, Marqués de Samaranch (Spain)
2001–	Jacques Rogge (Belgium)

*During World War I, between December 1915 and February 1917, Baron Godefroy de Blonay of Switzerland served as an interim president of the IOC. This was at the request of Baron de Coubertin, who felt that the IOC president should represent a country that was neutral during the war.
§The IOC presidency was technically vacant from 1942–1946; however, J. Sigfrid Edström served as de facto president during that time.

Appendix B: The Games of the Olympiads: Sites, Dates, Nations, and Athletes

	Site	Dates	Nations	Athletes	Men	Women
1896	Athens	6–15 Apr.	15	246	246	–
1900	Paris	20 May–28 Oct.	28	1,616	1,594	22
1904	St. Louis	1 Jul.–23 Nov.	12	662	656	6
1906	Athens	22 Apr.–2 May	19	842	836	6
1908	London	27 Apr.–31 Oct.	22	2,024	1,980	44
1912	Stockholm	5 May–27 Jul.	27	2,381	2,328	53
1920	Antwerp	23 Apr.–12 Sep.	29	2,663	2,586	77
1924	Paris	4 May–27 Jul.	44	3,068	2,933	135
1928	Amsterdam	17 May–12 Aug.	46	2,867	2,593	274
1932	Los Angeles	30 Jul.–14 Aug.	38	1,326	1,200	126
1936	Berlin	1–16 Aug.	49	3,955	3,626	329
1948	London	29 Jul.–14 Aug.	59	4,073	3,680	393
1952	Helsinki	19 Jul.–3 Aug.	69	4,916	4,395	521
1956	Total		72	3,347	2,964	383
	Stockholm	10–17 Jun.	29	159	146	13
	Melbourne	22 Nov.–8 Dec.	67	3,188	2,818	370
1960	Rome	25 Aug.–11 Sep.	83	5,337	4,725	612
1964	Tokyo	10–24 Oct.	93	5,132	4,452	680
1968	Mexico City	12–27 Oct.	112	5,555	4,771	784
1972	Munich	26 Aug.–11 Sep.	122	7,116	6,057	1,059
1976	Montreal	17 Jul.–1 Aug.	92	6,074	4,812	1,262
1980	Moscow	19 Jul.–3 Aug.	80	5,252	4,132	1,120
1984	Los Angeles	28 Jul.–12 Aug.	140	6,799	5,224	1,575
1988	Seoul	17 Sep.–5 Oct.	159	8,447	6,251	2,196
1992	Barcelona	25 Jul.–9 Aug.	169	9,386	6,663	2,723
1996	Atlanta	20 Jul.–4 Aug.	197	10,323	6,815	3,508
2000	Sydney	14 Sep.–1 Oct.	200	10,647	6,579	4,068
2004	Athens	13–29 Aug.	201	10,560	6,255	4,305

Appendix C: The Olympic Winter Games: Sites, Dates, Nations, and Athletes

	Site	Dates	Nations	Athletes	Men	Women
1908	London	28–29 Oct.	6	21	14	7
1920	Antwerp	23–29 Apr.	10	86	74	12
1924	Chamonix	25 Jan.–4 Feb.	16	291	278	13
1928	St. Moritz	11–19 Feb.	25	463	435	28
1932	Lake Placid	4–15 Feb.	17	252	231	21
1936	Garmisch-Partenkirchen	6–16 Feb.	28	668	588	80
1948	St. Moritz	30 Jan.–8 Feb.	28	668	591	77
1952	Oslo	14–25 Feb.	30	693	584	109
1956	Cortina d'Ampezzo	26 Jan.–5 Feb.	32	821	689	132
1960	Squaw Valley	18–28 Feb.	30	664	520	144
1964	Innsbruck	29 Jan.–9 Feb.	36	1,093	894	199
1968	Grenoble	6–18 Feb.	37	1,158	947	211
1972	Sapporo	3–13 Feb.	35	1,008	802	206
1976	Innsbruck	4–15 Feb.	37	1,129	898	231
1980	Lake Placid	13–24 Feb.	37	1,072	837	235
1984	Sarajevo	8–19 Feb.	49	1,273	996	277
1988	Calgary	13–28 Feb.	57	1,425	1,110	315
1992	Albertville	8–23 Feb.	64	1,801	1,313	488
1994	Lillehammer	12–27 Feb.	67	1,738	1,216	522
1998	Nagano	7–22 Feb.	72	2,180	1,391	789
2002	Salt Lake City	8–24 Feb.	77	2,399	1,513	886

Appendix D: Members of the International Olympic Committee

Dates of Service	Member (Nation)
1894–1895	Ferdinando Lucchesi Palli (ITA)
1894–1897	Demetrios Vikelas (GRE)
1894–1898	Arthur Oliver Russell, Lord Ampthill (GBR)
1894–1898	Duke Riccardo d'Andria Carafa (ITA)
1894–1900	General Aleksey Butowsky (RUS)
1894–1901	Count Maxime de Bousies (BEL)
1894–1905	Leonard Albert Cuff (NZL)
1894–1906	Charles Herbert (GBR)
1894–1907	Dr. Ferenc Kémény (HUN)
1894–1907	José Benjamin Zubiaur (ARG)
1894–1913	Ernst Callot (FRA)
1894–1921	General Viktor Gustaf Balck (SWE)
1894–1924	Professor William Milligan Sloane (USA)
1894–1925	Pierre Frédy, Baron Pierre de Coubertin (FRA)
1894–1943	Dr. Jiří Guth-Jarkovský (BOH/TCH)
1896–1909	Karl August Willibald Gebhardt (GER)
1897–1919	Count Eugenio Brunetta d'Usseaux (ITA)
1897–1925	Count Alexandros Merkati (GRE)
1897–1927	Reverend Robert Stuart de Courcy Laffan (GBR)
1898–1924	Baron Frederik Willem Christiaan Hendrik van Tuyll van Serooskerken (NED)
1899–1902	Prince Gheorghe Bibesco (ROM)
1899–1903	Count Archambauld Talleyrand de Perigord (GER)
1899–1906	Niels Vilhelm Sophus Holbeck (DEN)
1899–1937	Baron Godefroy de Blonay (SUI)
1900–1903	Theodore Stanton (USA)
1900–1904	Caspar Whitney (USA)
1900–1908	Prince Sergey Beloselsky-Belotsersky (RUS)
1900–1911	Henri Hébrard de Villeneuve (FRA)
1900–1916	Count Nikolao Ribeaupierre (RUS)
1900–1948	Count Carl Clarence von Rosen (SWE)
1901–1903	Robert François Joseph Nicolas Ghislain Reyntiens (BEL)

Dates of Service	Member (Nation)
1901–1905	Prince Eduard Max Vollrath Friedrich of Salm-Horstmar (GER)
1901–1908	Sir Charles Edward Howard Vincent (GBR)
1901–1931	Miguel de Beistegui (MEX)
1902–1921	Antonio de Mejorada del Campo, Marquis de Villamejor (ESP)
1903–1908	James Hazen Hyde (USA)
1903–1914	Count Caesar Erdmann von Wartensleben Carow (GER)
1903–1942	Count Henri de Baillet-Latour (BEL)
1904–1920	Count Albert Bertier de Sauvigny (FRA)
1905–1907	Henrik August Angell (NOR)
1905–1909	Alexander, Prince von Solms Braunfels (AUT)
1905–1909	Count Egbert Hoyer von der Asseburg (GER)
1905–1913	William Henry Grenfell, Lord Desborough of Taplow (GBR)
1905–1922	Don Carlos F. de Candamo (PER)
1905–1932	Richard Coombes (AUS)
1906–1912	Dimitri Tzokov (BUL)
1906–1912	Duke Antonio de Lancastre (POR)
1906–1912	Torben Grut (DEN)
1907–1908	Thomas Thomassen Heftye (NOR)
1907–1910	Manuel de la Quintana (ARG)
1907–1938	Count Géza Andrassy (HUN)
1908–1909	Prince Scipione Borghese (ITA)
1908–1910	Prince Simon Trubetskoy (RUS)
1908–1919	Baron Reinhold Felix von Willebrand (FIN)
1908–1920	Allison Vincent Armour (USA)
1908–1927	Johan Tidemann Sverre (NOR)
1908–1930	Selim Sirri Bey Tarcan (TUR)
1908–1939	Count Albert Gautier Vignal (MON)
1908–1949	Gheorghe A. Plagino (ROM)
1909–1914	Attilio Brunialti (ITA)
1909–1914	Baron Karl von Wenningen-Ullner von Diepburg (GER)
1909–1915	Sir Theodore Andrea Cook (GBR)
1909–1938	Jigoro Kano (JPN)
1909–1946	Gyula von Muzsa (HUN)
1910–1919	Count Adalbert von Francken-Sierstorpff (GER)
1910–1929	Jean-Maurice Pescatore (LUX)
1910–1933	Prince Léon Durusov (RUS)
1910–1963	Angelos Khristos Bolanaki (EGY)
1911–1914	Abel Ballif (FRA)
1911–1914	Oscar N. Garcia (CHI)
1911–1917	Evert Jansen Wendell (USA)

(continued)

Dates of Service	Member (Nation)
1911–1919	Otto, Prince zu Windisch-Gritz (AUT)
1911–1919	Rudolf, Count Colloredo-Mansfield (AUT)
1911–1921	John Hanbury-Williams (CAN)
1912–1921	Fritz Hansen (DEN)
1912–1940	Count José Carlos Peñha Garcia (POR)
1912–1949	Svetomir V. Đukić (SER/YUG)
1913–1915	Georges Aleksandrovich Duperron (RUS)
1913–1919	Count Adolf von Arnim-Muskau (GER)
1913–1920	Algernon St. Maur Somerset, Duke of Somerset (GBR)
1913–1929	Dimitri Stanciov (BUL)
1913–1938	Baron Edouard-Émile de Laveleye (BEL)
1913–1938	Raul de Rio Branco (BRA)
1913–1944	Albert Glandaz (FRA)
1914–1919	Sydney Howard Farrar (RSA)
1914–1939	Carlo Montu (ITA)
1914–1950	Marquis Melchior de Polignac (FRA)
1918–1922	Bartow Sumter Weeks (USA)
1918–1929	Eduardo Dorn y de Alsua (ECU)
1918–1940	Pedro Jaime de Matheu (ESA/Central America)
1919–1922	Carlos Silva-Vildosola (CHI)
1919–1925	Arthur Marryatt (NZL)
1919–1929	Marquis Giorgio Guglielmi (ITA)
1919–1933	Count Justinien de Clary (FRA)
1920–1927	Sir Dorabji Jamsetji Tata (IND)
1920–1943	Henry Nourse (RSA)
1920–1946	Franjo Bučar (YUG)
1920–1948	Ernst Edvard Krogius (FIN)
1921–1923	Henrique Echevarrieta (ESP)
1921–1923	Nizzam Eddin Khon (IRI)
1921–1932	Marcelo T. de Alvear (ARG)
1921–1933	Reginald John Kentish (GBR)
1921–1936	Francisco Ghigliani (URU)
1921–1946	James George Bower Merrick (CAN)
1921–1952	Johannes Sigfrid Edström (SWE)
1921–1954	Baron Guell de Santiago (ESP)
1921–1957	Wang Chengting (CHN)
1922–1924	Prince Stefan Lubomirski (POL)
1922–1931	Ivar Nyhölm (DEN)
1922–1936	Charles Hitchcock Sherrill (USA)
1922–1948	William May Garland (USA)
1922–1951	John Joseph Keane (IRL)
1923–1924	José Carlos Rincon Gallardo, Marquis de Guadalupe (MEX)

Dates of Service	Member (Nation)
1923–1927	Joseph Pentland Firth (NZL)
1923–1927	Prince Samad Khan Momtazos Saltaneh (IRI)
1923–1929	Gerald Oakley, Earl of Cadogan (GBR)
1923–1936	Porfirio Franca y Alvarez de la Campa (CUB)
1923–1939	Jorgé Matte Gormaz (CHI)
1923–1949	Ricardo Camillo Aldao (ARG)
1923–1957	Alfredo Benavides (PER)
1923–1961	Arnaldo Guinle (BRA)
1923–1962	José Ferreira Santos (BRA)
1924–1927	David Kinley (USA)
1924–1927	Fernando Alvarez, Duke d'Alba (ESP)
1924–1927	Jorgé Gomez de Parada (MEX)
1924–1928	Dr. Martin Haudek (AUT)
1924–1929	Oskar Ruperti (GER)
1924–1930	Prince Kasimierz Lubomirski (POL)
1924–1933	Seichi Kishi (JPN)
1924–1938	Theodor Lewald (GER)
1924–1944	James Taylor (AUS)
1924–1957	Pieter Wilhelmus Scharroo (NED)
1925–1943	Baron Alphert Schimmelperminck van der Oye (NED)
1925–1953	Count Alberto Bonacossa (ITA)
1926–1930	Giorgios Averof (GRE)
1926–1947	Jānis Dikmānis (LAT)
1926–1956	Duke Adolf Friedrich von Mecklenburg-Schwerin (GER)
1927–1933	George Kemp, Lord Rochdale (GBR)
1927–1936	Ernest Lee Jahncke (USA)
1927–1950	Sir Thomas Fearnley (NOR)
1928–1930	Bernard Cyril Freyberg (NZL)
1928–1930	Marquis François Manuel de Pons (ESP)
1928–1932	Friederik Akel (EST)
1928–1932	Miguel Moises Saenz (MEX)
1928–1938	Theodor Schmidt (AUT)
1928–1939	Ignasz Matuszewski (POL)
1928–1939	Sir George McLaren Brown (CAN)
1929–1933	Don Alfredo Ewing (CHI)
1929–1944	Stepan G. Shaprachikov (BUL)
1929–1957	Clarence Napier Bruce, Lord Aberdare of Duffryn (GBR)
1929–1964	Karl Ferdinand Ritter von Halt (GER)
1930–1931	Augusto Turati (ITA)
1930–1932	Kremalettin Sami Pascha (TUR)
1930–1933	Nikolaos Politis (GRE)
1931–1933	Cecil J. Wray (NZL)

(continued)

Dates of Service	Member (Nation)
1931–1945	Stanisław Rouppert (POL)
1931–1952	Count Federico Suarez de Vallelano (ESP)
1932–1952	Horacio Bustos Moron (ARG)
1932–1958	Axel Kristian George, Prince of Denmark (DEN)
1932–1964	Count Paolo Thaon di Revel (ITA)
1932–1966.	Guru Dutt Sondhi (IND)
1933–1936	Jotaro Sugimoura (JPN)
1933–1950	Sir Francis Noel Curtis Bennett (GBR)
1933–1951	Sir Harold Daniel Luxton (AUS)
1933–1952	Rechid Saffet Atabinen Bey (TUR)
1933–1981	David George Brownlow Cecil, Lord Burghley, the 6th Marquess of Exeter (GBR)
1934–1948	Count Michimasa Soyeshima (JPN)
1934–1966	François Piétri (FRA)
1934–1967	Lord Arthur Espie Porritt (NZL)
1934–1968	Mohamed Taher Pascha (TUR)
1934–1973	Segura Marte Rodolfo Gomez (MEX)
1936–1939	Prince Iesato Tokugawa (JPN)
1936–1942	Joakhim Puhk (EST)
1936–1972	Avery Brundage (USA)
1936–1980	His Royal Highness Prince Franz-Josef II (LIE)
1936–1980	Jorgé B. Vargas (PHI)
1937–1939	Henri Guisan (SUI)
1937–1948	Frédéric René Coudert (USA)
1937–1956	Joaquin Serratosa Cibils (URU)
1938–1942	Walther von Reichenau (GER)
1938–1955	Antonio Prado (BRA)
1938–1967	Johan Wilhelm Rangell (FIN)
1938–1969	Miguel Angel de los Dolores Amado de Jesus Moenck y Peralta (CUB)
1939–1939	Albert Victor Lindbergh (RSA)
1939–1948	Miklós von Horthy (HUN)
1939–1949	Giorgio Vaccaro (ITA)
1939–1950	Matsuzo Nagai (JPN)
1939–1955	Kong Xiangxi (CHN)
1939–1957	Baron Gaston de Trannoy (BEL)
1939–1967	Shingoro Takaishi (JPN)
1946–1951	Sydney Charles Dowsett (RSA)
1946–1954	John Coleridge Patteson (CAN)
1946–1955	Rodolphe William Seeldrayers (BEL)
1946–1956	José Joaquim Fernandes Pontes (POR)
1946–1964	Charles Ferdinand Pahud de Mortanges (NED)
1946–1965	Ioannis Ketseas (GRE)
1946–1965	Josef Gruss (TCH)

Dates of Service	Member (Nation)
1946–1966	Benedikt G. Waage (ISL)
1946–1968	Albert Roman Mayer (SUI)
1946–1970	Armand Émile Massard (FRA)
1946–1975	Hugh Richard Weir (AUS)
1946–1982	Reginald Honey (RSA)
1946–1998	His Royal Highness Grand Duke Jean (LUX)
1947–1958	Shou Tungyi (CHN)
1947–1967	Sidney Dawes (CAN)
1947–1969	Manfred Mautner Ritter von Markhof (AUT)
1947–1992	Raja Bhalindra Singh of Patiala (IND)
1948–1952	Enrique O. Barbosa Baeza (CHI)
1948–1952	Miguel Ydigoras Fuentes (GUA)
1948–1959	Stanko Bloudek (YUG)
1948–1961	Ferenc Mezö (HUN)
1948–1961	Jerzy Loth (POL)
1948–1965	Bo Daniel Ekelund (SWE)
1948–1967	Olaf Christian Ditlev-Simonsen (NOR)
1948–1968	John Jewett Garland (USA)
1948–1976	Erik von Frenckell (FIN)
1949–1950	Rainier Grimaldi III, Prince of Monaco (MON)
1949–1956	Ahmed E. H. Jaffer (PAK)
1950–1951	James Brooks Bloodgood Parker (USA)
1950–1964	Pierre Grimaldi, Prince of Monaco (MON)
1950–1968	Ryotaro Azuma (JPN)
1951–1974	Lewis Luxton (AUS)
1951–1988	Ian St. John Lawson Johnston, the Lord Luke of Pavenham (GBR)
1951–1988	Konstantin Andrianov (URS)
1951–1990	Count Jean Robert Maurice Bonin de la Bonninie de Beaumont (FRA)
1951–1992	Giorgio de Stefani (ITA)
1952–1959	Enrique Alberdi (ARG)
1952–1967	Augustin A. Sosa (PAN)
1952–1968	Julio B. Bustamente (VEN)
1952–1970	Gustaf Peder Wilhelmsson Dyrssen (SWE)
1952–1971	Aleksey Romanov (URS)
1952–1971	José de Jesús Clark de Flores (MEX)
1952–1980	Sir Michael Morris, the Lord Killanin of Dublin and Spiddal (IRL)
1952–1984	Douglas Fergusson Roby (USA)
1952–1985	Pedro Ybarra y McMahon, the Second Marquis de Guell (ESP)
1952–1986	Julio Gerlein Comelin (COL)

(continued)

Dates of Service	Member (Nation)
1952–1987	Sheik Gabriel Gemayel (LIB)
1952–1987	Vladimir D. Stoychev (BUL)
1955–1960	Lee Ki-Poong (KOR)
1955–1980	Prince Gholam Reza Pahlavi (IRI)
1955–1984	Suat Erler (TUR)
1955–1985	Alejandro Rivera Bascur (CHI)
1955–1998	Alexandru Siperco (ROM)
1956–1991	Willi Daume (GER)
1957–1962	Saul Cristovão Ferreira Pires (POR)
1958–1964	His Royal Highness Prince Albert of Liege (BEL)
1958–1977	Ivar Emil Vind (DEN)
1958–1982	Eduardo Dibos de Lima (PER)
1959–1996	Syed Wajid Ali (PAK)
1960–1974	Mario Luis Jose Negri (ARG)
1960–1987	Boris Bakrać (YUG)
1960–1990	Reginald Stanley Alexander (KEN)
1960–1993	Ahmed El-Demerdash Touny (EGY)
1961–1997	Mohamed Ben Hadj Addelouahed Benjelloun (MAR)
1961–1996	Włodzimierz Reczek (POL)
1963–1974	His Majesty King Konstantinos (GRE)
1963–1975	Alfredo Inciarte (URU)
1963–1985	Sir Adetokunbo Ademola (NGR)
1963–1989	Raúl Cordiero, Pereira de Castro (POR)
1963–	João Marie Godefrois Faustin Havelange (BRA)
1963–	Marc Hodler (SUI)
1964–1966	Lee Sang-Beck (KOR)
1964–1977	Jonkheer Herman Adriaan van Karnebeek (NED)
1964–1983	Arpád Csánadi (HUN)
1964–1983	Giulio Onesti (ITA)
1964–2002	Prince Alexandre de Merode (BEL)
1964–1995	Sylvio Magalhães de Padilha (BRA)
1965–1969	Amadou Barry (SEN)
1965–1981	František Kroutil (TCH)
1965–1981	Pyrros Lappas (GRE)
1965–1996	Gunnar Lennart Vilhelm Ericsson (SWE)
1965–	Mohamed Mzali (TUN)
1966–1971	Georg von Opel (FRG)
1966–1971	His Royal Highness, Prince George Wilhelm von Hanover (IOA)
1966–1980	Heinz Schöbel (GDR)
1966–2001	Juan Antonio Samaranch Torrelo, Marquis de Samaranch (ESP)
1967–1977	Chang Key-Young (KOR)

Dates of Service	Member (Nation)
1967–1981	Paavo Honkajuuri (FIN)
1967–1981	Prince Tsuneyoshi Takeda (JPN)
1967–1989	James Worrall (CAN)
1967–2000	Jan Staubo (NOR)
1968–1971	Henri René Rakotoke (MAD)
1968–1976	Hamengku Buwono, IX (INA)
1968–1981	José A. Bercasa (VEN)
1968–1982	Abdel Mohamed Halim (SUD)
1968–1999	Agustin Carlos Arroyo Yeroui (ECU)
1969–1976	Rudolf Nemetschke (AUT)
1969–1988	Sir Cecil Lancelot Stewart Cross (NZL)
1969–1989	Masaji Kiyokawa (JPN)
1969–1991	Raymond Gafner (SUI)
1969–1994	Virgilio E. de Léon (PAN)
1969–1999	Louis Guirandou-N'Diaye (CIV)
1970–1976	Sven Alfred Thofelt (SWE)
1970–1988	Henry Heng Hsu (TPE)
1970–1994	Maurice Herzog (FRA)
1971–1974	Prabhas Charusathiara (THA)
1971–1987	Ydnekatcheu Tessema (ETH)
1971–	Vitaly Smirnov (URS/RUS)
1972–1988	Berthold Beitz (GER)
1972–1994	Pedro Ramírez Vázquez (MEX)
1973–1993	Manuel Gonzalez Guerra (CUB)
1973–2000	Ashwini Kumar (IND)
1973–2002	Kéba M'Baye (SEN)
1973–2000	Roy Anthony Bridge (JAM)
1974–1981	David Henry McKenzie (AUS)
1974–1986	Julian Kean Roosevelt (USA)
1974–1990	Dawee Chullasapya (THA)
1974–1991	Eduardo Hay (MEX)
1974–2001	Mohamed Zerguini (ALG)
1975–1977	Epaminondas Petralias (GRE)
1976–1993	Matts Wilhelm Carlgren (SWE)
1976–1994	Kevin Patrick O'Flanagan (IRL)
1976–1995	José Dalmiro Vallarino Veracierto (URU)
1976–	Peter Julius Tallberg (FIN)
1977–1983	Kim Taik-Soo (KOR)
1977–1986	Cornelis Lambert "Kees" Kerdel (NED)
1977–1999	Roberto Guillermo Peper (ARG)
1977–1989	Dadang Suprayogi (INA)
1977–1990	German Rieckehoff (PUR)

(continued)

Dates of Service	Member (Nation)
1977–1999	Bashir Mohamed Attarabulsi (LBA)
1977–1999	Lamine Keita (MLI)
1977–2002	Niels Holst-Sørensen (DEN)
1977–2000	Philipp von Schöller (AUT)
1977–	Richard Kevan Gosper (AUS)
1977–	Shagdarjav Magvan (MGL)
1978–1986	Nikolaos Nissiotis (GRE)
1978–1994	Kim Yu-Sun (PRK)
1978–1998	René Essomba (CMR)
1978–2004	Honorable Tan Seri Hamzah bin Haji Abu Samah (MAS)
1978–	Richard William Duncan Pound (CAN)
1981–1990	Sheik Fahad Al-Ahmad Al-Sabah (KUW)
1981–1992	Günther Heinze (GDR/GER)
1981–1999	Pirjo Vilmi-Häggman (FIN)
1981–2002	Flor Isava-Fonseca (VEN)
1981–	He Zhenliang (CHN)
1981–	Nikolaos Filaretos (GRE)
1981–2002	Vladimir Cernušak (TCH/SVK)
1982–1993	Dame Mary Alison Glen Haig (GBR)
1982–	Chiharu Igaya (JPN)
1982–	Franco Carraro (ITA)
1982–	Ivan Dibos (PER)
1982–	Philip Walter Coles (AUS)
1983–1999	Zein El-Abdin Mohamed Ahmed Abdel Gadir (SUD)
1983–1999	His Royal Highness Prince Faisal Fahd Abdul Aziz (KSA)
1983–	Anani Matthia (TOG)
1983–	Pál Schmitt (HUN)
1983–	Roque Napoleon Muñoz Peña (DOM)
1984–1985	Park Chong-Kyu (KOR)
1984–1988	Turgut Atakol (TUR)
1984–1999	David Sikhulumi Sibandze (SWZ)
1984–	Her Royal Highness Princess Nora (LIE)
1985–1991	Robert Hanna Helmick (USA)
1985–1998	Carlos Ferrer Salat (ESP)
1985–	Albert Grimaldi, Prince of Monaco (MON)
1985–	Francisco J. Elizalde (PHI)
1985–	Henry Edmund Olufemi Adefope (NGR)
1986–1999	Jean-Claude Ganga (CGO)
1986–	Anita Luceete DeFrantz (USA)
1986–	Kim Un-Yong (KOR)
1986–	Lambis V. Nikolaou (GRE)
1987–1999	Seuili Paul Wallwork (SAM)
1987–	Antonius Johannes Geesink (NED)
1987–	Ivan Borissov Slavkov (BUL)

Dates of Service	Member (Nation)
1987–1995	Slobodan Filipović (YUG)
1988–1992	Marat V. Gramov (URS/RUS)
1988–	Borislav Stanković (YUG)
1988–	Fidel Mendoza Carrasquilla (COL)
1988–	Francis Were Nyangweso (UGA)
1988–	Princess Anne Windsor, Her Royal Highness the Princess Royal (GBR)
1988–	Rampaul Ruhee (MRI)
1988–2003	Sinan Erdern (TUR)
1988–	Tennant Edward "Tay" Wilson (NZL)
1988–	Willi Kaltschmitt Lujan (GUA)
1988–	Wu Ching-Kuo (TPE)
1989–	Fernando F. Lima Bello (POR)
1989–	Walther Tröger (GER)
1990–1996	Philippe Chatrier (FRA/ITU)
1990–1999	Charles Nderitu Mukora (KEN)
1990–	Antonio Rodriguez (ARG)
1990–2001	Carol Anne Letheren (CAN)
1990–	Nat Indrapana (THA)
1990–	Richard L. Carrion (PUR)
1990–	Shun-Ichiro Okano (JPN)
1991–	Denis Oswald (SUI)
1991–	Dr. Jacques Rogge (BEL)
1991–	Mario Vázquez Raña (MEX)
1991–	Thomas Bach (GER)
1992–1994	Olaf Poulsen (NOR)
1992–1999	Sergio Santander Fantini (CHI)
1992–1999	Primo Nebiolo (ITA/IAAF)
1992–	Sheik Ahmad Al-Fahad Al-Sabah (KUW)
1994–	Alex Gilady (ISR)
1994–	Alpha Ibrahim Dialio (GUI)
1994–	Arne Ljungqvist (SWE)
1994–	Austin L. Sealy (BAR)
1994–	Craig Reedie (GBR)
1994–	Gerhard Heiberg (NOR)
1994–	James Leland Easton (USA)
1994–	Mario Pescante (ITA)
1994–2004	Mohamed "Bob" Hasan (INA)
1994–	Robin Mitchell (FIJ)
1994–	Shamil Tarpichev (RUS)
1994–	Valery Borzov (UKR)
1995–1996	Yury Titov (RUS/FIG)
1995–	Antun Vrdoljak (CRO)

(continued)

Dates of Service	Member (Nation)
1995–	Jean-Claude Killy (FRA)
1995–	Mustapha Larfaoui (ALG/FINA)
1995–	Olegario Vázquez Raña (MEX)
1995–	Patrick Joseph Hickey (IRL)
1995–	René Fasel (SUI/IIHF)
1995–	Reynaldo González López (CUB)
1995–	Sam Ramsamy (RSA)
1995–	Toni Khouri (LIB)
1995–2001	Věra Čáslavská (CZE)
1996–1998	George Killian (USA/FIBA)
1996–	Gunilla Lindberg (SWE)
1996–	Guy Drut (FRA)
1996–	Hein Verbruggen (NED/UCI)
1996–	Julio Cesar Maglione (URU)
1996–	Lee Kun-Hee (KOR)
1996–2001	Lu Shengrong (CHN)
1996–	Ottavio Cinquanta (ITA/ISU)
1996–	Princess Doña Pilar de Borbon (ESP/FEI)
1996–	Syed Shahid Ali (PAK)
1996–2003	Tomas Amos Ganda Sithole (ZIM)
1996–	Ung Chang (PRK)
1998–	His Royal Highness Prince Henri (LUX)
1998–	His Royal Highness Prince of Orange (NED)
1998–	Irena Szewińska-Kirszenstein (POL)
1998–	Leopold Wallner (AUT)
1998–	Melitón Sánchez Rivas (PAN)
1998–	Mohammad Samih Moudallal (SYR)
1998–	Mounir Saleh Sabet (EGY)
1998–	Nawal El-Moutawakel Bennis (MAR)
1998–	Ser Miang Ng (SIN)
1999–2004	Roland Barr (GER/Athlete)
1999–2000	Hassiba Boulmerka (ALG/Athlete)
1999–	Sergey Bubka (UKR/Athlete)
1999–2004	Charmaine Crooks (CAN/Athlete)
1999–	Robert Ctvrtlik (USA/Athlete)
1999–	Manuela Di Centa (ITA/Athlete)
1999–2001	Johann Olav Koss (NOR/Athlete)
1999–	Aleksandr Popov (RUS/Athlete)
1999–2001	Vladimir Smirnov (KAZ/Athlete)
1999–2001, 2004–	Jan Železný (CZE/Athlete)
1999–	Josep S. Blatter (SUI/FIFA)
1999–	Lamine Diack (SEN/IAAF)
2000–2004	Ruben Acosta Hernández (MEX/FIVB)
2000–	Tamas Ajan (HUN/IWF)

Dates of Service	Member (Nation)
2000–2002	Alfredo Goyeneche Moreno (ESP/Spain OC)
2000–	Bruno Grandi (SUI/FIG)
2000–2004	Seyed Mostafa Hashemi Taba (IRI/Iran OC)
2000–2004	Paul Henderson (CAN/ISAF)
2000–2002	William J. Hybl (USA/United States OC)
2000–	Gian-Franco Kasper (SUI/AIWF)
2000–	Kipchoge Keino (KEN/Kenya OC)
2000–	Carlos Arthur Nuzman (BRA/Brazil OC)
2000–	Lassana Palenfo (CIV/Côte d'Ivoire OC)
2000–	Henri Serandour (FRA/France OC)
2000–2003	Robert Steadward (CAN/IPC)
2000–	Yu Zaiqing (CHN/China OC)
2000–	Susan O'Neill (AUS/Athlete)
2000–2004	Manuel Estiarte Duocastella (ESP/Athlete)
2000–2003	Giovanni Agnelli (ITA/Honor)
2000–	Alain Danet (FRA/Honor)
2000–	Kurt Furgler (SUI/Honor)
2000–	Henry Alfred Kissinger (USA/Honor)
2000–	Yoshiaki Tsutsumi (JPN/Honor)
2001–	Tsun-Ting "Timothy" Fok (HKG)
2001–	Randhir Singh (IND)
2001–	John Dowling Coates (AUS/Australia OC)
2001–	Issa Hayatou (CMR)
2001–	Juan Antonio Samaranch Jr. (ESP)
2001–	Els van Breda-Vriesman (NED/FIH)
2002–	Kai Holm (DEN)
2002–	Youssoupha Ndiaye (SEN)
2002–	Patrick S. Chamunda (ZAM)
2002–	Nawaf Faisal Fahad Abdul Aziz (KSA/Saudi Arabia OC)
2002–	Kikis N. Lazarides (CYP/Cyprus OC)
2002–	Park Yong-Sung (KOR/Korea OC)
2002–	Tamim bin Hamad Al-Thani (QAT/Qatar OC)
2002–	François Narmon (BEL/Belgium OC)
2002–2003	Sandra Baldwin (USA/United States OC)
2002–	Pernilla Wiberg (SWE/Athlete)
2002–	Jari Kurri (FIN/Athlete)
2002–	Ådne Søndrål (NOR/Athlete)
2002–2004	Matthew Pinsent (GBR/Athlete)
2003–	Phil Craven (GBR/IPC)
2004–	Jan Železný (CZE/Athlete)
2004–	Hicham El Guerroj (MAR/Athlete)
2004–	Frank Fredericks (NAM/Athlete)
2004–	Rania El-Wani (EGY/Athlete)

Appendix E: Awards of the International Olympic Committee

The International Olympic Committee has given out several awards, outside of the medals and diplomas given to Olympic athletes. Currently, the IOC presents only two awards, the Olympic Order and the Olympic Cup.

The IOC discontinued the other awards at the 75th IOC session in Vienna in 1974. These included the Olympic Diploma of Merit (first awarded in 1905), the Sir Thomas Fearnley Cup (donated in 1950), the Mohammed Taher Trophy (donated in 1950), the Count Alberto Bonacossa Trophy (presented in 1954), the Tokyo Trophy (presented in 1964), and the Prix de la Reconnaissance Olympique (presented in 1972).

RECIPIENTS OF THE OLYMPIC ORDER

The Olympic Order is the supreme individual honor accorded by the International Olympic Committee. It was created in 1974 and is to be awarded to "Any person who has illustrated the Olympic Ideal through his/her action, has achieved remarkable merit in the sporting world, or has rendered outstanding services to the Olympic cause, either through his/her own personal achievement(s) or his/her contribution to the development of sport." Originally, the Olympic Order was separated into three categories—gold, silver, and bronze. The bronze Olympic Order was discontinued in 1984, and currently, there are only gold and silver categories. Only the recipients of the Olympic Order in Gold are listed below. Through 2004, there have been over 900 recipients of the Olympic Order in Silver and 111 recipients of the Olympic Order in Bronze.

Gold (74 recipients)

| 1975 | Avery Brundage | USA |
| 1980 | Lord Killanin of Dublin and Spiddal | GBR |

1981	Lord Burghley, the Marquess of Exeter	GBR
	His Majesty King Olaf of Norway	NOR
	Amadou Mahtar M'Bow	SEN
	Pope John Paul II	VAT
1982	His Majesty King Pertuan Agung of Malaysia	MAS
1983	Indira Gandhi	IND
1984	François Mitterrand	FRA
	Peter Victor Ueberroth	USA
	Branko Mikulić	YUG
1985	His Majesty King Juan Carlos de Borbon	ESP
	Erich Honecker	GDR
	Nicolae Ceauçescu	ROM
1986	Li Wan	CHN
1987	Todor Zhivkov	BUL
	His Majesty King Bhumibol Adulyadej	THA
	His Excellency Kenan Evren	TUR
1988	Frank W. King	CAN
	Mario Vázquez Raña	MEX
	His Royal Highness Prince Rainier III	MON
	His Royal Highness Prince Bertil Bernadotte	SWE
1989	Chevalier Raoul Mollet	BEL
	His Imperial Majesty Emperor Akihito	JPN
	His Excellency Raphael Hernandez Colon	PUR
1990	Giulio Andreotti	ITA
1991	Count Jean de Beaumont	FRA
	Yoshiaki Tsutsumi	JPN
	Willi Daume	FRG
1992	Josep Miguel Abad	ESP
	Michel Barnier	FRA
	Javier Gomez-Navarro	ESP
	Jean-Claude Killy	FRA
	Pasqual Marragal	ESP
	Jordi Pujol	ESP
	Leopoldo Rodes	ESP
	Carlos Salinas de Gortari	MEX
	Narcis Serra	ESP
	Javier Solana	ESP
	Boris Yeltsin	RUS
1993	None	
1994	Joaquin Leguina	ESP
	Richard von Weizsäcker	GER
	Dr. Mauno Koivisto	FIN
	His Majesty King Harald of Norway	NOR
	Gerhard Heiberg	NOR
	Her Majesty Queen Sonja of Norway	NOR

1995	Arpád Goncz	HUN
	Robert Mugabe	ZIM
1996	Konstantino Stephanopoulo	GRE
	Adolphus Drewery "A. D." Frazier	USA
	Andrew Young	USA
	William Porter Payne	USA
	Islam Karimov	UZB
1997	Blaise Compaore	BUR
	El-Hadj Omar Bongo	GAB
	Nursultan Nazarbaev	KAZ
	Elias Hrawi	LIB
	Ernesto Zedillo Ponce de Léon	MEX
	Aleksander Kwaśniewski	POL
	Suleyman Demirel	TUR
1998	Eishiro Saito	JPN
	Grand Duke Jean	LUX
1999	Eduardo Shevardnadze	GEO
	Helmut Kohl	GER
	Petru Lucinschi	MDA
	Yury Luzhkov	RUS
2000	Michael Knight	AUS
	David Richmond	AUS
	John Dowling Coates	AUS
	Adolf Ogi	SUI
2001	Juan Antonio Samaranch	ESP
	Goh Chok Tong	SIN
2002	Mitt Romney	USA
2003	John Howard	AUS
2004	Gianna Angelopoulos-Daskalaki	GRE
	Johannes Rau	GER

RECIPIENTS OF THE OLYMPIC CUP

The Olympic Cup was instituted by Baron Pierre de Coubertin in 1906. It is awarded to an institution or association with a general reputation for merit and integrity, that has been active and efficient in the service of sport, and that has contributed substantially to the development of the Olympic movement. In reality, it has been given to individuals three times (1927, 1942, and 1947).

| 1906 | Touring Club de France |
| 1907 | Henley Royal Regatta |

1908	Sveriges Centralförening för Idrottens Främjande
1909	Deutsche Turnerschaft
1910	Česka obec Sokolska
1911	Touring Club Italiano
1912	Union des Sociétés de Gymnastique de France
1913	Magyar Athletikai Club
1914	Amateur Athletic Union of America
1915	Rugby School, England
1916	Confrérie Saint-Michel de Gand
1917	Nederlandsche Voetbal Bond
1918	Equipes Sportives du Front Interallié
1919	Institut Olympique de Lausanne
1920	YMCA International, Springfield, Massachusetts, USA
1921	Dansk Idræts Forbund
1922	Amateur Athletic Union of Canada
1923	Associación Sportiva de Cataluña
1924	Finnish Gymnastic and Athletic Federation
1925	National Physical Education Committee of Uruguay
1926	Norges Skiforbund
1927	Colonel Robert M. Thomson (USA)
1928	Junta Nacional Mexicana
1929	Y.M.C.A. World's Committee
1930	Association Suisse de Football et d'Athlétisme
1931	National Playing Fields Association, Great Britain
1932	Deutsche Hochschule für Leibesübungen
1933	Société Fédérale Suisse de Gymnastique
1934	Opera Dopolavoro Roma
1935	National Recreation Association of the USA
1936	Union of Hellenic Gymnastics and Athletics Associations, Athens
1937	Österreichischer Eislauf Verband
1938	Königlich Akademie für Körpererziehung in Ungarn
1939	"Kraft durch Freude"
1940	Svenska Gymnastik—och Idrottsföreningarnas Riksförbund
1941	Finnish Olympic Committee
1942	William May Garland (USA)
1943	Comité Olímpico Argentino
1944	City of Lausanne
1945	Norges Fri Idrettsførbund, Oslo
1946	Comité Olímpico Colornbiano
1947	J. Sigfrid Edström (SWE), IOC President
1948	The Central Council of Physical Recreation, Great Britain
1949	Fluminense Football Club, Rio de Janeiro
1950	Comité Olympique Belge; New Zealand Olympic and British Empire Games Association
1951	Académie des Sports, Paris

1952	City of Oslo
1953	City of Helsinki
1954	Ecole Fédérale de Gymnastique et de Sports, Macolin (SUI)
1955	Organizing Committee of the Central American and Caribbean Games, Mexico; Organizing Committee of the Pan-American Games, Mexico
1956	Not awarded
1957	Federazione Sport Silenziosi d'Italia, Milano
1958	Not awarded
1959	Panathlon Italiano, Génève
1960	Centro Universitario Sportivo Italiano
1961	Helms Hall Foundation, Los Angeles
1962	IV Juegos Deportivos Bolivarianos, Barranquilla
1963	Australian British Empire and Commonwealth Games Association
1964	City of Tokyo
1965	Southern California Committee for the Olympic Games (USA)
1966	Comité International des Sports Silencieux, Liège (BEL)
1967	Juegos Deportivos Bolivarianos
1968	City of Mexico
1969	Polish Olympic Committee
1970	Organizing Committee of the Asian Games in Bangkok (THA)
1971	Organizing Committee of the Pan-American Games in Cali (COL)
1972	Turkish Olympic Committee; City of Sapporo
1973	Population of Munich
1974	Bulgarian Olympic Committee
1975	Comitato Olímpico Nazionale Italiano (CONI)
1976	Czechoslovak Physical Culture and Sports Association
1977	Comité Olympique Ivoirien
1978	Comité Olympique Hellenic
1979	Organizing Committee of the 1978 World Rowing Championships in New Zealand
1980	Ginasio Clube Português
1981	Confédération Suisse; International Olympic Academy
1982	Racing Club de France
1983	Puerto Rico Olympic Committee
1984	Organizing Committee of the 1st World Championships in Athletics at Helsinki
1985	Chinese Olympic Committee
1986	City of Stuttgart
1987	L'Équipe (French sporting daily newspaper)
1988	The People of Australia
1989	City of Calgary; City of Seoul; La Gazzetta dello Sport (Italian sporting daily newspaper)
1990	Panhellenic Athletic Club of Athens
1991	Japanese Olympic Committee

1992	Département de la Savoie (Région Rhône-Alpes); City of Barcelona
1993	Comité Olympique Monégasque
1994	Comité National Olympique et Sportif Français; The Norwegian People
1995	Korean Olympic Committee
1996	City of Baden-Baden (GER)
1997	Not awarded
1998	People of Nagano (JPN)
1999	Leon Štukelj (YUG/SLO)
2000	People of Sydney
2001	Kip Keino School Eldoret
2002	People of Salt Lake City
2003	Team Alinghi (2003 America's Cup Crew)
2004	People of Athens

Appendix F: Final Olympic Torchbearers within the Olympic Stadium

GAMES OF THE OLYMPLADS

1936	Fritz Schilgen (GER)
1948	John Mark (GBR)
1952	Hannes Kolehmainen (lit main flame) (FIN)
	Paavo Nurmi (lit auxiliary flame) (FIN)
1956	Ron Clarke (AUS)
1960	Giancarlo Peris (ITA)
1964	Yoshinori Sakai (JPN)
1968	Enriqueta Basilio de Sotelo (MEX)
1972	Günter Zahn (FRG)
1976	Stéphane Prefontaine (lit flame concurrently) (CAN)
	Sandra Henderson (lit flame concurrently) (CAN)
1980	Sergey Belov (URS)
1984	Rafer Johnson (lit flame) (USA)
	Gina Hemphill (USA)
1988	Sohn Kee-Chung (lit flame) (KOR)
	Lim Chun-Ae (KOR)
	Chung Sun-Man (KOR)
	Kim Won-Tak (KOR)
	Sohn Mi-Chung (KOR)
1992	Antônio Rebollo (archer, lit flame) (ESP)
	Herminio Menéndez Rodriguez (ESP)
	Juan Antônio San Epifanio Ruiz (ESP)
1996	Muhammad Ali (lit flame) (USA)
	Janet Evans (USA)
	Paraskevi "Voula" Patoulidou (GRE)
	Evander Holyfield (USA)
	Al Oerter (USA)
2000	Catherine Freeman (lit flame) (AUS)
	Raelene Boyle (AUS)
	Betty Cuthbert (AUS)
	Shirley Strickland de la Hunty (AUS)
	Dawn Fraser (AUS)

	Shane Gould (AUS)
	Debbie Flintoff-King (AUS)
2004	Nikolaos Kaklamanakis (lit flame) (GRE)
	Dimitrios "Mimis" Domazos (GRE)
	Nikos Gallis (GRE)
	Akakios Kakiashvili (GRE)
	Ioannis Melissanidis (GRE)
	Paraskevi Patoulidou (GRE)

OLYMPIC EQUESTRIAN GAMES

1956	Hans Wikne (lit flame) (SWE)
	Karin Lindberg (SWE)
	Henry Eriksson (SWE)

OLYMPIC WINTER GAMES

1952	Eigil Nansen (NOR)
1956	Guido Caroli (ITA)
1960	Kenneth Henry (USA)
1964	Joseph Rieder (AUT)
1968	Alain Calmat (FRA)
1972	Hideki Takada (JPN)
1976	Christl Haas (lit main flame) (AUT)
	Josef Feistmantl (lit auxiliary flame) (AUT)
1980	Charles Morgan Kerr (USA)
1984	Sandra Dubravčić (YUG)
1988	Robyn Perry (CAN)
1992	Michel Platini (lit flame) (FRA)
	François-Syrille Grange (lit flame) (FRA)
1994	Crown Prince Haakon Magnus (lit flame) (NOR)
	Stein Gruben (ski jumper) (NOR)
	Catherine Nottingnes (NOR)
1998	Midori Ito (lit flame) (JPN)
	Hiromu Suzuki (JPN)
	Takanori Kono (JPN)
	Masaki Chiba (JPN)
	Chris Moon (NZL)
2002	The 1980 United States' Ice Hockey Team (lit flame)
	Dick Button (USA)
	Dorothy Hamill (USA)

Scott Hamilton (USA)
Peggy Fleming (USA)
Bill Johnson (USA)
Phil Mahre (USA)
Dan Jansen (USA)
Bonnie Blair (USA)
Jim Shea (USA)
Jim Shea Jr. (USA)
Picabo Street (USA)
Cammi Granato (USA)

Appendix G: Speakers of the Olympic Oath

GAMES OF THE OLYMPIADS—ATHLETES

1920	Victor Boin (Water Polo/Fencing)
1924	Georges André (Athletics)
1928	Harry Dénis (Football)
1932	George Calnan (Fencing)
1936	Rudolf Ismayr (Weightlifting)
1948	Donald Finlay (Athletics)
1952	Heikki Savoläinen (Gymnastics)
1956	John Landy (Athletics)
1960	Adolfo Consolini (Athletics)
1964	Takashi Ono (Gymnastics)
1968	Pablo Garrido (Athletics)
1972	Heidi Schüller (Athletics)
1976	Pierre St. Jean (Weightlifting)
1980	Nikolay Andrianov (Gymnastics)
1984	Edwin Moses (Athletics)
1988	Huh Jae (Basketball)
	Son Mi-Na (Handball)
1992	Luis Doreste Blanco (Yachting)
1996	Teresa Edwards (Basketball)
2000	Rechelle Hawkes (Hockey (Field))
2004	Zoi Dimoskhaki (Swimming)

OLYMPIC EQUESTRIAN GAMES—ATHLETE

1956	Henri Saint Cyr (Equestrian)

OLYMPIC WINTER GAMES—ATHLETES

1924	Camille Mandrillon (Nordic Skiing)
1928	Hans Eidenbenz (Nordic Skiing)

1932	Jack Shea (Speed Skating)
1936	Wilhelm Bögner (Alpine Skiing)
1948	Riccardo "Bibi" Torriani (Ice Hockey)
1952	Torbjørn Falkanger (Ski Jumping)
1956	Guilliana Chenal-Minuzzo (Alpine Skiing)
1960	Carol Heiss (Figure Skating)
1964	Paul Aste (Bobsledding)
1968	Leo Lacroix (Alpine Skiing)
1972	Keichi Suzuki (Speed Skating)
1976	Werner Delle Karth (Bobsledding)
1980	Eric Heiden (Speed Skating)
1984	Bojan Križaj (Alpine Skiing)
1988	Pierre Harvey (Nordic Skiing)
1992	Surya Bonaly (Figure Skating)
1994	Vegard Ulvang (Nordic Skiing)
1998	Kenji Ogiwara (Nordic Combined)
2002	Jim Shea Jr. (Skeleton)

GAMES OF THE OLYMPIADS—OFFICIALS

1972	Heinz Pollay (Equestrian official)
1976	Maurice Fauget (Track and Field Athletics official)
1980	Aleksandr Medved (Wrestling official)
1984	Sharon Weber (Gymnastics official)
1988	Lee Hak-Rae (Judo official)
1992	Eugeni Asensio (Water Polo official)
1996	Hobie Billingsley (Diving official)
2000	Peter Kerr (Water Polo official)
2004	Lazaros Voradis (Basketball Official)

OLYMPIC WINTER GAMES—OFFICIALS

1972	Fumio Asaki (Ski Jumping official)
1976	Willi Köstinger (Nordic Skiing official)
1980	Terry McDermott (Speed Skating official)
1984	Dragan Perović (Alpine Skiing official)
1988	Suzanne Morrow-Francis (Figure Skating official)
1992	Pierre Bornat (Alpine Skiing official)
1994	Kari Karing (Nordic Skiing official)
1998	Junko Hiromatsu (Figure Skating official)
2002	Allen Church (Nordic Skiing Official)

Appendix H: Official Openings of the Olympic Games

GAMES OF THE OLYMPIADS

1896	King Giorgios I (Greece)
1900	None
1904	President David Rowland Francis (Louisiana Purchase Exposition/United States)
1906	King Giorgios I (Greece)
1908	King Edward VII (England)
1912	King Gustaf V (Sweden)
1920	King Albert I (Belgium)
1924	President Gaston Doumergue (France)
1928	His Royal Highness Prince Hendrik (The Netherlands)
1932	Vice President Charles Curtis (United States)
1936	Reichsführer Adolf Hitler (Germany)
1948	King George VI (England)
1952	President Juho Kusti Paasikivi (Finland)
1956	His Royal Highness Philip, the Duke of Edinburgh (United Kingdom)
1960	President Giovanni Gronchi (Italy)
1964	Emperor Hirohito (Japan)
1968	President Dr. Gustavo Díaz Ordaz (Mexico)
1972	President Dr. Gustav Heinemann (Federal Republic of Germany)
1976	Queen Elizabeth II (England)
1980	President Leonid Ilyich Brezhnev (Soviet Union)
1984	President Ronald Wilson Reagan (United States)
1988	President Roh Tae-Woo (Korea)
1992	King Juan Carlos I (Spain)
1996	President William Jefferson Clinton (United States)
2000	Governor-General Sir William Patrick Deane (Australia)
2004	President Kostas Stephanopoulos (Greece)

OLYMPIC EQUESTRIAN GAMES

1956	King Gustaf VI Adolf (Sweden)

OLYMPIC WINTER GAMES

1924	Undersecretary for Physical Education Gaston Vidal (France)
1928	President Edmund Schulthess (Switzerland)
1932	Governor Franklin Delano Roosevelt (New York, United States)
1936	Reichsführer Adolf Hitler (Germany)
1948	President Enrico Celio (Switzerland)
1952	Her Royal Highness Princess Ragnhild (Norway)
1956	President Giovanni Gronchi (Italy)
1960	Vice President Richard Milhous Nixon (United States)
1964	President Dr. Adolf Schärf (Austria)
1968	President General Charles de Gaulle (France)
1972	Emperor Hirohito (Japan)
1976	President Dr. Rudolf Kirchschläger (Austria)
1980	Vice President Walter Frederick Mondale (United States)
1984	President Mika Spiljak (Yugoslavia)
1988	Governor-General Jeanne Sauvé (Canada)
1992	President François Mitterrand (France)
1994	King Harald V (Norway)
1998	Emperor Akihito (Japan)
2002	President George Walker Bush (United States)

Appendix I: Most Olympic Medals Won: Summer, Men

Medals	Athlete (Nation–Sport)
15	Nikolay Andrianov (URS–GYM)
13	Edoardo Mangiarotti (ITA–FEN)
13	Takashi Ono (JPN–GYM)
13	Boris Shakhlin (URS–GYM)
12	Sawao Kato (JPN–GYM)
12	Paavo Nurmi (FIN–ATH)
12	Aleksey Nemov (RUS–GYM)
11	Matthew Biondi (USA–SWI)
11	Viktor Chukarin (URS–GYM)
11	Carl Osburn (USA–SHO)
11	Mark Spitz (USA–SWI)
10	Aleksandr Dityatin (URS–GYM)
10	Raymond Ewry (USA–ATH)
10	Aladár Gerevich (HUN–FEN)
10	Carl Lewis (USA–ATH)
10	Akinori Nakayama (JPN–GYM)
10	Vitaly Shcherbo (EUN/BLR–GYM)
10	Hubert Van Innis (BEL–ARC)

Appendix J: Most Olympic
Medals Won: Summer, Women

Medals	Athlete (Nation–Sport)
18	Larisa Latynina (URS–GYM)
12	Birgit Schmidt-Fischer (GDR/GER–CAN)
12	Jennifer Thompson (USA–SWI)
11	Věra Čáslavská (TCH–GYM)
10	Polina Astakhova (URS–GYM)
10	Ágnes Keleti (HUN–GYM)
10	Franziska Van Almsick (GER–SWI)
9	Nadia Comăneci (ROM–GYM)
9	Dara Torres (USA–SWI)
9	Lyudmila Turishcheva (URS–GYM)
8	Shirley Babashoff (USA–SWI)
8	Kornelia Ender (GDR–SWI)
8	Dawn Fraser (AUS–SWI)
8	Sofiya Muratova (URS–GYM)
8	Susan O'Neill (AUS–SWI)
8	Merlene Ottey (JAM–ATH)
8	Margit Plachyné-Korondi (HUN–GYM)

Appendix K: Most Olympic Gold Medals Won: Summer, Men

Golds	Athlete (Nation–Sport)
10	Raymond Ewry (USA–ATH)
9	Carl Lewis (USA–ATH)
9	Paavo Nurmi (FIN–ATH)
9	Mark Spitz (USA–SWI)
8	Matthew Biondi (USA–SWI)
8	Sawao Kato (JPN–GYM)
7	Nikolay Andrianov (URS–GYM)
7	Viktor Chukarin (URS–GYM)
7	Aladár Gerevich (HUN–FEN)
7	Boris Shakhlin (URS–GYM)
6	Gert Fredriksson (SWE–CAN)
6	Rudolf Kárpáti (HUN–FEN)
6	Reiner Klimke (FRG–EQU)
6	Pál Kovács (HUN–FEN)
6	Edoardo Mangiarotti (ITA–FEN)
6	Nedo Nadi (ITA–FEN)
6	Akinori Nakayama (JPN–GYM)
6	Michael Phelps (USA–SWI)
6	Vitaly Shcherbo (EUN/BLR–GYM)
6	Hubert Van Innis (BEL–ARC)

Appendix L: Most Olympic Gold Medals Won: Summer, Women

Golds	Athlete (Nation–Sport)
9	Larisa Latynina (URS–GYM)
8	Birgit Schmidt-Fischer (GDR/GER–CAN)
8	Jennifer Thompson (USA–SWI)
7	Věra Čáslavská (TCH–GYM)
6	Kristin Otto (GDR–SWI)
6	Amy Van Dyken (USA–SWI)
5	Polina Astakhova (URS–GYM)
5	Nadia Comăneci (ROM–GYM)
5	Ágnes Keleti (HUN–GYM)
5	Nelli Kim (URS–GYM)
5	Krisztina Egerszegi (HUN–SWI)

Appendix M: Most Olympic Medals Won: Winter, Men

Medals	Athlete (Nation–Sport)
12	Bjørn Dæhlie (NOR–NSK)
9	Sixten Jernberg (SWE–NSK)
7	Ivar Ballangrud (NOR–SSK)
7	Veikko Hakulinen (FIN–NSK)
7	Eero Mäntyranta (FIN–NSK)
7	Bogdan Musiol (GDR–BOB)
7	Clas Thunberg (FIN–SSK)
7	Vladimir Smirnov (URS/RUS–NSK)
6	Johan Grøttumsbråten (NOR–NSK)
6	Wolfgang Hoppe (GDR–BOB)
6	Roald Larsen (NOR–SSK)
6	Eugenio Monti (ITA–BOB)
6	Gunde Anders Svan (SWE–NSK)
6	Vegard Ulvang (NOR–NSK)
6	Mika Myllylä (FIN–NSK)
6	Harri Kirvesniemi (FIN–NSK)

Appendix N: Most Olympic Medals Won: Winter, Women

Medals	Athlete (Nation–Sport)
10	Raisa Smetanina (EUN/URS–NSK)
9	Stefania Belmondo (ITA–NSK)
9	Larisa Lazutina (EUN/RUS–NSK)
9	Lyubov Yegorova (EUN/RUS–NSK)
8	Ursula "Uschi" Disl (GER–NSK)
8	Karin Kania-Enke (GDR–SSK)
8	Galina Kulakova (URS–NSK)
8	Gunda Niemann-Stirnemann-Kleemann (GER–SSK)
7	Andrea Ehrig-Schöne-Mitscherlich (GDR–SSK)
7	Marja-Liisa Kirvesniemi-Hämäläinen (FIN–NSK)
7	Manuela Di Centa (ITA–NSK)
7	Claudia Pechstein (GER–SSK)
7	Yelena Välbe (EUN/URS/RUS–NSK)
6	Bonnie Blair (USA–SSK)
6	Lidiya Skoblikova (URS–SSK)

Appendix O: Most Olympic Gold Medals Won: Winter, Men

Golds	Athlete (Nation–Sport)
8	Bjørn Dæhlie (NOR–NSK)
5	Ole Einar Bjørndalen (NOR–BIA)
5	Eric Heiden (USA–SSK)
5	Clas Thunberg (FIN–SSK)
4	Thomas Aalsgard (NOR–NSK)
4	Ivar Ballangrud (NOR–SSK)
4	Yevgeny Grishin (URS–SSK)
4	Sixten Jernberg (SWE–NSK)
4	Johann Olav Koss (NOR–SSK)
4	Matti Nykänen (FIN–NSK)
4	Gunde Anders Svan (SWE–NSK)
4	Aleksandr Tikhonov (URS–BIA)
4	Thomas Wassberg (SWE–NSK)
4	Nikolay Zimyatov (URS–NSK)

Appendix P: Most Olympic Gold Medals Won: Winter, Women

Golds	Athlete (Nation–Sport)
6	Lidiya Skoblikova (URS–SSK)
6	Lyubov Yegorova (EUN/RUS–NSK)
5	Bonnie Blair (USA–SSK)
5	Larisa Lazutina (EUN/RUS–NSK)
4	Chun Lee-Kyung (KOR–STK)
4	Galina Kulakova (URS–NSK)
4	Claudia Pechstein (GER–SSK)
4	Raisa Smetanina (EUN/URS–NSK)
3	17 athletes tied with three

Appendix Q: Positive Drug Tests at the Olympic Games

Listed after each athlete's name is his or her country, sport and event, finish before disqualification, and the name of illegal drug detected.

1968 MEXICO CITY (1)

Hans-Gunnar Liljenvall (SWE)—Modern pentathlon; 3rd—alcohol (depressant).

1972 SAPPORO (1)

Alois Schröder (FRG)—Ice hockey; 7th—Ephedrine (stimulant). (Note: The team doctor, Franz Schlickenrieder, was disqualified from serving in that capacity for life.)

1972 MUNICH (7)

Bakhaava Buida (MGL)—Judo, 63 kg. class; 2nd—drug unknown.
Miguel Coli (PUR)—Basketball; 6th—Ephedrine (stimulant).
Richard DeMont (USA)—Swimming, 400 meter freestyle; 1st—Ephedrine (stimulant).
Jamie Huelamo (ESP)—Cycling, individual road race; 3rd—Coramine (stimulant).
Walter Legel (AUT)—Weightlifting, 67½ kg. class; 15th—Amphetamines (stimulant).
Arjomand Mohamed Nasehi (IRI)—Weightlifting, 52 kg. class; 10th—Ephedrine (stimulant).

Aad van den Hoek (NED)—Cycling, 100 km. team time trial; 3rd—
Coramine (stimulant) (team disqualified).

1976 INNSBRUCK (2)

Galina Kulakova (URS)—Nordic skiing, 5 km.; 3rd—Ephedrine (stimulant). (Note: Kulakova also finished 3rd in the 10 km. and 1st on the
4 × 5 km. relay team at these Olympic Winter Games, but was allowed to keep those medals.)

František Pospíšil (TCH)—Ice hockey; 2nd—Codeine (narcotic pain
medication). (Note: The team doctor, Treffný, was disqualified from
serving in that capacity for life.)

1976 MONTREAL (11)

Blagoi Blagoev (BUL)—Weightlifting, 82½ kg. class; 2nd—Anabolic
steroid.

Mark Cameron (USA)—Weightlifting, 110 kg. class; 5th—Anabolic
steroid.

Paul Cerutti (MON)—Shooting, Trap shooting; 43rd—Amphetamines.

Valentin Khristov (BUL)—Weightlifting, 110 kg. class; 1st—Anabolic
steroid.

Dragomir Ciorislan (ROM)—Weightlifting, 75 kg. class; 5th—
Fencanfamine (stimulant).

Phillip Grippaldi (USA)—Weightlifting, 90 kg. class; 4th—Anabolic
steroid.

Zbigniew Kaczmarek (POL)—Weightlifting, 67½ kg. class; 1st—
Anabolic steroid.

Lorne Leibel (CAN)—Yachting, Tempest class; 7th—Phenylpropanolamine (stimulant).

Ame Norback (SWE)—Weightlifting, 60 kg. class; eliminated—Anabolic
steroid.

Petr Pavlagek (TCH)—Weightlifting, 110 kg. class; 6th—Anabolic
steroid.

Danuta Rosani-Gwardecka (POL)—Track and field athletics, Discus
throw; 14th in qualifying (DNQ)—Anabolic steroid.

1980 LAKE PLACID (0)

No positive drug tests.

1980 MOSCOW (0)

No positive drug tests.

1984 SARAJEVO (1)

Purevjalyn Batsukh (MGL)—Nordic skiing, 15 km. 69th; 30 km. 65th; 4 × 10 km. relay, 15th—Methandienone (anabolic steroid).

1984 LOS ANGELES (12)

Serafim Grammatikopoulos (GRE)—Weightlifting, Unlimited class; did not finish—Nandrolone (anabolic steroid).

Vesteinn Hafsteinsson (ISL)—Track and field athletics, Discus throw; 14th in qualifying round—Nandrolone (anabolic steroid).

Thomas Johansson (SWE)—Wrestling, Unlimited Greco-Roman class; 2nd—Methenolone (anabolic steroid).

Stefan Laggner (AUT)—Weightlifting, Unlimited class; 4th—Nandrolone (anabolic steroid).

Göran Petterson (SWE)—Weightlifting, 110 kg. class; 6th—Nandrolone (anabolic steroid).

Eiji Shimomura (JPN)—Volleyball; 7th—Testosterone (anabolic steroid).

Mikiyasu Tanaka (JPN)—Volleyball; 7th—Ephedrine (stimulant). (Note: The trainer of the Japanese volleyball team was banned from the Olympics for life.)

Ahmed Tarbi (ALG)—Weightlifting, 56 kg. class; 9th—Nandrolone (anabolic steroid).

Mahmoud Tarha (LBA)—Weightlifting, 52 kg. class; 4th—Nandrolone (anabolic steroid).

Gian-Paolo Urlando (ITA)—Track and field athletics, Hammer throw; 4th—Testosterone (anabolic steroid).

Martti Vainio (FIN)—Track and field athletics, 10,000 meters; 2nd—Methenolone.

Anna Verouli (GRE)—Track and field athletics, Javelin throw; 13th in qualifying round—Nandrolone.

1988 CALGARY (1)

Jaroslav Morawiecki (POL)—Ice hockey; 10th—Testosterone (anabolic steroid).

1988 SEOUL (11)

Alidad (AFG)—Wrestling, 62 kg. freestyle class; eliminated third round—Furosemide (Lasix) (diuretic, masking agent).

Kerrith Brown (GBR)—Judo, 71 kg.; 3rd—Furosemide (Lasix) (diuretic, masking agent).

Kálmán Csengeri (HUN)—Weightlifting, 75 kg. class; 4th—Stanozolol (anabolic steroid).

Angel Genchev (BUL)—Weightlifting, 67½ kg. class; 1st—Furosemide (Lasix) (diuretic, masking agent).

Mitko Grablev (BUL)—Weightlifting, 56 kg. class; 1st—Furosemide (Lasix) (diuretic, masking agent).

Ben Johnson (CAN)—Track and field athletics, 100 meters; 1st—Stanozolol (anabolic steroid).

Fernando Mariaca (ESP)—Weightlifting, 67½ kg. class; 13th—Pemoline (stimulant).

Jorge Quezada (ESP)—Modern pentathlon; 24th—Propranolol (ß-agonist/blocker).

Andor Szányi (HUN)—Weightlifting, 100 kg. class; 2nd—Stanozolol (anabolic steroid).

Alexander Watson (AUS)—Modern pentathlon; 61st—Caffeine (stimulant).

Sergiusz Wolczaniecki (POL)—Weightlifting, 90 kg. class; 3rd—Stanozolol (anabolic steroid).

1992 ALBERTVILLE (0)

No positive drug tests.

1992 BARCELONA (5)

Madina Biktagirova (EUN)—Track and field athletics, Marathon; 4th—Norephedrine (stimulant).
Bonnie Dasse (USA)—Track and field athletics, Shot put; 14th in qualifying round—Clenbuterol (ß-agonist).
Judson Logan (USA)—Track and field athletics, Hammer throw; 4th—Clenbuterol (ß-agonist).
Nijole Medvedeva (LTU)—Track and field athletics, Long jump; 4th—Meziocarde (stimulant).
Wu Dan (CHN)—Volleyball; 7th—Stimulant with a strychnine base.

1994 LILLEHAMMER (0)

No positive drug tests.

1996 ATLANTA (2)

Iva Prandzheva (BUL)—Track and field athletics, Long jump, 7th; Triple jump, 4th—Methadienone (stimulant).
Nataliya Shekhodanova (RUS)—Track and field athletics, 100 meter hurdles, 7th—Stanozolol (anabolic steroid).

Two noncompetitors were disqualified, a coach and physician to the Lithuanian cycling team, as several of their athletes did test positive for Bromantan:

Boris Vasilyev (LTU)—coach of Lithuanian cycling team
Vitaly Slionsarenko (LTU)—physician to the Lithuanian cycling team

Both were expelled from the Olympics because of offenses involving performance-enhancing drugs.

There were an additional six positive tests, but four of these were for the controversial drug Bromantan. The four athletes were originally disqualified, but on appeal, all were reinstated because the drug was new, it was not certain if it was an ergogenic aid, and it had not been announced in advance. A sixth positive test for phenylpropanolamine was announced, but the athlete was given only a warning, as that drug is commonly found in cold medications. These were as follows:

Estella Rodriguez Villanueva (CUB)—Judo, Unlimited class; 1st—Furosemide (Lasix). (It is unclear why this decision was made).
Zafar Gulyev (RUS)—Greco-Roman wrestling, 48 kg; 3rd—Bromantan.
Andrey Korneyev (RUS)—Swimming, 200 meter breaststroke; 3rd—Bromantan.
Rita Ražmaitė (LTU)—Cycling, Match sprint; 13th—Bromantan.
Marie McMahon (IRL)—Track and field athletics, 5,000 meters; 14th/heat two/round one—Phenylpropenolamine (an OTC cold remedy).
Marina Trandenkova (RUS)—Track and field athletics, 100 meters; 5th—Bromantan.

1998 NAGANO (0)

There were no drug disqualifications. However, in men's giant slalom snowboarding, the winner, Ross Rebagliati (CAN), was disqualified two days after winning the event, when he tested positive for marijuana use. He was reinstated as the gold medalist on 12 February after a ruling by the Court of Arbitration for Sport (CAS).

2000 SYDNEY (10)

Fritz Aanes (NOR)—Wrestling, 85 kg. Greco-Roman; 4th—Nandrolone (anabolic steroid).
Ashot Danielyan (ARM)—Weightliftng, Unlimited class; 3rd—Stanozolol (anabolic steroid).
Izabela Dragneva (BUL)—Weightlifting, 48 kg. class; 1st—Furosemide (Lasix) (diuretic, masking agent).
Ivan Ivanov (BUL)—Weightlifting, 56 kg. class; 2nd—Furosemide (Lasix) (diuretic, masking agent).
Alexander Leipold (GER)—Wrestling, 76 kg. freestyle; 1st—Nandrolone (anabolic steroid).
Svetlana Pospelova (RUS)—Track and field athletics, 400 meters; 4th in heat of round one—Stanozolol.

Oyunbileg Puervbaatar (MGL)—Wrestling, 58 kg. freestyle; 5th—Furosemide (Lasix) (diuretic, masking agent).

Andreea Raducan (ROM)—Gymnastics, Individual all-around; 1st—Pseudoephedrine (stimulant).

Andris Reinholds (LAT)—Rowing, Single sculls; 8th—Nandrolone (anabolic steroid).

Minchev Angelov Sevdalin (BUL)—Weightlifting, 62 kg. class; 3rd—Furosemide (Lasix) (diuretic, masking agent).

2002 SALT LAKE CITY (7)

Alain Baxter (GBR)—Alpine skiing, Slalom; 3rd—Methamphetamine (stimulant).

Olga Danilova (RUS)—Cross-country skiing, 30 kilometers; 8th—Darbopoietin (Erythropoietin [EPO] analog).

Larisa Lazutina (RUS)—Cross-country skiing, 30 kilometers; 1st—Darbopoietin (Erythropoietin [EPO] analog).

Marc Mayer (AUT)—Cross-country skiing, 50 kilometers, 24th; Pursuit, 50th; Sprint, 21st—Blood doping

Johann Mühlegg (ESP)—Cross-country skiing, 50 kilometers; 1st—Darbopoietin (Erythropoietin [EPO] analog).

Vasily Pankov (BLR)—Ice hockey; 4th—Nandrolone (anabolic steroid).

Achim Walcher (AUT)—Cross-country skiing, 30 kilometers, 45th; Pursuit, 43rd—Blood doping.

2004 ATHENS (14 COMPETITORS; 23 TOTAL ATHLETES)

Adrian Annus (HUN)—Track and field athletics, Hammer throw; 1st—Tampering with urine sample, and then refusing to submit to a second test.

Maria Luisa Calle Williams (COL)—Cycling, Points race; 3rd—Heptaminol (stimulant).

Robert Fazekas (HUN)—Track and field athletics, Discus throw; 1st—Refusal to provide a urine sample.

Mabel Fonseca (PUR)—Wrestling, freestyle, 55 kg. class; 5th—Stanozolol (anabolic steroid).

Anton Galkin (RUS)—Track and field athletics, 400 meters, 4th in semifinal—Stanozolol (anabolic steroid).

Ferenc Gyurkovics (HUN)—Weightlifting, 105 kg.; 2nd—Oxandrolone (anabolic steroid).

Irina Korzhanenko (RUS)—Track and field athletics, Shot put; 1st—Stanozolol (anabolic steroid).

Zoltán Kovács (HUN)—Weightlifting, 105 kg.; DNQ—Refusal to provide a urine sample.

Aleksey Lesnichiy (BLR)—Track and field athletics, High jump; DNQ, Group B of qualifying—Clenbuterol (ß-agonist).

Aye Khine Nan (MYA)—Weightlifting, 56 kg. class; 4th—Anabolic steroid (not released).

Olena Olefirenko (UKR)—Rowing, Quadruple sculls; 3rd—Etamivan (stimulant).

Leonidas Sambanis (GRE)—Weightlifting, 62 kg. class; 3rd—Testosterone (anabolic steroid).

Thing Baijan Sanamacha Chanu (IND)—Weightlifting, 53 kg. class; 4th—Furosemide (Lasix) (diuretic, masking agent).

Olga Shchukina (UZB)—Track and field athletics, Shot put; 18th in Group A of qualifying—Clenbuterol (ß-agonist).

In addition to the above, there were nine athletes disqualified for positive doping tests prior to the start of their competitions, and they were excluded from the Olympic Games and never competed, as follows:

Andrew Brack (GRE)—Baseball—Stanozolol (anabolic steroid)

Derek Nicholson (GRE)—Baseball—Hydrochlorothiazide (HCTZ) (Diuretic, masking agent)

David Munyasi (KEN)—Boxing—Cathine (stimulant)

Viktor Chislean (MDA)—Weightlifting—substance not released

Zoltán Kecskes (HUN)—Weightlifting—substance not released

Sule Sahbaz (TUR)—Weightlifting—substance not released

Pratime Kumari (IND)—Weightlifting—substance not released

Wafa Ammouri (MAR)—Weightlifting—substance not released

Albina Khomich (RUS)—Weightlifting—Anabolic steroid

Appendix R: Attempts at Olympic Revival Prior to 1896

1612   Robert Dover's Games, also known as the Cotswold Olimpick Games, are first contested in the Cotswold Hills in England, during Whitsun (Pentecostal) Week. The Games continued to 1642 and then were discontinued until the 1660s. They were held intermittently from the 1660s to the 1850s, resumed again a few decades later, then continued to be held sporadically. Rather than true sporting contests, the Games resembled more a medieval country fair.

1834   Ramlösa, Sweden (near Helsingborg)—"Olympic Games" organized under the initiative of Professor Gustav Johann Schartau of the University of Lund.

1836   Ramlösa, Sweden—second, and last, Swedish attempt at revival.

1830–1840s   Olympic-type festivals held in Montreal, Quebec, Canada.

1850   First Much Wenlock Olympian Games held in Much Wenlock, a small town near Shrewsbury, Shropshire, England. Altogether, 45 in number were held consecutively, failing only 1874, through 1895. They were later held sporadically and continued to the 1990s.

1859   First Zappas Olympic Games in Athens, Greece, sponsored by the Greek philanthropist Evangelis Zappas.

1860   First Shropshire Olympic Games organized in Much Wenlock, England, by the Shropshire Olympic Society.

1861   Second Shropshire Olympic Games held in Wellington, Shropshire, England.

1862   Third Shropshire Olympic Games held in Much Wenlock, Shropshire, England.

     First Grand Olympic Festival held in Liverpool, England, sponsored by the Liverpool Olympian Society.

1863   Second Grand Olympic Festival held in Liverpool, England, sponsored by the Liverpool Olympian Society.

1864   Fourth, and last, Shropshire Olympic Games held in Much Wenlock, England.

     Third Grand Olympic Festival held in Liverpool, England, sponsored by the Liverpool Olympian Society.

1866	First Olympic Games sponsored by England's National Olympian Association, held in London, England.
	Fourth Grand Olympic Festival held in Llandudno, Wales, sponsored by the Liverpool Olympian Society.
1867	Second Olympic Games sponsored by the National Olympian Association, held in Birmingham, England.
	Fifth, and last, Grand Olympic Festival held in Liverpool, England, sponsored by the Liverpool Olympian Society.
1868	Third Olympic Games sponsored by the National Olympian Association, held in Wellington, Shropshire, England.
1870	Second Zappas Olympic Games in Athens, Greece.
1873	First Morpeth Olympic Games held in Morpeth, England. The Games were held almost annually until 1958.
1874	Fourth Olympic Games sponsored by the National Olympian Association, held in Much Wenlock, England.
1875	Third Zappas Olympic Games in Athens, Greece.
1877	Fifth Olympic Games sponsored by the National Olympian Association, held in Shrewsbury, England.
1880	First Olympic Games at Lake Palić, in Palić, a spa eight kilometers east of Subotica, then in Hungary and now in the Vojvodina province of Serbia. The Games were held sporadically from 1880 until 1914.
1883	Sixth, and last, Olympic Games sponsored by the National Olympian Association, held in Hadley, Shropshire, England.
1889	Fourth Zappas Olympic Games in Athens, Greece.
1891	First Panhellenic Gymnastic Society Games, modeled after the Zappas Olympics, held in Athens.
1893	Second Panhellenic Gymnastic Society Games, modeled after the Zappas Olympics, held in Athens.
April 1896	Games of the Ist Olympiad, celebrating the First Olympiad of the Modern Era, held in Athens, Greece, signaling the final resurrection of the Olympic Games after 15 centuries.

Bibliography

INTRODUCTION

Within each section, the books are listed first by Olympic Games, then alphabetically, and then chronologically, in cases where one author has several books listed. Also included are dissertations specifically concerned with the Olympic Games or certain aspects of them. In addition, where no comprehensive book on a certain subject is available, a very few pertinent articles are listed. All transliterated titles are from the native alphabet, using the *Encyclopaedia Britannica* as the source of the transliteration table.

CONTENTS

I. Official Reports of the Games of the Olympiad
    A. 1896   380
    B. 1900   381
    C. 1904   381
    D. 1906   381
    E. 1908   381
    F. 1912   382
    G. 1916   382
    H. 1920   382
    I. 1924   382
    J. 1928   382
    K. 1932   382
    L. 1936   382
    M. 1940   383
    N. 1944   383
    O. 1948   383
    P. 1952   383

Q.   1956   383
R.   1956 Equestrian Games   383
S.   1960   383
T.   1964   384
U.   1968   384
V.   1972   384
W.   1976   384
X.   1980   384
Y.   1984   385
Z.   1988   385
AA. 1992   385
BB. 1996   385
CC. 2000   385
II. Official Reports of the Olympic Winter Games   385
A.   1924   385
B.   1928   386
C.   1932   386
D.   1936   386
E.   1940   386
F.   1944   386
G.   1948   386
H.   1952   387
I.   1956   387
J.   1960   387
K.   1964   387
L.   1968   387
M.   1972   387
N.   1976   388
O.   1980   388
P.   1984   388
Q.   1988   388
R.   1992   388
S.   1994   389
T.   1998   389
U.   2002   389
III. Ancient Olympic Games   389
IV. Attempts at Revival   390
V. Works on Specific Olympic Games   390

A.   All Olympiads   390
B.   1896   392
C.   1900   392
D.   1904   393
E.   1906   393
F.   1908   393
G.   1912   393
H.   1916   394
I.   1920   394
J.   1924   394
K.   1932   394
L.   1936   394
M.   1956   394
N.   1960   395
O.   1964   395
P.   1968   395
Q.   1972   395
R.   1976   395
S.   1980   396
T.   1984   396
U.   1988   396
V.   1992   396
W.   1994   397
X.   2000   397
Y.   2002   397
VI. General Sporting Histories of the Olympic Games   397
VII. General Political and Sociological Histories of the
      Olympic Games   399
VIII. Histories of National Participation in the Olympic Games   401
A.   Australia   401
B.   Bulgaria   402
C.   Canada   402
D.   Cuba   402
E.   Czechoslovakia   402
F.   Estonia   403
G.   France   403
H.   German Democratic Repbulic   403
I.   Germany   403

	J.	Great Britain	403
	K.	Greece	403
	L.	Hungary	404
	M.	India	404
	N.	Ireland	404
	O.	The Netherlands	404
	P.	New Zealand	404
	Q.	Poland	404
	R.	Slovenia	405
	S.	Soviet Union	405
	T.	Sweden	405
	U.	Ukraine	405
	V.	United States	405
IX.		Biographies of International Olympic Committee Presidents	406
	A.	Demetrios Vikelas	406
	B.	Pierre de Coubertin	406
	C.	Henri de Baillet-Latour	406
	D.	Johannes Sigfrid Edström	407
	E.	Avery Brundage	407
	F.	Lord Killanin	407
	G.	Juan Antonio Samaranch	407
X.		Olympic Works by Coubertin	407
XI.		Miscellaneous Olympic Works	408
XII.		Websites of Interest	409

I. OFFICIAL REPORTS OF THE GAMES OF THE OLYMPIAD

Current official reports (at least since 1960) are issued in both English and French, and usually in the language of the host nation. These are sometimes issued with parallel texts, and sometimes as separate editions for each language. In the following, COJO is the acronym that stands for Comité d'Organisateur des Jeux Olympiques, the French equivalent for Organizing Committee of the Olympic Games (OCOG).

A. 1896

The Baron de Coubertin; Timoleon Philemon; Spiridon P. Lambros; and Nikolaos G. Politis, eds. *The Olympic Games 776 B.C.–1896 A.D.; With the ap-*

proval and support of the Central Council of the International Olympic Games in Athens, under the Presidency of H. R. H. the Crown Prince Constantine. Athens: Charles Beck, 1896. [This was issued in various versions, including several in parallel texts, as follows: Greek/English; Greek/French; Greek/French/English; and German/English. Also, multiple reprints of this first Official Report have been produced, most notably a 1966 edition with English/French/Greek parallel texts published by the Hellenic Olympic Committee; also a 1971 German edition entitled *Die Olympischen Spiele 1896. Offizieller Bericht,* published by the Carl-Diem-Institut in Cologne, Germany, and most recently, with annotations by various historians, *Die Olympischen Spiele 1896 in Athen: Erläuterungen zum Neudruck des Offiziellen Berichtes,* edited by Karl Lennartz, published by AGON Sportverlag, Kassel, Germany, in 1996.

B. 1900

Merillon, Daniel, ed. *Concours Internationaux d'Exercices Physiques et de Sport: Rapports Publiés sous la Direction de M. D. Merillon, Délégué Général.* 2 vols. Paris: Imprimerie Nationale, 1901 (Vol. 1) and 1902 (Vol. 2). Strictly speaking, this was a report of the physical culture section of l'Exposition Internationale in Paris in 1900.

C. 1904

Lucas, Charles J. P. *The Olympic Games 1904.* St. Louis: Woodward & Tiernan Printing, 1905.

Sullivan, James E., ed. *Spalding's Official Athletic Almanac for 1905: Special Olympic Number, Containing the Official Report of the Olympic Games of 1904.* New York: American Sports Publishing, 1905.

D. 1906

Savvidis, Panagiotis S., ed. *Leukoma ton en Athenais B'Diethnon Olympiakon Agonon 1906/Jeux Olympiques Internationaux 1906.* Athens: Estia, K. Maisner, N. Kargadouris, 1907.

E. 1908

Cook, Theodore Andrea, ed. *The Fourth Olympiad. Being the Official Report of the Olympic Games of 1908 Celebrated in London Under the Patronage of His Most Gracious King Edward VII and by the Sanction of the International Olympic Committee.* London: British Olympic Council, 1909.

F. 1912

Bergvall, Erik, ed. *The Official Report of the Olympic Games of Stockholm 1912* and *V. Olympiaden. Officiel redogorelse for olympiska spelen i Stockholm 1912*. Stockholm: Wahlstrom & Widstrand, 1913. Separate editions were published in Swedish and English.

G. 1916

COJO Berlin 1916. *Denkschrift zur Vorbereitung der VI. Olympiade 1916, veranstaltet im Deutschen Stadion zu Berlin*. Berlin: COJO Berlin 1916, n.d.

H. 1920

Verdyck, Alfred, ed. *Rapport officiel des Jeux de la VIIème Olympiade, Anvers 1920*. Brussels: COJO Antwerp 1920, 1922.

I. 1924

Avé, M. A., ed. *Les Jeux de la VIIIè Olympiade Paris 1924. Rapport officiel du Comité Olympique Français*. Paris: Librairie de France, 1925.

J. 1928

Rossem, George van, ed. *IXe Olympiade. Officiel gedenkboek van de spelen der IXe Olympiade Amsterdam 1928; The Ninth Olympiad—Being the Official Report of the Olympic Games of 1928 Celebrated at Amsterdam Issued by the Netherlands Olympic Committee;* and *Olympiade Amsterdam 1928. Rapport officiel des Jeux de la IXè Olympiade Amsterdam 1928*. Amsterdam: J. H. de Bussy, 1930. Separate editions were published in Dutch, English, and French.

K. 1932

Browne, Frederick Granger, ed. *The Games of the Xth Olympiad, Los Angeles, 1932: Official Report*. Los Angeles: COJO Los Angeles 1932, 1933.

L. 1936

COJO Berlin 1936. *XI Olympiade, Berlin 1936: Amtlicher Bericht; Les XIè Jeux Olympiques, Berlin 1936. Rapport official;* and *The XIth Olympic Games, Berlin 1936—Official Report*. Berlin: W. Limpert, 1937. Separate editions were published in German, French, and English.

M. 1940

COJO Tokyo 1940. *XIIth Olympic Games, Tokyo, 1940. Report of the Organizing Committee on Its Work for the XII. Olympic Games of 1940 in Tokyo Until the Relinquishment.* Tokyo: Isshiki, 1940.

COJO Helsinki 1940. *XII Olympiad Helsinki 1940;* and *Olympische Vorbereitungen für die Feier der 12. Olympiade Helsinki 1940.* Helsinki: COJO Helsinki 1940, 1940. Separate editions were issued in English and German.

N. 1944

No report was ever issued.

O. 1948

Lord Burghley, ed. *The Official Report of the Organizing Committee for the XIV Olympiad.* London: McCorquodale, 1951.

P. 1952

Kolkka, Sulo, ed. *The Official Report of the Organizing Committee for the Games of the XV Olympiad Helsinki 1952; Le Rapport officiel du comité d'organisateur pour les Jeux Olympiques de la XVè Olympiade Helsinki 1952;* and *XV Olympiakisat Helsingissa 1952. Jarjestelytoimikunnan virallinen kertomus.* Porvoo, Finland: Werner Soderström Osakeyhtio, 1955. Three separate editions published in English, French, and Finnish.

Q. 1956

Doyle, E. A., ed. *The Official Report of the Organizing Committee for the Games of the XVI Olympiad, Melbourne 1956.* Melbourne: W. M. Houston, Government Printer, 1958.

R. 1956 Equestrian Games

COJO Stockholm 1956. *Ryttaroolympiaden: The Equestrian Games of the XVIth Olympiad. Stockholm 1956.* Stockholm: Esselte Aktiebolag, 1959. Parallel texts in Swedish and English.

S. 1960

Giacomini, Romolo, ed. *The Games of the XVII Olympiad, Rome 1960; Giochi della XVII Olimpiada Roma 1960;* and *Les jeux de la XVIIè Olympiade,*

Rome 1960. 2 vols. Rome: COJO Rome 1960, 1960. Three separate editions published in English, Italian, and French.

T. 1964

COJO Tokyo 1964. *The Games of the XVIII Olympiad, Tokyo 1964. The Official Report of the Organizing Committee*. 2 vols. Tokyo: COJO Tokyo 1964, 1964.

U. 1968

Trueblood, Beatrice, ed. *Mexico 1968. Mémoire officiel des Jeux de la XIX Olympiade/Commemorative Volumes of the Games of the XIX Olympiad*. 4 vols. Mexico City: COJO Mexico City 1968, 1968. Two separate editions were issued, one with parallel texts in French and English and one with parallel texts in Spanish and German. A fifth volume was also issued which contained entry tickets, programs, and other memorabilia. A supplement was also issued to the second volume.

V. 1972

Diem, Liselott, and Ernst Knoesel, eds. *Die Spiele: The Official Report of the Organizing Committee for the Games of the XXth Olympiad, Munich 1972*. 3 vols. Munich: ProSport, 1974. Separate editions of volumes 1 and 2 were issued in English, German, and French. Volume 3 (the results) was issued with parallel texts in English, French, and German.

W. 1976

Rousseau, Roger, ed. *Games of the XXI Olympiad, Montreal 1976: Official Report*, and *Jeux de la XXIè Olympiade, Montréal 1976. Rapport officiel*. 3 vols. Montreal: COJO Montreal 1976, ca. 1978. Separate editions were issued in English and French.

X. 1980

Novikov, I. T., ed. *Games of the XXIInd Olympiad Moscow 1980: Official Report of the Organizing Committee of the Games of the XXIInd Olympiad;* and *Jeux de la XXIIè Olympiade Moscou 1980: Rapport officiel du Comité d'organisation des Jeux de la XXIIè Olympiade*. 3 vols. Moscow: Fizkultura i Sport, 1981. Separate editions were issued in English and French.

Y. 1984

Perelman, Richard B., ed. *Official Report of the Games of the XXIIIrd Olympiad Los Angeles, 1984.* 2 vols. Los Angeles: COJO Los Angeles 1984, 1985. Separate editions were issued in French and English.

Z. 1988

Roh Sang-Kook, Lee Kyong-Hee, and Lee Bong-Jie, eds. *Official Report: Games of the XXIVth Olympiad Seoul 1988.* 2 vols. Seoul: Korean Textbook, 1989. Separate editions were issued in French, English, and Korean.

AA. 1992

Cuyàs, Romà, ed. *Official Report: Games of the XXV Olympiad Barcelona 1992.* 4 vols. Barcelona: COJO Barcelona 1992, 1992. Separate editions were issued in English, French, Castilian Spanish, and Catalan Spanish. Note that this Official Report, unlike most of them, did not contain complete results. Volume 4 of the Official Report listed results, but only the top eight finishers in each event. The results were issued as a separate volume, entitled *Games of the XXV Olympiad Barcelona 1992: The Results*, with the same editor and publisher. The results text was issued in parallel texts in English, French, Castilian Spanish, and Catalan Spanish.

BB. 1996

Watkins, Ginger T., ed. *The Official Report of the Centennial Olympic Games.* 3 vols. Atlanta: Peachtree, 1997. Separate editions were issued in English, French, Spanish, and German.

CC. 2000

COJO Sydney 2000. *Official Report of the XXVII Olympiad.* 3 vols. Sydney: Sydney Organizing Committee for the Olympic Games, 2001. Separate editions issued in English and French.

II. OFFICIAL REPORTS OF THE OLYMPIC WINTER GAMES

A. 1924

No separate official report of the Chamonix Winter Olympics was ever issued. The report is found at the end of the report for the 1924 Olympic Games in

Paris, *Les Jeux de la VIIIè Olympiade Paris 1924. Rapport officiel du Comité Olympique Français.* See above.

B. 1928

Swiss Olympic Committee. *Rapport général du Comité Exécutif des IIèmes Jeux Olympiques d'Hiver et documents officiels divers.* Lausanne: Swiss Olympic Committee, 1928. Results were not included in this report but were issued in a separate volume, as follows:
Swiss Olympic Committee. *Résultats des Concours des IIèmes Jeux Olympiques d'Hiver organisés à St. Moritz.* Lausanne: Swiss Olympic Committee, 1928.

C. 1932

Lattimer, George M., ed. *Official Report: III Olympic Winter Games, Lake Placid 1932.* Lake Placid: COJO Lake Placid 1932, 1932.

D. 1936

COJO Garmisch-Partenkirchen 1936. *IV. Olympische Winterspiele 1936. Garmisch-Partenkirchen 6. bis 16. Februar: Amtlicher Bericht.* Berlin: Reichssportverlag, 1936.

E. 1940

Diem, Carl, ed. *Vorbereitungen zu den V. Olympischen Winterspiele 1940 Garmisch-Partenkirchen.* Munich: Knorr und Hirth, 1939. The Games did not take place. They were originally scheduled for Sapporo, Japan, and were later scheduled for St. Moritz, Switzerland, before being rescheduled to Garmisch-Partenkirchen. Sapporo and St. Moritz did not issue reports.

F. 1944

No report was ever issued.

G. 1948

Swiss Olympic Committee. *Rapport Général sur les Vès Jeux Olympiques d'Hiver St-Moritz 1948.* Lausanne: Swiss Olympic Committee, 1951.

H. 1952

Petersen, Rolf, ed. *VI Olympiske Vinterleker/Olympic Winter Games: Oslo 1952.* English translation by Margaret Wold and Ragnar Wold. Oslo: Kirstes Boktrykkeri, 1956. Parallel texts in English and Norwegian.

I. 1956

Comitato Olimpico Nazionale Italiano. *VII Giochi Olimpici Invernali/VII Olympic Winter Games: Rapporto ufficiale/Official Report.* Rome: Comitato Olimpico Nazionale Italiano, ca. 1957. Parallel texts in Italian and English.

J. 1960

Rubin, Robert, ed. *VIII Olympic Winter Games, Squaw Valley, California 1960: Final Report.* Sacramento: California Olympic Commission, 1960. Issued in English only.

K. 1964

Wolfgang, Friedl, and Berd Neumann, eds. *Offizieler Bericht der IX. Olympischen Winterspiele Innsbruck 1964; Official Report of the IXth Olympic Winter Games, Innsbruck 1964;* and *Rapport du comité d'organisation des IXème Jeux Olympiques d'Hiver 1964.* Vienna: Osterreichischer Bundesverlag, 1967. Separate editions were issued in German, French, and English.

L. 1968

COJO Grenoble 1968. *Xème Jeux Olympiques d'Hiver: Grenoble 1968/Xth Olympic Winter Games Grenoble 1968: Official Report/X. Olympischen Winterspiele Grenoble 1968. Amtlicher Bericht.* Grenoble: COJO Grenoble 1968, 1968. Parallel texts in French, English, and German.

M. 1972

COJO Sapporo 1972. *Les XI Jeux Olympiques d'Hiver: Sapporo 1972. Rapport official;* and *The 11th Olympic Winter Games: Sapporo 1972. Official Report.* Sapporo: COJO Sapporo 1972, 1972. Separate editions were published in French and English.

N. 1976

Neumann, Bertl, ed. *Endbericht herausgegeben vom Organisationskomitee der XII. Olympischen Winterspiele Innsbruck 1976/Rapport final publié par le Comité d'Organisation des XIIèmes Jeux Olympiques d'Hiver 1976 à Innsbruck/Final Report Published by the Organizing Committee for the XIIth Winter Olympic Games 1976 at Innsbruck.* Innsbruck: COJO Innsbruck 1976. Parallel texts in German, French, English, and Russian.

O. 1980

Madden Robert, and Edward J. Lewi, eds. *Final Report/Rapport Final. XIII Olympic Winter Games/XIII Jeux Olympiques d'Hiver. Lake Placid, NY.* New York: Ed Lewi Associates, 1981. Parallel texts in English and French. Oddly, no results were given in the Official Report, as is common now, but they were issued separately, with no publishing information given, as: *Official Result/Résultats Officiels/Offizielle Ergebnisse.* No real text, but titles were given in English, French, and German.

P. 1984

COJO Sarajevo 1984. *Final Report Published by the Organising Committee of the XIVth Winter Olympic Games 1984 at Sarajevo/Rapport Final publié par le Comité d'Organisateur des XIVèmes Jeux Olympiques d'Hiver 1984 a Sarajevo/Završni Izvještaj Organizacionoh komiteta XIV zimskih olimipijskih igara Sarajevo, 1984.* Sarajevo: Oslobodjenje, 1985. Parallel texts in English, French, and Serbo-Croatian (but written in Latin alphabet, thus Croatian as opposed to Serbian, which is written in the Cyrillic alphabet).

Q. 1988

COJO Calgary 1988. *Rapport officiel des XVes Jeux Olympiques d'hiver/XV Olympic Winter Games Official Report.* Calgary: COJO Calgary 1988, 1988. Parallel texts in French and English.

R. 1992

Blanc, Claudie, and Jean-Marc Eysseric, eds. *Rapport officiel des XVIes Jeux Olympiques d'hiver d'Albertville et de la Savoie/Official Report of the XVI Olympic Winter Games of Albertville and Savoie.* Albertville: COJO Albertville 1992, 1992. Parallel texts in French and English.

S. 1994

Aune, Tor, Tom Fjellheim, Helge Mjelde, and Linda Verde, eds. *Official Report of The XVII Olympic Winter Games Lillehammer 1994*. 4 vols. Lillehammer, Norway: COJO Lillehammer, 1994, 1994. Separate editions were issues in English and French.

T. 1998

COJO Nagano 1998. *The XVIII Olympic Winter Games. Official Report*. 3 vols. A separate case volume containing a CD-ROM of the report was also issued. Nagano: COJO Nagano 1998, 1999. Separate editions were issued in English, French, Spanish, German, and Japanese.

U. 2002

COJO Salt Lake City 2002. *Salt Lake 2002. Official Report of the XIX Olympic Winter Games*. Salt Lake City: Salt Lake Organizing Committee, 2002. Separate editions were issued in English and French.

III. ANCIENT OLYMPIC GAMES

Diem, Carl. *Die Olympischen Spiele in Altertum und Gegenwart*. Eulau: n. p., 1933.
Finley, M. I., and H. W. Pleket. *The Olympic Games: The First Thousand Years*. London: Chatto & Windus, 1976.
Gardiner, E. Norman. *Athletics of the Ancient World*. Chicago: Ares, 1930.
Harris, H. A. *Sport in Greece and Rome*. Ithaca, N.Y.: Cornell University Press, 1972.
Matz, David. *Greek and Roman Sport: A Dictionary of Athletes and Events from the Eighth Century B.C. to the Third Century A.D.* Jefferson, N.C.: McFarland, 1991.
Miller, Stephen G. *Ancient Greek Athletics*. New Haven, Conn.: Yale University Press, 2004.
Poliakoff, Michael B. *Competition, Violence, and Culture: Combat Sports in the Ancient World*. New Haven, Conn.: Yale University Press, 1987.
Raschke, Wendy J., ed. *The Archaeology of the Olympics*. Madison: University of Wisconsin Press, 1988.
Renson, Roland, Manfred Lammer James Riordan, and Dimitrios Chassiotis, eds. *The Olympic Games through the Ages: Greek Antiquity and Its Impact on Modern Sport*. Athens: Hellenic Sports Research Institute, 1991.
Swaddling, Judith. *The Ancient Olympic Games*. London: British Museum Publications, 1980.

West, Gilbert. *Odes of Pindar, with Several Other Pieces in Prose and Verse, to Which Is Added a Dissertation on the Olympick Games*. London: R. Dodsley, 1753.

Young, David C. *The Olympic Myth of Greek Amateur Athletes*. Chicago: Ares, 1984.

IV. ATTEMPTS AT REVIVAL

Burns, Francis. *Heigh for Cotswold! A History of Robert Dover's Olimpick Games*. Chipping Campden, England: Robert Dover's Games Society, 1981.

Georgiadis, Konstantinos. *Olympic Revival: The Revival of the Olympic Games in Modern Times*. Athens: Ekdotike Athenon, 2003.

Kivroglou, A. Die Bemühungenn von Ewangelos Sappas um die Wiedereinführung der Olympischen Spiele in Griechenland unter besonderer Berücksichtigung der Spiele von 1859. Unpublished Diplomarbeit, Deutsche Sporthochschule Köln, 1981.

Lennartz, Karl. *Kenntnisse und Vorstellungen von Olympia und den Olympischen Spielen in der Zeit von 393-1896*. Schorndorf: Verlag Karl Hofmann, 1974.

Mullins, Sam. *British Olympians: William Penny Brookes and the Wenlock Games*. London: Birmingham Olympic Council and British Olympic Association, 1986.

Neumüller, B. Die Geschichte der Much Wenlock Games. Unpublished Diplomarbeit, Deutsche Sporthochschule Köln, 1985.

Redmond, Gerald. *The Caledonian Games in Nineteenth-Century America*. Rutherford, N.J.: Fairleigh Dickinson University Press, 1971.

Rühl, Joachim K. *Die "Olympischen Spiele" Robert Dovers*. Heidelberg: Carl Winter Universitätsverlag, 1975.

Svahn, Åke. "Olympiska Spelen" i Helsingborg 1834 och 1836. *Idrott Historia och Samhalle* (1983): 77–105. Text in Swedish but with an English summary.

Young, David C. *The Modern Olympics: A Struggle for Revival*. Baltimore, Md.: Johns Hopkins University Press, 1996.

Young, David C. Origins of the Modern Olympics. *International Journal of the History of Sport* 4 (1987): 271–300.

V. WORKS ON SPECIFIC OLYMPIC GAMES

A. All Olympiads

The Olympic Century: The Official History of the Modern Olympic Movement. 24 vols. Los Angeles: World Sport Research & Publications, Inc., 1995–2000.

Vol. #1—*The Ancient Olympiads & Bridges to the Modern Era: Ancient Olympia 2100 BC to AD 1894*, ed. James Lynch;

Vol. #2—*I Olympiad—Athens 1896*, eds. Gary Allison and Dietrich Quanz, not yet released;

Vol. #3—*II Olympiad—Paris 1900 and The Nordic Games*, ed. Carl Posey;

Vol. #4—*III Olympiad—St. Louis 1904 and Athens 1906*, ed. Carl Posey;

Vol. #5—*IV Olympiad—London 1908 and The International YMCA*, ed. George Constable;

Vol. #6—*V & VI Olympiads—Stockholm 1912 and the Inter-Allied Games*, ed. George Daniels;

Vol. #7—*VII Olympiad—Antwerp 1920 and Chamonix 1924*, ed. Ellen Phillips;

Vol. #8—*VIII Olympiad—Paris 1924 and St. Moritz 1928*, ed. Ellen Phillips;

Vol. #9—*IX Olympiad—Amsterdam 1928 and Lake Placid 1932*, ed. Ellen Phillips;

Vol. #10—*X Olympiad—Los Angeles 1932 and Garmisch-Partenkirchen 1936*, ed. Ellen Galford;

Vol. #11—*The XI, XII, & XIII Olympiads—Berlin 1936 to St. Moritz 1948*, ed. George Constable;

Vol. #12—*XIV Olympiad—London 1948 and Oslo 1952*, ed. George Daniels;

Vol. #13—*XV Olympiad—Helsinki 1952 and Cortina d'Ampezzo 1956*, ed. Carl Posey;

Vol. #14—*XVI Olympiad—Melbourne 1956 and Squaw Valley 1960*, ed. Carl Posey;

Vol. #15—*XVII Olympiad—Rome 1960 and Innsbruck 1964*, ed. Ellen Phillips;

Vol. #16—*XVIII Olympiad—Tokyo 1964 and Grenoble 1968*, ed. Carl Posey;

Vol. #17—*XIX Olympiad—Mexico City 1968 and Sapporo 1972*, ed. George Daniels;

Vol. #18—*XX Olympiad—Munich 1972 and Innsbruck 1976*, ed. George Daniels;

Vol. #19—*XXI Olympiad—Montréal 1976 and Lake Placid 1980*, ed. George Constable;

Vol. #20—*XXII Olympiad—Moscow 1980 and Sarajevo 1984*, ed. Roberta Conlon;

Vol. #21—*XXIII Olympiad—Los Angeles 1984 and Calgary 1988*, ed. Ellen Galford;

Vol. #22—*XXIV Olympiad—Seoul 1988 and Albertville 1992*, ed. Ellen Galford;

Vol. #23—*XXV Olympiad—Barcelona 1992 and Lillehammer 1994*, ed. George Constable;

Vol. #24—*XXVI Olympiad—Atlanta 1996 and Nagano 1998*, ed. Carl Posey.

The founder of the series and driving force behind its publication was Gary Allison, head of World Sport Research & Publications and chairman of the 1st Century Project. The publisher of the series was Robert G. Rossi, with associate publishers C. Jay Halzle and James A. Williamson. The series editor was

Christian D. Kinney. The senior consultant was Dietrich Quanz. Special consultants to the entire project were Walter Borgers (GER), Ian Buchanan (GBR), Dr. Karl Lennartz (GER), Wolf Lyberg (SWE), and Dr. Norbert Müller (GER). Statistical consultants were Bill Mallon (USA) and Walter Teutenberg (GER). Art editor for the series was Christopher M. Register. There were series of special contributors and consultants for each volume.

B. 1896

Georgiadis, Konstantinos. *Die Geschichte der ersten Olympischen Spiele 1896 in Athen—ihre Entstehung, Durchführung und Bedeutung*. Unpublished Diplomarbeit, Johannes Gutenberg Universität Mainz, 1986/87.

Kardasis, Vasilis. *The Olympic Games in Athens 1896–1906*. Athens: International Sport Publications, 2004.

Kluge, Volker, ed. *1896 Athens: The Pictures of the First Olympiad*. Berlin: Brandenburgisches Verlaghaus, 1996.

Koulouri, Christina. *Athens: Olympic City 1896–1906*. Athens: International Olympic Academy, 2004.

Lennartz, Karl. *Geschichte der Deutschen Reichsaußchußes für Olympische Spiele: Heft I—Die Beteiligung Deutschlands an den Olympischen Spielen 1896 in Athen*. Bonn: Verlag Peter Wegener, 1981.

Lennartz, Karl, and Walter Teutenberg. *Die deutsche Olympia-Mannschaft von 1896*. Frankfurt am Main: Kasseler Sportverlag, 1992.

Mallon, Bill, with Ture Widlund. *The 1896 Olympic Games: Results for All Competitors in All Events, with Commentary*. Jefferson, N.C.: McFarland, 1998.

Mandell, Richard D. *The First Modern Olympics*. Berkeley: University of California Press, 1976.

Smith, Michael Llewellyn. *Olympics in Athens 1896. The Invention of the Modern Olympic Games*. London: Profile Books, 2004.

Tsolakidis, Elias. *Die Olympischen Spiele von 1896 in Athen: Versuch einer Rekonstruktion*. Unpublished Diplomarbeit, Deutsche Sporthochschule Köln, 1987.

C. 1900

Bijkerk, Ton. *Nederlandse Deelnemers aan de Tweed Olympische Spelen. Tijdens de Wereldtentoonstelling Parijs 1900*. Haarlem, Netherlands: De Vrieseborch, 2000.

Drevon, André. *Les Jeux Olympiques Oubliés*. Paris: CNRS Editions, 2000.

Lennartz, Karl. *Geschichte des Deutschen Reichsaußchußes für Olympische Spiele: Heft 2—Die Beteiligung Deutschlands an den Olympischen Spielen 1900 in Paris und 1904 in St. Louis*. Bonn: Verlag Peter Wegener, 1983.

Lennartz, Karl, and Walter Teutenberg. *II. Olympische Spiele 1900 in Paris. Darstellung und Quellen*. Berlin: Agon Sportverlag, 1995.

Mallon, Bill. *The 1900 Olympic Games: Results for All Competitors in All Events, with Commentary*. Jefferson, N.C.: McFarland, 1998.

D. 1904

Lennartz, Karl. *Geschichte der Deutschen Reichsaußchußes für Olympische Spiele: Heft 2—Die Beteiligung Deutschlands an den Olympischen Spielen 1900 in Paris und 1904 in St. Louis*. Bonn: Verlag Peter Wegener, 1983.

Lucas, Charles J. P. *The Olympic Games 1904*. St. Louis: Woodward & Tiernan, 1905.

Mallon, Bill. *A Statistical Summary of the 1904 Olympic Games*. Durham, N.C.: author, 1981.

Mallon, Bill. *The 1904 Olympic Games: Results for All Competitors in All Events, with Commentary*. Jefferson, N.C.: McFarland, 1999.

E. 1906

Kardasis, Vasilis. *The Olympic Games in Athens 1896–1906*. Athens: International Sport Publications, 2004.

Koulouri, Christina. *Athens: Olympic City 1896–1906*. Athens: International Olympic Academy, 2004.

Lennartz, Karl, and Walter Teutenberg. *Die Olympischen Spiele 1906 in Athen*. Kassel: Kasseler Sportverlag, 1992.

Mallon, Bill. *The 1906 Olympic Games: Results for All Competitors in All Events, with Commentary*. Jefferson, N.C.: McFarland, 1999.

F. 1908

Lennartz, Karl, with Ian Buchanan, Volker Kluge, Bill Mallon, and Walter Teutenberg. *Olympische Spiele 1908 in London*. Berlin: Agon Sportverlag, 1999.

Mallon, Bill, and Ian Buchanan. *The 1908 Olympic Games: Results for All Competitors in All Events, with Commentary*. Jefferson, N.C.: McFarland, 2000.

G. 1912

Diem, Carl. *Die olympischen Spiele 1912*. Berlin: Bürger, 1912.

Hermelin, Colonel, Baron D. A. Sven, and Erik Peterson. *Den Femte Olympiaden. Olympiska Spelen i Stockholm 1912 i Bild och Ord*. Göteburg, Sweden: Åhlén & Åkerlund, 1912.

Mallon, Bill, and Ture Widlund. *The 1912 Olympic Games: Results for All Competitors in All Events, with Commentary*. Jefferson, N.C.: McFarland, 2000.

H. 1916

Lennartz, Karl. *Die VI. Olympischen Spiele Berlin 1916*. Cologne: Barz & Beienburg, 1978.

I. 1920

Mallon, Bill. *The Unofficial Report of the 1920 Olympics*. Durham, N.C.: MOST Publications, 1992.

Mallon, Bill. *The 1920 Olympic Games: Results for All Competitors in All Events, with Commentary*. Jefferson, N.C.: McFarland, 2001.

Renson, Roland. *The Games Reborn: The VIIth Olympiad Antwerp 1920*. Antwerp: Pandora, 1996. Also published in French as *La VIIiéme Olympiade Anvers 1920. Les Jeux Ressuscités*, in 1995.

J. 1924

Pallière, Johannès. *Les premiers jeux d'hiver de 1924: La grande bataille de Chamonix*. Chambéry, France: Société Savoisienne d'Histoire et d'Archéologie, 1991.

Vitalien, Pierre. *La mémoire des 1ers jeux Olympiques d'hiver. Chamonix 1924*. Sérignan, France: Imprimerie Nouvelle Chamonix/Sallanches, 2004.

K. 1932

Pieroth, Doris H. *Their Day in the Sun: Women of the 1932 Olympics*. Seattle: University of Washington, 1996.

L. 1936

Graham, Cooper. *Leni Riefenstahl and Olympia*. Metuchen, N.J.: Scarecrow Press, 1986.

Hart-Davis, Duff. *Hitler's Games: The 1936 Olympics*. London: Century, 1986.

Holmes, Judith. *Olympiad 1936: Blaze of Glory for Hitler's Reich*. New York: Ballantine, 1971.

Krüger, Arnd, and William Murray. *The Nazi Olympics: Sport, Politics, and Appeasement in the 1930s*. Urbana: University of Illinois Press, 2003.

Mandell, Richard D. *The Nazi Olympics*. New York: Macmillan, 1971.

M. 1956

Lechenperg, Harald. *Olympische Spiele 1956: Cortina, Stockholm, Melbourne*. Munich: Copress-Verlag, 1957.

N. 1960

Lechenperg, Harald. *Olympische Spiele 1960: Squaw Valley, Rome*. Munich: Copress-Verlag, 1960; and Zurich: Schweizer Druckerei und Verlagshaus, 1960. Also published in English as *Olympic Games 1960: Squaw Valley—Rome*. New York: A. S. Barnes, 1960.

O. 1964

Lechenperg, Harald. *Olympische Spiele 1964: Innsbruck, Tokyo*. Munich: Copress-Verlag, 1964; Zurich: Schweizer Druckerei und Verlagshaus, 1964; and Linz, Austria: Trauner, 1964. Also published in English as *Olympic Games 1964: Innsbruck—Tokyo*. New York: A. S. Barnes, 1964.

P. 1968

Bass, Amy. *Not the Triumph but the Struggle: The 1968 Olympics and the Making of the Black Athlete*. Minneapolis: University of Minnesota Press, 2002.
Lechenperg, Harald. *Olympische Spiele 1968*. Munich: Copress-Verlag, 1968.

Q. 1972

Groussard, Serge. *The Blood of Israel: The Massacre of the Israeli Athletes, The Olympics 1972*. New York: Morrow, 1975.
Lechenperg, Harald. *Olympische Spiele 1972*. Munich: Copress-Verlag, 1972.
Leebron, Elizabeth Joanne. An Analysis of Selected United States Media Coverage of the 1972 Munich Olympic Tragedy. PhD diss., Northwestern University, 1978.
Mandell, Richard D. *A Munich Diary: The Olympics of 1972*. Chapel Hill: University of North Carolina Press, 1991.
Reeve, Simon. *One Day in September: The Full Story of the 1972 Munich Olympics Massacre and the Israeli Revenge Operation "Wrath of God."* New York: Arcade, 2000.

R. 1976

Auf der Maur, Nick. *The Billion Dollar Game: Jean Drapeau and the 1976 Olympics*. Toronto: J. Lorimer, 1977.
Ludwig, Jack. *Five Ring Circus: The Montreal Olympics*. Toronto: Doubleday, 1976.

S. 1980

Barton, Laurence. The American Olympic Boycott of 1980: The Amalgam of Diplomacy and Propaganda in Influencing Public Opinion. PhD diss., Boston University, 1983.

Booker, Christopher. *The Games War: A Moscow Journal*. London: Faber & Faber, 1981.

Hulme, Derick L., Jr. The Viability of International Sport as a Political Weapon: The 1980 U.S. Olympic Boycott. PhD diss., Fletcher School of Law and Diplomacy, Tufts University, 1988.

Hulme, Derick L., Jr. *The Political Olympics: Moscow, Afghanistan, and the 1980 U.S. Boycott*. New York: Praeger, 1990.

Wilson, Harold Edwin, Jr. "Ours Will Not Go." The U.S. Boycott of the 1980 Olympic Games. Master's thesis, Ohio State University, 1982.

T. 1984

Perelman, Richard B. *Olympic Retrospective: The Games of Los Angeles*. Los Angeles: COJO Los Angeles 1984, 1985.

Reich, Kenneth. *Making It Happen: Peter Ueberroth and the 1984 Olympics*. Santa Barbara, California: Capra Press, 1986.

Shaikin, Bill. *Sport and Politics: The Olympics and the Los Angeles Games*. New York: Praeger, 1988.

Ueberroth, Peter V., with Richard Levin and Amy Quinn. *Made in America: His Own Story*. New York: Morrow, 1985.

Wilson, Harold Edwin, Jr. The Golden Opportunity: A Study of the Romanian Manipulation of the Olympic Movement during the Boycott of the 1984 Los Angeles Olympic Games. PhD diss., Ohio State University, 1993.

U. 1988

Kim Un-Yong. *The Greatest Olympics*. Seoul: Si-sa-yong-o-sa, 1990.

King, Frank W. *It's How You Play the Game: The Inside Story of the Calgary Olympics*. Calgary: Script, 1991.

Park She-Jik. *The Seoul Olympics: The Inside Story*. London: Bellew, 1991.

Pound, Richard W. *Five Rings over Korea: The Secret Negotiations behind the 1988 Olympic Games in Seoul*. Boston: Little, Brown, 1994.

V. 1992

Brunet, Ferrán. *Economy of the 1992 Barcelona Olympic Games*. Barcelona: Centre d'Estudis Olímpics Universitat Autónoma de Barcelona, 1993.

W. 1994

Klausen, Arne Martin, ed. *Olympic Games as Performance and Public Event: The Case of the XVII Winter Olympic Games in Norway.* New York: Berghahn, 1999.

X. 2000

Marichev, Gennadi. *Sydney 2000: The Figures, the Results, the Athletes.* Riga, Latvia: Demarko Sports Publishing, 2000.
McGeoch, Rod, with Glenda Korporaal. *The Bid: How Australia Won the 2000 Games.* Melbourne: William Heinemann Australia, 1994.

Y. 2002

Romney, Mitt. *Turnaround: Crisis, Leadership, and the Olympic Games.* Washington, D.C.: Regnery, 2004.

VI. GENERAL SPORTING HISTORIES OF THE OLYMPIC GAMES

Andersen, P. Chr., and Vagn. Hansen. *Olympiadebogen. De Olympiske Lege 1896–1948.* Copenhagen: Samlererns Forlag, 1948.
Associated Press and Grolier. *The Olympic Story: Pursuit of Excellence.* New York: Franklin Watts, 1979.
Gillmeister, Heiner. *Olympisches Tennis: Die Geschichte der olympischen Tennisturniere (1896–1992).* Sankt Augustin, Germany: Academia Verlag, 1993.
Georgiev, Nikolay. *Analyse du programme Olympique 1896–1996.* Lausanne: IOC, 1995.
Georgiev, Nikolay. *Analyse du programme des Jeux Olympiques d'hiver 1924–1998.* Lausanne: IOC, 1995.
Greenberg, Stan. *The Guinness Book of Olympics Facts & Feats.* Enfield, Middlesex, England: Guinness, 1983. Second edition issued as *Olympic Games: The Records,* Guinness, 1987. Third edition issued as *The Guinness Olympics Fact Book,* Guinness, 1991.
Greenberg, Stan. *Whitaker's Olympic Almanack. The Essential Guide to the Olympic Games.* 2nd ed. London: A. C. Black, 2003.
Gynn, Roger, and David Martin. *The Olympic Marathon.* Champaign, Ill.: Human Kinetics, 2000.
Henry, Bill. *An Approved History of the Olympic Games.* Four editions, 1948, 1976, 1981, and 1984. The last three editions were edited by Henry's daughter, Patricia Henry Yeomans. 1st ed.: New York: G. P. Putnam, 1948; 2nd ed.: New York: G. P. Putnam, 1976; 3rd/4th eds.: Sherman Oaks, Calif.: Alfred Publishing, 1981 and 1984.

Kahlich, Endre, László Gy. Papp, and Zoltán Subert. *Olympic Games 1896–1972*. Budapest: Corvina, 1972.

Kaiser, Rupert. *Olympia Almanach: Geshichten, Zahlen, Bilder. 90 Jahre Olympische Winterspiele*. Kassel, Germany: Agon Sportverlag, 1998.

Kaiser, Rupert. *Olympia Almanach: Geshichten, Zahlen, Bilder. 100 Jahre Olympische Spiele*. Kassel, Germany: Agon Sportverlag, 1996.

Kamper, Erich. *Lexikon der Olympischen Winterspiele*. Stuttgart, Germany: Union Verlag, 1964. Parallel texts in German, French, English, and Swedish.

Kamper, Erich. *Enzyklopädie der Olympischen Spiele*. Dortmund, Germany: Harenberg, 1972. Parallel texts in German, French, and English. American edition issued as *Encyclopaedia of the Olympic Games*, New York: McGraw-Hill, 1972.

Kamper, Erich. *Lexikon der 12,000 Olympioniken*. Graz, Austria: Leykam-Verlag, 1975. Second edition issued as *Lexikon der 14,000 Olympioniken*, Leykam-Verlag, 1983.

Kamper, Erich, and Bill Mallon. *The Golden Book of the Olympic Games*. Milan: Vallardi, 1993.

Kamper, Erich, and Herbert Soucek. *Olympische Heroen: Portraits und Anekdoten von 1896 bis heute*. Erkrath, Germany: Spiridon Verlag, 1991.

Kluge, Volker. *Die Olympischen Spiele von 1896 bis 1980*. Berlin: Sportverlag, 1981.

Kluge, Volker. *Winter Olympia Kompakt*. Berlin: Sportverlag, 1992.

Kluge, Volker. *Olympische Sommerspiele: Die Chronik I. Athen 1896—Berlin 1936*. Berlin: Sportverlag, 1997.

Kluge, Volker. *Olympische Sommerspiele: Die Chronik II. London 1948–Tokyo 1964*. Berlin: Sportverlag, 1998.

Kluge, Volker. *Olympische Sommerspiele: Die Chronik III. Mexico 1968–Los Angeles 1984*. Berlin: Sportverlag, 2000.

Kluge, Volker. *Olympische Sommerspiele: Die Chronik IV. Seoul 1988–Atlanta 1996*. Berlin: Sportverlag, 2000.

Kluge, Volker. *Olympische Sommerspiele: Die Chronik V. Sydney 2000–Athens 2004*. Berlin: Sportverlag, 2005.

Lord Killanin and John Rodda, eds. *The Olympic Games*. London: Queen Anne Press, 1976. Second edition published as *The Olympic Games 1984: Los Angeles and Sarajevo,* Salem, N.H.: Michael Joseph, 1983.

Lovett, Charlie. *Olympic Marathon: A Centennial History of the Games' Most Storied Race*. Westport, Conn.: Prager, 1997.

Mallon, Bill. *The Olympic Record Book*. New York: Garland, 1987.

Mallon, Bill. *Olympic Golden Data Retrieval System*. Baltimore: Datatrace, 2004.

Marichev, Gennadi. *Who Is Who at the Summer Olympics 1896–1992*. 4 vols. Riga, Latvia: Demarko Sport Publishing, 1996.

Marichev, Gennadi. *Winter Olympics 1924–2002: The Figures, the Results, the Athletes*. Riga, Latvia: Demarko Sport Publishing, 2002.

Messinesi, Xenophon. *The History of the Olympic Games*. New York: Drake, 1976.

Mezö, Ferenc. *The Modern Olympic Games*. Budapest: Pannonia Press, 1956. Multiple editions were issued in English, French, German, Spanish, and Hungarian.

Miller, David. *Athens to Athens: The Official History of the Olympics Games and the IOC, 1904–2004*. Edinburgh: Mainstream Publishing, 2003.

The Olympics. Athens to Athens 1896–2004. London: Weidenfeld & Nicolson, 2004.

Petrov, Prof. Raiko. *Olympic Wrestling throughout the Millennia*. Lausanne: FILA, 1993.

Schaap, Richard. *An Illustrated History of the Olympics*. Three editions, 1963, 1967, and 1975. The last two editions list author's name as Dick Schaap. New York: Alfred A. Knopf, 1963, 1967, 1975.

Soames, Nicolas, and Roy Inman. *Olympic Judo: History and Techniques*. Wiltshire, England: Crowood Press, 1990.

Wallechinsky, David. *The Complete Book of the Olympics*. Six editions, followed by separate editions for the Winter Olympics (see below). 1st ed.: Middlesex, England: Penguin Books, 1983; 2nd ed.: New York: Viking Penguin, 1988; 3rd ed.: London: Aurum, 1991; 4th ed.: Boston: Little, Brown, 1996; 5th ed.: Woodstock, N.Y.: Overlook Press, 2000; 6th ed.: London: Aurum Press, 2004. Probably the best-known book, and very complete, in English, on the results of the Olympic Games.

Wallechinsky, David. *The Complete Book of the Winter Olympics*. Three editions. 1st ed.: Boston: Little, Brown, 1993; 2nd/3rd eds.: Woodstock, N.Y.: Overlook, 1998, 2001.

Wasner, Fritz. *Olympia-Lexikon*. Bielefeld, Germany: Verlag E. Gunglach Aktiengesellschaft, 1939.

Weyand, Alexander M. *Olympic Pageant*. New York: Macmillan, 1952.

zur Megede, Ekkehard. *The Modern Olympic Century 1896–1996*. Berlin: Deutsche Gesellschaft für Leichtathletik-Dokumentation e.V., 1999.

VII. GENERAL POLITICAL AND SOCIOLOGICAL HISTORIES OF THE OLYMPIC GAMES

Barney, Robert K., Stephen R. Wenn, and Scott G. Martyn. *Selling the Five Rings: The International Olympic Committee and the Rise of Commercialism*. Salt Lake City: University of Utah Press, 2002.

Clark, Stanley James. Amateurism, Olympism, and Pedagogy: Cornerstones of the Modern Olympic Movement. EdD diss., Stanford University, 1975.

Da Costa, Lamartine P. *Olympic Studies. Current Intellectual Crossroads*. Rio de Janeiro: n.p., 2002.

Daniels, Stephanie, and Anita Tedder. *A Proper Spectacle: Women Olympians 1900–1936. Celebrating 100 Years of Women in the Olympics*. Bedfordshire, England: ZeNaNa Press, 2000.

Diem, Carl. *Ewiges Olympia*. Minden: n.p., 1948.

Espy, Richard. *The Politics of the Olympic Games*. Berkeley: University of California Press, 1979.

Findling, John E., and Kimberly D. Pelle. *Historical Dictionary of the Olympic Movement*. Westport, Conn.: Greenwood, 1996 and 2004.

Fuoss, Donald E. An Analysis of the Incidents in the Olympic Games from 1924 to 1948, with Reference to the Contribution of the Games to International Understanding. PhD diss., Columbia University, 1952.

Gafner, Raymond, and Norbert Müller. *The International Olympic Committee—One Hundred Years. The Idea—The Presidents—The Achievements.* 3 vols. Lausanne: IOC, 1995.

Graham, Peter J., and Horst Ueberhorst, eds. *The Modern Olympics*. Cornwall, N.Y.: Leisure Press, ca. 1975.

Guttmann, Allen. *The Olympics: A History of the Modern Games*. Urbana: University of Illinois Press, 1992.

Hill, Christopher R. *Olympic Politics: Athens to Atlanta 1896–1996*. 2nd ed. Manchester: Manchester University Press, 1996. First edition issued as *Olympic Politics*, Manchester University Press, 1992.

Hoberman, John. *Olympic Crisis: Sport Politics and the Moral Order*. New Rochelle, N.Y.: Caratzas, 1986.

Howard, Rachel. *The Truce Story, edited by the International Olympic Truce Centre*. Athens: Pallis ABEE, 2004.

Jennings, Andrew. *The New Lords of the Rings*. New York: Pocket, 1996. (See Vyv Simson and Andrew Jennings for the first edition.)

Kanin, David B. *A Political History of the Olympic Games*. Boulder, Colo.: Westview Books, 1981.

Landry, Fernand, Marc Landry, and Magdeleine Yerles, eds. *Sport: The Third Millennium/Le troisième millénaire*. Sainte-Foy, Quebec: Les presses de l'université Laval, 1991. A collection of papers with text in either French or English. Abstracts are provided in both languages.

Leiper, Jean Marion. The International Olympic Committee: The Pursuit of Olympism, 1894–1970. PhD diss., University of Alberta (Canada), 1976.

Lucas, John. *The Modern Olympic Games*. New York: A. S. Barnes, 1980.

Lucas, John. *The Future of the Olympic Games*. Champaign, Ill.: Human Kinetics, 1992.

Lyberg, Wolf. *The Book of Facts on the Olympic Winter Games 1924–1992: Part I: The Participants, the Medals, the Spectators*. Lausanne: IOC, 1992.

Lyberg, Wolf. *Fabulous 100 Years of the IOC: Facts, Figures, and Much, Much More*. Lausanne: IOC, 1996.

Lyberg, Wolf. *The History of the IOC Sessions*. 3 vols. Lausanne: IOC, 1994.

Lyberg, Wolf. *The Seventh President of the IOC: Facts and Figures*. Lausanne: IOC, 1997.

Messinesi, Xenophon Leon. *A Branch of Wild Olive*. New York: Exposition Press, 1973. Second edition issued as *A History of the* Olympics, New York: Drake Publishers, 1976.

Miller, Geoffrey. *Behind the Olympic Rings*. Lynn, Mass.: H.O. Zimman, 1979.

Multi-Media Partners. *Grace & Glory: A Century of Women in the Olympics*. Chicago: Triumph, 1996.

NOK für Deutschland and Kuratorium Olympische Akademie und Olympische Erziehung, eds. *Olympism: The Olympic Idea in Modern Society and Sport. Materialen für den Englischunterricht in der gymnasien Oberstufe*. Stuttgart: n.p., 2004.

Okafor, Udodiri Paul. The Interaction of Sports and Politics as a Dilemma of the Modern Olympic Games. PhD diss., Ohio State University, 1979.

Page, James A. *Black Olympian Medalists*. Englewood, Colo.: Libraries Unlimited, 1991.

Platt, Alan R. The Olympic Games and Their Political Aspects: 1952 to 1972. PhD diss., Kent State University, 1976.

Plowden, Martha Ward. *Olympic Black Women*. Gretna, La.: Pelican, 1996.

Pound, Dick. *Inside the Olympics: A Behind-the-Scenes Look at the Politics, the Scandals, and the Glory of the Games* . Baltimore, Md.: John Wiley & Sons, 2004.

Preuss, Holger. *Economics of the Olympic Games: Hosting the Games 1972–2000*. Petersham, South Wales, Australia: Walla Walla Press, 2000.

Preuss, Holger. *The Economics of Staging the Olympics: A Comparison of the Games 1972–2008*. Cheltenham, England: Edward Elgar, 2004.

Segrave Jeffrey O., and Donald Chu, eds. *The Olympic Games in Transition*. Champaign, Ill.: Human Kinetics, 1988.

Senn, Alfred E. *Power, Politics, and the Olympic Games: A History of the Power Brokers, Events, and Controversies That Shaped the Games*. Champaign, Ill.: Human Kinetics, 1999.

Simson, Vyv, and Andrew Jennings. *Lords of the Rings: Power, Money & Drugs in the Modern* Olympics. London: Simon & Schuster, 1991. Published in the United States as *Dishonored Games: Corruption, Money & Greed at the Olympics*. New York: S.P.I. Books, 1992. (See also Andrew Jennings for the second edition.)

Sun Byung-Kee, Lee Sei-Kee, Kim Sung-Kyu, and Kogh Young-Lee, eds. *Olympics and Politics*. Seoul: Hyung-Seul, ca. 1984.

Tait, Robin. The Politicization of the Modern Olympic Games. PhD diss., University of Oregon, 1984.

Tomlinson, Alan, and Garry Whannel, eds. *Five Ring Circus: Money, Power, and Politics at the Olympic Games*. London: Pluto Press, 1984.

VIII. HISTORIES OF NATIONAL PARTICIPATION IN THE OLYMPIC GAMES

A. Australia

Atkinson, Graeme. *Australian & New Zealand Olympians: The Stories of 100 Great Champions*. Canterbury, Victoria: Five Mile Press, 1984.

Australian Olympic Committee. *The Compendium: Official Australian Olympic Statistics 1896–2002*. St. Lucia, Queensland: University of Queensland Press, 2003.

Blanch, John, and Paul Jenes. *Australia at the Modern Olympic Games*. Coogee, New South Wales: John Blanch Publishing, 1984.

Gordon, Harry. *Australia and the Olympic Games*. Queensland: University of Queensland Press, 1994.

Howell, Reet, and Max Howell. *Aussie Gold: The Story of Australia at the Olympics*. South Melbourne: Brooks Waterloo, 1988.

Lester, Gary. *Australians at the Olympics: A Definitive History*. Sydney: Lester-Townsend, 1984.

Phillips, Dennis H. *Australian Women at the Olympic Games*. Kenthurst, New South Wales: Kangaroo Press, 1992.

B. Bulgaria

Tsigur Petfur Beron. *Olimpiyskite Igry 1896–1980 Shravochnyuk* [Transliterated title]. Sofia: Meditsina i fizkultura, ca. 1982.

C. Canada

Bryden, Wendy. *The Official Sports History and Record Book: Canada at the Olympic Winter Games*. Edmonton: Hurtig, 1987.

Cosentino, Frank, and Glynn Leyshon. *Olympic Gold: Canadian Winners of the Summer Games*. Toronto: Holt, Rinehart and Winston, 1975.

Cosentino, Frank, and Glynn Leyshon. *Winter Gold: Canada's Winners in the Winter Olympic Games*. Markham, Ontario: Fitzhenry & Whiteside, 1987.

Roxborough, Henry. *Canada at the Olympics*. Three editions in 1963, 1969, and 1975. Toronto: Ryerson Press, 1963, 1969, 1975.

D. Cuba

Forbes, Irene, Ana Maria Luján, and Juan Velázquez. *Cubanos en Juegos Olímpicos*. 2nd ed. Havana: Editorial Pueblo y Educación, 2003.

E. Czechoslovakia

Klír, M., Jiří Kössl, and AaM Martíkovi. *Almanach Ceskoslovenskych Olympionikü*. Prague: Stráz, 1987.

Kolář, František a kolektiv. *Kdo byl Kdo. Naši olympionici*. Prague: Nakladatelství Libri, 1999.

Kössl, Jiří, ed. *Český Olympijský Výbor. Olympijská knihovnička. Dokumentace K Dějinám Českého Olympismu.* Prague: Czech Olympic Committee, 1998. 4 vols. Vol. 1 covers 1891–1918, vol. 2 covers 1918–1945, vol. 3 covers 1945–1971, and vol. 4 covers 1971–1998.

F. Estonia

Kivine, P. *Estonikie sportsmeny prisery Olimpiyskikh/Estonian Olympic Medal Winners/Die estnischen Olympiamedaillen-gewinner/Les Médaillés olympiques d'Estonie.* Tallinn: Perioodika, 1980. Parallel texts in Estonian, English, German, and French.

G. France

Charpentier, Henri. *La Grande Histoire des Médaillés Olympiques Français de 1896 à 1988.* Paris: Editions Robert Laffont, ca. 1989.
Pellissard-Darrigrand, Nicole. *La Galaxie Olympique III: D'Athènes 1896 à Sydney 2000.* Biarritz: Atlantica, 2000.
Pellissard-Darrigrand, Nicole. *La Galaxie Olympique d'Hiver.* Biarritz: CNOSF, 1998.

H. German Democratic Republic

Gilbert, Doug. *The Miracle Machine.* New York: Coward, McCann & Geoghegan, 1980.
Kluge, Volker. *Das große Lexikon der DDR-Sportler.* Berlin: Schwarzkopf & Scwarzkopf, 2001.

I. Germany

NOK für Deutschland von Manfred Lämmer. *Deutschland in der Olympischen Bewegung. Eine Zwischenbilanz.* Frankfurt/Main: NOK für Deutschland, 1999.

J. Great Britain

Buchanan, Ian. *British Olympians: A Hundred Years of Gold Medallists.* London: Guinness, 1991.

K. Greece

Tarasouleas, At[hanassios]. *Helliniki Simmetokhi Stis Sinkhrones Olympiades* [Transliterated title]. Athens: Athanassios Tarasouleas, 1990.

L. Hungary

Mezö, Ferenc. *Golden Book of Hungarian Olympic Champions/Livre d'Or des Champions Olympiques Hongrois.* Budapest: Sport Lap. És Könyvkiadö, 1955. Parallel texts in English and French.

Tamás, Aján, István Szekres, Dr. Pál Hencsei, Tibor Ivanics, Dr. Ferenc Takács, Dr. Lajos Szabó, Vad Deszö, and Dr. Lászlo Kun. *Magyarok az Olimpai Játékokon: 1896–2000.* Budapest: Magyar Millenium, 2001.

M. India

Ezekiel, Gulu, and K. Arumugam. *Great Indian Olympians.* New Delhi: Field Hockey Publications, 2004.

Sanyal, Saraduni. *Olympic Games and India.* New Delhi: Metropolitan Book, 1970.

N. Ireland

Naughton, Lindie, and Johnny Watterson. *Irish Olympians.* Dublin: Blackwater Press, 1992.

O. The Netherlands

Bijkerk, Ton. *Olympisch Oranje van Athene 1896 tot en met Athene 2004.* Haarlem: De Vrieseborch, 2004.

Bijkerk, Ton, and Rudd Paauw. *Gouden Boek van ed Nederlandse Olympiers.* Haarlem: De Vrieseborch, 1996.

P. New Zealand (*see also* Australia)

Atkinson, Graeme. *Australian & New Zealand Olympians: The Stories of 100 Great Champions.* Canterbury, Victoria, Australia: Five Mile Press, 1984.

Q. Poland

Gluszek, Zygmunt. *Polscy Olimpijczycy 1924/1984.* 2nd ed. Warsaw: Sport i Turystyka, 1988. First edition published in 1980 as *Polscy Olimpijczycy 1924/1976.*

Tuszyński, Bogdan. *Polscy Olimpijczycy XX Wieku.* 2 vols. Wrocław: Europa, 2004.

R. Slovenia

Levovnik, Tomo, Marko Račić, and Marko Rozman. *1920–1988—Nasi olimpijci*. Ljublana: Grafos, 1992.

S. Soviet Union

Brokhin, Yury. *The Big Red Machine: The Rise and Fall of Soviet Olympic Champions*. New York: Random House, 1977 and 1978.

Khavin, B[oris]. *Vsyo ob Olimpiyskikh Igrakh* [Transliterated title]. Moscow: Fizkultura i sport, 1979.

Pavlov, S. P. *Olimpiyskaya Entsiklopediya* [Transliterated title]. Moscow: Fizkultura i sport, 1980.

Pavlov, S. P. *Olimpiyskaya Komanda SSSR* [Transliterated title]. Moscow: Fizkultura i sport, 1980.

T. Sweden

Glanell, Tomas, Gösta Huldtén, et al., eds. *Sverige och OS*. Stockholm: Brunnhages Förlag, 1987.

Pettersson, Ulf, ed. *1896–1980 Guldboken om alla Våra Olympiamästare*. Stockholm: Brunnhages Förlag, 1980.

U. Ukraine

Zinkewych, Osyp. *Ukrainian Olympic Champions*. 3rd ed. Baltimore, Md.: V. Symonenko Smoloskyp, 1984.

V. United States

Bortstein, Larry. *After Olympic Glory: The Lives of Ten Outstanding Medalists*. New York: Frederick Warne, 1978.

Carlson, Lewis H., and John J. Fogarty. *Tales of Gold: An Oral History of the Summer Olympic Games Told by America's Gold Medal Winners*. Chicago: Contemporary, 1987.

Johnson, William O., Jr. *All That Glitters Is Not Gold: An Irreverent Look at the Olympic Games*. New York: Putnam, 1972.

Mallon, Bill, and Ian Buchanan. *Quest for Gold: The Encyclopaedia of American Olympians*. New York: Leisure, 1984.

IX. BIOGRAPHIES OF INTERNATIONAL OLYMPIC COMMITTEE PRESIDENTS

A. Demetrios Vikelas

Young, David C. Demetrios Vikelas: First President of the IOC. *Stadion* (1988): 85–102.

B. Pierre de Coubertin

Boulongne, Yves-Pierre. *La vie et l'œuvre de Pierre de Coubertin*. Ottawa, Ontario: Lemeac, 1975.

Durántez, Conrado. *Pierre de Coubertin: The Olympic Humanist*. Lausanne, Switzerland: International Olympic Committee and International Pierre de Coubertin Committee, 1994.

Durry, Jean. *Le Vrai Pierre de Coubertin*. Paris: Comité français Pierre de Coubertin, 1994.

Éyquem, MarieThérése. *Pierre de Coubertin. L'Épopée Olympique*. Paris: Calman-Lévy, 1966.

Lucas, John Apostal. Baron Pierre de Coubertin and the Formative Years of the Modern International Olympic Movement 1883–1896. EdD diss., University of Maryland, 1962.

MacAloon, John J. *This Great Symbol: Pierre de Coubertin and the Origins of the Modern Olympic Games*. Chicago: University of Chicago Press, 1981.

Müller, Norbert, ed. *Pierre de Coubertin: Textes Choisis*. 3 vols. Zurich: Weidmann, 1986.

Navacelle, Geoffroy de. *Pierre de Coubertin: Sa vie par l'Image*. Lausanne: IOC, 1986.

Wassong, Stephan. *Pierre de Coubertin's American Studies and Their Importance for the Analysis of His Early Educational Campaign*. English translation and web published by the Amateur Athletic Foundation of Los Angeles at www.aafla.org. German version—*Pierre de Coubertins US-amerikanische Studien und ihre Bedeutung für die Analyse seiner frühen Erziehungskampagne*. Würzburg: n.p., 2002.

C. Henri de Baillet-Latour

Boin, Victor. Graf Baillet-Latour. *Olympische Rundschau* 17 (1942): 6–11.

Diem, Carl. Die Beisetzung (Graf Baillet-Latour). *Olympische Rundschau* 17 (1942): 24.

Polignac, Melchior Marquis de. Gedanken über Graf Baillet-Latour. *Olympische Rundschau* 17 (1942): 17–22.

D. Johannes Sigfrid Edström

Bratt, K. A. *J. Sigfrid Edström—En Levnadsteckning*. 2 vols. Stockholm: P. A. Nordstedt & Söner, 1950 (Vol. 1) and 1953 (Vol. 2).

Bring, Samuel E., ed. *J. Sigfrid Edström: Vänners hyllning på 75-årsdagen 21 november 1940*. Uppsala: Almqvist & Wicksell, 1940.

Edström, Ruth Randall. *J. Sigfrid Edström*. Viisteris: Vistmanlands Allehanda, 1946.

E. Avery Brundage

Gibson, Richard Lee. Avery Brundage: Professional Amateur. PhD diss., Kent State University, 1976.

Guttmann, Allen. *The Games Must Go On: Avery Brundage and the Olympic Movement*. New York: Columbia University Press, 1984.

Schöbel, Heinz. *The Four Dimensions of Avery Brundage*. Trans. Joan Becker. Leipzig, Germany: Offizin Anderson Nexo, 1968.

F. Lord Killanin

Lord Killanin. *My Olympic Years*. London: Secker & Warburg, 1983.

G. Juan Antonio Samaranch

Miller, David. *Olympic Revolution: The Olympic Biography of Juan Antonio Samaranch*. London: Pavilion Books, 1992.

X. OLYMPIC WORKS BY COUBERTIN

(Only his books on sport and the Olympic movement)

Coubertin, Pierre de. *L'éducation athlétique*. Paris: Imprimerie de Chaix, 1889.

Coubertin, Pierre de. *Notes sur l'Education publique*. Paris: Hachette, 1901.

Coubertin, Pierre de. *L'Education des Adolescents au XXe siècle. I: L'Education physique: La Gymnastique utilitaire. Sauvetage-Défense-Locomotion*. Paris: Alcan, 1905.

Coubertin, Pierre de. *Une campagne de vingt-et-un ans (1887–1908)*. Paris: Librairie de l'Education Physique, 1909.

Coubertin, Pierre de. *Une olympie moderne*. Lausanne: Olympic Review, 1909.

Coubertin, Pierre de. *Leçons de Gymnastique Utilitaire. Sauvetage-Défense Locomotion. A l'Usage des Instituteurs, Moniteurs, Instructeurs militaires, etc*. Paris: Payot, 1916.

Coubertin, Pierre de. *Leçons da Pédagogie sportive*. Lausanne: La Concorde, 1921.

Coubertin, Pierre de. *Mémoires olympiques*. Lausanne: Bureau international de pédagogie sportive, 1931.

XI. MISCELLANEOUS OLYMPIC WORKS

Bell, Daniel. *Encyclopedia of International Games*. Jefferson, N.C.: McFarland, 2003.

Borgers, Walter. *Olympic Torch Relays: 1936–1994*. Berlin: Agon Sportverlag, 1996.

Durántez, Conrado. *The Olympic Flame*. Burlada, Spain: I. G. Castuera, 1998.

Gadoury, Victor, and Romolo Vescovi. *Olympic Medals and Coins: 510 B.C.–1994*. Monaco: Victor Gadoury, 1996.

Greensfelder, Jim, Oleg Vorontsov, and Jim Lally. *Olympic Medals: A Reference Guide*. Saratoga, Calif.: GVL Enterprises, 1998.

Jackson, R., and T. McPhail, eds. *The Olympic Movement and the Mass Media: Past, Present, and Future Issues*. Calgary: Hurford Enterprises, 1989.

Leigh, Mary Henson. The Evolution of Women's Participation in the Summer Olympic Games, 1900–1948. PhD diss., Ohio State University, 1974.

Lennartz, Karl. *Bibliographie: Geschichte der Leibesübungen, Band 5, Olympische Spiele*. 2nd ed. Bonn: Verlag Karl Hofmann, 1983.

Mallon, Bill. *The Olympics: A Bibliography*. New York: Garland, 1984.

Moragas Spà, Miquel de, Montserrat Llinés, and Bruce Kidd, eds. *Olympic Villages: Hundred Years of Urban Planning and Shared Experiences*. Lausanne: IOC, 1997.

Moragas Spà, Miquel de, John MacAloon, and Montserrat Llinés. *Olympic Ceremonies: Historical Continuity and Cultural Exchange*. Lausanne: IOC, 1996.

Moragas Spà, Miquel de, Nancy K. Rivenburgh, and James F. Larson. *Television in the Olympics*. London: John Libbey, 1995.

Müller, Norbert. *One Hundred Years of Olympic Congresses 1894–1994*. Lausanne: IOC, 1994.

Pappas, Nina K. History and Development of the International Olympic Academy, 1927–1977. PhD diss., University of Illinois, 1978.

Stanton, Richard. *The Forgotten Olympic Art Competitions: The Story of the Olympic Art Competitions of the 20th Century*. Victoria, Canada: Trafford, 2000.

Welch, Paula Dee. The Emergence of American Women in the Summer Olympic Games, 1900–1972. EdD diss., University of North Carolina at Greensboro, 1975.

Wenn, Stephen Robert. A History of the International Olympic Committee and Television, 1936–1980. PhD diss., Pennsylvania State University, 1993.

Wilson, Wayne, and Edward Derse. *Doping in Elite Sport: The Politics of Drugs in the Olympic Movement*. Champaign, Ill.: Human Kinetics, 2000.

XII. WEBSITES OF INTEREST

www.olympic.org—official website of the International Olympic Committee; this will also direct you to websites for the various International Federations and the National Olympic Committees

www.isoh.org—official website of the International Society of Olympic Historians (ISOH)

www.aldaver.com/nocs.html—direct links to multiple National Olympic Committee websites

www.athens2004.com/athens2004/—official website of the Athens 2004 Olympic Games

www.torino2006.org—official website of the Torino 2006 Olympic Winter Games

www.beijing-2008.org—official website of the Beijing 2008 Olympic Games

www.vancouver2010.com—official website of the Vancouver 2010 Olympic Winter Games

www.aroundtherings.com—newsletter of current Olympic-related issues

www.gamesbids.com—website reviewing current status of host city bids

www.internationalgames.net—website covering the various regional and international sporting events

About the Authors

Bill Mallon, a former professional golfer, is an orthopedic surgeon whose lifelong interest in the Olympic Games became a second career while he was in medical school at Duke University. This third edition is his 21st book on the Olympic Games. He is the editor of the *Olympic Gold Data Retrieval System*. With Erich Kamper, he coauthored *The Golden Book of the Olympic Games*, and with Ian Buchanan he wrote *Quest for Gold: The Encyclopaedia of American Olympians*. He is the author of a series of books on the earliest Olympic Games (1896–1920), is a founding member and past president of the International Society of Olympic Historians, and is a former editor of the ISOH journal, *Journal of Olympic History*. For his contributions to the Olympic movement, he was awarded the Olympic Order in Silver in 2001.

Ian Buchanan has now retired from a business career in the Far East where he spent many years as a director of a reinsurance company and compiled the first authoritative history of the Far Eastern and Asian Games. This is the sixth book he has coauthored with Bill Mallon, and his many other published works include *British Olympians: A Hundred Years of Gold Medallists*. He is a founding member, an honorary member, and the first president of the International Society of Olympic Historians (ISOH) and a member of the British Olympic Association, the British Society of Sports History, and the Association of Track and Field Statisticians. For his contributions to the Olympic movement, he was awarded the Olympic Order in Silver in 1997.